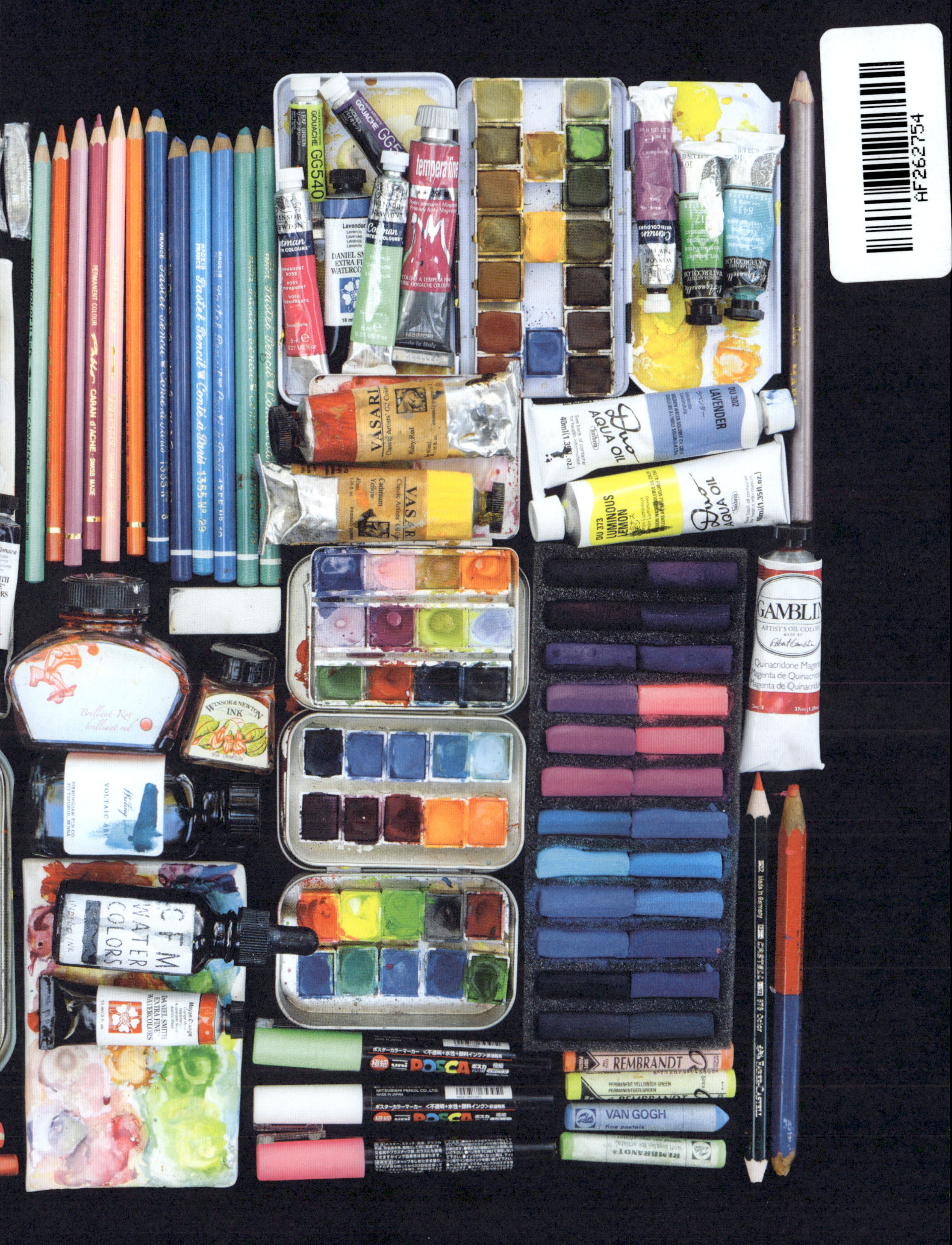

AF292754

Color Curious

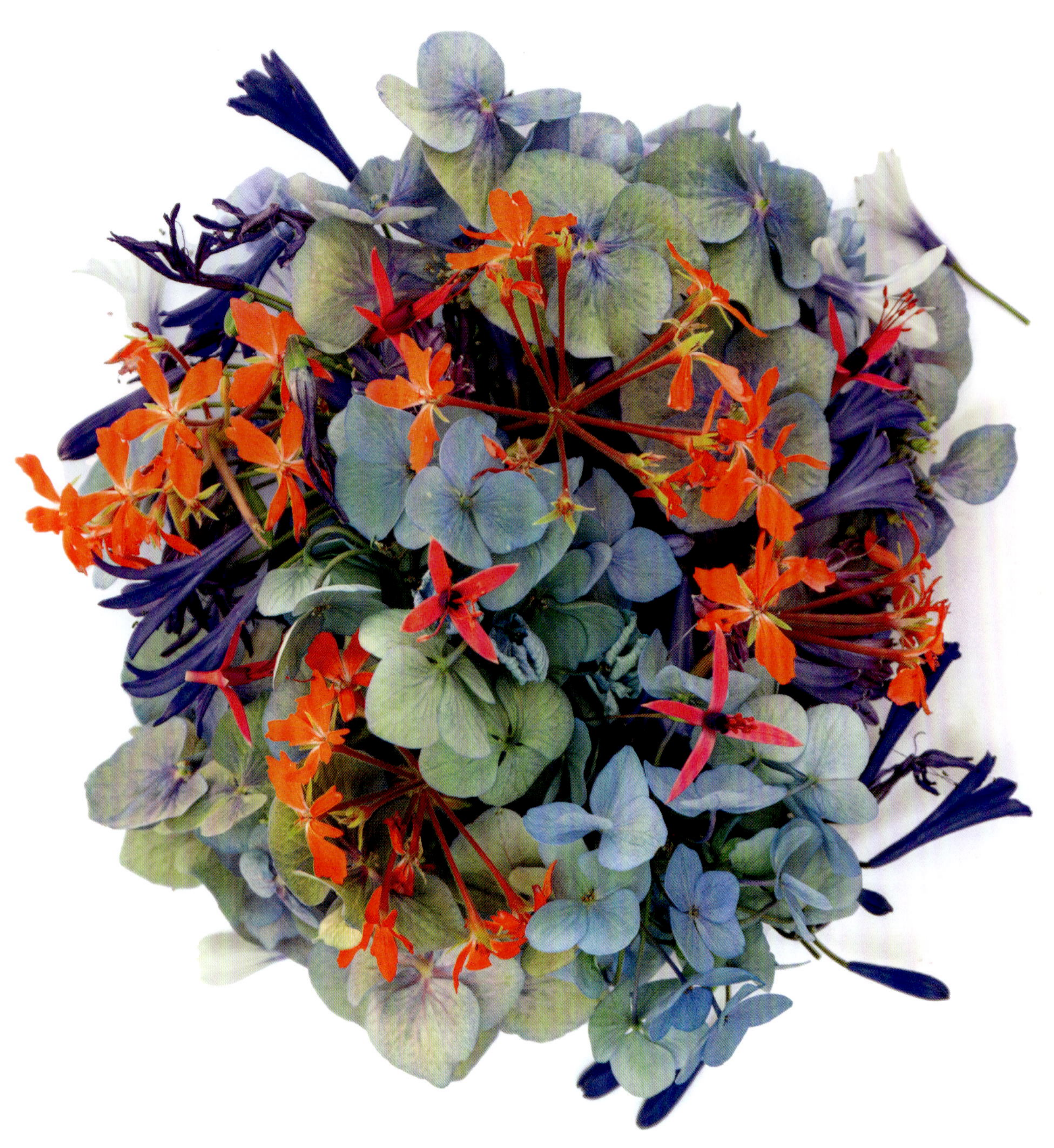

*"I found I could say things with color
and shapes that I couldn't say any other
way—things I had no words for."*
—Georgia O'Keeffe[1]

Ana Bianchi

Color Curious

Find Color Inspiration All Around You for Art, Design, and Life

CHRONICLE BOOKS

SAN FRANCISCO

Library of Congress Cataloging-in-Publication Data available.

ISBN 978-1-7972-3615-5

Manufactured in China.

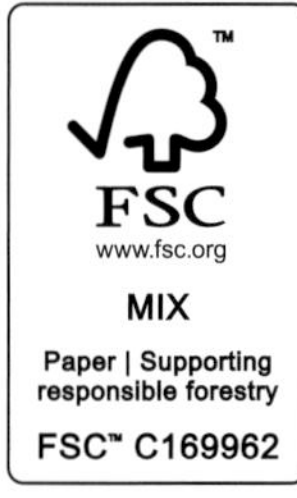

Design by Liz Li.
Typeset in BN Bergen St, Montserrat, and Newsreader.

10 9 8 7 6 5 4 3 2 1

Chronicle books and gifts are available at special quantity
discounts to corporations, professional associations, literacy
programs, and other organizations. For details and discount
information, please contact our premiums department at
corporatesales@chroniclebooks.com or at 1-800-759-0190.

Chronicle Books LLC
680 Second Street
San Francisco, California 94107
www.chroniclebooks.com

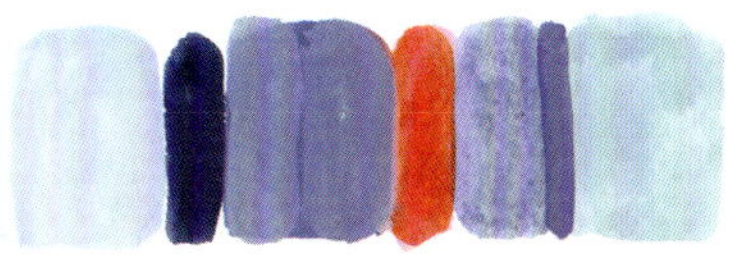

With love and gratitude
to my husband, Alberto, and my daughter, Florencia,
for they always gift me the sunshine
and a full spectrum of joy.

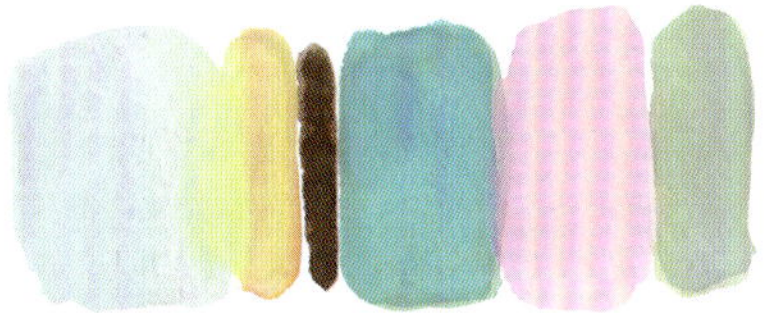

CONTENTS

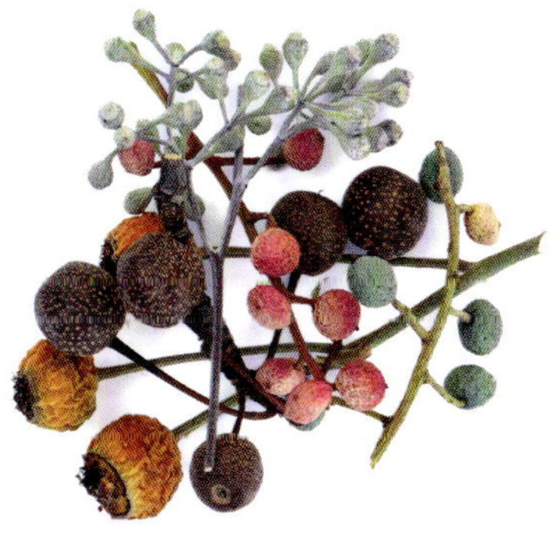

AN EYE FOR COLOR

BY DANIELLE KRYSA, THE JEALOUS CURATOR

I am honored to be a small part of this beautiful book about one of my favorite subjects. And so, it only makes sense to begin this preface by sharing my best, and most hilarious, joke from when I was two years old. Are you ready?

The sky . . . is PINK!

Ah, classic color joke! You're welcome.

From the time I was little, I've been knee-deep in color. Probably much like you, I was an artsy kid who constantly made stuff, hoarded art supplies, and then organized my stash into the always dreamy ROYGBIV rainbow standard. Then I grew up—but the color obsession didn't slow down!

I am an artist, and I also write about other contemporary artists through my platform, *The Jealous Curator*. When I started what was meant to be a solely personal project way back in 2009, I truly was jealous of anyone making art, showing work, living a creative life—because I was doing absolutely none of those things! After a terrible experience in art school during the mid-1990s, I had quit making art completely. I tried to start again but felt lost when it came to my own visual voice, and I changed directions every time a new artist crossed my path. I certainly didn't want to copy anyone, but I didn't know how to find my personal style—until I started writing blog posts. After writing every day for about a month, I scrolled back through everything I'd shared, and wouldn't you know it, a pattern had emerged. While the work was all quite different, there was one uniting factor. I'll give you a guess—yes, it was COLOR! From paintings and sculptures to fiber installations and photographs, it was the common palettes that had my artsy heart racing and finally feeling excited to create again. After a twenty-year hiatus from making anything, I had a starting place. I went back to the studio, armed with my favorite colors, ready to experiment. (FYI: I'm happy to report that the jealousy I'd been

overwhelmed by quickly and miraculously transformed into admiration as soon as I started celebrating the other artists and their work.)

I now have my own art practice, and I still love to watch for emerging patterns. I believe being as present as possible in the world around us is key to creativity. For example, you might walk the same way to work each day, so you think you've seen everything this route has to offer. You put on a podcast, let your mind wander, and magically arrive at work without noticing much of anything. But if you give yourself a simple daily assignment, you'll see something new every single day. So, staying with our color theme, on Monday you could challenge yourself to find and photograph five different shades of green; on Tuesday, look for five things that are black and white; and so on throughout the week. You might notice a flowering shrub you've hurried past a million times, or maybe there's a storm rolling in and the clouds aren't actually gray—they're a perfect palette ranging from charcoal to icy lavender. Unless you're paying attention, you'll probably just put up your umbrella and walk faster.

That is one of my most favorite things about this gorgeous book. I absolutely love that Ana is asking us to *really* look at the world around us. There are inspiring color palettes everywhere—in nature, on bookshelves, in our closets, and, yes, even on a mundane daily walk. So once you find all of these exciting new color combinations, are you done? Nope, that's just the beginning!

Color Curious delivers so many beautiful ideas, insights, and practical tips on how to bring this way of seeing the world into your art practice. This book is filled with techniques for mixing hues, interesting color-themed did-you-knows from the pages of art history, and a whole bunch of inspiring art projects to help jump-start your creativity.

Color isn't a new subject, but Ana shares her ideas and inspirations in such a beautiful, fun, and accessible way that I cannot wait to roll up my sleeves and get mixing. Are you ready to get color curious? Me too!

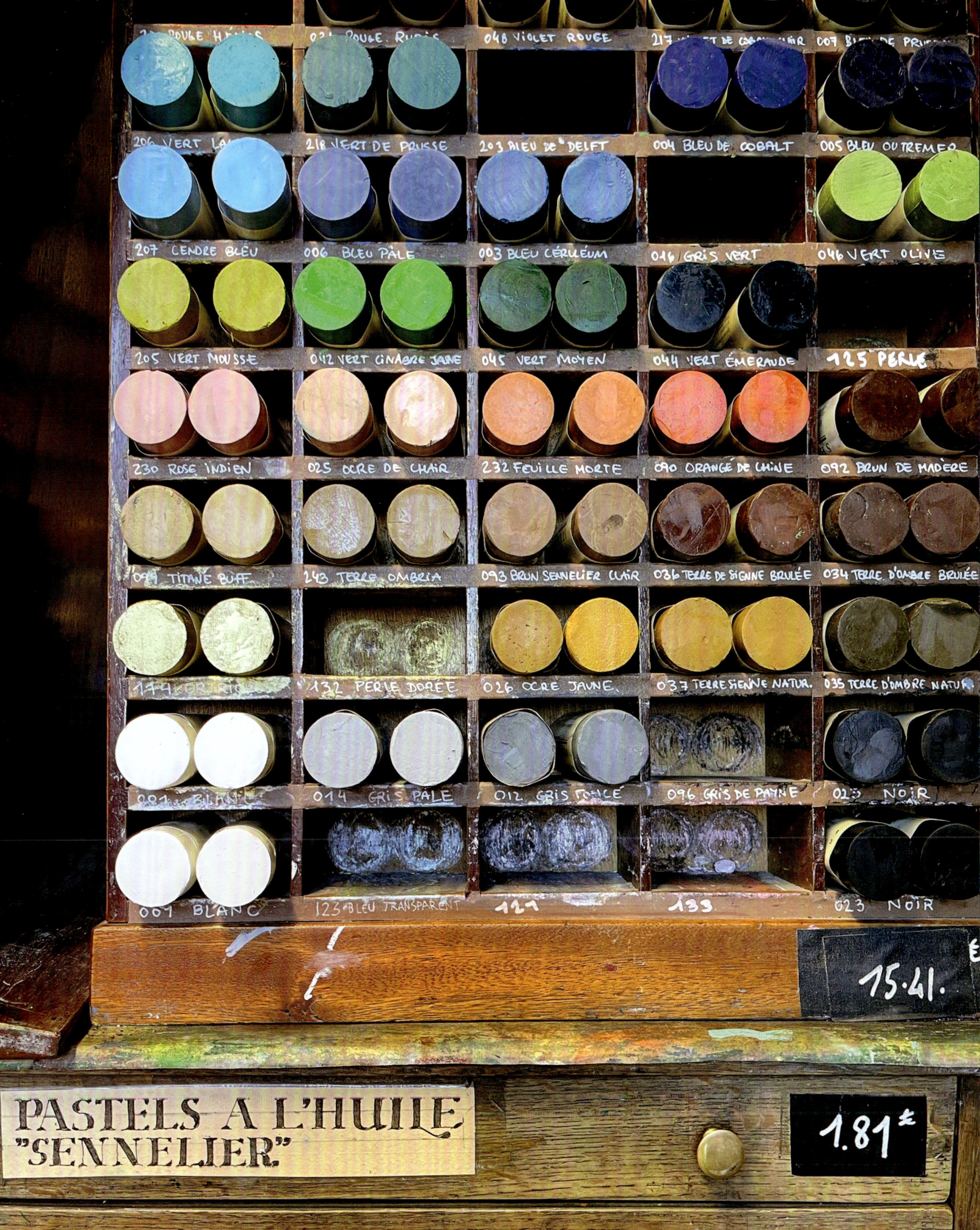
ROUGE HÉLIOS
021 ROUGE RUBIS
048 VIOLET ROUGE
217 VERT DE COBALT CLAIR
007 BLEU DE PRUSSE
206 VERT LAC
218 VERT DE PRUSSE
203 BLEU DE DELFT
004 BLEU DE COBALT
005 BLEU OUTREMER
207 CENDRE BLEU
006 BLEU PÂLE
003 BLEU CÉRULÉUM
016 GRIS VERT
046 VERT OLIVE
205 VERT MOUSSE
042 VERT CINABRE JAUNE
045 VERT MOYEN
044 VERT ÉMERAUDE
125 PERLE
230 ROSE INDIEN
025 OCRE DE CHAIR
232 FEUILLE MORTE
090 ORANGÉ DE CHINE
092 BRUN DE MADÈRE
099 TITANE BUFF
243 TERRE OMBRIA
093 BRUN SENNELIER CLAIR
036 TERRE DE SIENNE BRULÉE
034 TERRE D'OMBRE BRULÉE
114 OR GRIS
132 PERLE DORÉE
026 OCRE JAUNE
037 TERRE SIENNE NATUR.
035 TERRE D'OMBRE NATUR.
001 BLANC
014 GRIS PÂLE
012 GRIS FONCÉ
096 GRIS DE PAYNE
023 NOIR
009 BLANC
123 BLEU TRANSPARENT
121
133
023 NOIR
15.41.
€
PASTELS À L'HUILE
"SENNELIER"
1.81€

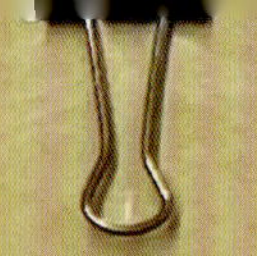

Aquarelle japonaise

Teppachi - Gansai

1 Enji	2 Ohdo	3 Senkoh Ki	4 Aka Daidai	5 Hana Byakuroku	6 Rokusho	7 Gunjo
9 Yoh Koh	10 Taisha	11 Kuro	12 Gofun	13 Yamabuki	14 Shu	15 Susu Dake
17 Asagi	18 Murasaki	19 Kawatetsu	20 Wakaba	21 Byakugun	22 Koge Cha	23 Gin Nezumi
25 Shinsha	26 Uguisu Charoku	127 Ao Kusa	28 Seiji	29 Koh Bai	30 Kurikawa Cha	31 Aka Murasaki
33 Beiju	34 Hana Iro	35 Seidoh	36 Kin Ohdo	37 Senkoh Chu	38 Kodai Murasaki	139 Hon Ai
41 Botan	42 Kuro Cha	43 Sango Iro	44 Gunroku Iro	45 Kincha	46 Sora Iro	47 Hatoba
49 Byakuroku	50 Ochiba Cha	51 Nohr Yoku	52 Gara Cha	53 Fuji Murasaki	54 A-ai Shu	

BECOMING COLOR CURIOUS

HOW TO START THINKING ABOUT COLOR AS PART OF A PERSONAL CREATIVE JOURNEY

I have led a colorful life, and I intend to continue.

Color is something I fell in love with very early on, around when I decided to become an artist at age five.

Color has always been an anchor in my creative work—from making art as a kid to making art for kids' books, from graphic design to fine art, and from dressing myself to dressing my home. In my mind, any creative project always has a color idea at its core or relies on some kind of color story.

Noticing color is a daily practice for me, even if it is merely an observation that delights me, like the color of my gray dog next to the sand of the path and some pink flowers we pass on our walk. Observing color can also be a way to entertain myself while I am in an otherwise boring situation—such as checking out the clothes of everyone in the New York subway and finding *that* person with a great sense of color. Currently, where I live in Walnut Creek, California, I look out for the Monochrome Lady, an older lady who is always dressed head to toe (hat and shoes included) in various shades of the same hue. She has become a color talisman for me. When I see her dressed all in lilac, mustard, or tan, it makes my day.

Observing color is something I do all the time. It trains my eye, increases my visual awareness, helps me think about color, and leads to more purpose and intention in my art.

It is also a mindfulness practice, a form of active meditation and awareness. I see the constantly changing colors of my surroundings, and I bask in their fleeting beauty. So even if I don't apply all my observations to actual pieces of art, the simple act of noting these colorful moments and thinking about them helps me strengthen my eye for color.

Over the years, I have been fortunate enough to have conversations with many fellow artists and have learned lessons (and tricks) from many teachers and mentors who have shared my color love. The nuggets of wisdom they have given me have opened my eyes to color in new ways and have piqued my curiosity. All these ideas about color fell, like seeds, into fertile ground with me: I ran to the hills, planted them, and grew my own colorful forest. Because ideas are meant to be shared and seeds spread, I am passing them all to you, along with my own experiences, experiments, moments of discovery, and curiosity about color.

At the risk of sounding bookish, I've also dedicated many hours and lots of shelf space to observing the work of artists and crafters, known and anonymous, from all eras and around the world. When I cannot see the art live at a museum, I sink into my red chair to look at the photos in my art books. I pay attention to color, examine the images in detail, and try to connect with the thoughts of the person who made the art. All these artists are my mentors.

As a self-taught art history student, I'm deeply interested in certain periods and places, while others are just a big hole in my learning. I am okay with it since I'm on my own journey of curiosity and color love, as you should be on yours.

As you go through the pages of this book, you will discover many ways to find, observe, analyze, and apply color. Take them and make them your own.

I hope you see this book as a springboard from which to jump into whatever creative practice you are interested in and learn that you can do so in both novel and age-old ways. Above all, may this book lead you to become more color curious and help you develop a strong eye for color.

Ana Bianchi

@AnaLovesColor

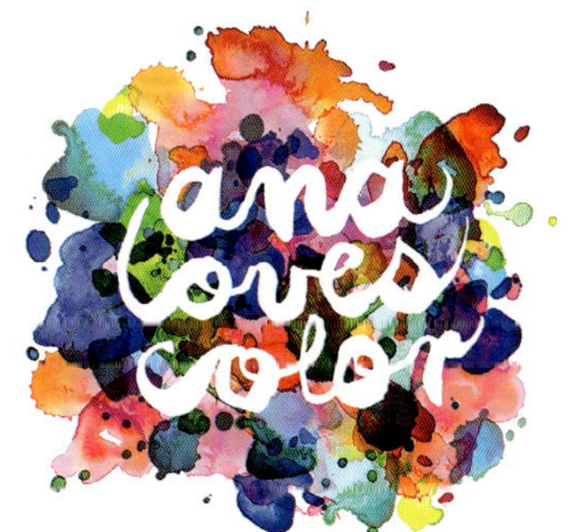

HOW DO YOU TRAP THE RAINBOW?

There is a pot of gold at the end of the rainbow, right? Have you ever gone toward it and found that proverbial pot of gold? I'd guess not. I think this is a good metaphor for understanding color.

Isaac Newton explained light and color, and we all studied them at some point in school: the prism tricks, the light diffracted from white to the full spectrum, the wavelengths, and how the eye perceives them.

Every time I see a science documentary about light, I find it fascinating. I must say, I don't fully understand it all. One thing is certain, though: gaining a full scientific understanding of color is not necessary to make me a better artist. Observing it as I show in these pages is what gave me my eye for color.

Newton was not the only one to try to explain and harness the color around us. Through the centuries, artists and scientists (such as the chemists who make pigments) have tried to organize color and make it consistent and replicable. While this book is not about understanding these systems or explaining them in depth, these are their stories in a nutshell.

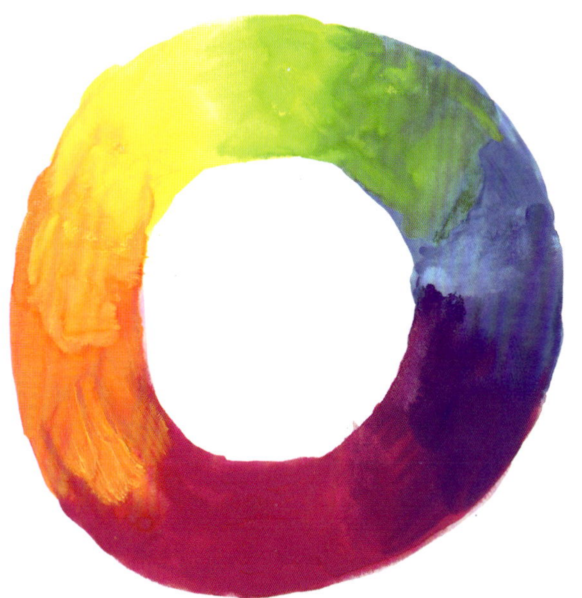

THE COLOR WHEEL

The first thing people usually think about when talking about color is the color wheel. That circle with the rainbow organized around it, followed by concepts like primary colors and secondary colors or complementary colors. The wheel also introduces concepts like

- **Hue:** the color itself—yellow, green, and others—encompassing its full range (e.g., all the yellows)
- **Chroma:** the level of purity of the color itself (e.g., How blue is that blue?)
- **Value:** how light or dark a color is
- **Shade:** the variations of any color toward its darkest version
- **Tint:** the variations of any color toward its lightest version
- **Tone:** how the color moves from pure and saturated toward gray and desaturated

Newton's color wheel from 1666 is the first iteration of this color system. Derived from his rainbow studies, it would be the standard for learning about the science of light optics for centuries, and in a way, it still is the gold standard of color charts, serving both scientists and artists.

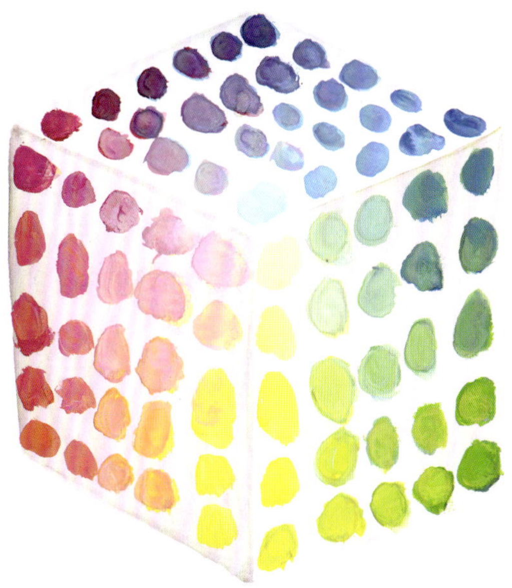

This color wheel eventually evolved into a 3D version, the Munsell color system, which Albert Henry Munsell created in 1904. This more complete version relies on three axes: hue (blue, red, green, yellow, etc.), value (how light or dark a color is), and chroma (how saturated it is). This is basically Newton's wheel on steroids.

If you studied graphic design like I did or trained for another creative career, you were likely taught about Munsell's wheel and may have progressed into having to color mix the whole Munsell model. In my case, I was assigned a different color-mixing exercise, the color cube. This monthlong project consisted of creating a cube covered by ninety-six color swatches mixed using only the true primary colors of gouache paint: cyan, magenta, yellow, and white. Each corner of the cube had a pure hue, and from there we had to make incremental progress toward the other corners. This grueling exercise is a great practice for precise color mixing but not for color ideation or personal expression.

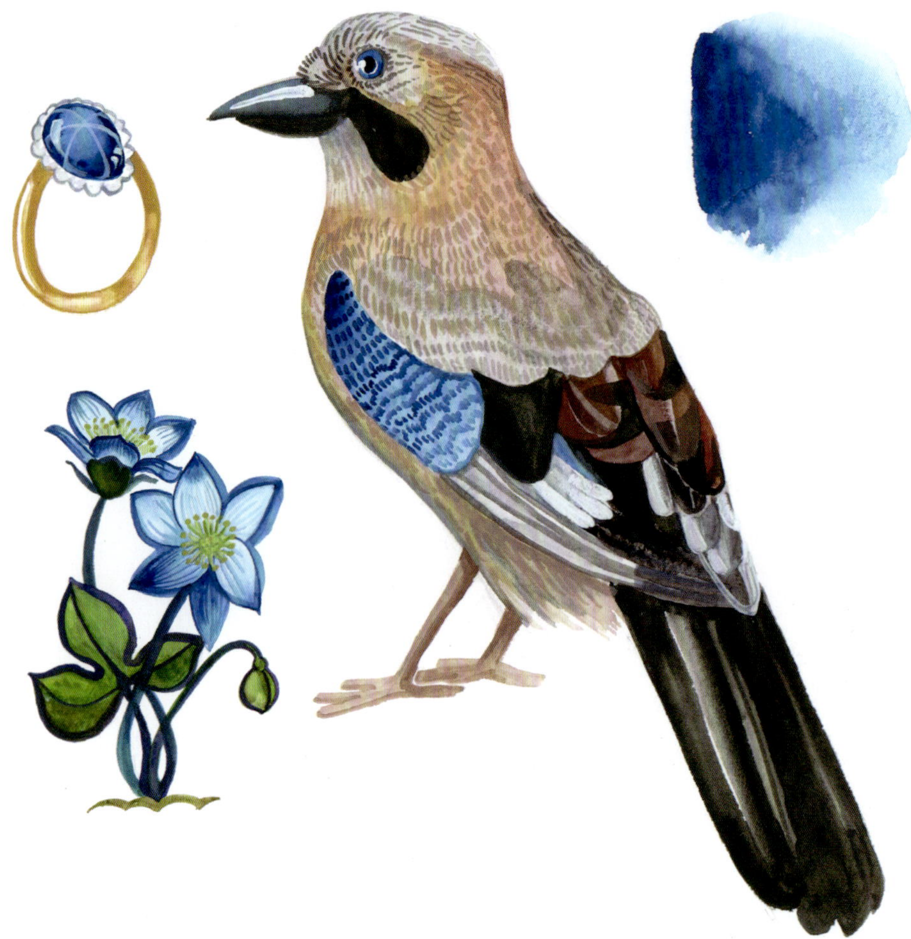

SYSTEMS BASED ON

NAME

Werner's Nomenclature of Colours started in 1774 as a way to catalog colors by comparing their appearance to rocks and minerals, and eventually also to plants and animals.

Abraham Gottlob Werner was a geologist, and his first book contained fifty-four minerals for which color was one of the important data points for identification. Over the years, with the help of his students, Werner's catalog gradually grew. In 1814, Scottish artist Patrick Syme expanded Werner's book to contain 108 minerals, and then, in 1821, 110 minerals.

Syme took Werner's mineral references and added comparisons in the animal and plant kingdoms. He also made the little color swatches and wrote the mixing recipes where needed.

For example, Berlin blue (a basic blue for Werner) was described as a blue with a certain portion of velvet black, adding a bit of gray plus a dash of carmine red. Then Syme would provide the natural world references: the wing feathers of a jay, the hepatica flowers, and blue sapphires.

Then, upping the game, along came Robert Ridgway. His very rigorous *Color Standards and Color Nomenclature* from 1912 was also aimed at naturalists and contained a whopping 1,115 distinct swatches, each with its own name. He intended his nomenclature to become the gold standard in color naming, but he also provided a few caveats in his introduction: "It should also be borne in mind that almost any object or substance varies more or less in color; and that therefore if the 'orange,' 'lemon,' 'chestnut' or 'lilac' does not exactly match in color a particular orange, lemon, chestnut, or lilac which one may compare it with, it may (in fact does) correspond with other specimens."[2]

While very evocative and poetic, these nomenclatures offer an inconsistent and inefficient way to standardize color, for the obvious reason that things in the natural world are varied and changing, and not all visual references are available to everyone in the same manner. However, this was the system used by nineteenth-century naturalists, including Charles Darwin, when describing their observations.

Maybe because of Werner's system or several that followed, or because of the imagination of art material makers, we still recall some colors based on their names. In my case, I reference several colors using the names from boxes of Crayola crayons or Prismacolor pencils. I have even come up with names for certain colors I like to use or look for but that I have not found in other naming systems—names that would not mean anything to you, but that sure work for me. So feel free to name a color you like for your enjoyment!

SYSTEMS BASED ON PIGMENT

The first known book dedicated to color-mixing based on pigments is a rare 1692 Dutch book titled *Traité des couleurs servant à la peinture à l'eau* (Treatise on colors used for water painting). The author, A. Boogert, of whom little is known, demonstrated diligently—across eight hundred handwritten pages with hand-painted swatches of color—how pigments change with precise dilutions and when mixed with other colors. This little book is the result of the paintings of the Dutch Golden Age, when lots of new pigments were developed and used by masters like Rembrandt and Vermeer. However, at the time it was impossible to reproduce a color book, so it is assumed there is only one copy of the book. Few artists would have been able to benefit from it.

Traité des couleurs servant à la peinture à l'eau has been dubbed the original Pantone book. But sadly, since it is

written in Old Dutch, which I cannot read, all I can do is swoon over the colors swatches of the facsimile copy I own.

While the mighty little Dutch book was not able to be disseminated due to the lack of printing technology, the well-known Pantone book's origin story is actually the result of a problem with modern printing. In the 1960s and before, each printer mixed their colors as they saw fit, trying to match colors without a standard. Everyone who has ever used a film camera remembers the ubiquitous yellow boxes of Kodak film. But Kodak Yellow, its brand color, did not always appear the same due to differences in production and printing of the boxes, and photographers buying film would perceive boxes with slightly darker variations of yellow as "old product." This problem led Dr. Lawrence Herbert, a chemist, to develop in 1963 what became the Pantone Matching System (PMS). Based on ten basic inks and precise recipes, it allows any designer to deliver color instructions for their client's projects and allows any printer to achieve uniform color across the board.

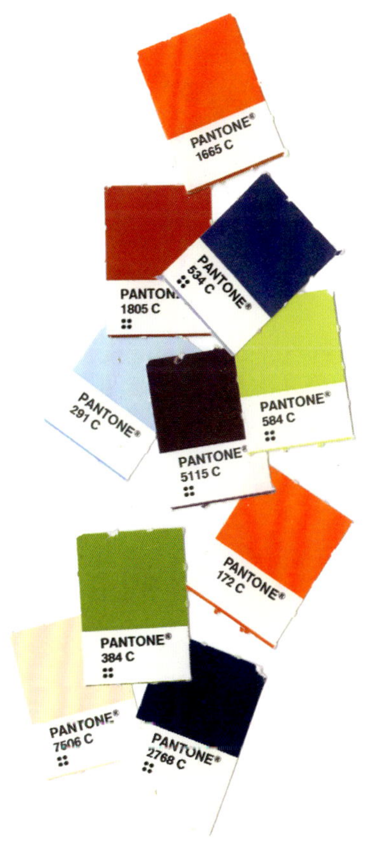

PRINTING COLOR: CMYK ROSETTE

A variety of printing methods, from woodcuts to etching, lithography to chromolithography, have allowed artists and bookmakers to create multiple copies of the same page or image. It was not until technology combined with photography through the invention of fast rotary press machines that offset printing—and the use of CMYK— came about. Fast, convenient, and reliable, offset printing uses four basic colors of inks—cyan, magenta, yellow, and black (represented by the letter *K*, standing for *key*)—to create the whole range of printed colors. Sometimes a spot color or two, or a unique ink referenced by Pantone, can be added for special effects, like neon ink.

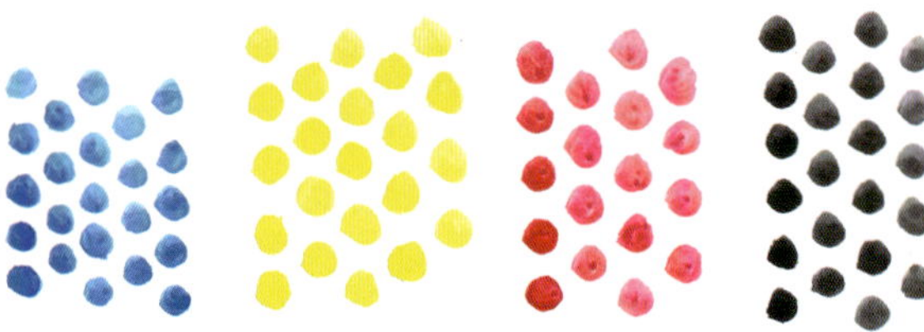

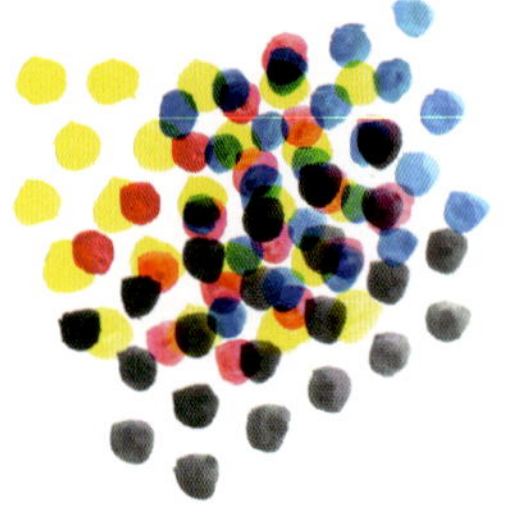

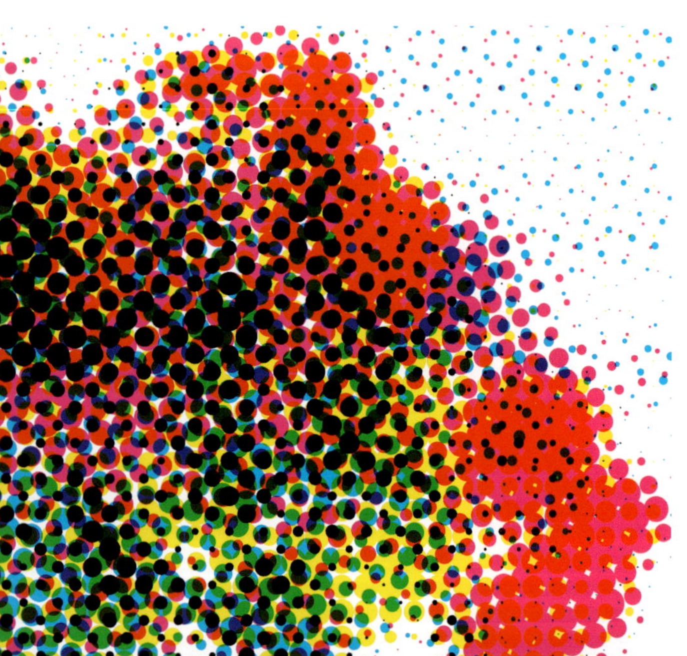

COLOR ON-SCREEN: RGB/HEX

RGB and HEX are the online cousins of CMYK. RGB stands for *red, green, blue*, the colors of light used on any screen, from color TVs to all our devices. These colored light beams combine to form all the colors we see. If CMYK inks combined get you to black, RGB lights combined lead you to white light.

Hex, or hexadecimal, colors are the very precise expression of RGB in digital media for consistent color matching on screens.

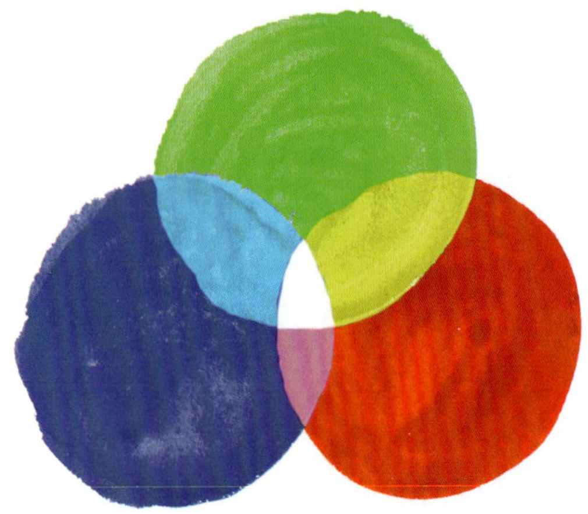

COLOR COLLECTIONS

Last but not least, there are those fabulous places that house huge color collections. Some are museum archives and others are art stores where shelves full of tens, hundreds, or thousands of little jars of pigment can be seen.

Some on my bucket list are

- The Harvard Art Museums' Forbes Pigment Collection, with over 2,500 samples
- Pigment Tokyo, an art supply store that is the stuff of color dreams
- A tour into the Kremer Pigmente archive in Germany

Maybe one day.... A girl can dream ... in color.

COLOR AS PERSONAL EXPERIENCE

Understanding color theory, following color nomenclature as a reference, and identifying color with precision for printing or screens are useful tools and knowledge, but they are not sufficient or even necessary to get you to a place of full color love.

That can only happen if color is approached as a personal experience, as something coming from within, as an extension and expression of your authentic, unique self.

A well-developed color point of view includes understanding and applying color while being aware of how it relates to mood, memory, place and time, and the story being told. Getting to this place involves an ever-changing personal experience resulting from your unique eye for color.

What matters most in developing your eye for color is really making it your own journey derived from who you are, your memories, your places, your imagination, the attention and curiosity with which you observe your surroundings, and the experimentation and ongoing practice with color you develop as a result. Here, through these pages, I present some bits of my own color journey. May they become useful seeds for you to cultivate.

Carl Jung

Carl Jung, in his exploration and explanations of the human psyche, created a color-coding system to help interpret dreams and visions. Each color, he explained, had a symbolic aspect and psychological meaning. While these codes are not as universal as he believed, I find them interesting and occasionally amusing. For example, regarding red, he says that the psychological experience of it will connect you with primal instincts, desires, and emotions. While we often connect red with anger, the primal aspect feels too wild to my taste, as not all reds feel that raging to me. Picture a glorious field of summer poppies or a perfectly ripe tomato: not aggressive at all.

However, we all can generally agree on how meditative and tranquil blue is.

The painter Wassily Kandinsky also looked into the connections between color, mood, and spirituality in his book Concerning the Spiritual in Art. *While he does go through the general symbolisms of each color—red and passion, white and silence, black and death—he also goes beyond, to the uniqueness of each artist. Kandinsky says that artists should create from their "inner necessity," where color choices reflect their individual experience, perception, and spiritual systems of beliefs. Something that makes Kandinsky and his relationship with colors interesting is that he experienced synesthesia, a sensorial condition in which one sense is engaged in perceiving and, involuntarily, a second sense jumps in. Kandinsky would see colors when hearing music, and vice versa. Thus, his color explorations and paintings had a soundtrack he could hear! He painted so that it would also be harmonious for him to "listen" to his painting. How I'd love to be a synesthete!*

THE COLOR-HARVESTING LIFESTYLE

Creating the Habit of Observing, Analyzing, and Creating with Color

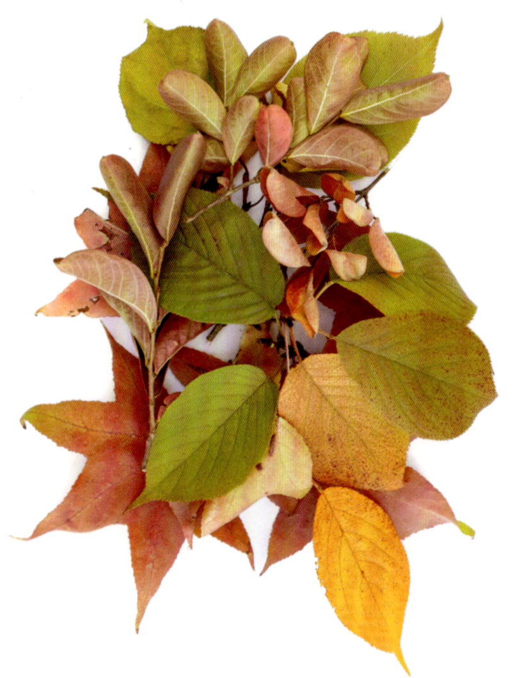

"You are what you do. . . .

If you think about becoming an artist all the time, then you are a thinker.

If you dream about being an artist, you are a dreamer.

If you read about becoming an artist, then you are a reader.

If you study art, you are a student.

If you do the dishes, or vacuum or declutter your house to avoid making art, then you are a cleaning crew.

But if you show up every day and make a little bit of art, however incomplete, or unsatisfying or misguided or not how Georgia O'Keeffe would have done it, you are an artist."

—*Mary Jo Hoffman,* Still: The Art of Noticing[3]

Fear color not . . .
. . . and you will never have a color rut.
All these years as a color-curious person have helped me develop a level of color fluency that prevents me from falling into the nefarious rut. It pains me to see people paralyzed by not knowing what to do with color, or being so afraid of color that they succumb, for example, to the cozy, safe blanket of a beige house or think they must hire a color consultant to paint their home.

While I agree that there is sometimes a need for color professionals—I am one—to be hired for their expertise, I think everyone should feel comfortable enough to experiment with and apply their color ideas to their everyday lives. And while there are no bad colors, there are bad color ideas, so training your eye will empower you to develop *good* color ideas that speak in your voice.

The worst argument people offer for staying in a beige mind space is when they say "I am not an artist" or "I am not creative." Granted, not everyone is a professional artist, but we all have a creative side and a sensitivity for color, just waiting to be nurtured and unleashed. This is not a creativity problem but a mindset problem that can be overcome. Even professional artists fall into color humdrum—always using the same colors, over and over, without true conviction, sometimes under the guise of having a "signature palette."

My favorite way to search for color is what I have come to call *color harvesting*. You could also call it scavenging, picking, plucking, or foraging. It does not necessarily involve flowers, fruits, and veggies, though those are some of my favorite chromatic sources. Basically, I am always on the lookout for interesting colors and color combinations around me. And by becoming truly observant of color—anywhere and everywhere—I have developed a strong eye and true personal color love. And so can you.

How do I do this? Wherever I am, without my computer or my art materials, I have the best color tools: my eyes, which are always curious and ready to find interesting combinations. Sometimes I browse my surroundings, scanning for a specific color. Sometimes I cherry-pick with my eyes a variety of tones, tints, and shades that might look good together, or I stumble upon something already made up of combined colors: a flower,

a shop window, a well-designed package, a piece of clothing, a magnificent sunset. I make a mental note of what I saw and why I liked it, or I get back in the studio and quickly scribble a palette representing it, to be used later when the opportunity arises. Sometimes I bump into a really interesting and unique color, something I normally don't use, and I linger on that idea, trying to find a place for it in my work. Needless to say, over the decades, I have amassed A LOT of color notes and palettes, both on paper and in my head.

You can jump into your own color harvesting in a heroic way, like doing a one hundred day project or a full year or more of daily practice—that is how I started creating the images in this book—or it can just be something you incorporate gradually but consistently into your life.

"The more one looks, the more one sees and the more one sees, the better one knows where to look."
—attributed to Pierre Teilhard de Chardin

Developing a color-harvesting habit, for me, is also a form of mindful meditation. It is a mental state of being aware, ready to catch a fleeting moment, and unwilling to risk missing it—visual FOMO? It prevents me from walking through the world on visual autopilot. It anchors me in the present and quiets my monkey mind. When I am deep into color-harvesting mode, I am in that blissful state of focus also known as *being in the zone*. I also practice sit-down breathing meditation, but when I involve color and turn the moment into active meditation, I know I am doing something good for my art, not only for my brain.

I must say, color harvesting is also a really good remedy for boredom! Think of all those color combinations you can find by observing people's clothes while going on a stroll, or leafing through a magazine at a doctor's office, or perusing a seed catalog. It is just a matter of shifting your mindset from bored to curious, and it is the curious, observant eye that will reap the reward.

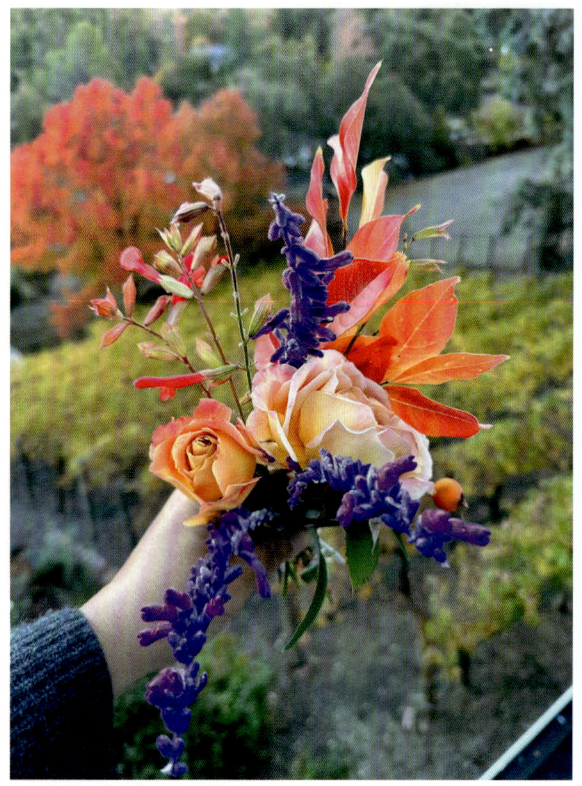

"The universe is full of magical things patiently waiting for our wits to grow sharper."
—Eden Phillpotts[4]

When do I color harvest? At this point, it is something I do daily, anywhere, everywhere. It is my modus operandi, my default way to take in the view. It is also the way I access any creative project; I usually start by thinking about what colors I will use, either from my imagination or from my palette archive.

Sometimes my daily color-harvesting practice is just about observing and making mental notes. Sometimes I pull out my phone camera and take a snapshot of something I stumble upon—in a book, in a painting, in the garden, in the street—as a memento of that fleeting impression.

Sometimes, I actually color harvest with pruners and scissors or rummage around my house for spontaneous or specific colors I want to work with, and then I produce a still life photo of the gathered elements. This photo can be the finished piece of my Abstract Naturalism creative project—a lot of which you will see in the pages of this book—or it can be the starting point to finding really interesting colors I might not have normally used. After observing and analyzing them, I can go ahead and create something else: a design project for a client, an illustration or surface pattern design, or a piece of art.

Hmmmm . . . I see a process here: I OBSERVE, then ANALYZE, then CREATE.

This process is what has come to be the backbone of this book, with each chapter structured accordingly:

- **Observe:** Each chapter opens with an essay about observing and being observant using examples from art history and personal learning experiences. These essays are quite nutrient dense and meant to be a source of food for thought.
- **Analyze:** Then come the pages containing photography and color palettes. The photos are the result of my constant "color harvesting," completed weekly, consistently, over the past several years. They are created from both natural and human-made things found in my garden and my house (oh! all those drawers!). Once I've collected them, not for what they are but for their colors, I forget they are flowers or toys. I randomly arrange them to observe their coloring and analyze them in combination with other colors. Creating a matching painted color palette from the photos is a way to take the analysis a

step further. It allows me to synthesize the colors found in the gathered objects I've photographed. The best part of finding color this way is that I sometimes discover colors I would never have thought of using if I had just pulled out my watercolor box. The palettes resulting from the analysis of the images become ready-made color ideas looking for a story.

- **Create:** The last part of each chapter is about applying these color observations and analyses to a creative project. I have come up with one or two project suggestions in each chapter inspired by a variety of creative disciplines. Even if you are not a professional in those disciplines or are just starting a creative journey, I encourage you to give the exercises a try anyway. Be a textile or interior designer for a day!

I am, of course, not the first one to follow this simple, three-step method; my inspiration comes from the brilliant, timeless minds of the Bauhaus teachers. The Bauhaus was the legendary early-twentieth-century school where art, design, craft, and architecture were first taught under one roof. The aim of teaching was not to produce fancy, beautiful objects for the upper classes, but to design for everyone. "Artist and artisan united!" was their motto. The Bauhaus served as a catalyst of modernity in all these disciplines, with the technology of the time at their service to produce beautiful, quality pieces for all. Sadly, the school only lasted for fourteen years; it was forced to close in Berlin in 1933. Yet its many teachings are timeless and continue to be thoroughly current. I have deep admiration for those brilliant teachers and their art and design, but above all, their ideas are a continued source for me. I strongly encourage you to dig deep into anything Bauhaus related—it is a treasure trove!

I first learned about the Bauhaus in history class while attending graphic design school, but it was a few years later, when I was doing an art installation in Germany, that some fellow artists and I decided to take a road trip to Dessau to visit the school. It was almost a pilgrimage! Upon arriving, there it was, the legendary vertical signage spelling *BAUHAUS*, the wall of windows with the interesting opening mechanism, and the balconies with the rounded tubular railings from the

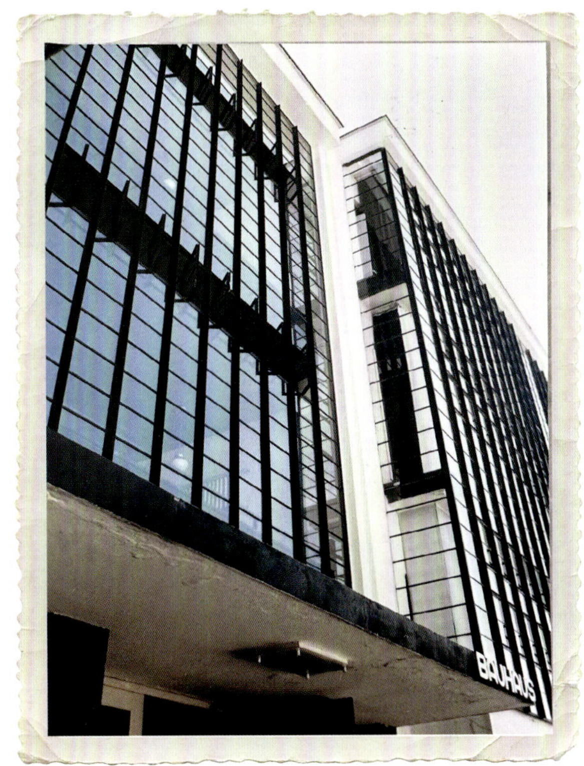

1930s posters. We even sat in the auditorium in the same poses as our Bauhaus heroes: Gropius, Kandinsky, Klee, Albers, Moholy-Nagy, Delaunay, Mies van der Rohe, Itten, and others. Oh, how I wished I had been able to attend this school!

While the building is still there, it is now occupied by a different school. But the teachings of the Bauhaus are what have really lived on.

Most notably, the teachers and students at the Bauhaus followed an intuitive method that celebrated individual vision and artistry. It was similar to the scientific method, but for art and design. Proponents believed that every creative project should be worked on in three successive steps: OBSERVE → ANALYZE → CREATE.

OBSERVE

At the Bauhaus, students were encouraged to constantly keep their eyes open to both the natural world and human-made environments and their contents. Whether their observations were meant to enrich their visual language or to be used in a specific project, the students noted and collected them as a researcher would do. Observations could include artistic or cultural artifacts. The students also worked on exercises and projects designed to develop their powers of observation. There were no preconceived notions of what one was hunting for. The goal was simple: Keep your eyes open and note what catches your eye.

Following these recommendations, I started color harvesting. What the students at the Bauhaus were doing for all aspects of design became my way to engage with color. This eyes-open, no-preconceived-notions way of finding color all around me allowed me to see new combinations I hadn't previously noticed. The random colors surrounding me—from the plants and human-made objects that I used to create the images in this book to the whole vast universe of art in museums, books, and world cultures I have been noticing for years—became a wide panorama for me to observe and train my eye.

When observing, you become a hunter-gatherer: You may be gathering at random whatever appears ripe to your eyes, or you may hunt for a specific color.

A good way to start this practice is to purposefully challenge yourself to be extremely color observant for a week while taking notes or snapshots with your phone of things that catch your eye because of their color. After a week, go back and notice if there is any pattern or any surprise. This does not need to turn into a major project; it is just a warm-up for your eyes to jump-start the color-harvesting habit.

One of my favorite ways to hunt for color is something I used to do when I lived in New York City: Before leaving my apartment, I would mentally pick a color of the day, and then as I walked, in the subway, all around, I would search for that color and sort of blur, or gray out, with my imagination the rest of the colors. The objects in my chosen color became like the colored fish in the black-and-white movie *Rumble Fish*.

Try doing this; no need to make an illustration, just do it with your mind.

Later, when I started gathering and photographing color palettes, I used what I could find just outside my studio. As an avid gardener, I turned to everything growing, blooming, fruiting, or decaying within the fence of my yard through the seasons. I called this series Color/Flora or Abstract Naturalism. For me, it was a way to catch a fleeting moment, because certain things were in peak in my yard for just a few days a year.

No garden? No problem! I used botanicals from my yard because I have them, I love them, and they are a part of my own story. But you can color harvest in many places and with all kinds of things, especially those that are meaningful to you. I eventually moved indoors, expanding the series to use trinkets, tchotchkes, and toys I found everywhere in my home. Go ahead and be observant; you may need to squint to get rid of unnecessary details that distract from color. Make it a habit and you will develop a keen eye. The following are a few examples of great places to find color.

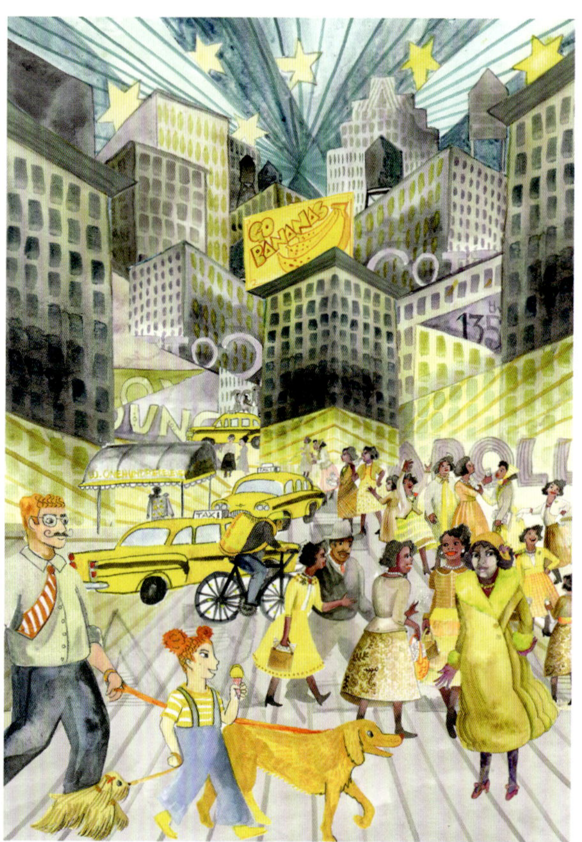

1. **A landscape, seascape, or cityscape,** like the view of Mount Diablo in front of my house: a gradient from green to golden, with a streak of vermilion and cobalt shadows.

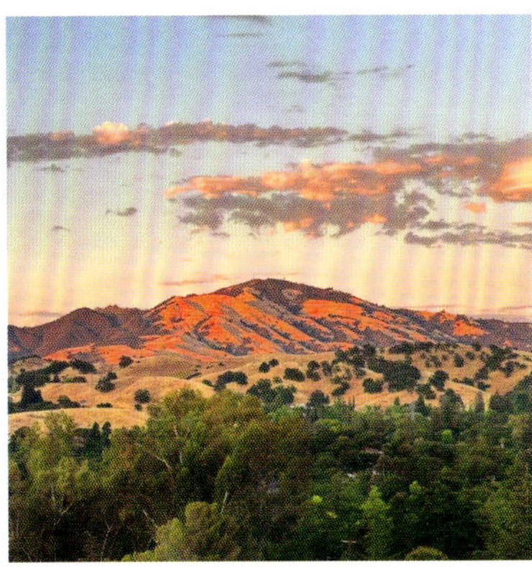

2. **Out on the town.** Look for people with interesting clothes, the overlap of cars, or signs.

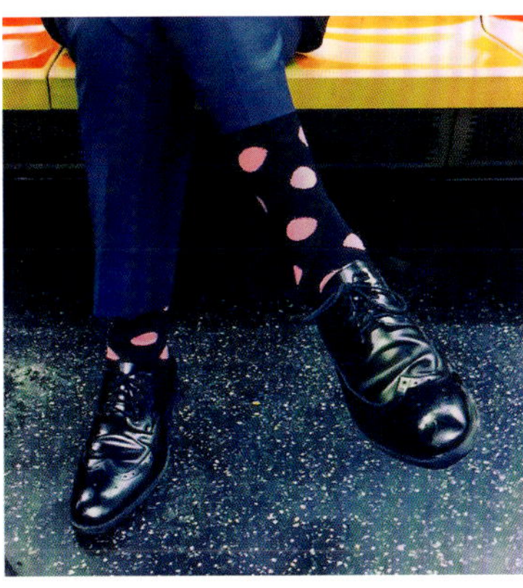

3. **New and old things—** trinkets of all kinds, with bright new colors or dirty, peeling paint.

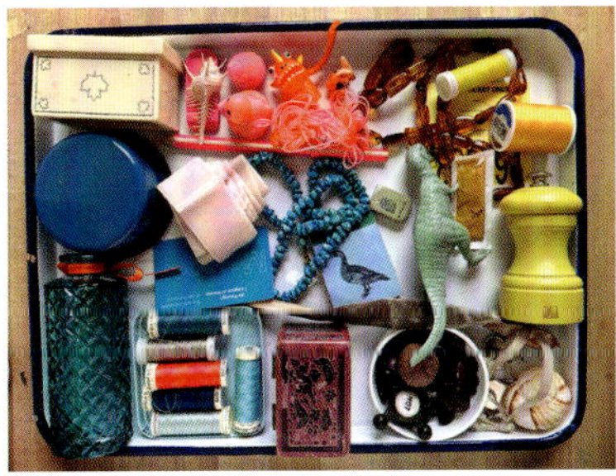

4. **The farmers market** and the veggie aisle. When you cook or prepare ingredients, try cooking in full color!

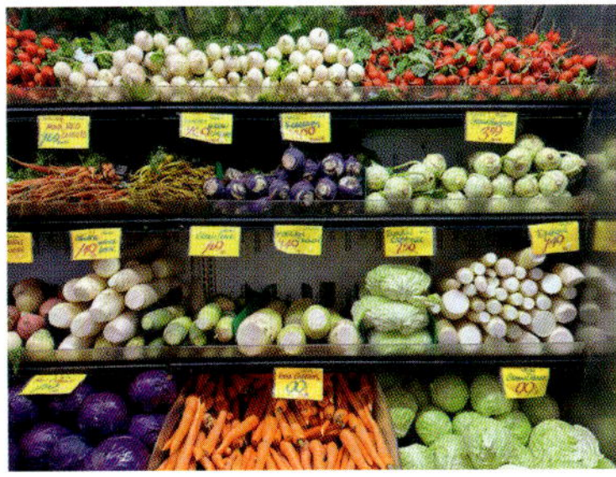

5. **At fashion shows** or fashion museum exhibits, and on clothing racks, in your closet and in stores.

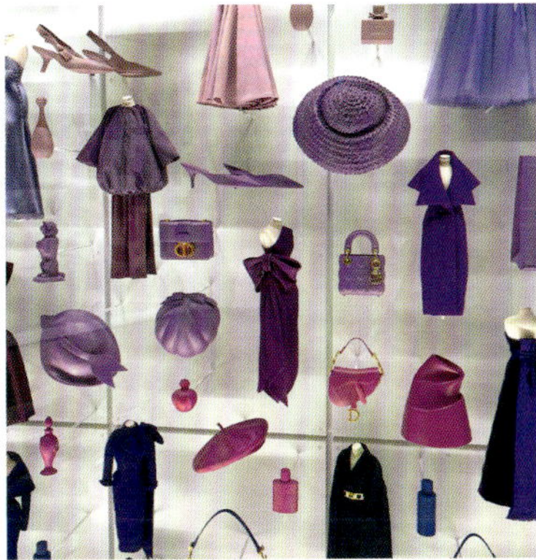

6. **A museum:** Rather than photographing whole paintings, collect little close-ups to get you into the artist's color mindset, close enough to see their hand in the brushstrokes.

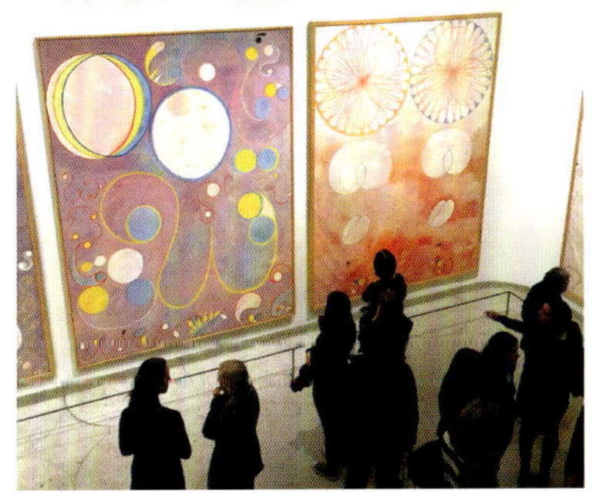

7. **The books on your bookshelf.**

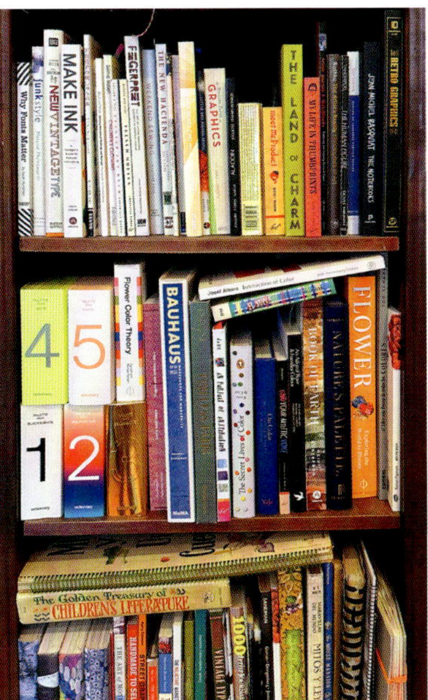

8. **Photos and souvenirs** you bring home from your travels.

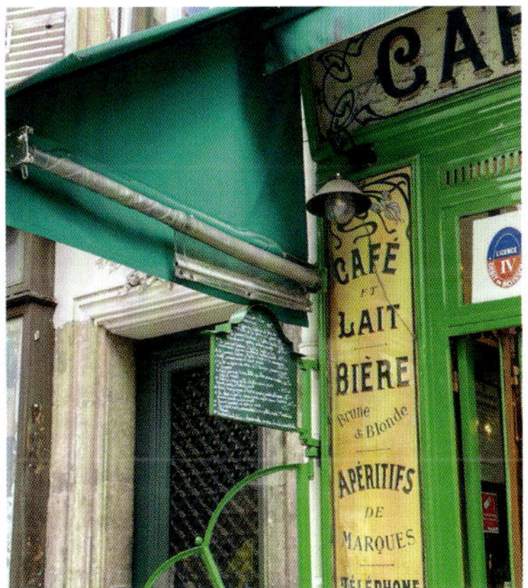

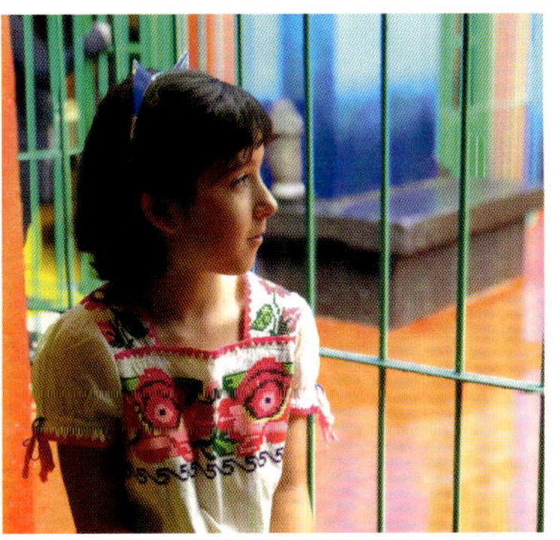

ANALYZE

Time to become a color judge and make sense of the interesting bits and pieces you've gathered.

You should collect your observations with an open mind, a bit aimlessly, in search of whatever catches your eye. In contrast, you *analyze* using critical thinking to evaluate, move things around, discard what does not work, and look for connections between the parts you keep.

Throwing random things together, like dice in a game, and then observing and analyzing them is one of my favorite ways to understand color. Sometimes, a basketful of botanicals from the garden will render a single photo, but sometimes it will multiply in tens of variations: monochrome groupings, tone-on-tone versions, or contrasting combinations. I have used a lot of these contrasting pairings in my branding and graphic design projects, and I've used color triads extensively in my paintings and illustrations. The analysis that comes after color harvesting has created a chromatic library for me to access when I need it.

As I analyze what I call my orbs of Abstract Naturalism (the photos of botanical colors from the garden) or my flat-lay photographs of objects, I am also coming to understand color relationships and interactions, as the Bauhaus taught. Throughout this book, I will give you a range of ways to approach this analysis and think about color relationships.

The included annotations and color palettes represent my conclusions and a reference library of my color thoughts for future use. While this process is a bit more left-brained, more rational and structured, making color palettes is not an exact science; it is an intuitive process. As with every creative expression, color combinations will always be the result of the artist's keen eye, good taste, imagination, intuition, and personal point of view.

"For me, color is a vibe. I don't do color of the year. Having a single color as a guide is not enough. It is like having a one-word poem. One color is not a vibe; an intuitively put-together palette is what projects this vibe. Color work is a completely intuitive process. With color, one cannot be an intellectual. When I am making a piece of art and I'm working with color, my hands and brush just go to the colors. I smoosh them down, and then I take another color and I smooth that one down. I just know intuitively what I want next: another muddy or vivid or big color, or small one, or dark one.

We respond to art viscerally. Color is the immediate way we connect to a piece of art.

An artist's color palette is a reflection of who they are at the deepest level because it is so intuitive. Finding your color style and your color palette is an essential part of developing your art style. Just think of great artists and you immediately think about their use of color.

I always recommend artists to work on a variety of color ranges. If all you show is bright colors, a client is never going to hire you for a moody piece. They hire from what they see, so it is important to show a variety of pieces with different color vibes to open up the possibilities.

Color can be bold and aggressive, it can be soft and understated. Mysterious. Magical. It is the most powerful psychological tool that we have as creatives."

—Lilla Rogers, artist, art agent, art teacher, and founder of Make Art That Sells

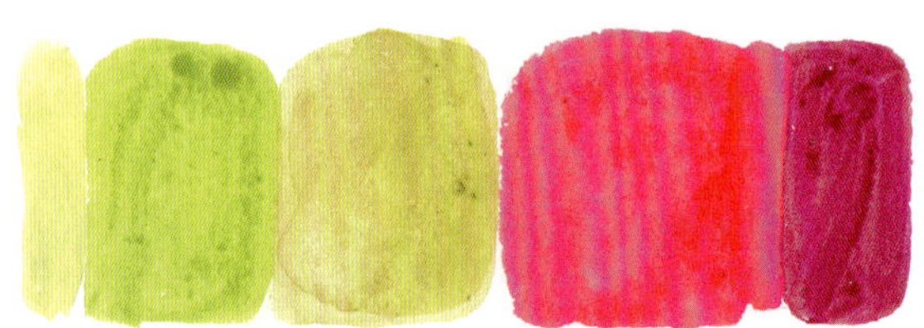

CREATE

While all the observing and analyzing can just be an eye–brain practice, the way to mature your instinct and explore ideas and opinions that form your aesthetic taste is to actually apply your observation and analysis onto a new creation. The Bauhaus emphasized that the process is not complete until a tangible object is created based on the previous steps.

But creativity does not only happen in the studio while doing client work or personal design or art projects like the ones in this book. Color harvesting can also become, as happened for me, a lifestyle: I cook in color, I apply my color palettes to my home and my clothing, I do garden experiments by color planting (obsessively cultivating blue flowers), I do flower bouquets . . . You get the point. My eye is now always on the lookout for color!

My little OBSERVE → ANALYZE → CREATE practice has also served me in major life transitions and helped me connect more deeply with people in my life.

For gratitude: I visited my friend Claude's beach house on Fire Island, and as a thank-you for his hosting I made these images with what I found and gathered (with his permission) around his property. I set up the objects on his weathered wooden deck instead of my normal white background since it better captured the spirit of the place. We shot the photos together, and the memory of that moment lives on.

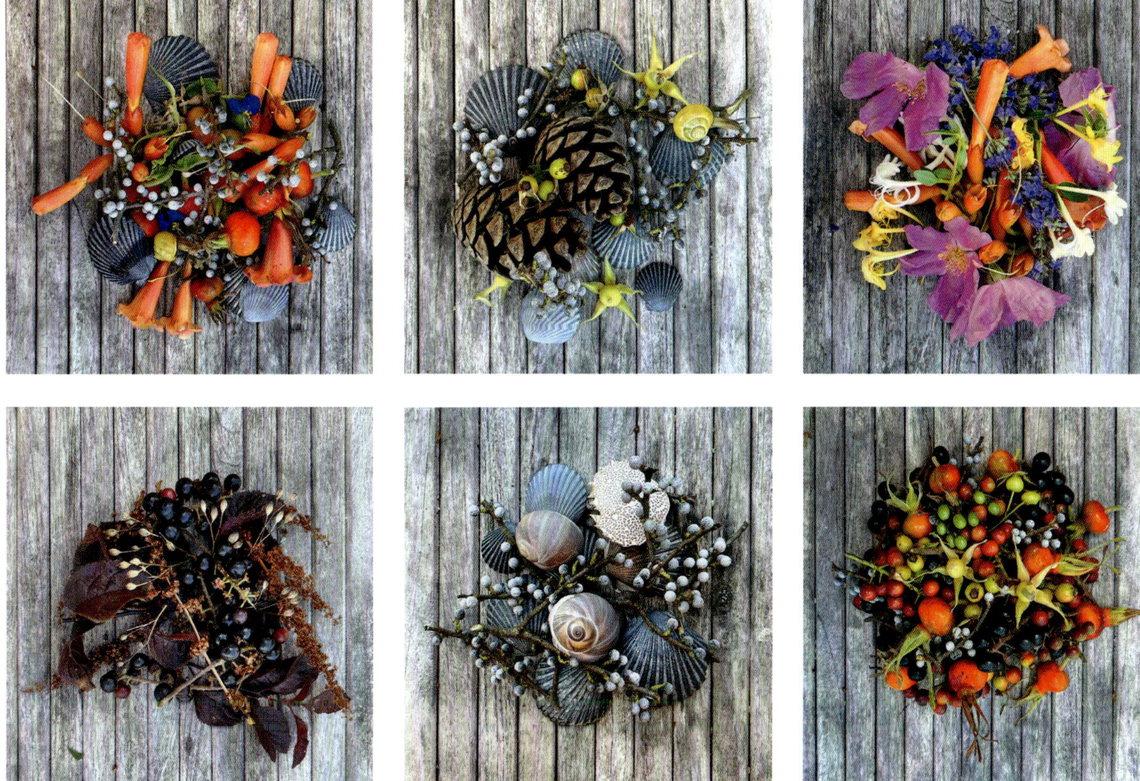

For solace: While my father was in his final days in hospice care in Salamanca, Spain, I took short walks around the fields surrounding the hospital. In these fields I color harvested the wildflowers of the Castillian spring, and the beauty of making these color orbs and leaving them in the fields brought comfort to my sadness.

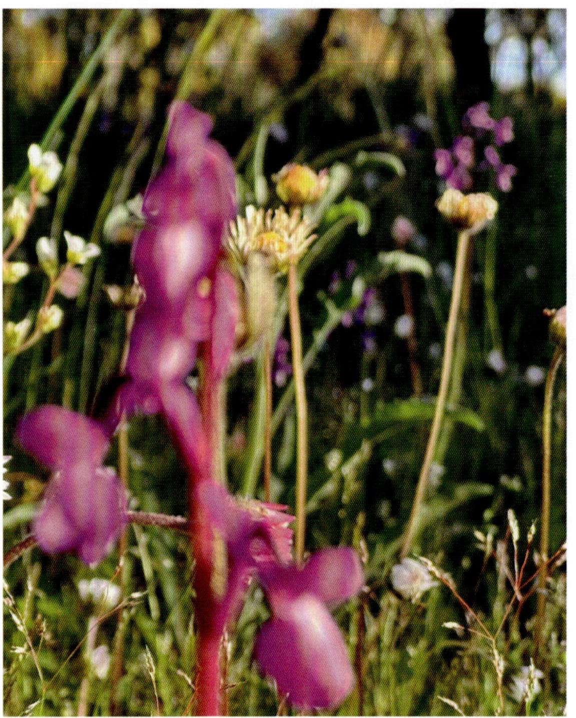

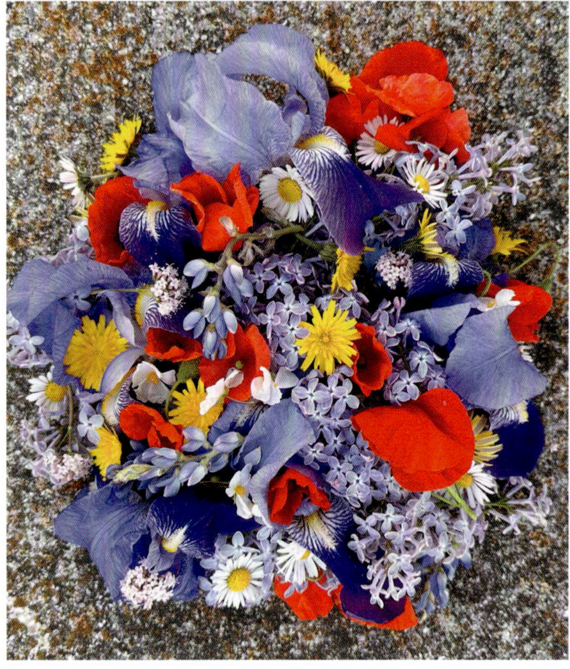

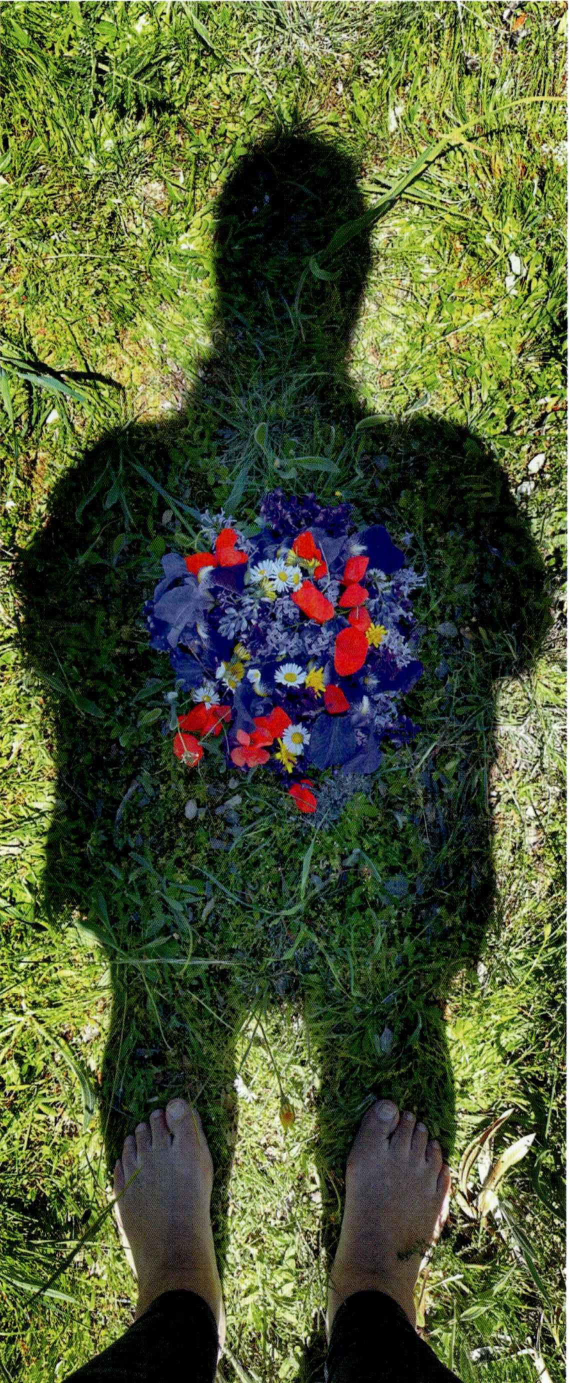

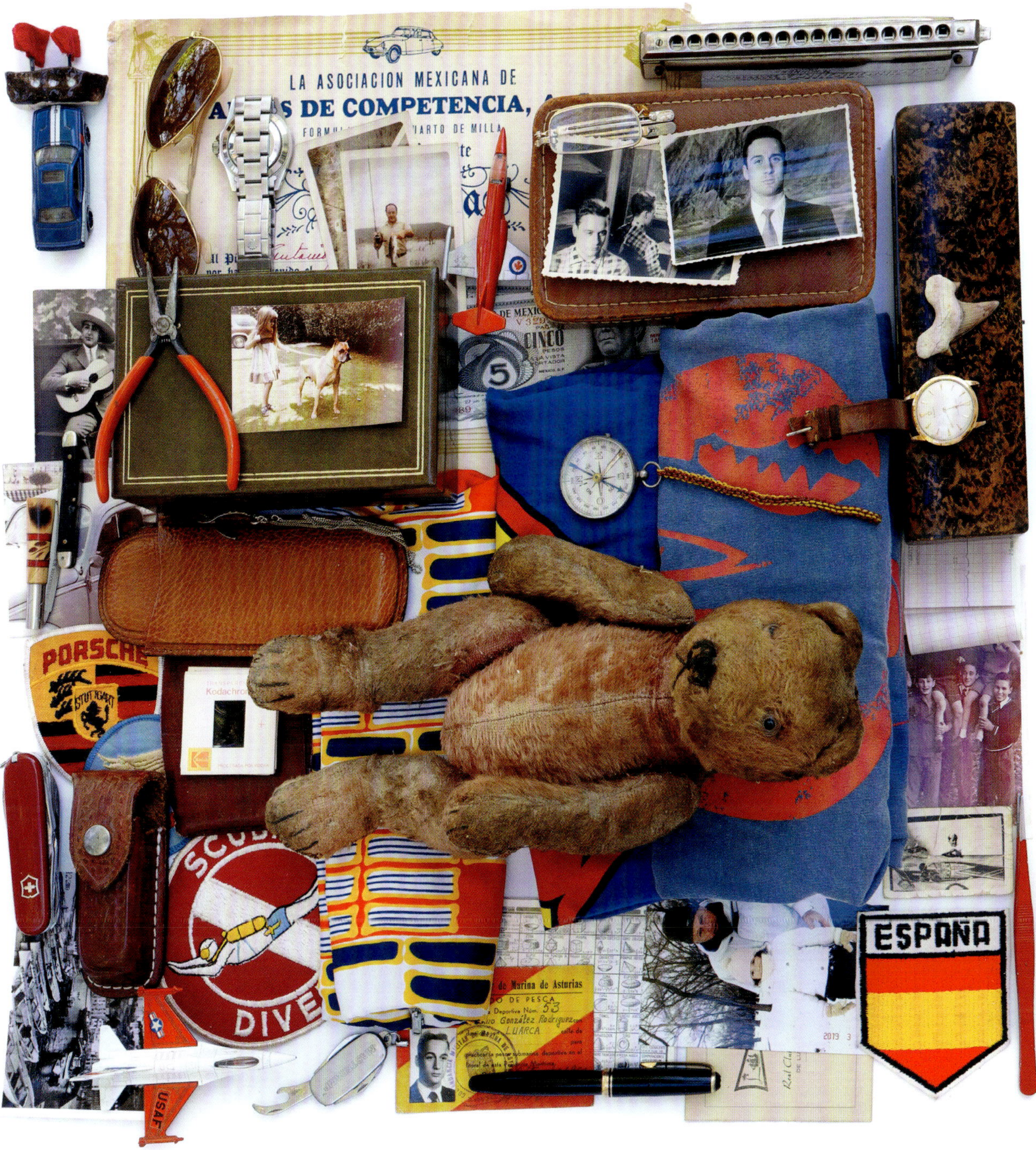

For remembrance: Back in California, after my father's passing, I opened my suitcase containing a final set of his personal belongings. I noticed the color of these things and was blown away by how much these colors reminded me of him. I made this flat-lay portrait of him.

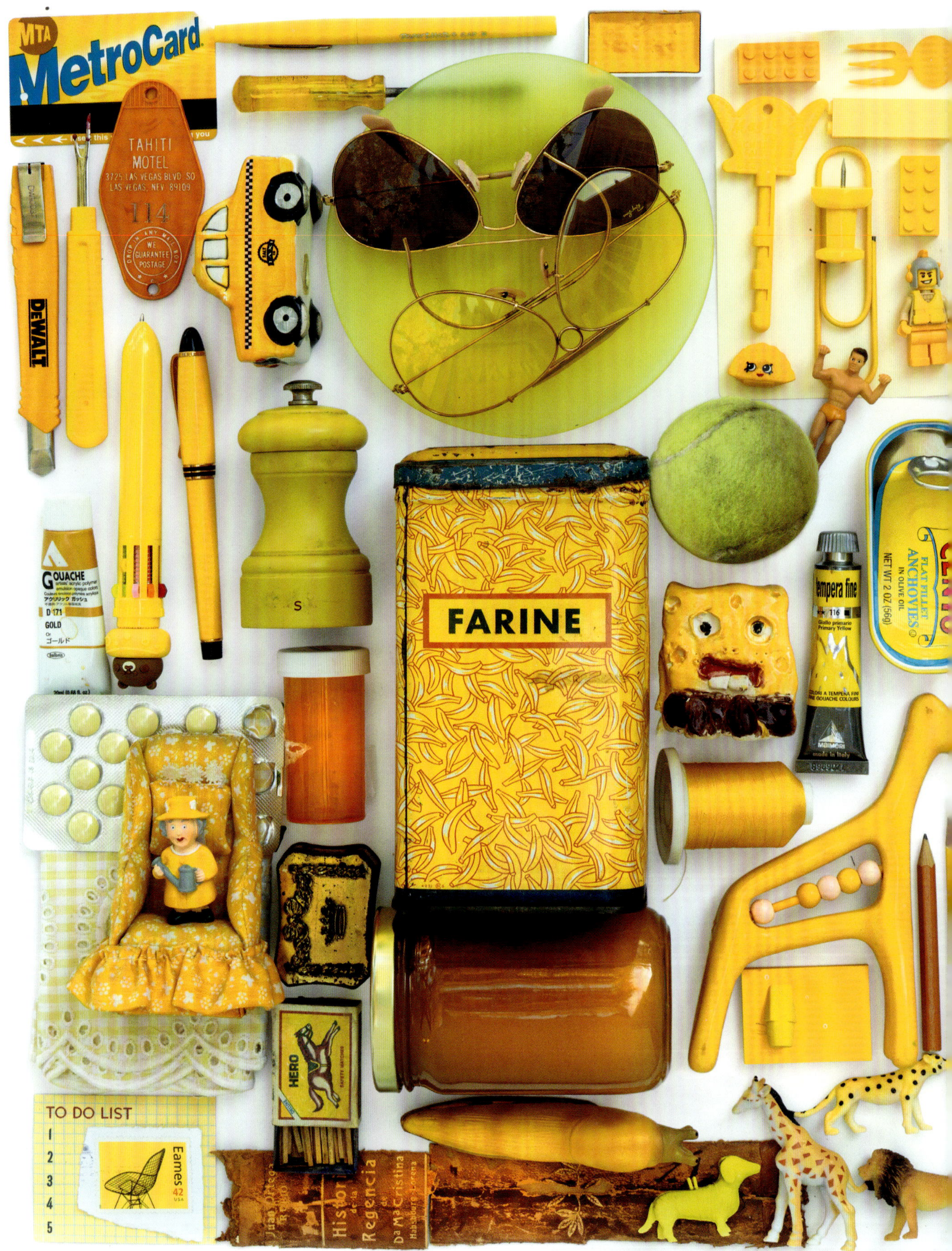

MTA
MetroCard
TAHITI
MOTEL
3725 LAS VEGAS BLVD. SO.
LAS VEGAS, NEV. 89109
114
WE
GUARANTEE
POSTAGE
DeWALT
GOUACHE
GOLD
FARINE
tempera fine
Primary Yellow
ANCHOVIES
IN OLIVE OIL
NET WT 2 OZ (56g)
HERO
SAFETY MATCHES
TO DO LIST
1
2
3
4
5
Eames
42
USA
Regencia

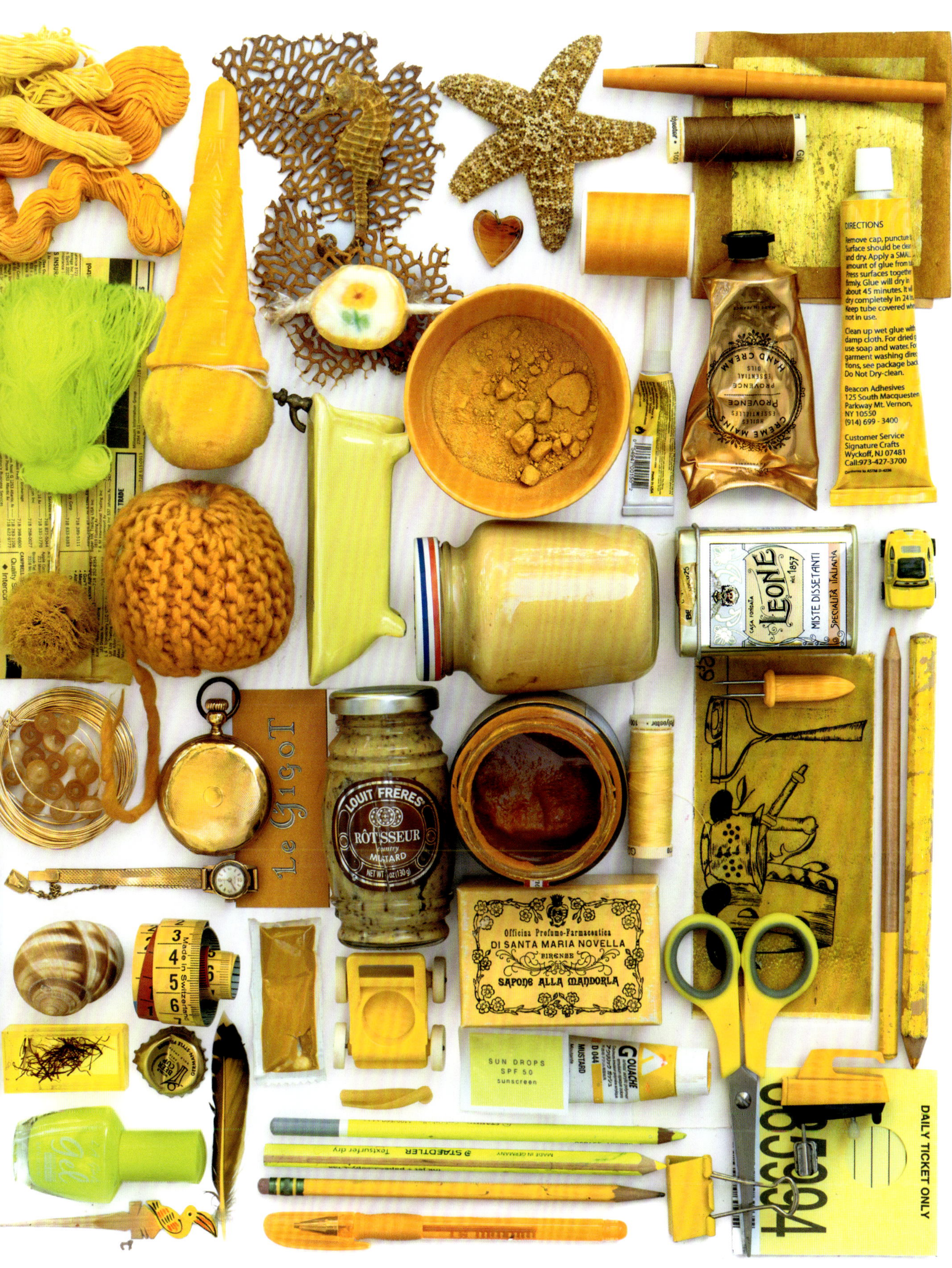
DIRECTIONS
Remove cap, puncture
Surface should be clean
and dry. Apply a SMALL
amount of glue from the
Press surfaces together
firmly. Glue will dry in
about 45 minutes. It will
dry completely in 24 hours
Keep tube covered when
not in use.

Clean up wet glue with a
damp cloth. For dried glue
use soap and water. For
garment washing direc-
tions, see package back.
Do Not Dry-clean.

Beacon Adhesives
125 South Macquesten
Parkway Mt. Vernon,
NY 10550
(914) 699 - 3400

Customer Service
Signature Crafts
Wyckoff, NJ 07481
Call:973-427-3700

CRÈME MAINS
HUILES ESSENTIELLES
PROVENCE
PROVENCE
ESSENTIAL OILS
HAND CREAM

CASA FONDATA
LEONE
NEL 1857
MISTE DISSETANTI
SPECIALITÀ ITALIANA

Le GigoT

LOUIT FRÈRES
RÔTISSEUR
country
MUSTARD
NET WT 4 oz (130 g)

Officina Profumo-Farmaceutica
DI SANTA MARIA NOVELLA
FIRENZE
SAPONE ALLA MANDORLA

Made in Switzerland

SUN DROPS
SPF 50
sunscreen

GOUACHE
D 044
MUSTARD

STAEDTLER   Textsurfer dry
MADE IN GERMANY

05304
DAILY TICKET ONLY

1.

NOT THE BASIC FOUR-CRAYON BOX

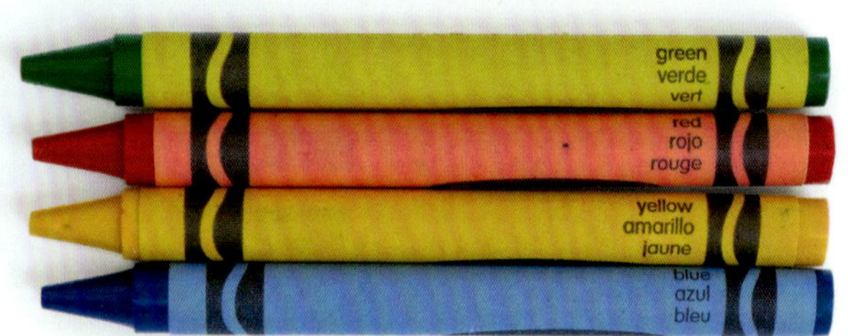

How to Make the Most out of Monochromes

N owadays, we all generally start in the same place: making art in kindergarten. We learn the basic color names: blue, yellow, red—green, orange, and purple come later. We get those kid-safe paints; we have that original crayon box with first four, then eight, then eventually more colors.

We start making art with very basic colors, which gets us painting the sky blue, the trees green, and the sun yellow. I was always an artistic kid and very color curious; every chance I had, I asked for painting classes, so by age five I was already taking classes with a *real* artist, a printmaker. That is where I first fell in love with painting. With the abundance of little jars of paint, I set out to discover what basic colors could do, and that is how I uncovered, in my mind, the big kindergarten lie that blue, red, and yellow are the primary colors that can be mixed to create all the other colors. I vividly remember the day I mixed blue and yellow to create green—my childhood favorite color—and red and yellow to create orange. But when I mixed blue and red, the result was not the lovely purple I had been told to expect: It was muddy. What I really needed was magenta; red, with its little bit of yellow, was not the right thing to make purple.

I continued making color mixes to find the colors I liked and the ones I didn't, such as various muddy, gloomy purples, browns, and not-too-black blacks. What I remember most and carry with me is the feeling of being a color alchemist. That was a game-changing moment for me.

The other thing we got as kids, especially when the crayon box expanded beyond the basic eight colors, was the imagery and poetry of evocative color names.

Let's take yellow. My favorites are canary yellow, lemon yellow, sunflower yellow, mustard yellow, gold, honey, daffodil, corn, straw, wheat, and saffron. These names immediately put an image in your mind; they help you see many yellows beyond the basic, pure yellow. You can buy these colors, or you can mix them by using the name as a mental note for reference: Picture something, then replicate the nuances of that color in your palette.

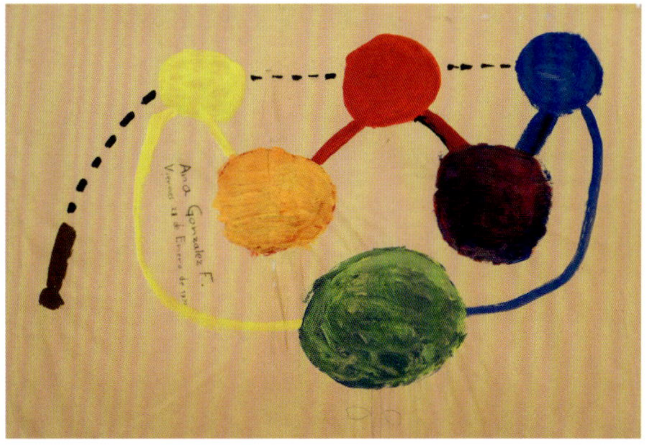

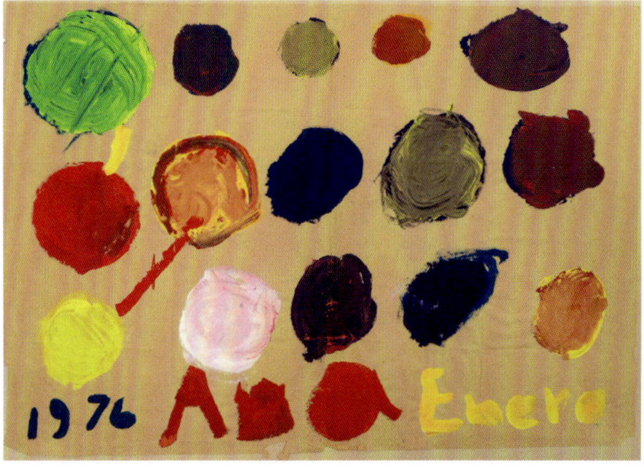

↑ These are the color experiments I did back then in my art class in the artist's garage. This is the moment when I discovered I did not have to use the paint out of a tube, that I could mix colors at will. I was hooked! However, I also discovered the need to use magenta instead of red to really get all the colors.

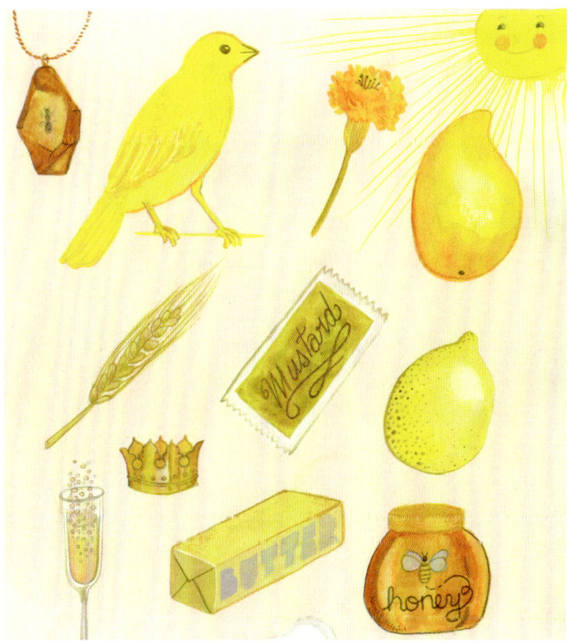

MONOCHROME ART

In art, a monochrome piece uses a single color within this wide range of potential. It can use one or two variations or as many as desired. Many artists have created art using monochrome palettes either by necessity or by a self-imposed aesthetic limitation.

Ellsworth Kelly made numerous abstract paintings and sculptures using a single bright color: a pure yellow, a bright red, an emerald green, a cobalt blue. While he used commercially available paints and pigments, he carefully and masterfully selected these hues and mixed them himself. His approach was highly intuitive and personal. He chose his colors with precision and intention. The beautiful emerald green he used was so personal to his work that it is also known as Kelly green.

Kelly also worked extensively with yellow, and while a majority of his pieces are flat abstract shapes, there are some that explore vibrancy, light, and shadow using two or three variations of yellow. Sometimes the variations are very subtle, as in *Yellow over Yellow*; sometimes he contrasted the brightest yellow with a slightly orange yellow or ochre to denote volume, as in his cube painting or his *Two Yellows* patterned panels.

When I think of an artist who committed his whole body of work to a single color and applied it purposefully, as a signature, with full intensity and consistency, I think of Yves Klein and his namesake blue. From paintings to sculptures to performance pieces, he always used the same blue, a super-intense custom color made with synthetic ultramarine and resin. It is velvety and matte, yet it seems to glow. The only true way to fully take in Klein's ode to blue is to see these pieces in person; that is how rich it is!

For Klein, this particular color provided him with a spiritual and mystical quality that he described as immaterial. It gave his art pieces a transcendence that reflected his philosophical ideas about the cosmos. The pureness of the color and its consistent use also served to eliminate distractions and focus him on the spirit of the piece. Plus, this color became an immediate identifier of his work.

Since each color has certain mood associations, a monochrome palette (whether simple or highly nuanced) can be used for emotional aesthetic choices.

The Blue Period of Pablo Picasso's extensive oeuvre is a good example of monochrome moodiness. Blue carries feelings of nostalgia, sadness, and loneliness. Picasso chose to paint with mostly blue to reflect his sadness and loneliness after moving to Paris; the social environment surrounding him in his impoverished neighborhood; and especially, the dramatic loss of his friend Carlos Casagemas, who committed suicide due to unrequited love. Then Picasso moved to Montmartre, made friends, and fell in love with Fernande Olivier. His mood improved, and his palette went from blue to pink. He discovered a new, playful subject matter: circus acrobats and harlequins. Also, he was not a starving artist anymore; he had started selling his art and finding support from gallerists and art dealers. This would make any artist change their palette from blue to pink!

Regardless of which palette Picasso used, or the subject matter, the paintings of both the blue and pink periods are full of nuances. Looking at them in detail, one can see how the colors were mixed and stretched for intentional expression.

A contemporary artist working with highly nuanced monochromes is Lisa Yuskavage. Her subject matter explores feminine themes of beauty, gender, and sexuality. Her women, voluptuous and occasionally grotesque, exist in settings that are sensual and intimate, yet sometimes uncomfortable. But aside from her provocative approach to the subject matter, it is her use of color that I find most fascinating.

Her paintings tend to have a dominant color—red, green, or yellow—that is richly expanded into all possible variations to create a luminous effect in the settings and subjects. Throughout the soft surfaces of the bodies and the multiple objects in the rooms, the color is mixed and applied in a nuanced, layered manner, stretching a hue to its full range. On a yellow painting, Yuskavage will take the color from the palest cream to the richest golden to create a vibrant atmosphere, full of warmth, intimacy, and sensuality. Similarly, in the green or red paintings, each hue is mixed in all tones and levels of saturation and applied to create maximum narrative depth, drawing viewers in. The color range in Yuskavage's paintings carries and sustains the theme, creates the mood, and fills the air of the rooms where her female subjects exist. This is the power of color.

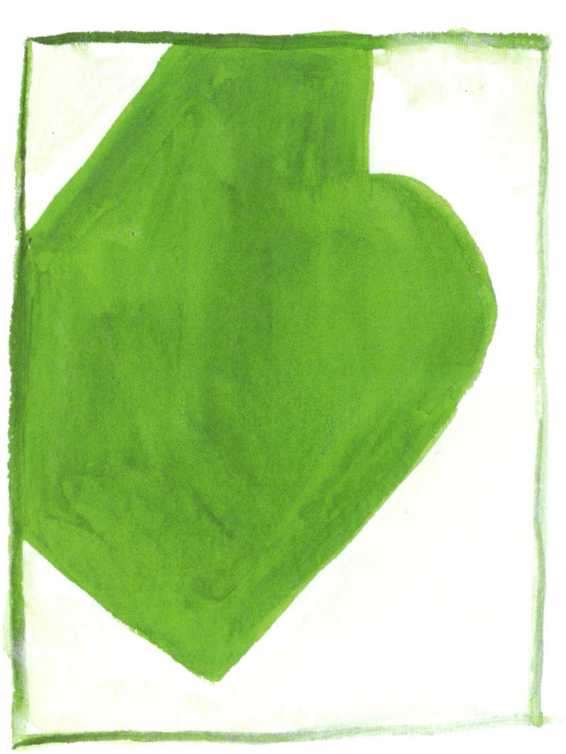

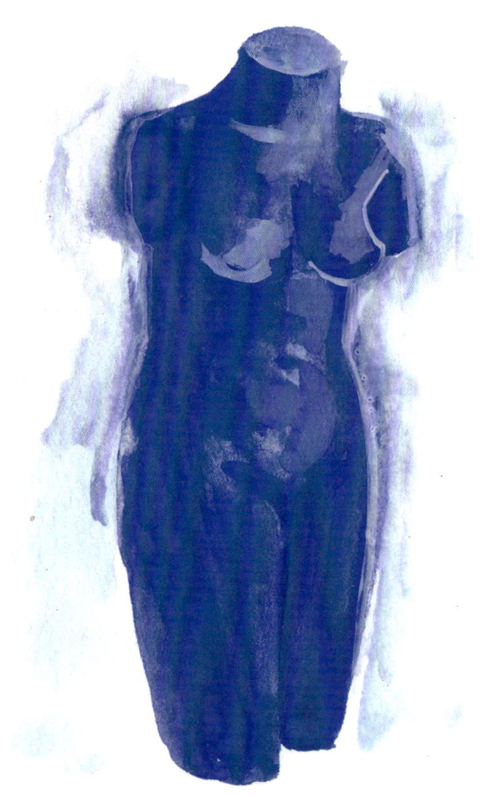

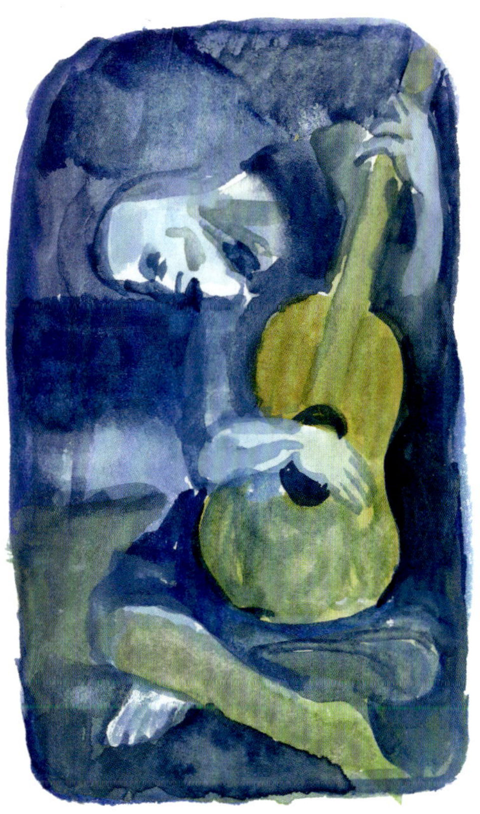

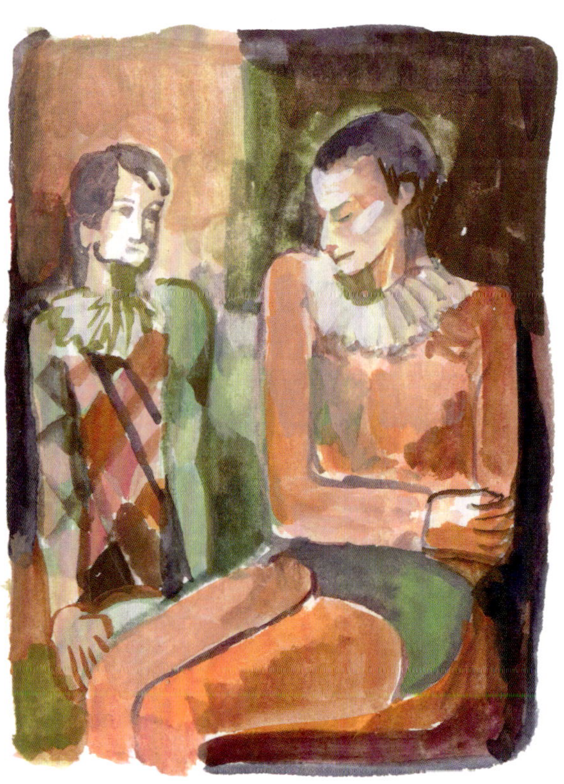

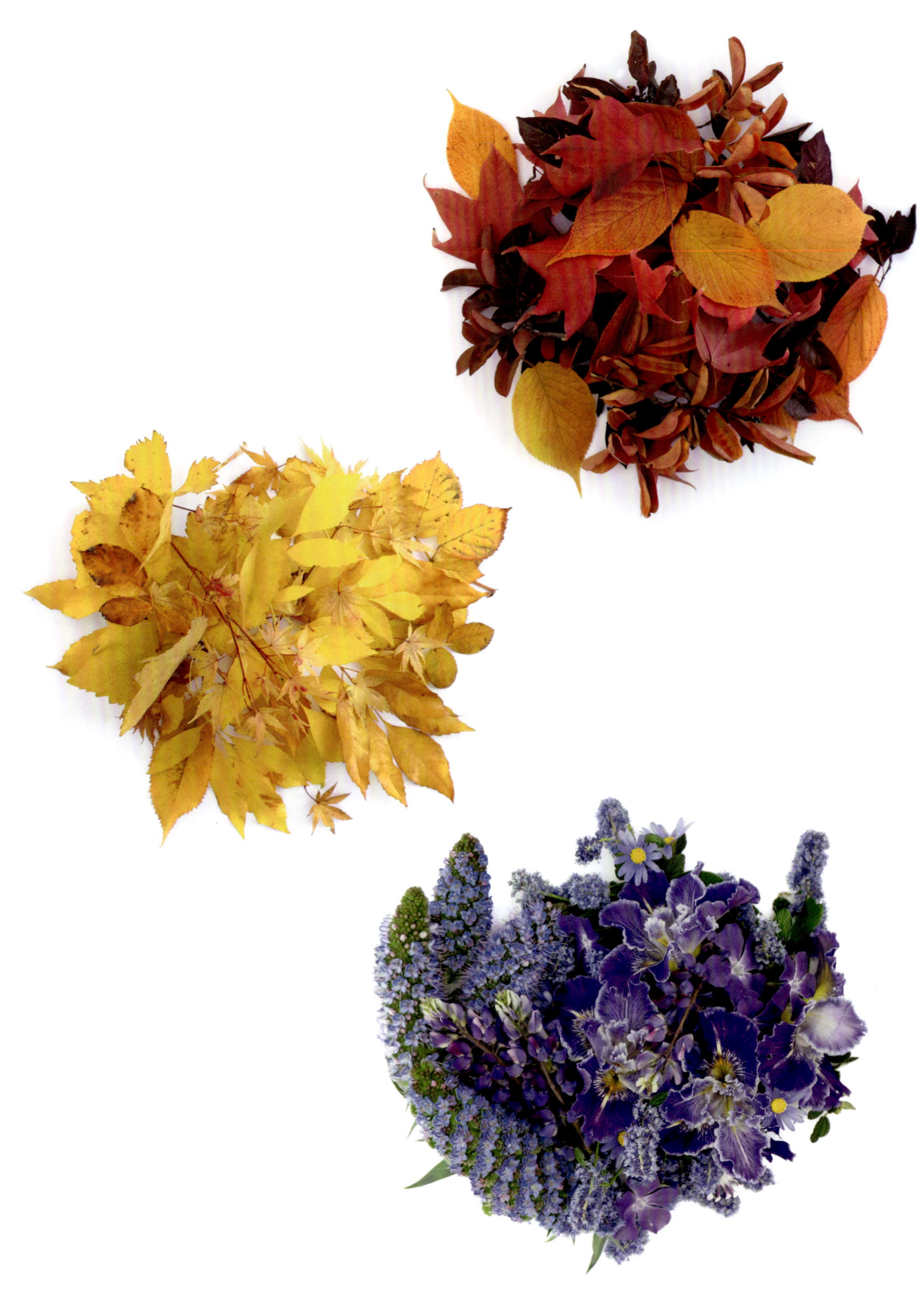

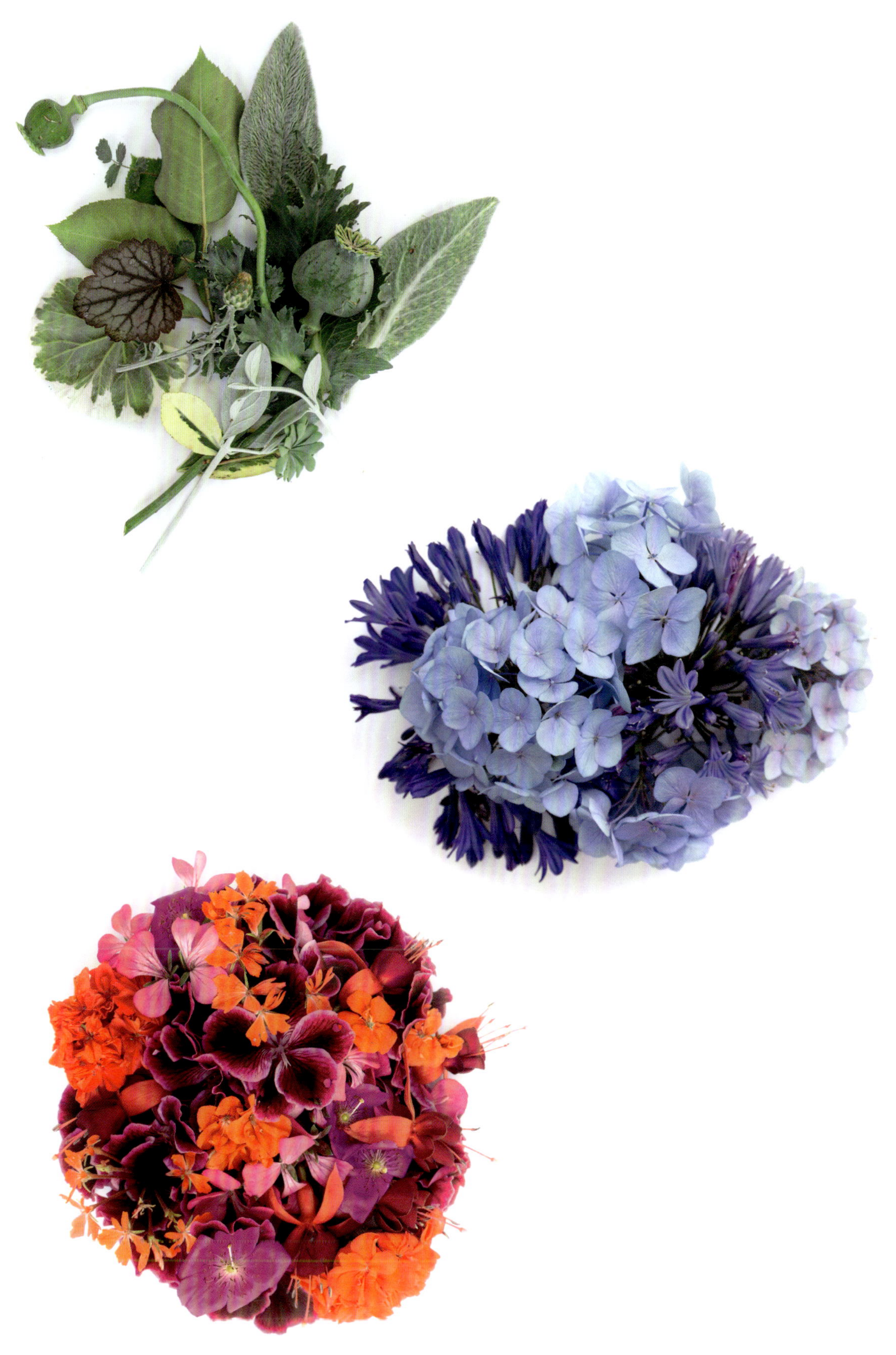

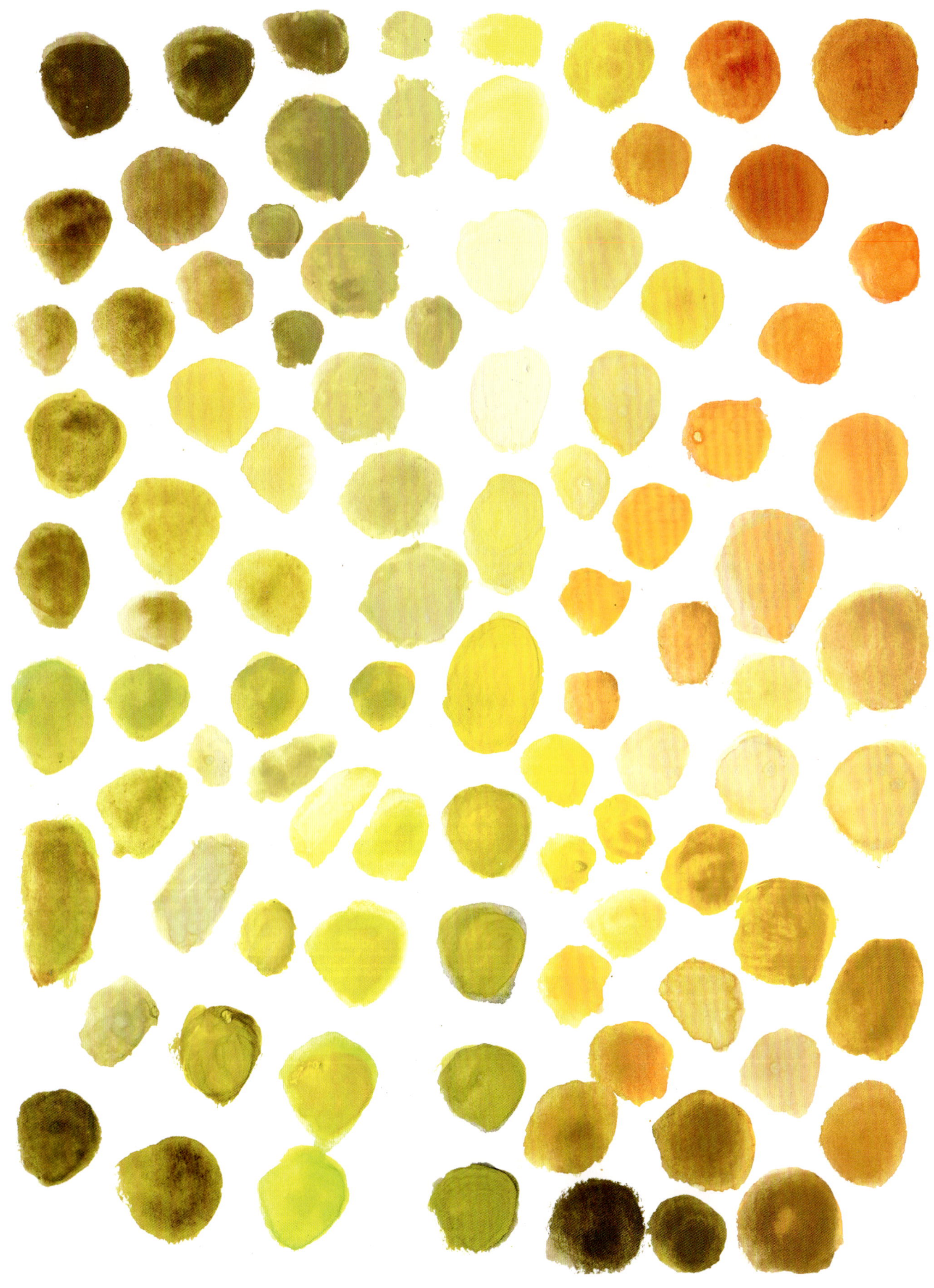

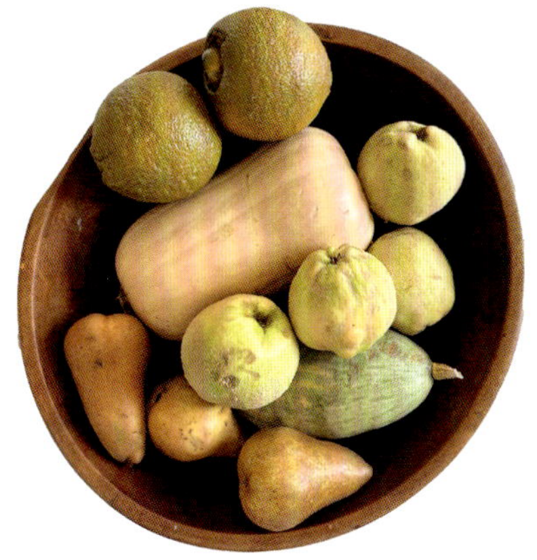

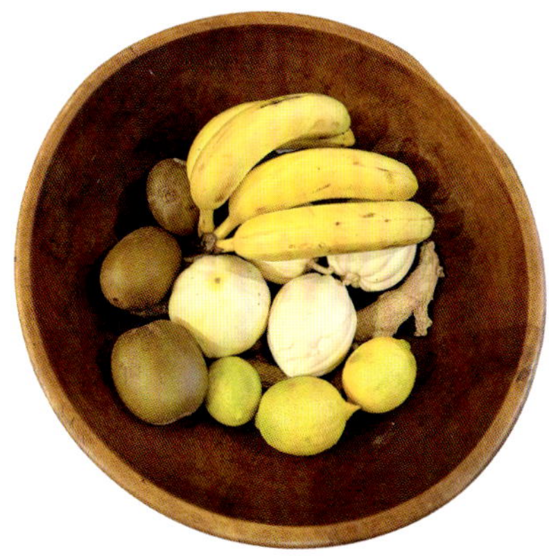

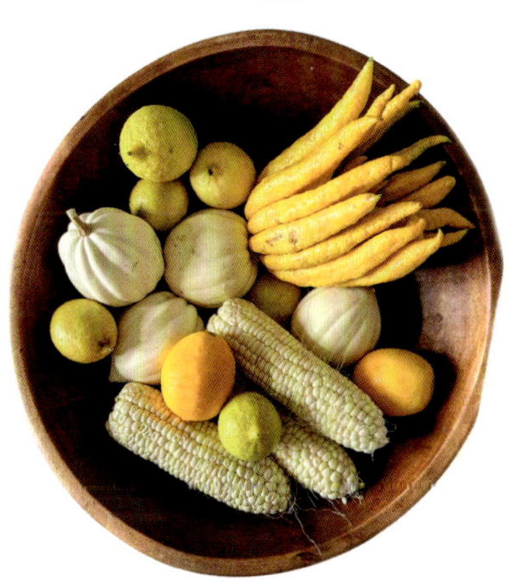

EXPANDING A COLOR
TO ITS FULL POTENTIAL

Using color straight from the tube is A-OK to a certain degree, but if you want to have a whole range of yellows, you'll need an awful lot of tubes of paint, pencils, and inks to cover the whole spectrum of the color.

Or you can practice how to push a basic color in all directions to get those nuances and find a color's full potential.

Again, let's take yellow. Starting with a basic pure yellow—a primary yellow, in gouache nomenclature, or a canary in more evocative naming—incrementally mix it with white, then with black.

Then mix it with other colors, such as red, magenta, green, cyan (a pure form of blue for mixing). Mix it gradually to bring the original pigment to the last frontier of yellow, to the place where it is about to stop being yellow but before it becomes a definite orange or green.

Then take those colors—the greenest yellow, the orangiest yellow, the darkest and the lightest yellows—and combine them together to see what you get.

Step back and look at all that you just created: a wide sample of the whole potential of yellow! Maybe even name some of the new tints. Try doing this with other hues; flex your color muscle!

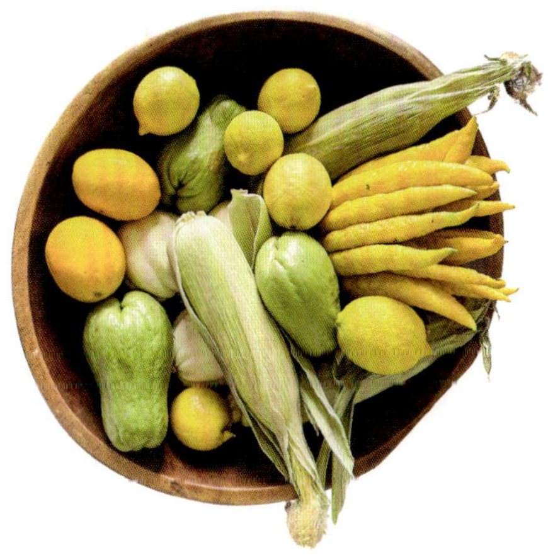

A TALE OF THREE YELLOWS

Yellow pigments, like those of any color, can come from a variety of sources: mineral or botanical, natural or synthetic. Myriad plants can be used as dyes, from calendula and marigold petals to the precious stamens of the saffron flower and the rich bright yellow of the turmeric root. These botanicals are beautiful as dyes but not stable enough to paint with.

Here are three yellows paints and their stories.

Yellow Ochre: The Original Yellow

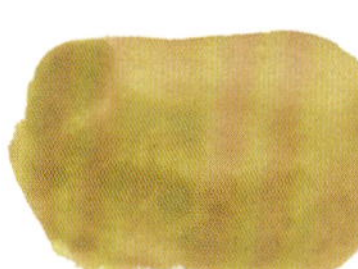

Think of cave paintings and recall the reddish-yellow figures of bison and humans and the silhouettes of hands. They were all painted using pigments ground from rocks or naturally occurring compounds found on the walls of the same caves. Early humans figured out a way to grind these colored minerals and mix them with water to make the first-ever paints. These paints let them depict hunting scenes in rich detail. Maybe they used the paintings to plan the hunt, or maybe the images worked as a protective spell against the big animals they were planning to pursue. Regardless, painting gave them a way to harness the magical power of their imagination. This was the beginning of art, and yellow ochre was there.

This naturally occurring color, made of iron oxide mixed into clay, is readily available most everywhere. You can find it in cliffs and soil. You can even harvest it to make your own paints while hiking (if allowed by the park ranger, and always being careful not to disturb the landscape). Its coloration depends on the amount of iron oxide and the composition of the locally occurring clay, along with other factors: a fire will change yellow iron oxide (limonite) into red ochre (hematite), and browner, darker shades are found when manganese is in the mix. This is why ochre can range from paler yellow to green to deep orange.

If you went around the world collecting ochre samples, you would have a rich palette of colors. That is what Heidi Gustafson of Early Futures[5] has done. She has spent years collecting and grinding soil and naturally occurring pigments, and her vast archive of more than six hundred pigments includes a glorious chart of ochres from around the world:

- **Ochre from the UK,** sourced near Oxford, is pale, muted, and earthy.
- **Ochre from Australia** is rich and saturated.
- **Ochre from France,** specifically from the Roussillon region, is intense and warmer in tone, with a wide range from yellow to reddish.
- **Ochre from Cyprus** has a lemony green tint.
- **Spanish ochre** from Andalusia is golden, almost the color of saffron.
- **Arizona** and the dryland of the Southwest provide a full range, from bright yellow to deep red.

Really, there is ochre to be found everywhere! Whenever you go on a hike or walk by the ocean where there is a cliff with layers of color, you can harvest this iron oxide–tinted clay and make paint.

Indian Yellow: The Controversial Yellow

Imagine a hot day in India; imagine you are a cow looking for shade; imagine how nice it would be to spend the day under the shade of the mango trees, so green and luscious. Those green leaves and maybe the occasional green mango seem like the perfect food for you.

The herder likes that their cow rests under the mango trees, because they know that the cow will produce something that they can collect and sell: the dried-up cow urine.

Indian yellow is an intense, rich, golden yellow, used in Indian painting and later exported to Europe, to other artists' and dyers' delight. Nowadays it is produced synthetically, but for centuries it was made with the dried-up urine of those cows eating mango leaves. All those leaves contain a compound that makes urine yellower, and the sun dries it to a crystalized form. Once dry, the little golden nuggets can be collected, then ground to create this bright yellow rarely seen elsewhere in art.

Over the years, improvements in synthetic color and the controversy of feeding mango leaves to the cows to the detriment of their health have led to the phasing out of Indian yellow's natural form. I would be curious to see how the natural paint compares to the synthetic.

Hansa Yellow: The Good Yellow

The advent of a wider range of synthetic colors in the early nineteenth century and the need for human-made yellow led to the formulation of cadmium yellow, first formulated by the German chemist Friedrich Stromeyer in 1817. It is bright, intense, saturated, and easy to mix into a variety of tones, from an almost neon, lemony yellow to golden orange and beyond into rich reds. Cadmium itself, however, is poisonous. As with other gorgeous colors that contain health-hazardous components, cadmium colors should be used with caution, with gloves and away from children and pets. Also, beware of how cadmium colors are disposed of, as they can have a negative environmental impact.

In 1904, the search for a safer yellow resulted in Hansa yellow: an organic paint (which means carbon-based), equally bright and vivid, a bit more translucent and versatile, and more affordable. But the main advantage over cadmium is its safety.

KEY TAKEAWAYS

1. Don't settle for a color straight out of the tube or from the pencil; purposefully mix or layer and expand its possibilities. In textiles, choose your threads or mix them as you embroider or knit to get the right tone. No matter what media you use to create, strive to look for that specific, more interesting color, not just the basics—unless that is your point: a basic, pure color.

2. Think of ways to use color for expression, mood, and atmosphere beyond the obvious.

3. Monochrome can be simple or nuanced.

4. Ponder this: If you were to do a monochrome piece of art or design, which color would you choose? Would your choice change based on the intended end piece, such as an illustration or painting, designing a room or fabric, or clothing yourself in monochrome? Would your choice be driven by a fascination with the color itself, or would the deciding element be the mood and evocative qualities that color conveys?

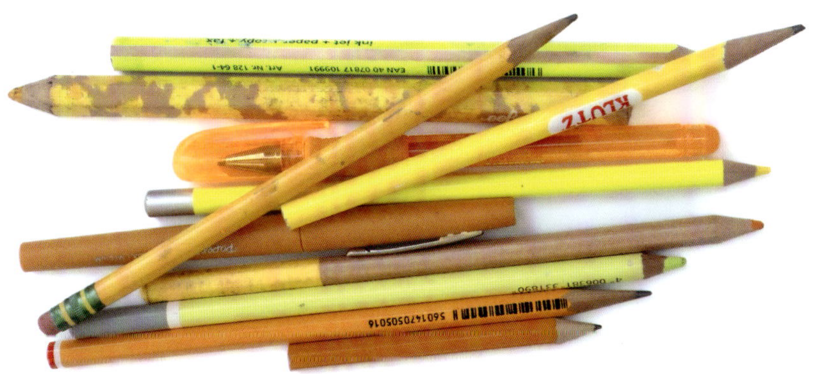

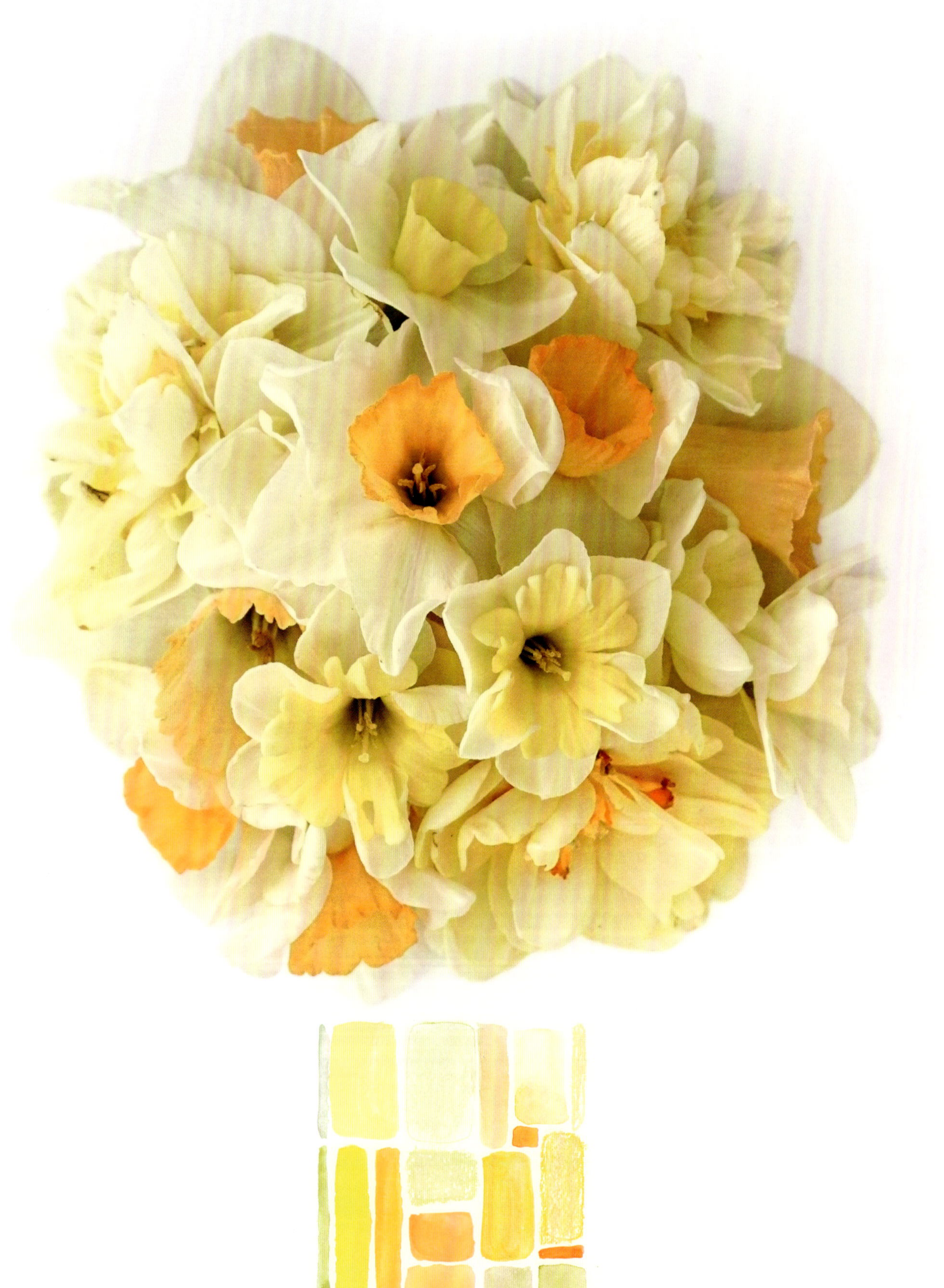

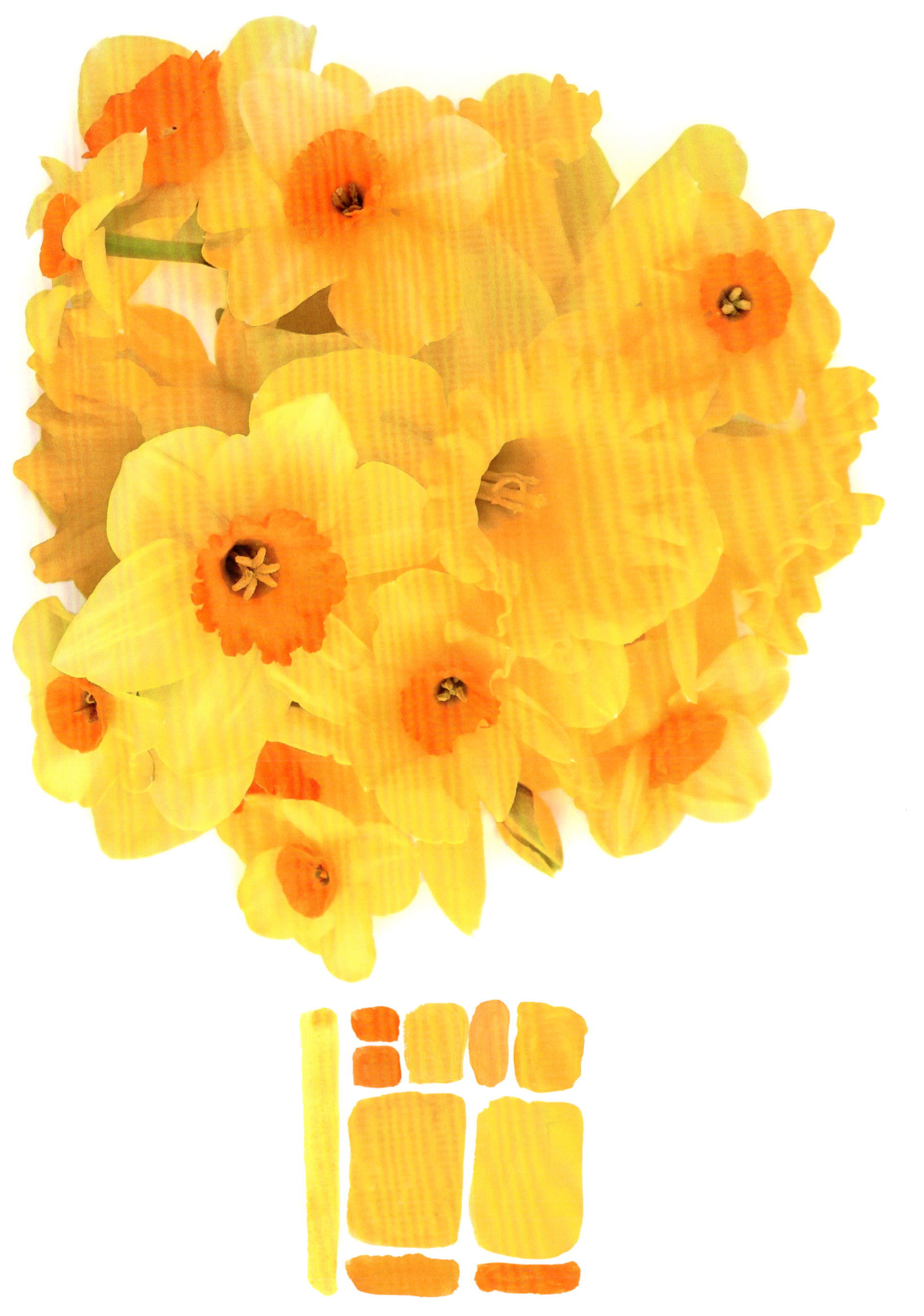

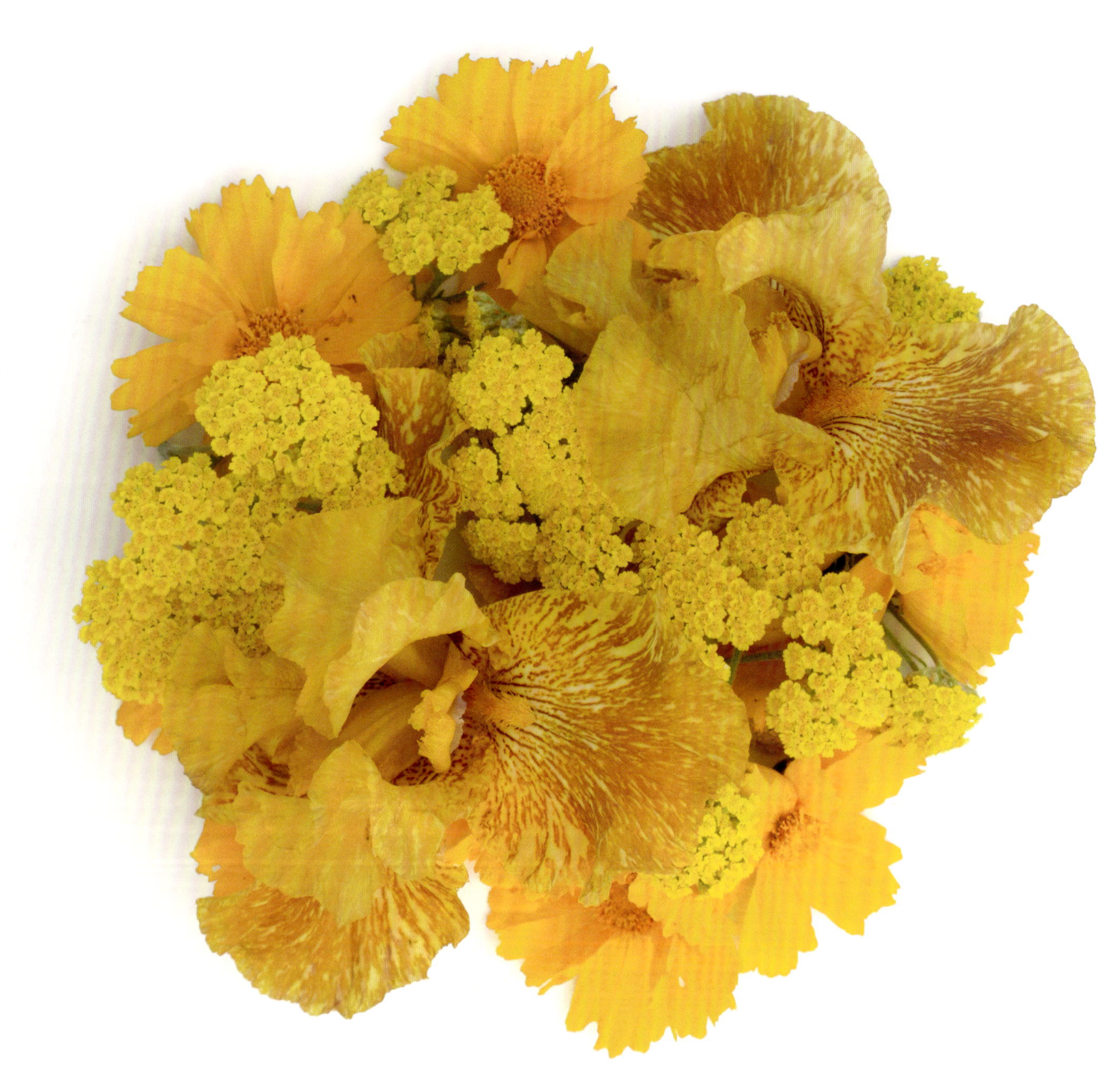

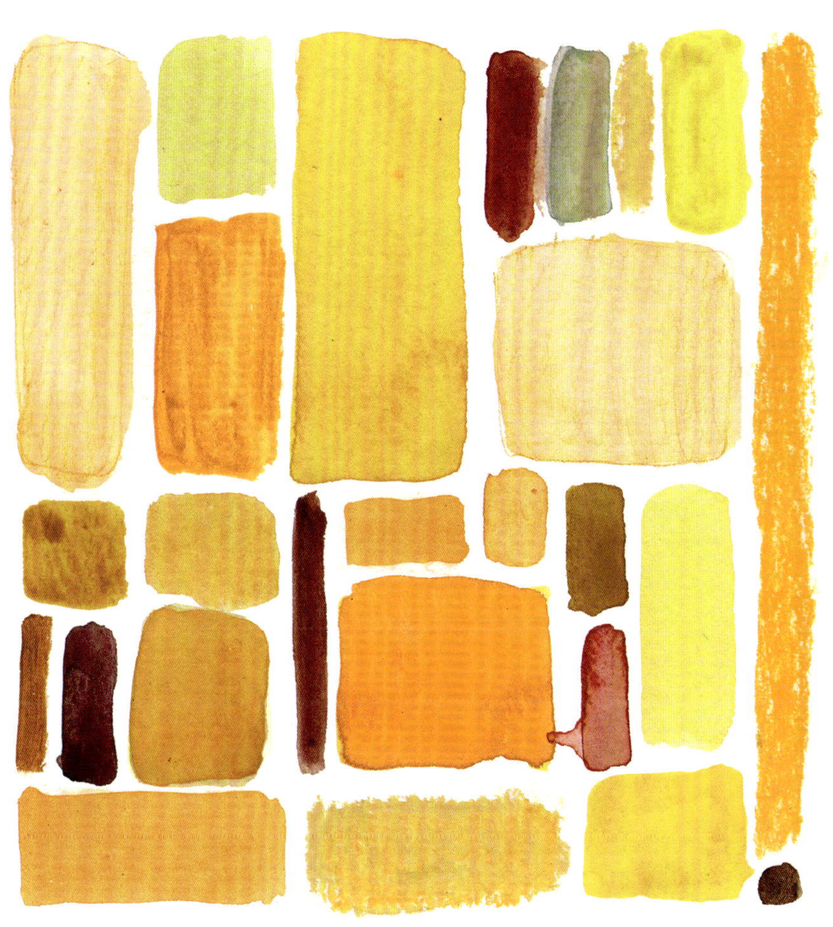

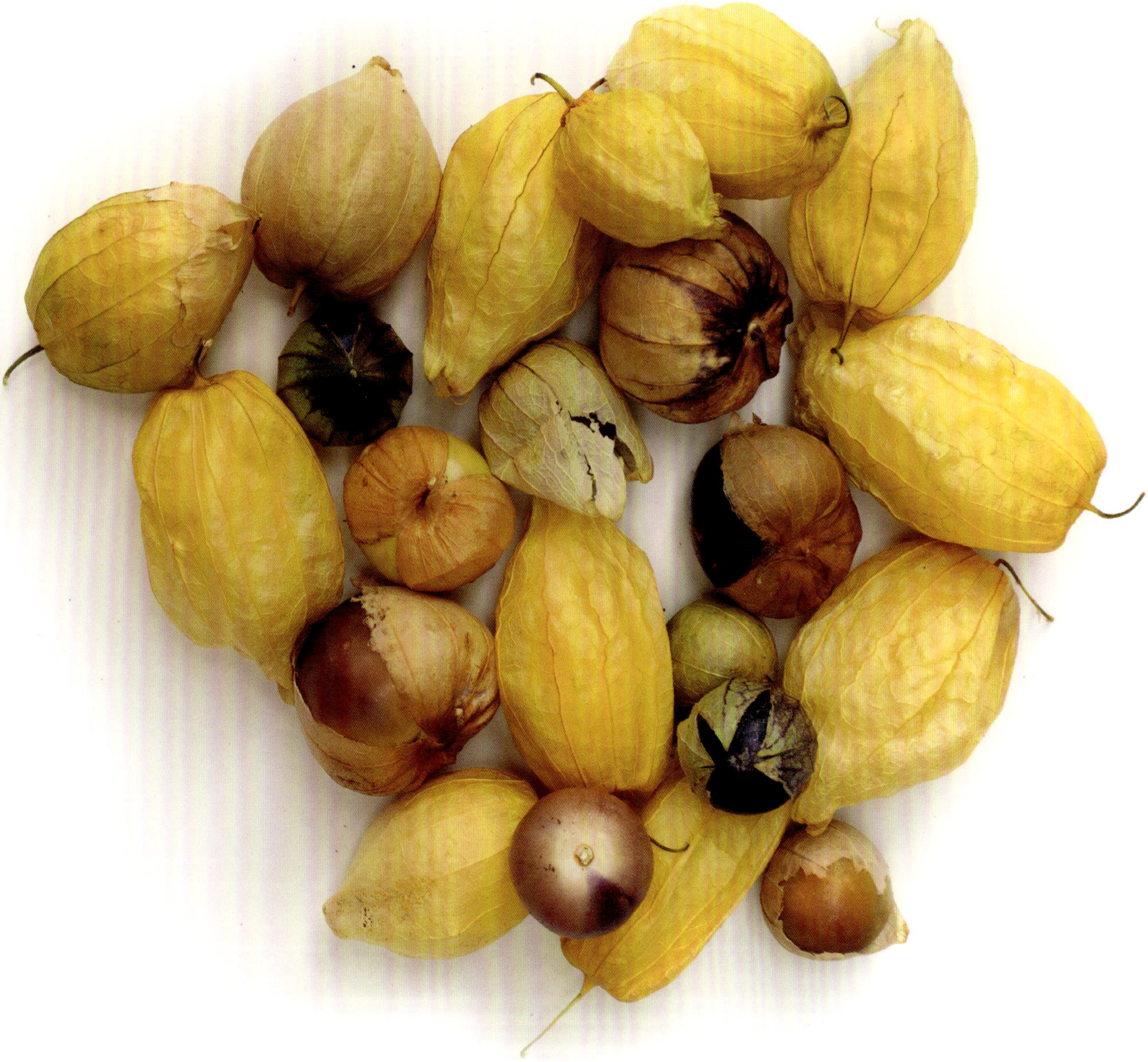

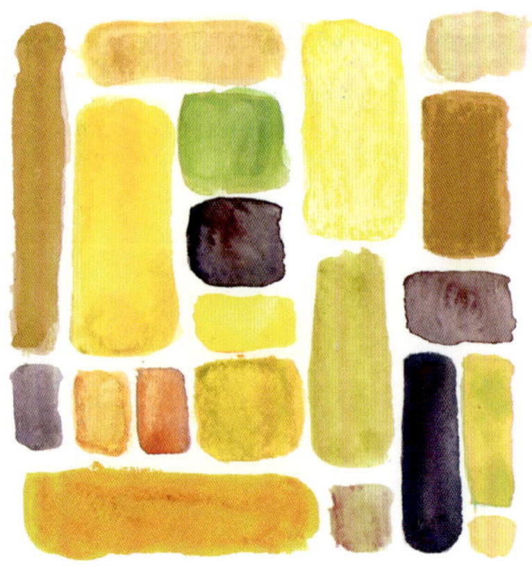

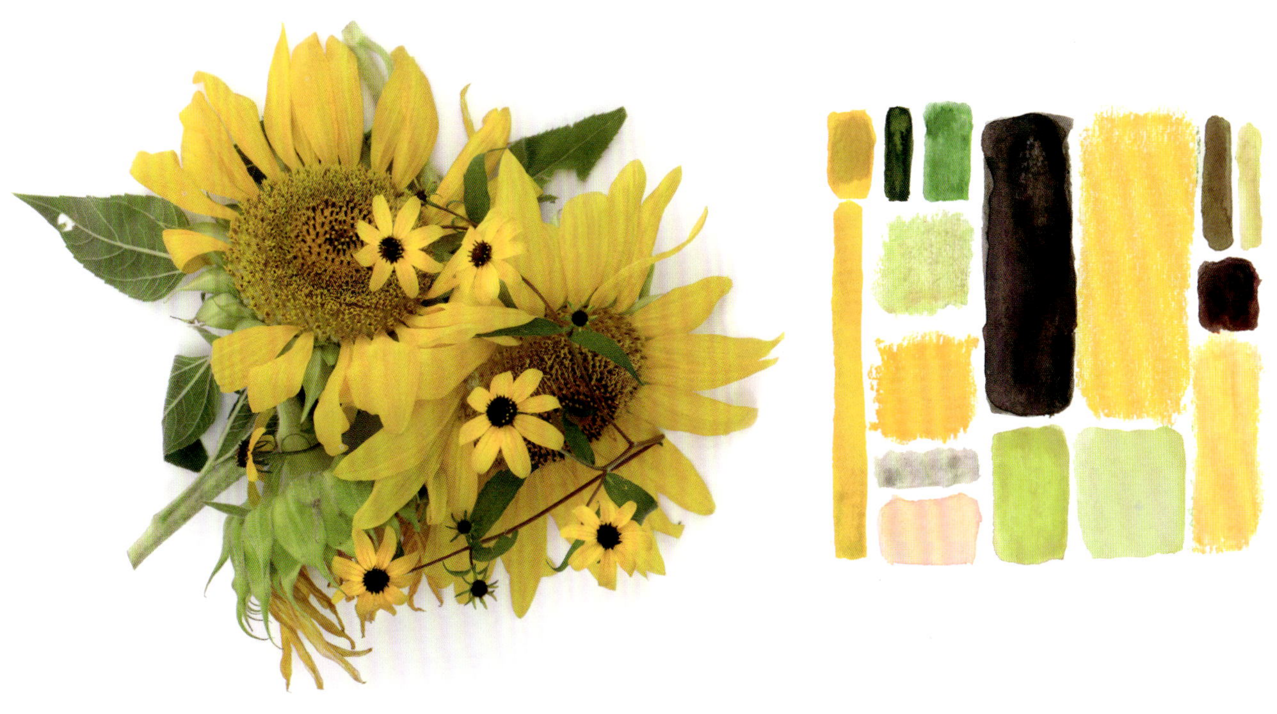

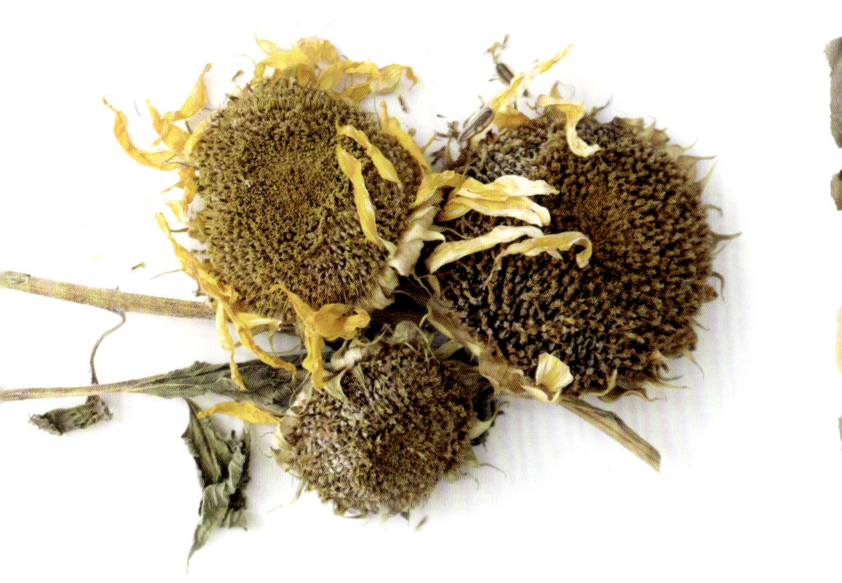

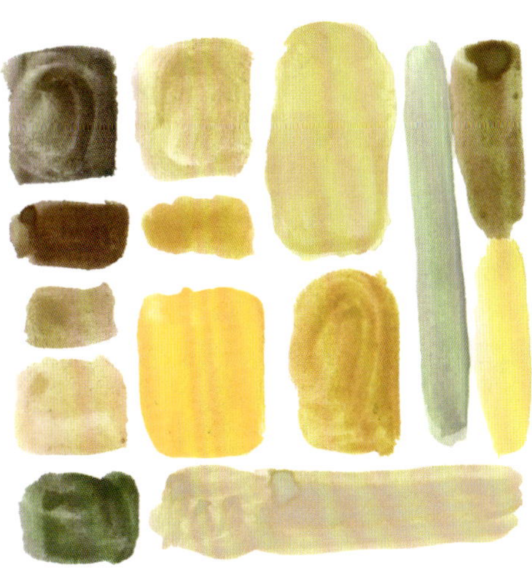

PROJECT

OBSERVE: Observe the range of yellows in the objects collected on pages 28–29 and pages 40–53.

ANALYZE: Analyze how the companion color palettes have synthesized the tints and hues of the objects. Think of the relationship between these colors and what they evoke when they are together.

CREATE: Create one or more pattern designs using the colors from the palettes in these pages, in a style that matches what those colors made you feel. You can use repeated patterns, like those of fabric and wallpaper, or placement patterns, such as what you would see on a dining plate. As you create each design, think of where the pattern would be used: clothes, wallpaper, home decor fabrics, tableware?

Ask yourself: Does the pattern match the mood of the colors?

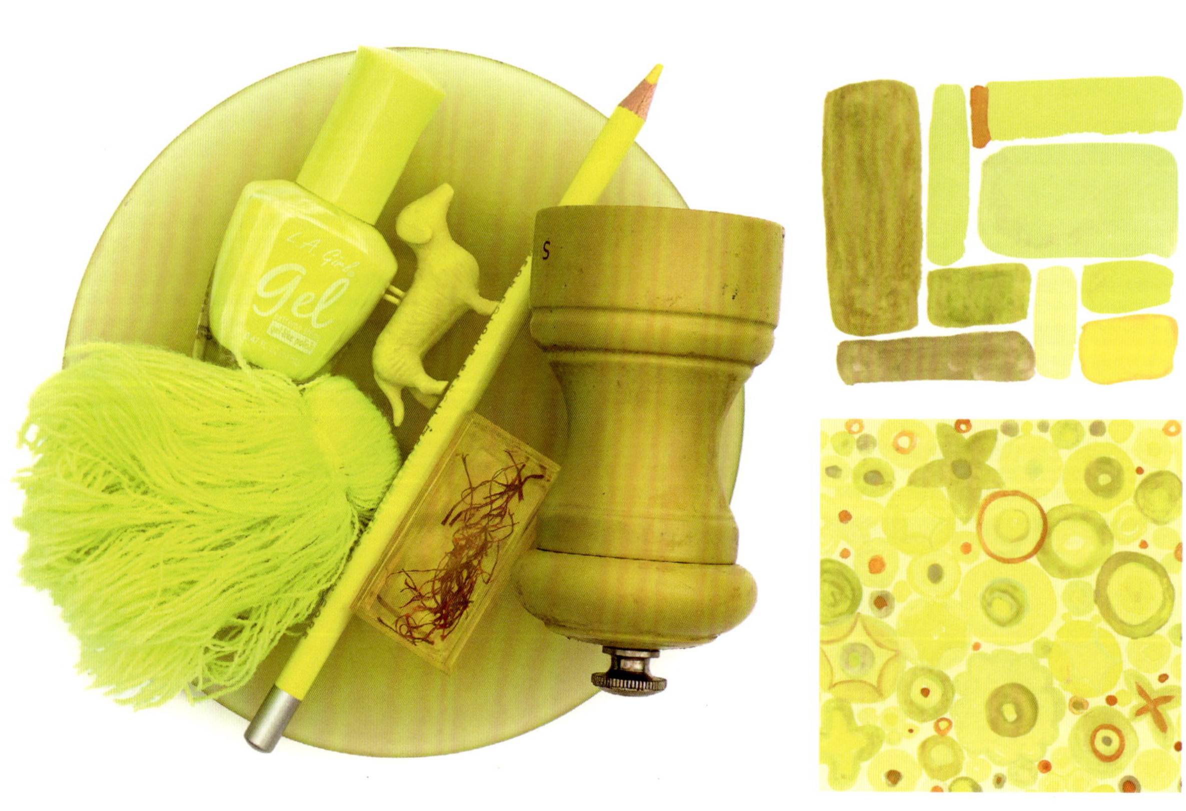

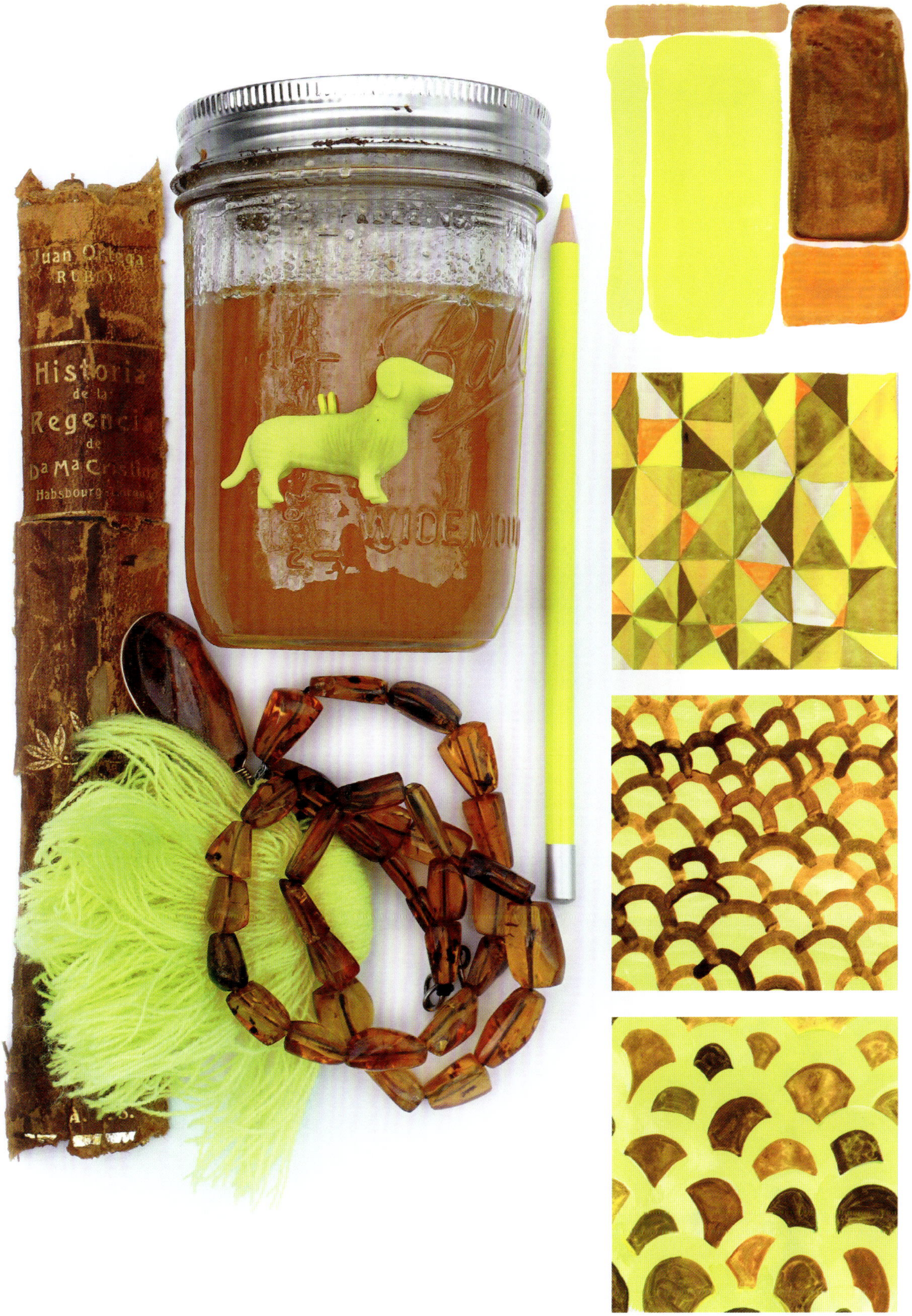

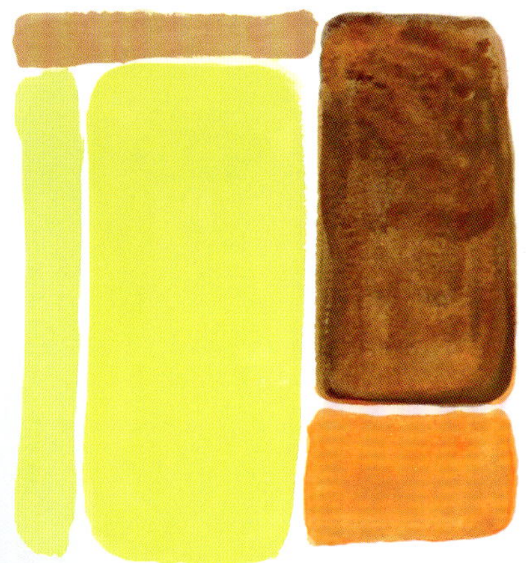
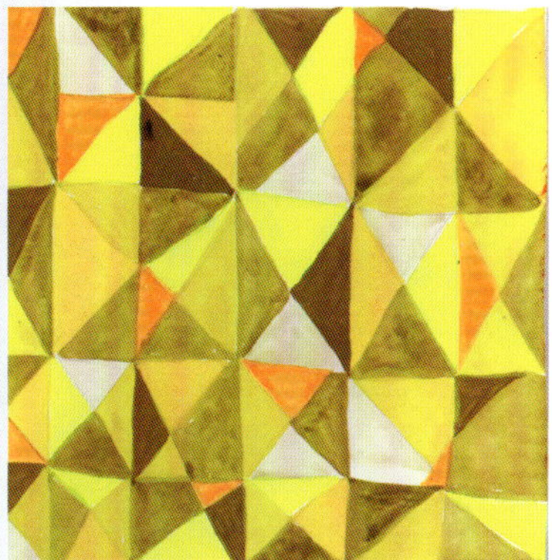
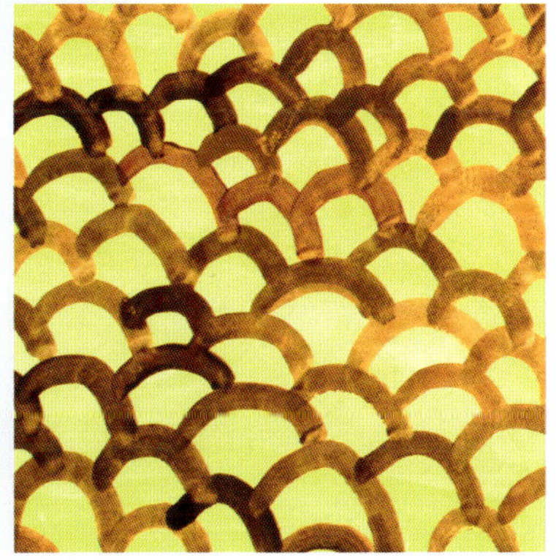
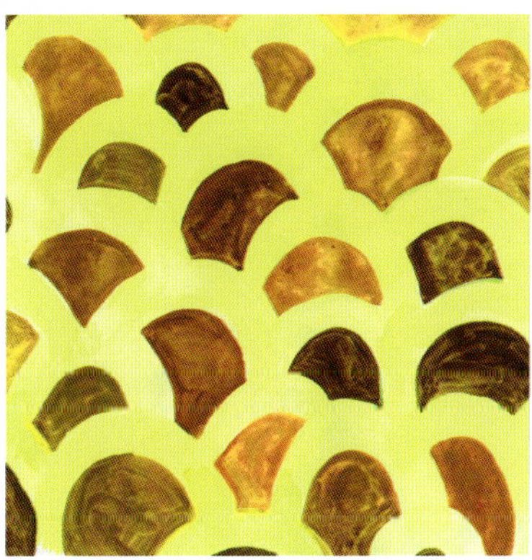

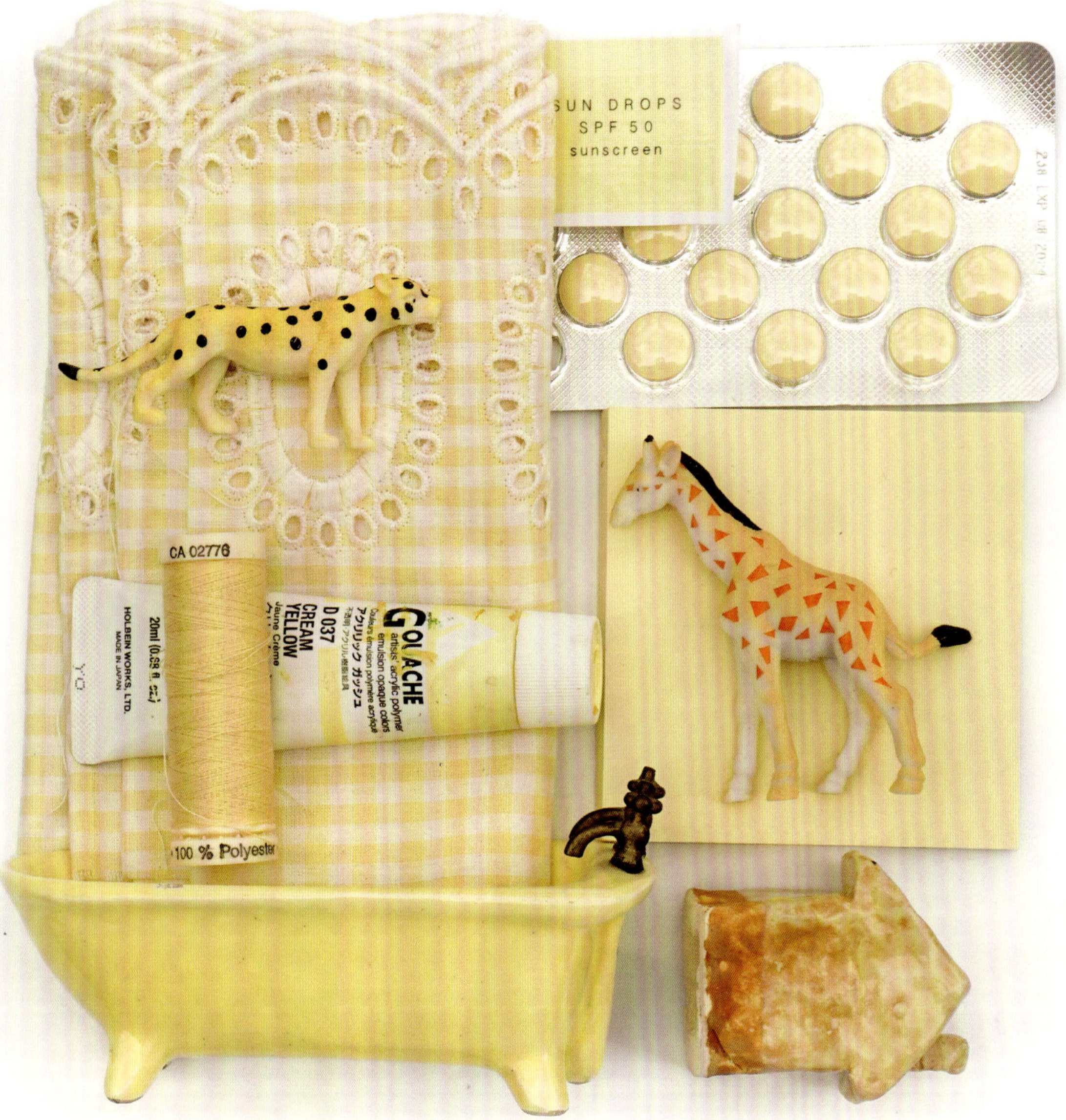

SUN DROPS
SPF 50
sunscreen
CA 02776
GOUACHE
artists' acrylic polymer
emulsion opaque colors
Couleurs émulsion polymère acrylique
D 037
CREAM
YELLOW
Jaune Crème
20ml (0.68 fl. oz.)
HOLBEIN WORKS, LTD.
MADE IN JAPAN
100 % Polyester

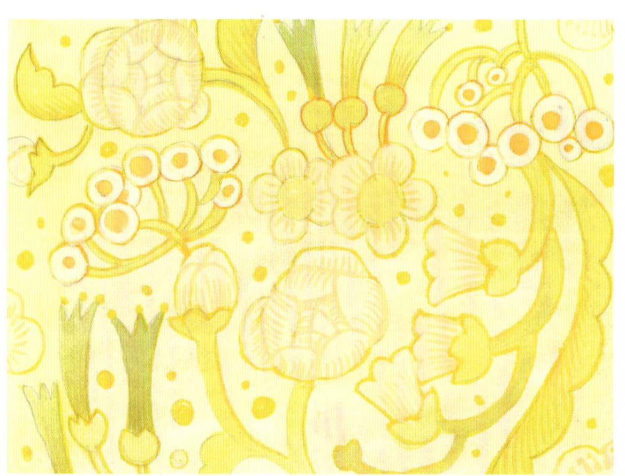

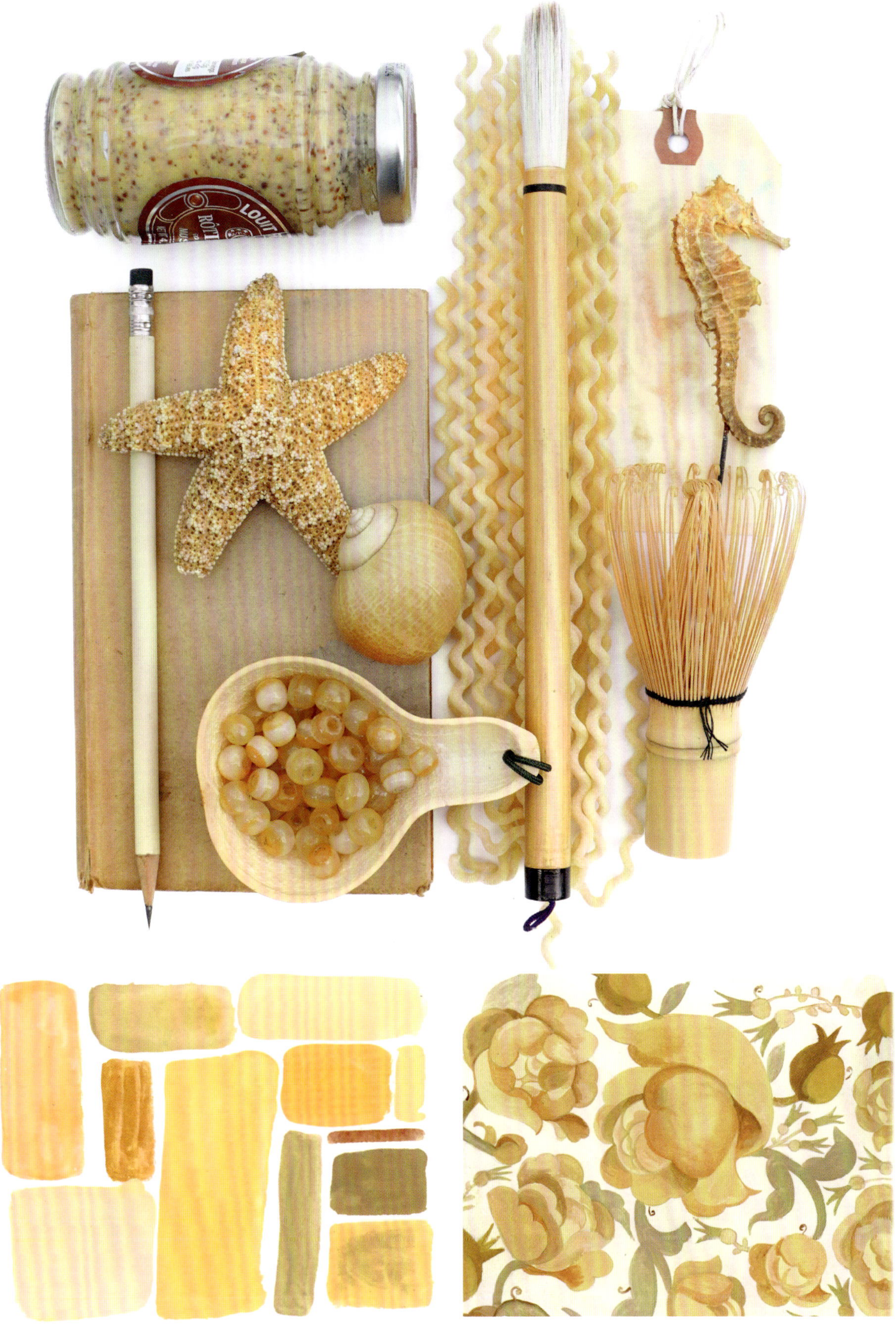

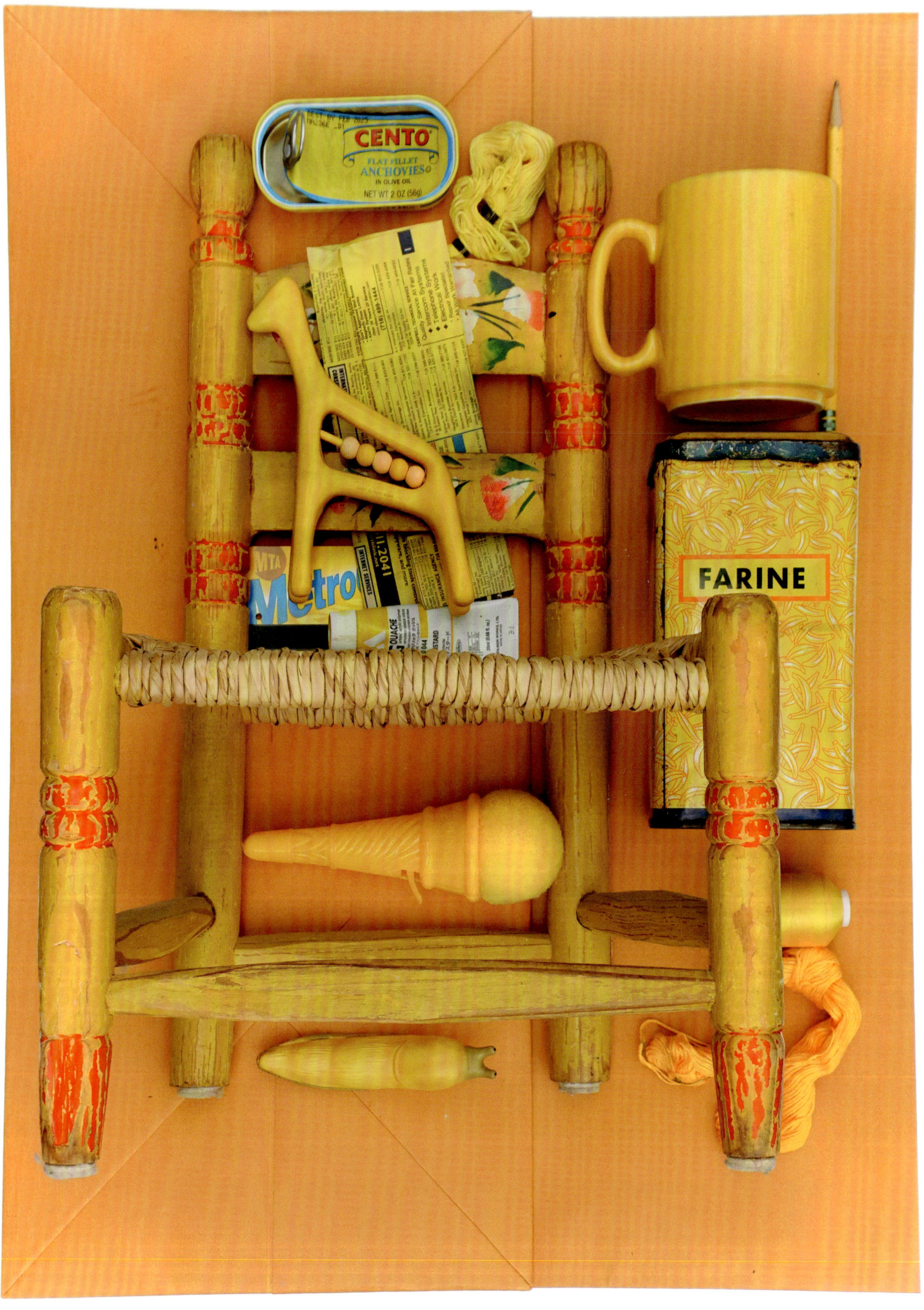

CENTO
FLAT FILLET
ANCHOVIES
IN OLIVE OIL
NET WT 2 OZ (56g)
MTA
Metro
FARINE

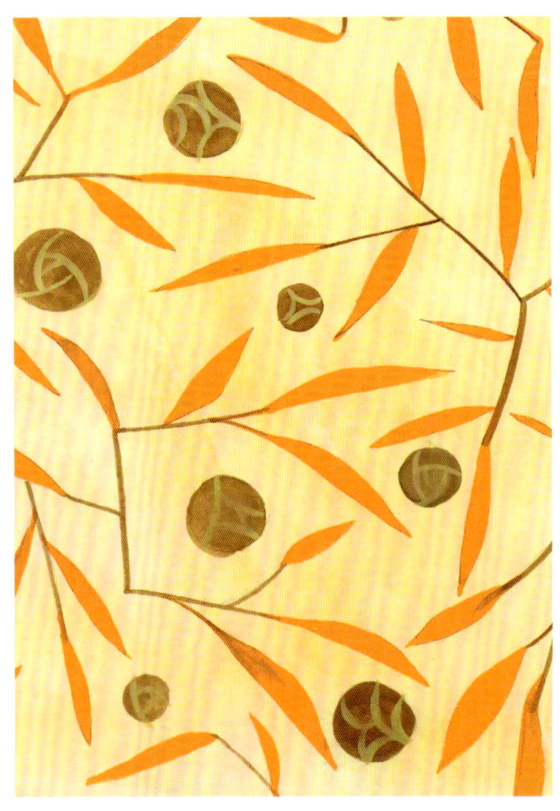
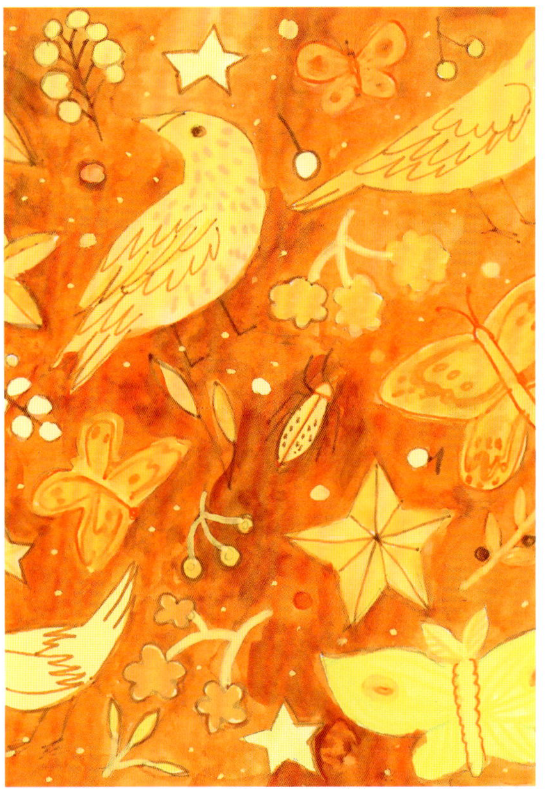
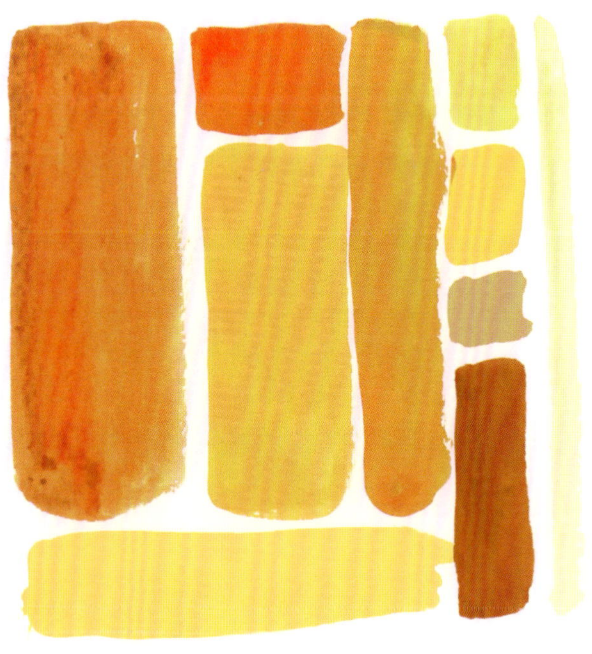
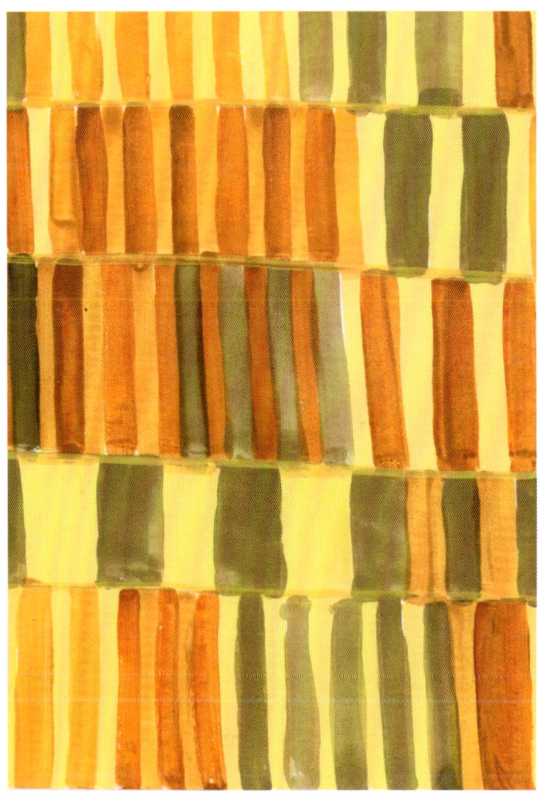

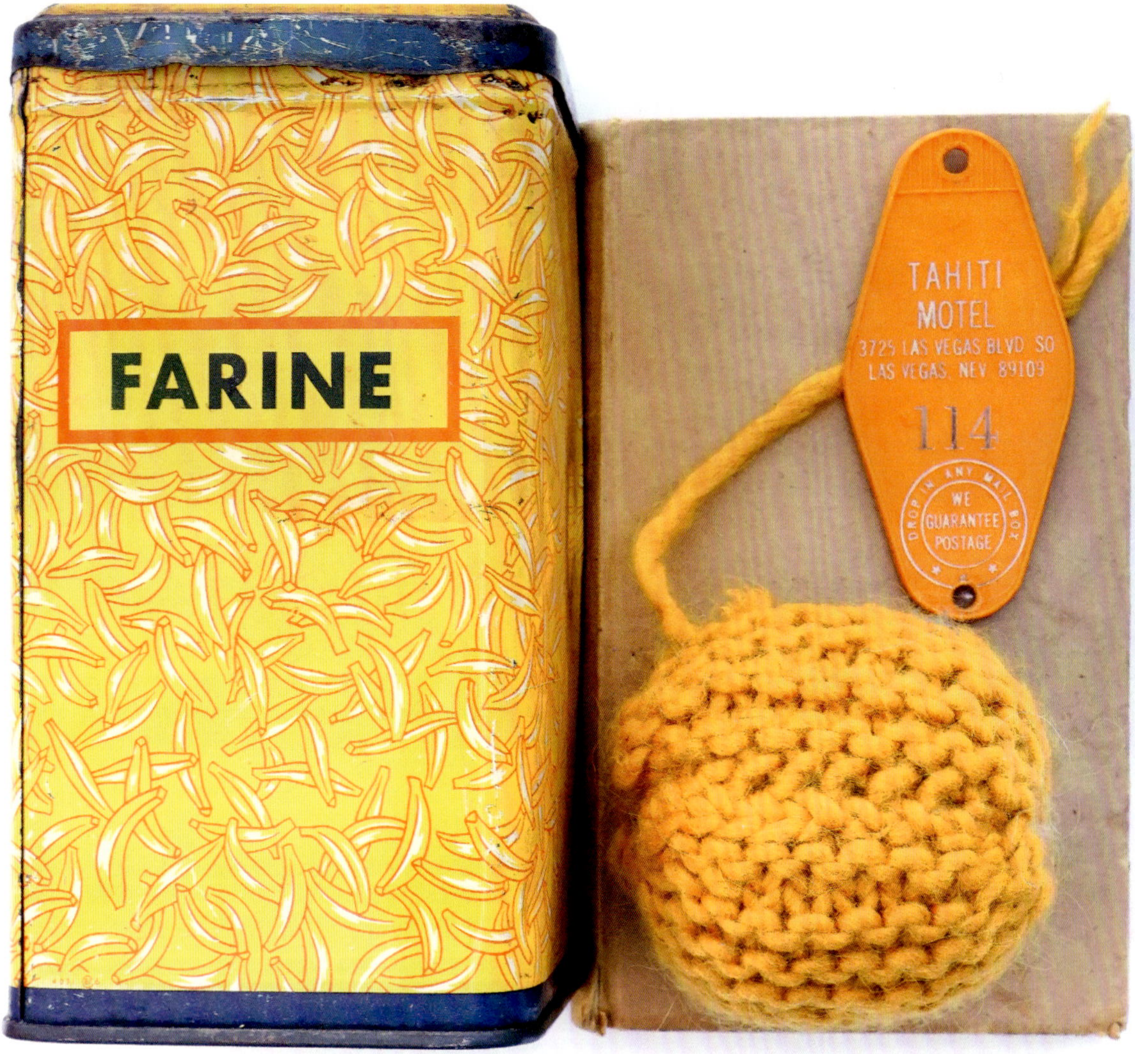

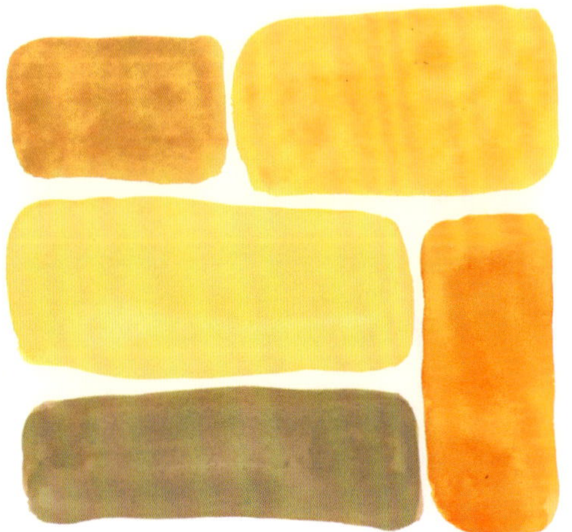

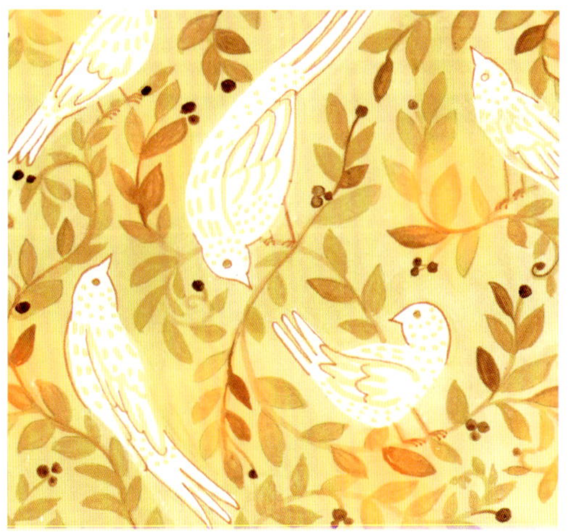

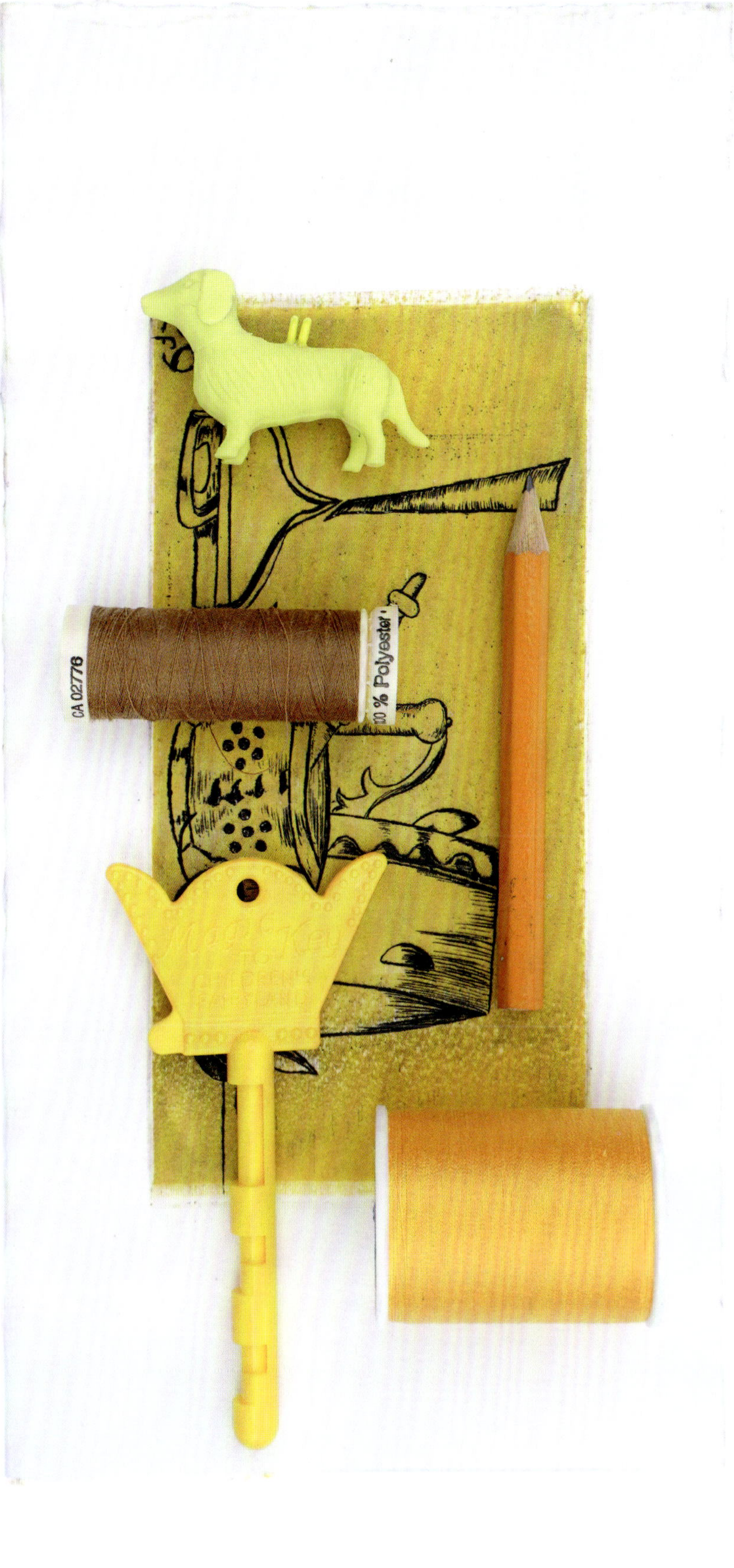

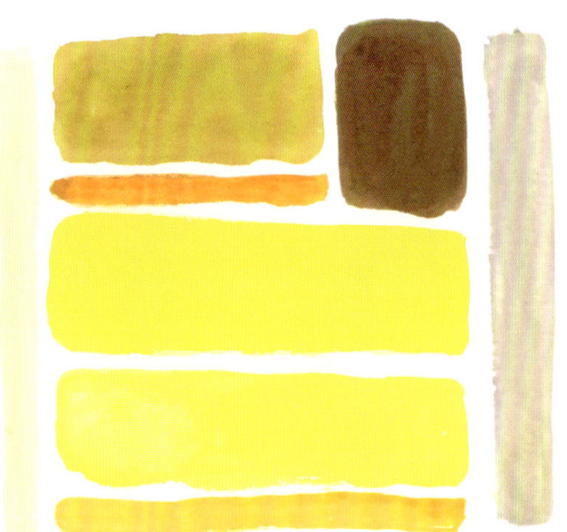
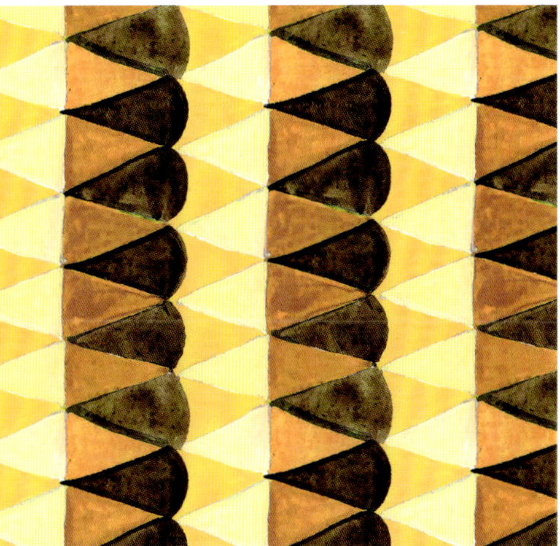

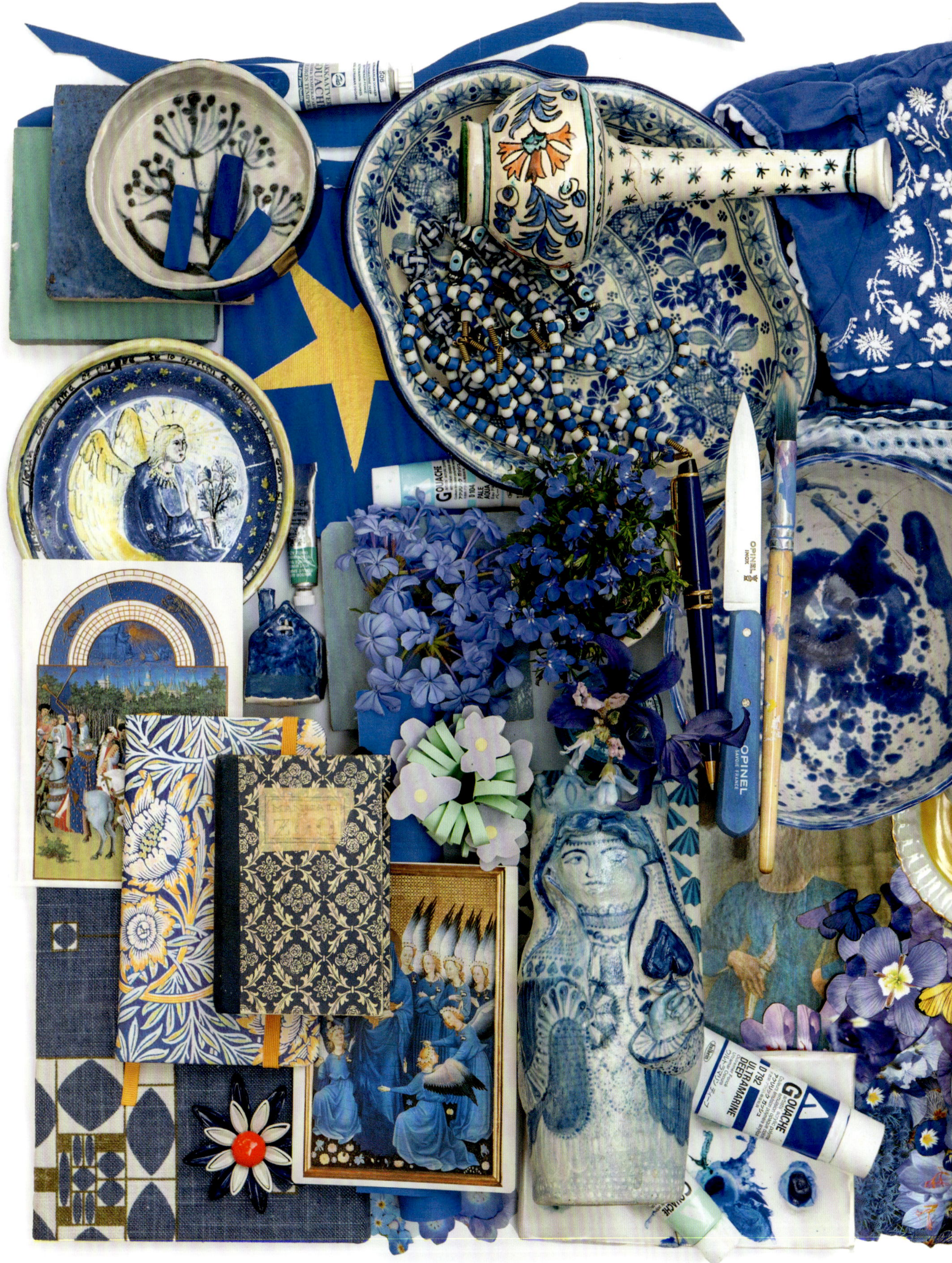

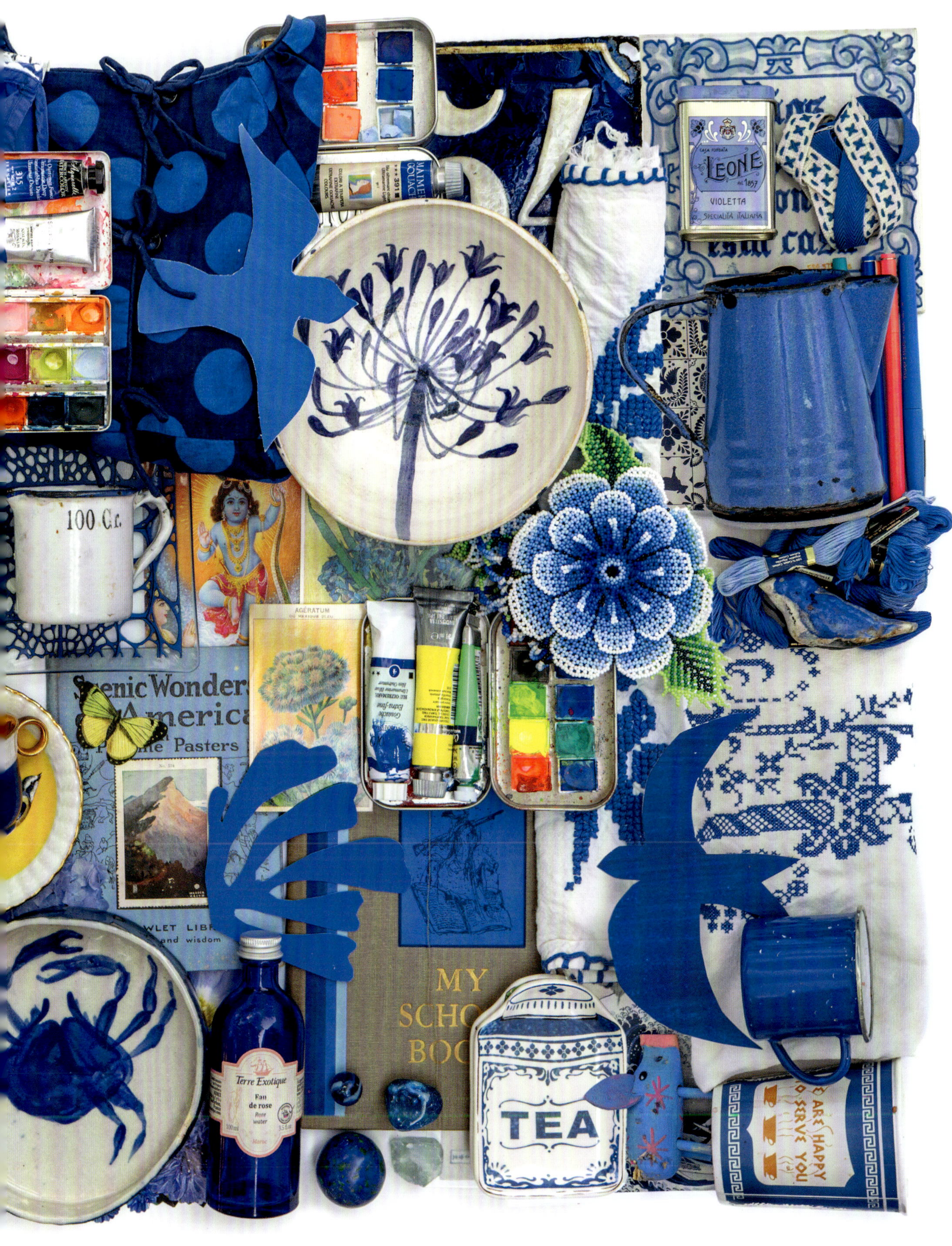

2.

COLOR AS A LEITMOTIF

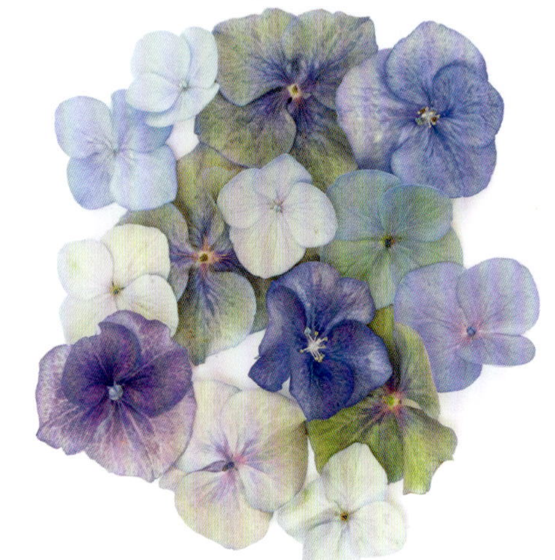

Using a Favorite Color to Explore
Color Interactions

One of the first questions we should ask when getting to know each other is "What is your favorite color?"

A favorite color tells a lot about a person. I was once surprised to learn from a close friend that her favorite color is purple; it changed my whole perception of her! Purple imparted an air of magic, mystery, and funkiness to her otherwise controlled and collected persona. I had never thought of her as a purple person, and suddenly there it was, in her clothing, her eyeliner, her collection of teapots. From that day on, knowing this also helped me be able to buy her gifts in her favorite lilac, violet, burgundy, and other purplish shades.

I think a favorite color is much more than a hue one likes a lot; it becomes a leitmotif. It leads and affects our color choices through life, or as long as it is favored.

Your favorite color may be influenced by gender, culture, or personality—extroverts tend to like brighter colors, and introverts favor paler colors. You may remain loyal to your childhood favorite, or it may change with age,

Leitmotif

German origin, from leit, "leading" (+) motiv, "motive"

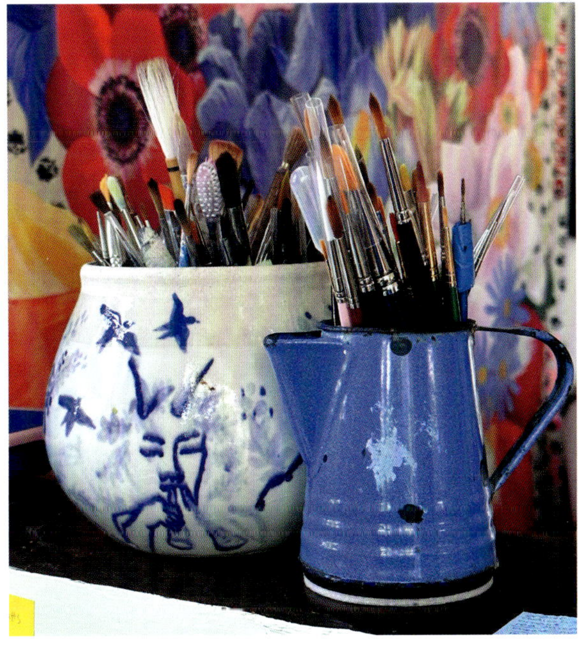

fashion, and the place you live in. Your favorite may even change after accidentally bumping into a new favorite color, or at least a color that makes you color curious for a while.

My all-time favorite color is green, all shades of it, from lime to aqua, from emerald to celadon, including all the greens in a garden or landscape. But I have stumbled upon other colors I've fixated on for a while. Scavenging for leftover art materials discarded by fellow students in Italy, I once stumbled upon a tube of Naphthol red—an intense, bright, really pure red—and I became obsessed. I still use it combined with pale minty greens or pale pinks in some paintings and as the central color in others. I also found the closest CMYK and Pantone equivalents so that I could use it in branding and graphic design projects. I even used it as a reference while directing a colorist to create paint colors for major airlines, including Air Canada and American Airlines, when I was designing liveries for them. This red made me reconsider my outlook on red as a whole.

More recently, a similar thing happened with a group of aubergine and amethyst watercolors: They took me through my own purple journey, expressed mostly in sweaters I bought and illustrations I made.

But loving green and Naphthol red and aubergine does not mean I would always dress in those colors or decorate my home in them. For textiles, fashion, and the home, I have another favorite: cobalt blue and its companions ultramarine, king's blue, and periwinkle (2727 in Pantone). Cobalt has become a leitmotif in my home, as well as a recurring theme in my art and ceramics and the things I buy and wear.

While I think of myself as a lover of all colors, when I see my artwork, I do see that there are colors I obsess over and repeat consistently: the ultramarine–cobalt spectrum, bright red and magenta, deep purples, and a range of greens. These are colors I come back to without even thinking. I sometimes wonder whether my color choices stem from a mindful decision about signature colors or if they are just a mindless default, the colors I automatically reach for. Thinking like this is a constant reminder to be intentional with my chromatic choices, and it encourages me to find new combinations for my favorites; returning to these leading colors as leitmotifs in my work creates the space to actively pursue keeping my favorite colors fresh and interesting—for me to use, and for others to see and enjoy.

OBSESSING OVER ARTISTS THAT SHARE YOUR TASTE IN COLOR

Welcome to the cobalt and friends club!

When I think of cobalt, ultramarine, periwinkle, and king's blue, I am immediately reminded of artists who use blues in their art. I am an imaginary member of their club, and I love to search for them in museums and books.

I find cobalt in Henri Matisse as much as in medieval art. I actually share a lot of colors with Matisse, such as his greens and reds. After all, he is one of my top three favorite artists. But it is the cobalt, which he uses especially in his cutouts, that I am always drawn to.

Maybe it was the Mediterranean Sea he observed during his stays in Nice or the textiles he collected when he was a starving artist in Paris or the time he spent in Morocco. Whatever the inspiration, Matisse's art is full of rich, deep blues.

I also find cobalt in Vincent van Gogh's skies and his irises (not unlike the blue irises I obsessively grow to have blue flowers in the garden); in David Hockney's American patios, gardens, and pools; and in the impressionist shadows in Claude Monet's haystacks and foggy mornings in London. I find it floating in Monet's beautiful ponds with waterlilies: thick, loose brushstrokes in all shades, from deep ultramarine to bright cobalt to pale, almost lilac periwinkle. Monet is also among my favorite painters.

Modern and contemporary art? Cobalt is also a magnet for me.

But before there was cobalt blue, the synthetic paint color we know, there was Smalt blue. Both are made of cobalt oxide but result in slightly different textures and tones. Modern cobalt is brighter, smoother, and more stable.

I love finding Smalt blue in Dutch Golden Age paintings. I see it in many textiles and dresses, in the small flowers among the tulips set in large vases, and in the Delft tiles and ceramics in those same paintings. But mostly, I love finding it in Johannes Vermeer's women in *The Art of Painting*, *Women in Blue Reading a Letter*, *The Milkmaid*, *Woman with a Water Jug*, and *Girl with a Pearl Earring*, where it frames the subject's face. All these rich blues, paired with pale yellow and crisp white linen and bathed in the light from the stained-glass window, are what I see when I close my eyes and think of the Dutch master.

Further back in history, in medieval and Renaissance art, I love finding the most luxurious of blues: the ultramarine made from crushed semiprecious lapis lazuli. It was so fancy that at the time, it was reserved only for painting the robes of the Virgin Mary and portraits of the superrich. Ground from real lapis lazuli from Afghanistan, the pigment was originally used in Persian miniatures as far back as the thirteenth century.

But one of my favorite ultramarine blue moments in art is a devotional, yearlong calendar journal from about 1411. Each page of the *Très Riches Heures du Duc de Berry* features a luscious semicircle of sky with gilded stars and zodiac signs hanging over beautiful scenes of the duke's dreamy castle and the seasonal activities surrounding it. While the illustrations are rich with detail, it is that rich blue that made me fall in love with this journal as a teenager.

So why do I search for blue in history, in museums, and in books?

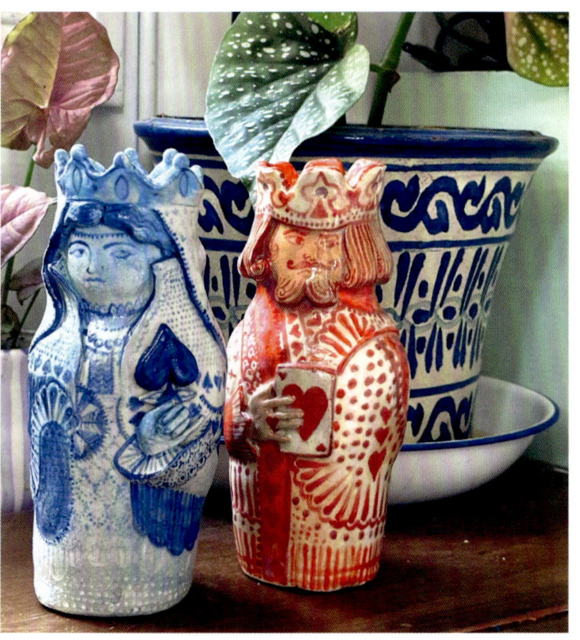

Finding my favorite color in art history connects me with bygone artists. I think, *How did they use the blue? Which blue did they favor?* And of course, I imagine them swooning over the preparation of the color, as I do. The color serves as an anchor that makes me a more engaged observer.

I see this search as a personal treasure hunt that keeps my eyes wide open when I visit museums or browse through books. It grabs my attention and it helps keep the art of sightseeing fresh. By finding the blue, I am drawn into the piece on the brushstroke level.

Blue has served as a common thread through history, through my favorite pieces, and through my relationship with art: ancient, modern, high art, design, and illustration.

If I am in a rush to make a quick but beautiful illustration, chances are there will be cobalt or ultramarine involved. When I travel, I always have a cobalt blue pencil or a bicolor pencil to sketch with. Sometimes I pair ultramarine with pastels or go monochromatic, mixing the watercolor with white to make it opaque and pale or transparent at will. Cobalt is a total leitmotif for me.

I love faience (or Talavera, as it is called in Mexico), the painted ceramics that use blue in the form of cobalt oxide or cobalt carbonate, which is especially beautiful painted over the white glaze called majolica. Many cultures around the globe seem to share my love for blue and white ceramic—sometimes with the addition of yellow or copper-oxide green. Interestingly, as it happens with most ceramic glazes, the real color reveals itself only after a piece is fired; when I first apply the cobalt carbonate on my own bisque-fired ceramics, the glaze looks like pale lilac. It is only after going through the high-temperature glaze firing that it becomes the rich dark blue I love.

In the garden, I obsess about planting anything that will produce blue (or blueish) flowers: irises, California lilac, sage, bachelor button, nigella, and more. My garden goal is cobalt blue, but the color is very elusive.

A focus on a favorite color can become a connecting thread between you and artists from around the world, both past and present. It can become a research project in your own art or a limiting creative prompt for a body of work. It can simply act as a training exercise for your eye for color. Eventually, you may even find a signature color and, with consistent, varied use, a leitmotif.

"Ultramarine blue is a color illustrious, beautiful, and most perfect, beyond all other colors; you may make it from lapis lazuli or from the azure stone."
—Cennino Cennini[6]

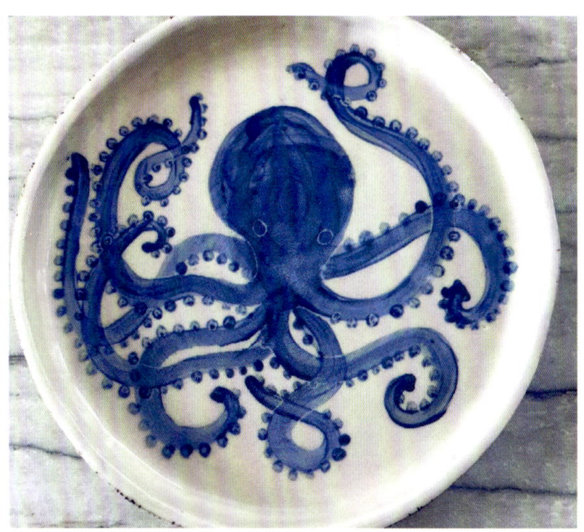

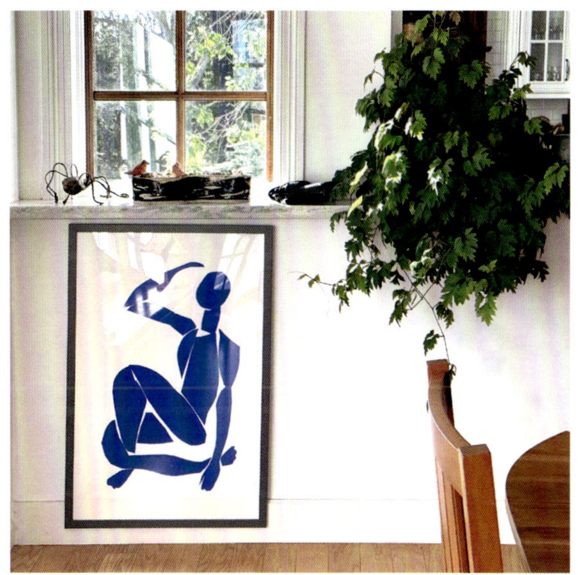

"I've been forty years discovering that the queen of all colors is blue. A certain blue enters your soul. A certain red influences your blood pressure."
—Henri Matisse[7]

JUST PICK A COLOR

Easier than it sounds, with so many beautiful or intriguing colors! How can we pick a color and commit to it?

A good starting point is to browse through your past creative work—or your clothing and other items in your home—and look for an already existing leitmotif, that color you keep on loving and wanting near you over and over again. Isolate that color and work with it to investigate how it interacts with other colors and discover the reactions it brings about in you.

The first time I heard about this idea was with my group of designer friends in the mid-1990s. They had all studied at Schule für Gestaltung Basel in Switzerland. They talked all the time about their legendary typography teachers and the grueling exercises in all principles of graphic design that they had gone through. I had studied fine arts in Italy, so my formative years, in contrast, had been much more intuitive and self-expressive. I was fascinated by the grand tales of their design school. But no design assignment of theirs exerted bigger fascination for me, not to mention a bit of jealousy, than a monthslong color exercise they had all submitted to.

For this color interaction exercise, they had to pick a color and custom mix it with attention and specificity, and in abundance, then paint pages upon pages of that color, without variation, applied as smoothly as possible, to use as a base.

Afterward, through months and months, they had to combine this hero color with all kinds of other colors—pastels, neutrals, and brights, similar colors and different ones, saturated and unsaturated—and then observe and analyze these pairings.

How lucky were they, I thought, to have been able to devote such attention to a single color! I wondered what they got out of it. I wished I had a full year to do such an exercise, but I still haven't found the time.

Like with many design principles, and specifically those related to color, this exercise links directly to the teachings of Josef Albers, first at the Bauhaus and later at Black Mountain College and Yale in the United States. Albers came up with a course to teach color unlike anything seen before. It was controversial at the time—criticized by many, praised by most.

Albers later compiled his revolutionary approach into the book *Interaction of Color*, based on hands-on experimentation, not theories. This experimentation renders no good or bad answers; the learning is in the observation and discovery of color combinations and one's reactions to them. The goal is never relying on a "safe" color system but the development of one's color taste.

Albers compares colors with sounds in music. A single color or pigment is nothing until it is put next to

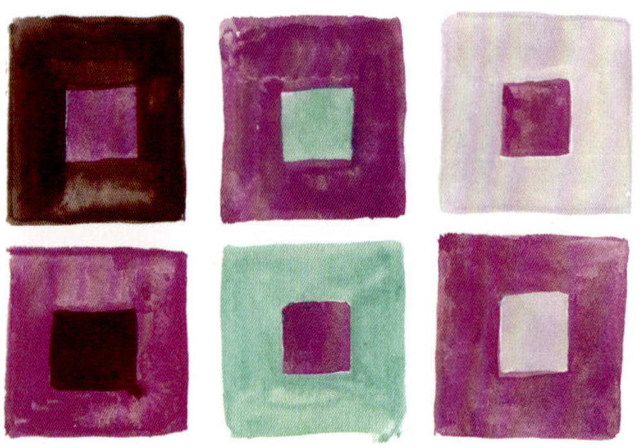

"In visual perception, a color is almost never seen as it really is—as it physically is. This fact makes color the most relative medium in art.

In order to use color effectively it is necessary to recognize that color deceives continually. First, it should be learned that one and the same color evokes innumerable readings.

The aim of such study is to develop … through experience—by trial and error— an eye for color.

This means, specifically, seeing color action as well as feeling color relatedness."
—Josef Albers[8]

another, just as it is not until you combine notes that you make music (or noise). It is not until you see two or more colors together that you can evaluate them. Albers developed a suite of color exercises that allows us, in many ways, to see the relationships, instabilities, harmonies, and dissonances of color when it interacts.

The benefits of observing color interactions are immense: You will gain insights about how a single color changes as it interacts with others and draw conclusions that range from aesthetic to emotional to mechanical, allowing you to make more intentional choices in the future. You will become inventive and precise at color mixing and move away from obvious combinations into more interesting ones, especially if you complete Albers's exercise for long periods of time.

You might even consider a meditative ten-minute daily practice for one hundred days or a yearlong project. It most certainly sharpens our eye for color, as Albers said.

I know that if I took a year to do the exercise my friends were assigned or to follow Albers's book, I would pick cobalt as my color. Choosing cobalt, the particular tint of it I love so much, would not mean I would not play with other hues. On the contrary, picking my favorite blue as a leitmotif would allow me to go deep into how it combines with all the other possible colors. This intimate look at cobalt as a hero color would teach me as much about it as about all the companion colors I observe in interaction.

"Our study of color differs fundamentally from a study which anatomically dissects colorants (pigments) and physical qualities (wavelength).

Our concern is the interaction of color; that is, seeing what happens between colors.

Colors present themselves in continuous flux, constantly related to changing neighbors and changing conditions."
—Josef Albers[9]

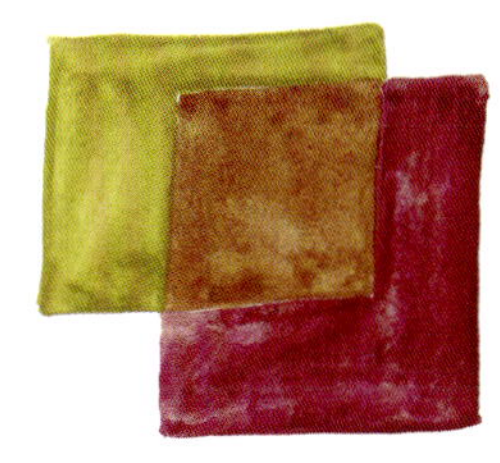

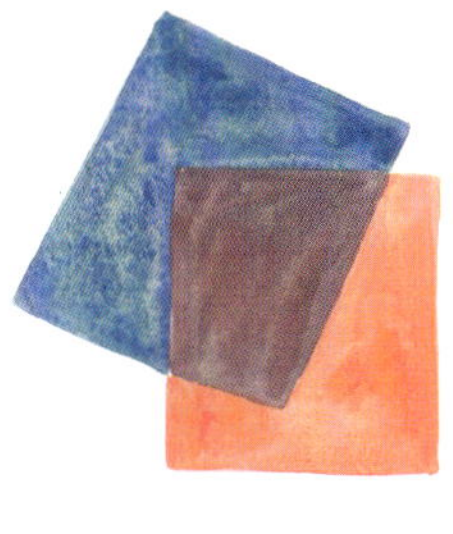

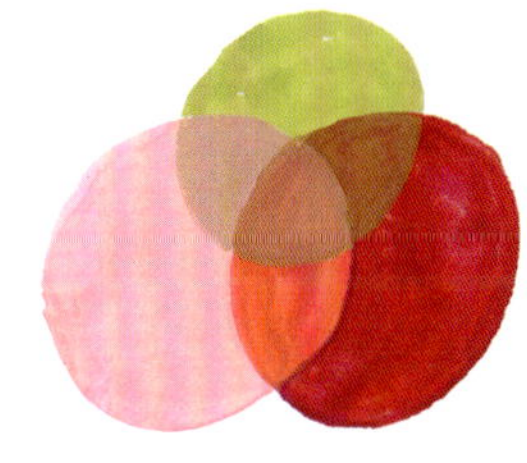

"There is no blue without yellow and without orange, and if you use cobalt blue, you must be aware of its delicate nature and its harmonious combination with other colors."
—Vincent van Gogh[10]

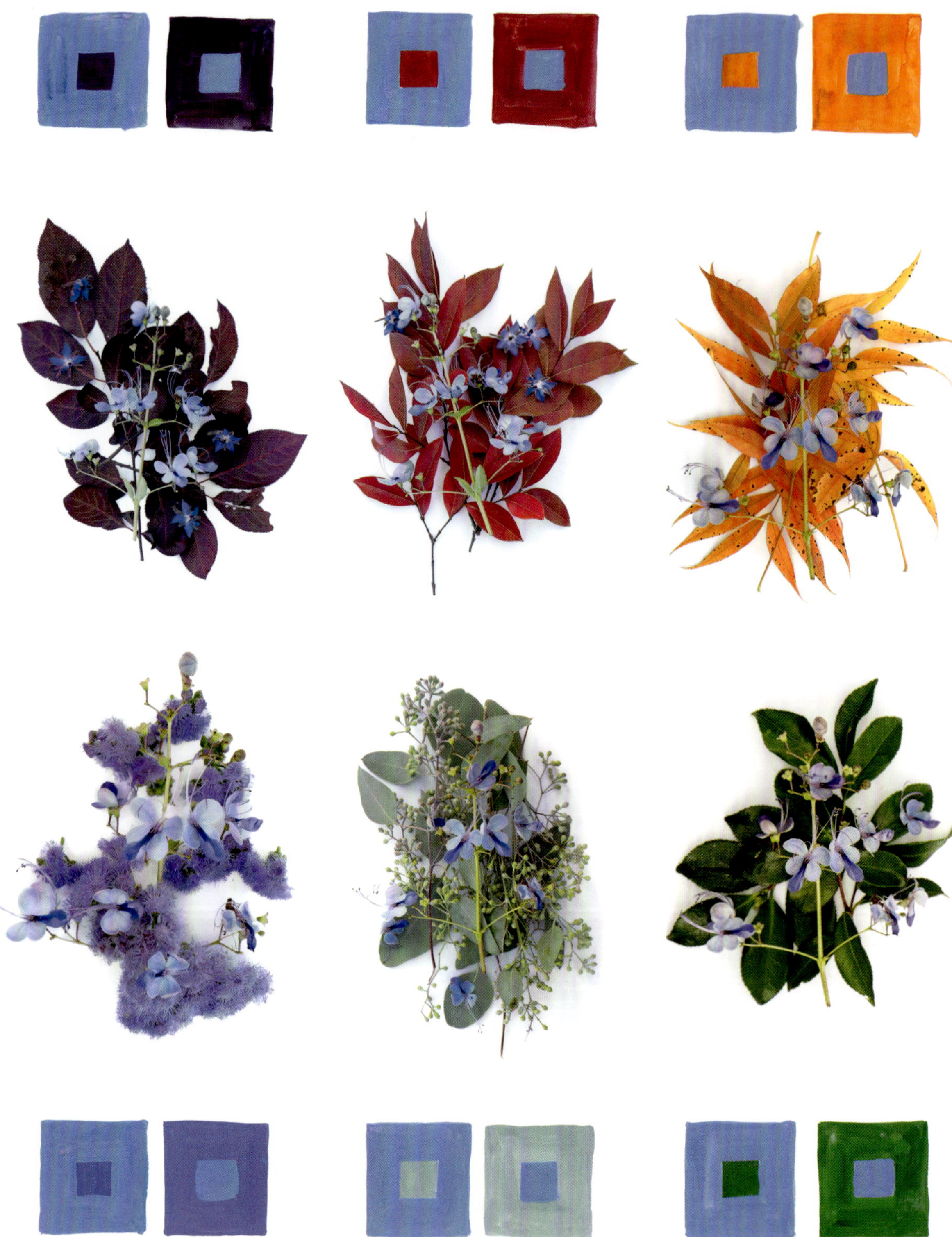

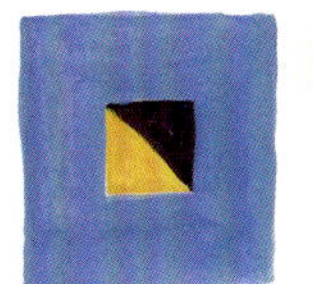 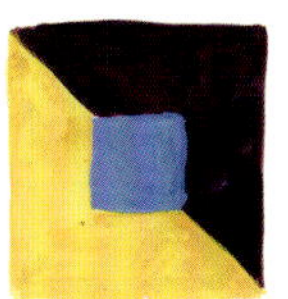 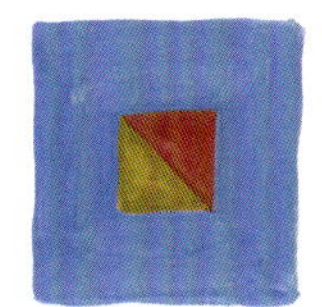 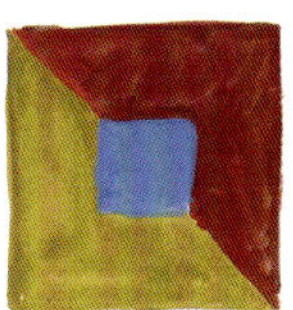 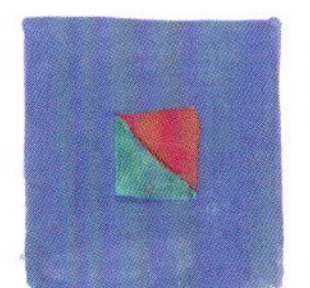 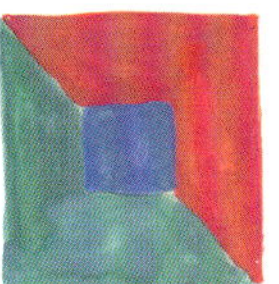

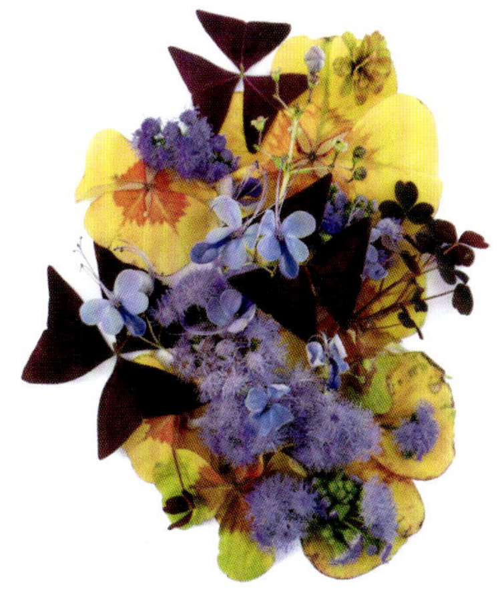 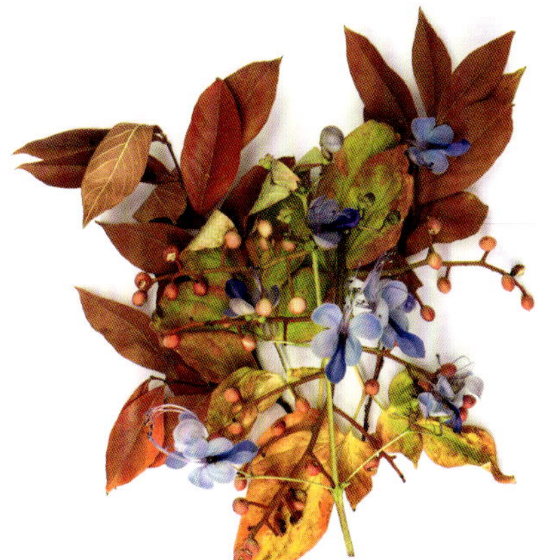 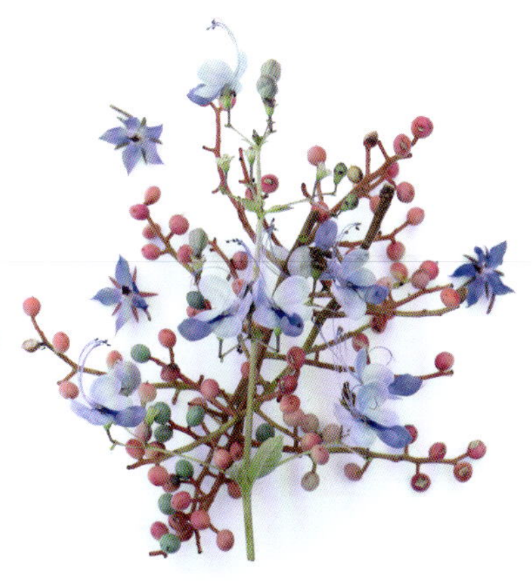

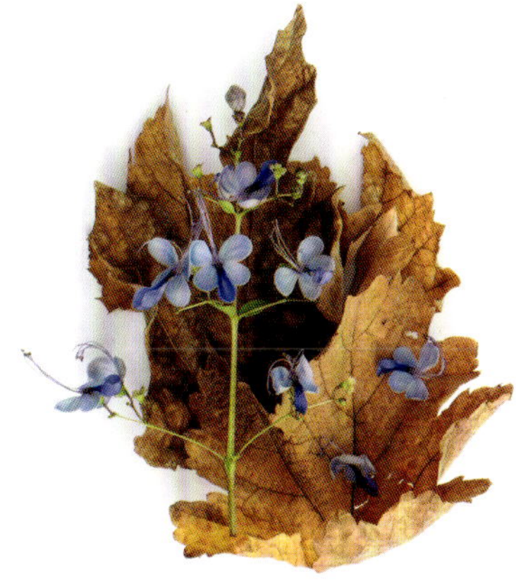 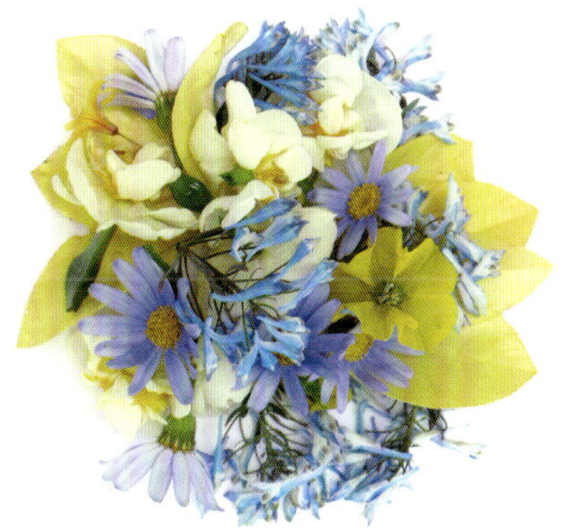

A STUDY SERIES

PERIWINKLE BLUE AS LEITMOTIF

I picked one of my favorite flowers from a bush; notice it has two tones of periwinkle. Then I placed it on all the different foliage I found around the yard to observe the interactions of the darker periwinkle with those other colors in a leitmotif exercise.

For each combination, I made two square variations: one with periwinkle dominating and one with it in a smaller amount. Then I analyzed how these sets of two and three colors look and which ones I like best.

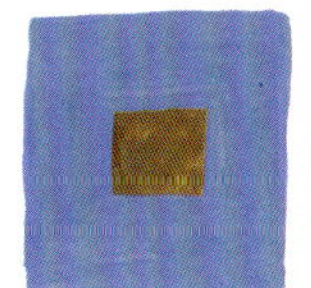  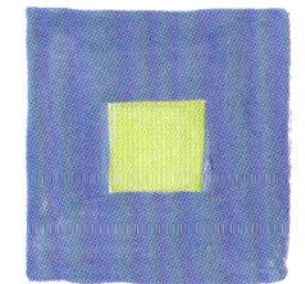 

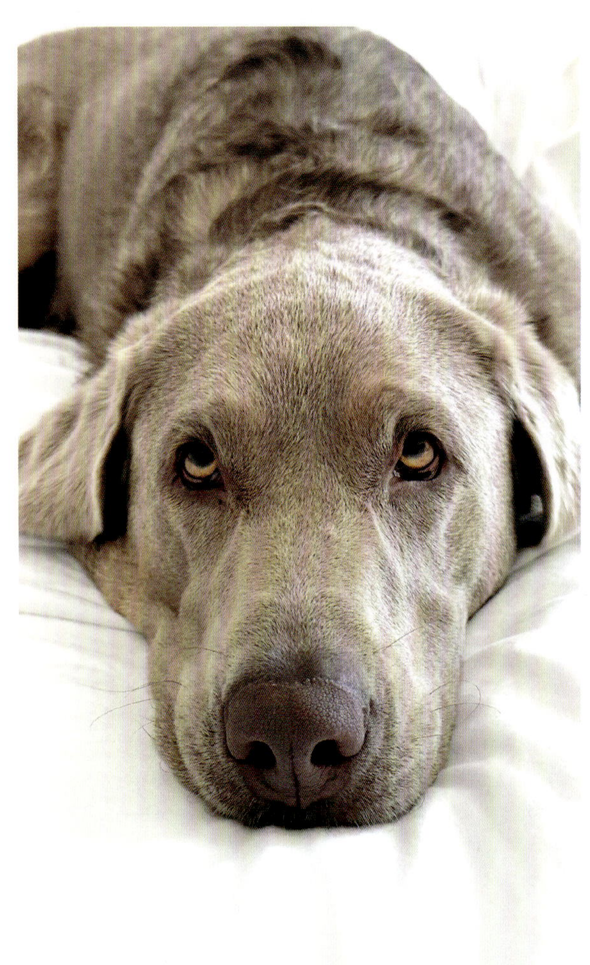

A SET OF COLORS BOTH INTRIGUING AND FAMILIAR

I observed and analyzed Bonnie, my Labrador dog, as her silver fur, her taupe nose, the lilac inside her ears, and her yellow mustard–colored eyes have become a recent obsession (not to mention her lilac-pink belly!). Everywhere we go, I can't help seeing her colors in relationship to her surroundings: the sofa, the rug, my clothes, the bed, the plants along our walks. This has resulted in many silver-toned mental notes and little palettes with her colors as a recurring theme.

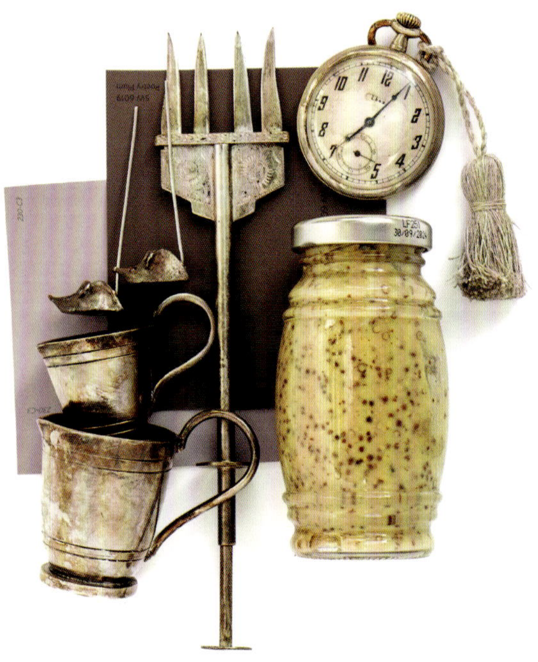

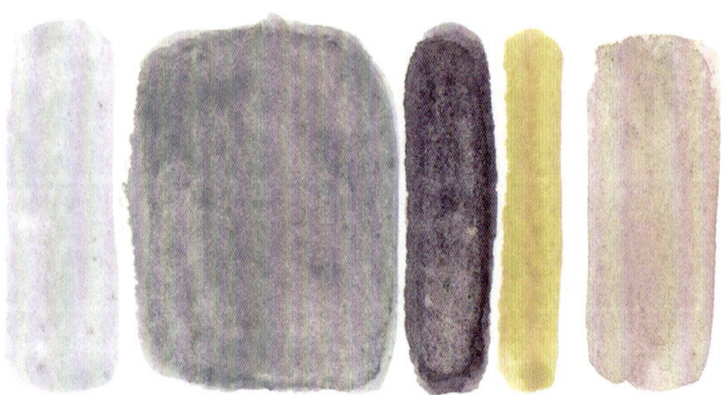

↓ Oxidized silver, grain mustard, taupe, and lilac.

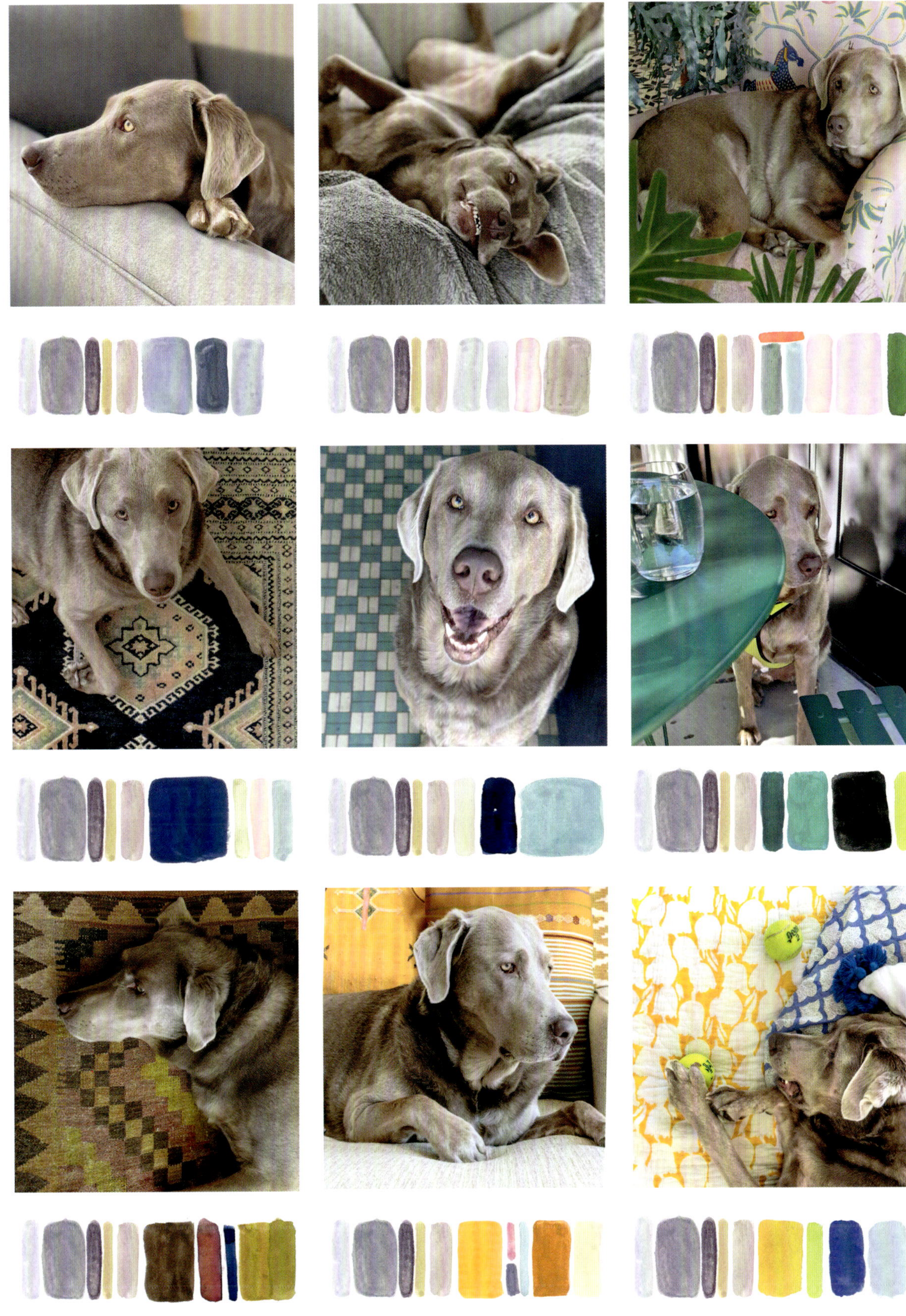

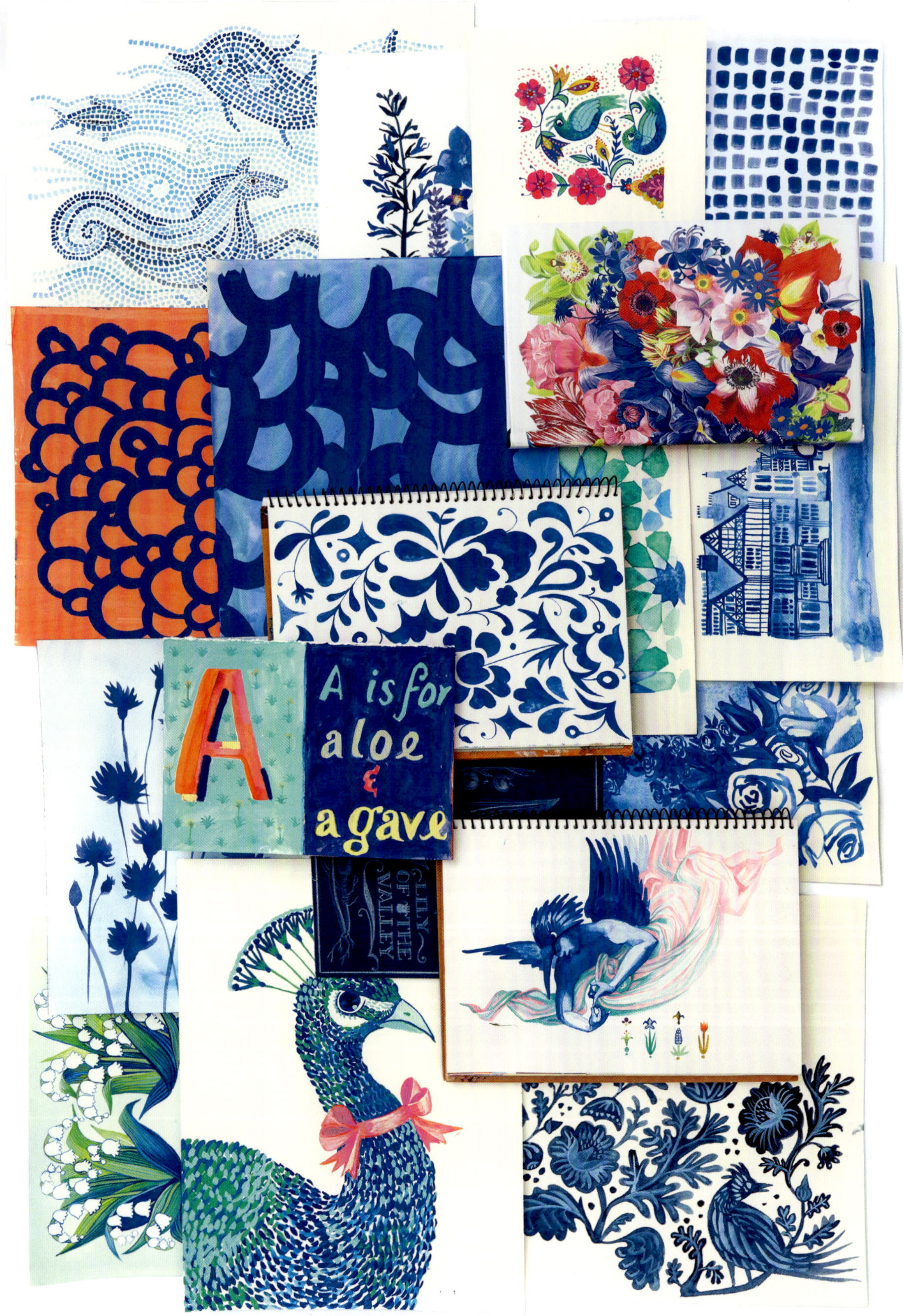

A is for
aloe
& agave
A
LILY OF THE VALLEY

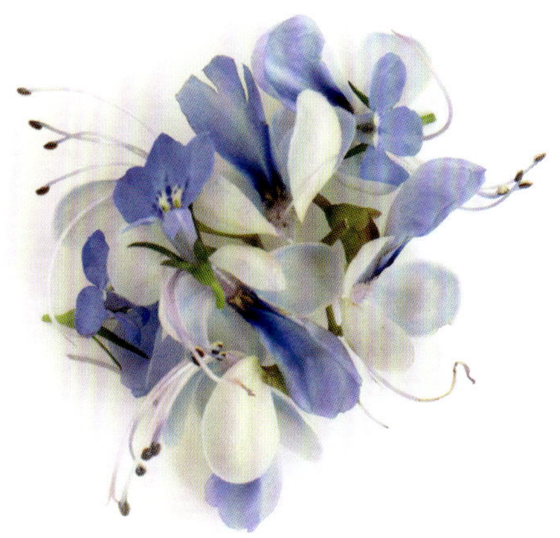

KEY TAKEAWAYS

1. A favorite color has a reason for being favored; notice it and then expand on it. It is okay to have many favorite colors, bask in them, refine them, and explore them to make them truly your own. They may end up recognized as part of your signature palette.

2. Take a chosen color through a visual scavenger hunt: Find it in museums and books, in crafts from around the world and the products in the supermarket, in the clothes in your closet, and in the streets and subway. Notice how others use and combine it.

3. Go deeper into the application of your favorite color, whether you follow Albers's exercise or create your own. Make your practice intentional, focused, and varied. The goal is to find new interactions for your favorite color and develop your own opinion of those combinations.

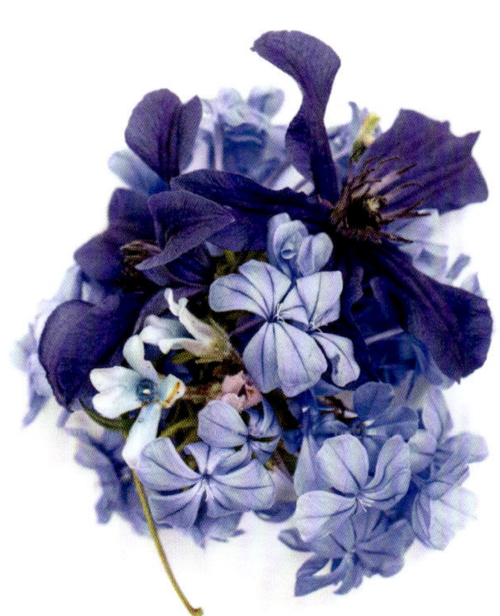

4. Notice each combination, how it looks, what it evokes, how it changes with light, and how it makes you and others feel.

PROJECT

OBSERVE: Observe the series of periwinkle interactions in the previous pages. These are eleven variants, but there could be one thousand, and each would provide more information about what this blue can do. Look for periwinkle or your favorite color all around your house, in your clothes, and in your creative work. Did you find your leitmotif?

For a second exercise, as I did with Bonnie, find a new unexpected color or interacting colors to obsess over. Look out for a hue or tone you usually don't favor but that you suddenly find intriguing, then try to notice it in various settings.

Pick up a little object, like a piece of fabric or clothing, or even a fruit or vegetable you find in the market. It can be something bigger, as long as you can move it around to observe its relationship in combination with other hues, shades, and tints.

Once you identify your favorite color and your unexpected new color, you can extend the observation to take a deep dive finding these colors in art books or at a museum or botanical garden. Notice how looking for your colors helps you become a better art observer.

ANALYZE: Analyze the chromatic mental notes you make while observing your selected colors in art, nature, or your own home. As you analyze a specific color, ask yourself how you would mix it with paint or colored pencils. Is it a straight-out-of-the-tube-of-paint color, like my cobalt? Do you have the exact thread in your sewing box? Or do you need to combine various colors to accurately use it?

In my case, I know my favorite periwinkle results from a mix of ultramarine blue with white. I can also find it ready to go in some tubes, pencils, and pastels, and I have a few spools of thread in that same color. I like combining it with other blues and various greens, with pale pink, with mandarin orange and yellow, and of course, with white and off-white.

As you create the leitmotif color exercise with a single color—ultramarine variations for me—analyze your combinations, considering which ones are most surprising and which ones you love most. Notice how they feel emotionally and think about how and where you would use them.

CREATE: Curate a gallery wall with your favorite color; I will use cobalt and periwinkle for mine. Collect or make a variety of pieces—postcards, textiles, posters, a shadow box, your own art, or your favorite art—that use the chosen color. This collection of art pieces will be featured on the gallery wall. Focus on your color not on its own but acting as a leitmotif in a variety of combinations. This collection can become a real gallery wall in your house, or it can be just a practice run as a digital collage.

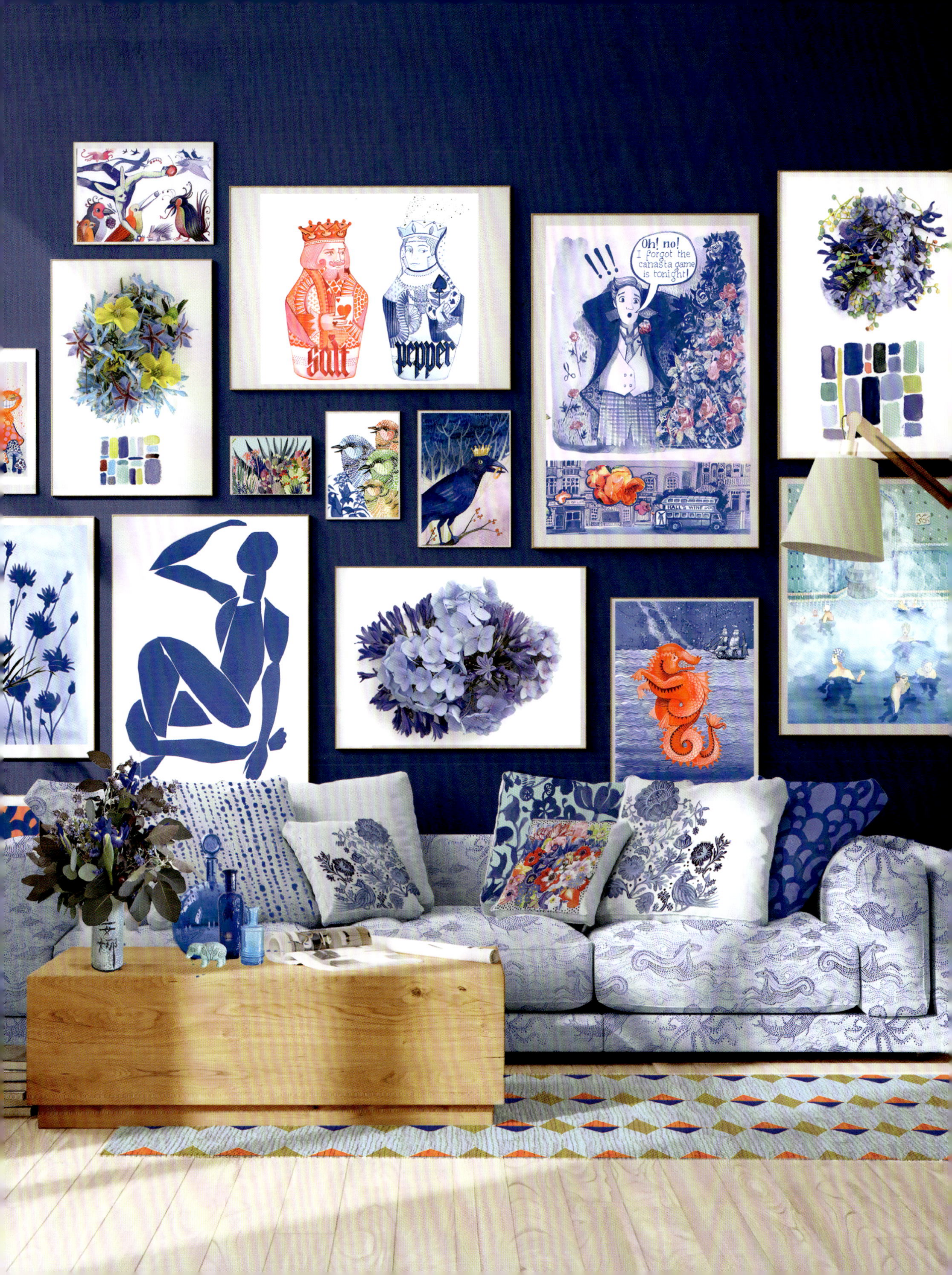

salt
pepper
Oh! no! I forgot the canasta game is tonight!
!!!

OBSERVE:

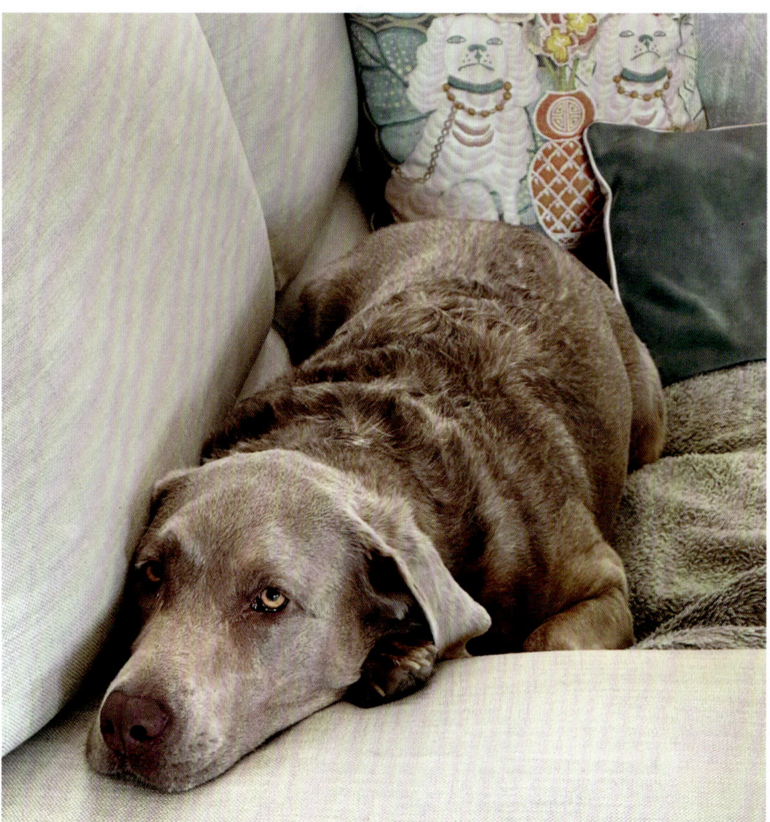

There are a variety of chromatic grays here, from all of Bonnie's grays, her yellow eyes, and her taupe nose, with the blueish and greenish grays of the sofa and her blanket.

For my unexpected color, I did not pick just the tarnished silver of Bonnie's fur. I created a mini palette of four of her colors to combine with the colors of her surroundings. This resulted in many palettes that are so interesting to me but I would have never found without her "help."

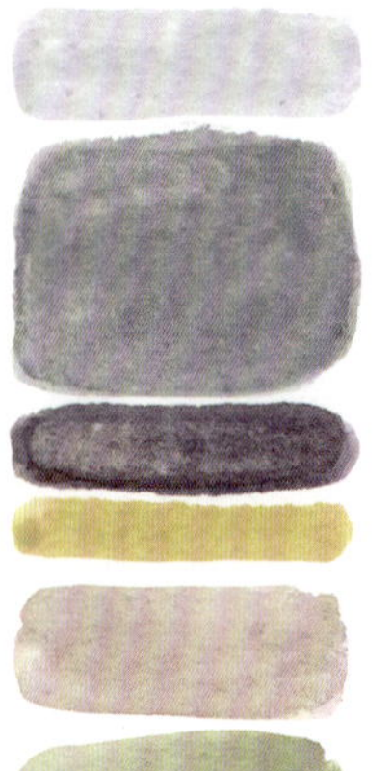

ANALYZE:

Where is the most neutral gray? From there, notice all the chromatic variations and their range of low saturation. Notice the slightly more saturated colors in the cushions. These wouldn't feel saturated if they were not surrounded by gray.

CREATE:

Create a table setting or a shelf display using your unexpected colors. I will use the Bonnie-on-the-sofa colors for mine.

Think of a 3D space: a table, console table, or mantle, and the objects, dishes, vases or containers, plant or flowers, wall covering, and so on that might go on it. It can be a real setting or a digital collage. It can be for a home or a store window, like a miniature Bergdorf Goodman window. What matters is that it features the unexpected colors you've just discovered and like, in combination with other tones, to convey a specific vibe or mood.

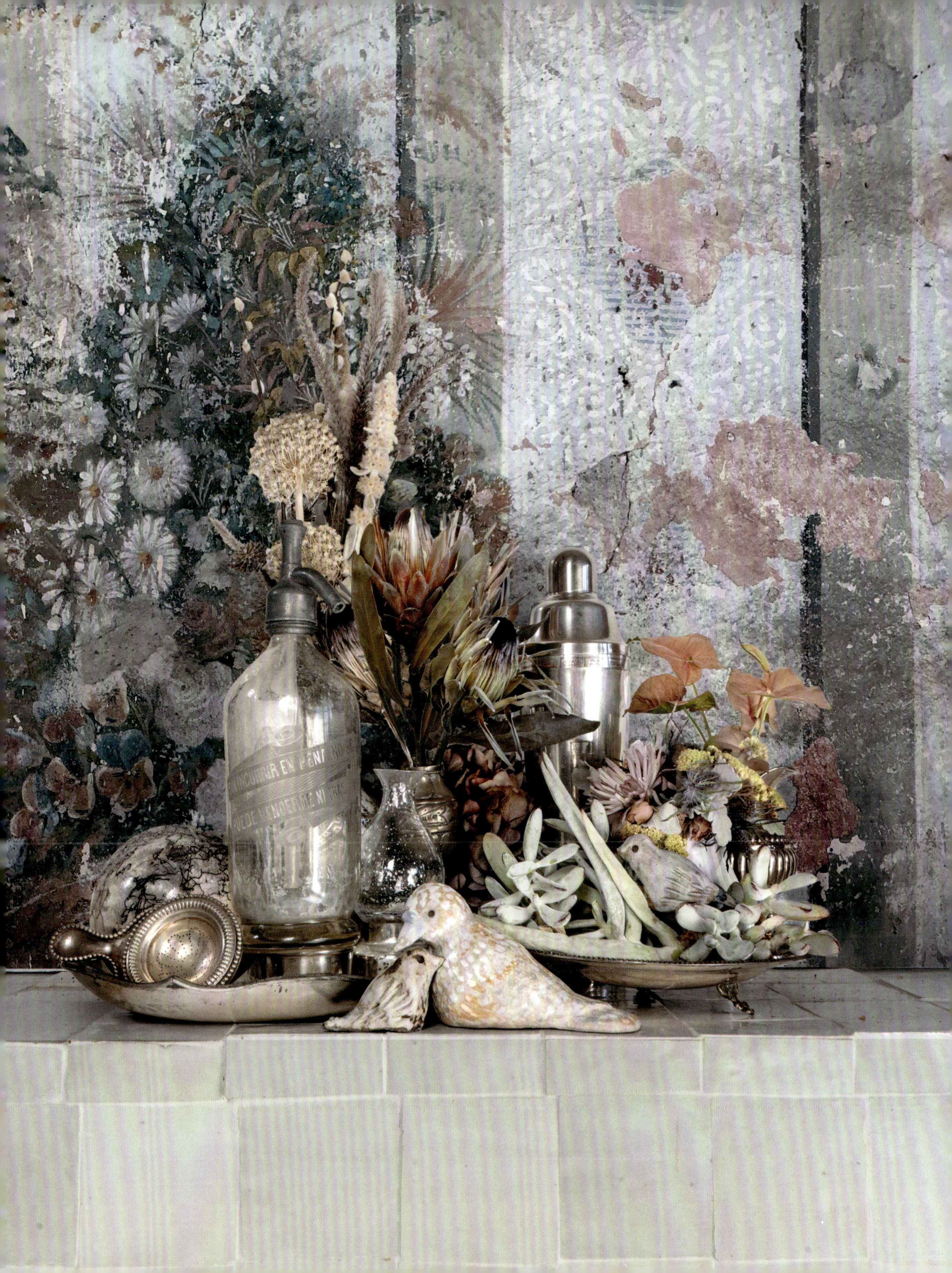

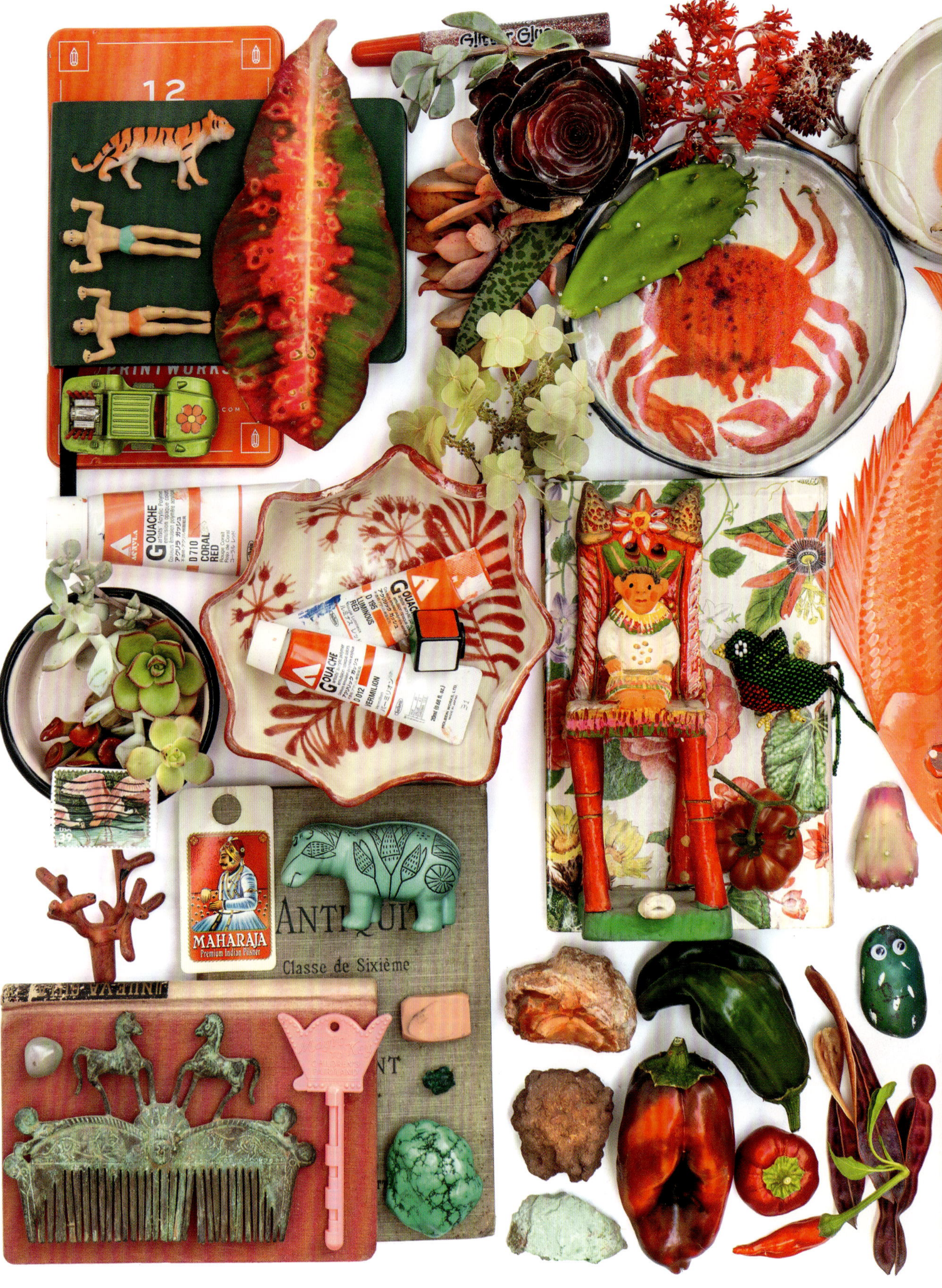

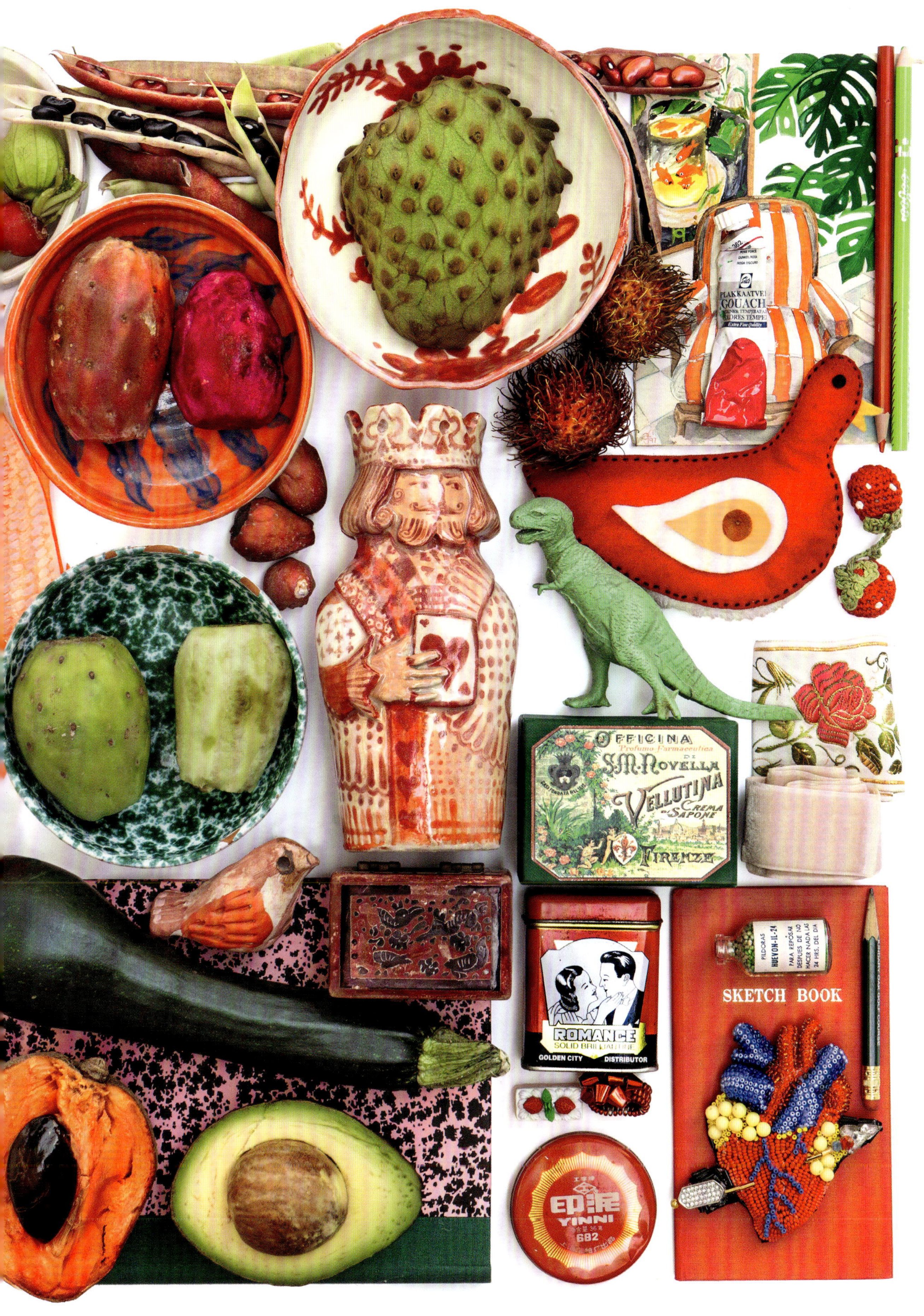

PLAKKAATVERF
GOUACHE
Extra Fine Quality
OFFICINA
Profumo Farmaceutica
DI
S·M·NOVELLA
VELLUTINA
CREMA
DA SAPONE
FIRENZE
ROMANCE
SOLID BRILLIANTINE
GOLDEN CITY   DISTRIBUTOR
SKETCH BOOK
YINNI
682

3.
SIDEWAYS AND ACROSS, NEIGHBORLY COLORS

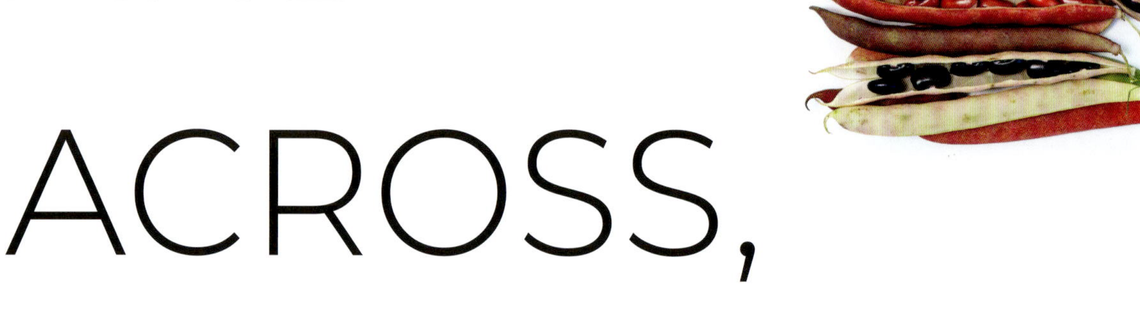

Ways to Create Color Systems and Expand the Potential of Color Pairs and Triads

O n Newton's color wheel, the round chart with rainbow colors all around, we can easily see colors that are opposite each other, or complementary: red and green, purple and yellow, blue and orange. If you pay attention, you'll find that these opposing colors coexist in nature. We appreciate the beauty of red poppies on a field of green, and with a closer look, we notice the long blue-green shadows cast by objects under the vermilion light of a low sun (more on the color of light and shadow in Chapter 5).

Think of complementary colors as protagonist and antagonist sitting on opposite sides of the wheel.

When combined in art and design, complementary colors balance each other, providing contrast and interest. We are not talking only about pure red and green or straight-out-of-the-tube cobalt and yellow. Using chromatic nuances, we can explore the full range of one color in combination with the full potential of a second: pale pink with a deep green, bright orange with midnight blue. Using complementary colors with intention, when every tone and shade is orchestrated masterfully, results in balance, depth, and nuanced beauty.

Jules Maidoff, my New York–born painting mentor in Florence, Italy, taught me about color systems in painting. After completing my training in graphic design, it was my dream to study art in Florence, and once I was there, I was eager to learn how to paint with oils. I set out to make a very large painting based on a photo I took of hens and roosters. Coming from Mexico—the land of saturated colors—I began to paint the scene in full intense technicolor. The black, green, red, and deep orange of the poultry were set against a green wall and perched over a tiled floor of cobalt and yellow. Intuitively I had used a complementary color system—red and green, blue and yellow—but my intensity was out of whack, since everything was painted at full saturation. Jules asked for permission to show me how to create chromatic nuances. In horror, I watched him tone down a corner of my lime-green background using carmine (complementary to the green), then mix it with white and a bit more green to make it paler, creamier, and less saturated.

Somehow, it worked.

He told me to do the same with all the walls, adding nuances of light and shadow—the tonal structure—but controlling the level of saturation. The important things—the hens and roosters—could be more saturated to help them stand out, while their surroundings could be less saturated so that they didn't distract from the fowl. As a result, the scene gained depth. In one single painting, under Jules's watchful eye, I learned three important tricks for using complementary colors:

- Keeping my brightest, most saturated colors on the main elements, in this case the greens and reds on the main birds. Regardless of how dark—the rooster's dark green feathers—or pale—part of the hens—if they belonged to the main characters, they were to be vibrant and saturated.

- Toning down and desaturating the rest of the colors to create depth, modulating colors to contrast pale areas with shadows, none of which should be saturated and, therefore, distracting.

- "Dirtying" colors with their complementary colors to create nuances. The modulated effect was not achieved by adding black; on the contrary, black was to be avoided, as it would make things gray and muddy. If I needed to tone down, desaturate, or darken a green, I would do so by mixing in red gradually. (White was okay to use in pale mixes.)

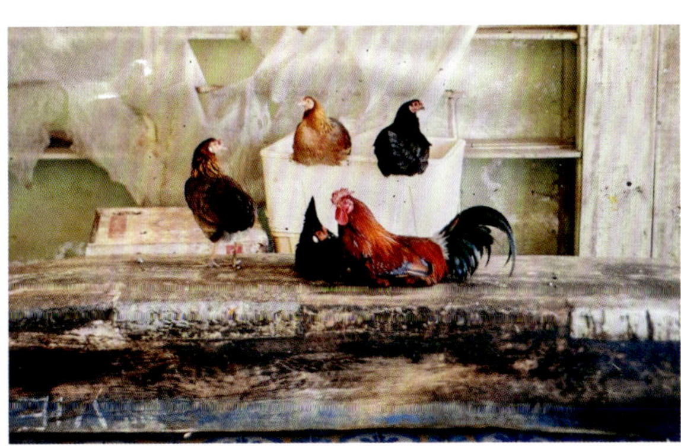

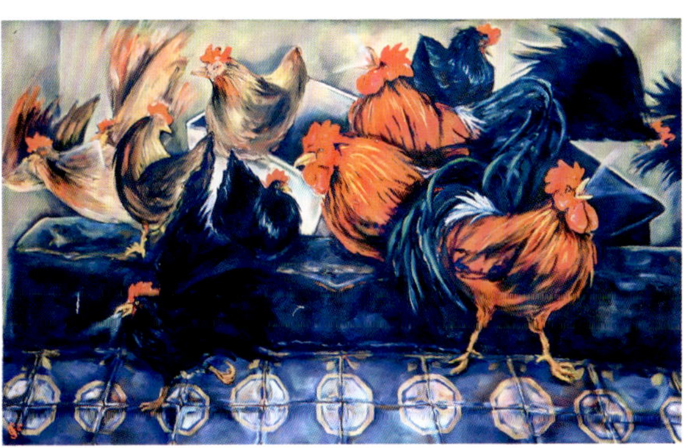

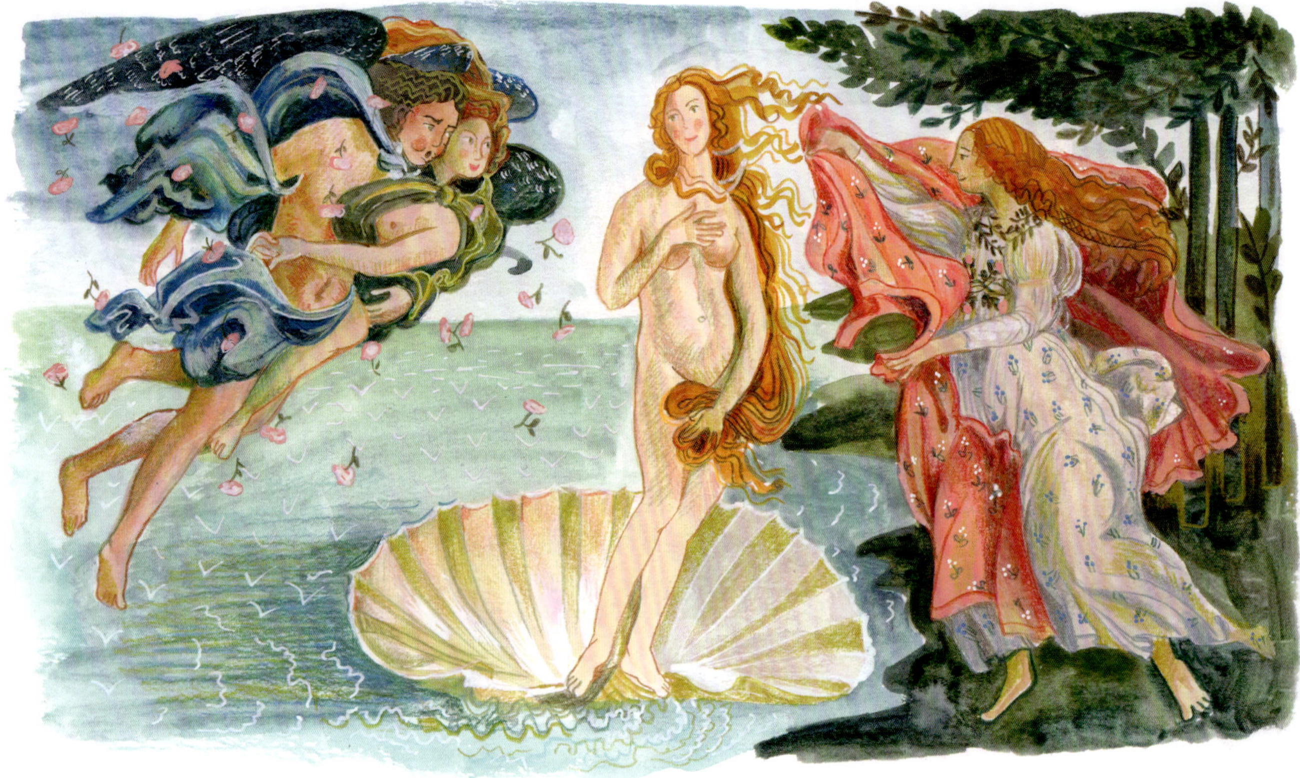

Then Jules told me to meet him at a museum in the center of Florence, which showed Renaissance paintings interspersed with some Amedeo Modigliani paintings—old and modern Italian art.

In front of each painting, he asked me these two questions: What is the complementary color system being used? What is the tonal structure?

Ignoring the story of the painting for a minute and focusing on the color used by the masters changed the way I see art and think of color. That was thirty years ago, and I still find myself asking those two questions in museums or when I make my own art.

On my own, I went to the Brancacci Chapel. I turned my eye away from the faces and the nakedness of one of the most beautiful Adam and Eve scenes ever and concentrated on the garments of the people in the piazza scenes. I saw groupings of blue and orange and accents of green and red. At the Uffizi, I saw Sandro Botticelli's *Birth of Venus* in a different light too; this time I paid attention to the pale green of the water contrasting with the dark green of the trees, the land, and the wings of the wind god. I noticed the lovely contrast of the pink roses everywhere and the salmon-colored towel. Red and green, but so nuanced!

What about Venus's golden hair? The blue sky and the periwinkle flowers on the woman's dress are there to complement it. All these colors served to offset Venus's milky naked skin and her scalloped shell.

USING COMPLEMENTARY COLORS FOR DRAMA AND LUMINOSITY

Once I learned about complementary color systems, I could not stop noticing them! From the Middle Ages through the Renaissance and on to the later, more dramatic Manierist style, the Italians were masters of using these systems. But there was another trick they had up their sleeves: a luminous color effect called cangiantismo, meaning *changing* in Italian. Cangiantismo is the technique of relying on contrasting colors to indicate a shift in volume without making one color darker than the next; one side of an object is blue and the other side is orange, for example. It's mostly used for clothes to make them look silky and luxe, but it is also used on the wings of angels and occasionally on faces. It was invented by none other than Giotto, that art genius who opened the door to Renaissance humanism.

I recall first observing this technique in Florence's Santa Croce frescoes and Padua's Arena Chapel, particularly in the suffering faces of the monks crying over the death of Saint Francis. I was intrigued and, I must say, almost moved to tears by the pale skin softly going from a greenish undertone to barely there purple to indicate shadows. The luminous vestments worn by the angels shifted from blue to yellow or green, giving them an almost iridescent quality of silk damask.

Fra Angelico, known for his golden panels full of angels, also used this luminous effect subtly in the clothing of his myriad figures.

But the apex of the cangiantismo color range was reached with Michelangelo, especially in the Sistine Chapel: purple to pale aqua blue, yellow to green, copper to yellow, lilac to turquoise, red to ultramarine. All these Italians really liked their luxe textiles!

Where else have I observed this technique recently? In many Pixar movies! Look at the monsters of *Monsters, Inc.* and the characters of *Toy Story*, especially when a scene is set in low light. See how the darker sides of the faces have a blue or purple tint; it's really not that dark, but it creates the effect of shadow. Look also to your own photos. When a portrait taken next to a window is lit by indoor light as well, the window side will be blue and cool, while the indoor side is orangey and warm.

Once you start seeing it, you won't be able to stop. The luminous light effects of cangiantismo are everywhere.

Do all artists use complementary color systems? Not all, but browse through your art books, visit a museum, or observe contemporary illustrations or beautiful children's books, and ask yourself Jules's two questions about the color system and tonal structures. You will see this intentional use of color everywhere. Once you find the complementary colors, ask yourself what they are doing to tell the story of the picture.

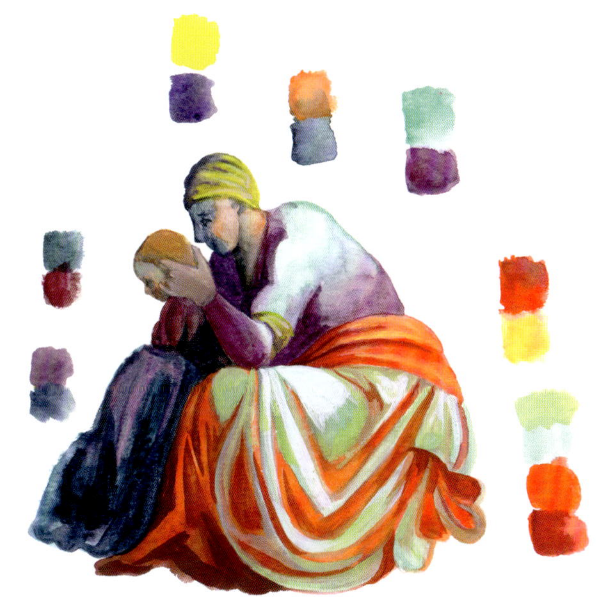

↑ This illustration is from a detail from Michelangelo's Sistine Chapel. Just in this scene of a woman and a child, there are seven pairs of complementary colors creating cangiantismo effects. Notice how not all colors are at full intensity: There are bright reds and oranges paired with minty greens, there are dark greens paired with dark reds, bright yellows with violets, and others.

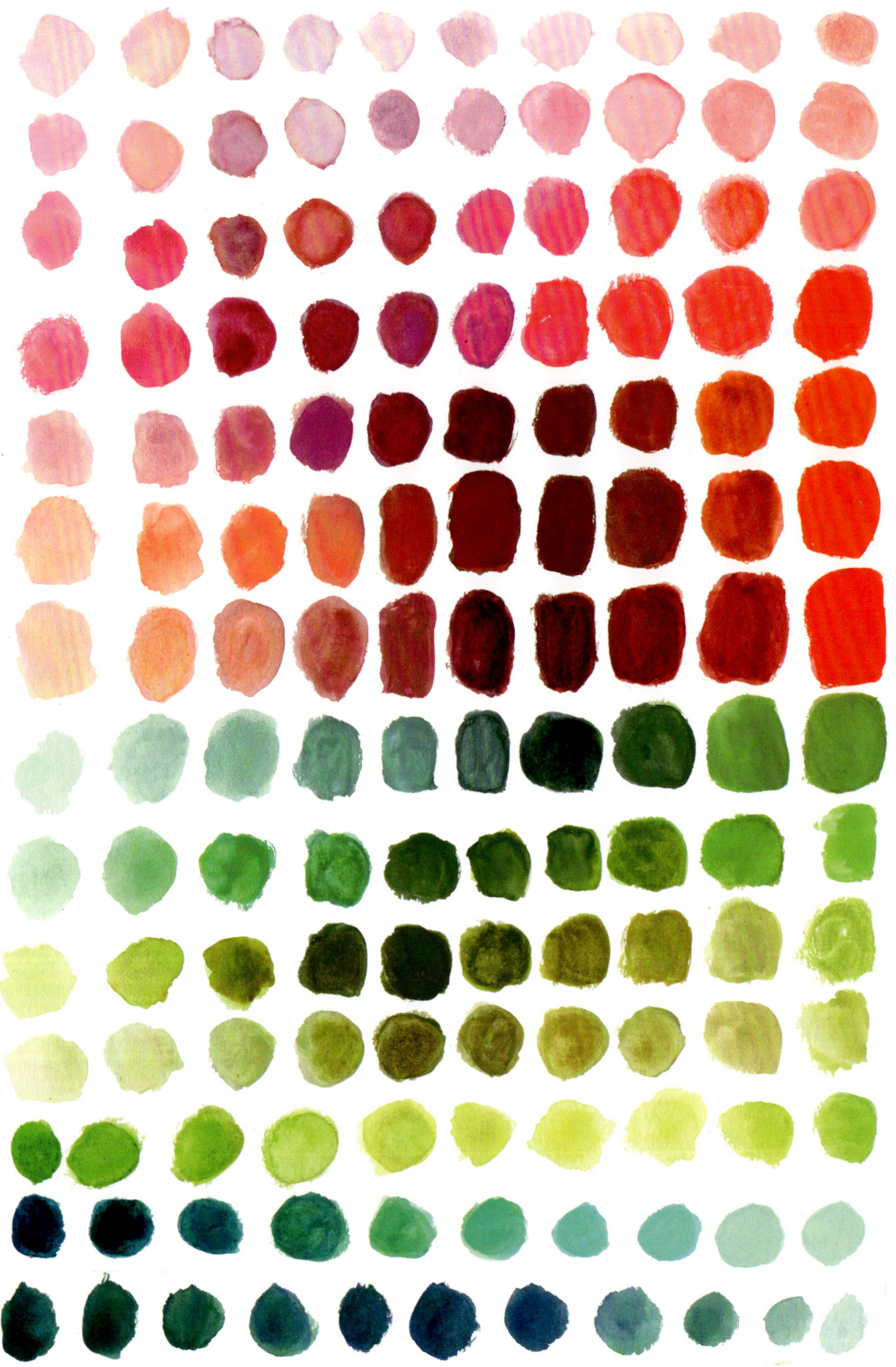

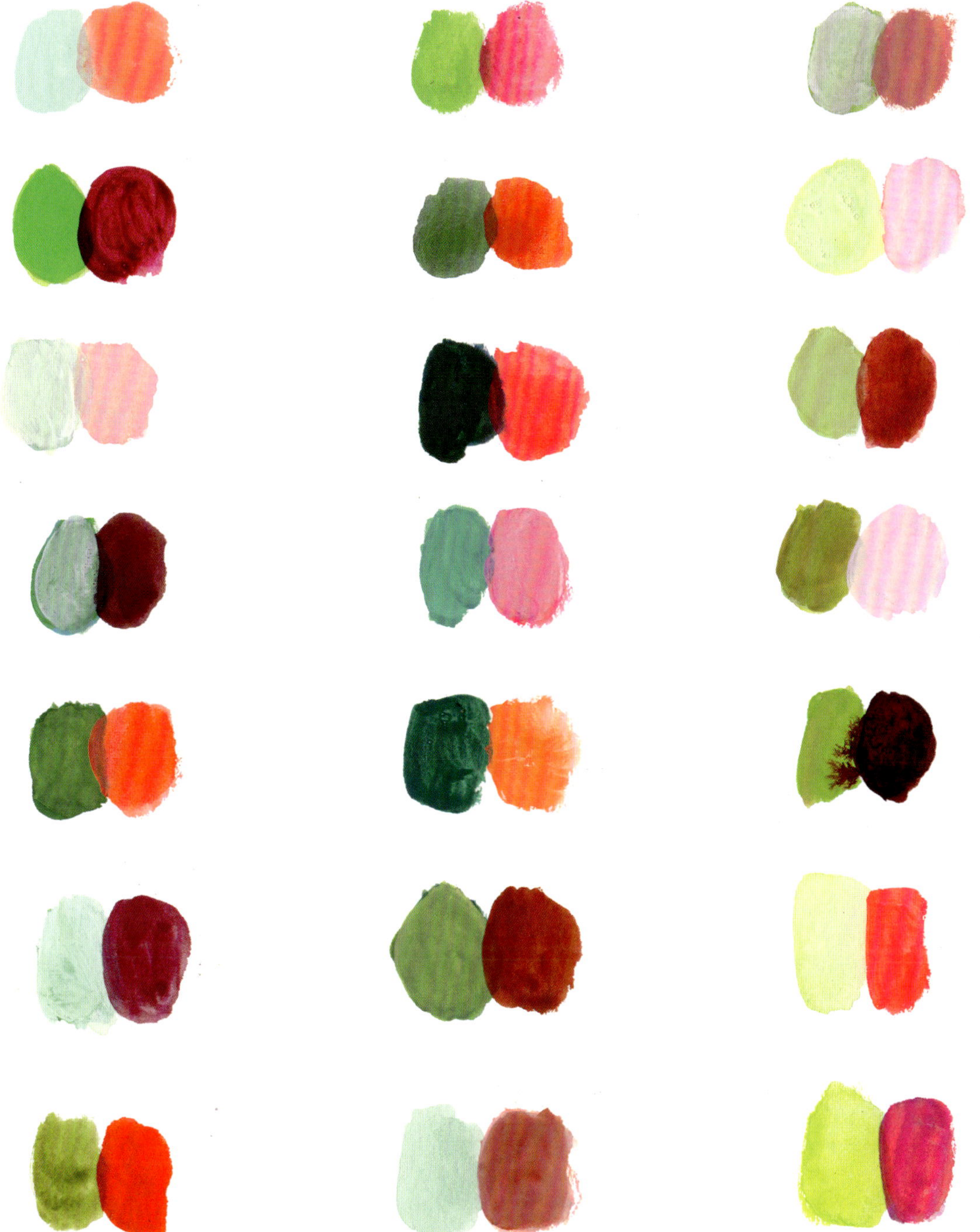

↑ Observe the full range of reds and greens:

When mixing color, complementary colors cancel each other, creating interesting neutrals when combined in equal amounts.

When searching for interesting nuances, skip the pure hue and try using variations of it that are closer to its adjacent colors: For example, red can move toward purple or orange, while green can move toward blue or yellow. Then experiment with those nuanced hues.

- Take a bright green and mix it with a deeper red, and you will get a jewel-tone deep green. The same thing happens with bright red mixed with deep greens. If you were to use black to darken a color, the effect would be different. Try it and compare.
- Consider using a pale tone with a bright tone (e.g., pale green with a bright red).
- Consider using a deep color with a bright color (e.g., deep green with a bright red).
- Pair saturated with desaturated. Try bright pastels together as well as dusty, desaturated pastels.

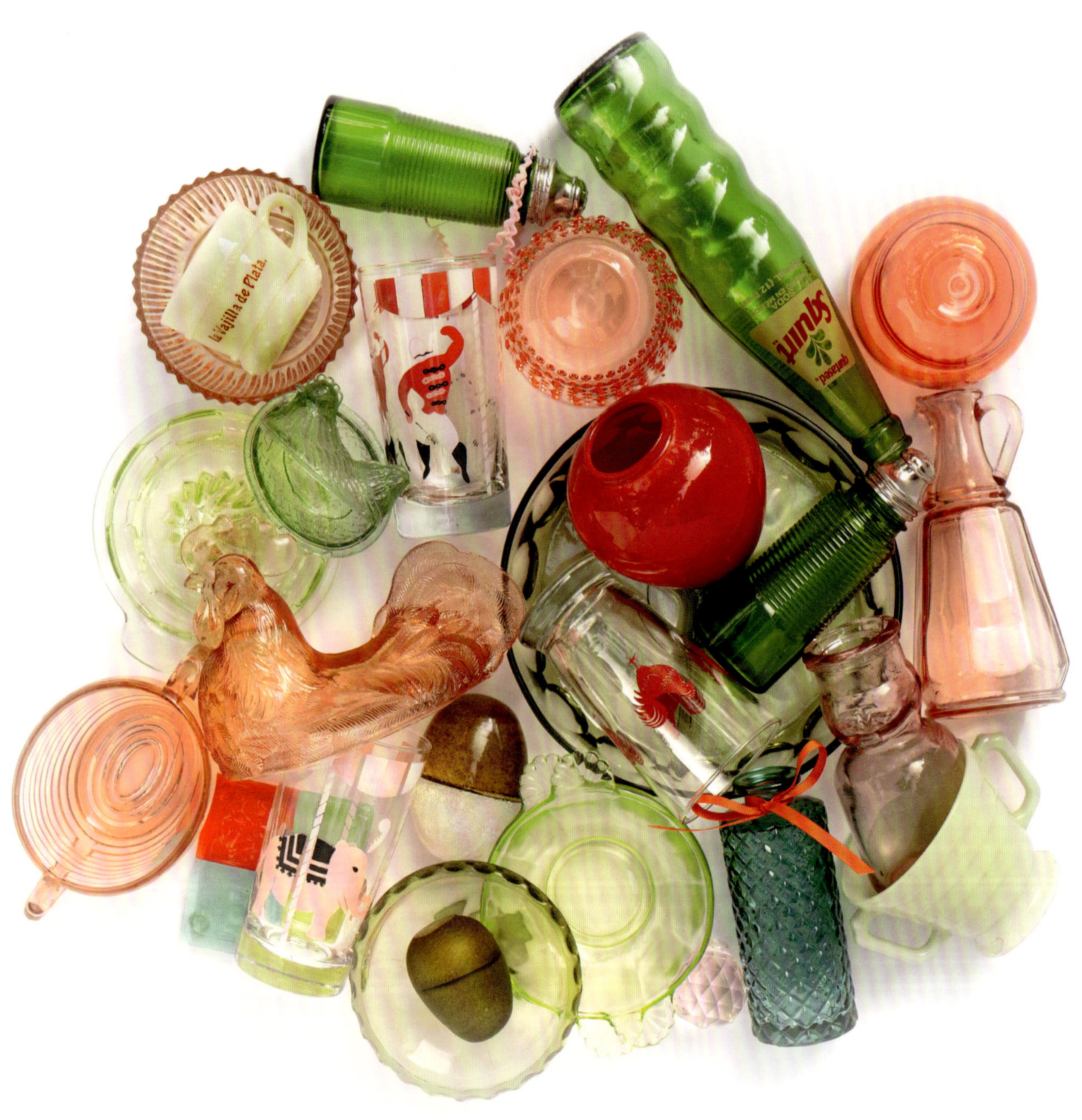

↑ When I think of green and red, it is not all "tomato and leaf"; I love to go from the palest green to the deepest, and with red from the brightest to the palest pink.

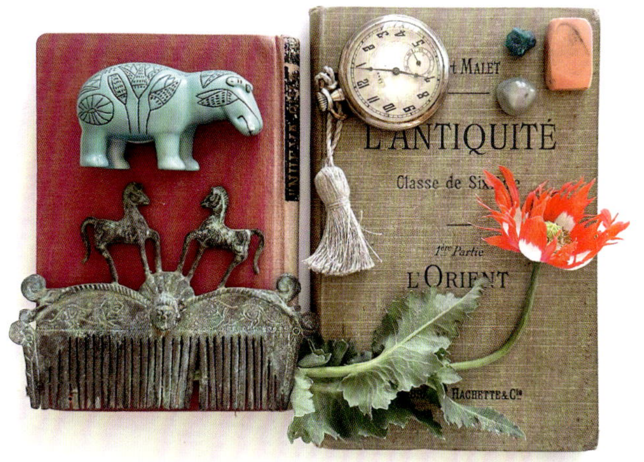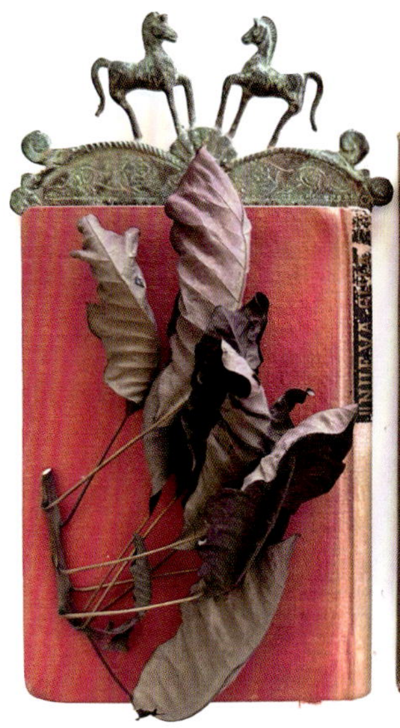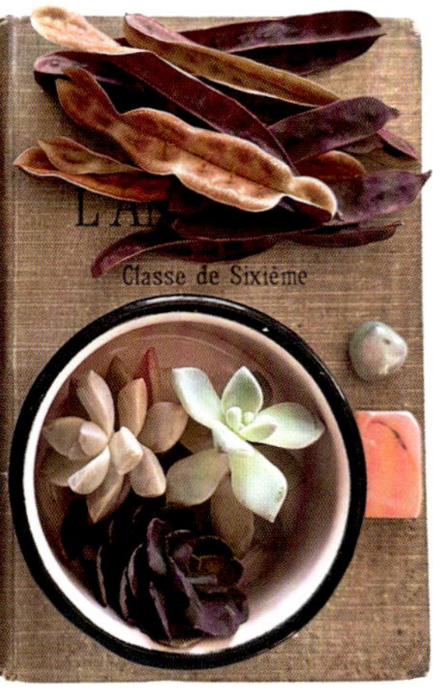

Remarkable Examples of Complementary Colors

There are endless examples in art of the use of complementary colors, but these are some of my favorites:

Henri de Toulouse-Lautrec in his scenes At the Moulin Rouge, *especially that wonderful green face. This painting features so much green and pink, with the red accents of lipstick and cancan dresses.*

Amedeo Modigliani, with his serene, elongated faces in blue and yellowy orange.

Paul Gaugin, who, even in his European paintings, was drawn to red and green systems. But once he made it to Tahiti, the temperature, the lush vegetation, and the ripe fruits and floral textiles consolidated this aspect of his art. Look at the red and green bananas in la Orana Maria *and the visual dialogue between the woman with the red pareo surrounded by green and the woman depicted in ultramarine and yellow in the background.*

Vincent van Gogh, who had two recurrent color systems: The first is blue (from greenish blue to violet-periwinkle blue) and yellow (from lemony to gold), present in so many of his night scenes and iris paintings. Forget that you've seen his paintings a million times and this time focus on the color pairings in them. I especially love:

- The Starry Night
- Wheatfield with Crows
- Irises
- Café Terrace at Night

His second pairing is green and red, which he used in several flower vase paintings and in portraits, including his own:

- Self Portrait *(1887)*
- The Gardener
- La Berceuse
- *The richly nuanced* Oleanders *(my favorite), which pairs green and pink with purple and yellow*

FROM PAS DE DEUX TO MÉNAGE À TROIS AND BEYOND

Complementary color systems are powerful and beautiful. Often, two colors, used in their full range with a few neutrals, are all that is needed. Or, instead of being complementary, the duo can be made with adjacent colors. Whereas complementary pairs appear across from each other on the color wheel, adjacent colors are next-door neighbors: red and purple, yellow and green, cyan and violet. These neighborly pairs can provide a more contemporary aesthetic. Same as with complementary colors, they can be used at full saturation or in the full range of nuanced tones, tints, and values.

But sometimes there is an appetite for more, a desire to invite a third color. That is called a triad. Picture the color wheel, then superimpose a triangle. The colors at the tips of the triangle are the colors you use in a triad, whether as pure chroma or toned down or tinted.

- **Primary triad:** the classic yellow, red, and blue. This combination is very childlike but also appears in fine art: Think of Piet Mondrian's *Broadway Boogie Woogie* and Matisse's *Red Room*.
- **Secondary triad:** the funkier green, orange, and purple. Visualize them in jewel tones—green emeralds, purple amethysts, and orange citrines—in high-end jewelry, or muted and rich in luxury fashion collections by Prada and in various Dries Van Noten print designs. Or pay close attention to the details of pointillist paintings like Georges Seurat's *A Sunday on La Grande Jatte*, which is made out of little dots of greens, oranges, and purples.

Yet the triangle does not need to be equilateral. It can be made of two adjacent colors and their opposite. Like with the pairs, think also about pale and dark variations or rich and muted tones, not just the pure chroma. The triangle can even be turned into a quad, using four colors by combining two color pairs. Beyond that, you would not be using a limited color palette; you would be entering the multicolor space.

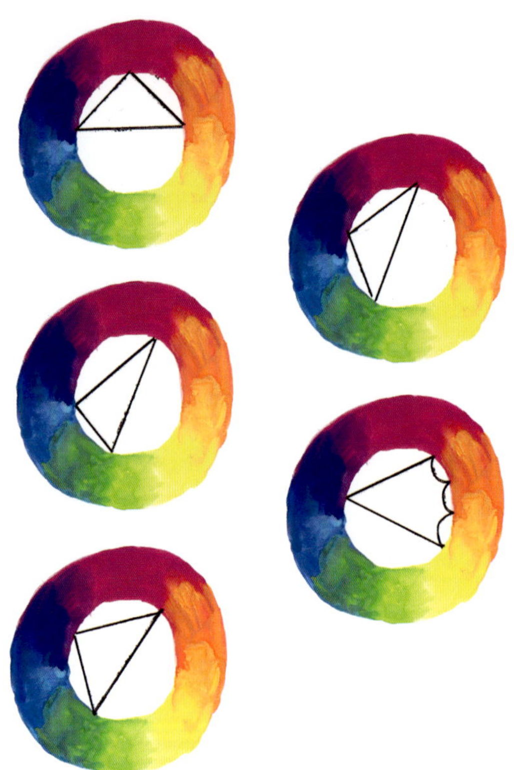

KEY TAKEAWAYS

1. When working with complementary colors, consider not only the basic hue pairings (red and green, blue and orange, yellow and violet) but also other, in-between colors. For example, a redder tangerine orange combined with a greenish blue.

2. The colors you choose to use do not need to be in their purest form. You can maintain the complementary quality but intentionally increase or decrease the intensity, tonality, or saturation of each specific color. For example, a very pale pistachio green can be paired with a deeper cherry or plum color, or a very desaturated lilac can be combined with a muted ochre.

3. Consider pairings of not only complementary but also adjacent colors.

4. Try some triads and think about what kind of mood each one creates.

5. Use the color wheel to get started, but then let it go. The more you practice observing and finding complementary colors (or adjacent colors, or triads) in your surroundings, the less you will need it, and the freer your eye for color will become.

6. In the following photos from my Abstract Naturalism series, observe how each hue is selected from its full range—the darkest and the lightest, the most saturated and the barely there. Then look at the groupings and ask Jules's two questions: What is the complementary color system being used? What is the tonal structure?

A STUDY SERIES

RED + GREEN & RED + PURPLE

When I was in graphic design school, I had a friend that had a fierce use of color. You could always tell which were her projects since she always used bright red accompanied by intense purple-violet and green. She also dressed in those colors! Back then, as today, I used a wide range of color combinations in my work, but that high-octane trio of her colors has always stayed with me.

RED + GREEN: complementary, like poppies in a field.
RED + PURPLE: adjacent, like a mixed berry tart.

Over the following pages, you will see how these two parings can be stretched and combined in a wide range of nuances. I start the series with the colors in their brightest, most saturated and intense versions. The kind of thing that comes to mind when someone says RED + GREEN or RED + PURPLE, but as the series continues, you will see what happens when the red is stretched toward orange or magenta, when colors become super pale and muted or deep and dark, like in the chart on page 78.

Then, we see the colors, in their full range, interact in triads and quads on pages 96 and 97. There are some botanical orbs with RED + GREEN + PURPLE, but also other kinds of triads: primary, secondary, and more. Spend time with each one and try coming up with a color palette based on them.

While each image is beautiful—just look at all those flowers!—try to see beyond the petals; observe colors. Look at each color orb as a whole or hyperfocus on a little corner or a couple of petals. Look at the color palette as an abstracted portrait of the botanicals, and like with the photo, take in the whole palette or focus on just a few of the components. Training your eye to see all these different color systems will make you more color fluent.

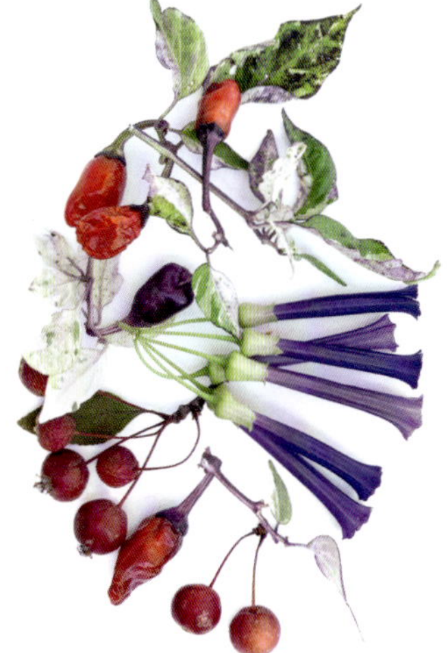

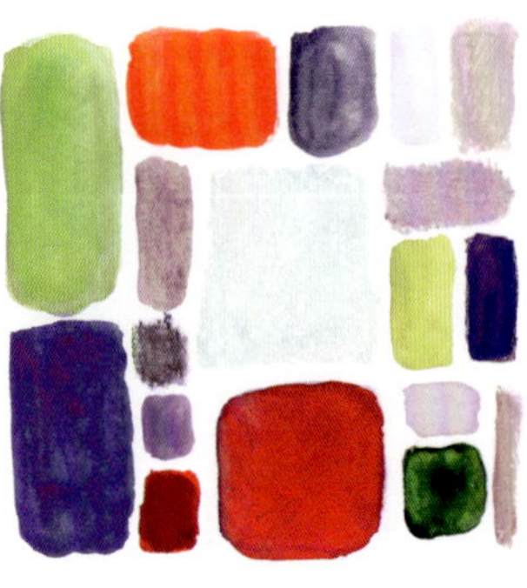

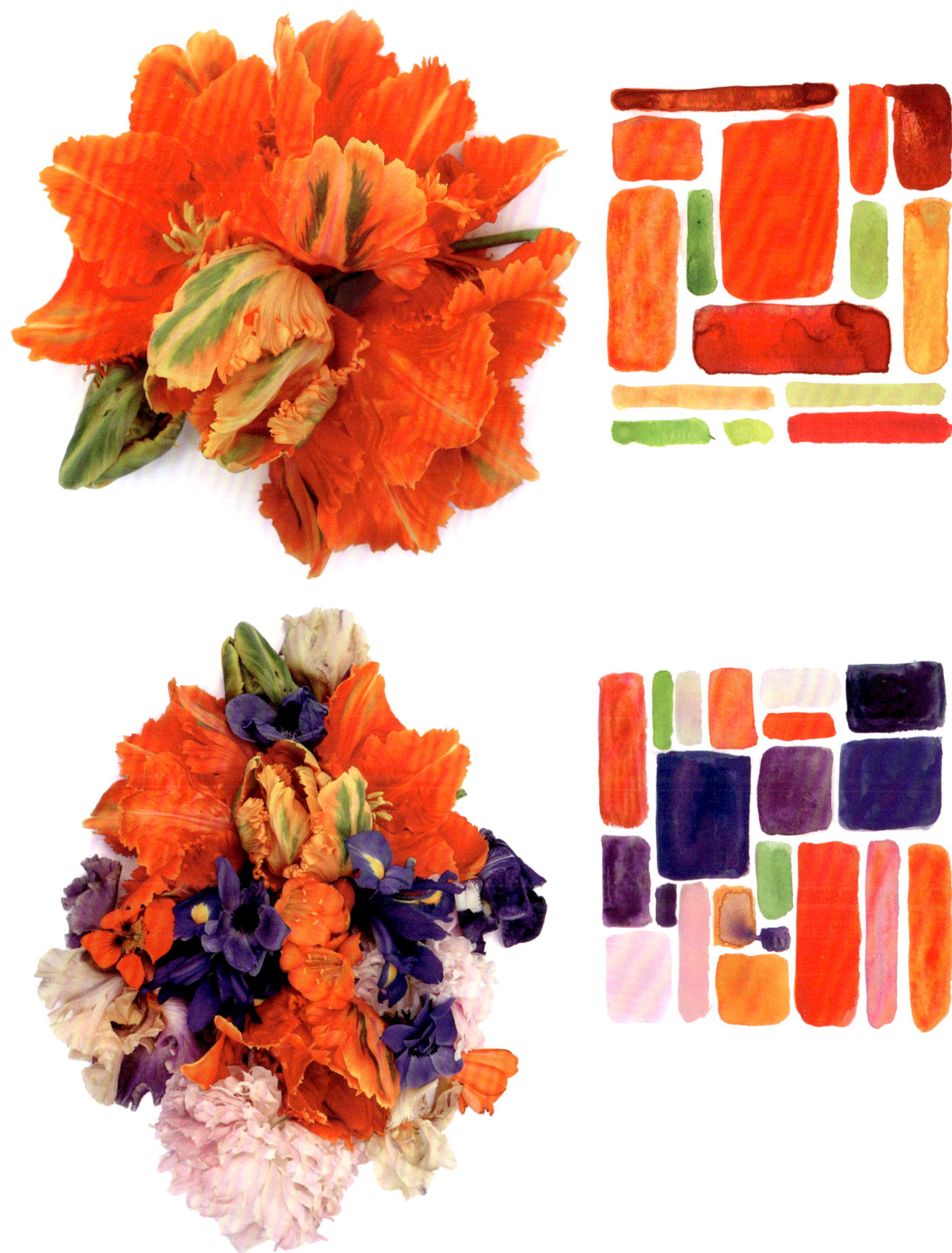

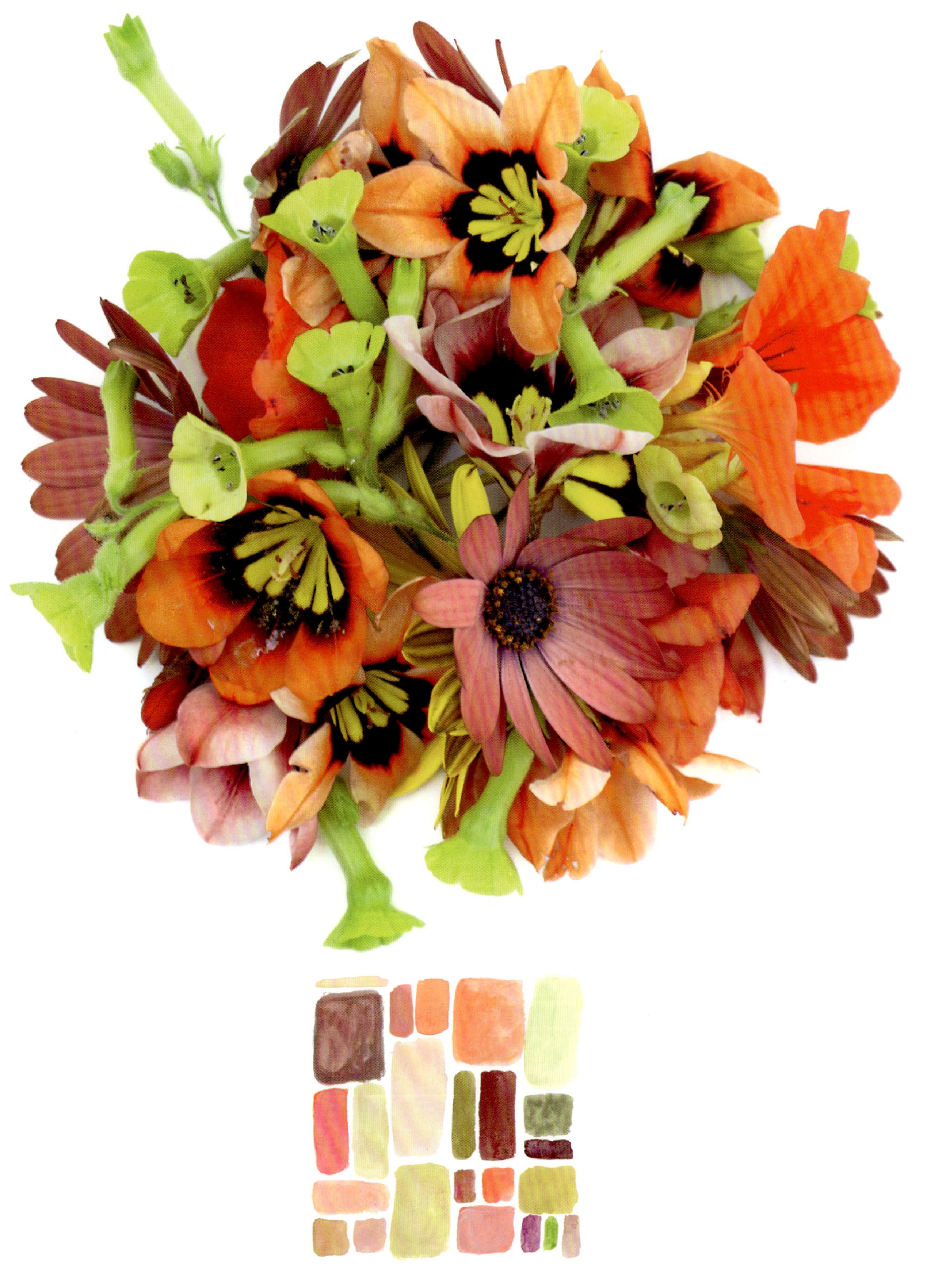

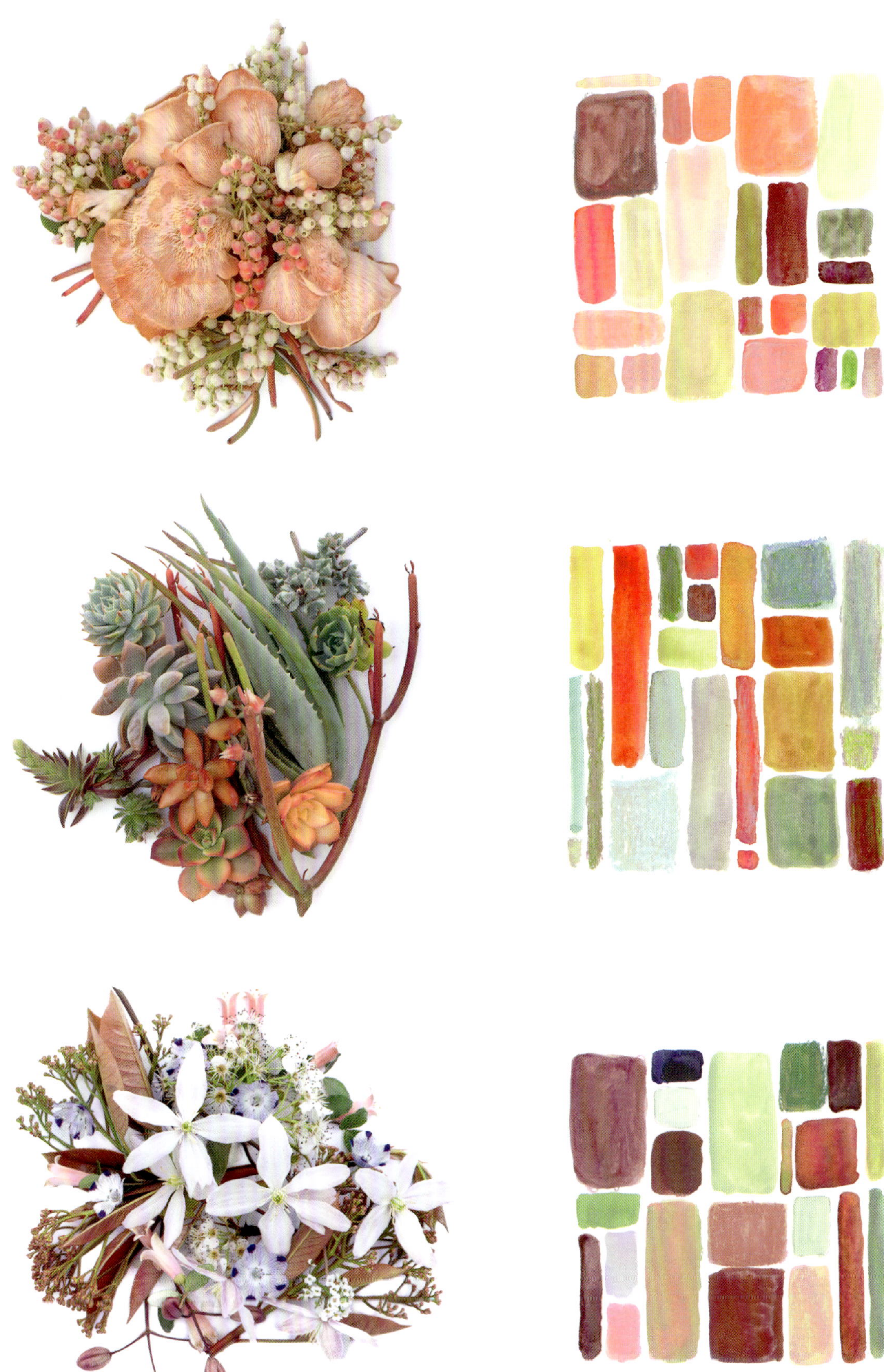

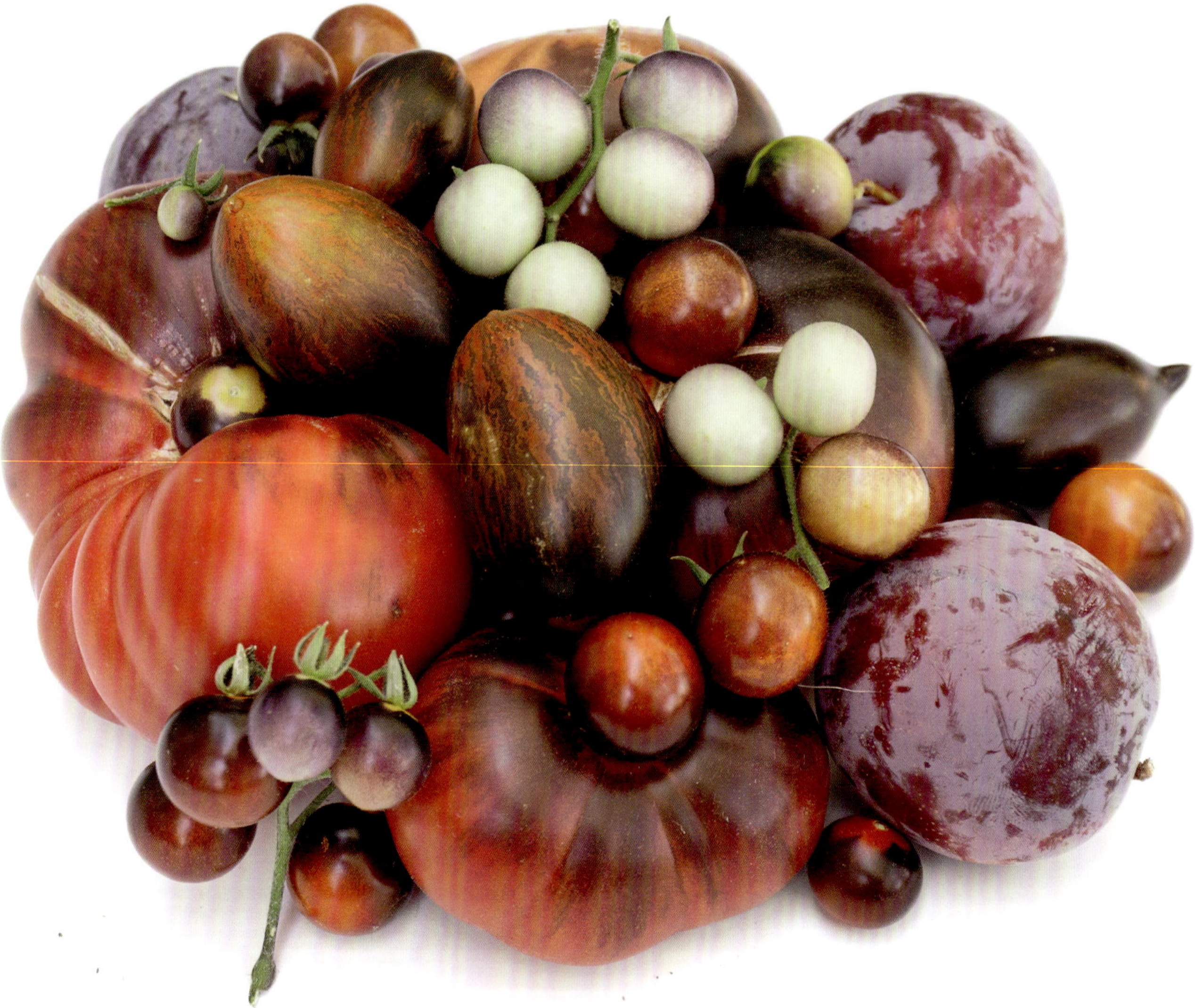

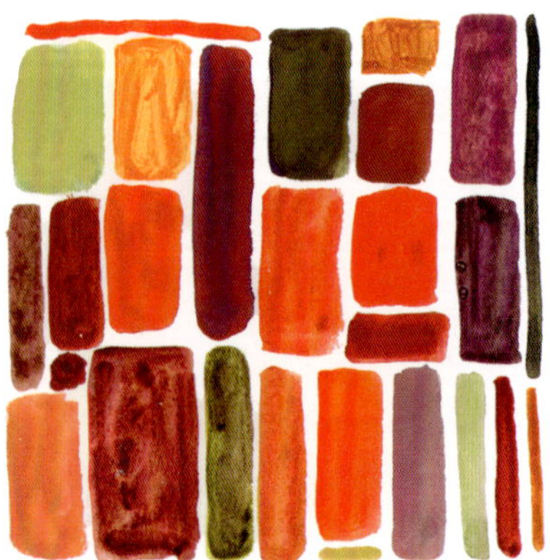

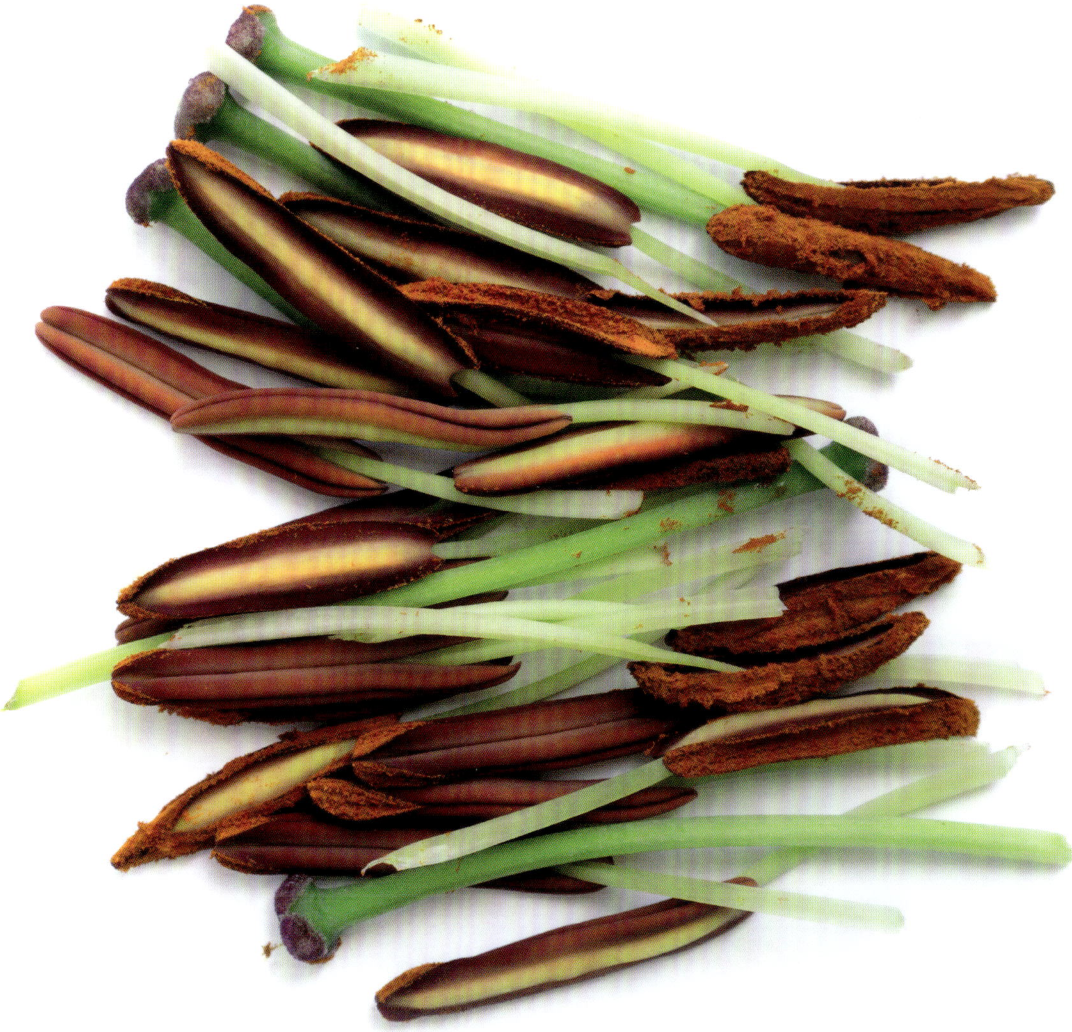

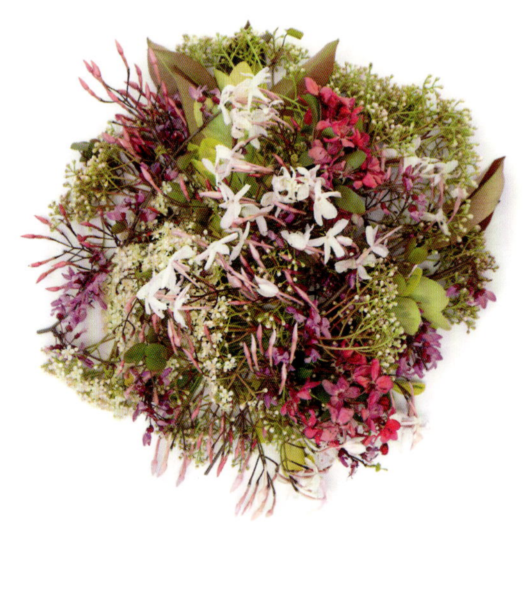
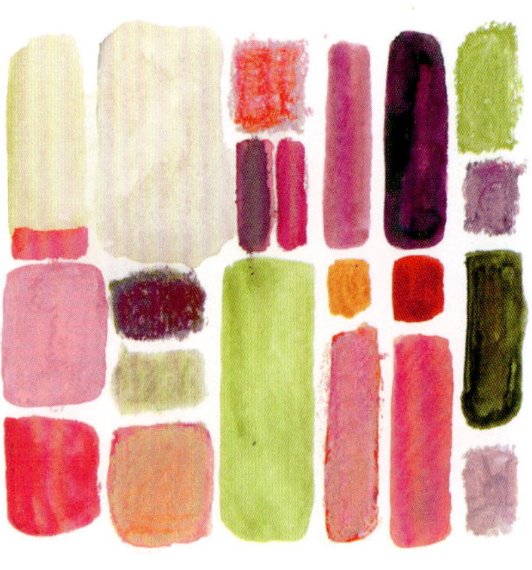
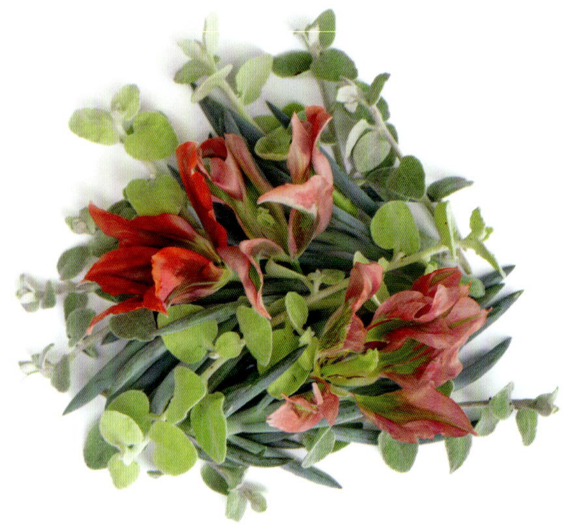
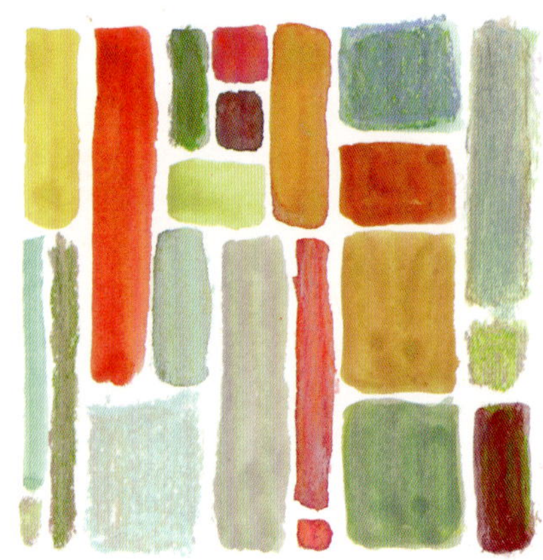
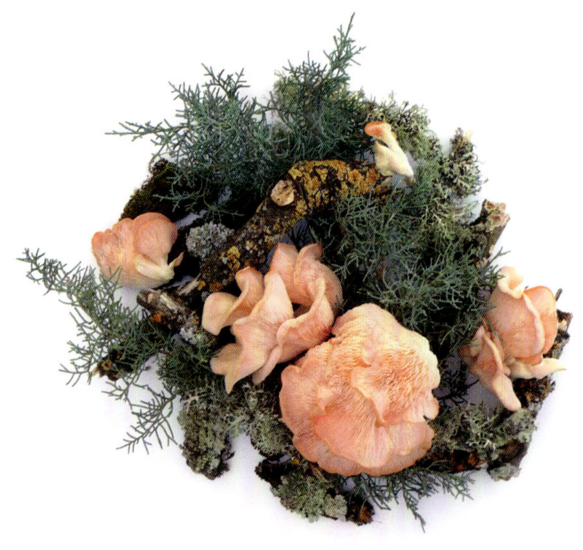
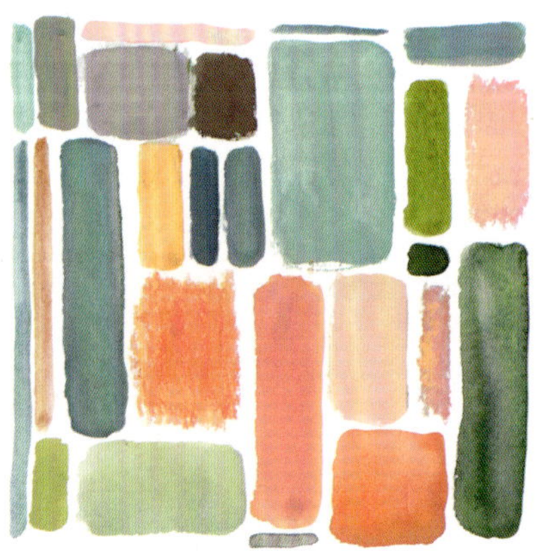

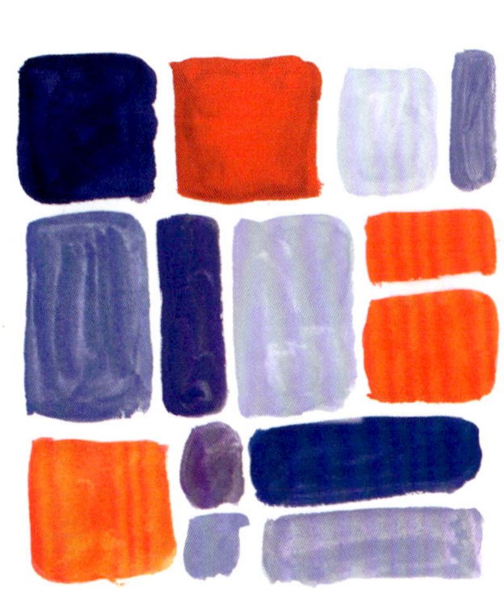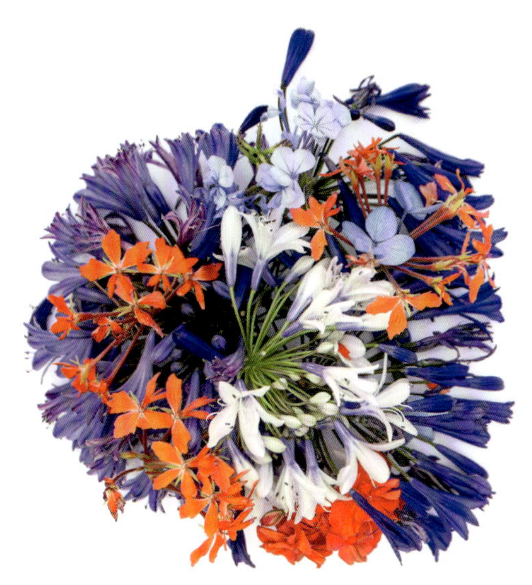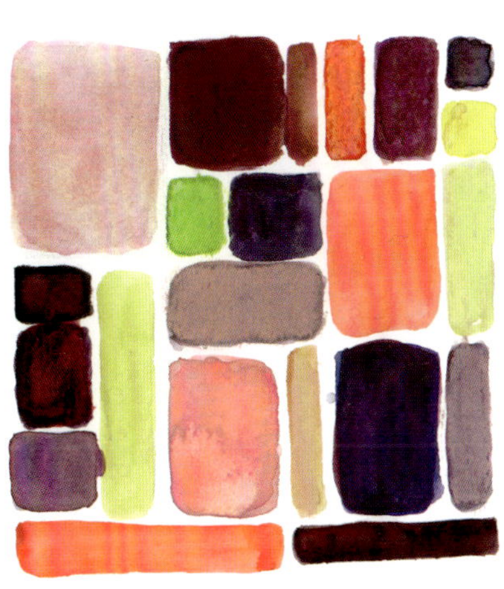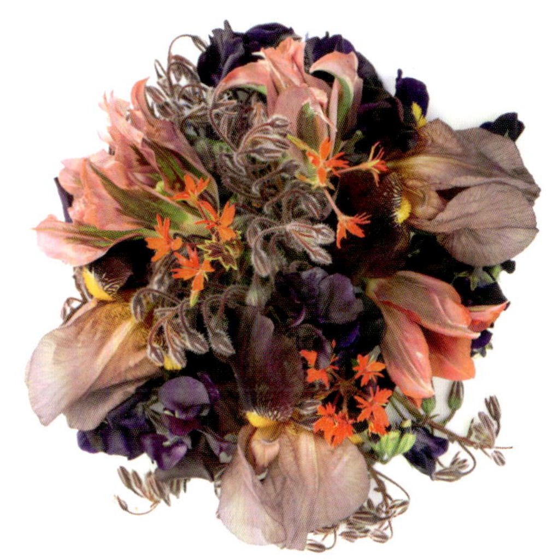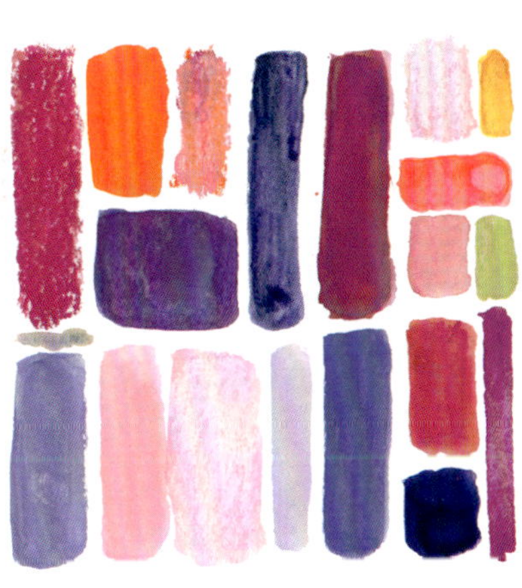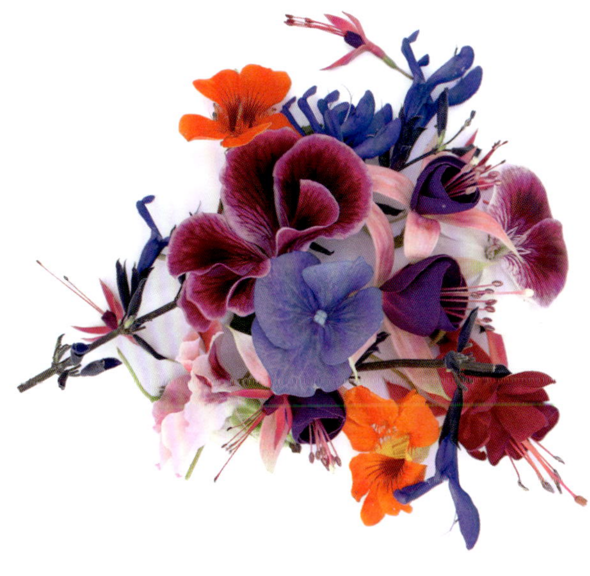

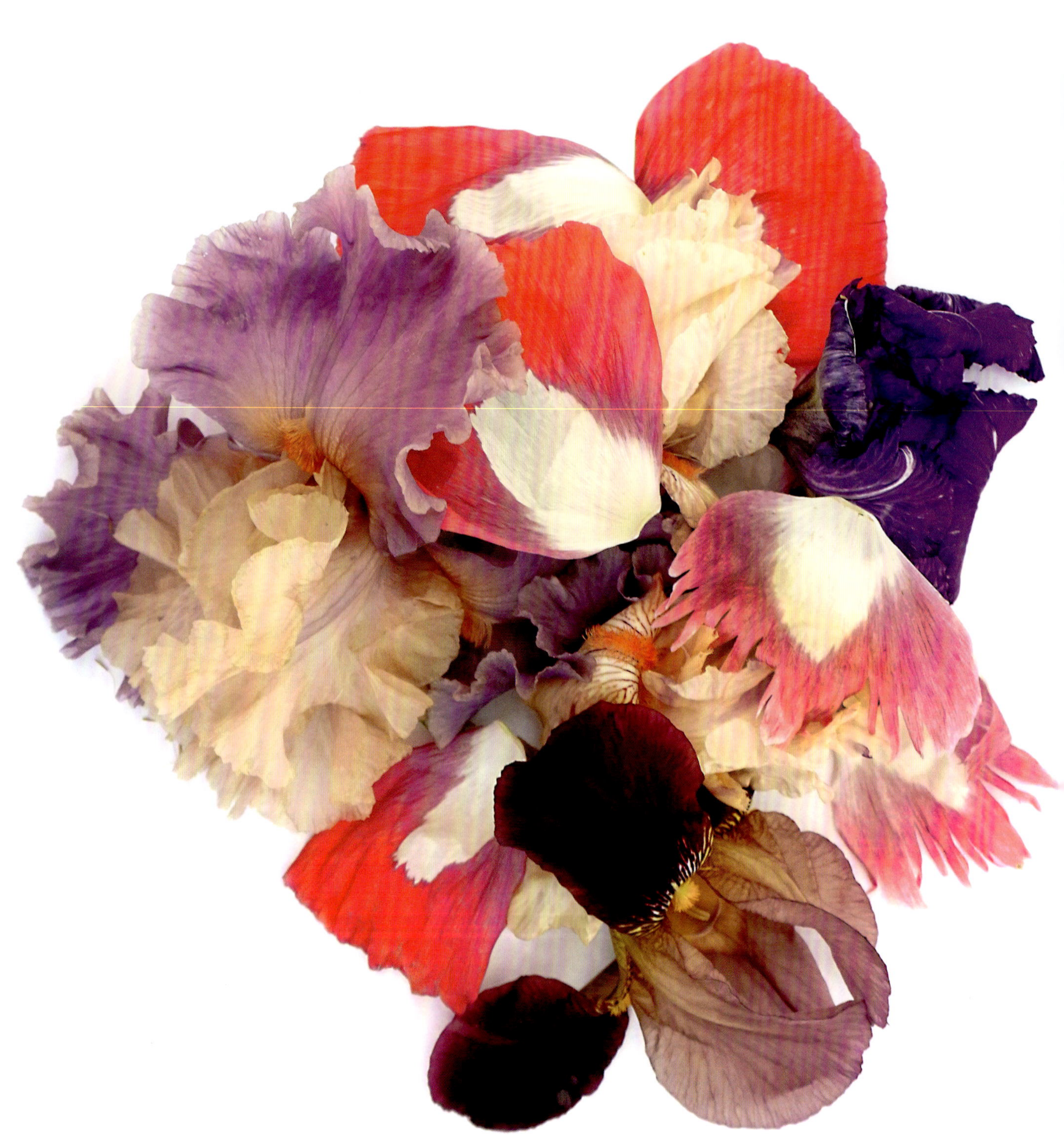

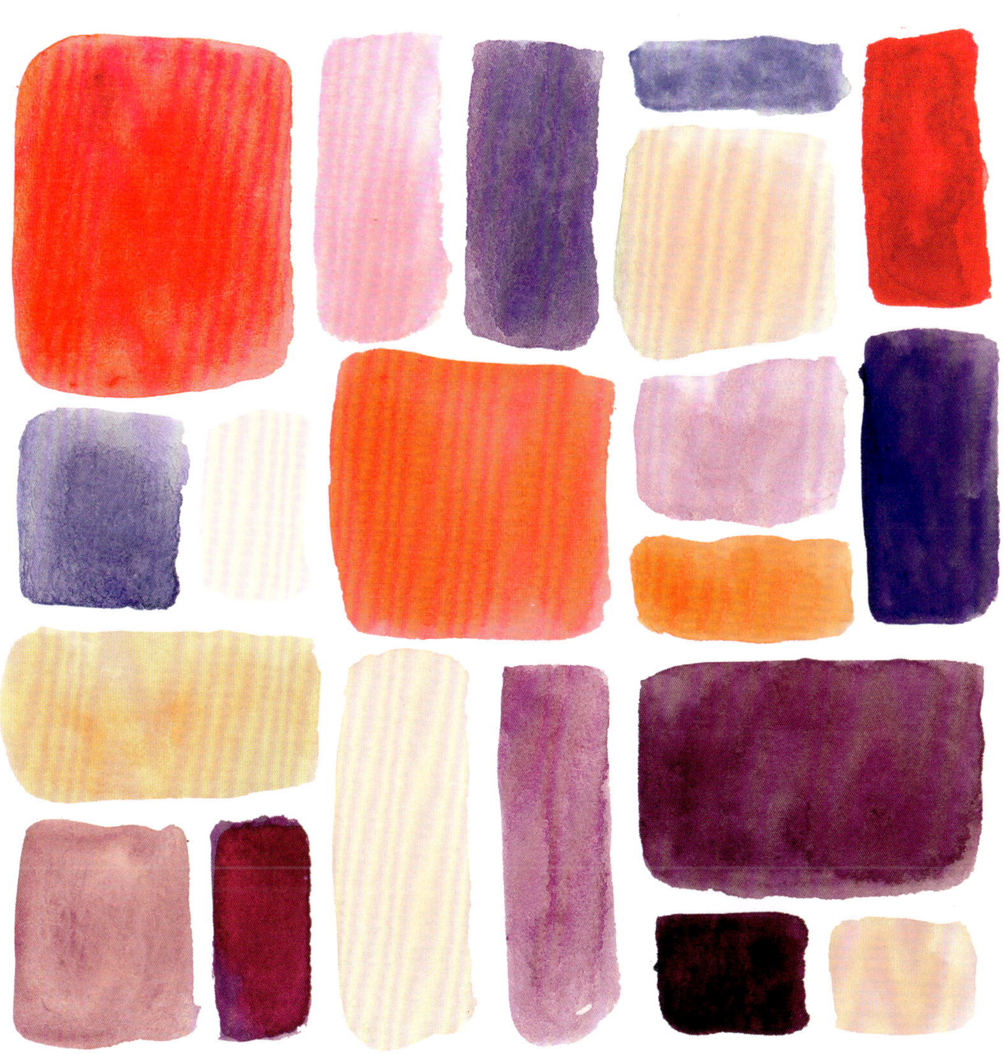

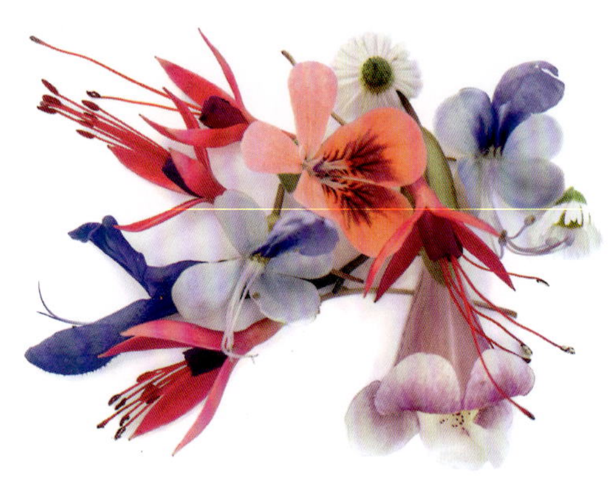

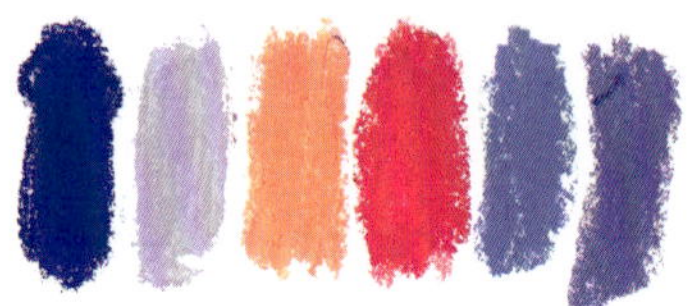

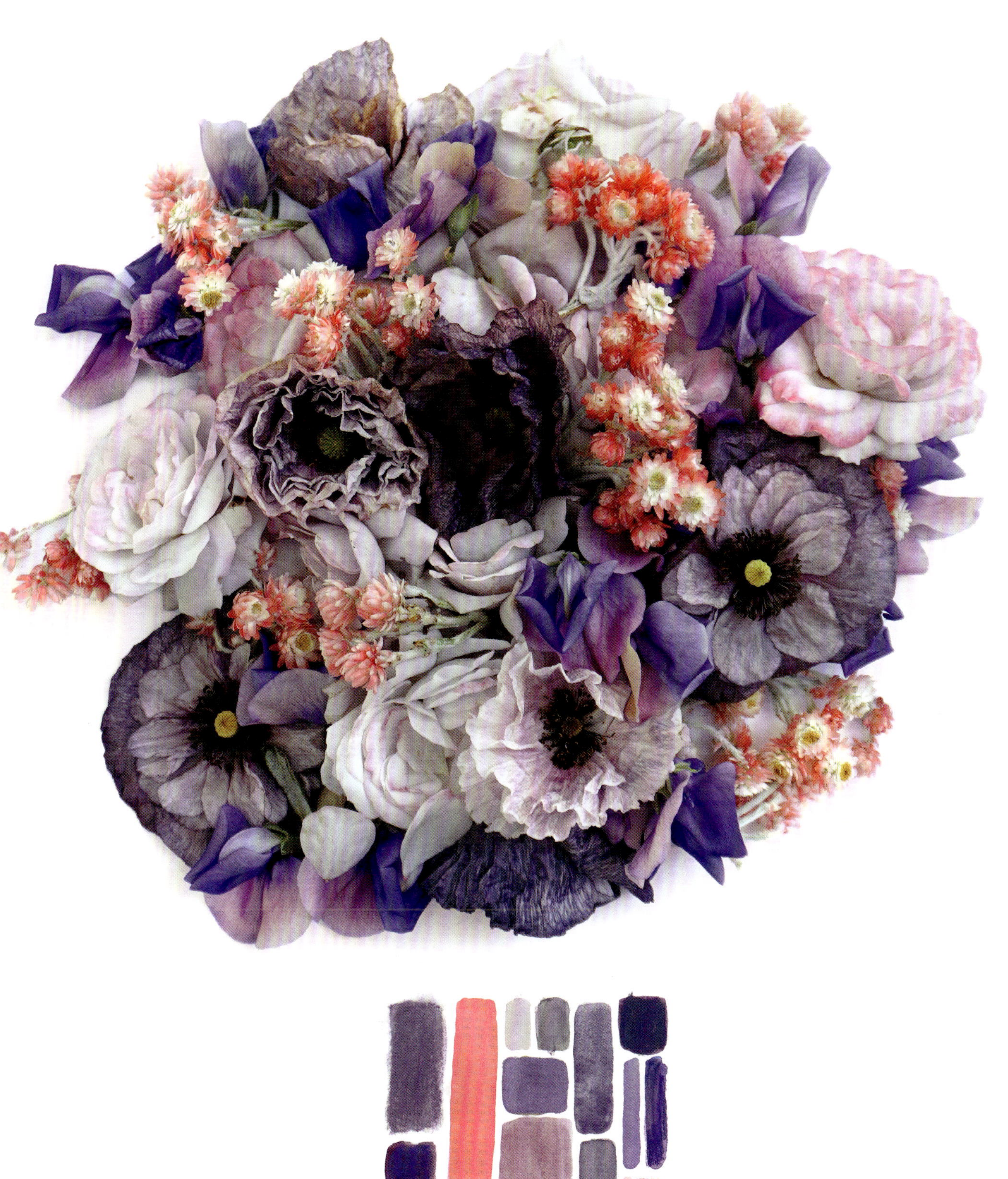

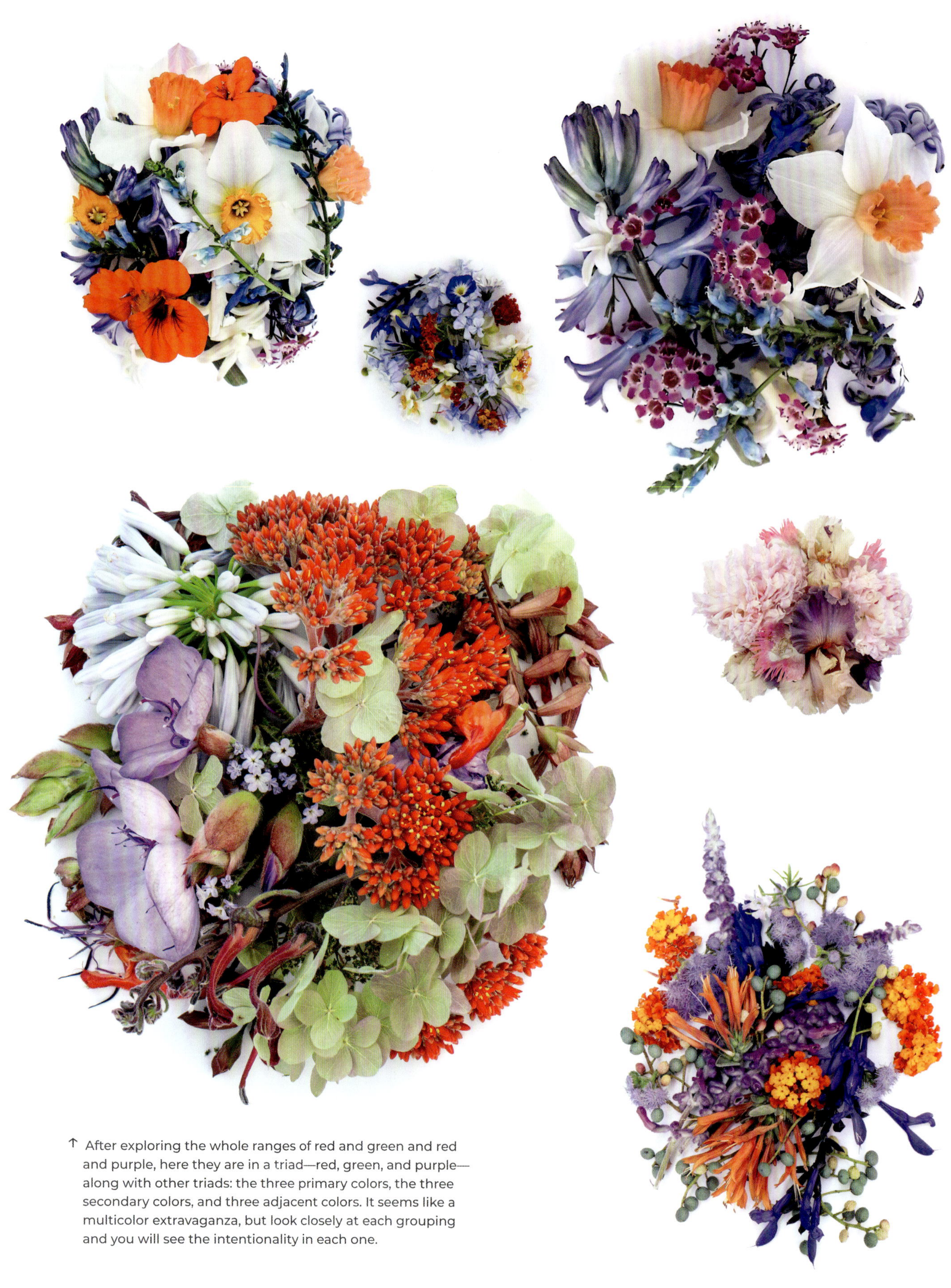

After exploring the whole ranges of red and green and red and purple, here they are in a triad—red, green, and purple— along with other triads: the three primary colors, the three secondary colors, and three adjacent colors. It seems like a multicolor extravaganza, but look closely at each grouping and you will see the intentionality in each one.

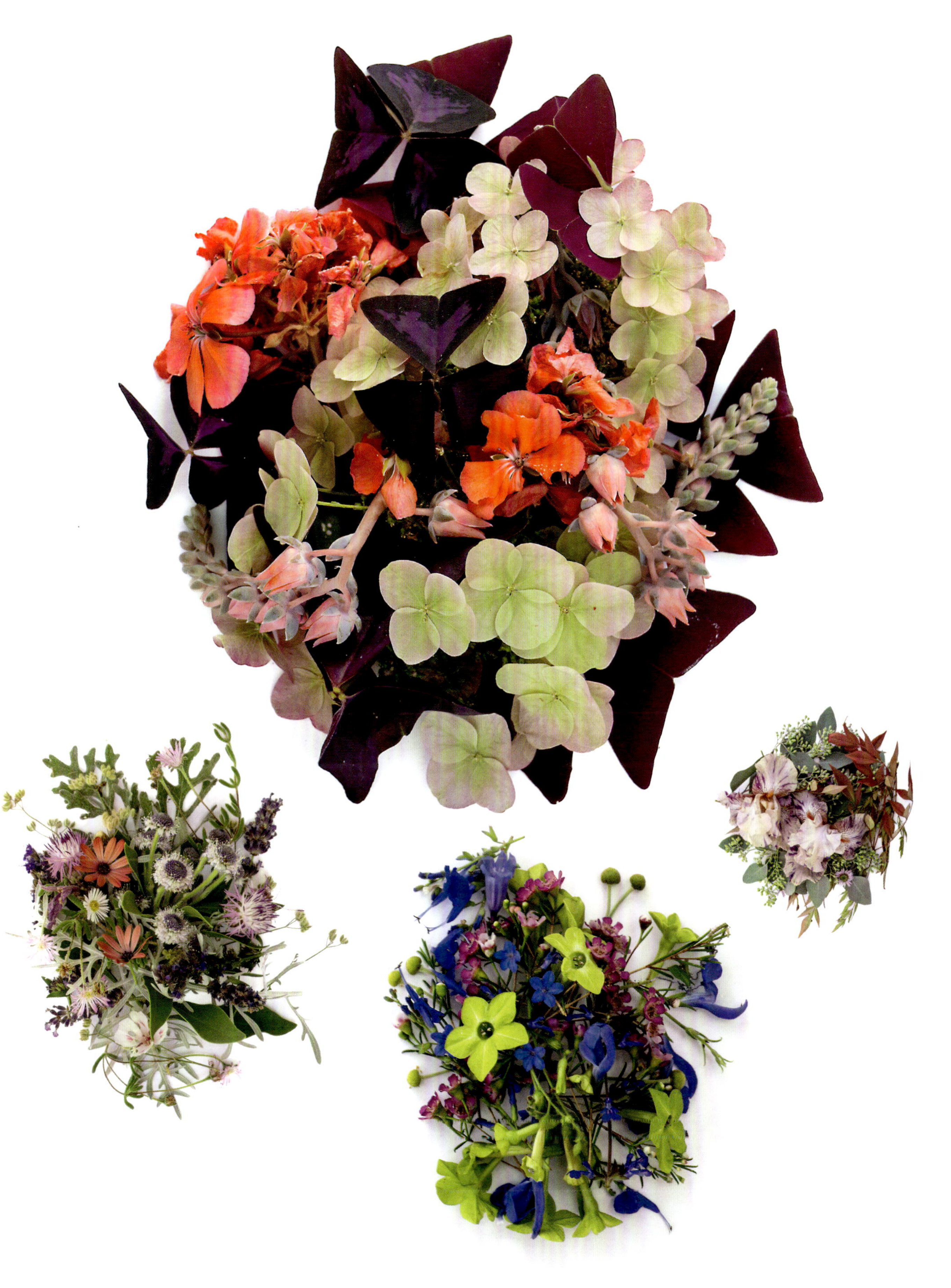

PROJECT

OBSERVE: Observe the complementary color combinations in the images of this chapter and spend some time out and about—in nature, in town—finding moments of complementary or adjacent pairs or triads. I recently went to a local boba place, and they had all these red-and-green or purple-and-yellow drinks! You might buy a box of macarons in complementary colors just for the pleasure of it, or complementary-colored fruits and veggies—there is so much red and green food! Take photos of your findings.

ANALYZE: Analyze the colors in the photos you took. Are the colors pure or deep or toned down or pale? Look back at the botanical colors in my photos on pages 85–97 and their matching palettes. Make notes about the color pairings that are most interesting to you for future use.

CREATE: OPTION A

Create an illustration of cloth with cangiantismo: Drape some fabric over a chair, choose an image from an art history book of a lady with a fabulous dress, or find a page in a fashion magazine. The main point is that you can observe lots of fabric draped with creases. An evening dress in silky damask or taffeta is ideal. Then ignore the colors in your source image and paint or draw it using any complementary color system, applying cangiantismo to create luminous effects.

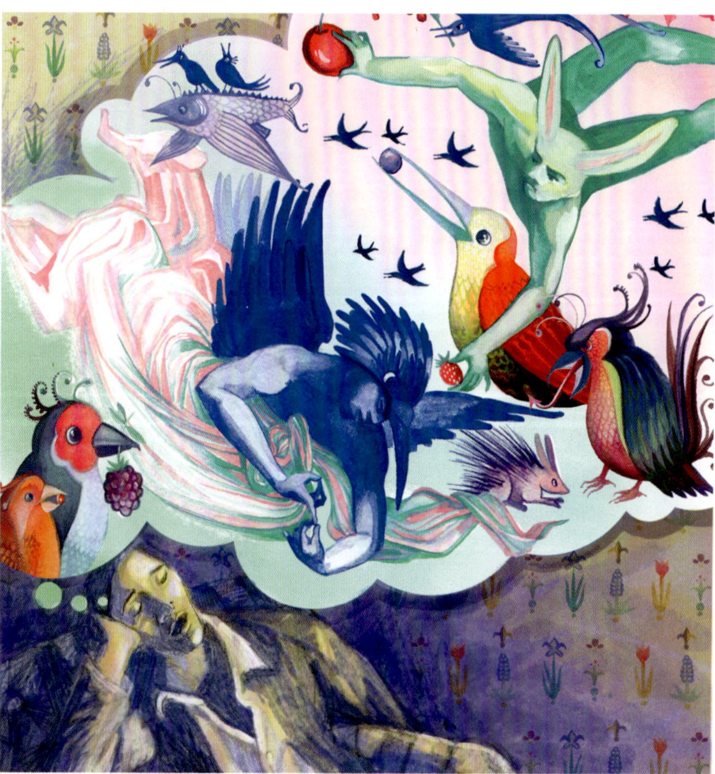

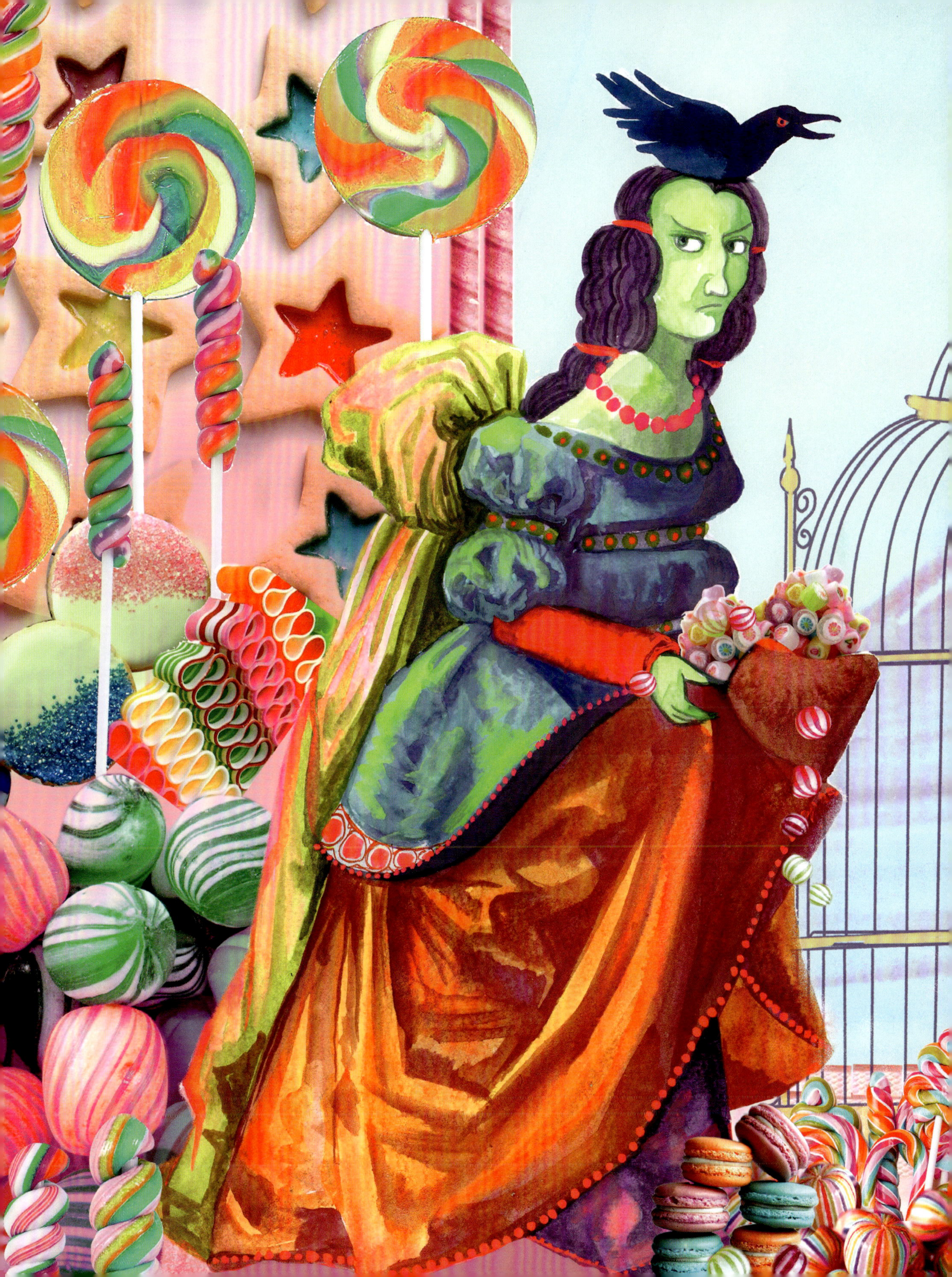

OPTION B

Now, let's work with triads and fashion design:

1. Go into your closet and pull out clothes and accessories you already have in interesting colors. Avoid multicolor prints, though you can use tone-on-tone elements. Combine them into triads that feel interesting and different than the usual combinations you make. Mix your clothes into a colorful ball of fabric like the ones in the following pages, or, if you prefer to avoid wrinkles, you can instead fold them and use them as mix-and-match tiles.

2. Take a photo for reference or go straight into creating a color palette based on your combinations. (Don't forget to fold or hang your clothes after you've documented the triad in all its nuances!)

3. Pick your favorite triad color palette. Remember, it can be all super dark and moody, or all bright, or all very pale and muted, or you can combine your three colors in a variety of intensities. You can also try making a variety of palettes and then pick "the one."

4. Time to design a five-day mini capsule collection with one of these triads. Even if you are not a fashion designer, pretend you are one; after all, we all interact with fabric and clothes every day, so give it a shot! Remember, this is an exercise to train your eye and maybe update your style. Your collection most likely won't go down any runway, but it will show you how to orchestrate a triad.

The collection should clearly show the triad and have cohesiveness yet allow for variety. It can be made all with solids or a combination of patterns and solid colors.

To create the variations in the capsule collection:

- **Mix and match your selected triad color clothes** into a week's worth of outfits using the clothes you already have. Sticking with the triad color palette, add accessories—shoes, bandanas, bags, belts, jewelry—to add accents within the triad.

- **If you like drawing and illustrating,** mimic fashion illustration to create an imagined collection with more freedom. Choose casual daytime clothes or throw in some eveningwear or a unique piece like a fabulous kaftan; perhaps think of styling a collection for a particular setting or occasion, like a resort collection or a collection with a Greek, Hawaiian, or Moroccan flair, all using your selected triad of colors.

If you are a surface pattern designer, go ahead and create a pattern collection for your clothes, applying your patterns to mockups or sketches to display your pattern collection.

If you are a children's book illustrator, create a collection for kids, drawing a playground with all the children dressed in a triad of colors.

If you are indeed a fashion designer, then go to town: Make a full collection based on a triad, sourcing fabrics and notions and even sewing a piece or two.

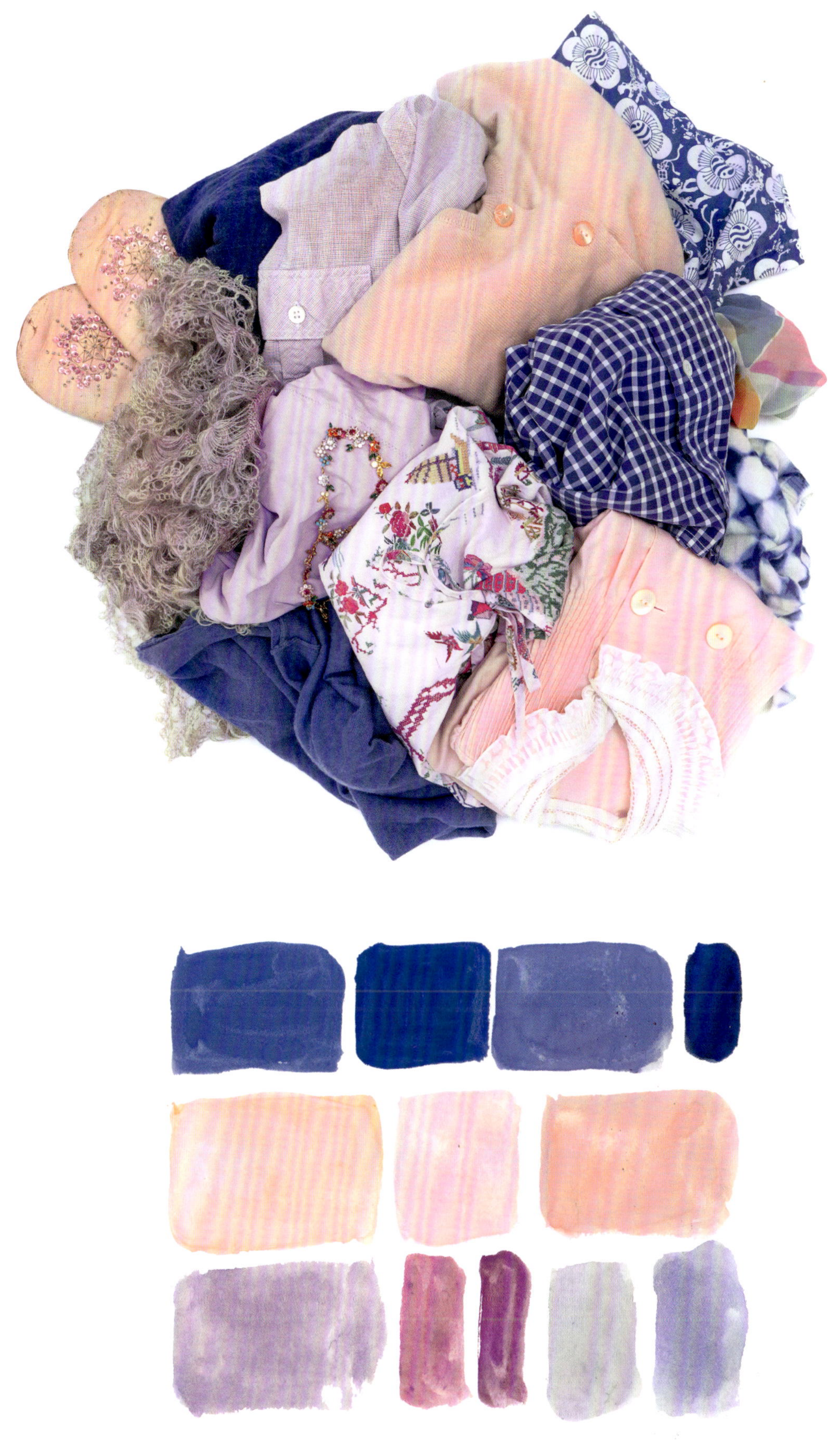

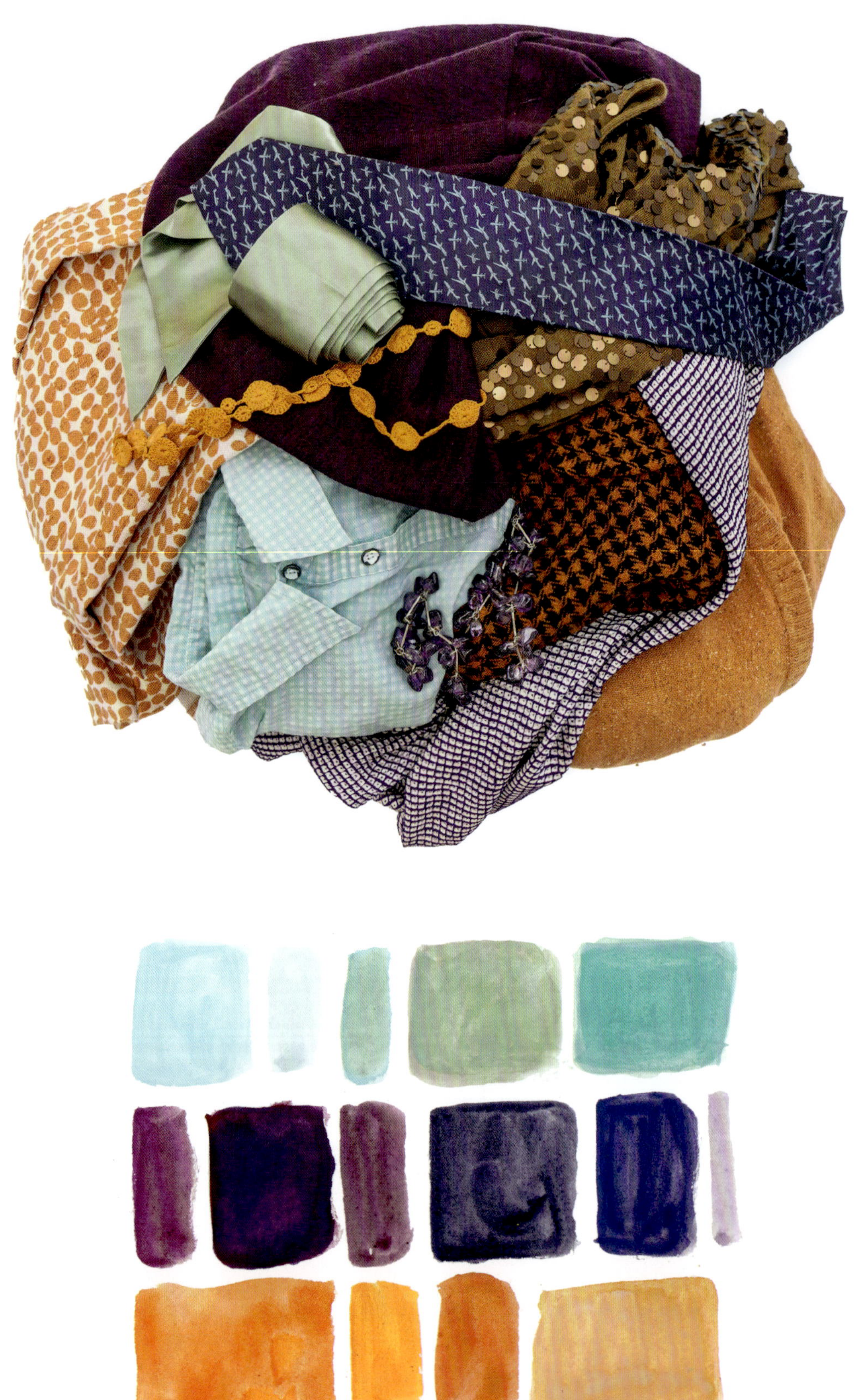

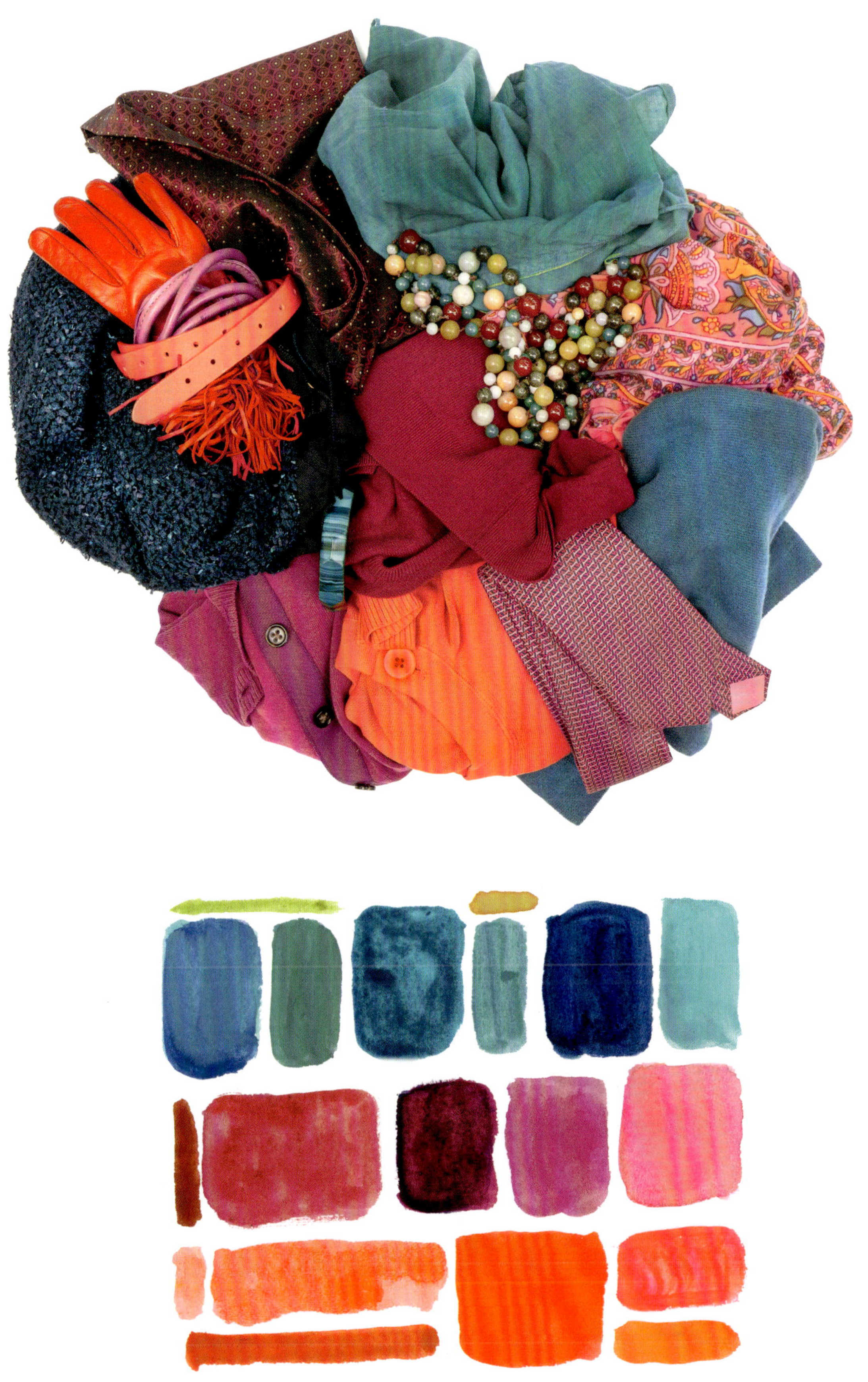

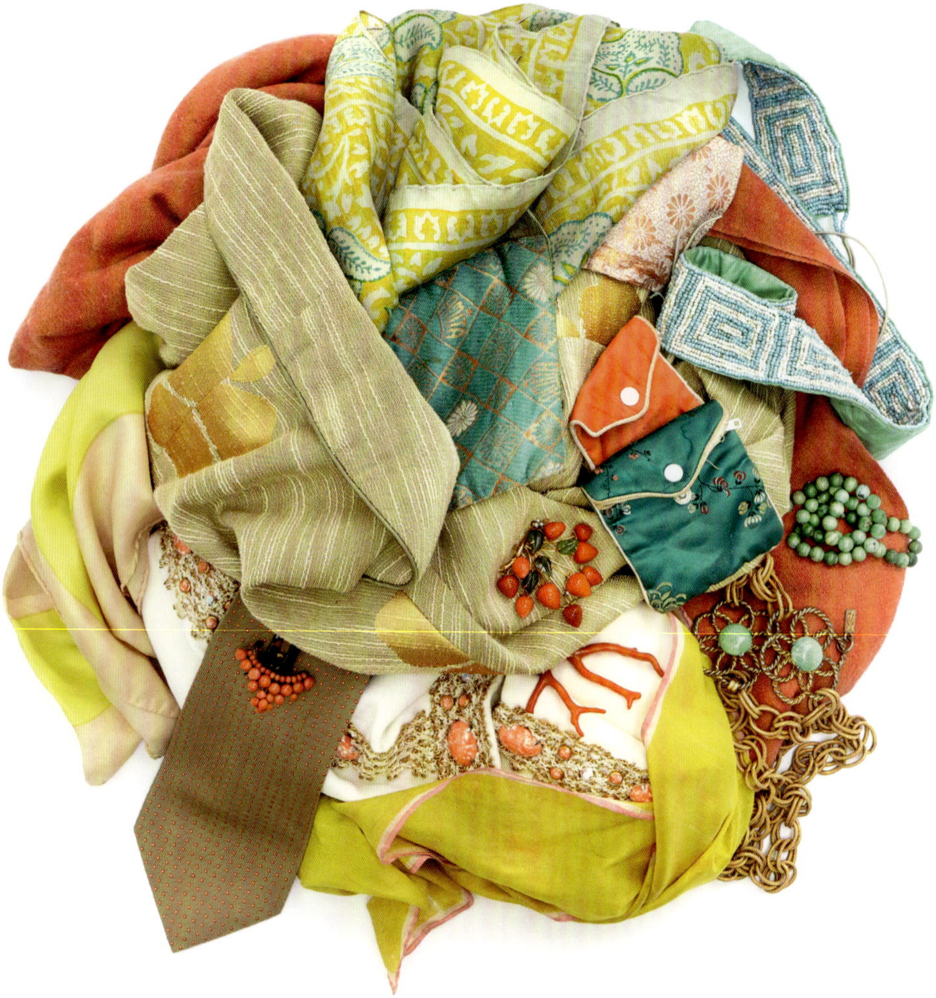

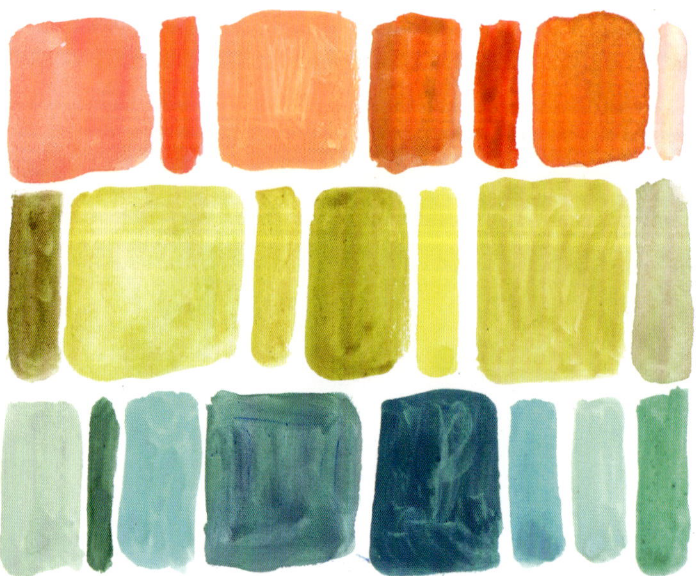

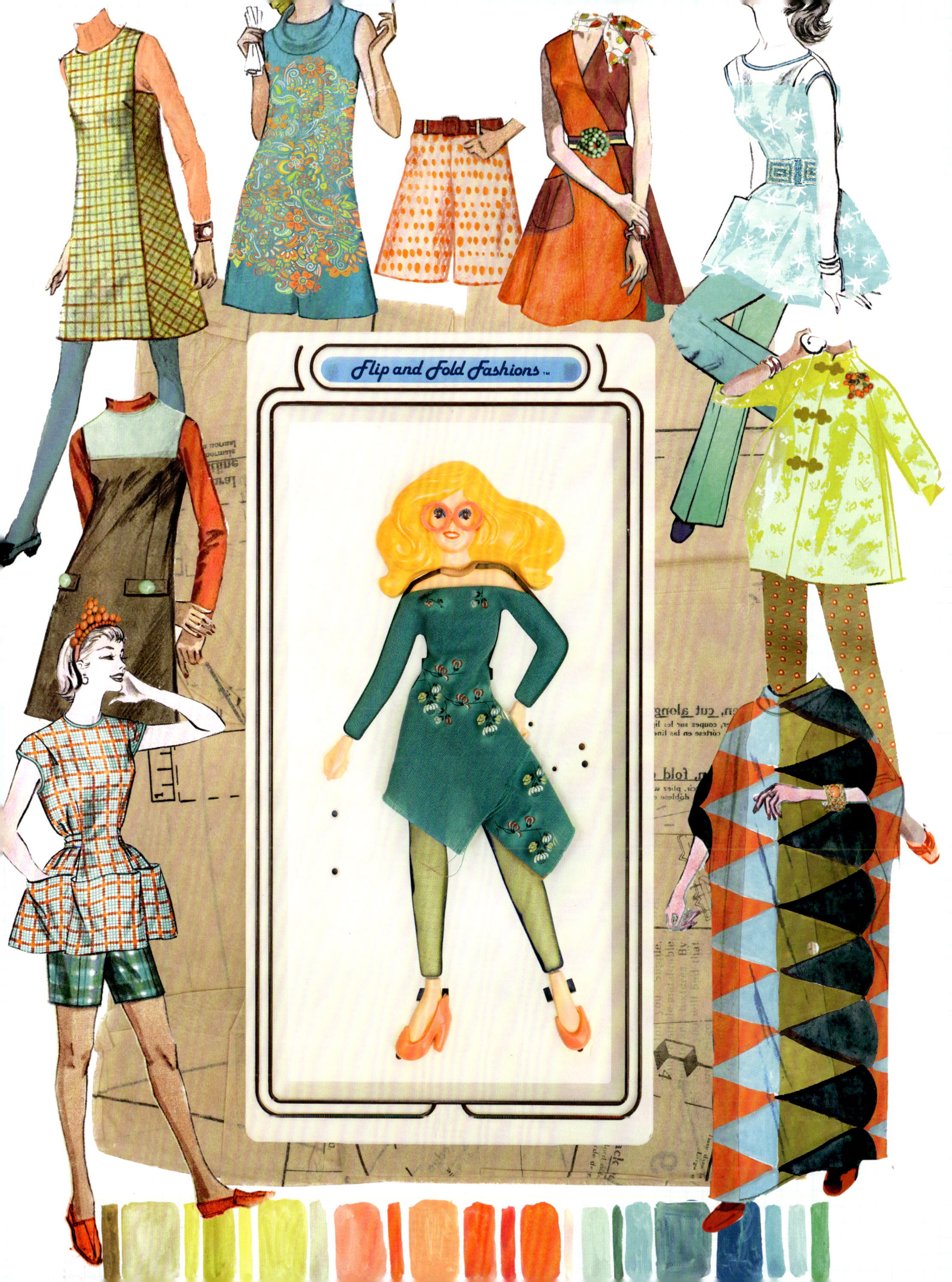
Flip and Fold Fashions ™

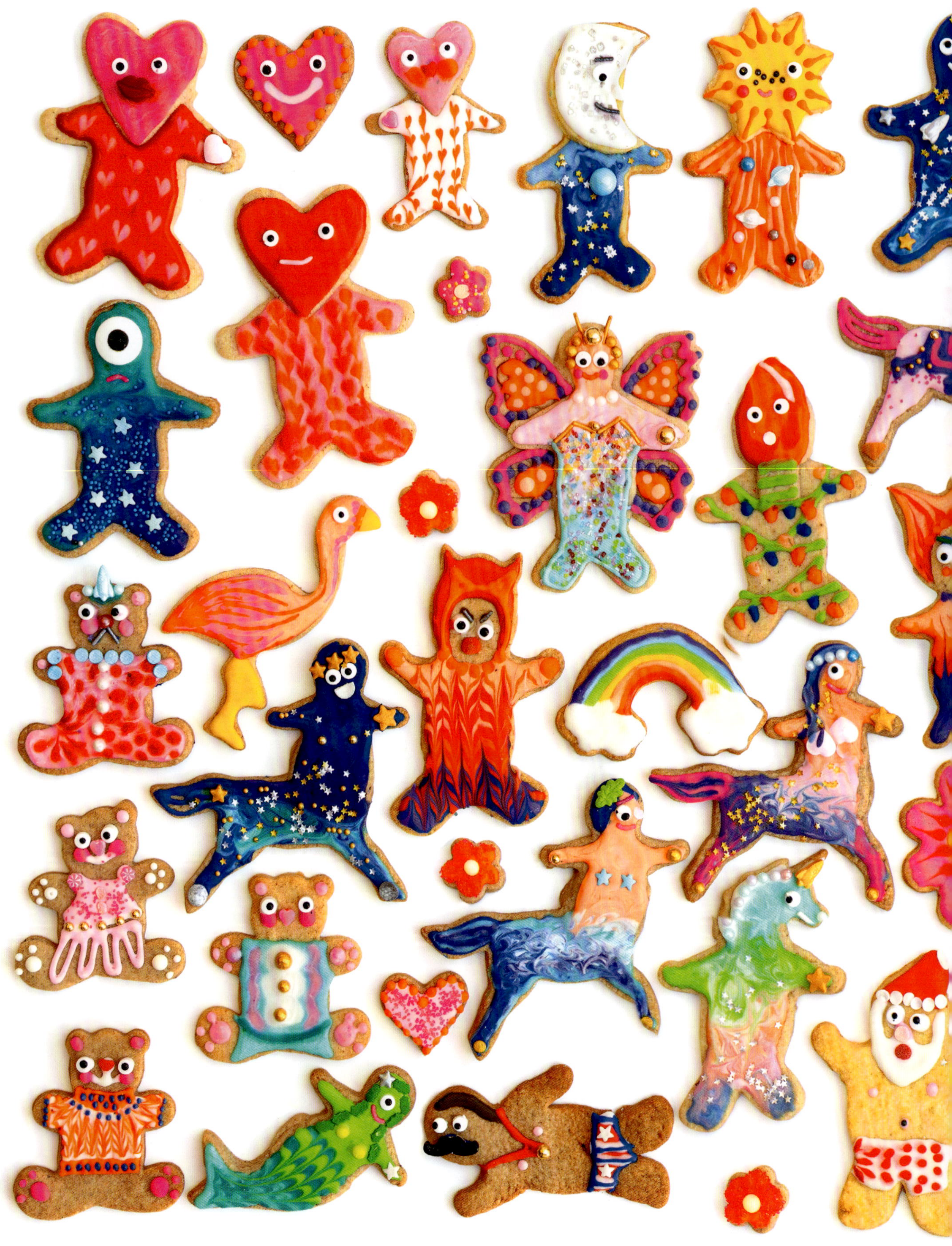

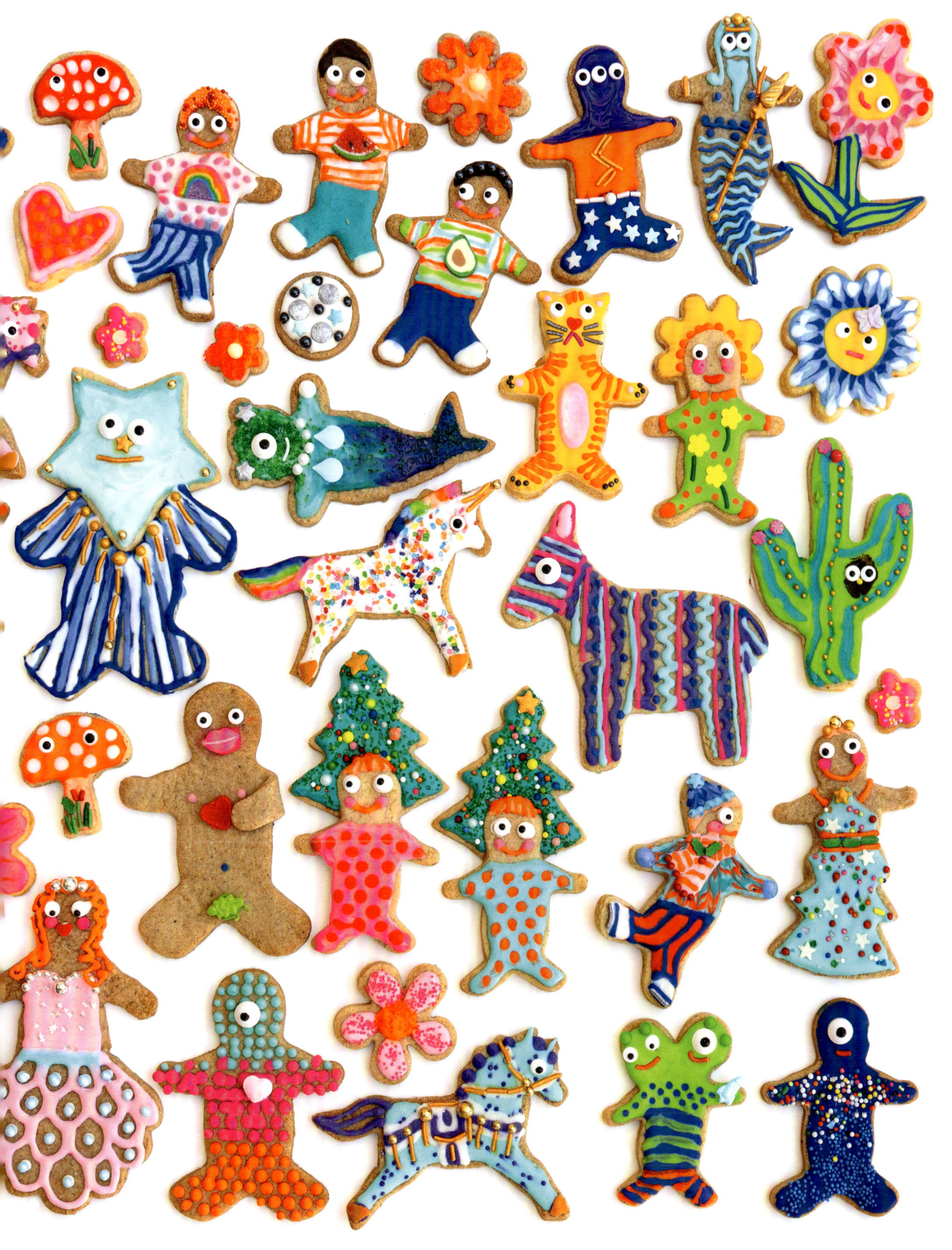

4.
THE JOY OF MULTI-COLOR EYE CANDY

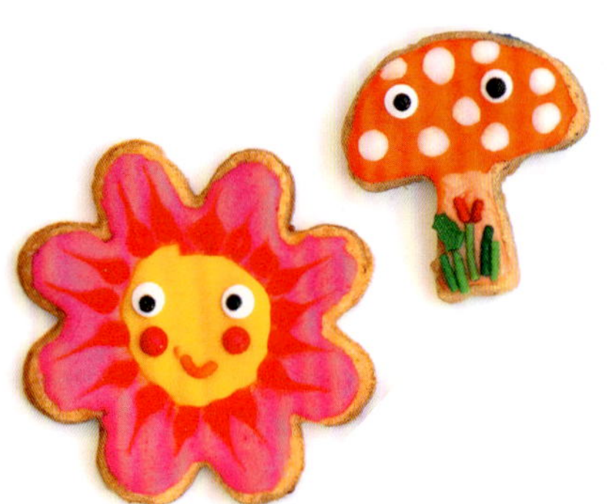

Loading Up the Palette for Maximum Expressiveness

W hat did you feel when you saw the previous page? I expect that you felt joy, or at least that my holiday cookies made you smile. Yes, my daughter and I bake a lot of pretty houses, cute and crazy characters, and more, but it is not the cookies' personalities but the many colors that make anyone receiving a box full of these happy. Cookies are tasty, but really the colors add that sprinkle of joy. The cookies don't have the same effect if we only use white royal icing for them.

Think of other many-colored things: rainbows, sprinkles, candy, confetti, and pompoms, for example. They all make you smile. If you think about it, pompoms are like sprinkles for fabric. A box of seventy-two crayons, or a visit to La Maison du Pastel in Paris to open their drawers of handmade pastels in all colors and intensities, or an afternoon pulling out all my little boxes of watercolors and paints on my worktable just for the joy and pleasure of observing them, or a glimpse of a person walking down the street in a really colorful outfit. All of these things make me so color happy.

Where you were born and raised likely formed your personal memories of multicolor joy. I grew up in Mexico—yes, quite multicolor—and that affected my lifelong love for colorful things. I would go to the weekly farmers market with my mom and see the market tables with all kinds of prints on their plastic tablecloths, contrasting with the produce, and stalls that were shielded from the sun with hot-pink fabric near jacaranda trees covered with pale violet flowers. Or we would go to Mercado de San Ángel, the indoor food market in my neighborhood, where the fruit stalls displayed multiple tiers of fruit and vegetable pyramids under multicolor star-shaped piñatas. One of my favorite paintings ever depicts this: *La vendedora de frutas* (*The Fruit Vendor)* by Olga Costa. Seeing this painting, even thinking about it, fills me with joy.

But regardless of where we grow up, evolution has made us enjoy multicolor. Somewhere in our brains, bright colors mean nourishment, satisfaction, and survival: Think of the joy of our ancestors upon finding a bounty of ripe fruits. I certainly get that "multicolor is healthy" happiness kick when I go to the farmers market in summer or harvest my tomatoes and spread this colorful bounty on my kitchen table. Being exposed to bright and vibrant colors—in food or otherwise—stimulates our brains; it tickles our pituitary and pineal glands into releasing dopamine and serotonin, the neurotransmitters associated, respectively, with wanting more of something and feeling good. If you submerge yourself in a world with no color stimuli, the goodness is gone, and your mood will sadden. Just think of the winter blues. A table with multicolor food can cure that.

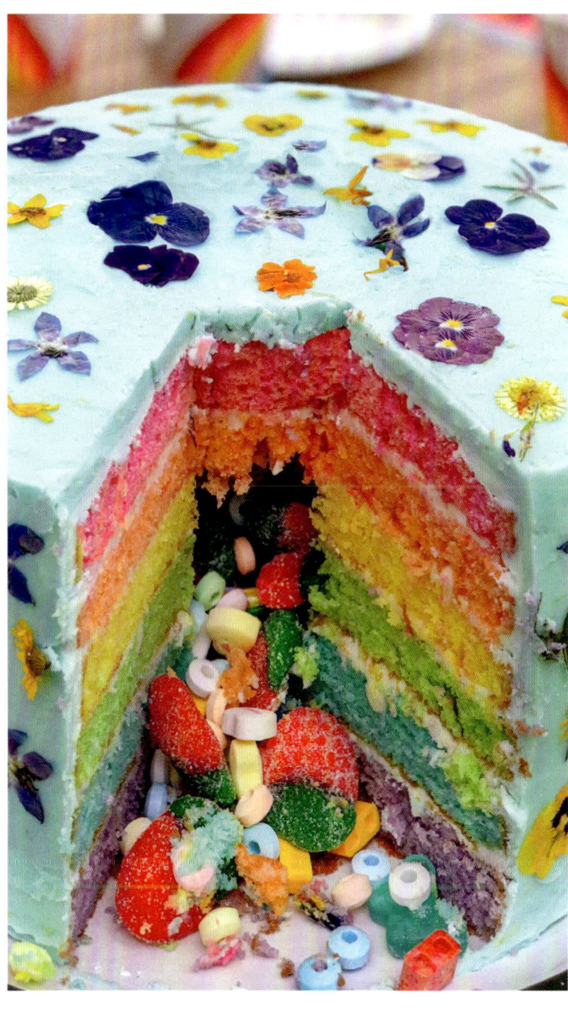

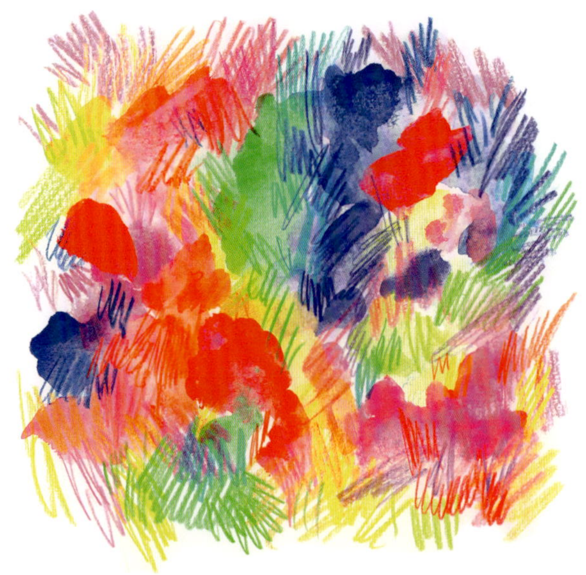

"Well, poor Duncan just wanted to color … and of course he wanted his crayons to be happy. And that gave him an idea.

When Duncan showed his teacher his new picture, she gave him an A for coloring and an A+ for creativity!"
—The Day the Crayons Quit *by Drew Daywalt, illustrated by Oliver Jeffers*[11]

LOTS OF COLOR EVERYWHERE

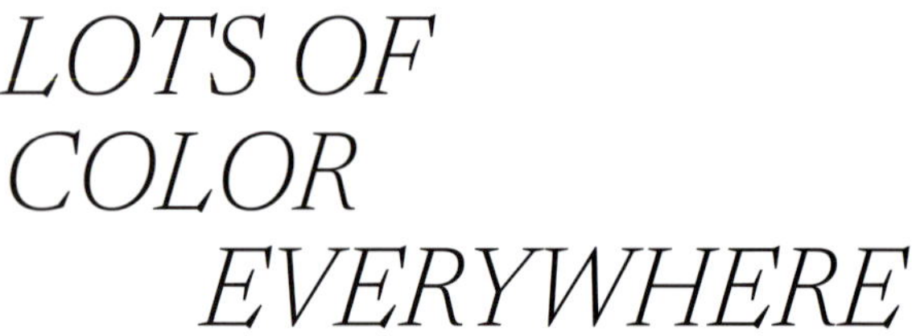

As artists and designers, we are taught a lot of concepts around color restraint and order. Color structures, conscious color parings, and a love for neutrals are all impressed upon us. We learn that too much color can be juvenile, frivolous, and even tacky and tasteless. (I am talking about you, minimalists of the world.) In design school we get too much color theory, then have to spend a lifetime deconstructing some of those restraints for a more personal, more fluid, and freer use of color.

I believe in a time to pull back and a time to let the colors explode. There is a place for limited, highly curated color, for black, gray, and white, but then there are moments when perfection includes an explosion of multicolor. As we develop a good eye for color, a personal color canon emerges that will guide us in when to be color restrained and when to let loose.

When you look at popular arts and crafts from around the world, you see that the artisans who made them are free from theories and the artifice of color restraint. They may be self-taught or apprentices of an older artisan, but they generally have in common a more exuberant and looser approach to color. Naive and spontaneous in their style and renderings, these master artisans relish their colors. Coming from Mexico, I have always enjoyed finding beautiful crafts and textiles from my country, and I learn from these artisans' keen eye for multicolor. I especially love

- **The long-stitch embroidery from Pátzcuaro, Michoacan,** that depicts multicolor scenes of people, fishing boats, mythical and farm animals, market flowers, and fruits, all combined in joyful plaza scenes stitched on simple white cotton cloth.
- **The imaginative, polychromed ceramics from Ocumicho, Michoacan,** that feature regular people playing with devils, angels, and monsters of all kinds and all colors.
- **The now-famous wooden alebrijes from Oaxaca,** which I first encountered while walking from house to house in the little town of San Martín Tejalapan. The artisans working on their patios made fantastic creations—dragons, animals, characters—following the capricious forms of the copal wood branches.
- **Any traditionally crafted toy from the various regions of Mexico,** which, whether created out of rag, wood, clay, tin, or more recently plastic, feature an explosion of color.

THE JOY AND FREEDOM OF NOT FOLLOWING COLOR RULES

Multicolor connects us to celebrations, happy times, birthday parties, gifts, cakes, and candies, also to silly playtime with toys, games (I still play memory matching with my same 1960s Milton Bradley kit), dress-up, and kids' crafts. It all connects us with carefree times when we had not yet become too serious or intellectual or contrived, when we still loved all things full of color: a room full of colorful toys; an outfit of clashing colors and patterns put together by a five-year-old; and the rainbows, unicorns, monsters, and all that a crayon box can create. More is more.

Along with toys and crafts, my childhood dose of color came from TV cartoons. I loved watching *Here Comes the Grump*, about a princess and a boy traveling across imaginary lands on a paisley-decorated balloon in what feels like a PG-rated LSD or mushroom trip. More recently, I LOVE *The Amazing World of Gumball*. There are no words to describe it, so just watch it . . . But above all, my favorite full-color animation is *Yellow Submarine*: the patterns, the clothes, the whole drama with the Blue Meanies, and of course the Beatles. I am not sure if it was this movie or missing out on the '60s, but I am always on the lookout for '60s fabrics—flowers, paisleys, wavy patterns, all of the above combined. The '60s brought an explosion of color, partly as a rebellion to muted traditions, partly because of the psychedelic trips. For me, it simply makes me very color happy.

Along with children and craft artisans from around the world, there is another group that often creates colorful art without restraint: people with psychological or developmental differences. Their work has been called outsider art, because they are, along with children and artisans, outside of the art and design establishment.

The first time I encountered the term *outsider* and saw this kind of art was at an exhibit in a former fifteenth-century sanatorium in Caldas da Raihna, Portugal. It featured the art of the residents of a nearby mental health treatment center showing work from both before and after their condition developed, when their art became freer and wilder with characters that were more imaginative and uninhibited and with a full-octane use of color. Reality blurred into imagination.

The artists were mostly people who suffered from schizophrenia, a condition known for, among other symptoms, heightened sensory perception, resulting in the use of intense multicolor and repetitive patterns.

Twentieth-century artist Jean Dubuffet, disillusioned with the establishment, fell under the colorful spell of art by neurodiverse people. He coined the term *art brut*, which roughly translates to *raw art*. He was enticed by the uninhibited themes, the imaginative figures, and the saturated colors he saw in the work of these artists. One of the artists whose work he collected was Aloïse Corbaz. This Swiss artist was institutionalized with schizophrenia after an incident at age thirty-three. She was well educated and had worked as a governess in the entourage of Kaiser Wilhelm II, but, unfortunately, she developed an infatuation with him that became problematic, especially as her symptoms got worse. This unrequited love became the backdrop of the art she made in the asylum. Her colorful work featured powerful, sensual women in fancy dresses or various degrees of undress surrounded by smaller royal suitors and admirers. These princess-over-prince imaginings are a joy to observe!

Other examples of outsider artists include Louis Wain, a turn-of-the-century British illustrator who went from cute cat characters to very eccentric-looking cats as his schizophrenia progressed, and Judith Scott, a deaf artist with severe Down syndrome whose gorgeous textile sculptures are made with tubes, ropes, and other fibers that her twin sister provided to her. Her pieces are so sophisticated, intriguing, and full of color! With her creations, Scott transcended the limiting perceptions people have of artists with disabilities. As a color lover and as the sister of a person with a mental disability, I can truly appreciate this.

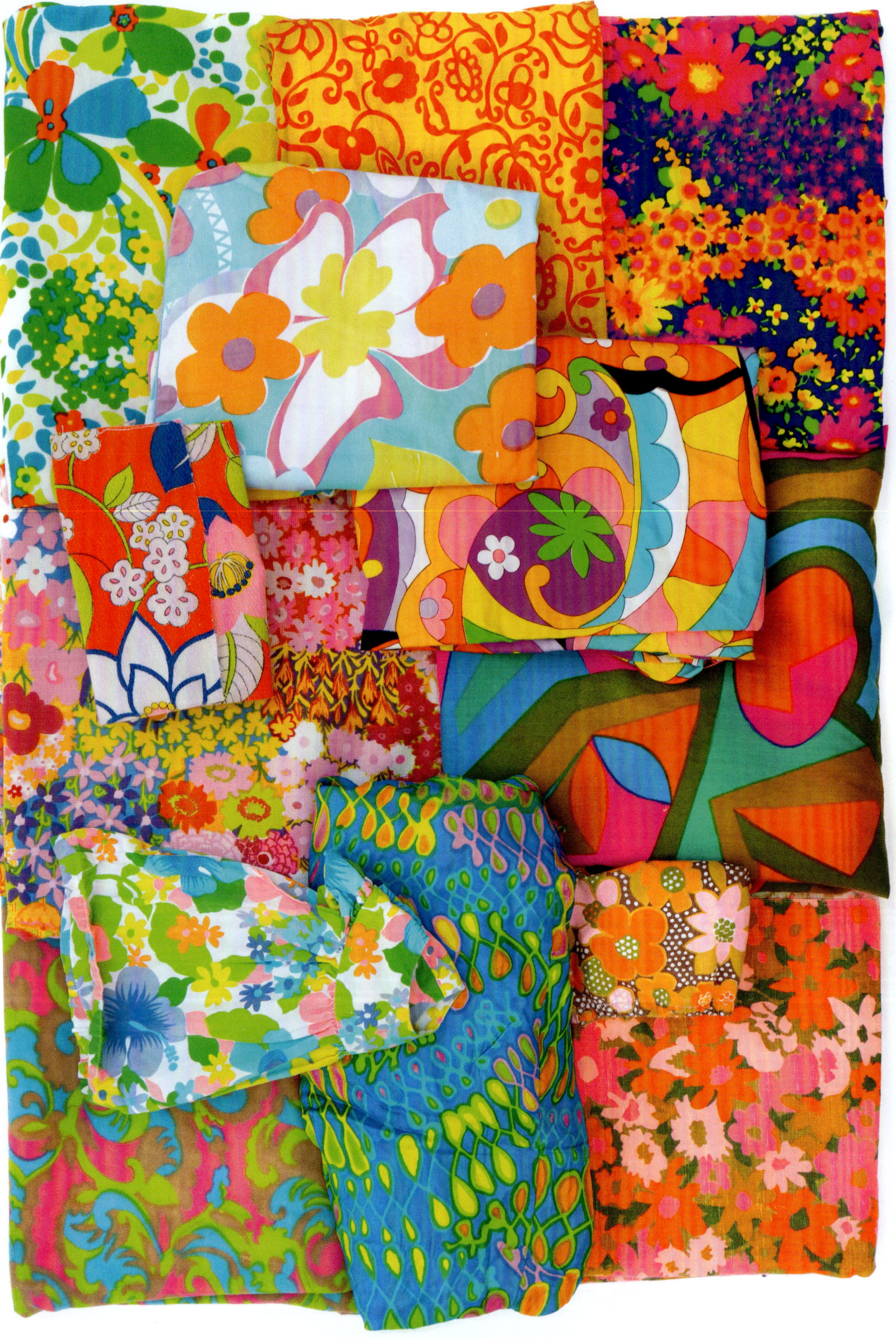

HOW TO HARNESS THE POWER OF MULTICOLOR

So, is multicolor frivolous? Naive? Tacky? Trippy? Or the result of a mind unleashed?

It can be all of these things! One of the best ways to educate your eye is to keep on the lookout for multicolor art, really examine it, and ask yourself how these artists and designers use it with fluency and full power. When you see something multicolor that you like, stop to observe it in more detail and analyze why it works for you. More than with any other color notion, multicolor is where personal voice and perspective really come through. By asking yourself color questions in the presence of multicolor, you will find the specific place where you draw the line between unhinged and fabulous.

Since there is no rule book for using multicolor correctly, your own experiences with multicolor really create the framework for how you can use lots of colors together. Creating colorful things is not just for kids or a modern phenomenon (though advances in synthetic colors, photography, and printing methods have definitely helped). Through history, there have been moments of rich multicolor. Look to artists of the past as a jumping-off point for your own observations and to develop your eye for multicolor.

When East met West via the Silk Road, commerce brought goods, plants, and spices to Europe, and with them came a whole new set of colors. Italian Renaissance frescoes look like a carnival of silk damask, where even the angels have multicolor peacock-feathered wings. The birds and flowers from the Persian gardens and the Chinese ceramics and silks reappeared in all their colorful glory in the tapestries, paintings, and frescoes of Italy, France, and Europe in general.

Recently, I have taken a deeper dive into Dutch florals. Tulips have always been my favorite flower, ever since I first saw a red one in Mexico, the land of tropical flowers. My mom brought it from a flower

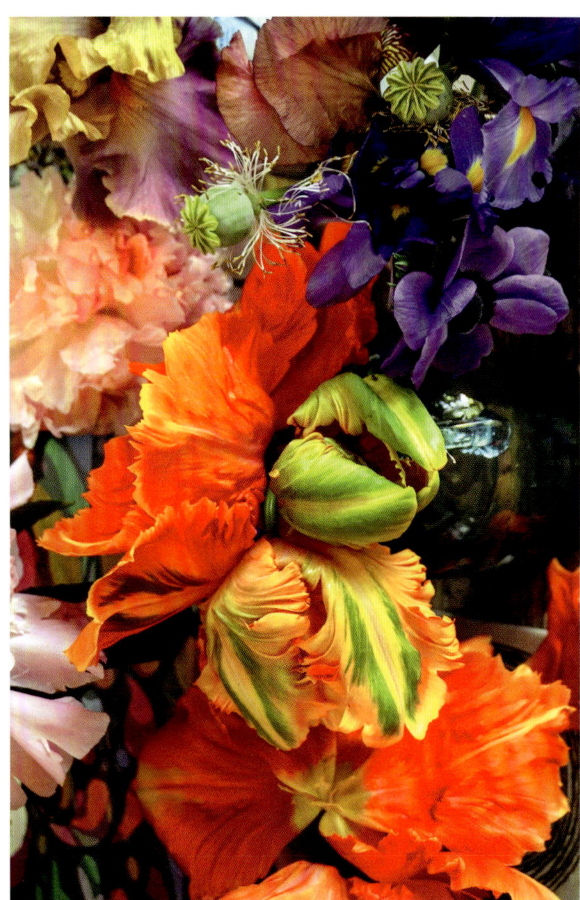

show; I was eight and had to sit down just to stare at it for a while. I had never seen anything so beautiful! Later, in New York, I passed by the longest, most beautiful multicolor parrot tulips at the now-gone Dean & Deluca. I could not afford them, so I would stop by to "visit" them every day on my way home. I still regret not buying them.

Tulips, of course, come in a myriad of hybrids. I love perusing the bulb catalogs I receive, and even more reading about how these flowers came from Persia and created Tulip Mania, the financial speculative bubble in the Netherlands in the seventeenth century. While I do not understand financial markets and the sale of futures, the yearning for the bulbs leading to exploding prices is a passion I can understand.

Once the merchants had their tulips, they'd put them in a vase, add other flowers—mindful of their symbolism—commission a painting, and walk away with a floral portrait that spoke of their worth and values. Imagine yourself in their shoes:

1. Start by showing off your wealth with a selection of tulips, preferably the striped varieties.
2. Add other bulbs, like blue hyacinths to represent playfulness.
3. For more depth, red and purple anemones remind viewers of the fleeting nature of life.
4. Add a dash of vanity with yellow and orange narcissi.
5. Include some pink by using peonies, which represent prosperity and honor.
6. For love and beauty, any color rose will do.
7. As a bonus, to show smarts, add irises—deep purple, lilac, yellow, or even green ones—to represent wisdom and valor.
8. Throw in some greenery and a few smaller flowers, some random bugs, a nest, and a lizard, and voilà! You have your Dutch multicolor floral family statement.

Do you see how these beautiful Dutch paintings used color and petals to deliver a message about the owner of the blooms? Look at Jan Brueghel the Elder, Jan Davidsz. de Heem, Ambrosius Bosschaert, and Rachel Ruysch (yes, a prominent woman painter). Observe the colors, think of what the person commissioning the painting wanted to display about their family, and bear in mind that these paintings often have aged with a varnish that obscures the radiance of the original colors. I think that, in this case, the key to harnessing the power of multicolor is to not only pay attention to the beauty of the flowers, but to see beyond into the symbolism of each element.

Skip a few centuries and enter modern art. The dotted multicolor of impressionism, best appreciated at close range with all its broken-color little dots and brushstrokes, laid the color-freedom foundation for fauvism. *Fauve* means *wild beast,* which is what the stupefied members of academia called the artists presenting their bold, colorful paintings in the 1905 Salon d'Automne in Paris. They thought the paintings were garish and unfinished. Yet art changed after this show; realistic, grandiose art lost steam as art became more of a personal expression and the critics increasingly shifted away from academia.

My favorite fauve of all time? Henri Matisse. My favorite multicolor piece? Hard to tell . . . maybe his wonderful painted paper cutout collage *Danseuse Créole,* or really, any of his seaweed collages. Once a fauve, always a fauve.

How did he harness multicolor so successfully?

Each color is interesting on its own, but combined, their powers multiply. Matisse was a master of each one of his colors and a wizard at combining them. He did not use just any bright green, red, purple, or blue thrown together mindlessly. He intentionally selected, carefully mixed, and purposefully placed each color, turning the art piece into a masterpiece.

It does not matter if you are a kid, a professional artist, a set designer, a florist, a crafter, an artisan, or a weaver, the approach is the same. The secret sauce for good use of color—from monochrome to multicolor—is intentionality. It happens when the artist selects or mixes colors that they love and trusts their intuition, combining them with conviction, freely and joyfully.

It is not unlike cooking, where you are balancing sweet, salty, sour, piquant, bitter, and umami; mixing herbs and spices; cooking the ingredients to the right temperature; and stopping to smell or taste along the way. When you stop to check, you are assessing what needs to happen next. The same mix of intuition and constant decision-making and adjusting goes into both multicolor visual arts and culinary arts.

There are so many modern artists of intentional multicolor! Abstract art lends itself well to explode in multicolor joy!

I grew up with an abstract painting by Benito Messeguer that was exactly that—an explosion of color, an abstract representation of a tropical night over a serene field of ultramarine blue, with a grouping of thickly painted blobs of multiple bright colors: lemon, red, orange, magenta, more blues. You see it and you feel tropical, hot, and humid, as if you were at the beach in Mexico; even the blue feels hot. I have photos of me as a baby next to this painting, and it still hangs in my home.

There are so many multicolor artists to observe! The following artists are particularly worth checking out for their use of color:

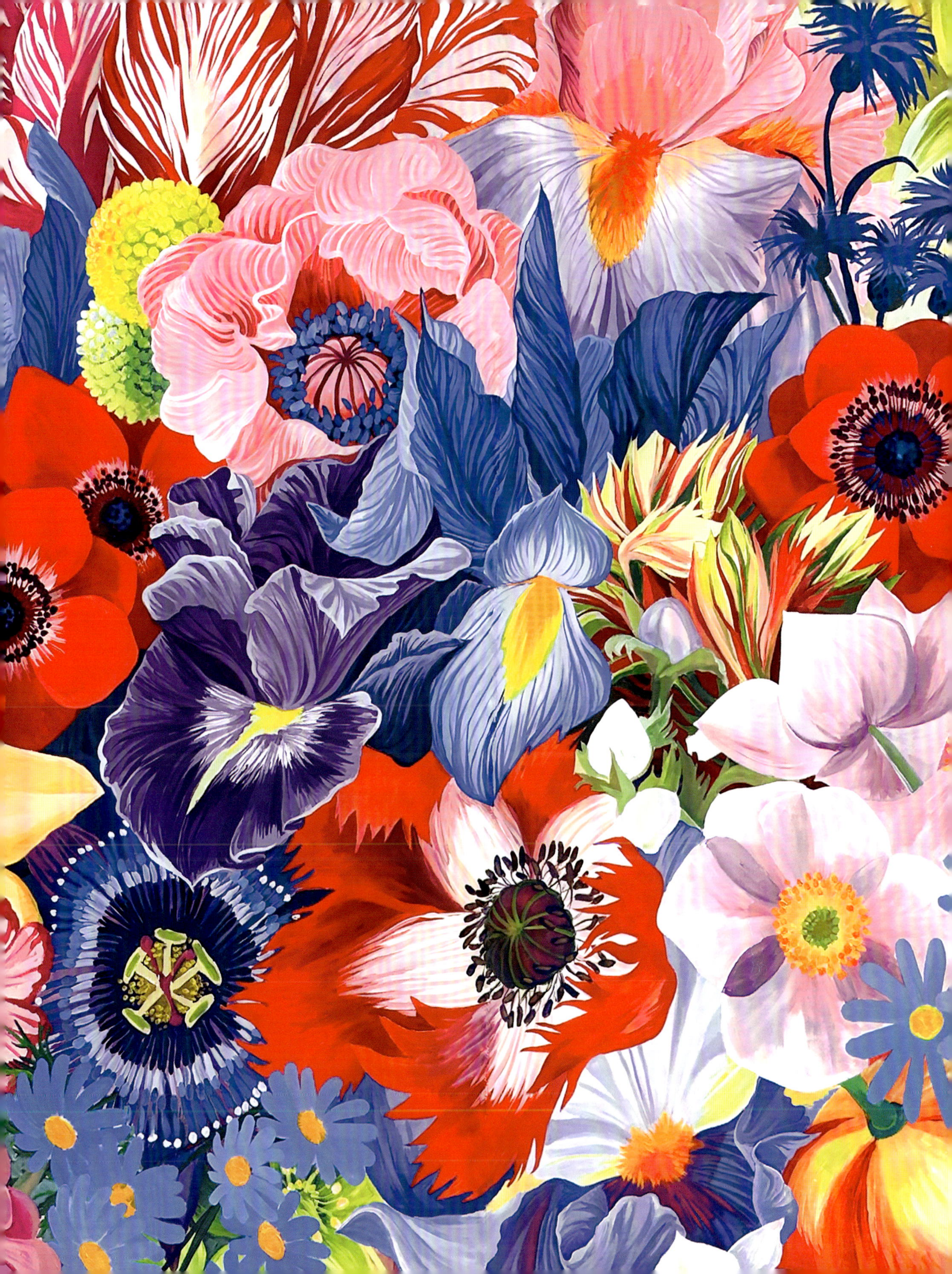

- **Dale Chihuly** and his gorgeous blown-glass sculptures, especially when they are installed in natural settings like botanical gardens.
- **Sonia Delaunay** and her multicolor circle compositions.
- **Willem de Kooning** and his wild brushed abstracts, such as *Untitled XXV.*
- **Jean-Michel Basquiat,** both on his own and when he collaborated, four hands on canvas, with Andy Warhol.
- **André Butzer** (born in 1973 in Germany), whose art I first saw recently. I was instantly blown away by his huge, widely colorful, expressive paintings. I could clearly see two moods: Several paintings looked to me like highly stylized representations of childhood extravaganza, in bright, happy, saturated colors, some with cheeky characters, some completely abstract. But then there were others, also multicolor, but dark, quite dark. Childhood nightmares and monsters? No idea—I need to learn more about him and his intentions, but just observing them without previous context or a bio or intellectuality was quite an experience!

Next time you find yourself looking at a piece of multicolor art or design, try to look beyond the joy and happiness, the beauty or fun of it. Ask yourself what kind of feelings arise in you and what the creator might have meant to provoke. Remember that not all multicolor is joyful. Was the artist spontaneous in their color choices, like a child, a naive artist, or a person with a psychiatric condition, or was this art or design piece the result of intentionality?

If you are in a garden full of flowers (add the Dutch Keukenhof garden to your bucket list!) or a spring meadow full of all kinds of wildflowers, don't just bask in the joy of the multicolor; observe the somewhat random mix and match of colors in nature and how well it works, and think about those Dutch painters and the meaning of each flower and color.

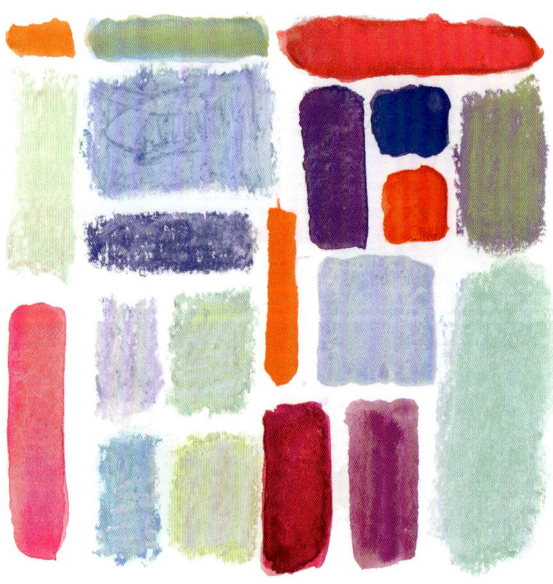

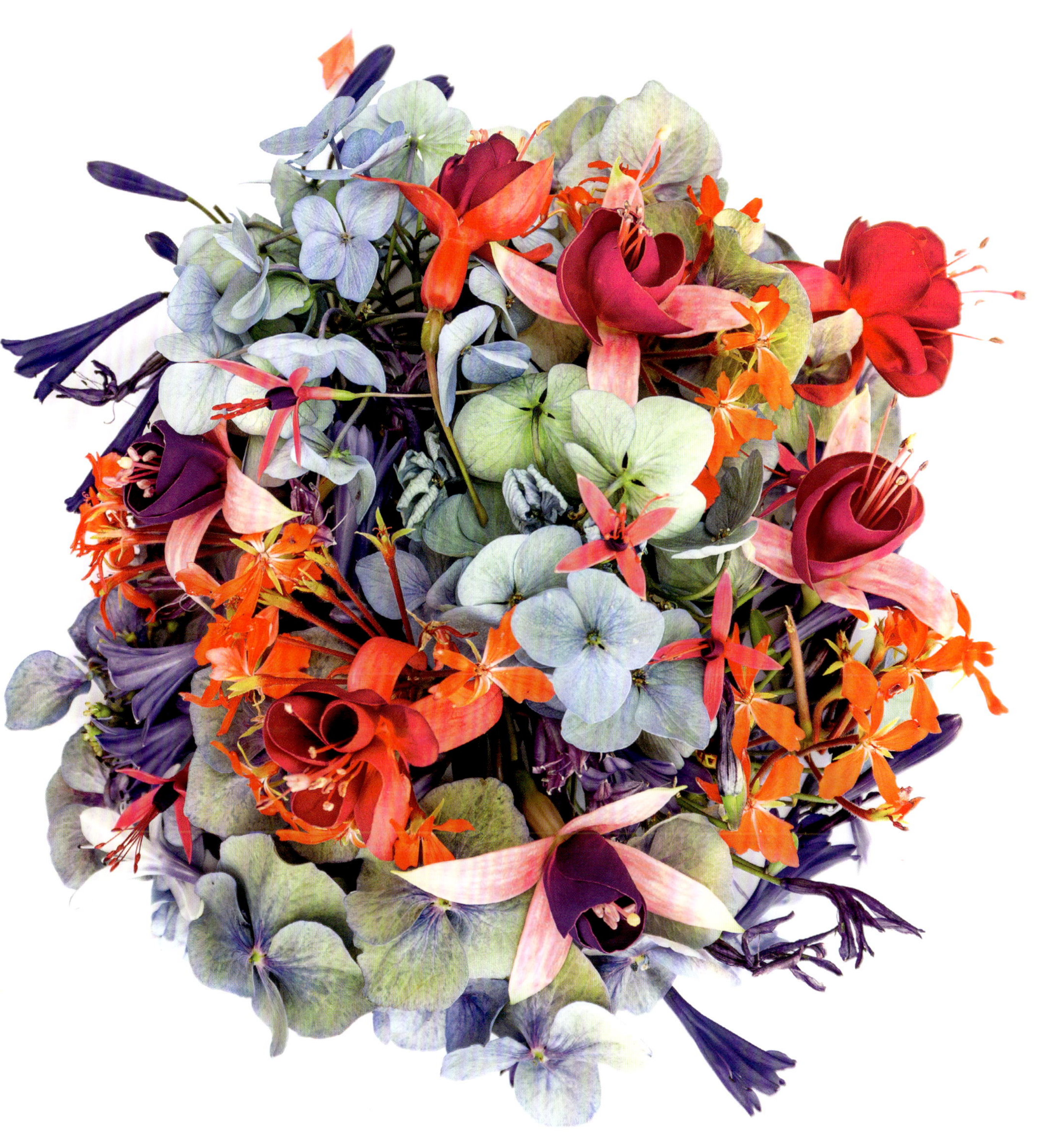

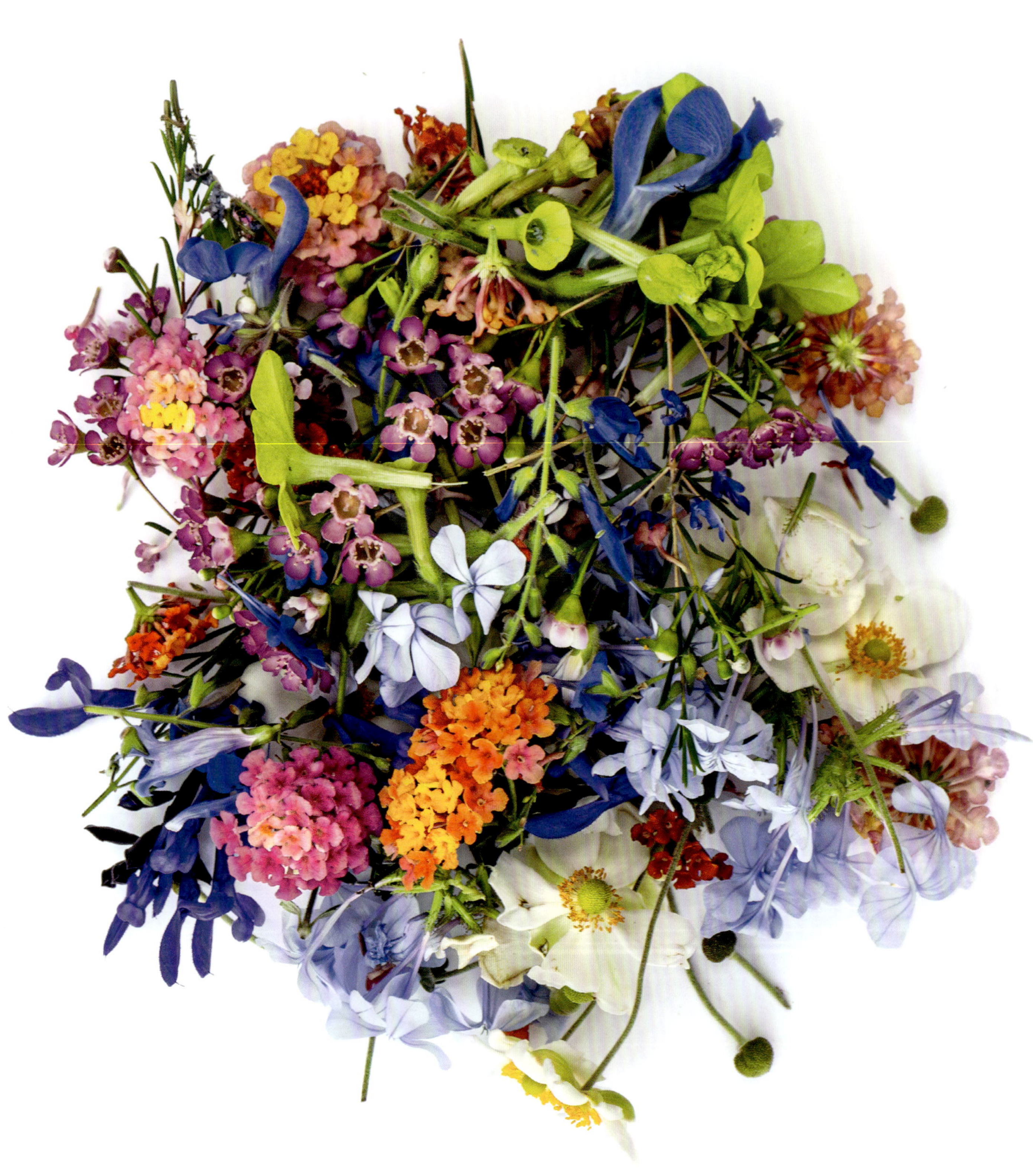

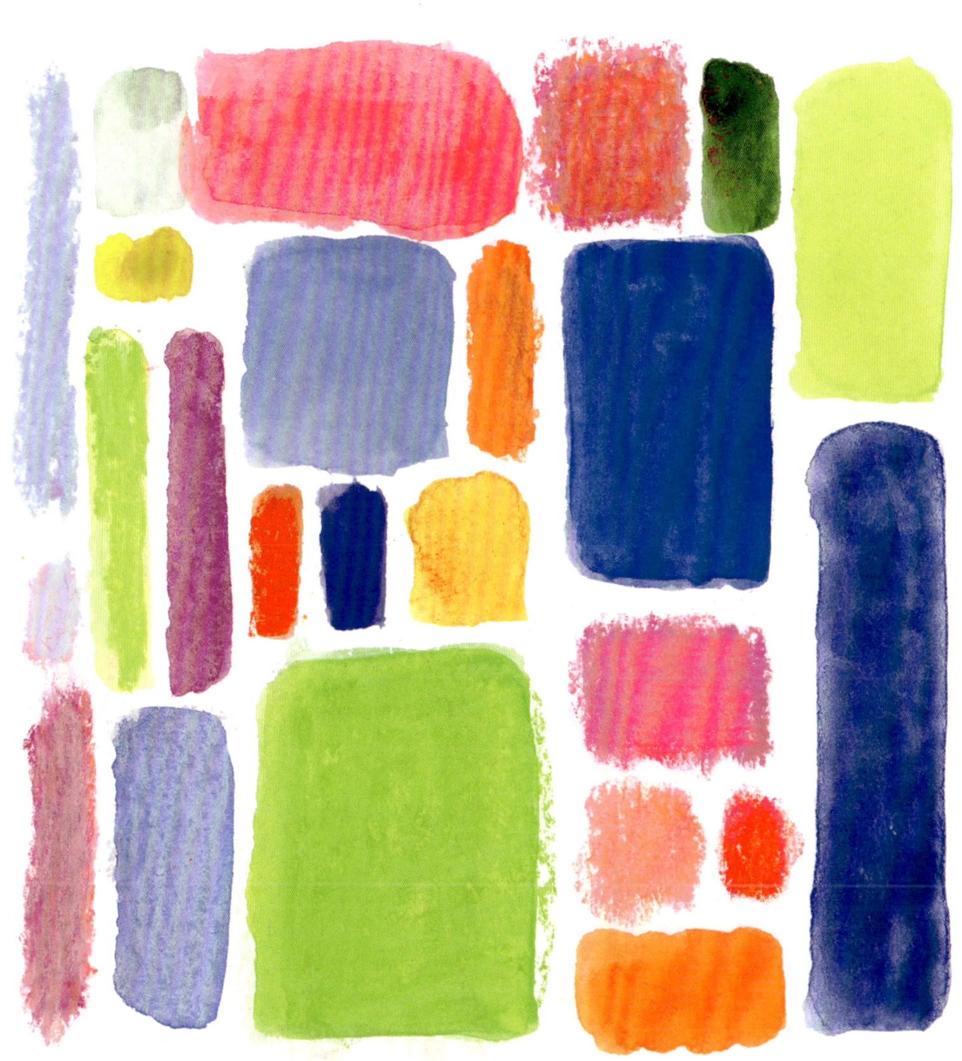

A CENTURY OF COLORFUL CHILDHOODS

No matter how old you are, you have childhood color memories, from the color of your room (I chose Prairie Green from a Formica catalog) to the clothes you wore over and over. You may recall the colors of your birthday cake (mine was always decorated with fluffy multicolor Swiss meringue, plus sugar cones filled with more colorful meringue to make them look like ice-cream cones), but nothing connects us more to the colors of childhood than toys.

Your favorite toys connected your imagination with the times. For '60s kids, there were spaceships and robots, and in the '70s, toys were very colorful and wacky. What about recent decades? Nowadays, most toys are branded, mass-market, and probably made of plastic.

At the end of this chapter's text, you will see some family heirlooms: toys from different decades with different personalities and changing colors. You will see my mom's Madame Alexander Doll from the '40s with all the dresses she made her (yes, my mom was quite an accomplished sewer from a young age!), some tin toys from the '50s and '60s along with a cowboy comic and my husband's favorite little book about a satellite (he is such a Space Age boy!). Then come my toys, all those plushies I just can't get rid of, especially Manolo, that Humpty-Dumpty-like character with red yarn hair that my grandmother crocheted for me. Next are lots of pastel teacups from the '90s and my daughter's toys from the 2010s. Each decade is so different in theme, but even more so in colors! As you look at the images, notice the changes in hues and tones. Try to recall the toys and objects from your childhood and how they compare with my family's.

→ Three different childhoods, three different styles of drawing, and most definitely three different multicolor palettes: the stickers and litho-printed chromes from the turn of the century, with detailed drawings and muted colors; the scratch-and-sniff stickers from my own childhood (yes, they still smell!!) with their bright colors and wacky cartoon faces; my daughter's collection from the late 2010s, glitter, avocados, yoga, and affirmations (very Gen Z).

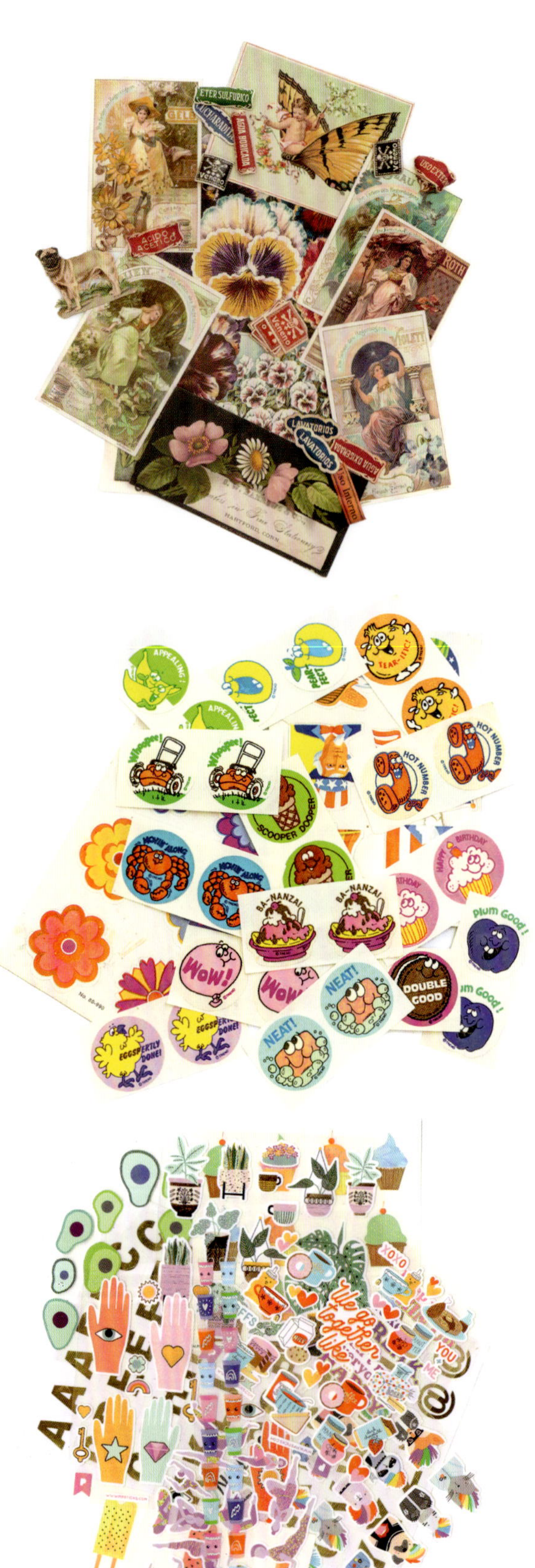

ON COLOR AND TOYS

IN CONVERSATION WITH RILEY WILKINSON

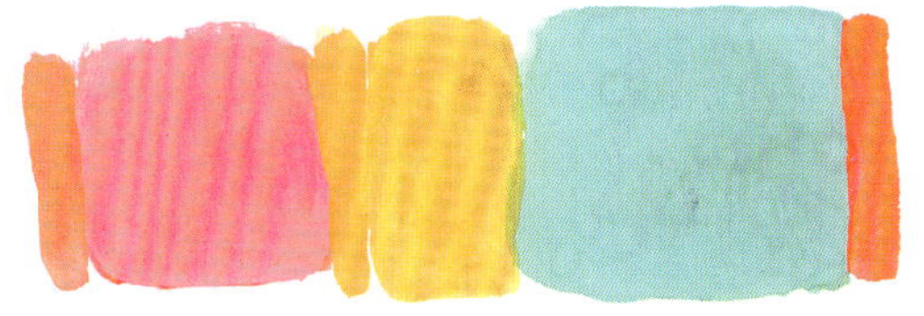

Riley Wilkinson is like a Willy Wonka of toys. For over thirty years he has designed and helped develop toys with companies like Mattel and American Girl and publishers like Scholastic and DK. He is currently an independent toy agent and creative director. His own Sneaky, Snacky Squirrel Game, fully conceived, designed, and developed by Riley, has sold more than two million sets and has over ten thousand five-star reviews.

Find him on Instagram @rileywilkinson or on his website at RileyWilkinson.com, and check out his Pinterest inspiration boards full of toys and multicolor joy. See the resource pages at the end of the book to learn about his toy design class.

"Let's start by saying that the '70s for me are all about aqua, bright red, and that yellow—both bright and mustardy—of the Fisher-Price Little People. That is why aqua is my personal color . . . and pink, not the Barbie pink but more of a bubble-gum pink."
—Riley Wilkinson

Nowadays, most of the toy properties involve one kind of licensing or another—from huge lines of products like Barbie to characters from animation that end up becoming toys and games. The colors of these toys are limited to the palettes that come with the trademarked characters. So those palettes can't change, and nowadays they form the majority of the mass-market toys.

In that space there are, however, some things that are gradually changing. Colors are much less binary; I love seeing pink gender-neutral toys! And there is more of a multicolor thing, lots of rainbows. Back in the '90s rainbows were only in pride flags, but now they are all over in toys, games, and decor for kids. That is multicolor joy.

Some of the best examples of this multicolor joy are the surprise-box toys, those little collectibles that come in packaging that does not let you know which one you are getting, prompting you to buy more—to continue building the collection or to find *the one*. These include stylish Japanese collectibles like Kidrobot and the mass-market wonder that was the Shopkins: the cute little surprise-box toys that came in a myriad of shapes representing everything you can possibly buy in a store, from food to shoes to cleaning materials turned into big-eyed characters.

Shopkins were a brilliant toy from the dollar perspective. Kids would buy these really affordable cute things by the dozen, and brands were coming in saying "We want our cereal on a toy," and would pay a licensing fee. So they were an explosion of colors that sometimes included the whole lineup of the cereal aisle with their inherited colors, like orange for Frosted Flakes.

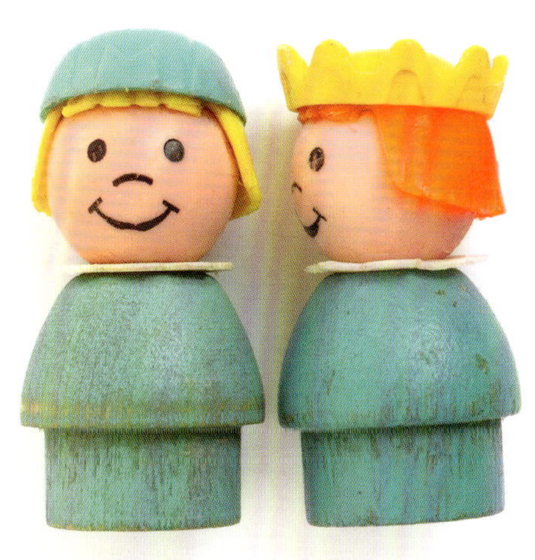

From the huge plastic explosion of the '80s and '90s to today, we are seeing more toys made out of wood. Wood and pastel colors: That is a very millennial thing, signaling that they are moving away from this mass-produced world. What's funny is that these are still mass-produced products, but now in wood tones with the addition of a more controlled color palette of pastels and muted colors, though lately fluorescents are coming back.

This reminds me of that awful trend of making children's rooms gray, which I don't get. The parents want a monochromatic home that looks like the catalog, and they extend that into the kids' rooms, but kids gravitate to color!

I love European toy stores and toy companies. They are unlike some big American companies that will only make toys out of plastic and envelop them with licensed characters. These European toy companies are all about pretend play and the play sets. I think kids need that. Fewer characters, because with licensed characters the play becomes prescribed instead of imaginative. Some of my favorites are

- **Londji:** Everything they make is muted wood or printed on cardboard with gorgeous illustrations. I specially love a giraffe balancing game.
- **Petit Collage:** Sweet, beautiful toys with a mission of sustainability.
- **Maileg:** So down to earth and wholesome, yet fabulous! All those fabric characters that live in matchboxes, and everything in dusty blue, old pink, sage green, and natural colors.
- **Marbushka:** Beautiful board games.
- **Uncle Goose:** Wooden toys, mostly based on wood blocks, painted with muted limited colors. So beautiful!

One more favorite source of multicolor joy: children's books! That is a great place to look at color and to see trends for kid products and toys.

KEY TAKEAWAYS

1. Feed your eyes all kinds of multicolor inspiration, not only in art but everywhere you go: the produce in the market, a flower shop, the playground at a school or park full of kids wearing fun colors, a boxful of threads or fabric scraps, the sprinkles next time you bake, crafts from around the world, a mass of toys in your kids' rooms (before you ask them to kindly clean up). When in the presence of multicolor, ask yourself: How does this make me feel? Why do these colors, as diverse as they are, look good together?

2. When working with lots of colors, make sure you are not doing so mindlessly. Ask yourself why a multicolor palette is the right choice for this particular piece or design.

3. Do not go for default, straight-out-of-the-tube colors; be purposeful about the hue, shade, and tone of every bit of your multicolor piece. Make each color special. Sometimes even preparing a little palette like the ones all throughout this book is a good practice before moving on to the final piece.

4. Remember, multicolor does not only mean full-octane chroma; you can have multicolor that is deep and jewellike, or very pale, or a mix of pastel and neon.

5. Dig into your childhood memories for color combinations. Use toys and children's books (or cartoons) from other decades to inspire your children's book illustrations or kid-product designs.

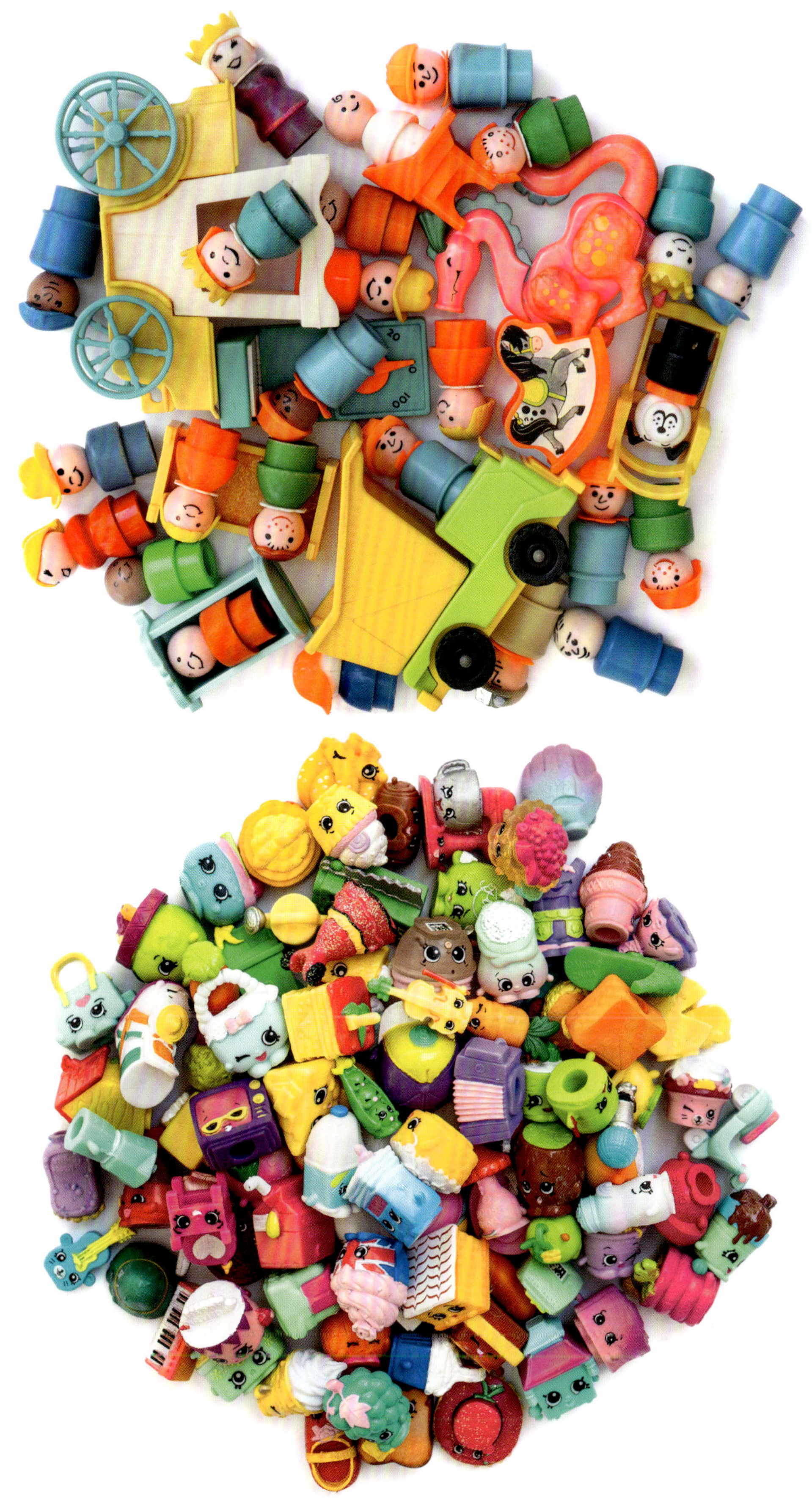

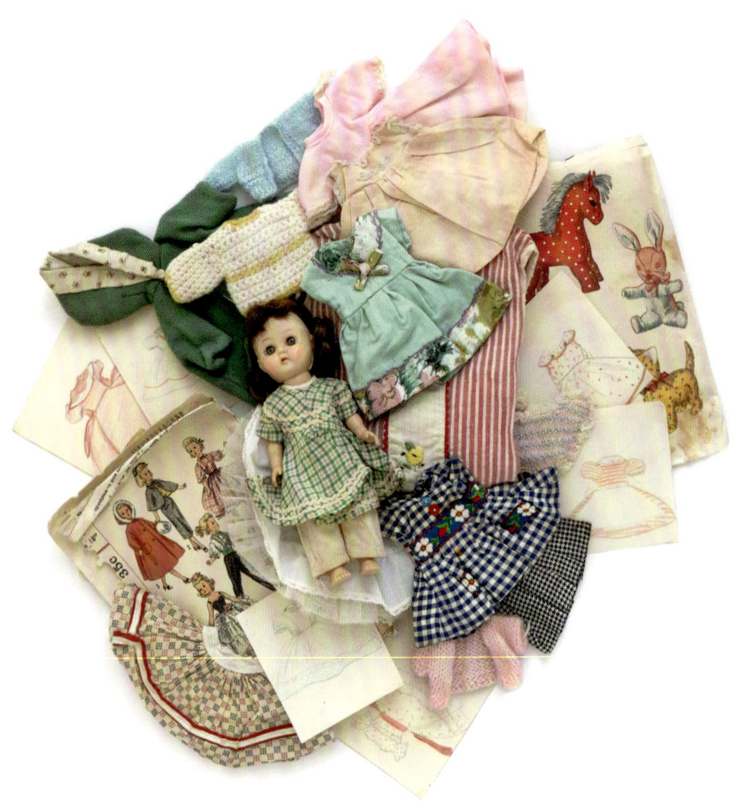

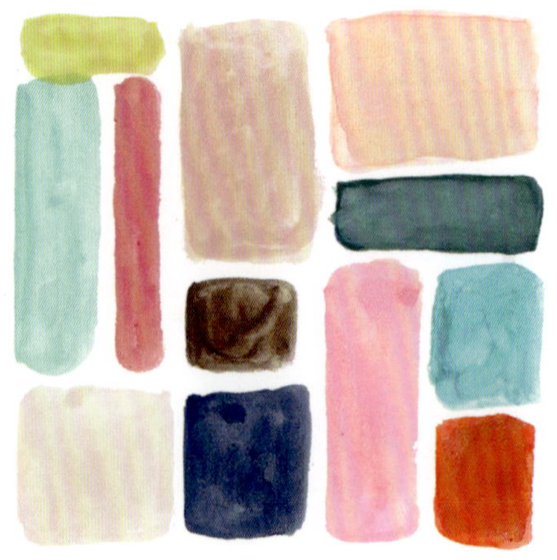

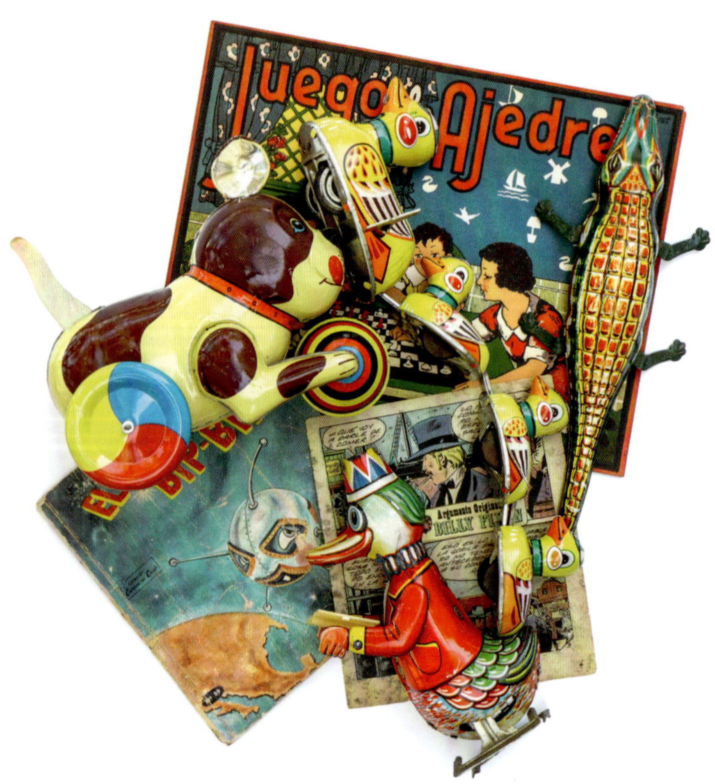
Juego Ajedre
EL BILI-BO
Argumento Original
BILLY P...

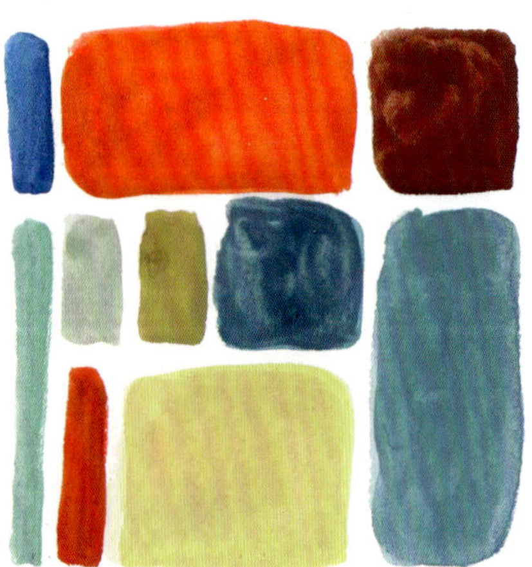

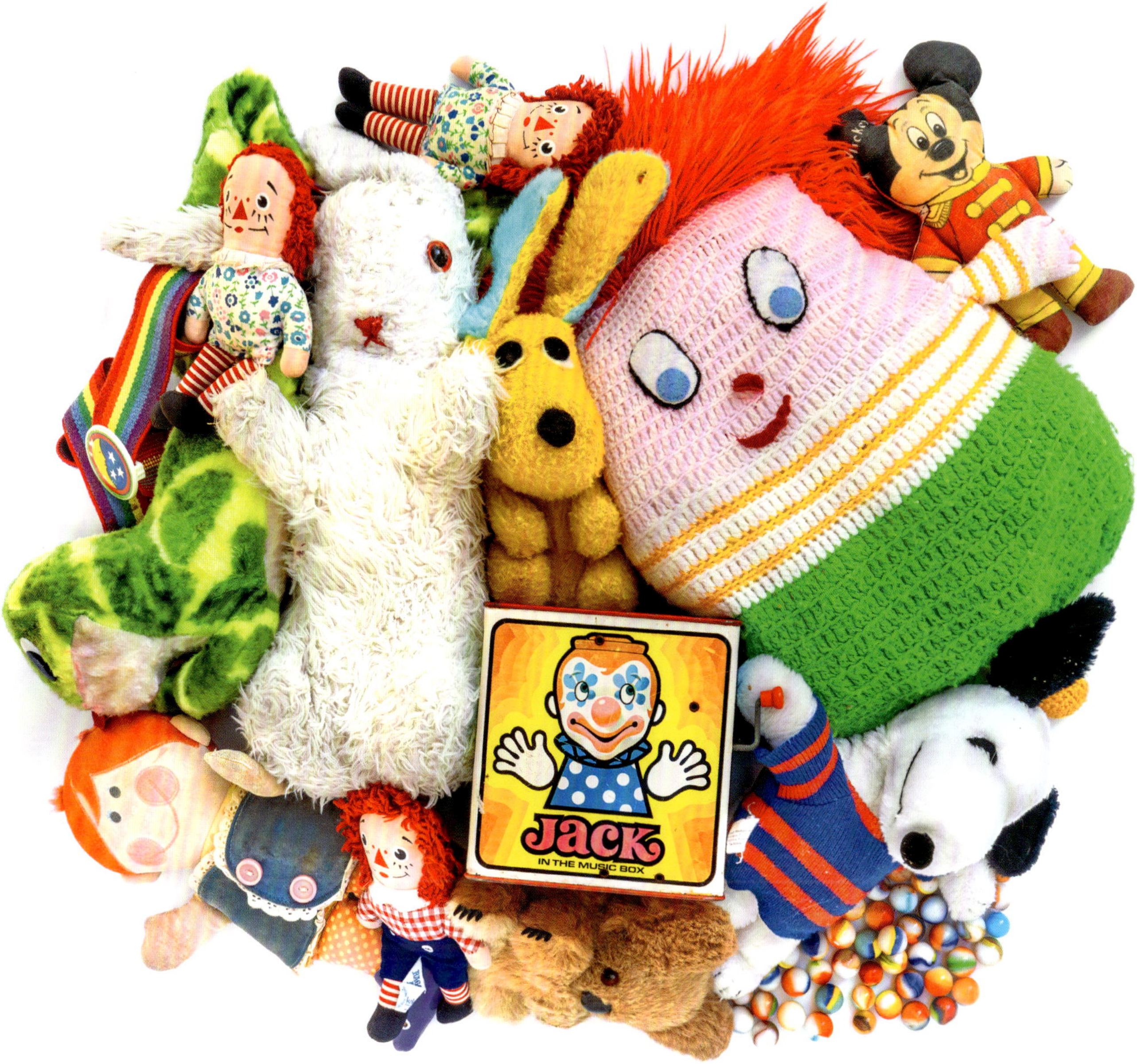

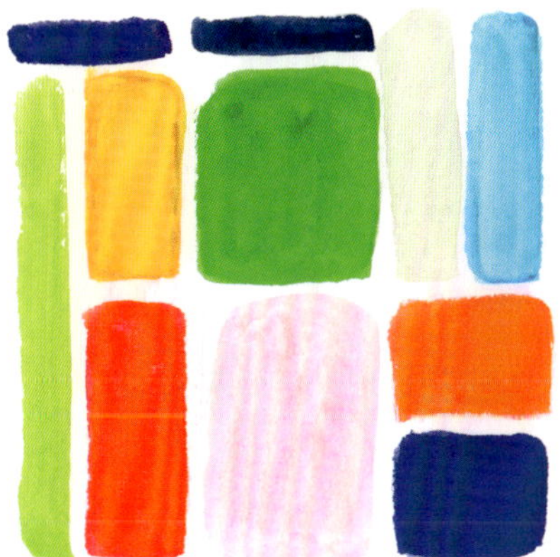

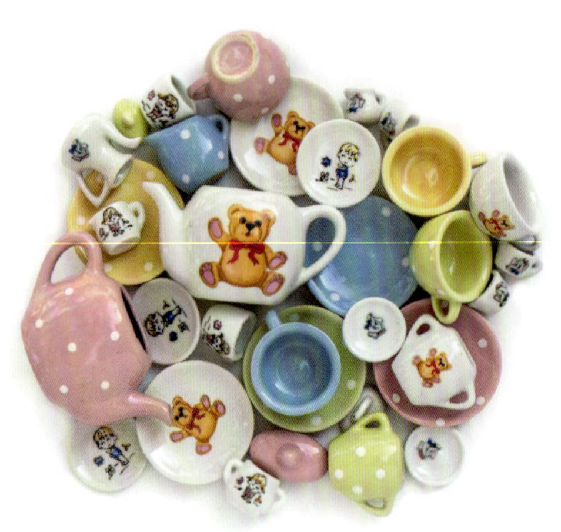

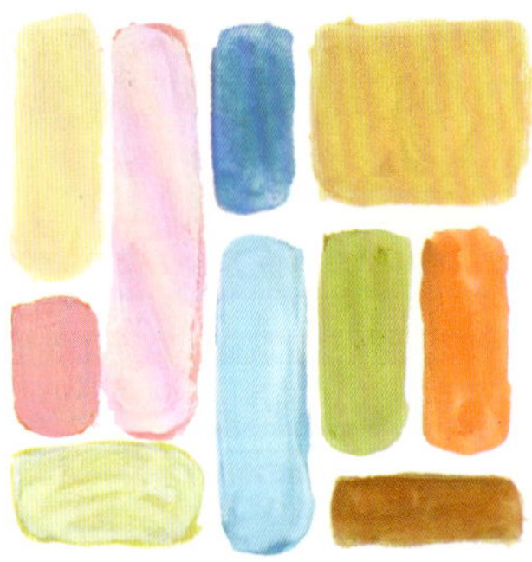

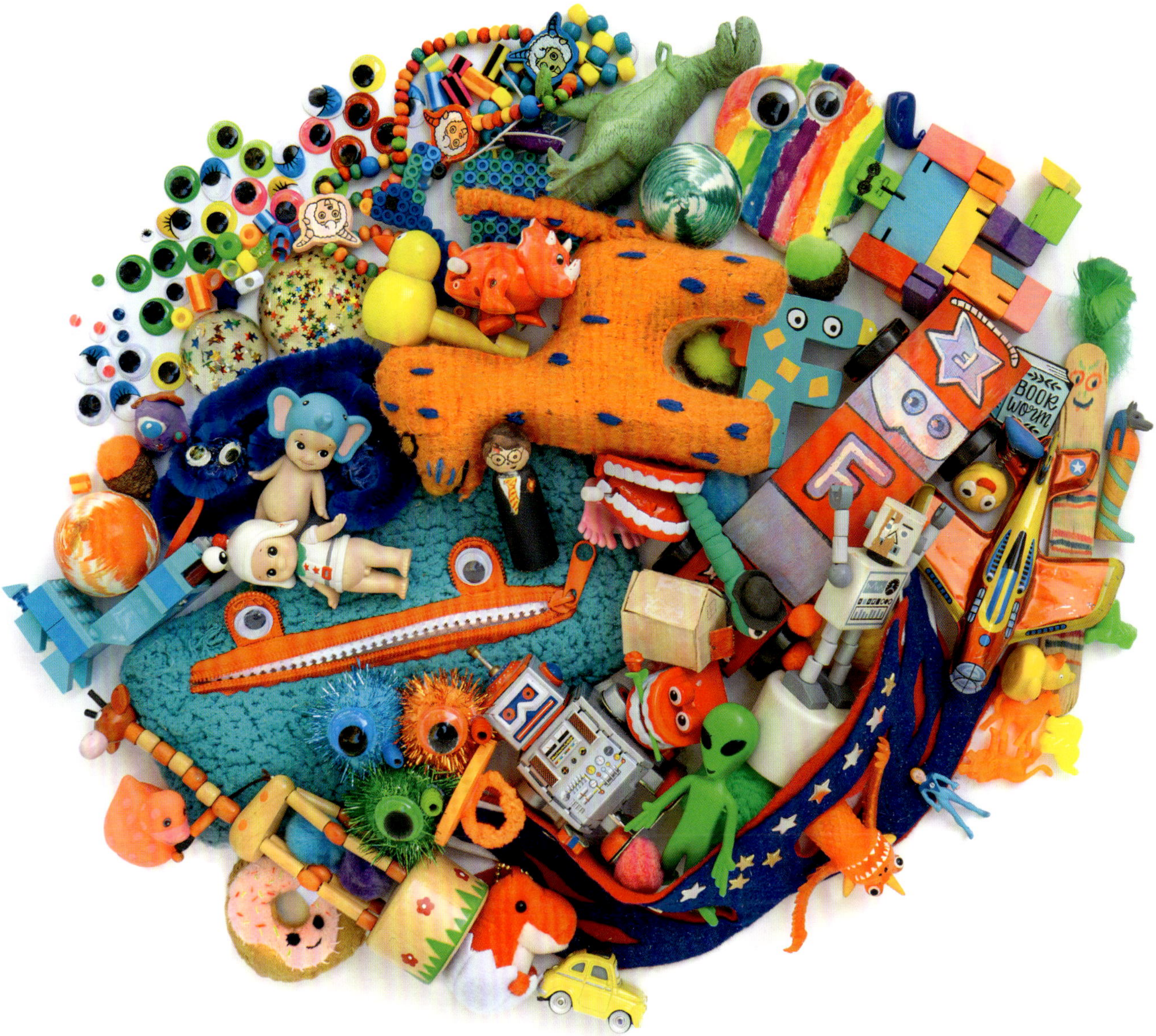

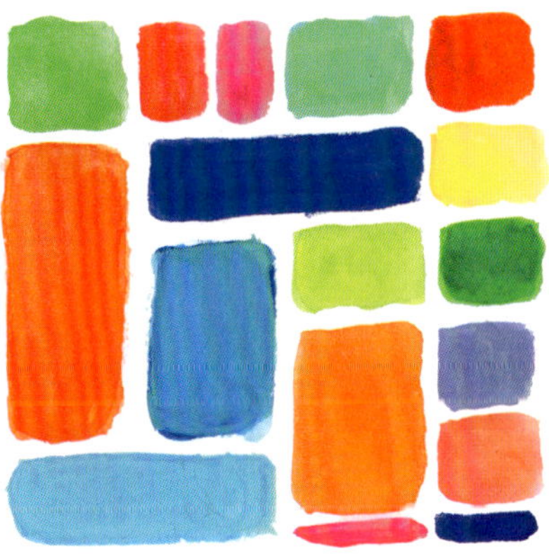

PROJECT

OBSERVE: Observing the color of childhood is a great way to play with multicolor, but not all childhoods have the same palette. Childhood colors change with the aesthetics of different decades, and they are affected by culture and the color trends of grown-up universes: fashion, home decor, fine art, and others. Even the idea of kid products looking different from the adult world is fairly new.

Observe the stickers on page 120. They are all meant for the same purpose: paper appliqués to use on stationery or crafts. One set is Victorian, the next one from the 1970s—from my personal collection of scratch-and-sniff stickers that still smell!—and the third one from my daughter's box of stickers, very 2010s. Three different palettes for three different childhood eras.

ANALYZE: Analyze in more detail how color evolves through the decades. Which is your decade? Are the colors of my objects similar to the toys of your childhood? Do you still have your favorite toys? What are their colors?

Notice the levels of saturation, the emergence of neon, and how some decades are bright and some are muted or pastel. Think of home decor and fashion of that time. Are the toys similar to grown-up things from that era?

CREATE: OPTION A

Create a collection of objects in a shadow box; no need to pull out the paints to experience multicolor joy! Collect your own childhood toys, or your kid's most memorable ones. How many you have and how small or big they are will determine the size of box you need. The idea is to fill the box with tightly packed toys so that we forget about each individual toy and all you see is a box of colors.

A version of this, on steroids, that I have often thought of recreating with my and my daughter's most colorful toys is the stuffed-animal chair by the Campana Brothers. Not to be missed!

OPTION B

Create a set of simple portraits of your childhood toys or your children's toys. You can also draw them from memory, if you don't have toys anymore, or visit a toy shop and photograph what you like the most. Imagine these would become a little gallery wall in a kid's room. Be purposeful with the colors and aim to end up with a multicolor grouping of portraits.

OPTION C

Create a new toy or game! It doesn't matter what it is, but just make sure your design starts with a strong multicolor palette.

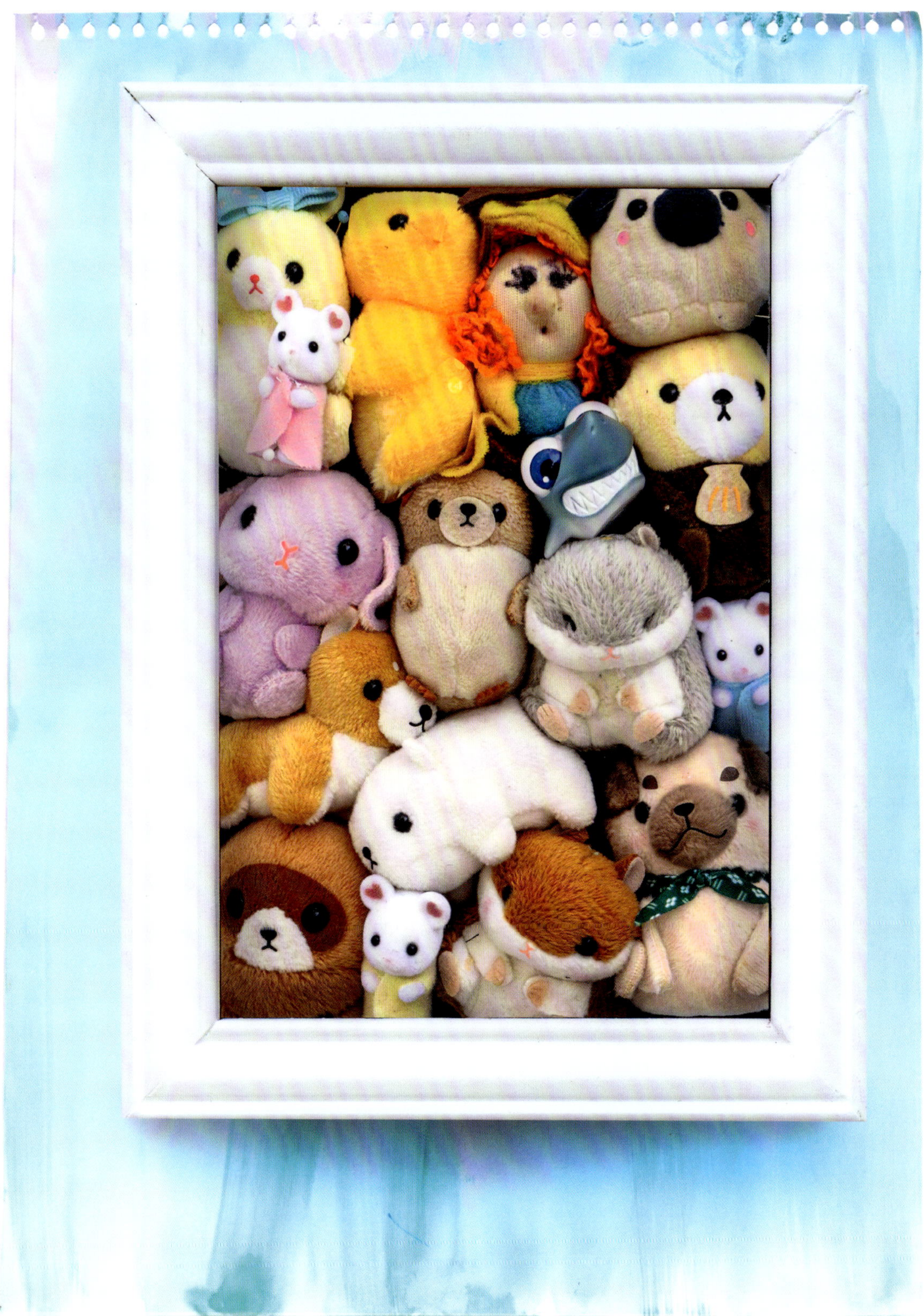

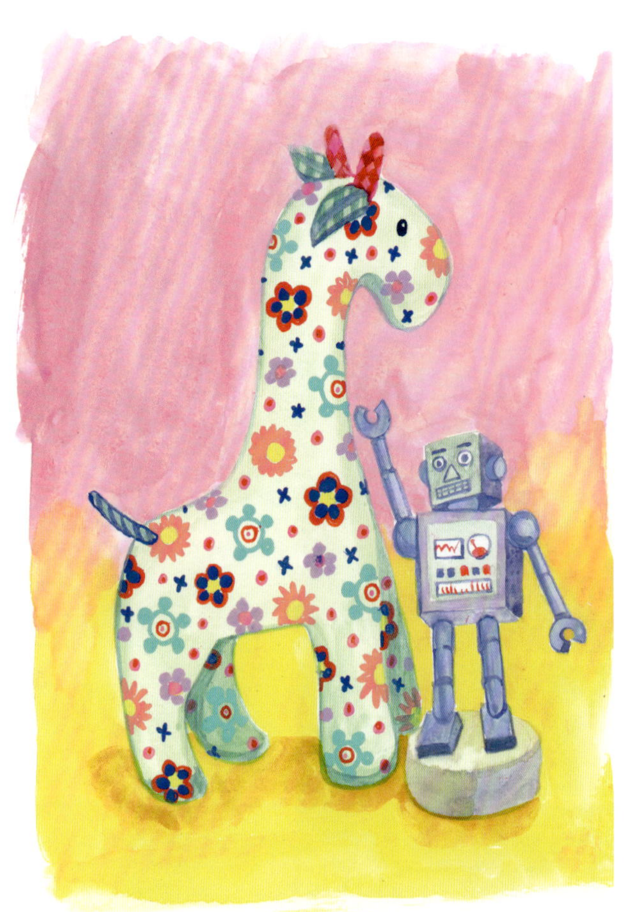
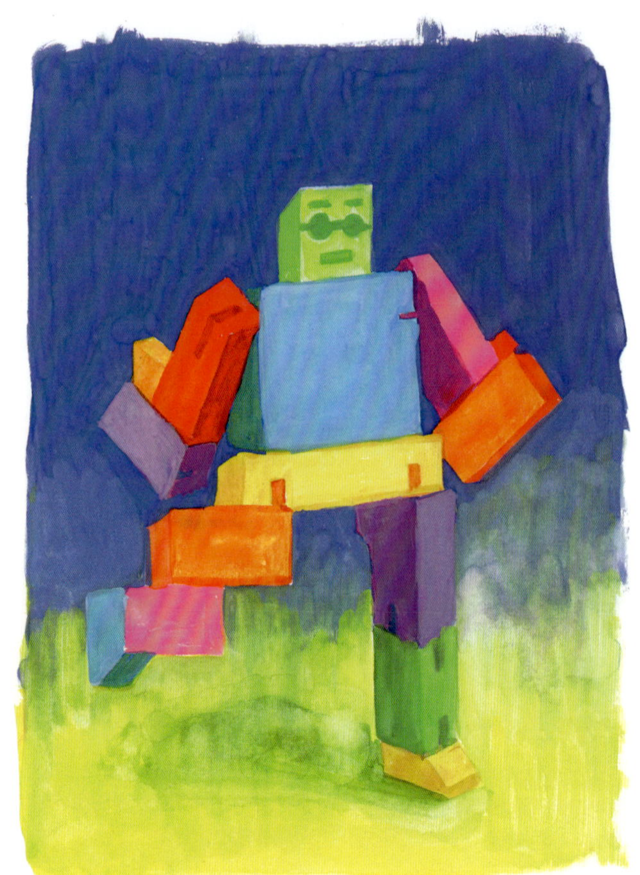
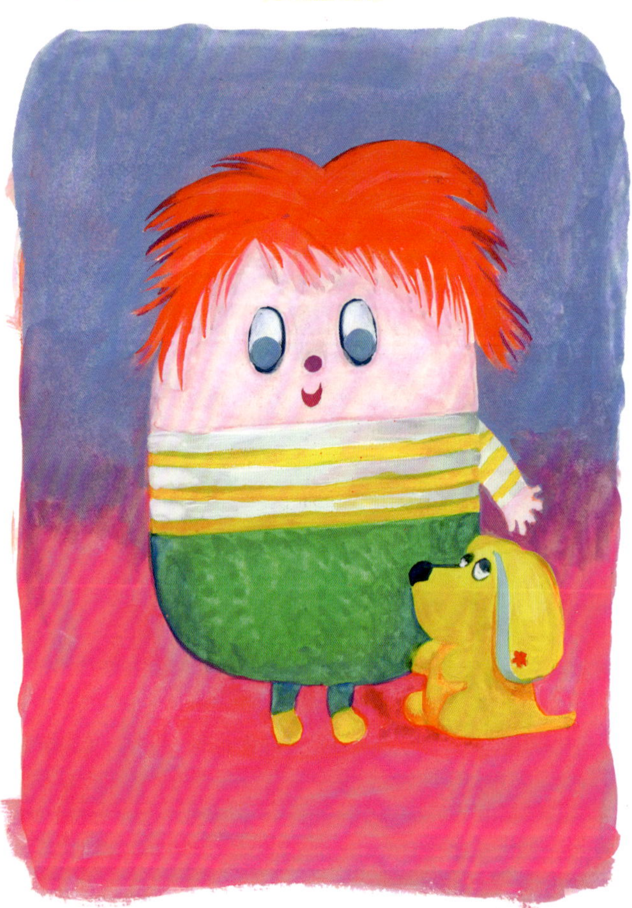
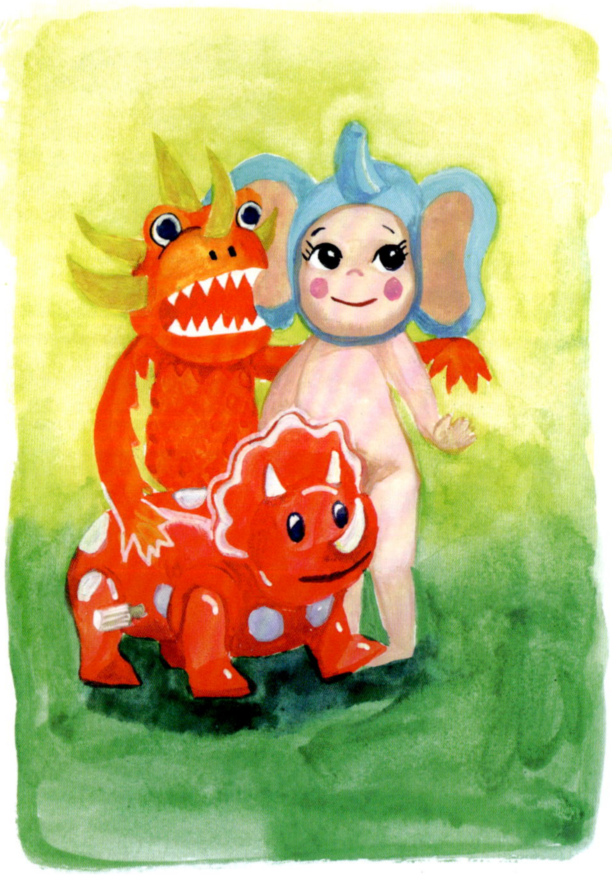

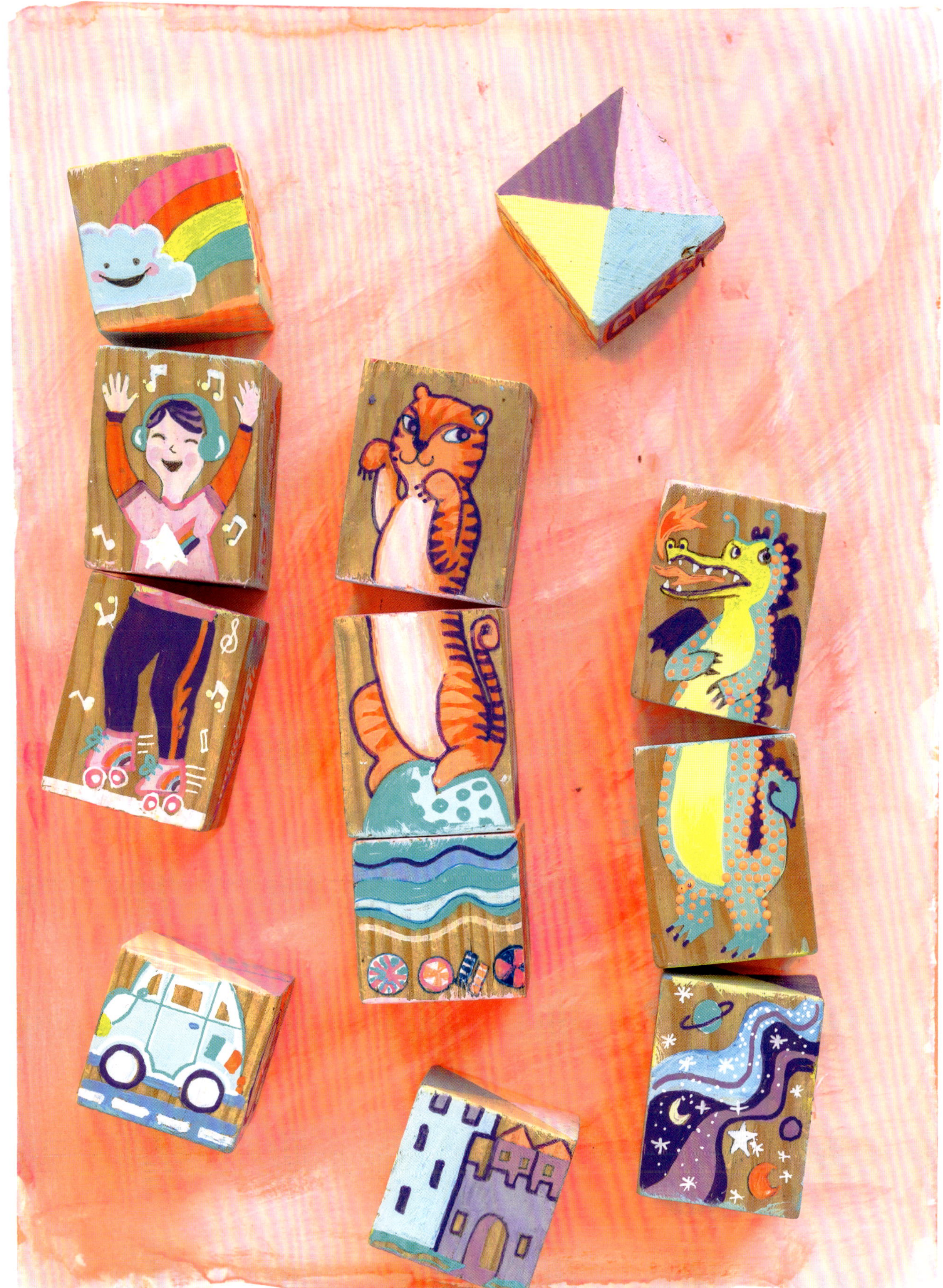

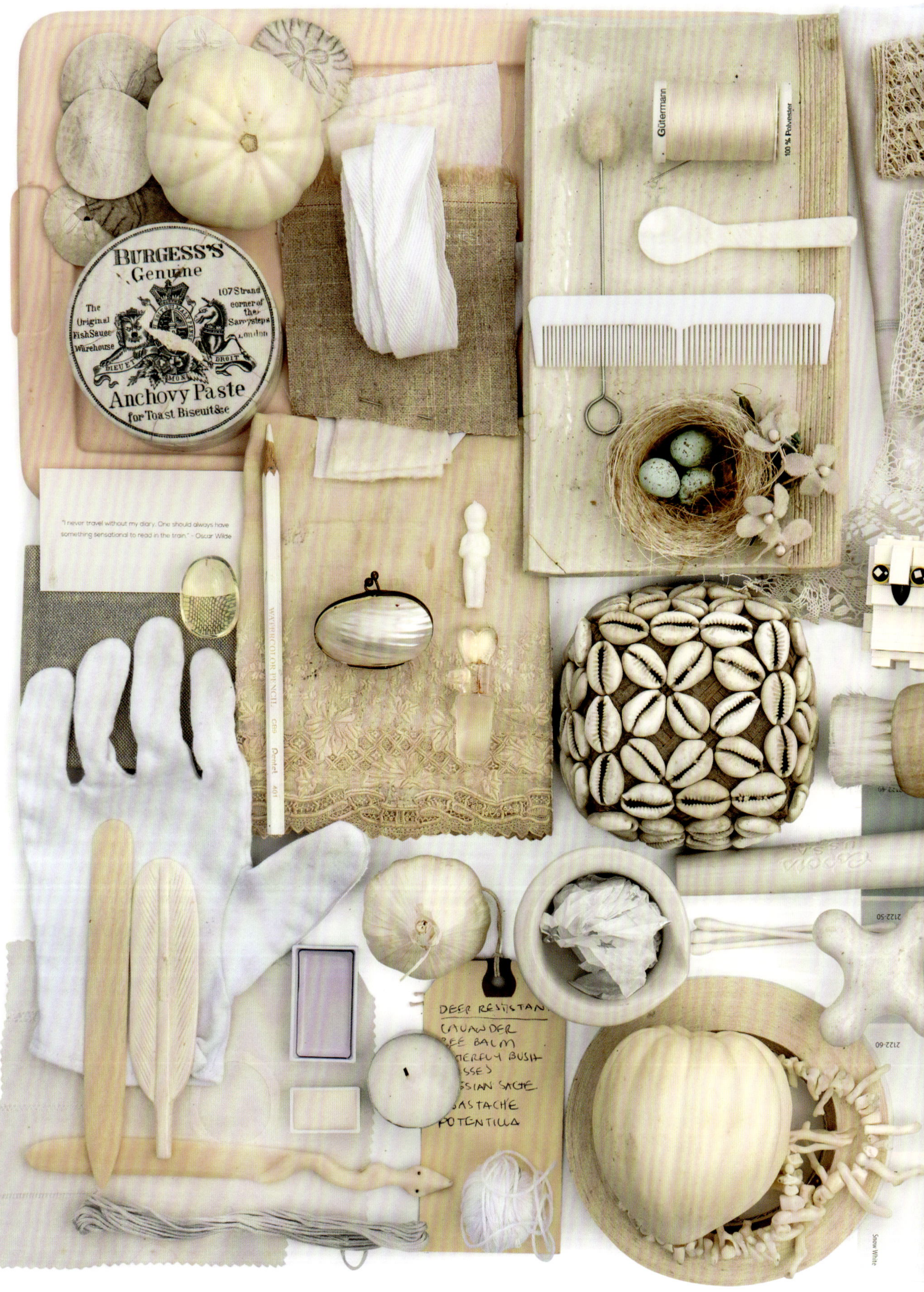

Gütermann
100 % Polyester
BURGESS'S
Genuine
107 Strand
corner of the
Savoy steps
London
The
Original
Fish Sauce
Warehouse
Anchovy Paste
for Toast Biscuit &c
"I never travel without my diary. One should always have
something sensational to read in the train." - Oscar Wilde
DEER RESISTANT
LAVANDER
BEE BALM
BUTTERFLY BUSH
IRISSES
RUSSIAN SAGE
AGASTACHE
POTENTILLA
Snow White

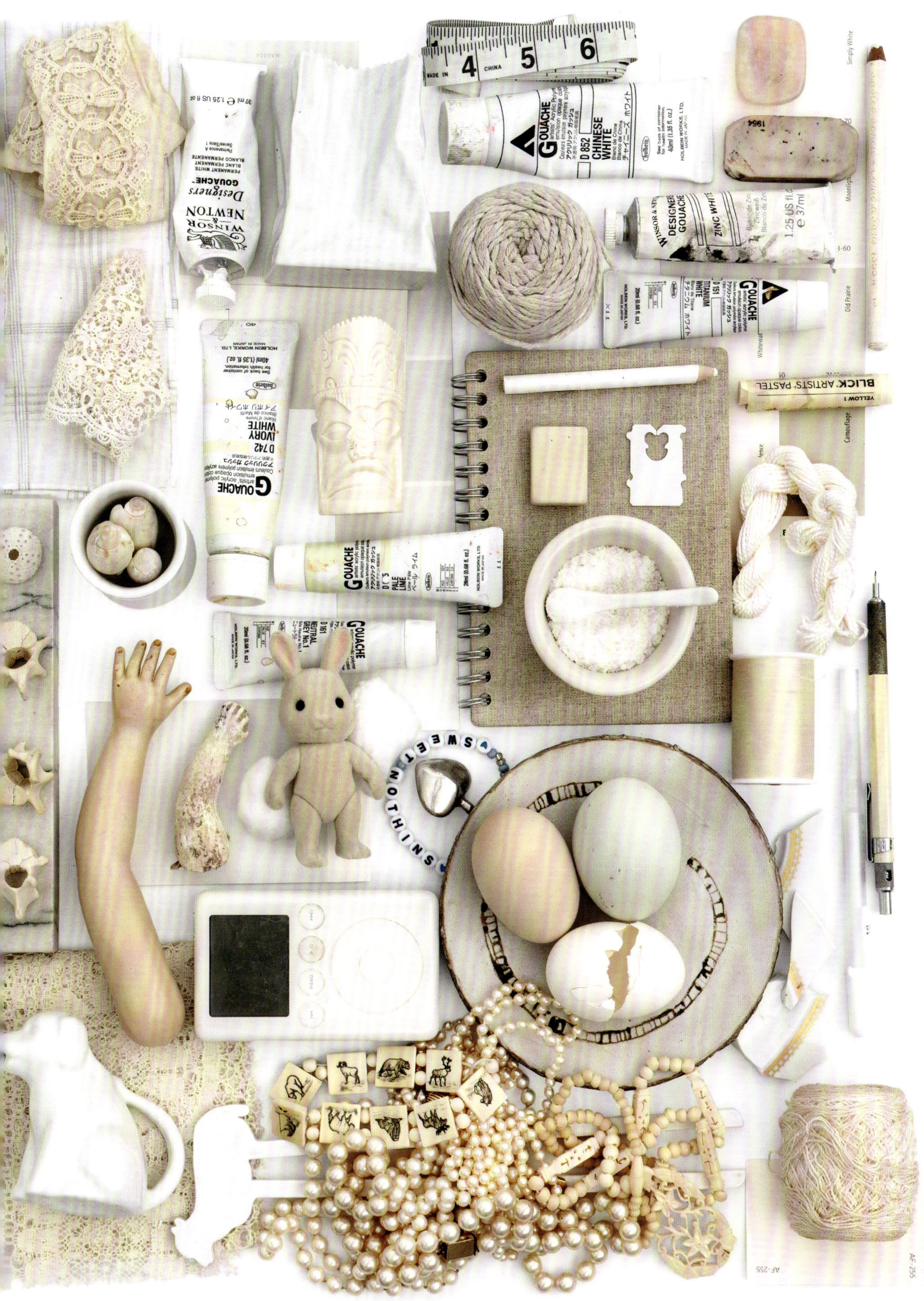

5.

THERE IS NO WHITE

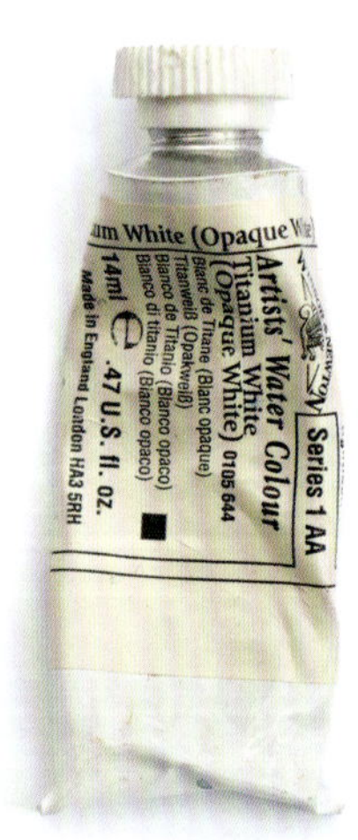

Discovering the Color of Light and Going from White Paint to Chromatic Whites to Pastels

Pure white light, as Newton demonstrated and we learned in school, is the whitest white, the sum of all colors. It breaks down into glorious ROYGBIV (red, orange, yellow, green, blue, indigo, and violet), also known as a rainbow. But most of us do not paint with light; we paint with *paint*, and that is where the problem of white starts—because there is no true white pigment.

If you have ever been to a hardware shop looking for paint for your white walls, you know what I am talking about: so many white options! And none of them, not even the so-called "whitest white," is truly devoid of a tint of something else. Your bright-white laundry? Well, detergent contains a hint of blue to make your clothes and linens appear very white instead of creamy.

In the drawers of my studio, where I hoard art materials, I have zinc white, titanium white, unbleached white, and the infamous flake white, made of lead oxide. When should I use one of these white paints unmixed, and when should I turn them into neutral off-whites or chromatic whites, those lovely whites with a barely there color? Which is the right white for each need? There are so many shades at the art store, and each one has a purpose.

Let's observe the basic whites in paint.

Titanium white, made of titanium dioxide, is the whitest of all. Dense and opaque, it covers whatever you apply it over. It is great for mixing very pale colors. I use it mostly with gouache and watercolor, and rarely with oil paint. Mixing it with other colors makes them look chalky, so if you use it for painting skin tones, it makes your figures look like they are in the highly powdered court of Louis XV. It's great for last-minute highlights to show the shine on glossy surfaces, like the wetness of dewdrops and the sparkle of a cheeky eye.

Unbleached titanium white, also made of titanium dioxide, has a buff undertone and looks similar to parchment, stones, or sand. A great desaturator, it makes colors interesting when mixed in with them. Pale colors get just a bit dirty, so unbleached titanium white is great for painting the natural world or conveying an aged or historical feeling.

Zinc white, made of zinc oxide, is a tiny bit cooler, with a barely there hint of blue. It was originally

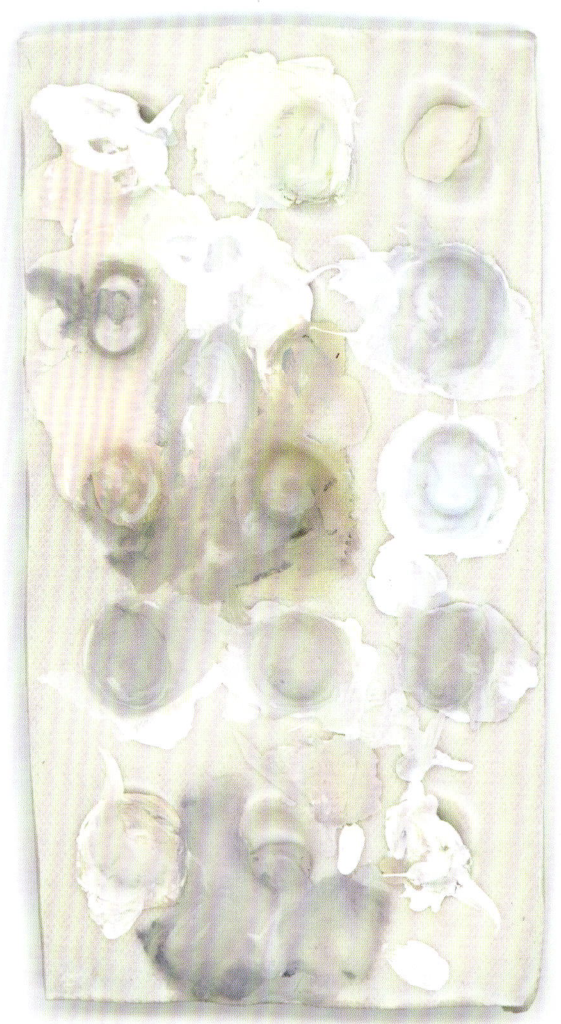

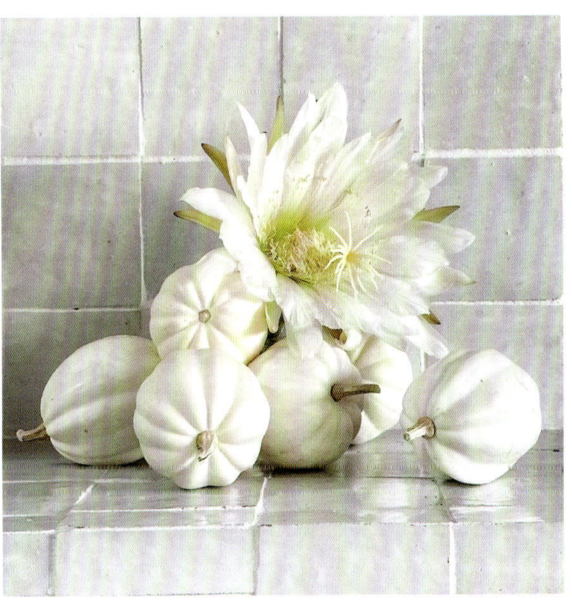

called Chinese white because it reminded Europeans of porcelain: Unlike titanium white, it has a bit of translucency. This is great when you want to create velatures or to give your art piece a certain atmospheric quality with a hint of fog, a sense of distance in the landscape, or a soft quality for skin, fur, or silk.

Now onto the most interesting white: the deadly and lovely flake white.

Yes, it is made with lead carbonate, and lead in any form is super poisonous. All paints made with lead oxide—flake white, Cremnitz white, Flemish white—contain enough lead to kill. The lives of many artists have been cut short because of them. There is proof that Caravaggio had enough lead in his bones for it to be counted as the probable cause of death; his lifetime of gorgeous lead-filled chiaroscuros proved lethal at age thirty-eight. Rembrandt, despite living a long life, is believed to have been seriously affected by his use of Flemish white. Francisco Goya's late-life madness? Most likely induced by often painting with his hands and, thus, absorbing lead through the skin.

Not only numerous artists—some of whom licked their brushes for the sweet-tasting lead paint—but also the people who made the paint and the fashionable gents and ladies of nobility who powdered their faces with lead-white makeup centuries ago died of many afflictions connected with exposure to lead.

Why use poison to paint? Because it produces one of the most gorgeous of all whites. Flake white is creamy and silky at the same time; it dries fast and is thus great for layering, and it has an opalescent transparency no other white has. Its undertone is a super-faint red-yellow, so it is inherently warm. When mixed with colors, it does not make them chalky. This is the best white for painting a variety of flesh tones and pale petals.

So poisonous! So lovely! What is an artist to do? Take extreme precaution with lead-based white:

- Never taste the paint or lick your brushes (obvious for a grown-up, but not for a sweet-toothed kid).
- Reserve a few brushes for painting with lead paint and spare the rest to avoid cross-contamination.

- Wear gloves while painting with lead white (weird at the beginning, but you get used to it; plus, it saves your manicure from all that paint and ink).
- To protect the environment, don't pour lead paint down the pipes or discard tubes in the trash. Bring it to the hazardous trash disposal facility near you.
- As an alternative, use a lead-free flake white. Not the same, but safer for sure.

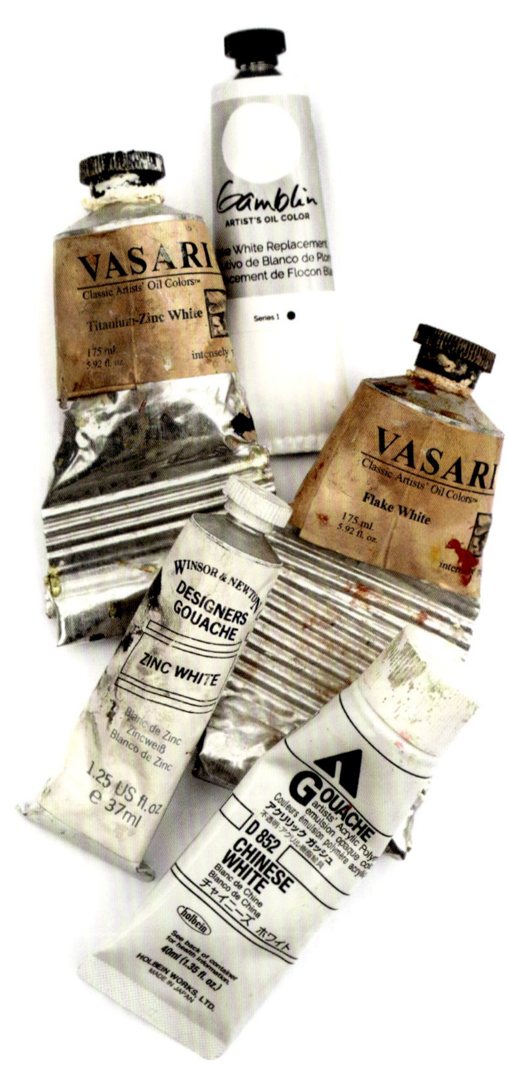

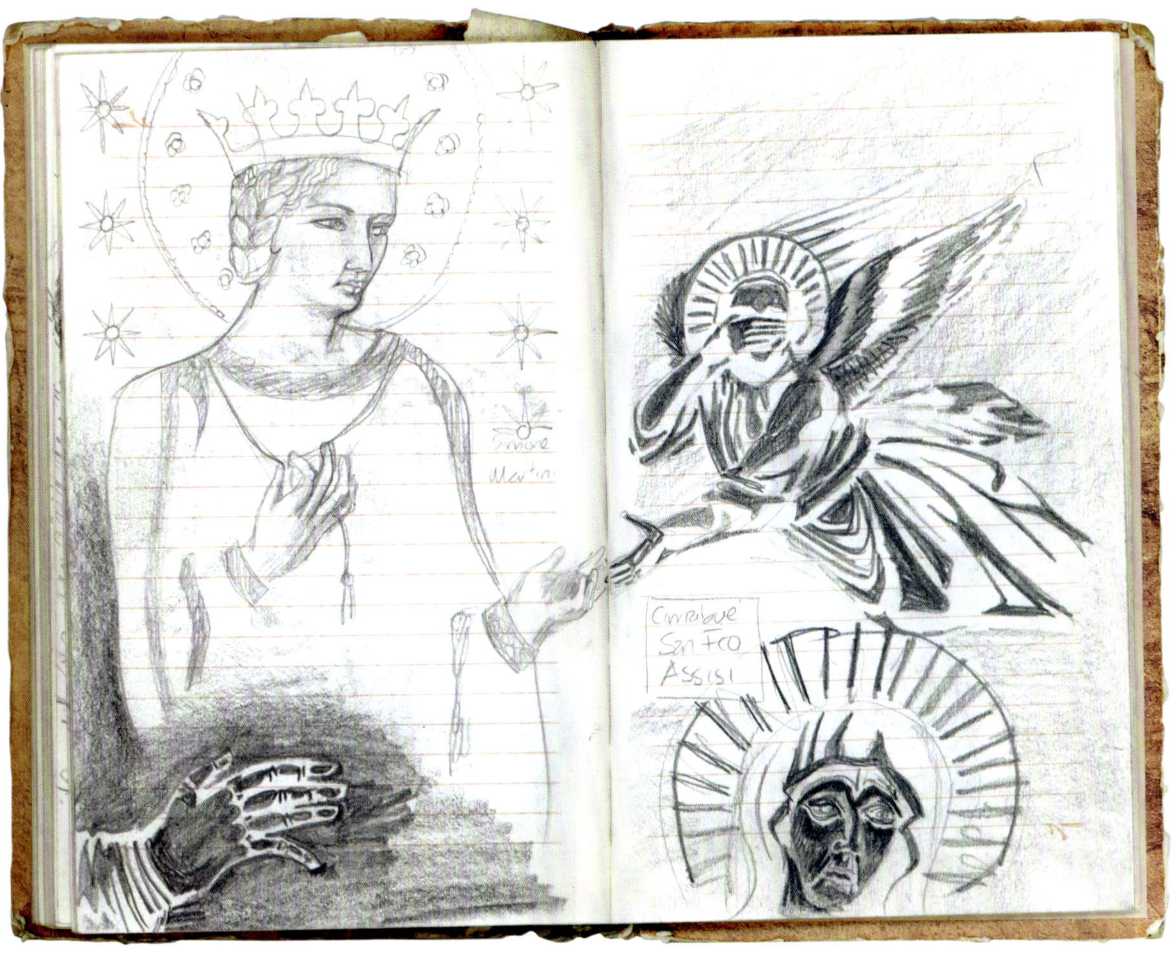

A Flake White Cautionary Tale

Cimabue, the thirteenth-century Italian master painter and mentor of Giotto, oversaw the painting of the frescoes for the Basilica of Saint Francis of Assisi. When I visited this basilica, I was particularly intrigued by a big Crucifixion scene that had none of the colors of the rest of the church. It looks like a black-and-white film negative! Lead white was the culprit. The whiteness of lead carbonate is stable only when encased in oil, like in an oil paint tube. But when used with a water base or exposed to humidity, it oxidizes.

Cimabue and his apprentices decided not to use their usual white, Bianco di San Giovanni (calcium carbonate, or chalk), and tried lead white instead. Shortly after the fresco was painted, however, the wetness of the mortar started to turn the white into oxidized deep brown-black. The painters came back and painted over the highlights with more lead white. But over time, the humidity of the air, the breath of people, and even other compounds like sulfites caused the extra layer to blacken as well. Sadly, this fresco and others were either severely damaged or destroyed by the powerful earthquakes of 1997, so only pictures survive. I sure treasure the sketches I made when visiting.

OBSERVING LIGHT

Not only can using white paint itself be a fraught endeavor, but pure white light can also be quite elusive. Observe how blue daylight is in the morning and how delightfully golden to red everything gets at dusk—and how that changes the mood of a scene.

As I photographed the botanical images in this book, I got to see how much white light changes through the year. Always photographing outdoors on whiteboards, I got to see all the colors "hidden" in (literally) plain daylight and had to adjust the settings of my camera to catch the pure white background I wanted. Winter was bluer, summer reflected a lot of green from the surrounding trees, spring was cleaner and brighter, and fall was tricky because my house dropped a big bluish shadow on the area outside my studio where I photographed everything. Daylight happens in all kinds of colors, never pure white light.

The first time I sat down to really search for the color of light was the summer of 1995 in the tiny, beautiful town of Óbidos, Portugal. I was working on a large-format drawing series for my graduate school final project. The town sits within a thirteenth-century Moorish fortification. From the top of it you can see the Atlantic Ocean, and all over town, the air smells of peaches from the surrounding orchards. The light is bright and clear in summer—as pure white as you can get it—and all the white houses, with their yellow or cobalt accents, provided me with the opportunity to observe the color of white.

During the weeks that I was in Óbidos, I sat on a wooden chair in front of those white houses and observed them—in the early morning, at midday, in the late afternoon, in bright sunlight, and on the only cloudy day of the summer. A few of the walls I observed had vines or the occasional birdcage casting shadows on them, which allowed me to see the white paint in direct sunlight and also with dropped shadows. This is where I got excited and started seeing more than a white wall. It was all very subtle, but I could see it clearly: If the sunlight had a tint of blue because it was early morning, the gray shadow had orange undertones in it; in the afternoon's pink- and red-tinted light, the shadows were greenish. While I am sure scientists interested in optics and light dynamics have talked about this before, I was excited to "discover" it on my own: The sunlit areas and the shadows had complementary color undertones, even when all I was supposedly looking at was white. This really changed the way I paint.

Try it: Pull up a chair and observe a white wall with shadows on it.

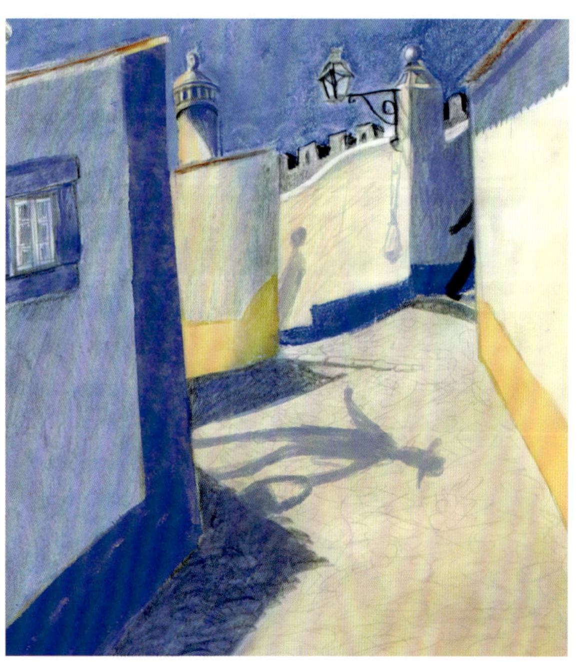

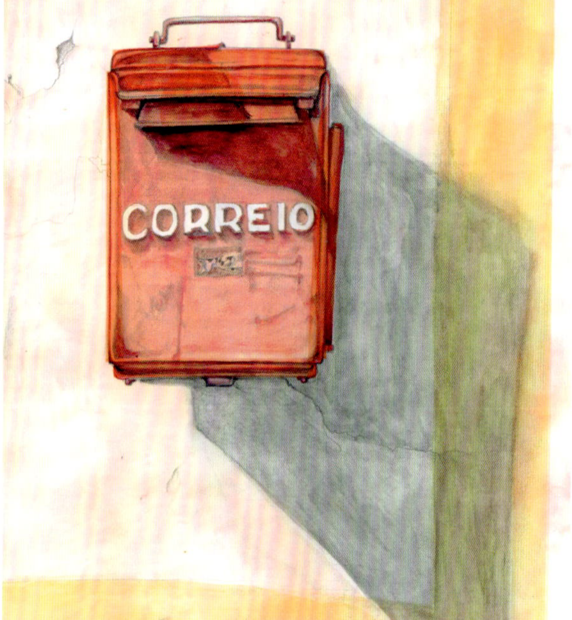

Someone I always look up to when thinking about white walls is Edward Hopper, a keen observer of light. He painted many houses and interiors with white walls. While a lot has been said about how his work is a cinematic portrait of American mid-century life, for me it has always been about his interesting use of light and shadow, especially on white buildings.

This is a list of my favorite Hopper paintings to observe how he painted light:

- *House by the Railroad* (which inspired the house in Alfred Hitchcock's film *Psycho*)
- *Seven A.M.*
- *Cape Cod Morning*
- *High Noon*
- *Coast Guard Station*
- *Second Story Sunlight*

And for white under artificial light:

- *Summer Evening*
- *Rooms for Tourists* (for white exterior at night and lit interiors)

Looking at Hopper's paintings, I can see the changes in the color of white throughout the day. The mood of the painting is set by the time of the day, and the story is told even if no people are shown in the scene. Like what I saw in Portugal, Hopper painted his deep shadows with blue-violet tints against sunny walls with a hint of golden yellow. His light is bluer in the early morning paintings like *Seven A.M.* and closer to pure white, bright and luminous, in *High Noon*.

The light and shadows in these paintings also convey a sense of place and time of the year. The light in most of them reminds me of summers on the East Coast when, during our family vacations on Long Island, we would say "Let's go for a walk to see the Hoppers," meaning the houses we would encounter on our walks around town bathed in early morning or early evening light.

Observing Hopper's work in detail will change the way you see white objects, and will in turn change your choice and use of color mixed into white. Shadows will not be dead gray spaces but vibrant darker areas that are in conversation with the bright areas around them.

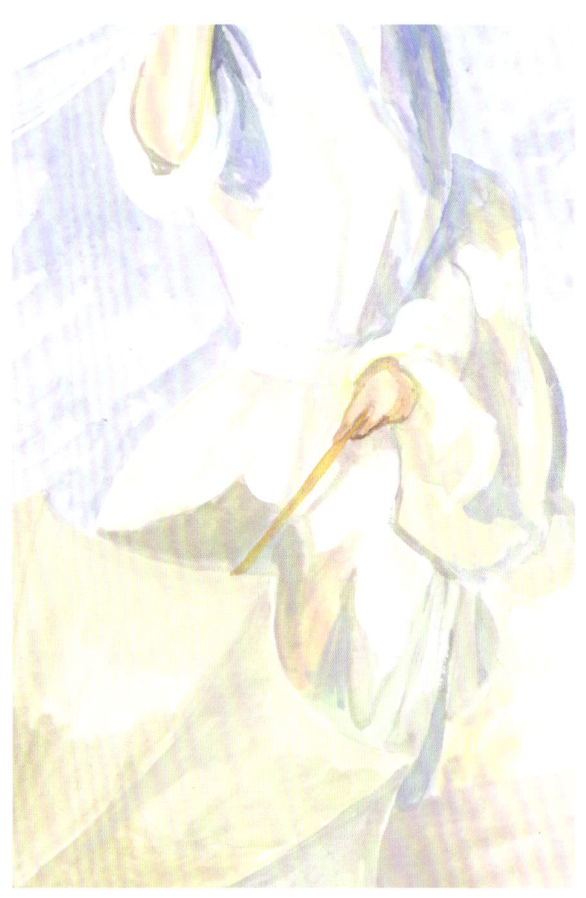

Another Painter of Light

Another painter of light in a different geography is the Spanish painter Joaquín Sorolla, who best portrayed Mediterranean light with its bright and slightly pink warmth. His outdoor scenes, especially the ones by the sea, have delightfully orchestrated light and shadow. Sitting under the dappled light of a pergola or under the Valencia orange trees or at the beach, most of Sorolla's subjects are wearing white clothes, and every dress is a study of white light and shade and of delightfully mixed chromatic whites—those whites that are just on the edge of becoming a pastel color.

PAINTING WHITE OBJECTS USING OFF-WHITES & NEUTRALS

I have always been fascinated by white on white, especially white objects on a white background: the simplicity and pureness of shapes, the mindful, meditative moods, and the subtleties of color dressed up as white. I am especially delighted when looking at Giorgio Morandi's paintings. He had shelves full of simple domestic objects—cups, bottles, bowls—that he painted in various arrangements and lighting, most often using whites, off-whites, creams, and grays, and occasionally adding a colorful object to the same composition to see how it impacted the white objects.

In these paintings, white brings a mood of timelessness, transcendence, and serenity. But Morandi's use of white is also a pragmatic approach to analyzing shapes in carefully constructed arrangements that feel almost architectural. He was on a mission to explore the relationship between object and background, between positive and negative space.

In addition to his paintings, he also created a series of watercolors where his focus sometimes changes from the subject to the background as he paints "around" the objects so that the white of the paper stands for the space occupied by those objects. This practice of using positive-negative space and subtracting the white objects from the painted areas is a simple yet challenging exercise. Some of these watercolor studies are representational, but some veer into abstraction, simplifying the forms to the extreme.

For me, with my love for color and tendency to use pattern and ornamentation, observing Morandi (and making art inspired by his works) brings serenity and calm to my practice. His works remind me of a beautiful book of poems by Pablo Neruda called *Odes to Common Things*—the salt shaker, the spoon, the broom. Morandi's paintings live in the same space as these poems. Both are simple and humble, yet deeply profound and interesting.

FROM PURE WHITES TO OFF-WHITE NEUTRALS TO CHROMATIC WHITES & PASTELS

When you start working with a full range of white to create nuances, you may start, like Morandi, by using the purest whites and mixing neutrals into them, or you may end up gradually adding bits of more saturated colors to progress to chromatic whites—the most colorful of whites—and then into pastels. One thing to keep in mind is that chromatic whites, off-whites, and pastel whites are not quite the same:

- **Neutral off-whites** tend to be muted—a bit gray, a bit beige—but still very light and unsaturated.
- **Chromatic whites,** like Sorolla's dresses, are the closest a color can get to white. It is barely there color, so pale that a distracted eye will perceive it as just white but a keen eye will see the hint of pink, or blue, or green.
- **Pastels,** while still very light, are more saturated—like Easter eggs. This is white mixed with a bit of a brighter color.

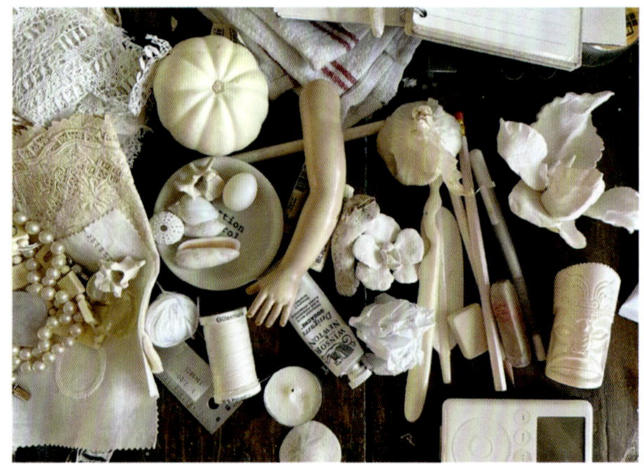

When I think of pastels, I always think of Wayne Thiebaud.

First, because pastel in Spanish means *cake*, and that is exactly what his subject matter often was, but also because he was a master of using bright but pale colors. Setting aside his pop art influences and his interest in mid-century Americana, the creamy frosting of his cakes and ice-cream desserts provided Thiebaud with the perfect subject matter to pursue his interest in light and color.

Thiebaud's baked goods and desserts, like Hopper's houses, set the mood with light. The light coming from a window we don't see bathes his sweet confections as they sit in the bakery. One side is illuminated, showing the creamy yellow or pale pink frosting in the light, and the shaded side is comprised of blue- or violet-tinted frosting and a bluer drop shadow on the table.

His pastel paintings are vibrant with color. On close observation, one can see that he did an underpainting for the whole surface, often in a pale yet saturated coral or pink. Then, as he laid on thicker layers of paint to depict frosting or the table or the background, he would let a bit of that underpainting show through and add lines of intense color to the plate or cake edges. This barely there saturated underpainting with the thin bright edges add vibrancy while everything still retains its creamy pastel palette.

In Thiebaud's paintings, the subjects become volumes and shapes sitting in a simple space. He was not a painter of confections; he was, like Hopper and Morandi, a painter of form and color in particular light situations.

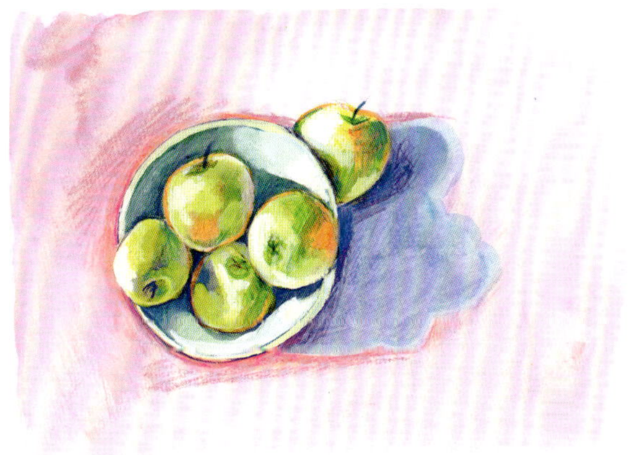

KEY TAKEAWAYS

1. Observe white objects in different light situations, paying attention to the highlights, midtones, and shadows. Make mental notes of the undertones. Discover the color of the light and what else in the surroundings affects the white of the objects. Analyze the changes of chroma and tone when the light changes.

2. Find and observe, ideally in person or in book, works by Hopper, Morandi, and Thiebaud.

3. Look at works of other artists, like Kazimir Malevich (the original white-on-white), Agnes Martin (white paintings using paint mixes, or thin lines to modify white), Gerhard Richter (magnificent atmospheric paintings of white objects, like candles and toilet paper), and Fra Angelico (not the gilded paintings, but the very white, ethereal frescoes in San Marco, Florence). Also, look at close-ups of pastel-toned impressionist paintings like Monet's haystacks to see how color is broken down into little paint blobs.

4. Set out to discover illustrations, graphic designs, textiles, and ceramics that use white-on-white, off-whites, chromatic whites, and pastels. Make notes on them or put together an inspiration board. Pull out some white paints—zinc, Chinese white, titanium, a lead white substitute, an off-white, a creamy white—then mix each with a bright color like cobalt and see how the different whites result in different variations of light blue.

5. Observe in the next pages how rare it is to find a pure white, even when we think we are looking at white flowers. Pay close attention and see all the color in those "white" flowers, especially as the the sequence progresses toward pastels.

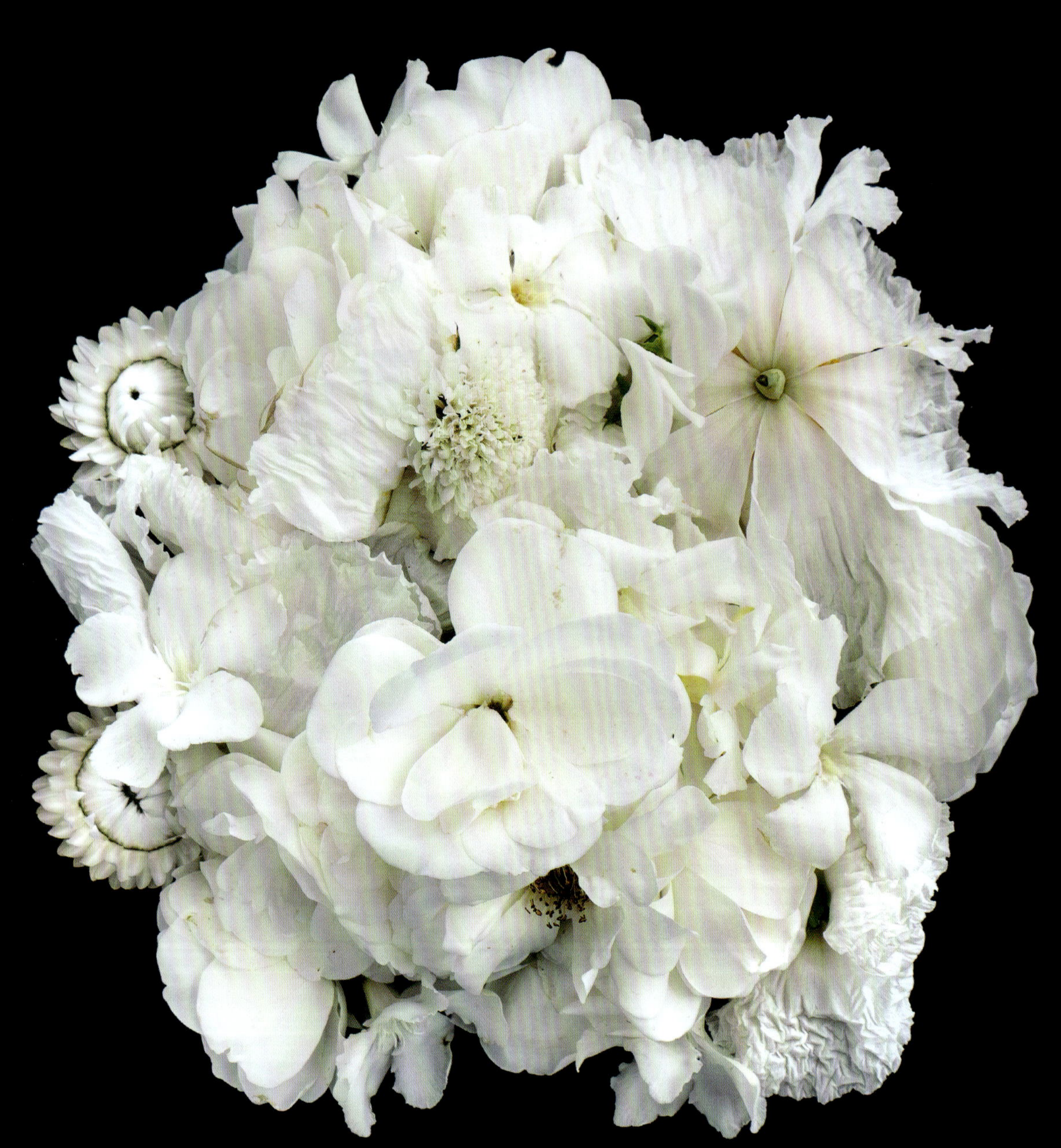

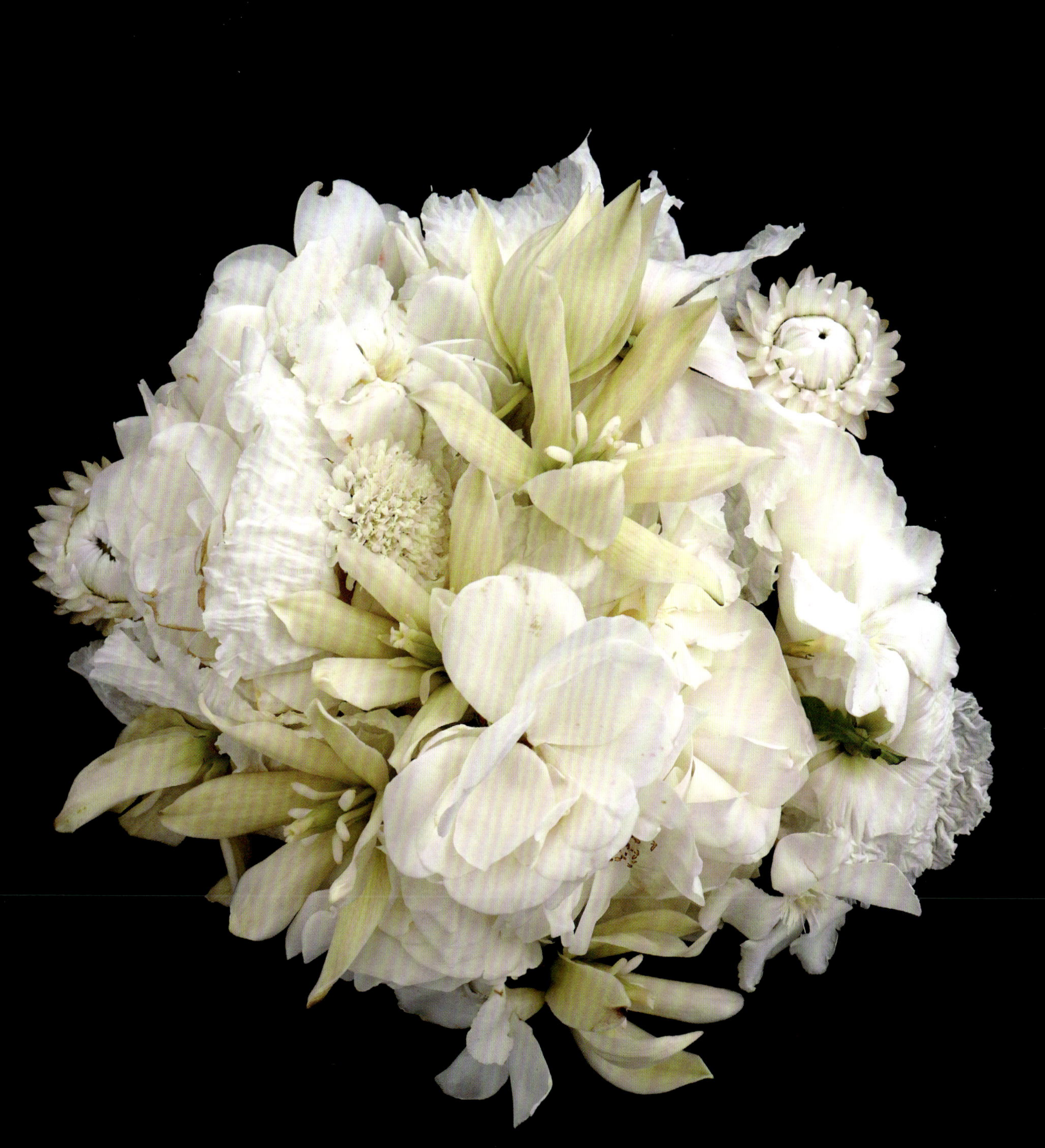

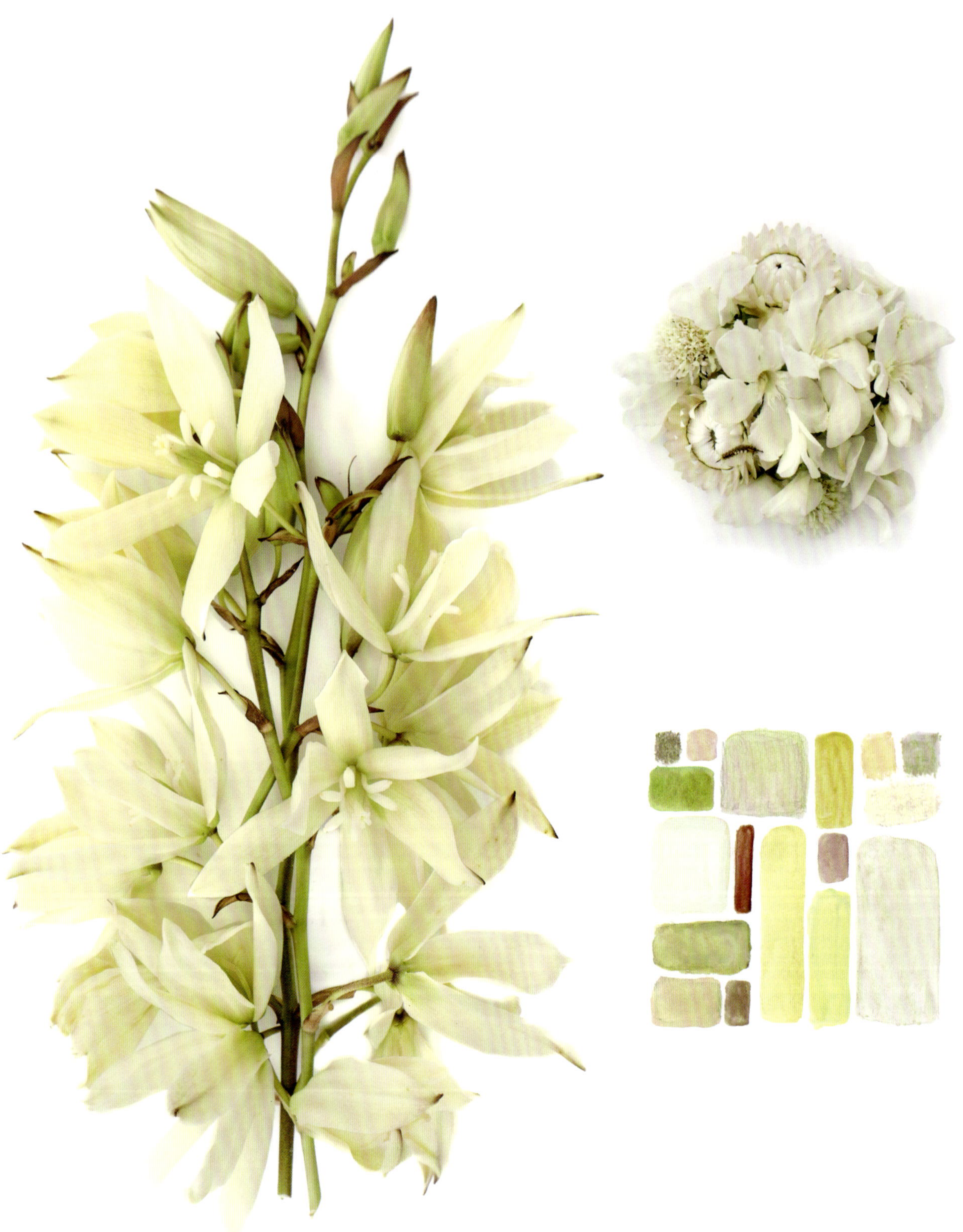

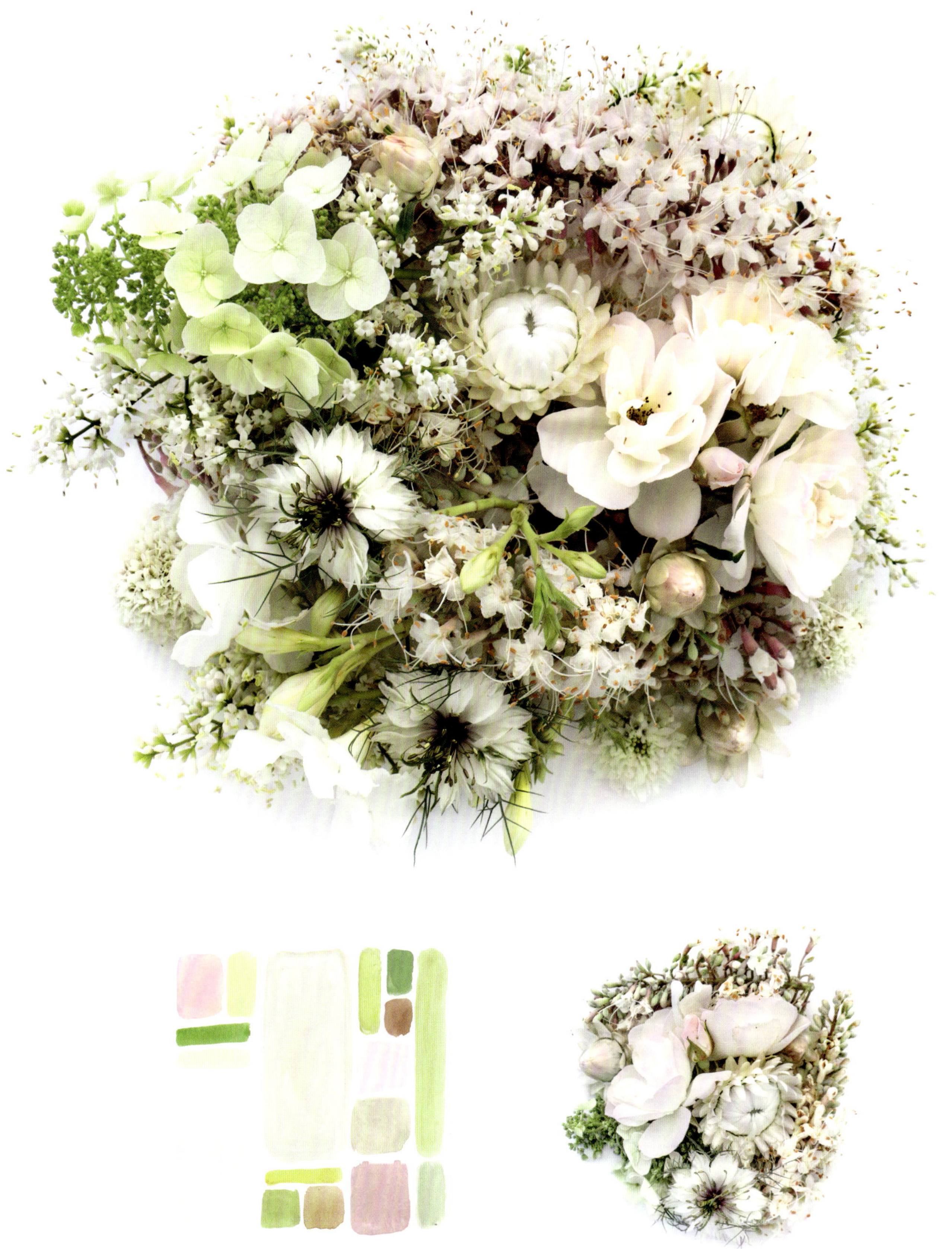

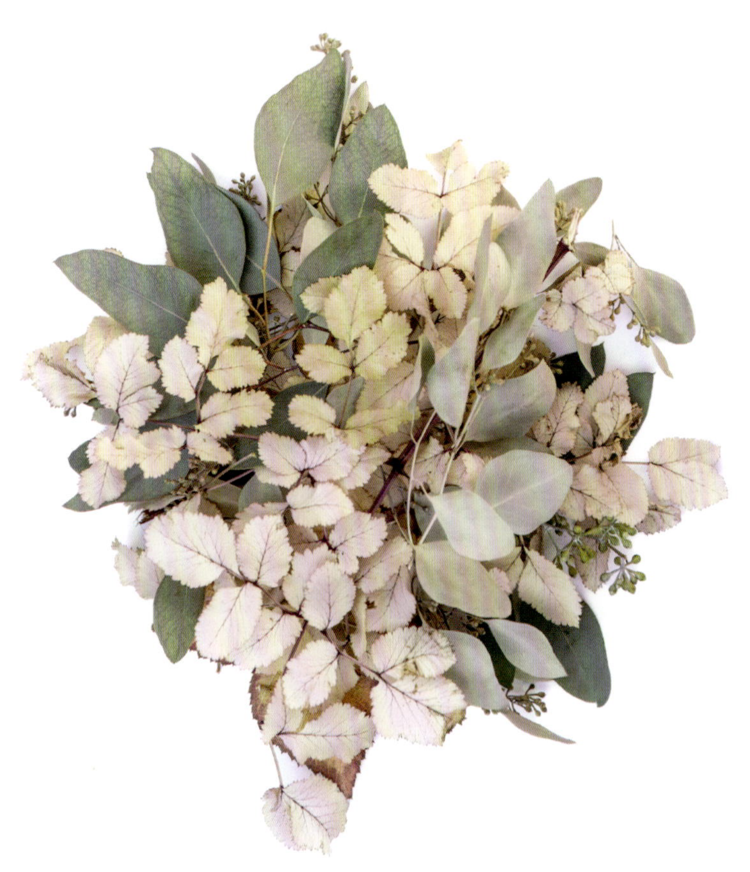
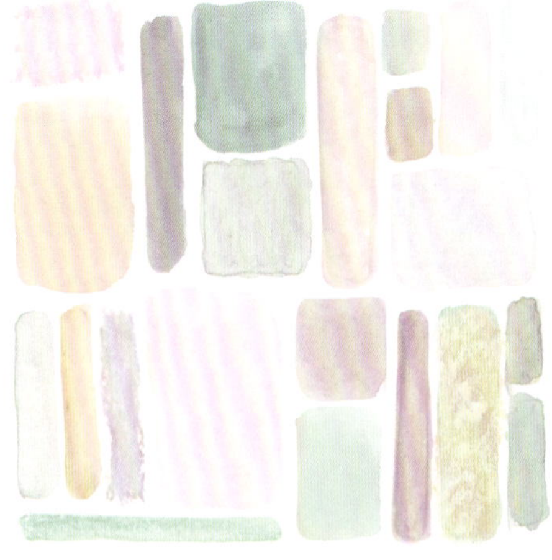
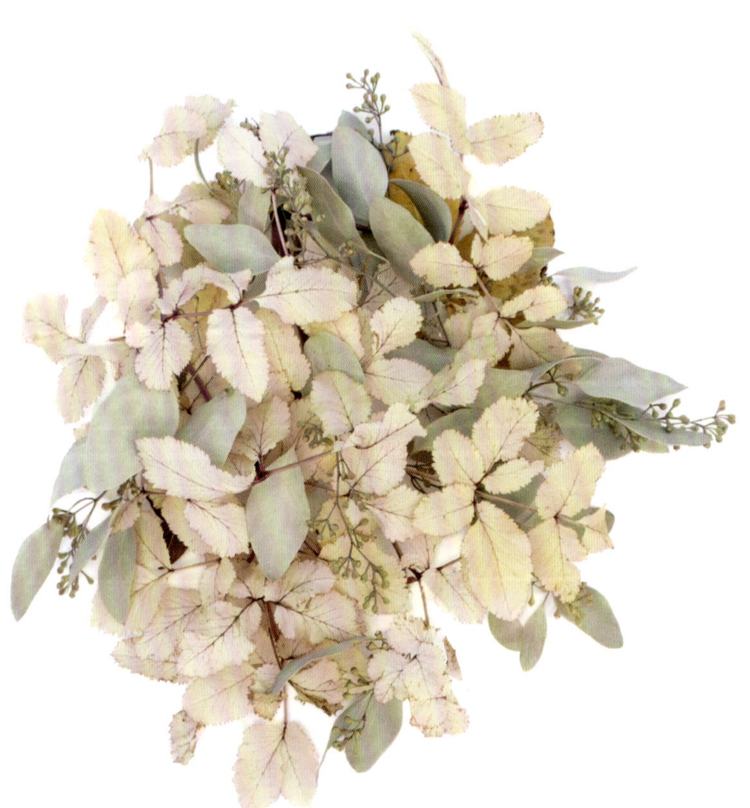
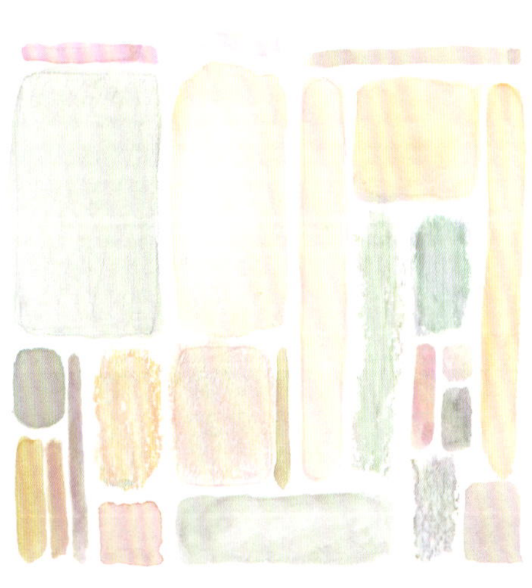

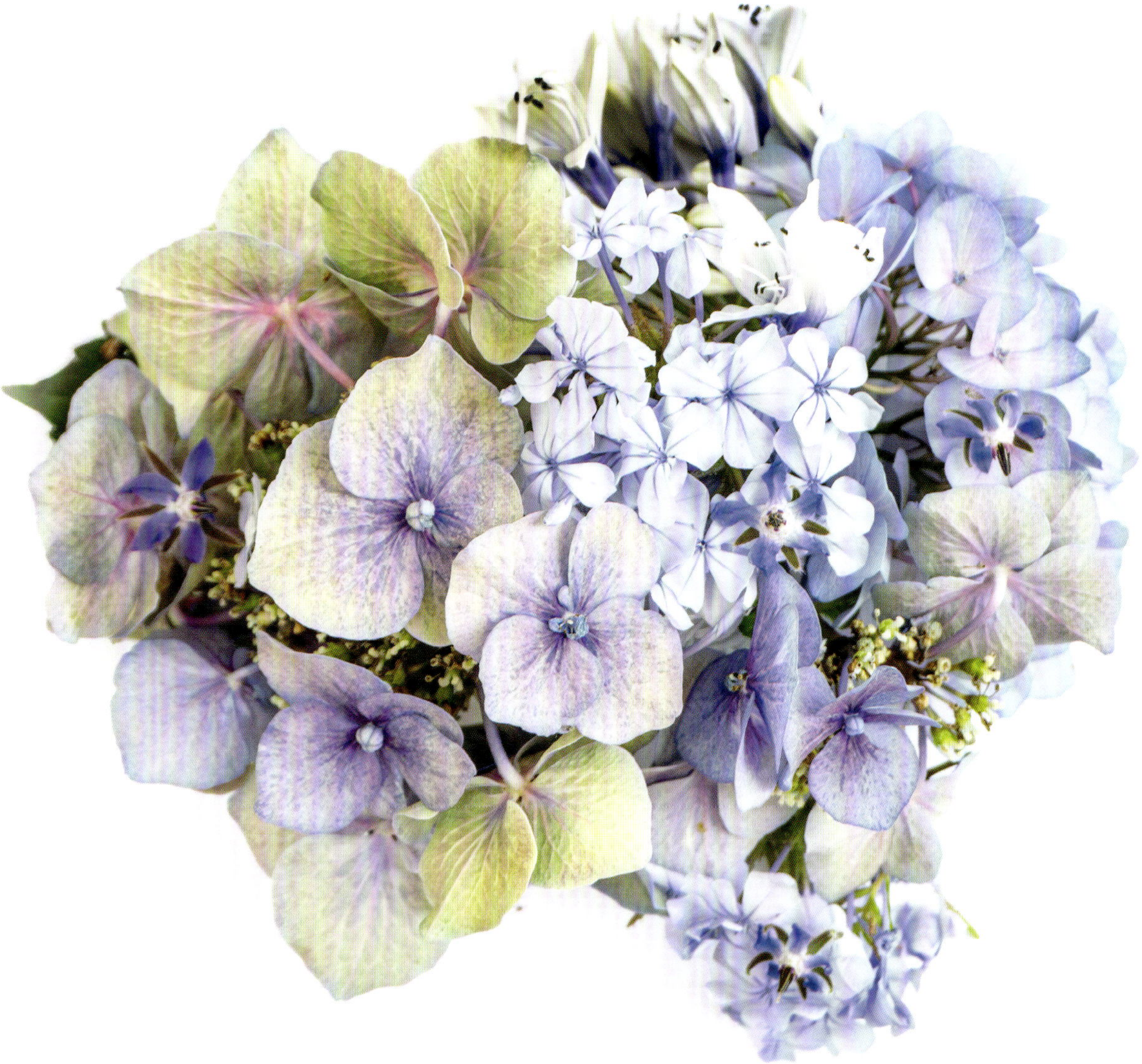

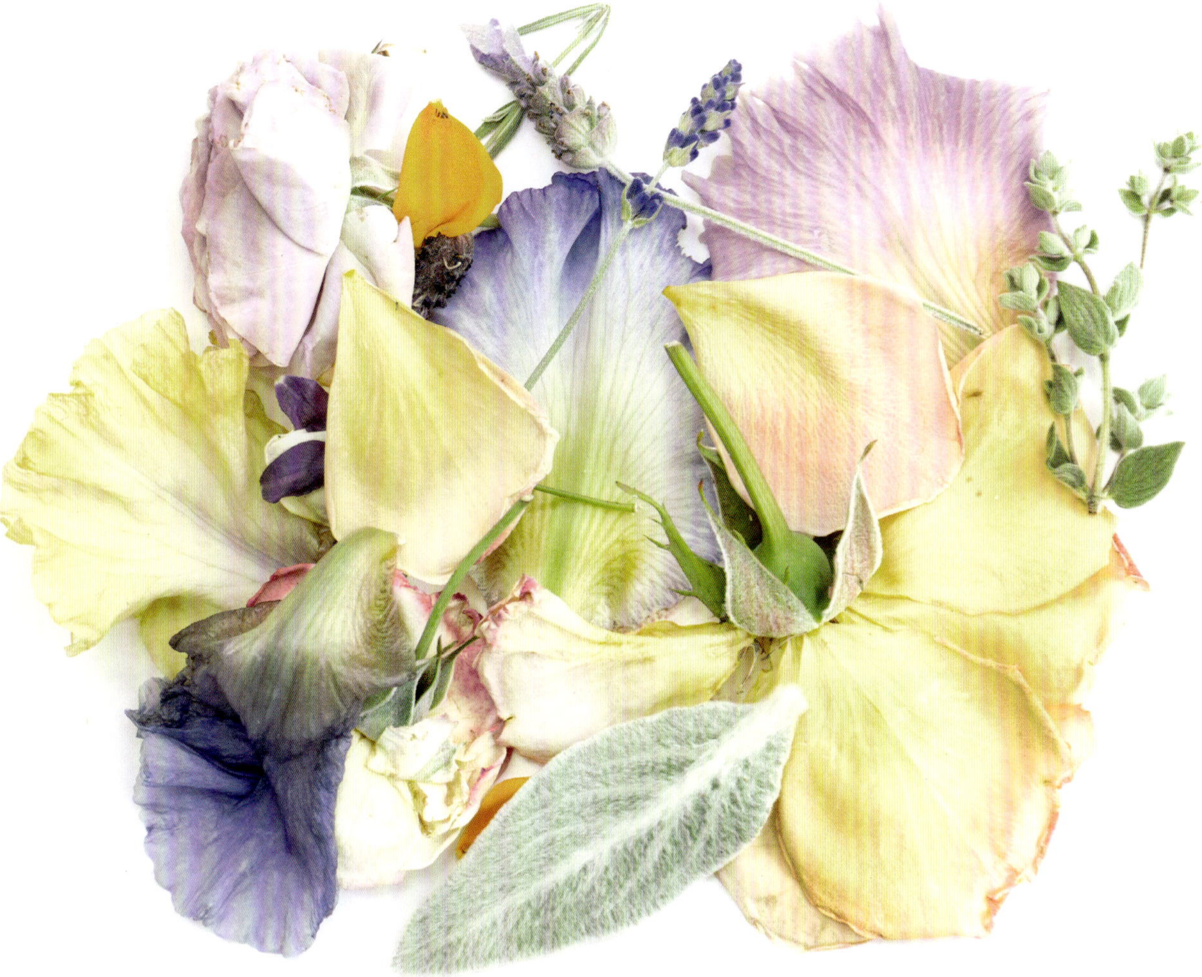

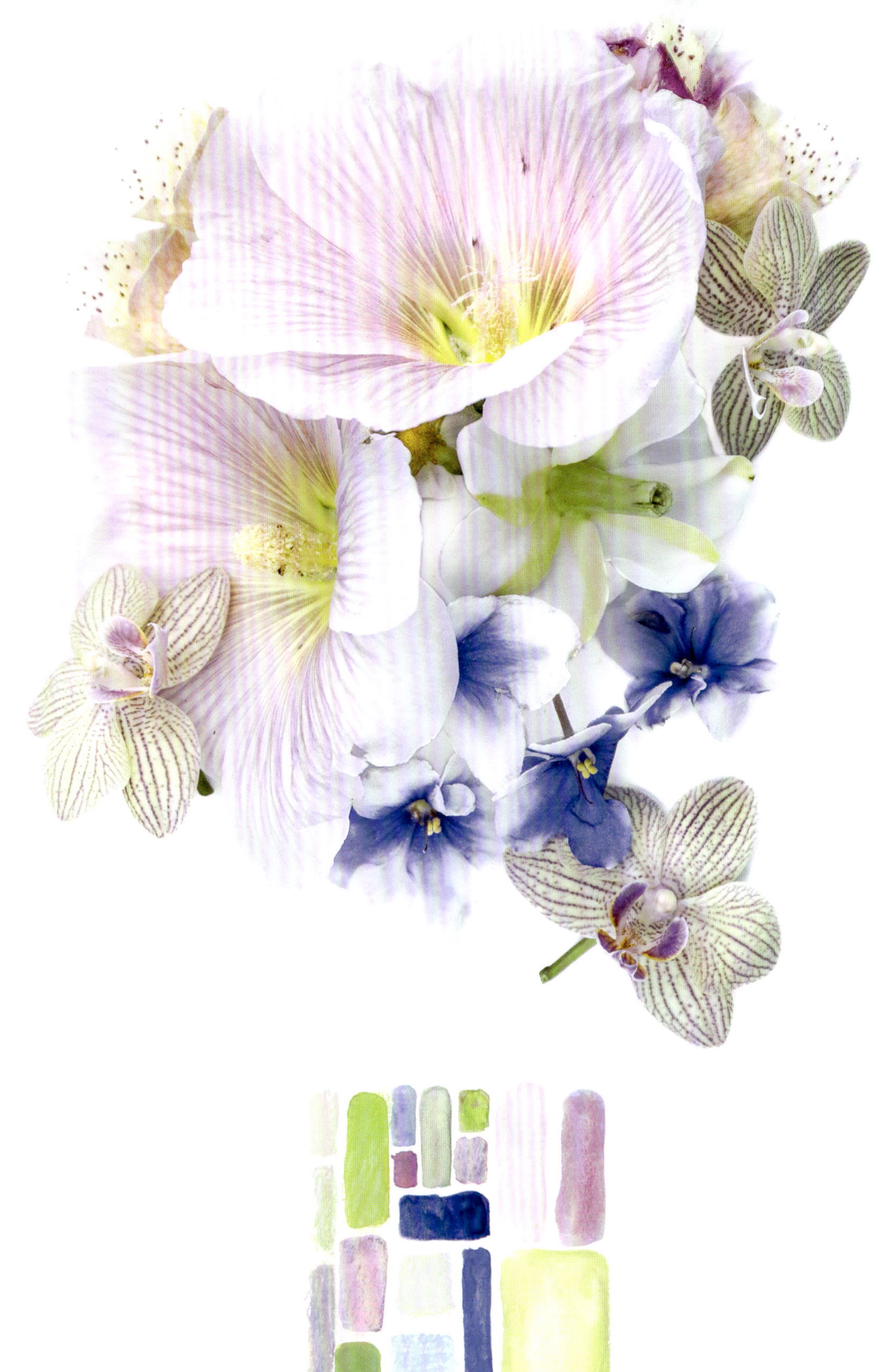

PROJECT

OBSERVE: Observe all the botanical (or abstract naturalist) images on pages 142–149 and their color palettes. Look at the whole or concentrate on a specific smaller area that catches your eye. Look also at Hopper, Sorolla, Morandi, and Thiebaud.

ANALYZE: Analyze how these non-whites came to be. In your mind, try to break down the colors in the images, forgetting about the subject matter and just looking at color. Take into account each color's hue, saturation, and relative lightness and brightness, and then consider how you would mix it in paint. Especially pay attention to how the light sources affect the whites in what you are observing.

CREATE: OPTION A

Create a series of photographic and painted still lifes inspired by Giorgio Morandi:

1. Take a moment to look at Morandi's white-object still lifes. Look in books or online; peruse paintings, etchings, and watercolors; and observe how he organizes the objects in the groups. Pay attention to shapes and the relationships among them as well as between them and the background (i.e., the negative space). Notice the variations of white through each piece: Are they neutral, chromatic, pastel, or pure white?

2. Go around your house and gather as many white objects as possible—undecorated, simple objects in a variety of shapes and sizes. Cups, vases, mugs, toiletries, or an egg holder with an egg are all great options. Find cylinders, spheres, cubes, and prism-shaped objects. Find variety within a limited range of sizes so that they sit well together.

3. Prepare your set in a place near a window. Let the natural light—but not direct sunlight—come from the right or the left, not from behind or in front. Your set will need a white surface and a white background (this is as simple as setting up two foam boards).

4. With your phone or camera, photograph as many variations as you like, changing and rearranging your objects. I recommend a full-frontal, low-angle position of the camera facing the objects.

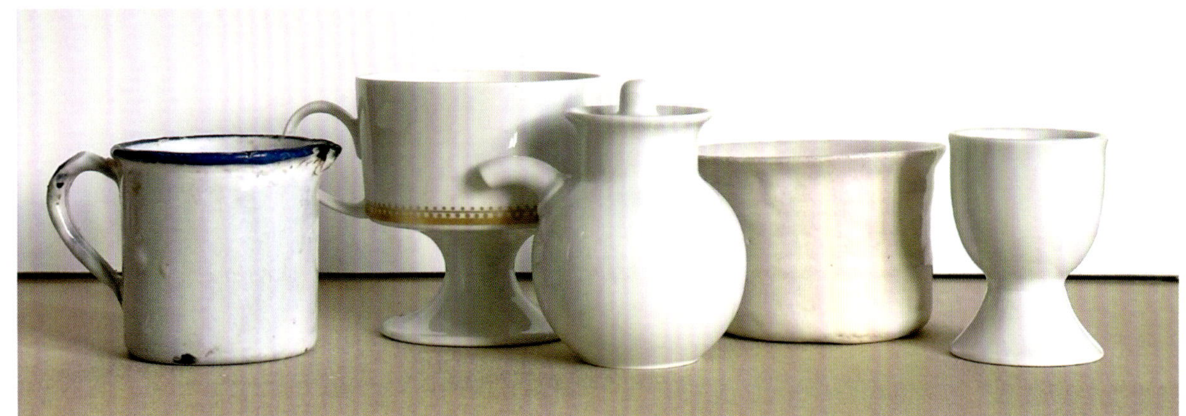

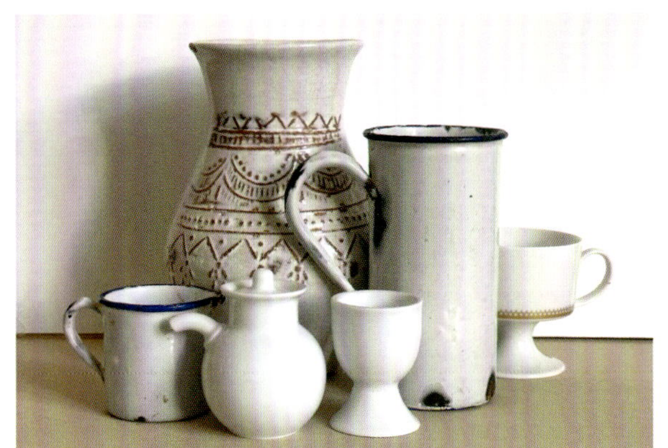

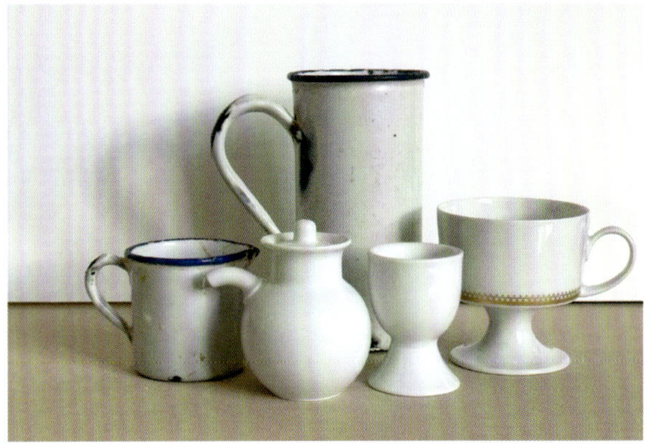

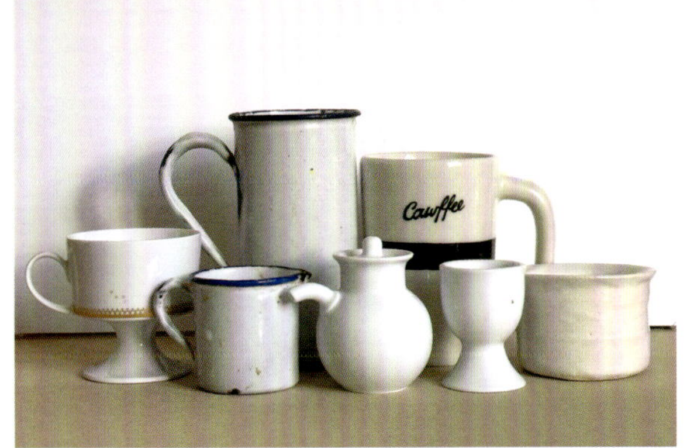
Cauffei

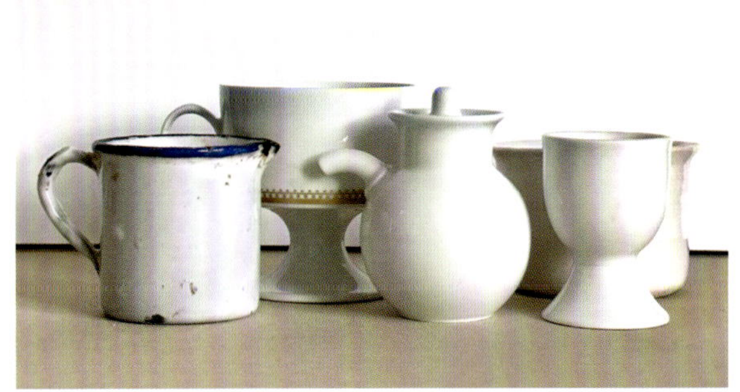

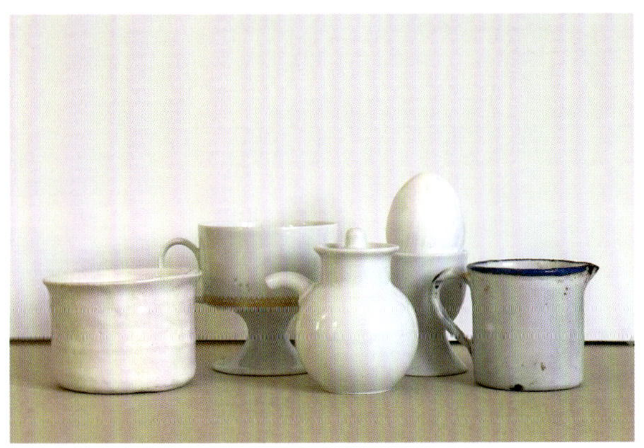

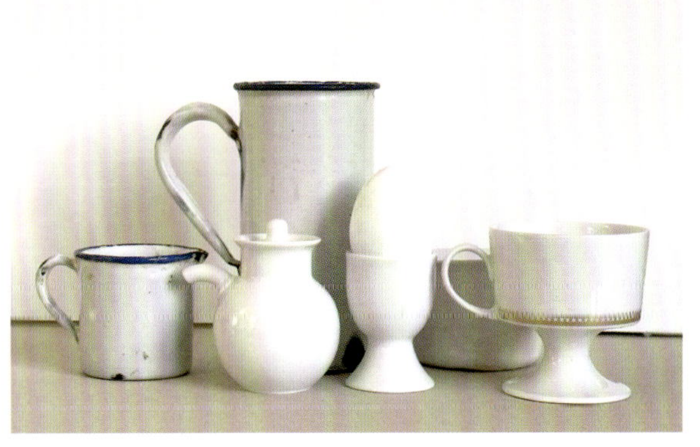

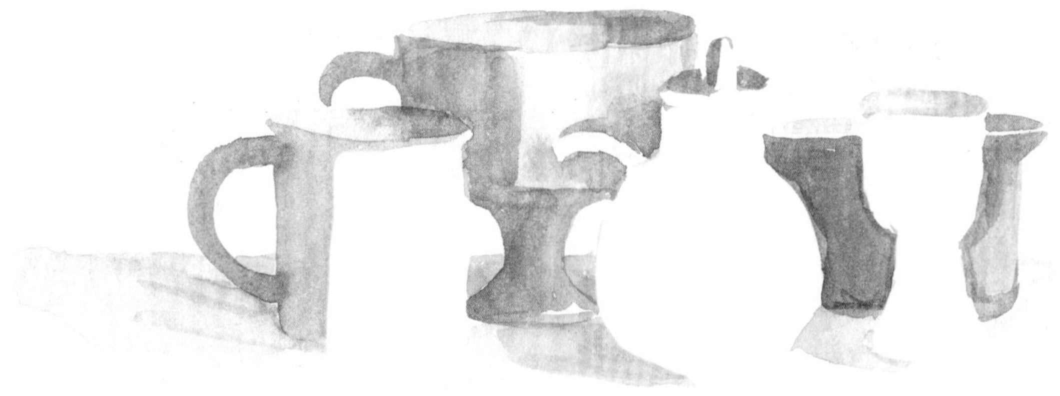

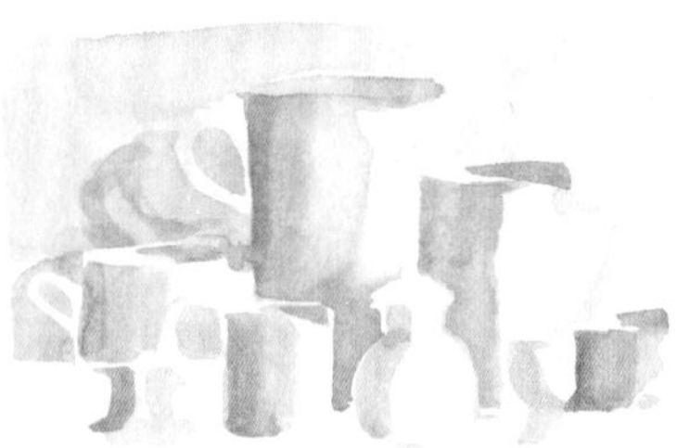

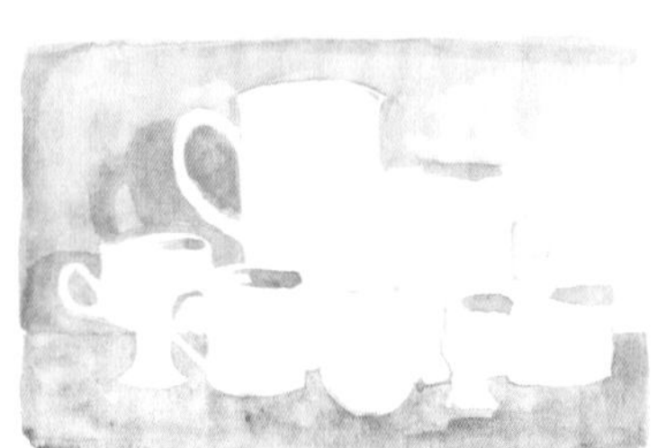

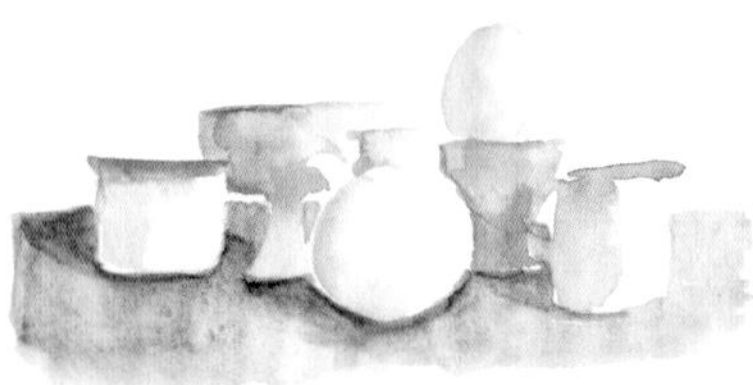

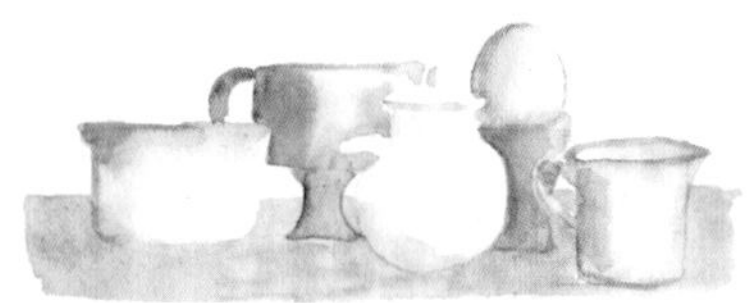

5. Observe and analyze your photos in the same way you observed Morandi's work in step 1. Then gather watercolors or inks in light neutral colors and watercolor paper. You can also use colored pencils or a simple graphite pencil. Do several very simple watercolor or pencil drawings of your groupings. Forget about details, don't strive for realism, and focus on shapes and negative space. Try to experiment around these variations:

- Do you have one very white object? Leave that object unpainted and paint the other shapes around it.
- Paint the background and the surface, leaving all the objects unpainted.
- Paint the background and the surface, leaving the objects unpainted, then add a shadow to depict one or two objects while leaving the rest and all the bright sides unpainted.
- Paint the collection of objects in fast, simple brushstrokes, still leaving some areas unpainted. Paint the same scene twice and notice how the second round is easier and you are not so stuck in details.
- "Burst the edges"; that is, do not outline each object, but let the whitest areas bleed into the background. Your mind's eye will complete the objects with the few shadows that you do paint.

Observe my watercolors of cups and other vessels as you review the suggestions on the bulleted list. Don't spend more than five minutes on each variation. Make many variations, for as you make them you will be learning to observe, analyze, and create with simple shapes. Some won't work, and some will be amazing in their simplicity. The more you make, the more you learn. Feel free to take more photos and rearrange the objects to visualize more negative and positive space as well as shape and volume variations.

OPTION B

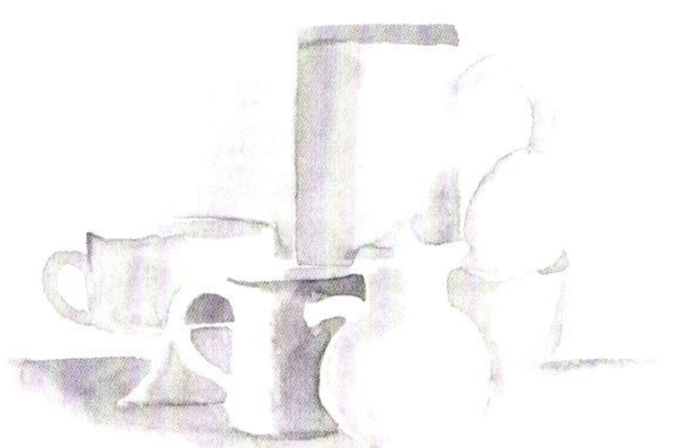

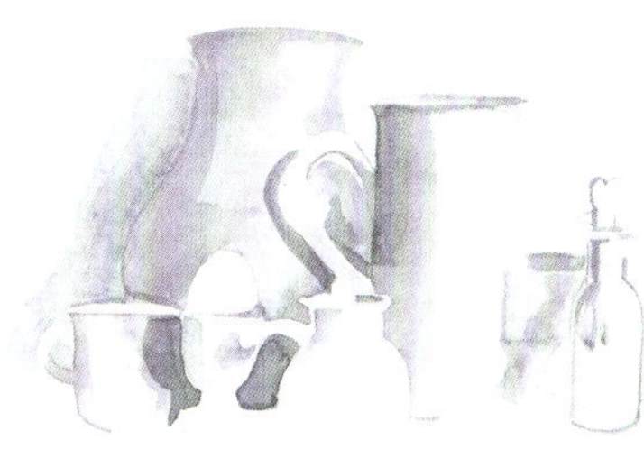

For an advanced exercise, paint a chromatic white still life. Observe and analyze the colors of your objects. Is one a bit bluish? or pinkish? or greenish? What color are the shadows? and the brighter areas? Look back at the photos and color palettes in previous pages and compare them with your still life.

Go ahead and paint the still life using gouache, oil paints, watercolors, or colored pencils. Any technique you prefer will do. Keep it simple, don't fret too much with details (unless you want to), and focus on getting the chromatic nuances of all those whites right. You can choose to capture everything in neutral, very pale grays or exaggerate the chroma in the whites you see and take the color from barely there to a definite pastel. Feel free to make more than one version, and remember, this is not meant to be the perfect "museum quality" piece; it is an exercise for applying on paper what you observe.

So remember to paint what your eyes see. Sounds simple, but only if you shut off the inner critic.

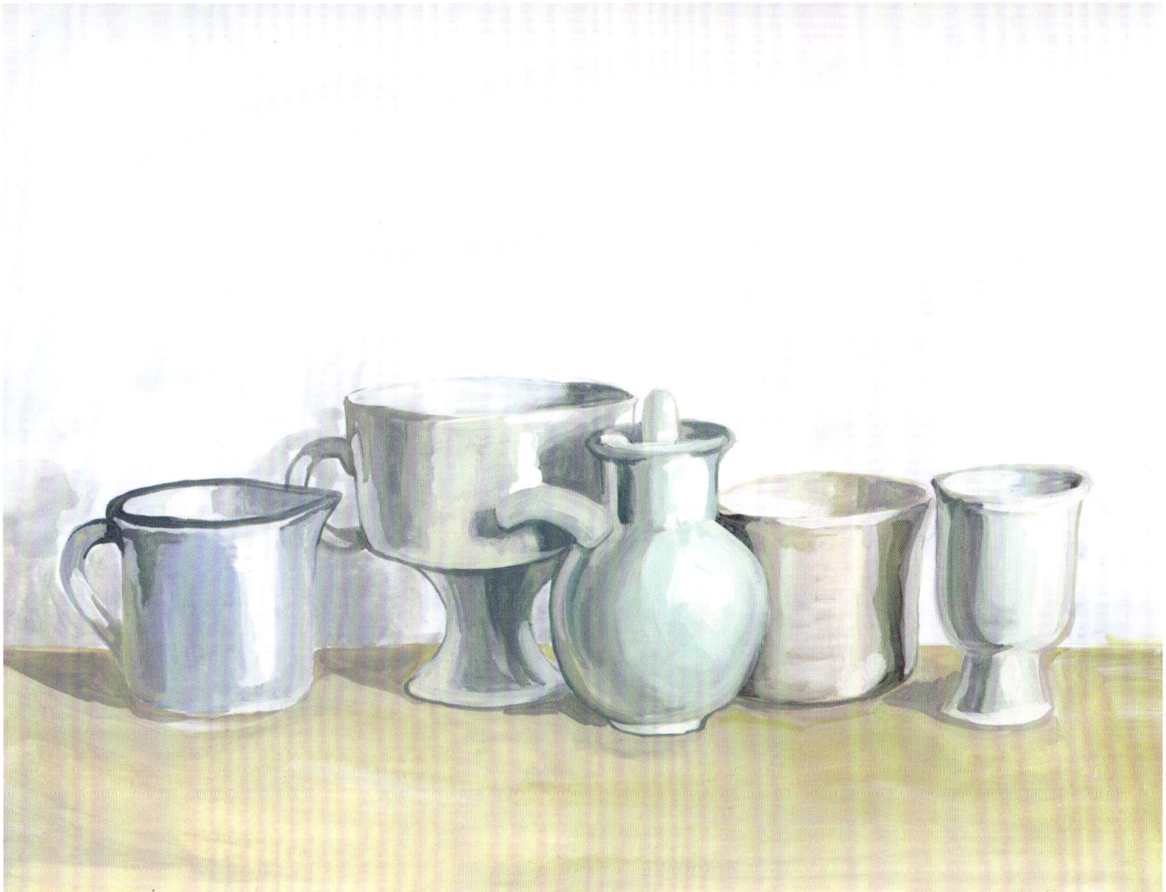

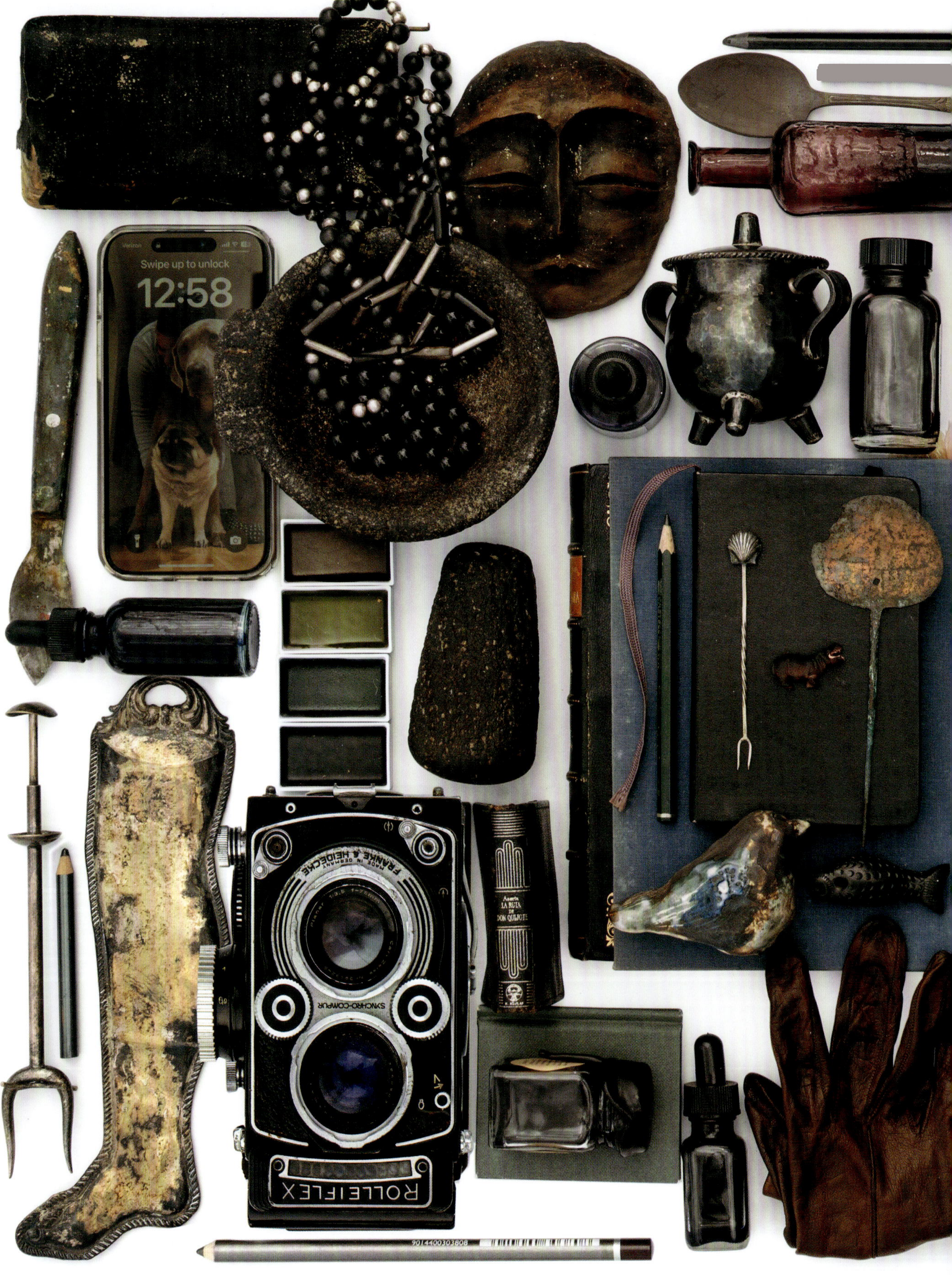

Swipe up to unlock
12:58

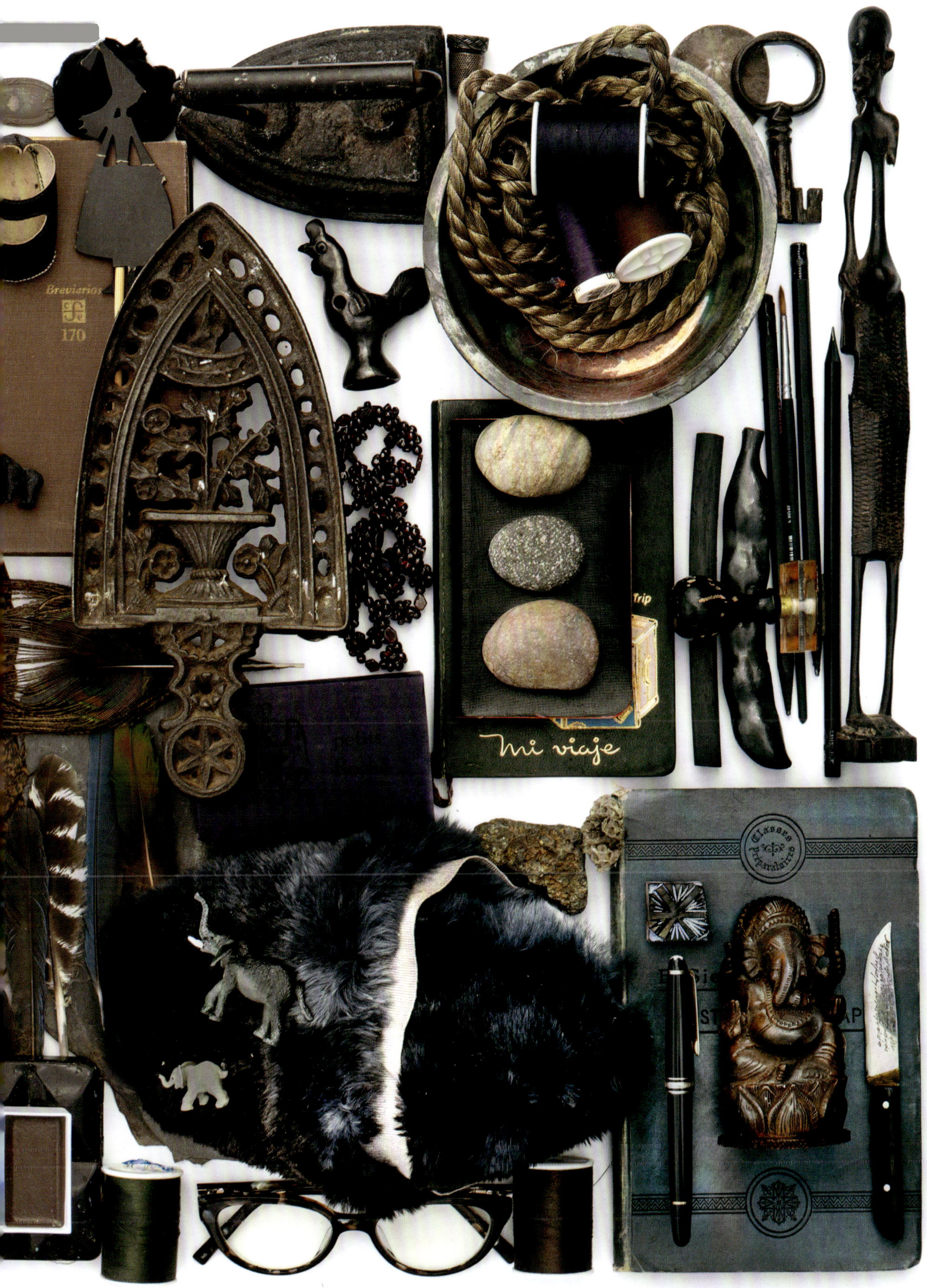
Breviarios
170
Mi viaje
Trip
Classes
Préparatoires

6.

THE COLOR IN ENRICHED BLACKS

Working with Chromatic Blacks and Deep Colors

Absolute black doesn't exist either, except maybe in Anish Kapoor's art pieces using his trademarked Vantablack. These are like looking into a black hole, a velvety black hole made out of tiny light-absorbing carbon nanotubes where nothing is reflected, all is absorbed.

Such an odd experience! But no other blacks are like that.

Have you ever dressed in black velvet with black silk? So luxe! But the two no longer look identical; the shine of the silk makes it look like a different shade of black from the nonreflective velvet.

Dressing all in black separates can be disastrous or it can be done by design, with each piece carefully selected based on its undertones, its shine, and, let's face it, how many times you have washed that favorite black garment.

For me, the line between washed-out, mismatched blacks and intentional black combinations is all in the undertone. That hint of hue, subtle or intense, behind all the darkness is the color that turns a black into an enriched black. Observing these undertones is the key to using black clothes and art materials.

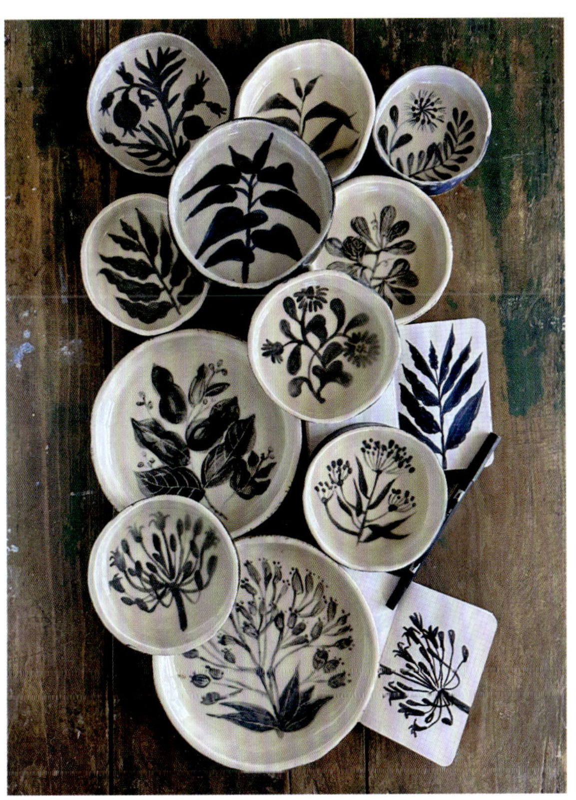

BLACK INK ON
WHITE PAPER

Picture this: A drop of black ink in a glass of water. Splash, swirl, and mix until there is a gray wash. So luscious! When thinking about the color black, an inevitable topic is ink. It is one of the oldest art materials, second only to pure pigment from soil and minerals. It is the conduit to all of humanity's written word.

One thing I love is when the same phenomenon occurs in places so far away from each other that people couldn't have gotten together to exchange thoughts. That is the story of ink: In all three ancient cradles of civilization (Egypt, India, and China), around 2,500 BCE, scribes and artists started using the OG ink: soot ink. The Japanese, also famous for their use of ink, learned from the Chinese a few centuries later and refined the process into their beautiful sumi-e ink, whose use is almost ceremonial.

Making ink with soot is an ancient practice, and in some places it is still made traditionally. I encourage you to find videos of people making ink—so messy and oddly satisfying. The traditional recipe is this:

1. Burn a lot of oil lamps in a small room.
2. Scrape the ceiling and walls and everything to collect the soot.
3. Mix the soot with gum Arabic (Egyptian-style) or gelatine from animal bones (Chinese-style).
4. Form a black blob. Grind, mix, and massage the blob using both feet (a good workout, bad for pedicures).
5. Fill molds with this thick paste and let it age and dry into solid blocks of ink.
6. Add water again, filter for impurities, and put it in jars to use as liquid ink.

Most likely you will never attempt this at home; you will buy your ink in an art store, where you may find India ink as a liquid and Chinese or China ink as both a liquid and a solid bar. They are essentially the same: soot ink nowadays is made industrially from carbon particles.

I first used India ink when I was about ten years

old. Using the ink both at full strength and diluted for a wide range of grays, I made my grandmother a gift of a painted pair of pigeons. She loved it, and I loved the possibilities with ink. One thing led to another: I eventually became fascinated by Asian calligraphy and ended up spending a year as a student with a Japanese calligraphy master. We used those bricks of ink described earlier. The first step was activating the ink by adding a bit of water and rubbing the solid ink onto a special washboard-shaped stone to grind it. Gradually adding water while continuously grinding (sometimes for more than thirty minutes!) resulted in perfect black sumi-e ink. Then it was time to start the practice, kneeling on the floor by a low table and using beautiful rice paper. I practiced holding the brush and repeated each kanji for hours. Funny enough, this was in Italy, so as I practiced the kanji for *child*, the Japanese teacher would say "bambino."

A year, of course, is not enough time to learn the language and become a calligrapher in the Japanese tradition—far from it. But I did learn how to hold a brush and work with the nuances of pressure, how to mix the ink, and, most importantly, how to settle in the calm and focused mindset of working with ink.

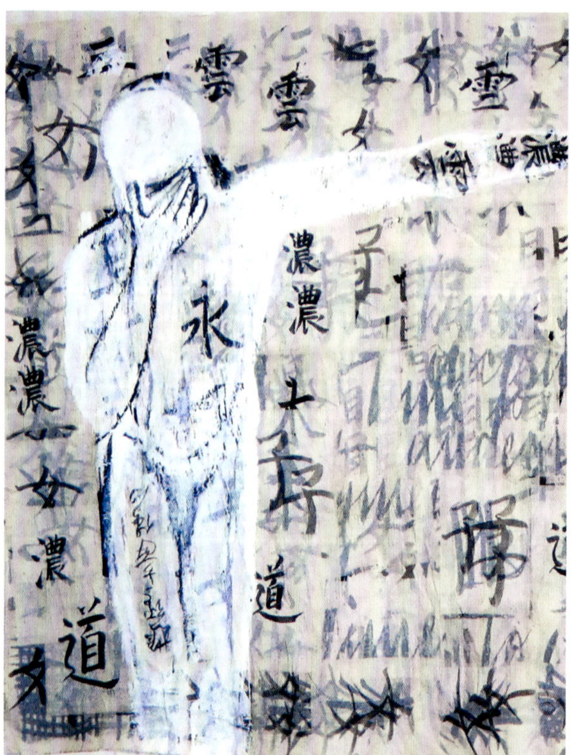

Many years later, at a Buddhist retreat focused on calligraphy as active meditation, I repeated this same experience. We started with normal-size brushes, but as the days progressed, the brushes got bigger. Following the tradition, we put three marks on the paper: one for the sky, one for the earth, one for humanity. The end of the week was the most physical of them all. The paper was fifteen by four feet, the brush as tall as me, and the inkwell . . . well, it was a five-gallon bucket of luscious black ink.

Putting black ink on white paper is a practice that never disappoints. No matter if you are using true ink, paint, or even cheap markers, focusing on black-and-white work sharpens one's eye without the jolly distractions of color. Whether they are used for centering one's mind or for illustration or calligraphy work, black lines, solid shapes, and washes train one's hands for precision, expression, and form. I was once told, and I truly believe it is true, that every logo design should be done in black first. Once its shape and form are settled, then you can move on to colors. By the same token, nice colors cannot save a bad logo. From design to illustrations to surface patterns for my ceramics, I use this approach in a lot of my silhouette work. To make a set of plates, for example, I challenged myself to sketch, with a black marker, as many plant and animal silhouettes as I could in an hour. I did so many! Fast, gestural, trying to capture in a minute the essence of that flower, bird, bug, lizard, crustacean. This little sketchbook of natural forms resulted in lots of black-and-white pieces, and some evolved into all kinds of colorful work.

For me, so much starts with black on white paper. But, as with white, there are many kinds of blacks, each with its undertone and level of richness. Besides making black ink from soot, called lampblack, there are other ways to achieve black. Observe each and keep them in your repertoire of black colors. Imagine orchestrating a piece of black-on-black art that uses all these different kinds

---

← After a year of calligraphy practice, I ended up with hundreds of rice-paper practice sheets with a single kanji each. I ended up collaging them to form a large 8 x 8 ft. painting surface onto which I painted a single figure in white. The subject—sad? tired?—was painted with white gouache using broad, fluid brushstrokes in the spirit of the calligraphy brushwork.

of blacks—from the art store, from the pantry, from the garden—then adding deep saturated color to enrich them.

- **jet black:** the blackest black commercially available; synthetic
- **lampblack (sumi-e):** made from soot, has a bluish undertone
- **ivory black:** originally made from charred bones, has a warm undertone
- **other carbon-based blacks** from fruit pits, each with a different-color undertone
- **ink made from oak galls,** like the one used for all books before Gutenberg
- **ink made with walnuts,** a rich dark brown
- **ink from squid and octopi**
- **ink made from berries,** beautiful, though not very lightfast
- **edible materials** such as black coffee, soy sauce, or Maggi sauce
- **graphite**
- **pigment-based pencils,** often iron oxide–based
- **oily inks** like printing inks and ballpoint pen inks
- **all kinds of markers,** from kid-safe water-based to permanent ink ones
- **vintage carbon paper,** made from burnt hydrocarbons—very rich black, but not very eco-friendly

Antoni Tàpies

Antoni Tàpies, an abstract expressionist Catalonian artist, took influence from this kind of very physical and minimalist approach to his work. Numerous pieces show big, bold, gestural brushstrokes that convey spirituality, force, and symbolism via big, spontaneous mark making.

- Gran creu negra shows a minimal yet powerful black cross on an off-white background.
- Gran Nus features a knot of black brushstrokes made with speed, movement, and variations in black.
- Espiral sobre negre is made with deep black combined with tones of gray.
- His various prints, lithographies, and etchings combine deep blacks in various textures.

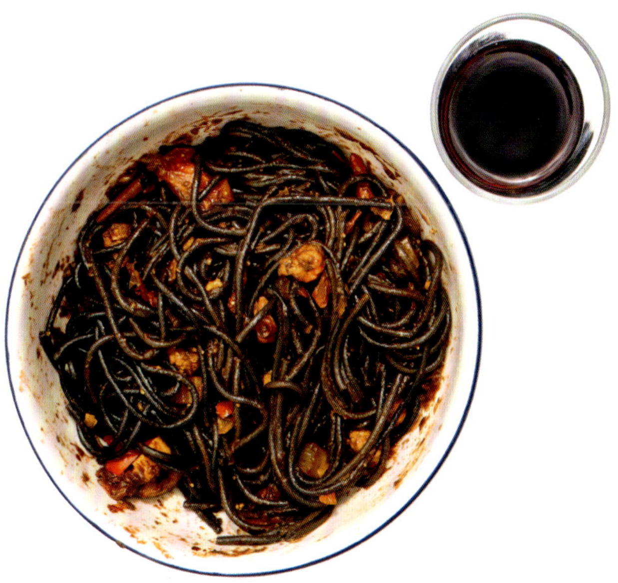

↑ Black dinner: glass of Syrah wine with black squid-ink pasta and homegrown Black Beauty tomato sauce.

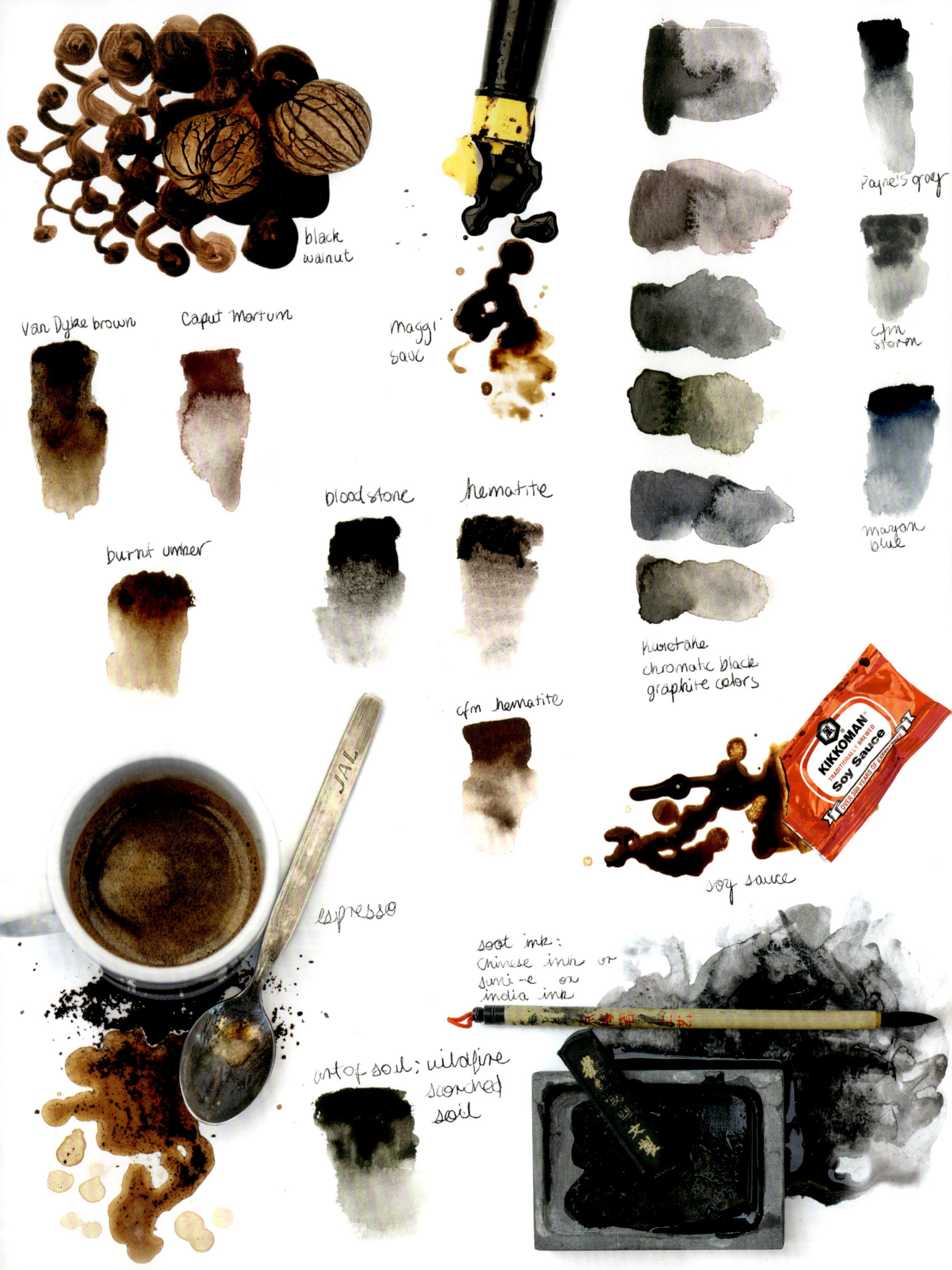

black walnut
Van Dyke brown
Caput Mortum
burnt umber
maggi sauce
blood stone
hematite
Payne's gray
cfm storm
cfm hematite
mayan blue
kuretake chromatic black graphite colors
JAL
espresso
soy sauce
soot ink: Chinese ink or sumi-e or india ink
art of soil: wildfire scorched soil
KIKKOMAN
Soy Sauce

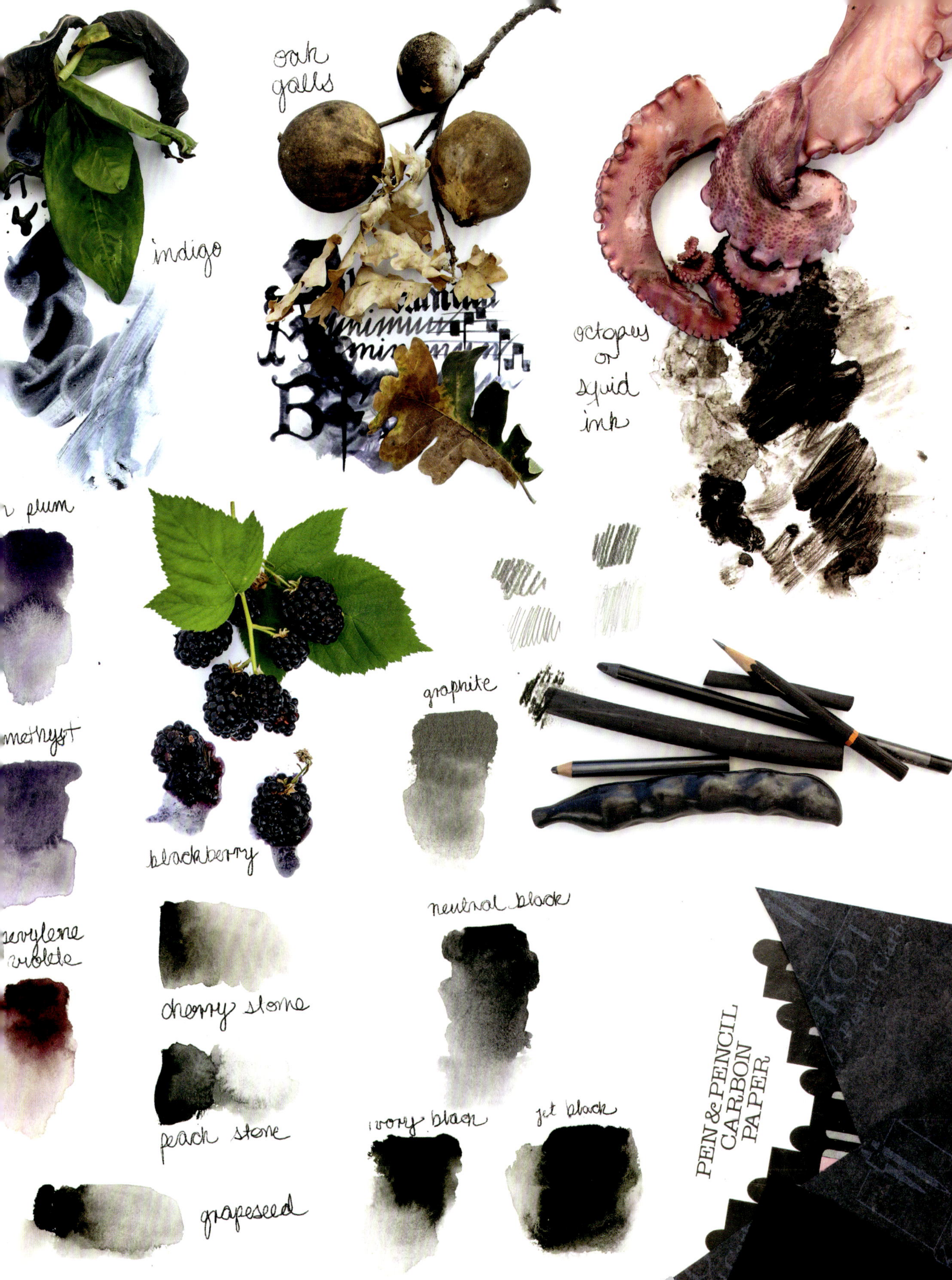
oak galls
indigo
octopus or squid ink
plum
amethyst
blackberry
graphite
perylene violet
neutral black
cherry stone
peach stone
ivory black
jet black
grapeseed
PEN & PENCIL CARBON PAPER

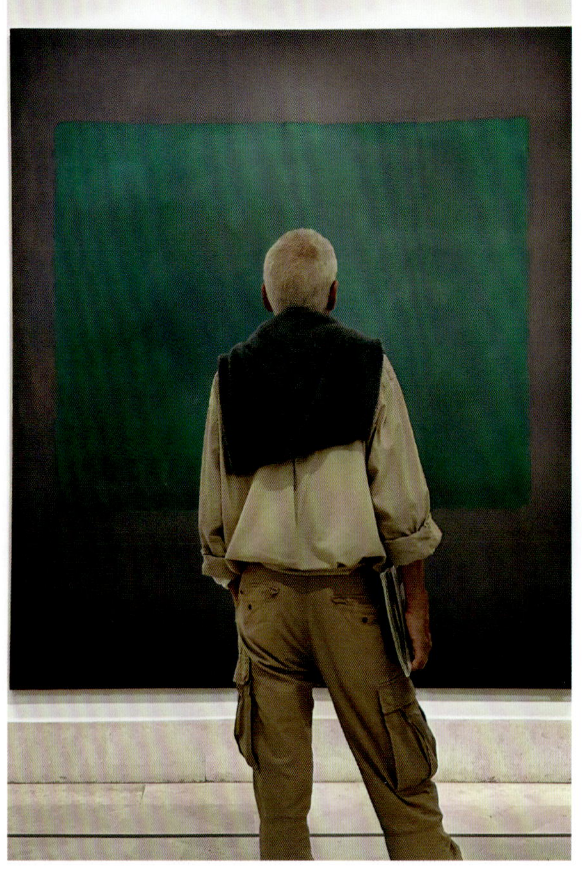

A PROFOUND EXPERIENCE WITH BLACK PAINT

My husband, an art-loving scientist, and I had talked about going to see the Menil Collection since we met. He had worked there as a volunteer during graduate school.

Next to the Menil Collection, there is a separate building alongside a reflecting pool. Its design intention was to serve as a nondenominational chapel; it holds no regular services and is a space for anyone, of any faith, to spend time in meditative, spiritual contemplation. It is known as Rothko Chapel for the artist's paintings on all interior walls. These fourteen paintings are also known as the Black Paintings since that is what they are.

Or are they?

I came into the octagonal space and sat on one of the backless benches. All around me were the paintings, flooded by the soft daylight coming from above. The paintings were very imposing, big and black; they almost had a sound to them. A grave, very low sound that reminded me of Buddhist chants in a temple I was invited into in Tibet. But there was actually no sound at all. Maybe it was a little moment of synesthesia.

I ended up staying in the room for over an hour. I changed benches, and I sat on the cushions on the floor so that I could really spend time with each of the paintings. Then the most remarkable thing happened: The paintings, black at first, started to glow from within. Not glow as in anything magical or electrical, but *color* glow as I observed them for longer periods. By staying and observing, in deep silence, my eyes adjusted from seeing only the obvious black to noticing the subtler violets and magentas.

Rothko created this effect intentionally so that the paintings would glow from within. How did he do it? For Rothko, "a painting is not a picture of an experience. It is an Experience."[13] If you were to visit the chapel, your experience would be different from mine, and if I return my experience may be unlike the first time. That is part of the power of a Rothko painting. He saw his paintings as something that "lives and breathes." Much could be

> *"Broad, unblemished, undifferentiated expanses of near formless color, free of readily observable figures, distinct marks and distractions. And of content? But this is not necessarily what Rothko thought of . . . the apparent emptiness is already filled with murmurs and shadows of what came before and what might be percolating just beneath the surface."*
> —Christopher Rothko[12]

said about the way he painted these and all his color field paintings: that he built his colors not with transparent layers of glaze or by alternating cool and warm colors like other abstractionists, but by building wispy layers of precisely selected tones and applying them, he would say, "as one breathes." The *how* he painted is really not what is relevant to me; it is the experience the final piece creates that matters.

Intellectually, reading or knowing about Rothko's work is one thing, but seeing and feeling the transcendence of his work within these black paintings in this serene place—well, it moved me to tears. It was grave but uplifting; it was severe yet comforting.

By the time I left, none of the paintings looked black anymore, and some were even vibrant and saturated to my eyes. All kinds of purples, magentas, and reds came afloat from the black. I kept all this in my mind, waiting for a design or art project where I could apply this memory. Eventually, I found the moment. I was hired to design a set of wine labels, and when I saw Syrah grapes being pressed, their dark juice dripping down the pressing machine, it reminded me of these deep-color paintings. I ended up making a lot of variations with watercolor, emulating Rothko.

For me, as a color lover, Rothko has always been top of my list, but after this experience with the black paintings, every time I have a chance to see a Rothko in person, especially those very dark ones, I take my time so that I can truly observe all the colors hiding underneath the surface. Also, as my husband did with me at the Menil, I like observing people observing the paintings, some in awe and some not quite there yet.

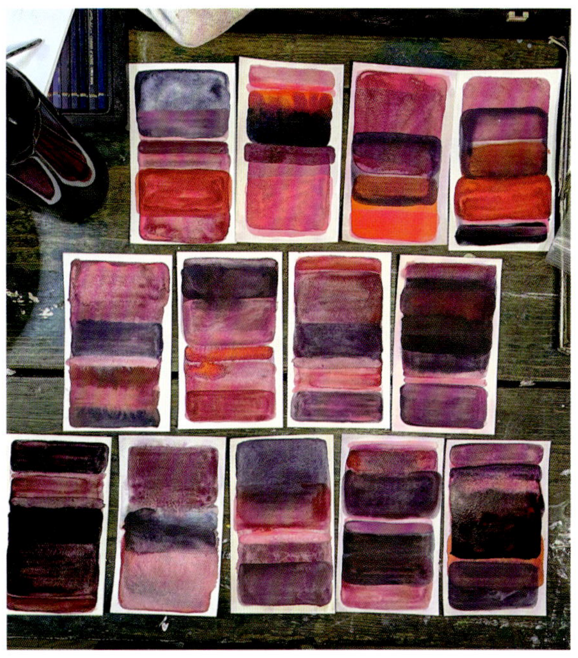

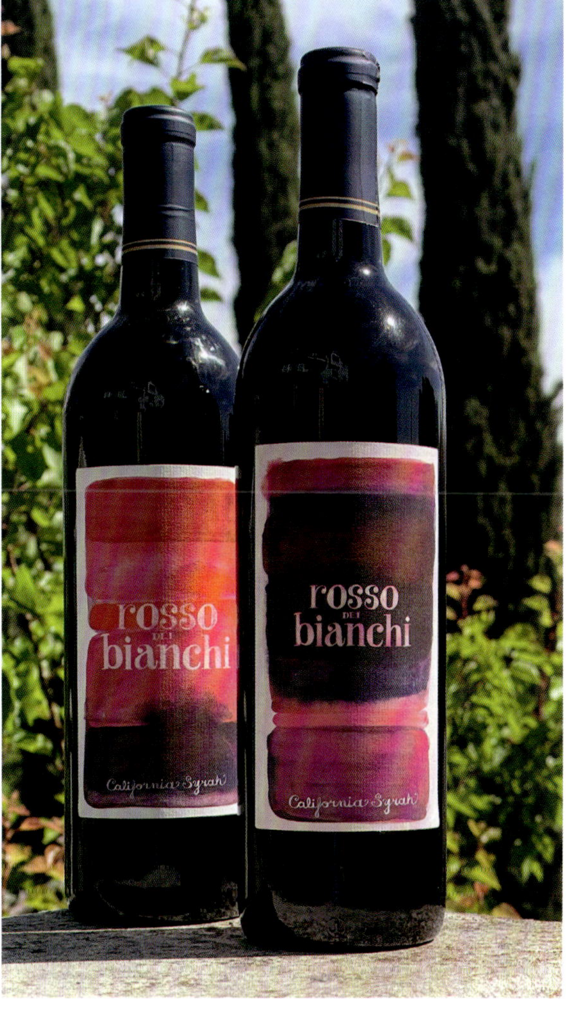

DARK ART

Looking at very dark art can be challenging. Not all museums have the right light, and there may be too many reflections, or our love for multicolor may drag our eyes somewhere else. It is even harder with books or internet photos of art in deep, dark colors since those colors are particularly hard to accurately reproduce in print or on-screen. I find it important to take my time with very dark paintings—both with modern art like Ed Reinhardt's black-on-black and any of the old masters, especially Dutch or Spanish. There is much more to observe: the tonal variations, the shine or opacity, but above all the color nuances and richness of chroma in some of them.

Francisco Goya

Francisco Goya enjoyed a happy life in the court. Rumor has it he even had an affair with the Duchess of Alba, the famous dressed and nude Maja of his paintings. He made candy-colored paintings of Spanish people in festive settings. But then everything changed. There was political turmoil under Ferdinand VII, and Goya lost his wife, his youth, and above all his hearing. He retreated to a country house called La Quinta del Sordo—the deaf man's manor—where, isolated, depressed, and full of pessimistic feelings, he painted some of his most expressive pieces directly on the walls. Goya's Black Paintings are dark in color and subject. His palette was lampblack (from soot) and bone black (from burnt animal bones), his undertones umber and various ochres. The palette fits the mood in color and material. The only saturated color is in Saturn, with the vermilion for blood as the god of time, angry, chomps up his child's head.

With Goya's Black Paintings, look at the dark brushstrokes, how they cover the underlying color, how deep and dark it gets, and how that reflects the painter's mood. My favorites are

- Witches' Sabbath *(1819) with its large hellish goat*
- A Pilgrimage of San Isidro *(1820)*

Look at these dark paintings and then check out Goya's early, colorful work, much of which is on display at Museo Nacional del Prado in Madrid. The contrast is so striking.

Always worth looking at, but especially for dark colors, are the shadows in Francisco de Zurbarán's paintings:

- Santa Casilda *(1630) for dark crisp, luxury textiles with red undertones*
- Saint Francis of Assisi in His Tomb *(1630) for deep browns and a face in deep shadows*
- *His various renditions of Christ on the cross and dark still lifes*

And, of course, the master of light and shadow is Caravaggio. Revisit any of his paintings, focusing not on the illuminated side but on the dark side. That is where all the enriched black nuances happen.

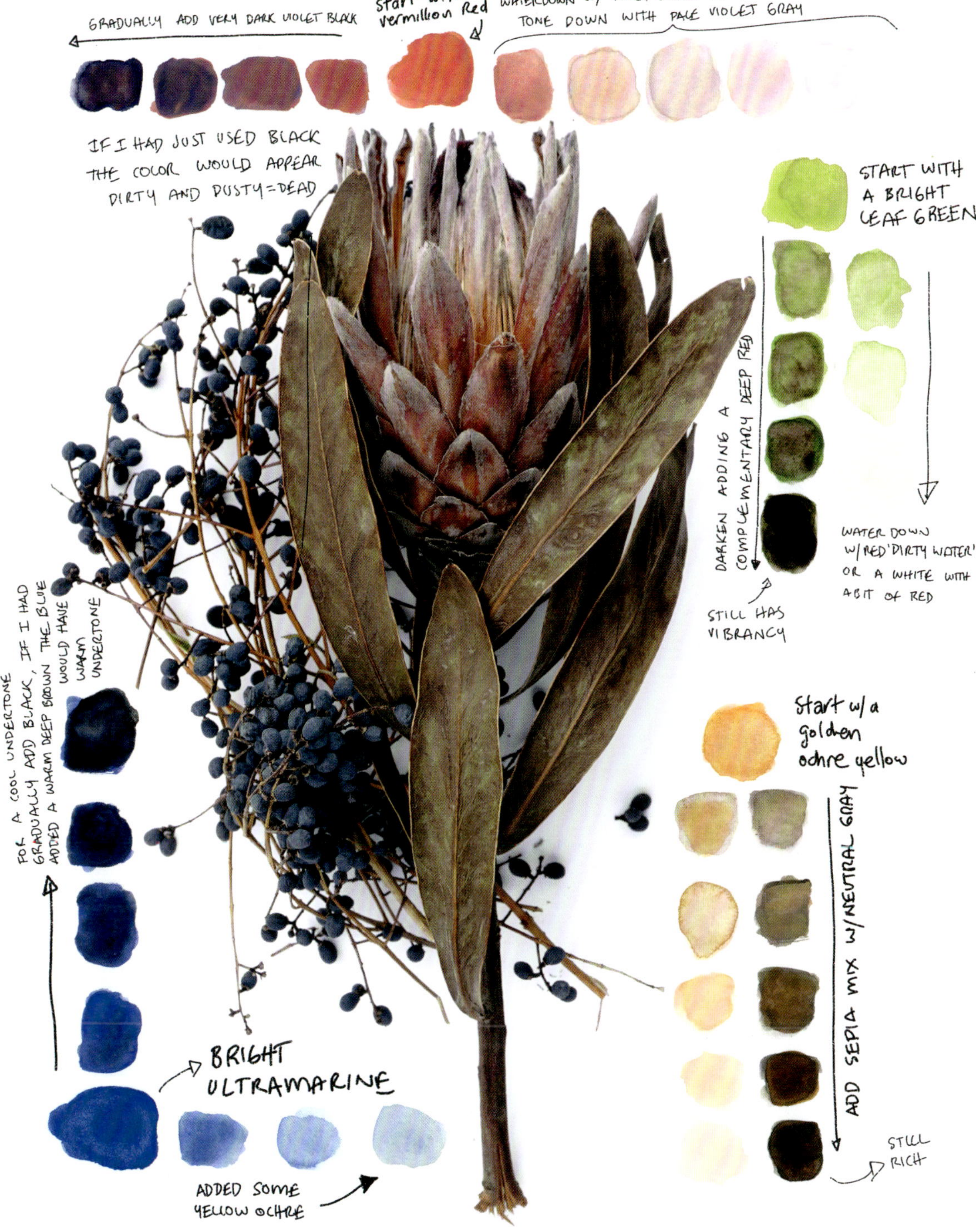

↑ How to Mix Richer Dark Colors

The first thing we think when trying to mix a dark color is simply to add a deep black, like jet black. Yes, that will definitely make it darker, but maybe not the right kind of deep shade. Black can make colors ashen, which may be what you are looking for, but maybe your goal is deep jewel tones. Look at the beautiful colors of this dry protea; to achieve those tones, there are ways other than adding black to make a color darker.

- **Try different types of black** or deep browns or grays; they will all render different kinds of cooler or warmer deep shades to a color.
- **Instead of blacks or dark neutrals,** use a deep shade in a complementary color—darken a green with a deep burgundy, for example. That will result in a more saturated, enriched black, something more jewel-toned, or even an unexpectedly rich, deep tone, like the dark violets resulting from mixing magenta with phthalo green.
- **Try using an adjacent dark color too;** for example, darken red with a deep violet.

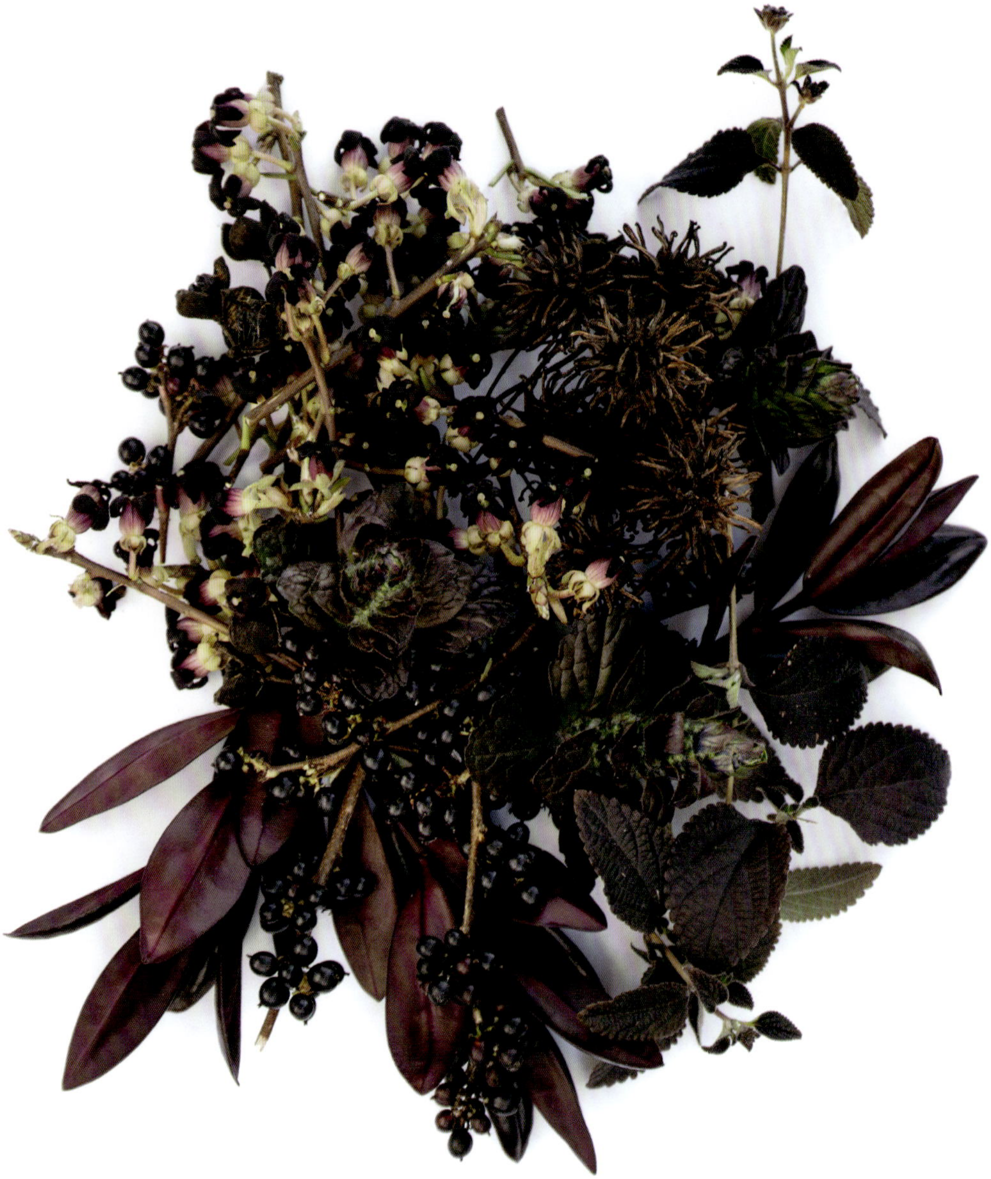

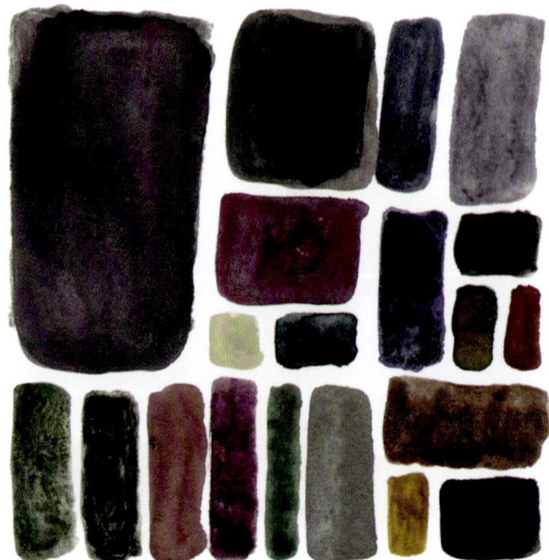

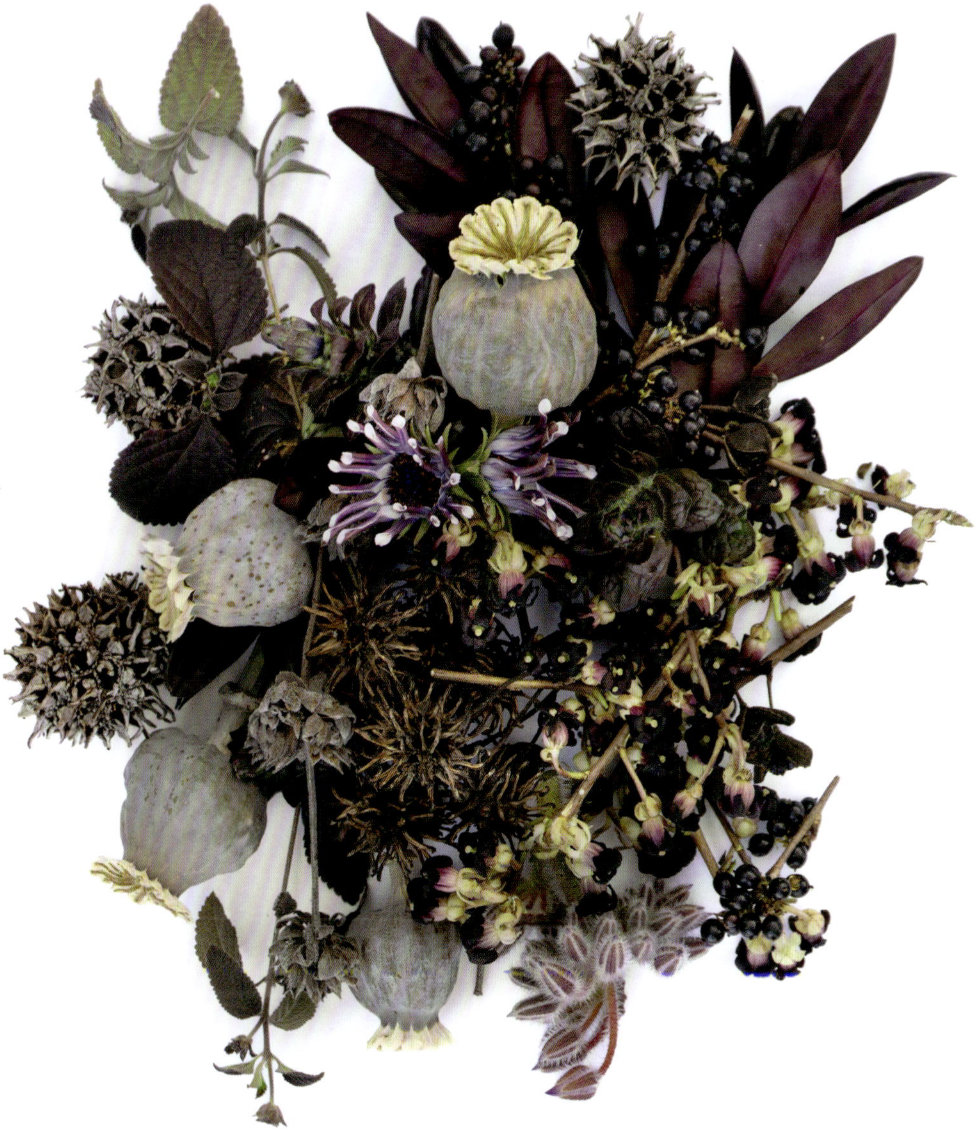

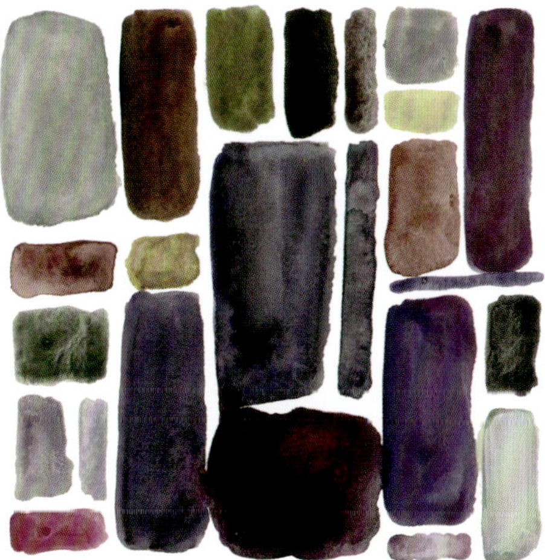

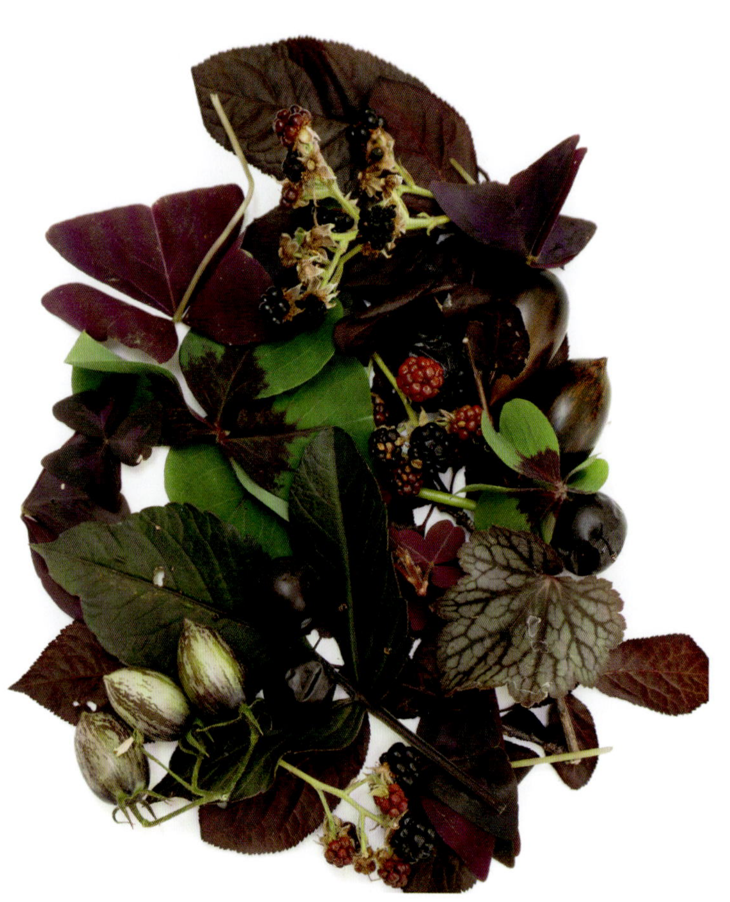
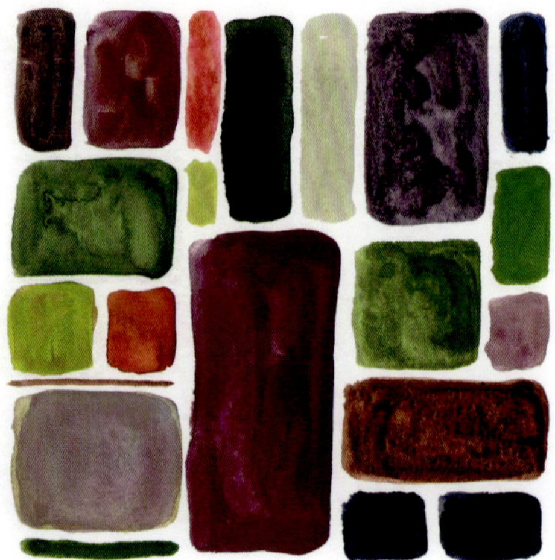
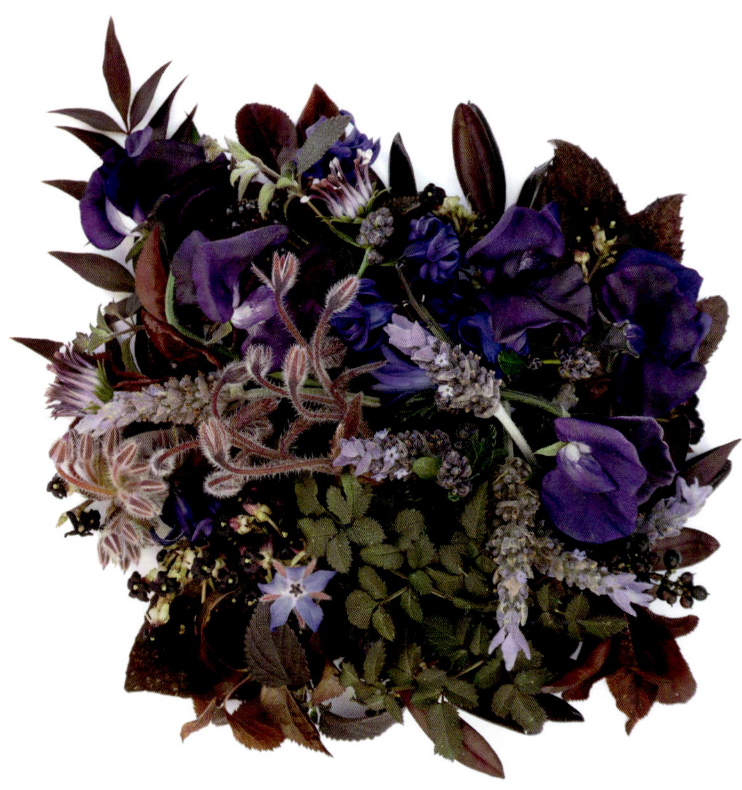
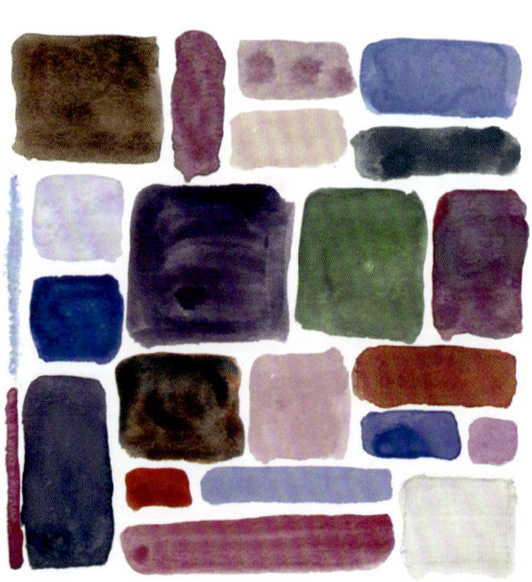

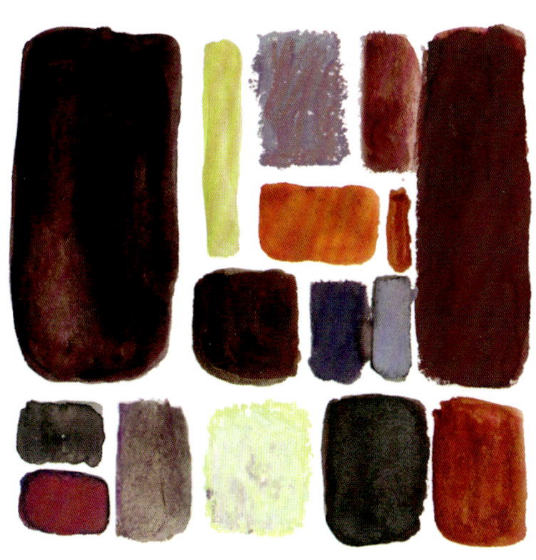

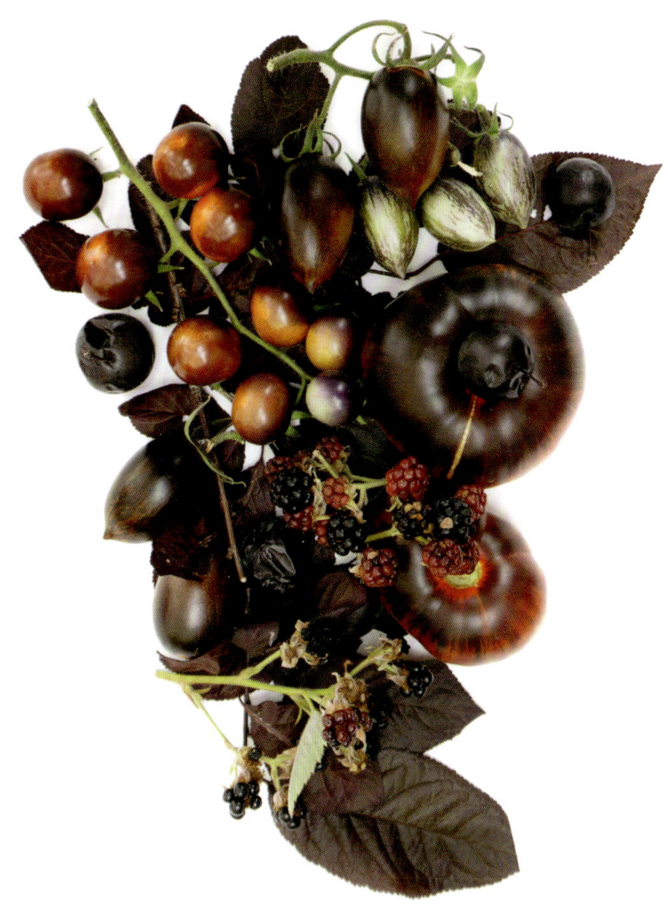

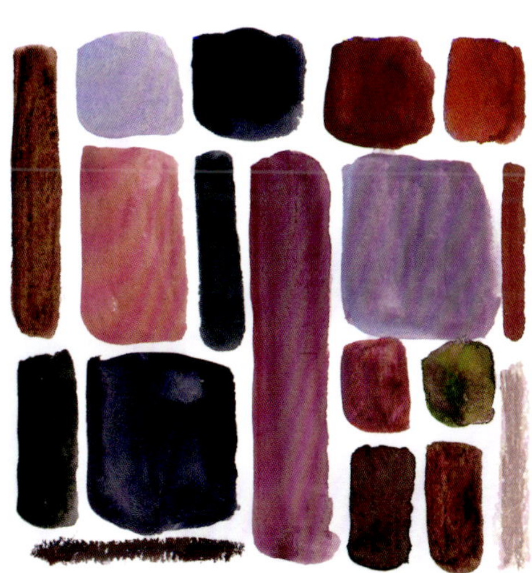

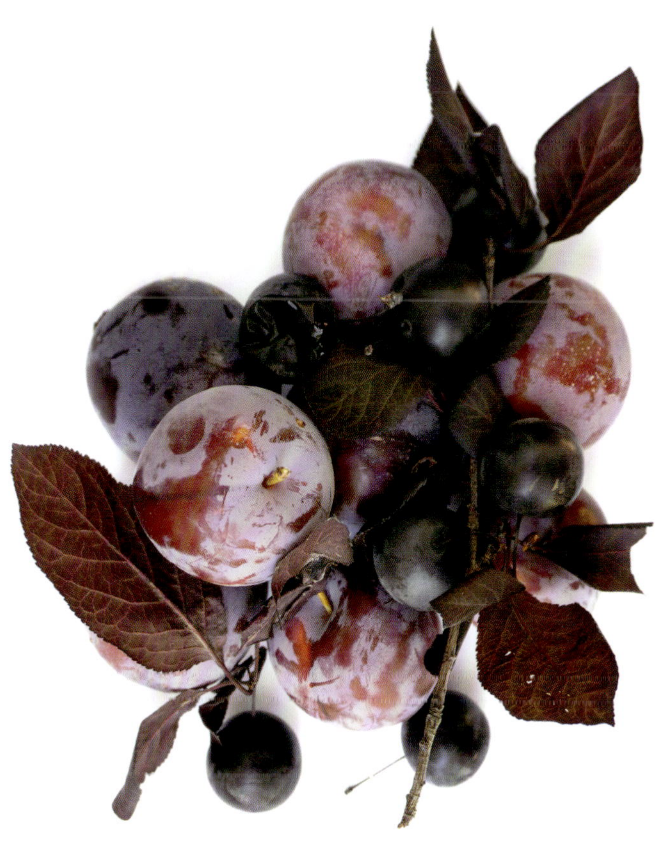

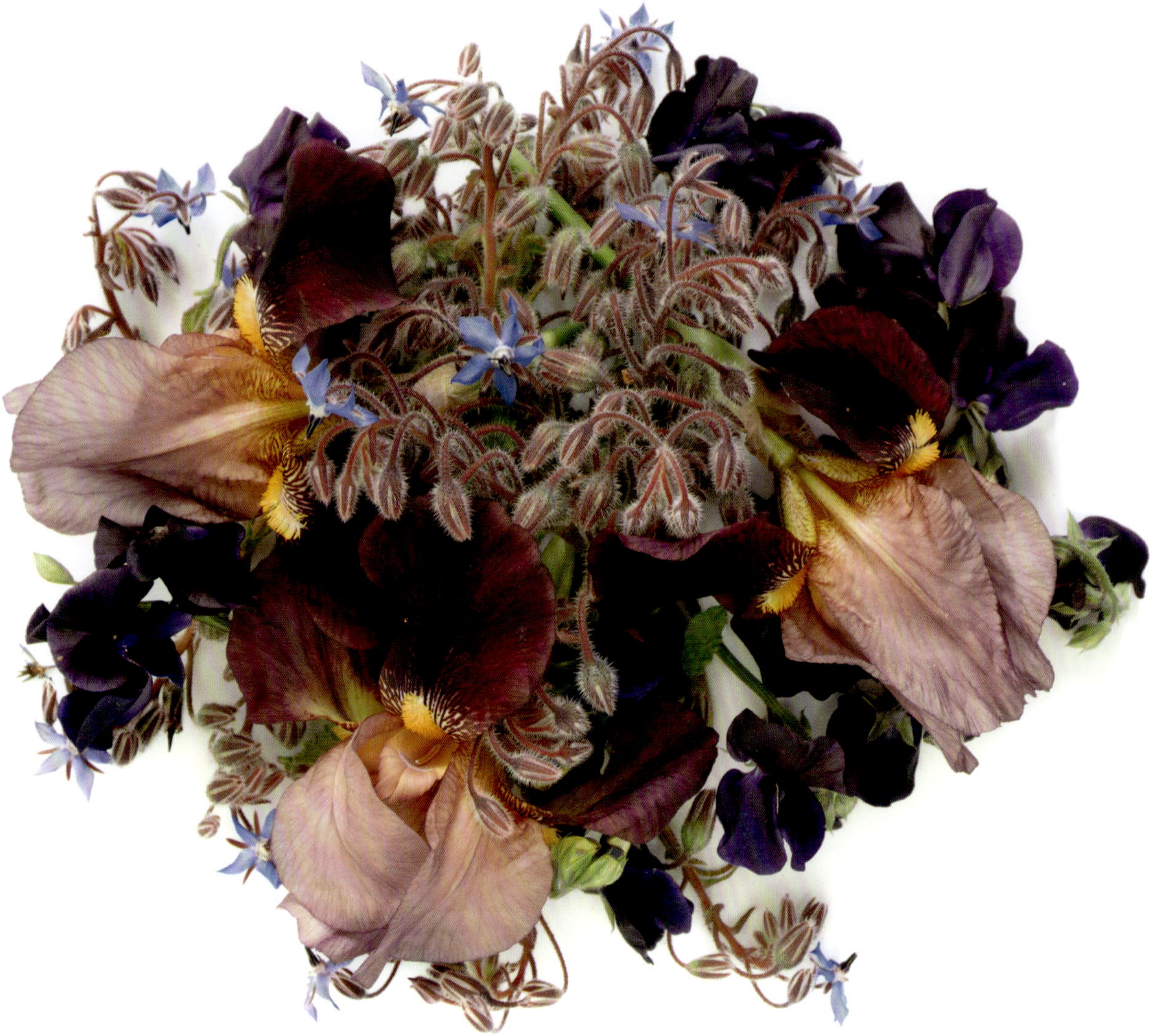

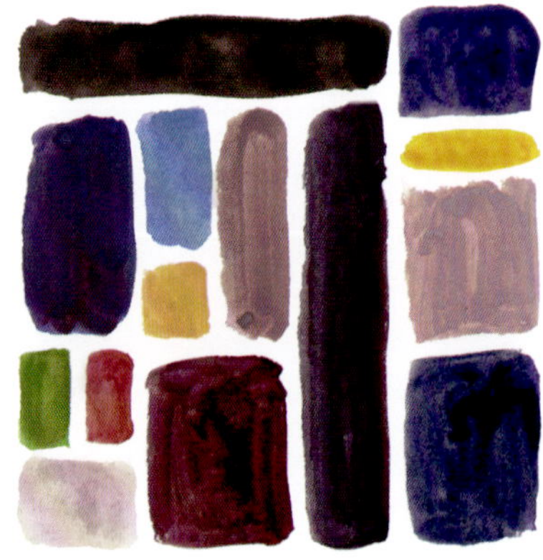

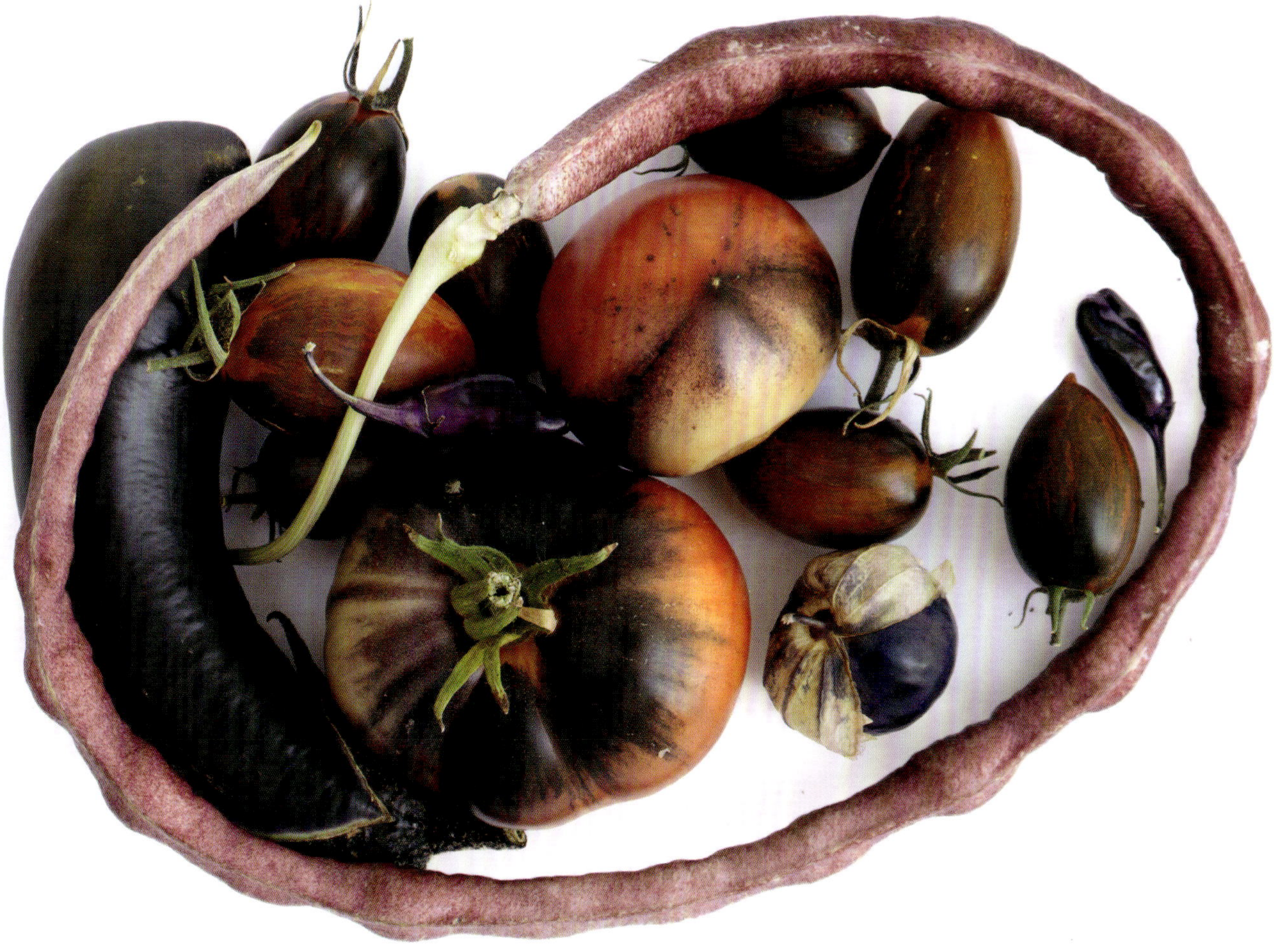

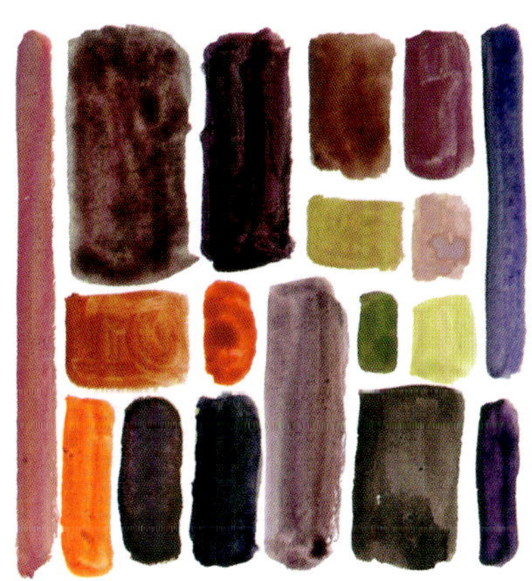

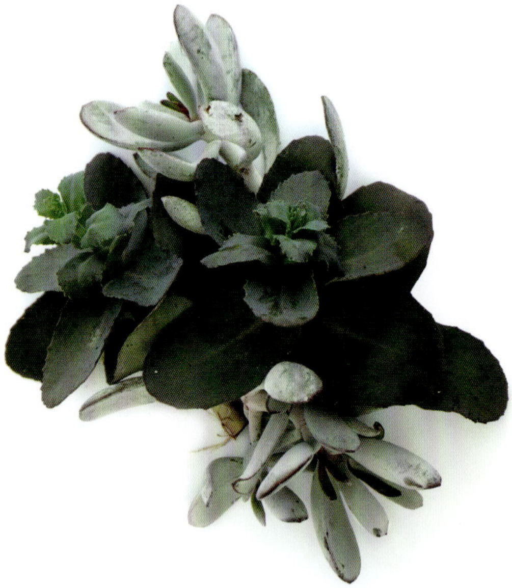

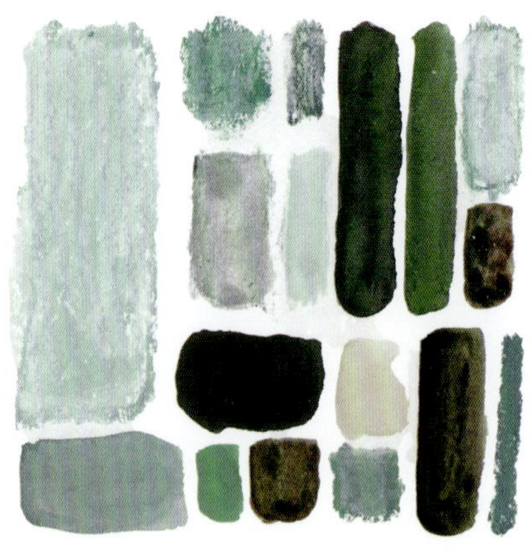

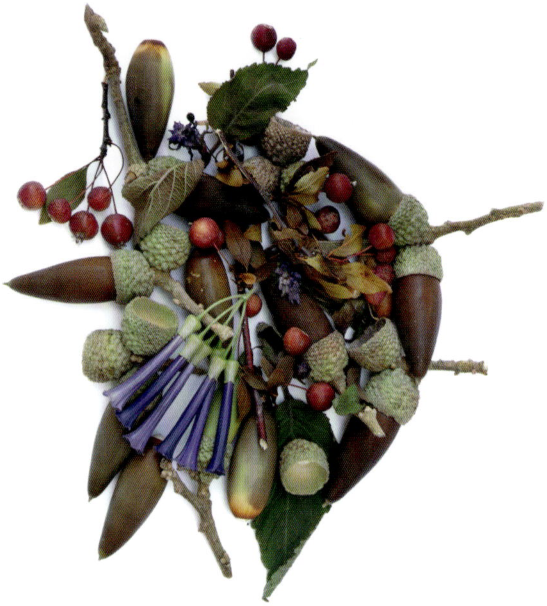

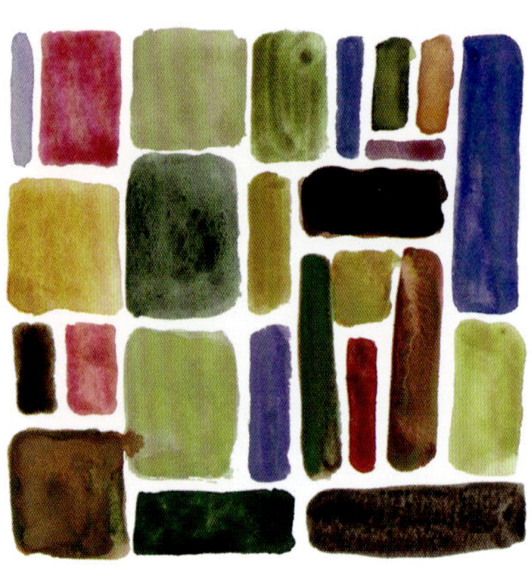

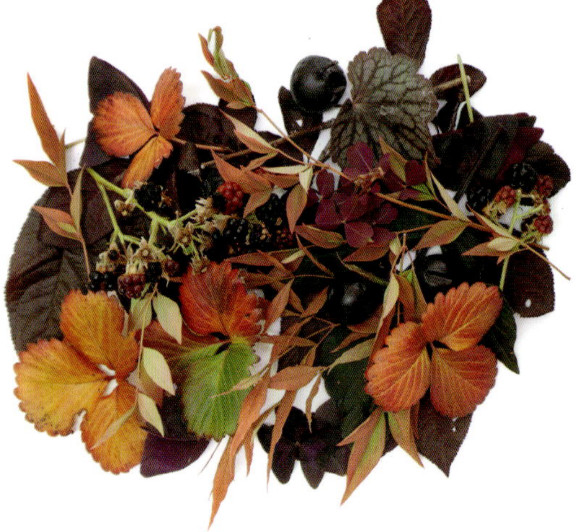

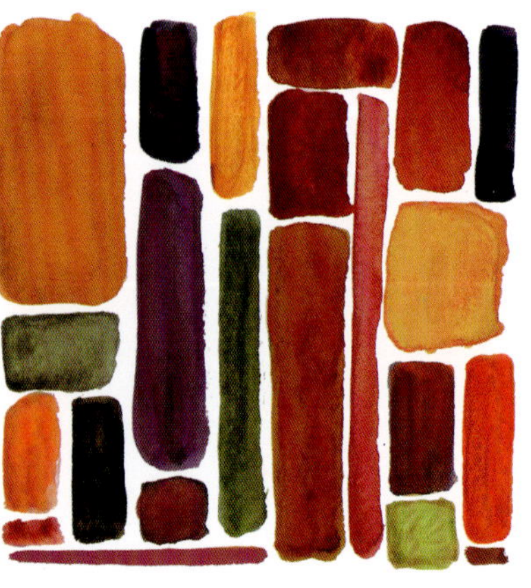

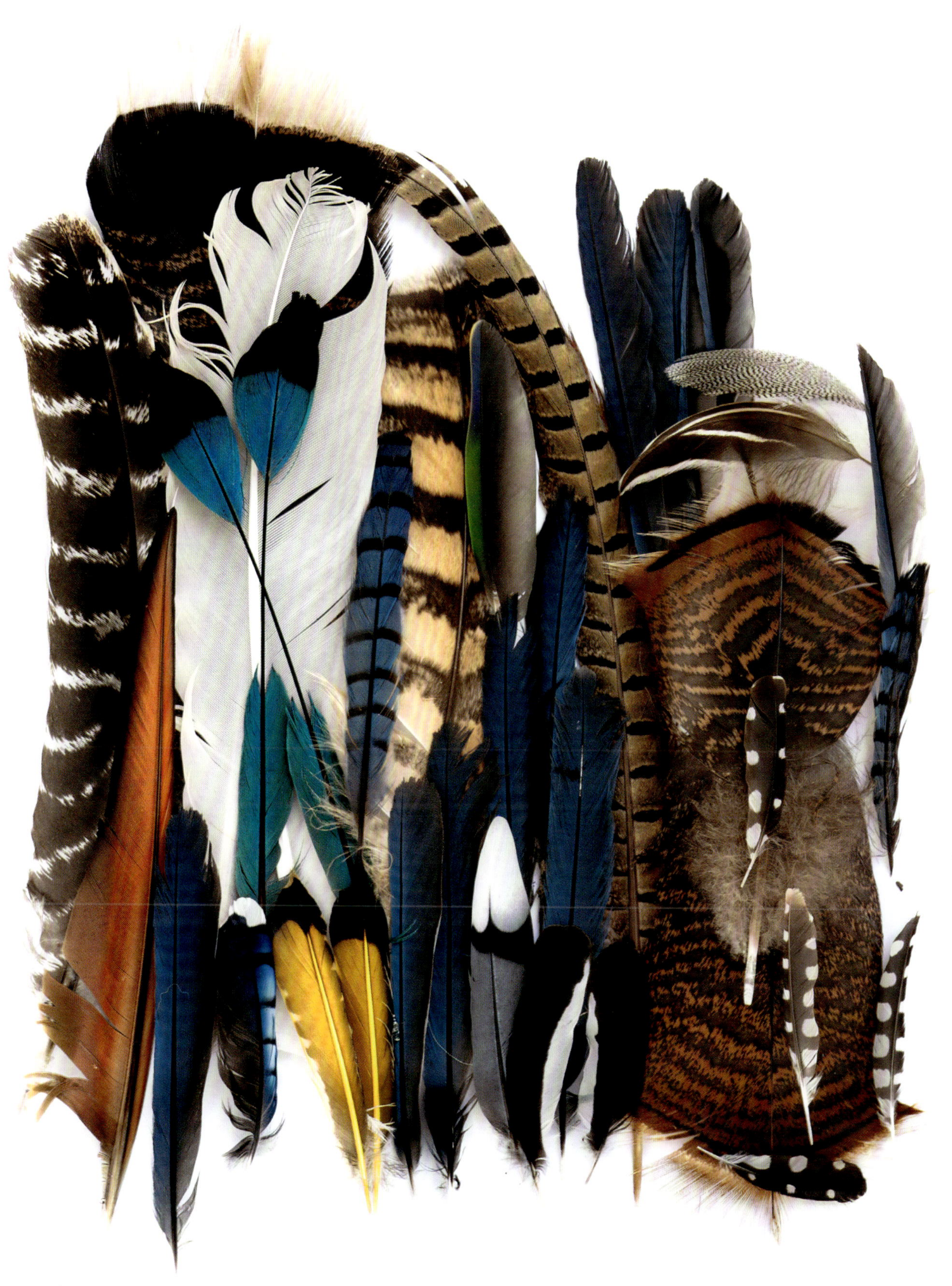

TWO STORIES OF BLACK IN PRINT

Pull out a magnifying glass and observe anything offset-printed in color: a magazine, a book, or a newspaper. See the dots in four colors, cyan, magenta, yellow, and black? This is CMYK. As explained earlier, K stands for *key*, the dark tone used to anchor text, outlines, and shadows; in most cases K is black, but not always. Most full-color printed matter is made by combining these four inks, while printing just words on a page requires only pure, 100 percent black (or key). However, to obtain enriched blacks in printing, there are other techniques.

Black on Black: The 9/11 New Yorker Cover

I had just moved to New York when 9/11 occurred. The smell and the image of the black smoke haunted me for months. Right after it all happened, Françoise Mouly and Art Spiegelman thought of how to represent it in the design for the cover of *The New Yorker*. The all-black cover only had the silhouette of the two towers on a black background. Black on black, but each black is distinct from the other. This cover was not printed with 100 percent black ink. It was made by enriching black with high percentages of cyan, magenta, and yellow. Changing the values of the four inks between the background and the towers rendered two different, super rich blacks. Then adding a varnish to the towers made that contrast even deeper.

Two brilliant designers displaying their knowledge of printing techniques at the most somber of moments.

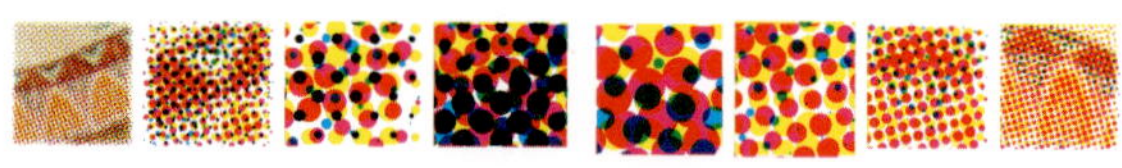

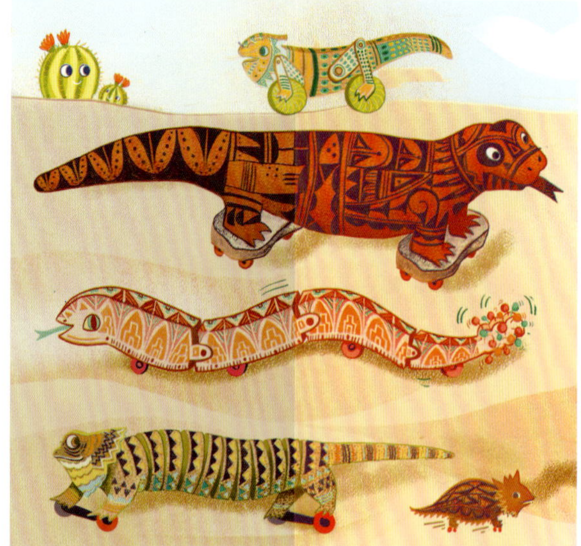

↑ The left side of this image is made with full CMYK, where K is black, and on the right side it is the same image without the black: only cyan, magenta, and yellow, and slightly adjusted for contrast. Look at the close-up of the printing dots to see the presence or absence of black. Notice how colors look different on each side, with the right side having the sunburnt feel Elaine describes. Cover one side while looking at the other, then observe both at the same time.

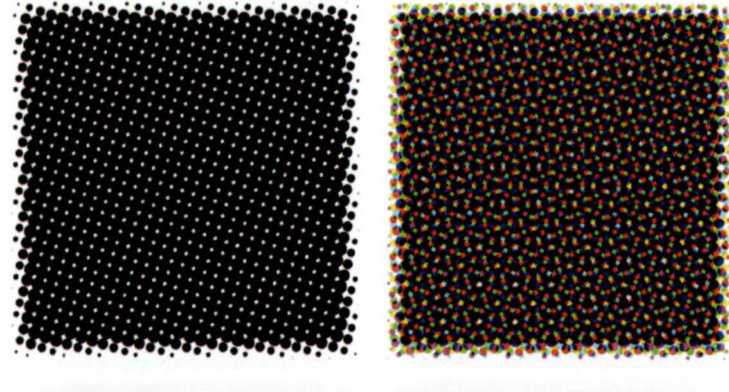

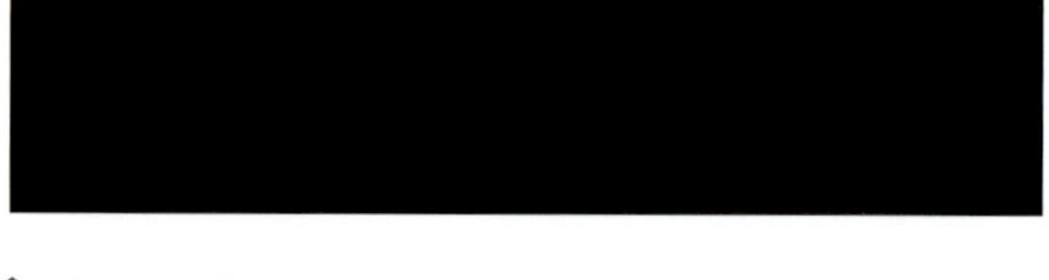

↑ Above, at first glance you see a deep black rectangle, but if you take a closer look you will see that it is actually two different kinds of black: On the left side is a black made with 100 percent black with no other color, and on the right side is a black actually made of equal amounts of CMYK for a richer, darker black. Here I did 70 percent for each of the colors, but if they were at 100 percent, that would be the blackest you can achieve on print. Above the rectangle are close-ups of what each looks like in print: all black dots on the left and CMYK dots on the right.

When K Is Not Black and When CMY Has No K

A few years ago, at the SCBWI (Society of Children's Book Writers and Illustrators) conference, I attended a session about color in graphic novels. The two presenting were the brilliant illustrator Raúl the Third, whose marvelous Lowriders books are drawn using ballpoint inks, and his colorist-collaborator wife, Elaine Bay, who is in charge of color in his Vamos series.

Elaine talked about when she was hired as a colorist by Stephen Hillenburg, the creator of SpongeBob, when he was converting the cartoons into comics. To create the desired look, there were several rules, one of which was not to use black for the key; a dark gray should be used instead. She went on to work on three SpongeBob comics, and in all of them the dark gray would be used only in text and for the outlines of bubbles and the main characters. The rest of the palette was formulated just with cyan, magenta, and yellow.

This idea of eliminating the black resonated with Elaine because of memories of her punk-rock days hand-printing concert posters, when the fewer colors she used, the cheaper the printing run would be and the faster she would be done printing. But now, the idea of getting down to the minimum with inks became a creative challenge: With three inks she needed to create a whole rainbow of colors. When the time came to do the colors in Raúl's books, she had the freedom to go all the way on this idea and eliminate the black ink entirely, formulating the color palettes for Vamos using only CMY and no K.

The effect is saturated, since adding any percentage of black usually dulls colors. At the same time, all the colors in Vamos acquire a certain sunburnt effect since the darkest color renders a sort of dark neutral brown.

Before talking to Elaine, I knew I could make black with only the primary colors. I had done that with the color cube exercise, and my painting mentor in Italy had instructed me not to mix black into my oil paint colors but to use complementary colors instead. But learning about how *The New Yorker* cover was printed and hearing Elaine talk about CMY-no-K in offset printing set me on a whole different path when working with my graphic design projects and even some of my illustrations.

- If I want vibrant colors, then I pick colors without black in the mix.
- If I want deep, blackest blacks in print, I use all CMYK to deepen the black, but I do not risk it in text, as any failure in the registration would render the text blurry.
- And then, of course, from observing Rothko, I learned how to enrich black paint with intense, layered undertones to bring color from within the black.

"I'm from El Paso, Texas, I grew up in a Hispanic community, and because it is the desert, everything is bleached out, color-wise. The reds and magentas are just not very resistant to the sun, and all those man-made things, left out in the sun, their colors get burned, and there are not a lot of plants, just cactus. So in my colors there are a lot of greens, but then they pop a bright magenta flower! And, well, I love a neon. So that is where I get a lot of my color inspiration for Raúl's Vamos books, this takes you to that place of the sunburnt things."
—Elaine Bay[14]

THE GREAT GRAYS

What about neutrals? The beautiful grays? As with whites and blacks, none of them are pure. Even if you are formulating them with only black and white, the type of black and the kind of white you choose will infuse them with a chromatic undertone.

Add a tiny bit of a cool color to the mix, and you will create cooler grays or a whole range of beautiful lichen and sage tones; add warmer colors and you will go from warm grays directly into browns.

From there, more white and you have your beige; less white and we get chocolate.

The Night of the Moonbow

Did you know the moon can also produce rainbows? The mechanics are the same as with rainbows: Light passes through rain and diffracts into a colorful arch, but in the case of moonbows, the light comes from the moon instead of the sun. These are very rare, but I was lucky enough to spot one!

It was Christmas Eve, and my husband and I were vacationing on an island, far from all sources of light. It looked like it might rain.

Soon a big, fat cloud above us started to rain, but as often happens in the tropics, the cloud moved—toward the beach, then toward the sea—and over the edge of the cliff behind us, a huge full moon came out.

Across the sea in front of us, I suddenly saw a beam . . . Was it a spotlight pointed up from another island? No, it was not straight, it was curved . . . "Wait, pass me the binoculars," I said, and I noticed that what at first just looked gray actually had all the colors of the rainbow—albeit faint and desaturated, but definitely there. An arch made of chromatic grays! It wasn't until later that I learned that this rare occurrence is called a moonbow.

KEY TAKEAWAYS

1. Experiment with a variety of black inks and paints. Different blacks will render different effects on the colors you mix them with.

2. When observing a piece of art or design or a very dark object, or when you are in a place with low light, try to find the colors infusing the darkness. Find the blue in the midnight sky and the hues of red and purple in your wine. Decipher the puzzle of why your black separates look mismatched when you wear them: Is it that one has a purplish undertone and the other one greenish? Can you make them work by adding a third, more chromatic shade, like a deep burgundy?

3. When mixing color, try to create very dark colors without using jet black. How dark can you get them to be? Do they still retain the richness and unctuousness of a chromatic black?

4. As you dilute the blacks or mix them with whites or pale colors, at what point do the neutral grays—both warm and cool ones—just become colors in unsaturated tones?

5. Depending on the desired effect, when working in CMYK or selecting Pantone colors to later turn into CMYK, try keeping your colors clean, without K, or using K strictly for text and outlines. Or try making a custom K. For example, instead of black, use a dark blue, or a gray, or a chocolate brown, and see what happens to your colors. This is a bit technical, but there are tutorials to learn how to modify the channels in Photoshop or other Adobe design applications. It's challenging but very worth experimenting with.

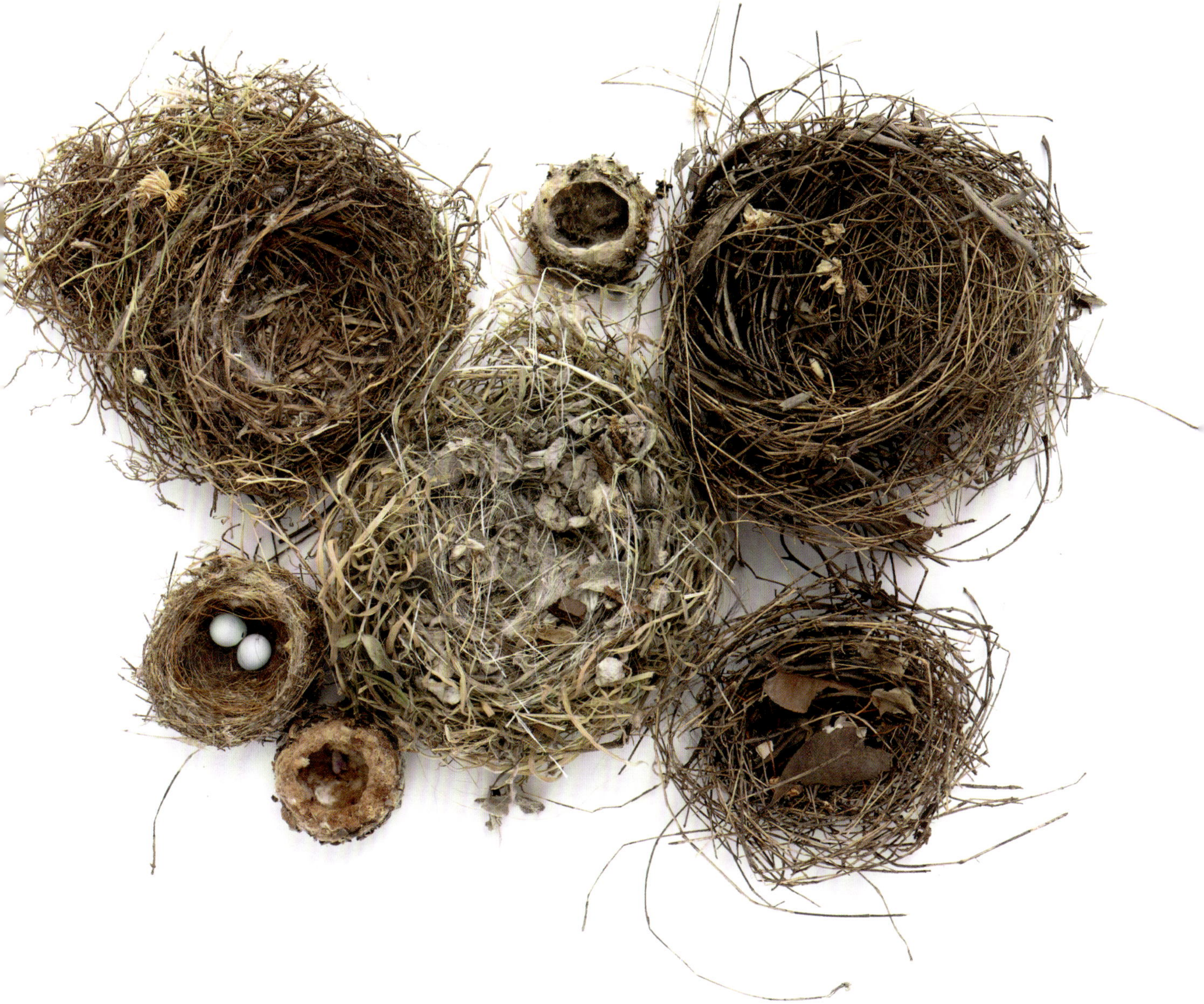

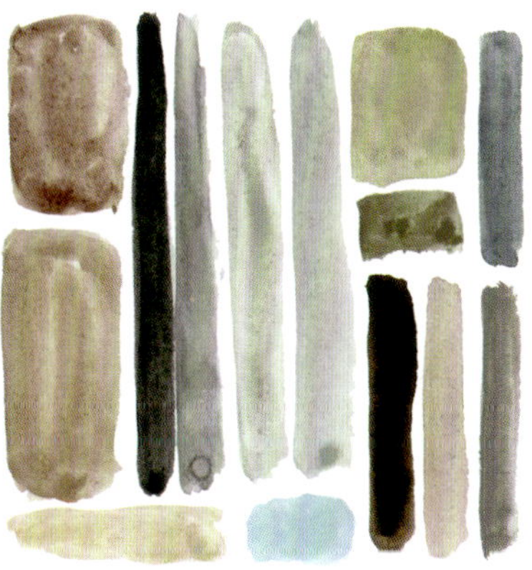

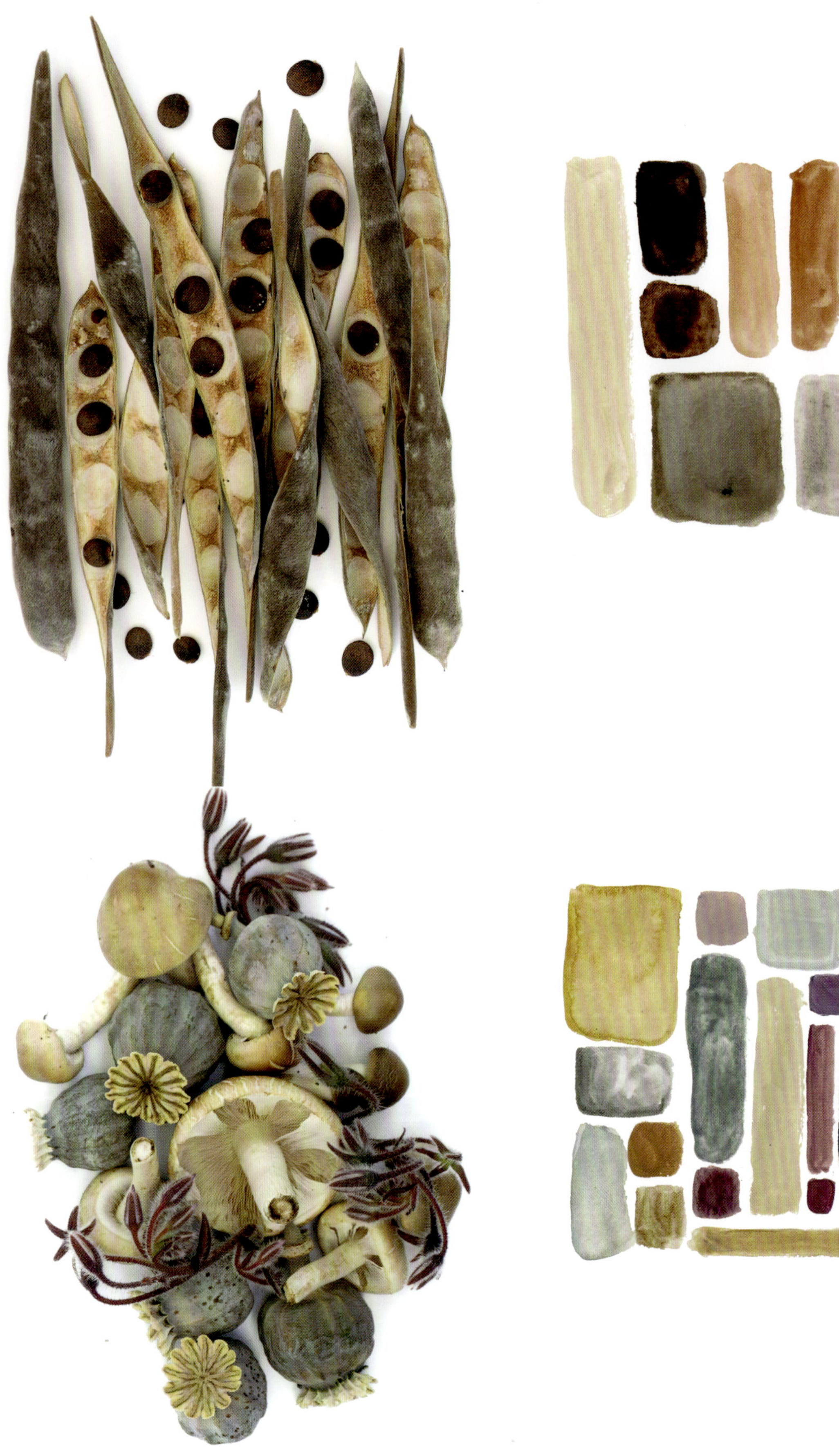

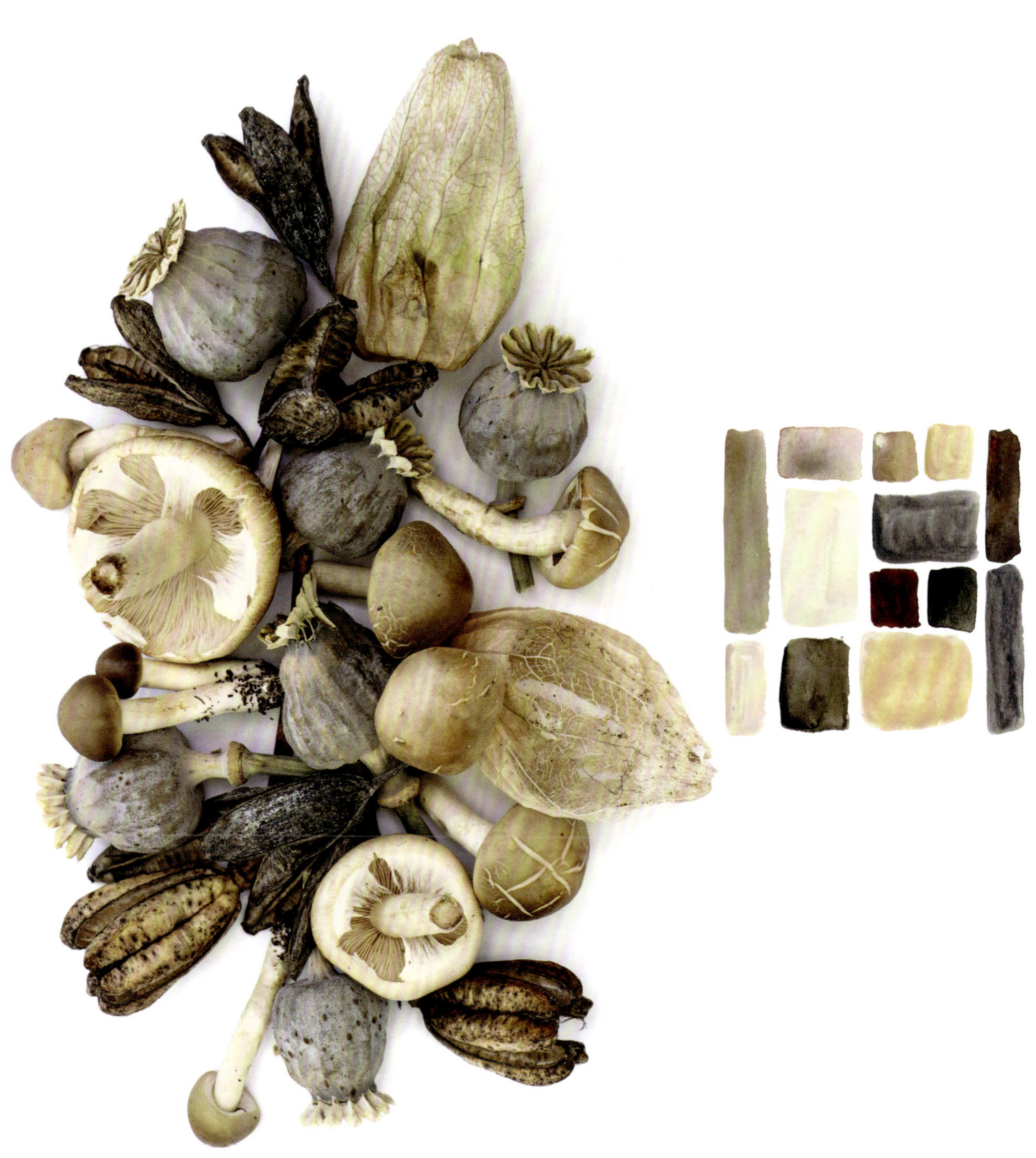

PROJECT

OBSERVE: Observe in detail the nuances behind all the dark natural colors in the previous pages. Notice how there is no true black.

Tonight, turn off the light, and when your eyes adjust to the darkness, make an effort to see the chroma in all the darkness. Do the same outdoors on a moonlit night.

ANALYZE: Analyze all those chromatic blacks and grays, those deep jewel tones, aubergines, and midnights.

Think of how you would mix those shades, whether you would use black in them or whether you could pull them off with deep and dark complementary colors, or CMY mixes if working digitally.

Observe dark art by the artists mentioned throughout this chapter and also by George de La Tour, the master of candlelight, or the contemporary artist Jeremy Miranda. Also, think of movies with night scenes. One I recall is in *The Remains of the Day*: a beautiful night scene when a character walks through a forest in pursuit of something—I don't remember what—and the forest floor is covered with blue bonnet flowers. Dreamy!

CREATE: OPTION A

Create an interior design for a room with deep, moody chromatic blacks. Think about who would live there, what they would collect or use to decorate, and which books they would read. Is this a bedroom, a living room, a home studio? Rather than actually decorating a room, you can just make, like I did, a mood board of materials: fabrics, woods, metals, wall paints, patterns, decor, and other inspiring elements. Be purposeful in your dark, moody color palette when selecting materials. Gather enough materials to get you to a point when you can fully furnish the surfaces and furniture of a room with this board.

Ready for a remodel? You can extend the project and move on to designing a real room (on your computer or in your actual home).

OPTION B

Create night scene illustrations.

Start with a dark blue background. Add darker details. Finish with any highlights—light in the windows, streetlights, moonlight, fireflies, stars—for contrast and to enhance the storytelling element.

Or gradually build the dark, mysterious night background around a dark central figure.

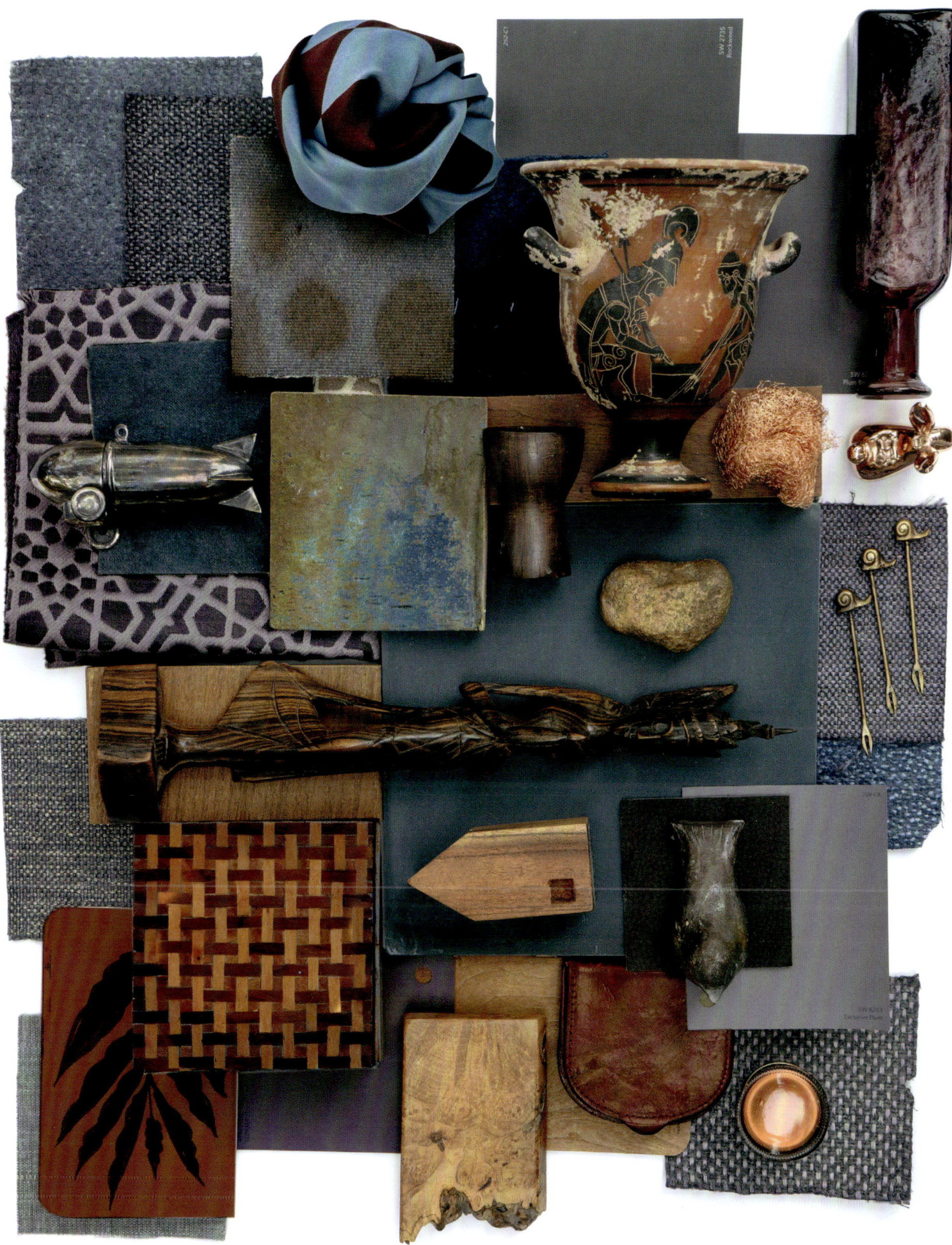

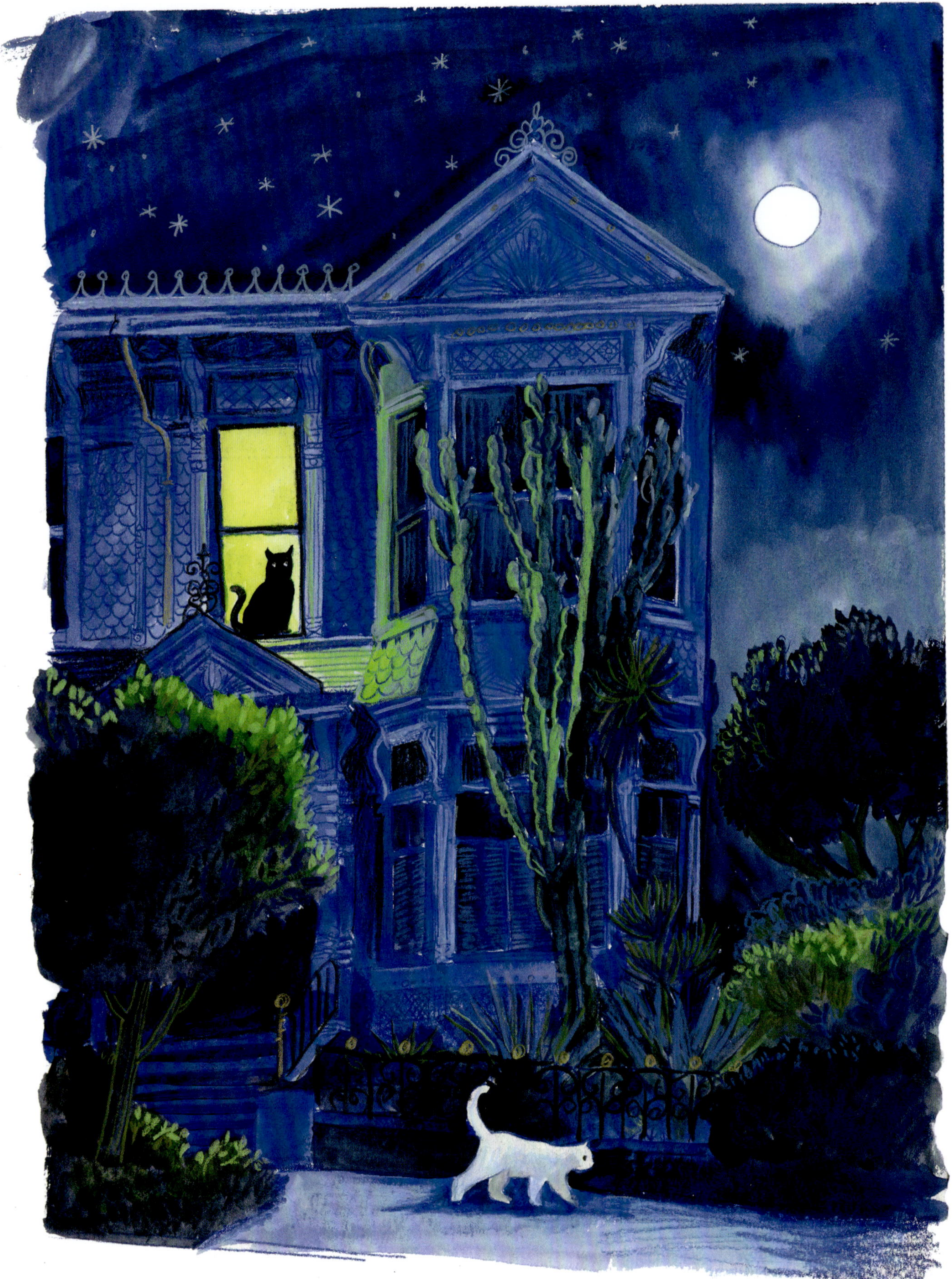

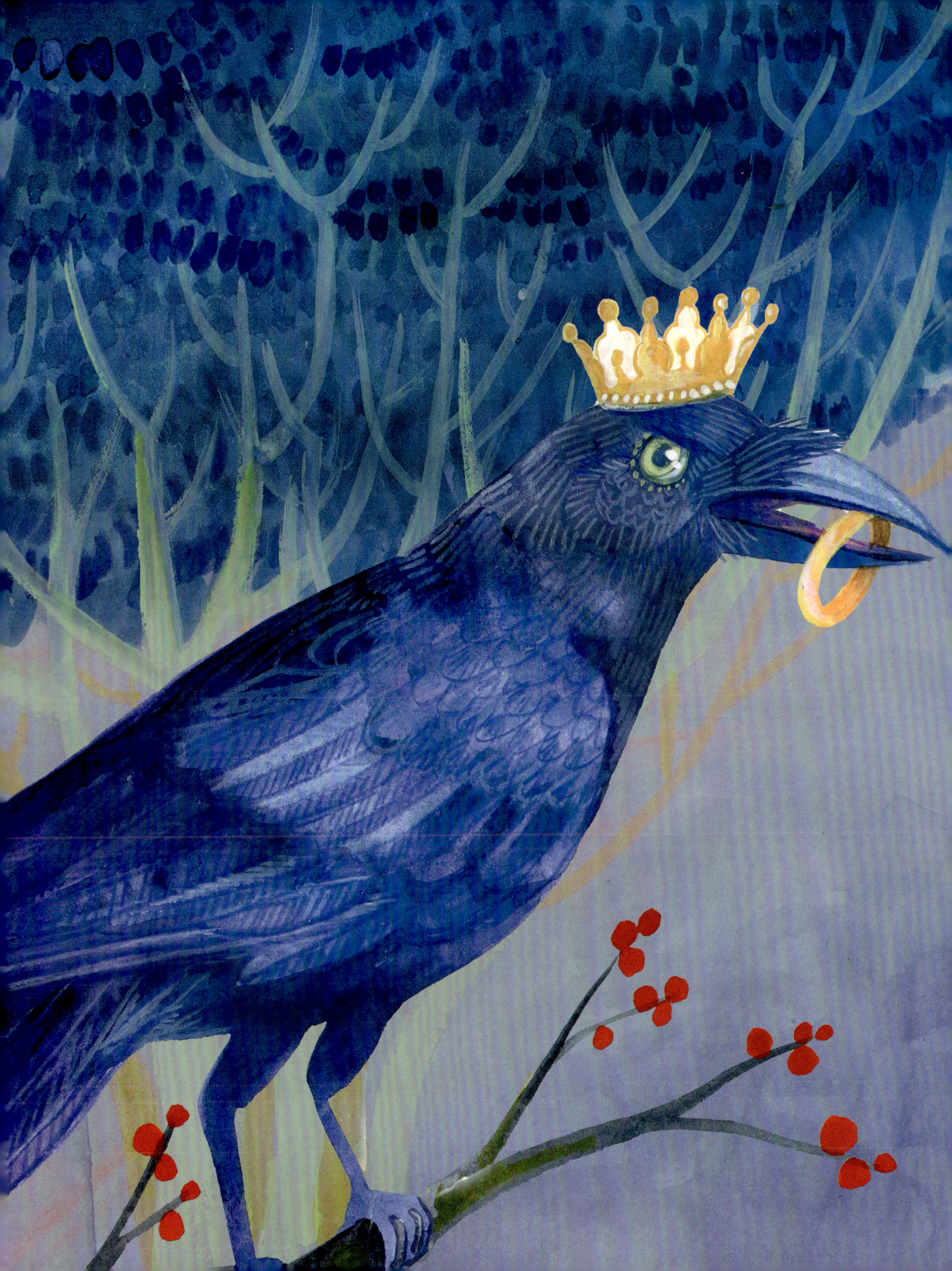

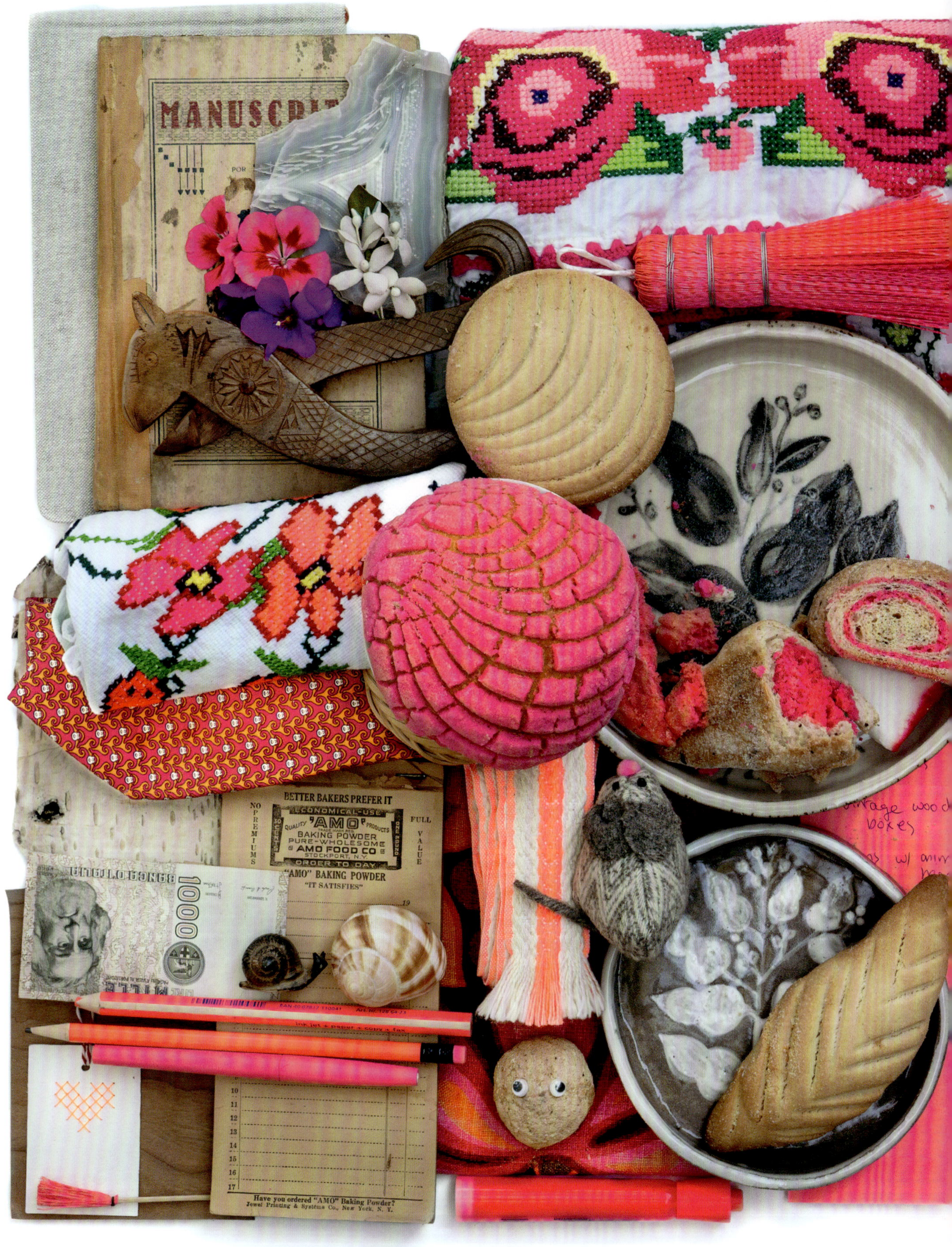

MANUSCRIT
POR
BETTER BAKERS PREFER IT
ECONOMICAL-USE
QUALITY 'AMO' PRODUCTS
TRADE MARK REG.
BAKING POWDER
PURE-WHOLESOME
AMO FOOD CO
STOCKPORT, N.Y.
ORDER TO DAY
NO PREMIUMS
FULL VALUE
"AMO" BAKING POWDER
"IT SATISFIES"
19
Have you ordered "AMO" Baking Powder?
Jewel Printing & Systems Co., New York, N. Y.
1000
MILLE
orange wood boxes
w/ anim

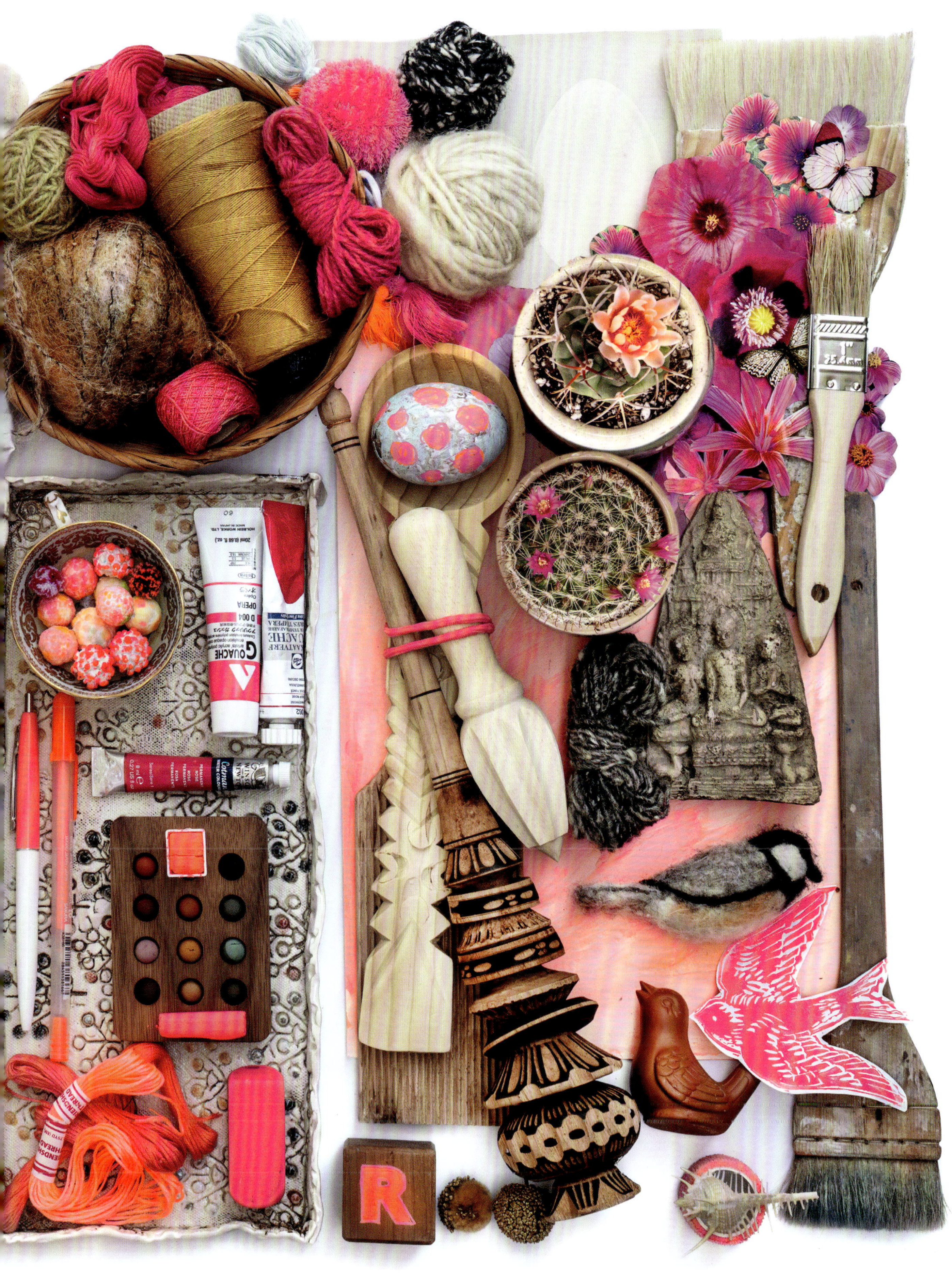

7.

SORRY FOR THE INTER-RUPTION

Using a Contrasting "Pop" with Intention to Make a Point

U sing a color accent interrupts the lull of a scene and captures our attention: the red balloon in the eponymous movie, the overcolored fish in the tank in the black-and-white '80s cult movie *Rumble Fish*, the red coat in *Schindler's List*.

Designers and movie fans alike were awed by these color accents back when we first saw these films. It was before VFX and CGI technology in film editing made color effects as easy as they are today.

The yellow brick road, the ruby slippers, the Emerald City: Those were a series of pops of color that aided the story of *The Wizard of Oz* and signaled a magical land away from black-and-white Kansas.

We have all heard the overused expression "pop of color" to reference accenting a color palette with a contrasting color. Muted colors can be paired with a sudden burst of magenta or red, pastels with bright cobalt, or dark colors with a bit of neon yellow. This kind of color conversation is not balanced in equal measurements; it is more like 90 percent for the main colors compared to 10 percent for the accent color, or even less, 97 percent to 3 percent in some cases.

The red-soled shoes, the red lips, the bright-colored scarf or necklace over a black outfit: We have all seen these in fashion editorials and on runways. On home decor TV, the accent-color wall and the pop of color from paint, throw blankets, or pillows are ubiquitous.

Pop here, pop there, pop! pop! everywhere. But what does it achieve?

WHAT IS IT FOR?

The main use of a pop of color is to add an element of surprise and contrast that breaks the stability of an otherwise monotone palette. It adds interest, force, focus, and even humor.

A pop of color is the ultimate interruption.

Think of it as the laughter that stands out in a room full of people, the voice that carries the conversation you are paying attention to at a party.

It can create a visual thread guiding the reader or viewer through a story, like in *The Red Balloon*, or it can serve to identify a specific character and their attributes throughout so many children's books.

The pop of color will add visual interest and tension—good tension—to the color story of the piece or design.

There are many ways to achieve the desired pop of accent color:

- **Tonal contrast:** By working with the tonal structure—how light and dark colors are distributed—find a place of contrast to put the accent. If the overall color story has a lot of light tones, add a contrasting dark, and vice versa. If there are already a variety of tones, then add the pop where it will contrast. Your color scheme can be all pale blues, pale mint, and off-white accented with a deep indigo or jewel tone, or this can be reversed, accenting deep rich colors with a pale and sweet pink. Think of this as contrast by level of lightness and darkness.

- **Difference in saturation:** Now think about the saturation level of the colors as a group—pale pinks and lilacs accented by bright magenta; aged, historic colors cut through with a strike of bright red; chromatic grays and blacks with a sudden high-octane green. As you do this, think about what this accent color is doing, what it means in the context of the piece, and what this disruption represents. Asking these questions may help you select the accent color better.

- **Reverse pop:** We usually think of the accent

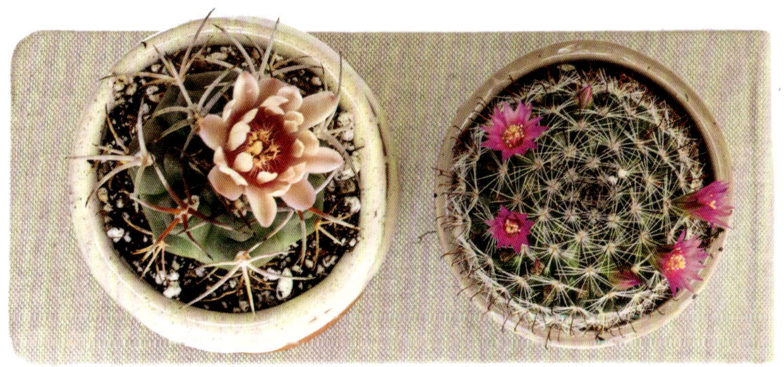

color as a bright color over a field of neutrals, or a saturated color or neon over pastels or even over a white. A reverse pop is the opposite: lots of bright colors with a muted accent, or a scheme of light colors accented with deep reds, dark blues, or purples. A reverse pop achieves the same element of surprise among the subtler nuances of other colors in the palette.

A Battle and the Advent of a Great Accent Color

On June 4, 1859, Vittorio Emmanuele II made a decisive win on his path to unifying Italy. He defeated the Austrians near a town called Magenta in Northern Italy. Around then, a French chemist formulated for the first time a vivid purplish-red synthetic dye, a type of aniline. This color was named magenta to celebrate the victors. It quickly became fashionable and widely used, in part because of an early case of branding and in part because it offered a much cheaper alternative to precious cochineal.

Personally, though I was not into Barbie or pink as a kid, I now love all variations and derivations of magenta: hot pink, neon pink, opera pink, raspberry, Mexican pink, fuchsia, and more. I love them for a pop of color. Magenta has a special place in my recurrent color palette, from the pinkest to the reddest variations, from pale to jewel tones.

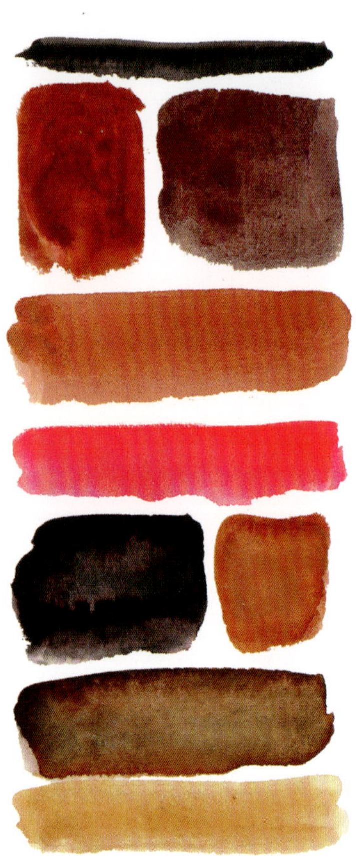

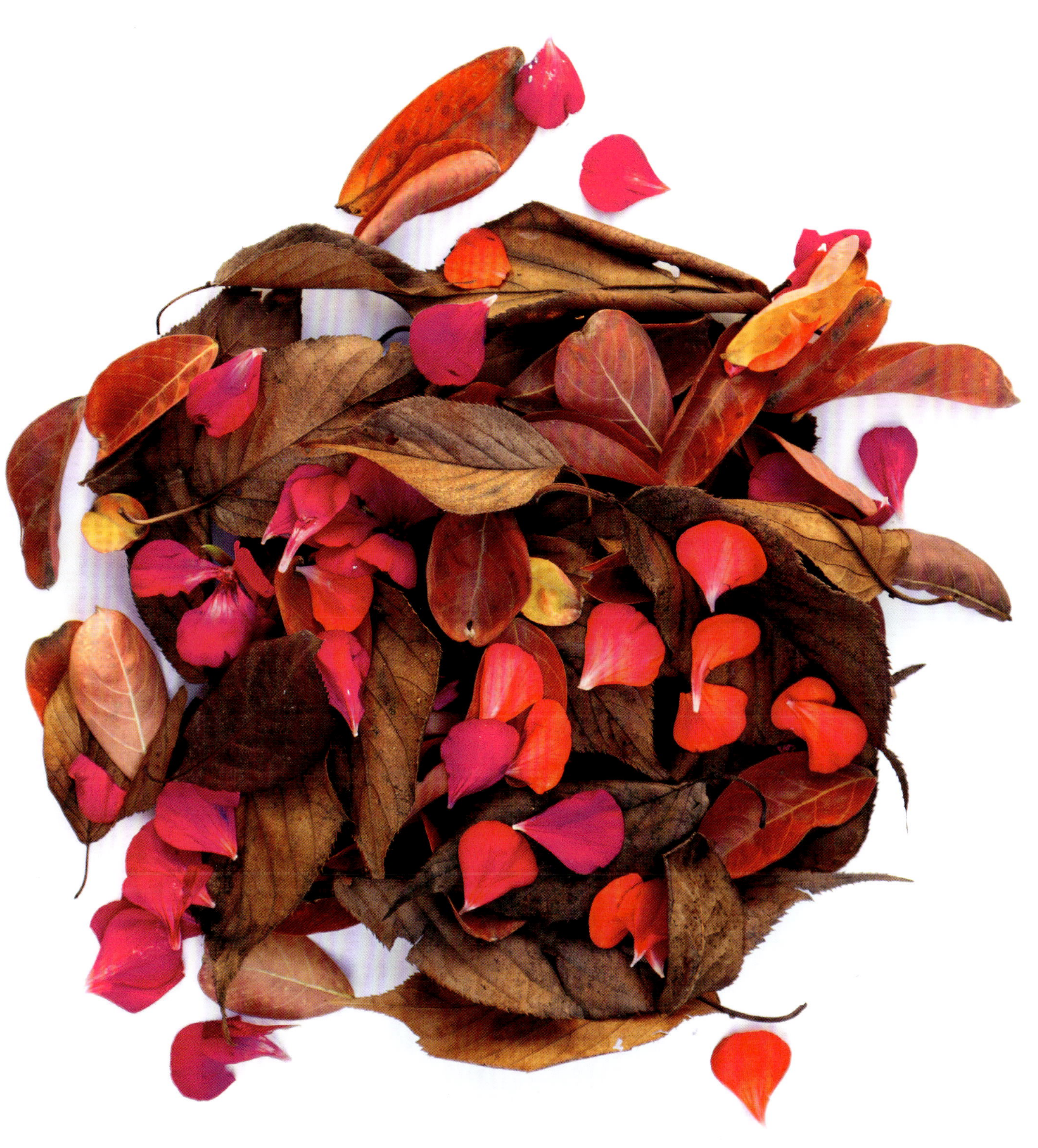

NEON: THE GREAT INTERRUPTER

While a pop of color or a contrasting accent can be created in many ways, few things catch our eye like neon. It is used in advertisements to announce *Sale! New! Buy now!* Those spiky stickers on a product or store shelf are there to distract us from the panorama of products and extend their neon hands into our wallets.

The neon orange cones on the roads signal to us that the traffic is interrupted or road work is happening; *PROCEED WITH CAUTION*, they say. This would not work with pale orange.

We use neon markers to highlight salient points in an ocean of black-on-white pages. Those pops of color facilitate fishing for ideas during a second browse.

Neon can be tacky if abused, but it can be quite powerful when used with restraint and intention, when it falls in the right place, ready to get our attention: the ultimate visual bait.

Fluorescence exists in nature. Fluorite is an element that has the special quality of absorbing light and sending it back amplified. Many minerals, rocks, and even corals contain elements that render them fluorescent. So many insects and fish are fluorescent! If you were to go out into the dark water with a black light flashlight, you would see their bodies glowing.

Many of us have enjoyed a humid summer night with fireflies signaling for love all around us with their bioluminescent bodies or seen videos of ocean life that glows at night. While bioluminescence is chemically different from fluorescence, the effect on the viewer is the same: a bright, luminous burst of life in the dark or in an otherwise bland landscape.

Inspired by the bright moments in nature and paired with advances in pigment chemistry, neon colorings were formulated in the early twentieth century as a dye mostly for scientific purposes. While neither these nor modern neon paints contain fluoride, the term *fluorescent* was used to describe them. Later, in the '30s, these bright paints were released commercially for use on safety signs

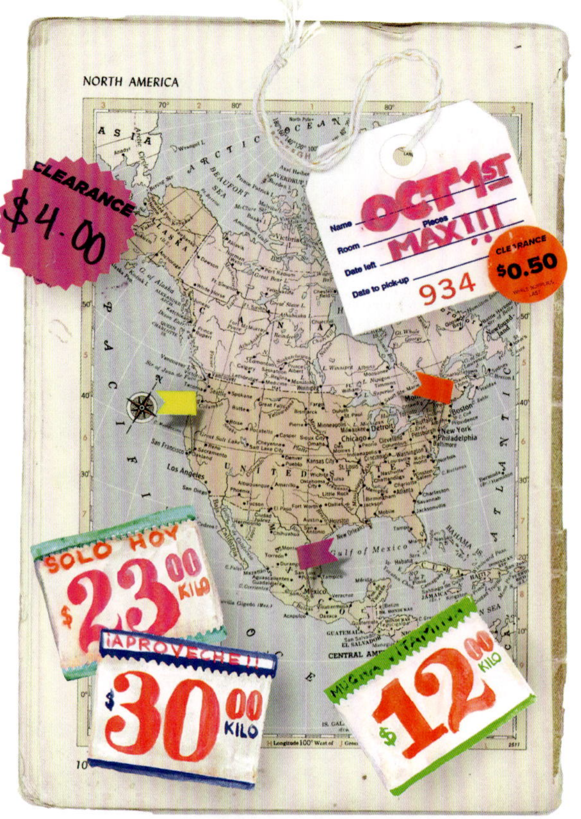

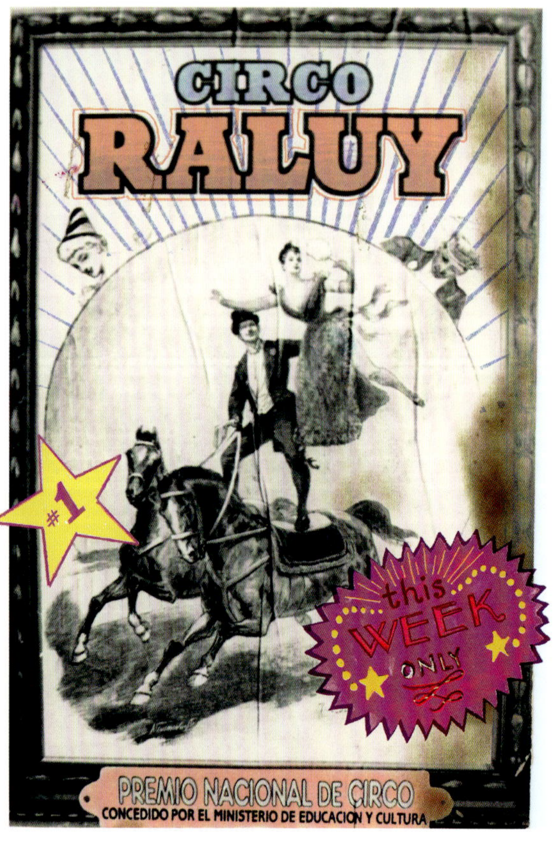

and in various industrial and scientific applications.

It was in the flower-powered '60s that neon colors really burst into popular culture and style. They marked a moment of convergence between chemistry and psychedelia. The chemists Robert and Joseph Switzer started their pigment company in 1946, developing a line of fluorescent colors called DayGlo. Over time, DayGlo became synonymous with fluorescence. The Switzers' dyes, pigments, and paints came in handy when a generation of young people wanted to create a new order contrary to their conservative parents. Ideological freedom and psychedelic experiences found the perfect ally in the bright DayGlo paints. From concert posters to groovy fashions (especially those made with all the new synthetic fabrics) to acrylic and plastic furnishings for modern homes, neon colors became all the rage, the color voice of a generation looking to shake up the conservative establishment and get society to notice their peace-and-love ideology.

Since then, the use of fluorescent colors has waxed and waned. It has lived on in the party scene in discos and nightclubs since the '70s, when clothes in luminous tones were the thing to wear under the black lights and strobes of the dance floor. In urban culture, streetwear designers and graffiti artists have always had an eye for spray paint in bright colors. Posters, books, and all kinds of graphic design applications often rely on fluorescents for a pop of color to catch someone's attention.

Fluorescent colors also have made a crossover into fine art with the development of a wider range of art materials available in neon. A friend of mine, the talented painter Dorielle Caimi, loves a neon accent. Her realistic oil paintings often feature DayGlo yellow and opera pink, the hottest pink gets before becoming neon. Once, out of curiosity or maybe research, to shock her audience and collectors, she took one of her beautiful Dutch-style floral portraits and added a strident yellow graffiti-style … ahem … penis, and then asked online if the painting was better with or without the fluorescent intervention. Surprisingly, most people agreed that this attention-grabbing addition did take the little painting into a whole new realm. The contrast between the beautiful and the sordid, the carefully painted florals and skin versus the graphic scribble of a phallus, made it quite contemporary

and powerful! I also think that in a gallery wall, that bright interruption would definitely have been an attention grabber even if it had just been a happy face.

I love hot-pink accents, including on Mexican pastries! (Just see the cover of this chapter.) I love to combine this color with neutrals, from the palest off-white to beiges and browns to dark gray, like the wool of a black sheep. I love bumping into it as a bright thread in an embroidered kitchen towel or in a vintage flower-power printed fabric. I saw it in graffiti in New York City and on walls in small Mexican towns announcing a banda concert in completely over-the-top lettering. I love it combined with both red and pale pink, or with dusty periwinkle and any blue green, from a pale lichen to the brightest turquoise. I once bought a sari in India that was pale pistachio with neon pink details and turned it into a dress for a wedding. When I travel, I always have a neon pink pencil in my portable art kit, lest the need for a pop in a drawing arise.

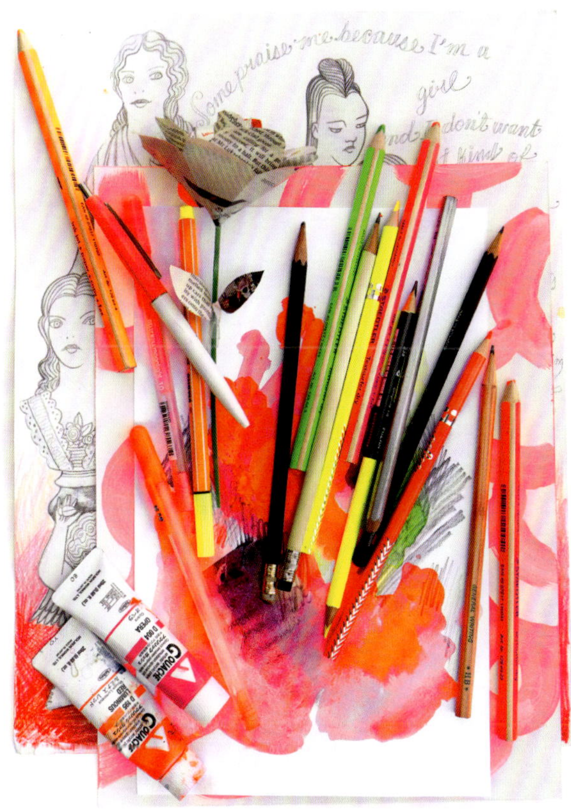

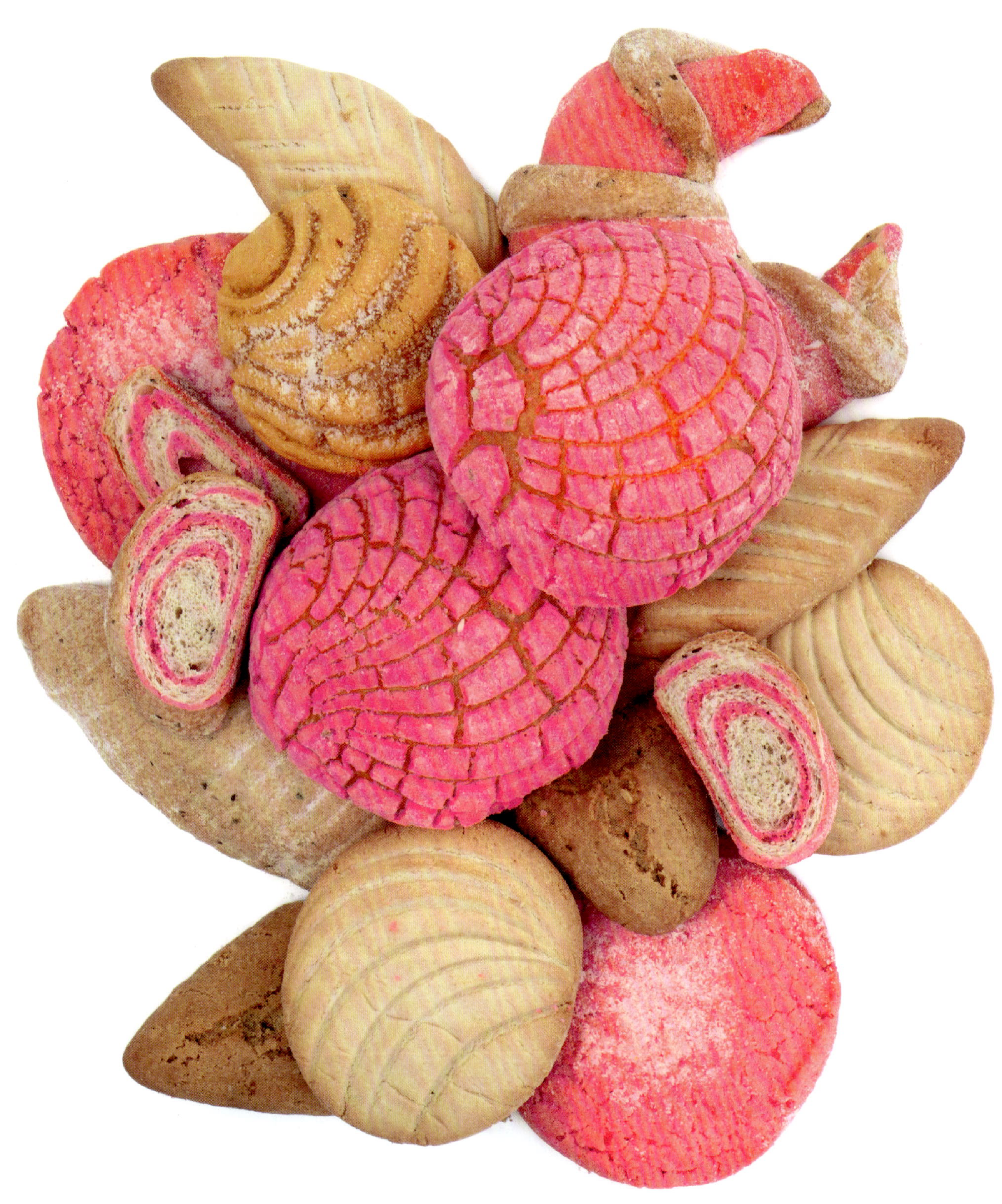

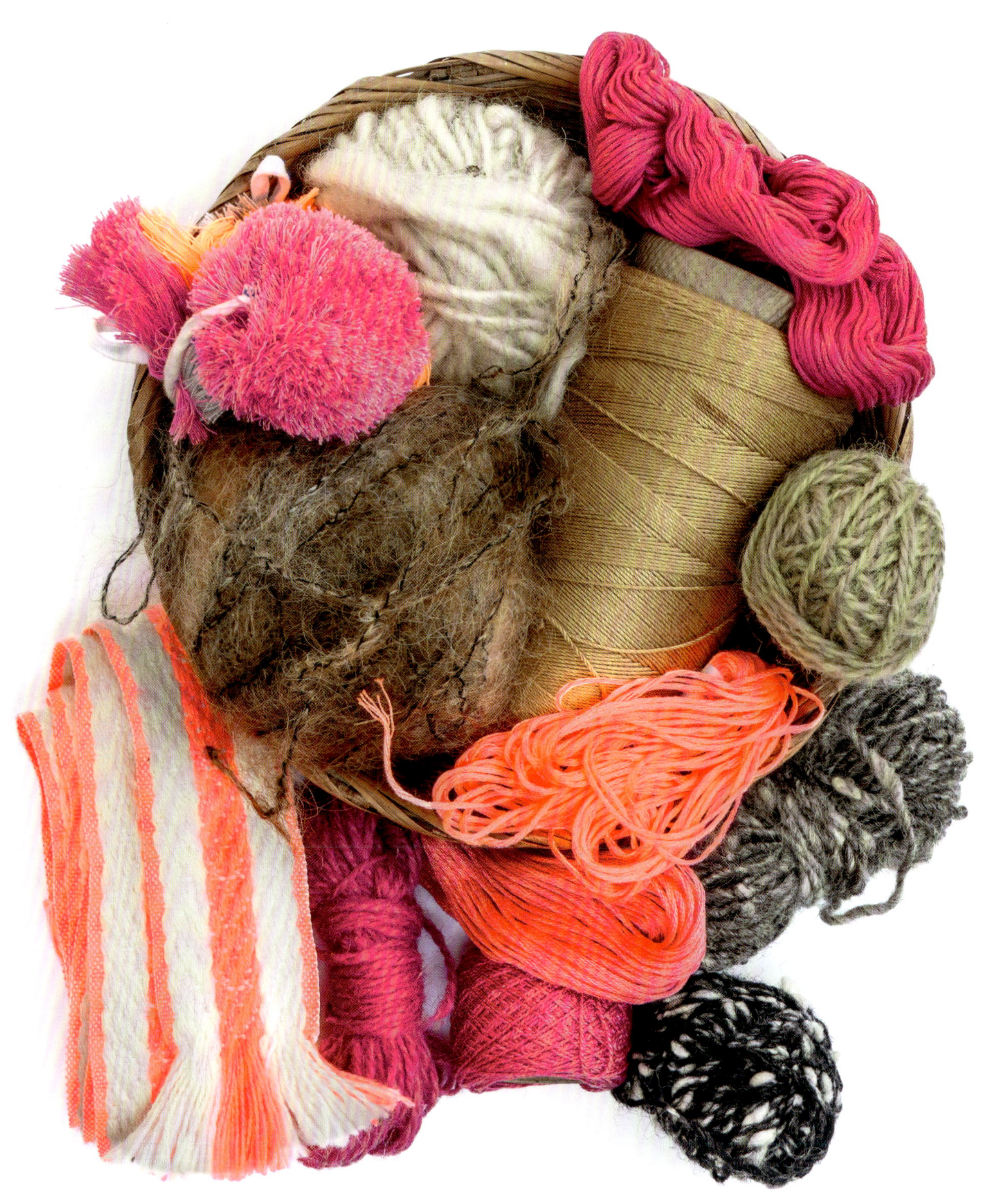

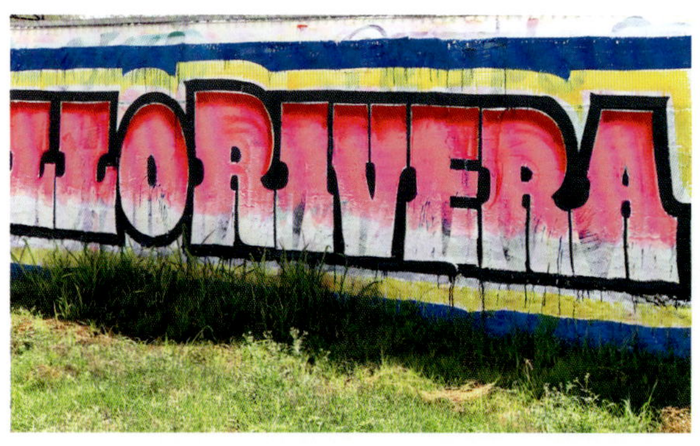

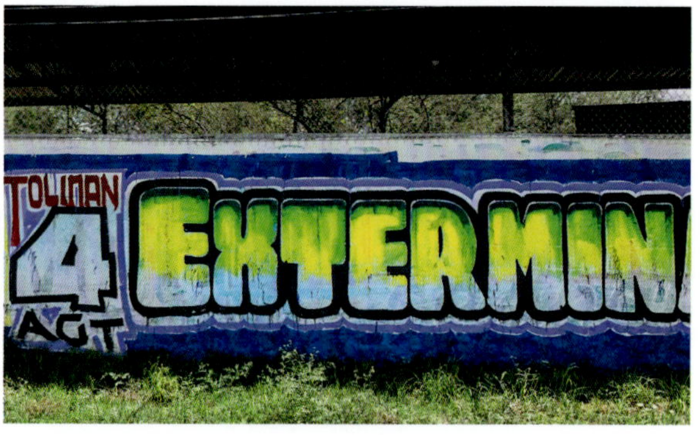

Phosphorescence: The Prolonged Glow

There are a few differences between fluorescence and phosphorescence.

Neons are bright in daylight or under black light, while phosphorescence only shines when it is dark. But the biggest difference between regular neons and phosphorescence is the duration of the glow: While fluorescence and bioluminescence are momentous, phosphorescence offers a prolonged emission of light. The object "charges" when there is light, natural or artificial, and that charge keeps it glowing for a while in the dark. Think of the dials on watches or the stars on the ceiling of your kid's room. In nature, only certain minerals and rocks have this kind of prolonged glow-in-the-dark ability, along with a few fungi that can absorb light and reemit it over a period of time. Lately, I heard of some GMO petunias with white flowers that can "charge" during the day and then emit a green glow all night. Just imagine having this in your garden or on your deck! Magical? Tacky? Well, definitely expensive, as each plant costs over twenty dollars.

For prolonged glow in print media, there is glow-in-the-dark ink, which I have seen used brilliantly—pun intended—in children's books to make ghosts appear or to present two books in one: the story with the light on and the story with the light off.[15]

Neon and CMYK

Occasionally seen in children's books[16] and rarely in others, neon printing can be a powerful companion to CMYK. It is done by preparing your design files with an extra channel in the image (in Photoshop) or an extra spot ink (in Illustrator or InDesign); this will indicate to the printer that besides the four basic inks, they will have to prepare a fifth inkwell with this extra neon ink.

Usually the neon spot color is applied first, and then on top of it the basic four, CMYK, are printed. Since CMYK inks are translucent, they will benefit from the neon underprinting for an extra boost in brightness and zing.

Neon can be printed as solid areas, with or without CMYK on top. Solid areas without any overprinting are especially bright and signal a place to rest our attention, such as the main character or something sudden that appeared in the story.

Neon can also be treated like any other ink, used at 100 percent or in a variety of tints. There is something quite amazing about a pastel that is also neon. This may sound like an oxymoron, but you can try it by getting a neon watercolor or acrylic paint and using it both at full strength and diluted, or mixed with white.

NATURAL VERSUS SYNTHETIC COLOR WITH NEON

The range of colors available nowadays is vast, larger than ever. From the natural colors of plants, animals, and minerals to the synthetic, human-made pigments—from the palest to the most high-powered bright neons. They are all there at our service.

I remember the first time I set foot in the legendary Zecchi, an art store in the center of Florence, and saw the wall of jars full of all the pigments. They had superfine pigments like real lapis lazuli and malachite green bought by art restorers working on medieval pieces. There was a whole range of mineral pigments and mason stains to be used in frescoes, and then there were those brilliant modern synthetic pigments, in general safer than the old counterparts (yes, vermilion and cinnabar, I am looking at you, with your mercury!). Like a kid in a candy store, I drooled.

My teachers had taught me how to use the pigments to create egg tempera (a technique historically used in religious iconography on gilded wood panels), how to mix them into watercolor to use on paper, and how to grind them in linseed oil to turn a pigment into oil paint. Like any art student, I barely had money for art materials, but I did save enough to buy some pigments before I left Florence. I still have those pigments, in vintage jars and bottles, so precious to me that I have barely used them. They are a color treasure I keep and may soon gather the courage to finally turn into watercolor pastilles.

The only time these pigments were fully used was when my boxer dog dropped the jar with magenta pigment, got her paws pink, and walked all over my studio's white floor. Talk about a pop of color! Those pink pawprints stayed forever, such is the magic of pure pigment: It is so concentrated and rich!

It is easy to go all the way down the rabbit hole of pigments and dyes. It would take a whole book to talk about them in depth, and probably a degree in chemistry too. But just for eye candy, here is a snapshot of some of my favorite pigments: natural colors, synthetic ones, dyes from plants, rocks, and animals, earthy colors from the soil, and bright, industrial-grade neon, in case I need to interrupt something subtle.

↓ Jars of pure pigment on the shelves of Zecchi in Florence.

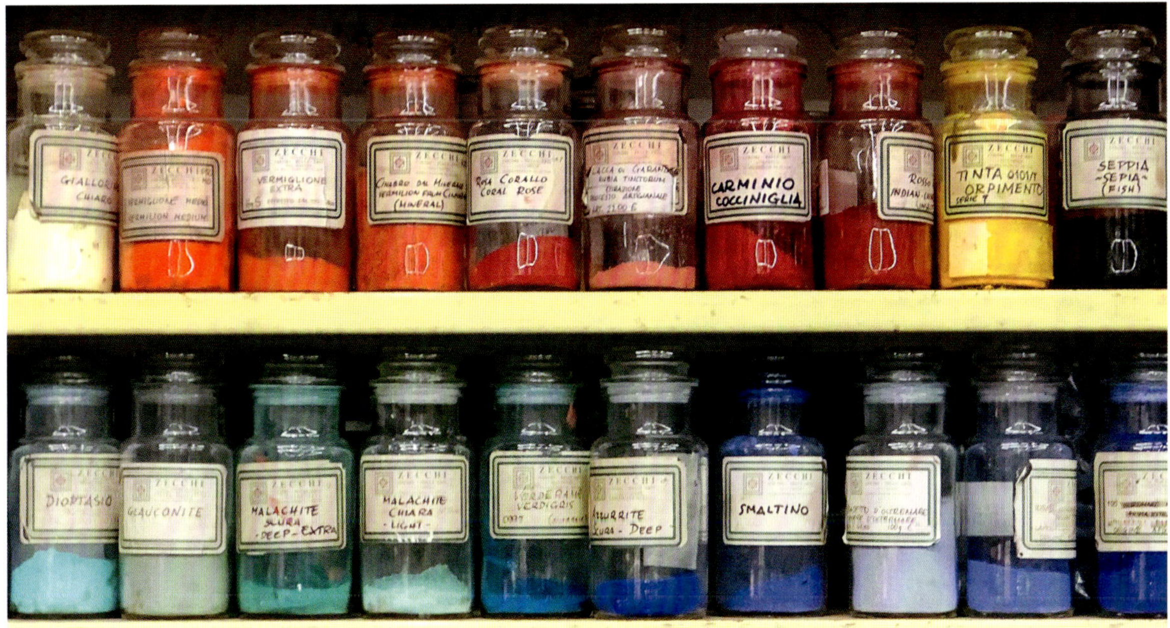

Going to the Tlapalería

In Mexico, a hardware store is not called ferreteria (related to fierros, *a Spanish word meaning* metals*); it is called tlapalería. This Aztec-derived word, very much used in Mexico, refers to a place to buy colors or paints. Tlapali was actually the name used for red, specifically the precious cochineal—the beautiful carmine-colored pigment obtained from crushing the little bugs that plague some varieties of cacti.*

In the Florentine Codex, *a sixteenth-century book written by the Spanish friar Bernardino de Sahagún as he was getting to know Mexico, he describes in detail in side-by-side columns—Castilian on one and Náhuat on the other—tlapali color vendors in the tianguis (markets). The book's original title is* The General History of the Things of New Spain, *and as truthfully and vividly as he saw in the market, the descriptions of pigments, from cochineal to minerals and botanicals, from the origin of each to their uses in murals and as textile dyes, are a delight to read.*

KEY TAKEAWAYS

1. One can create contrast in many ways, not only with neon or bright red. Think of the pop as the accent to break up the other colors' harmony. It calls attention to whatever is important. Observe the various ways to create an accent in the following pages.

2. This disruption will become a focal point; use it wisely and purposefully.

3. Neon colors are powerful showstoppers; they can be used with restraint as an accent or with full intensity, like in 1960s posters. When you use them, think about what the right dose is for the piece you are creating and what you are using them for.

4. When creating an illustration or a layout for a book, remember that in print, neon color can be underprinted to increase the intensity of CMYK.

5. Neon colors can be used at full intensity or tinted to create fluorescent pastels. They can also be mixed into other paint colors to intensify them.

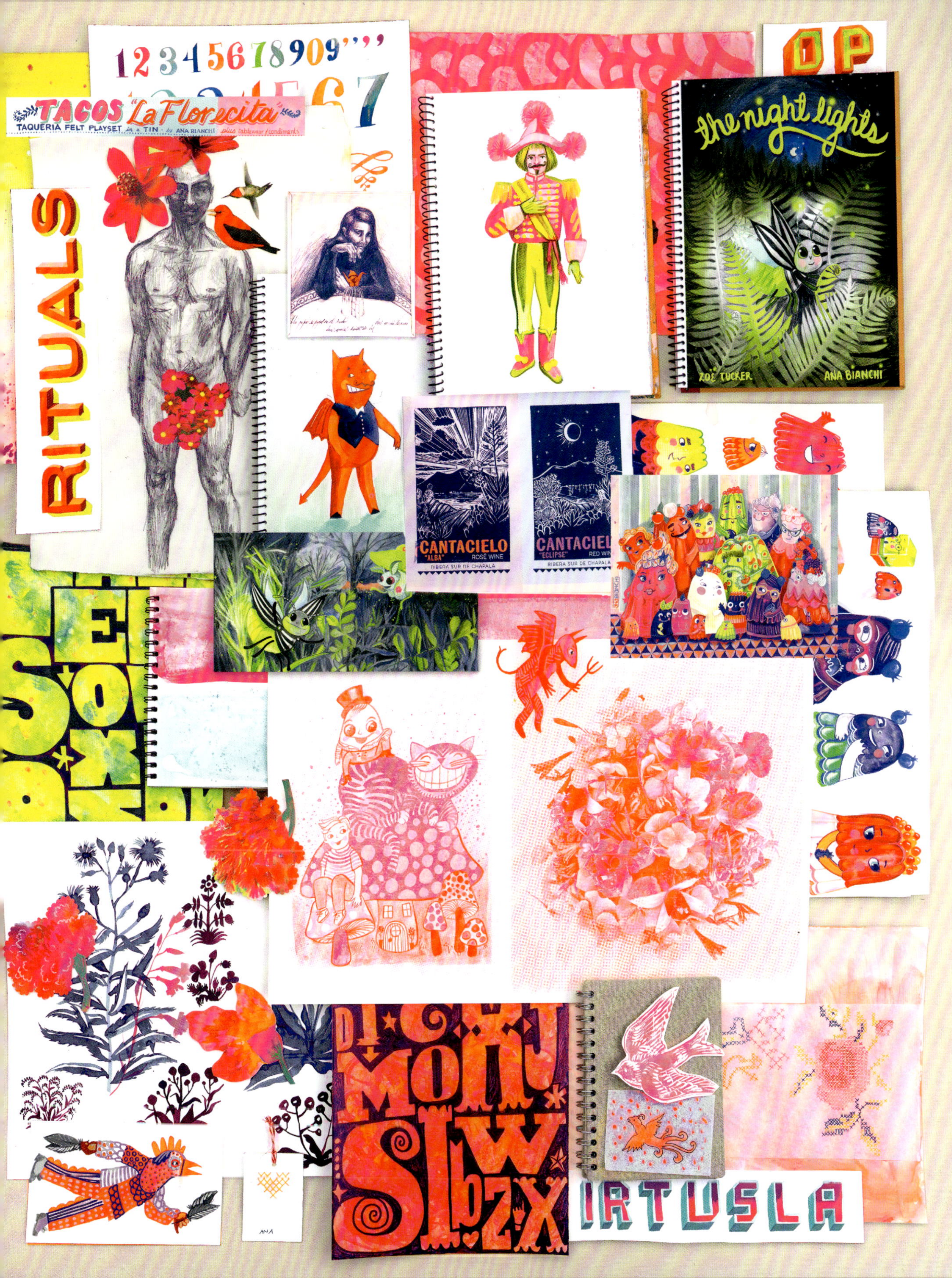

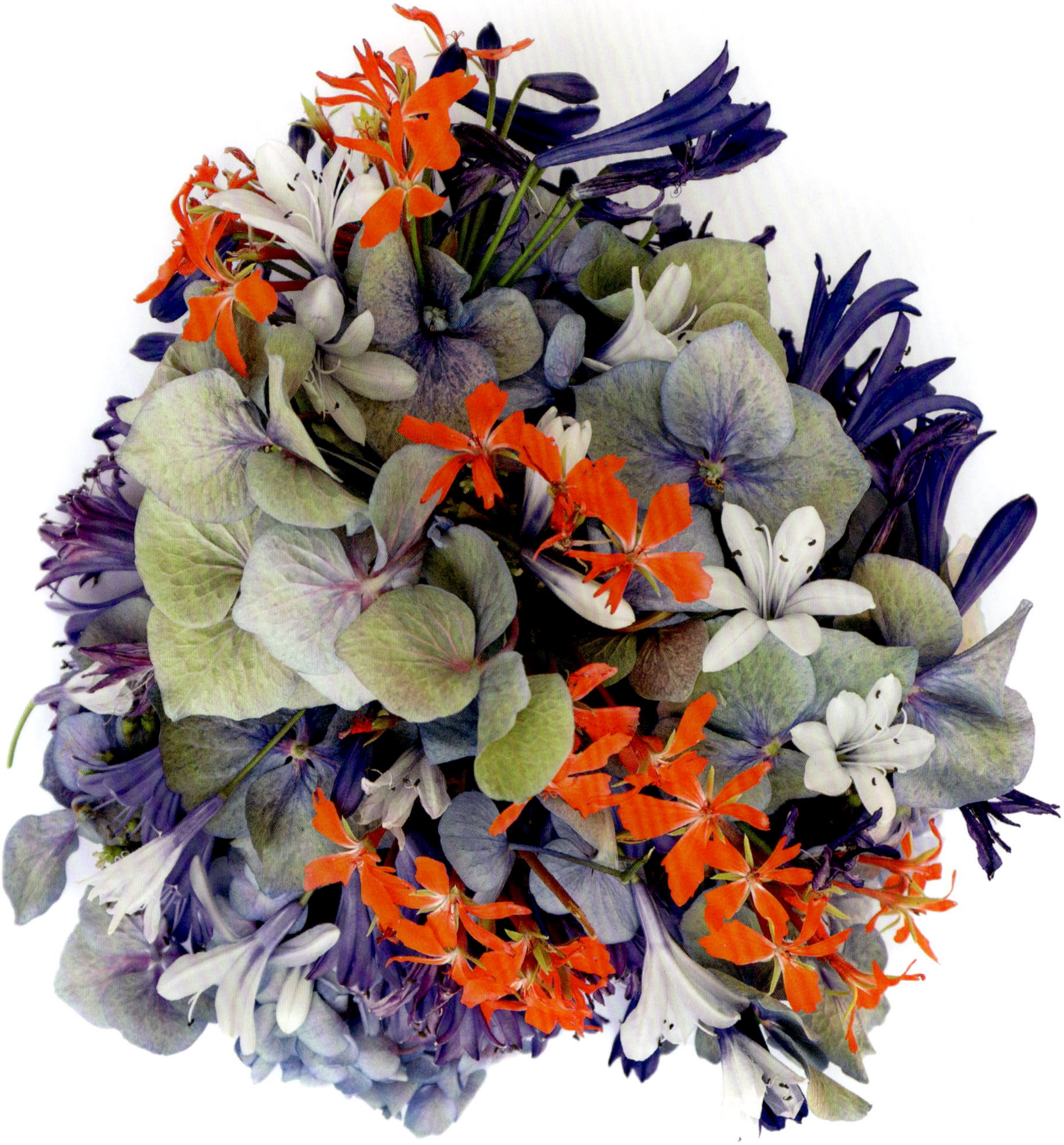

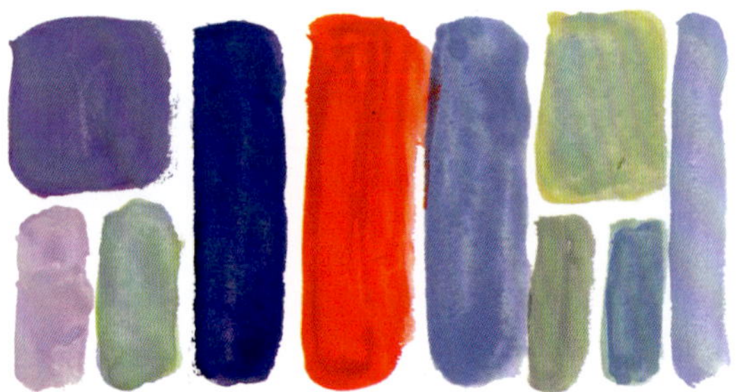

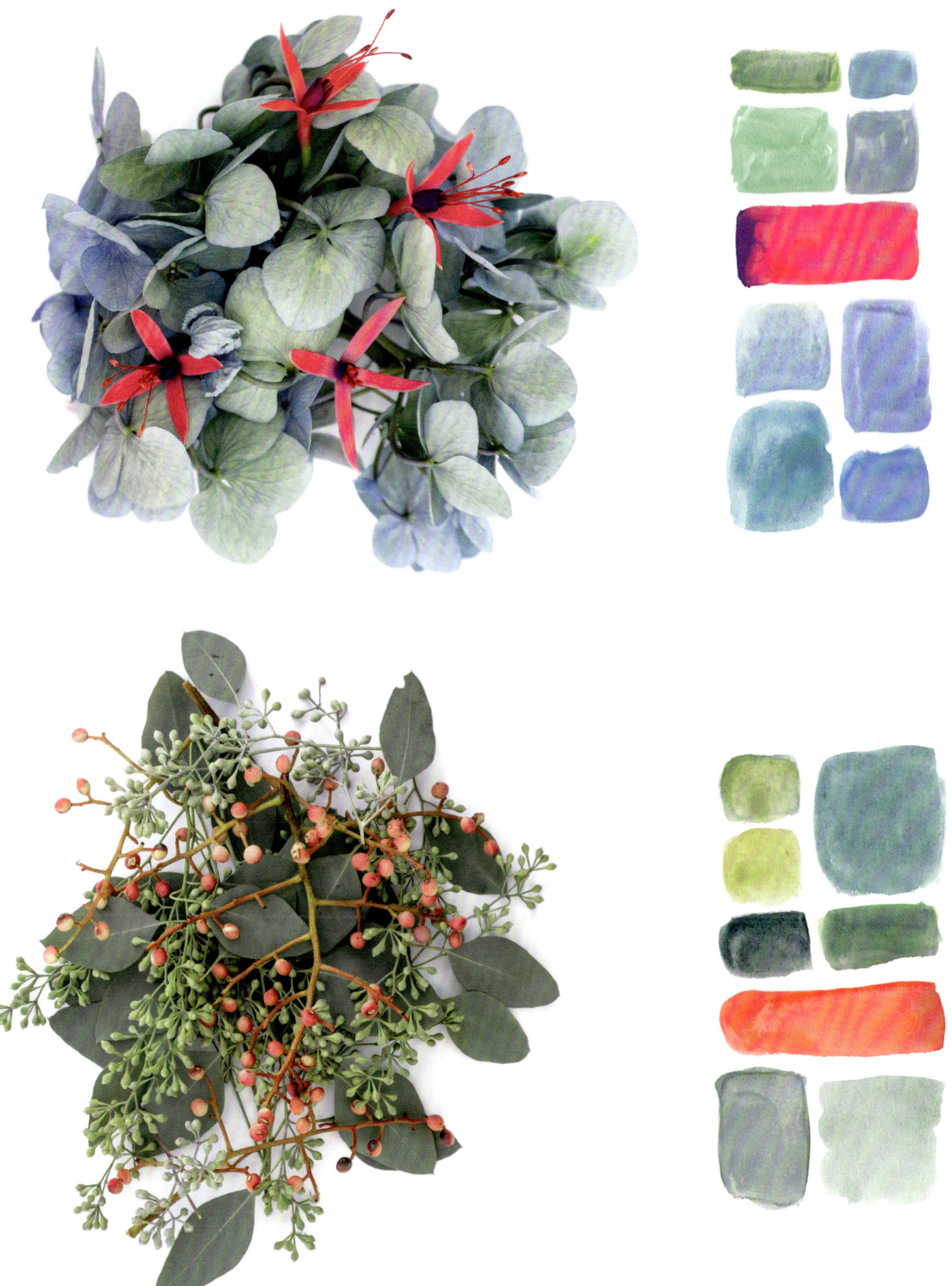

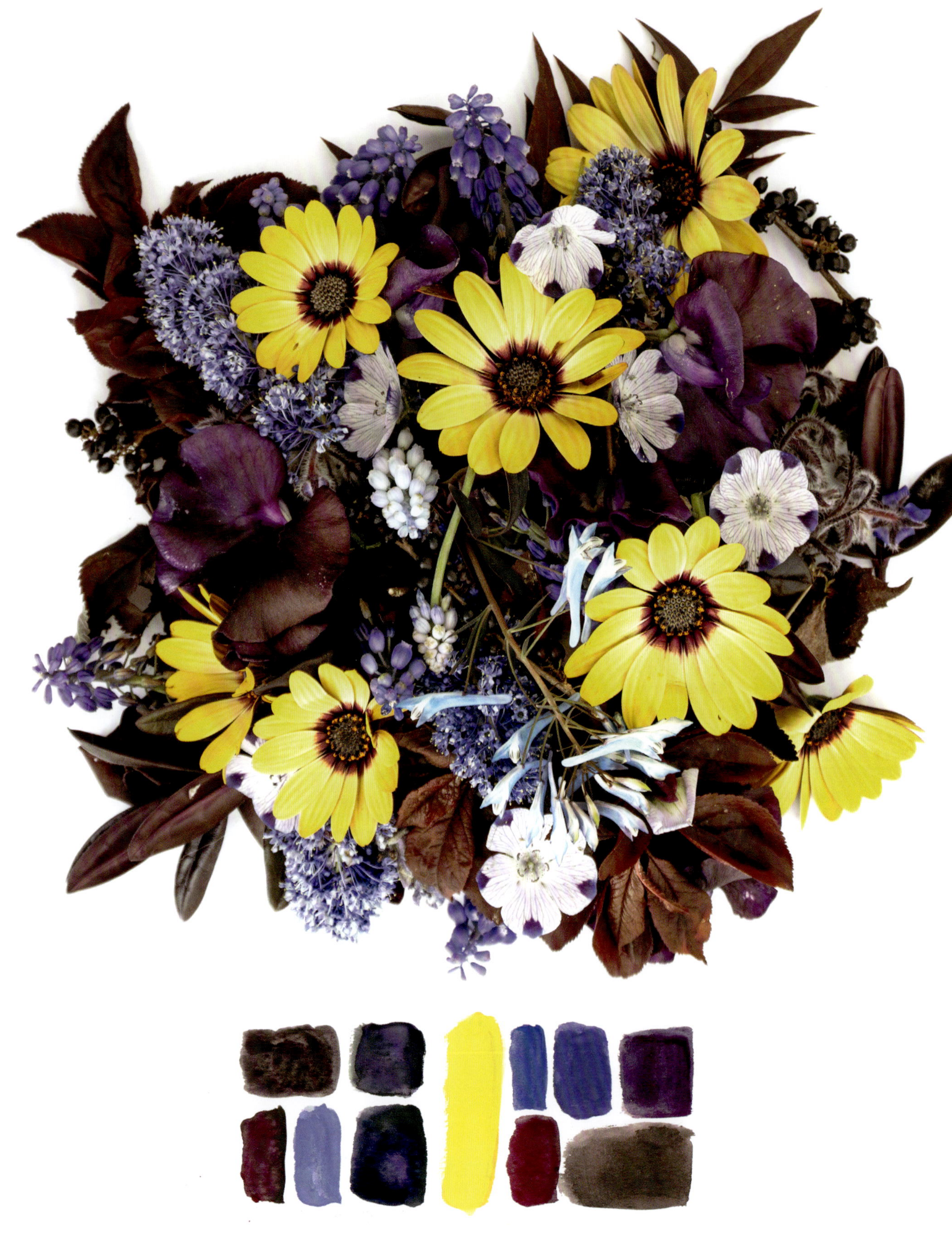

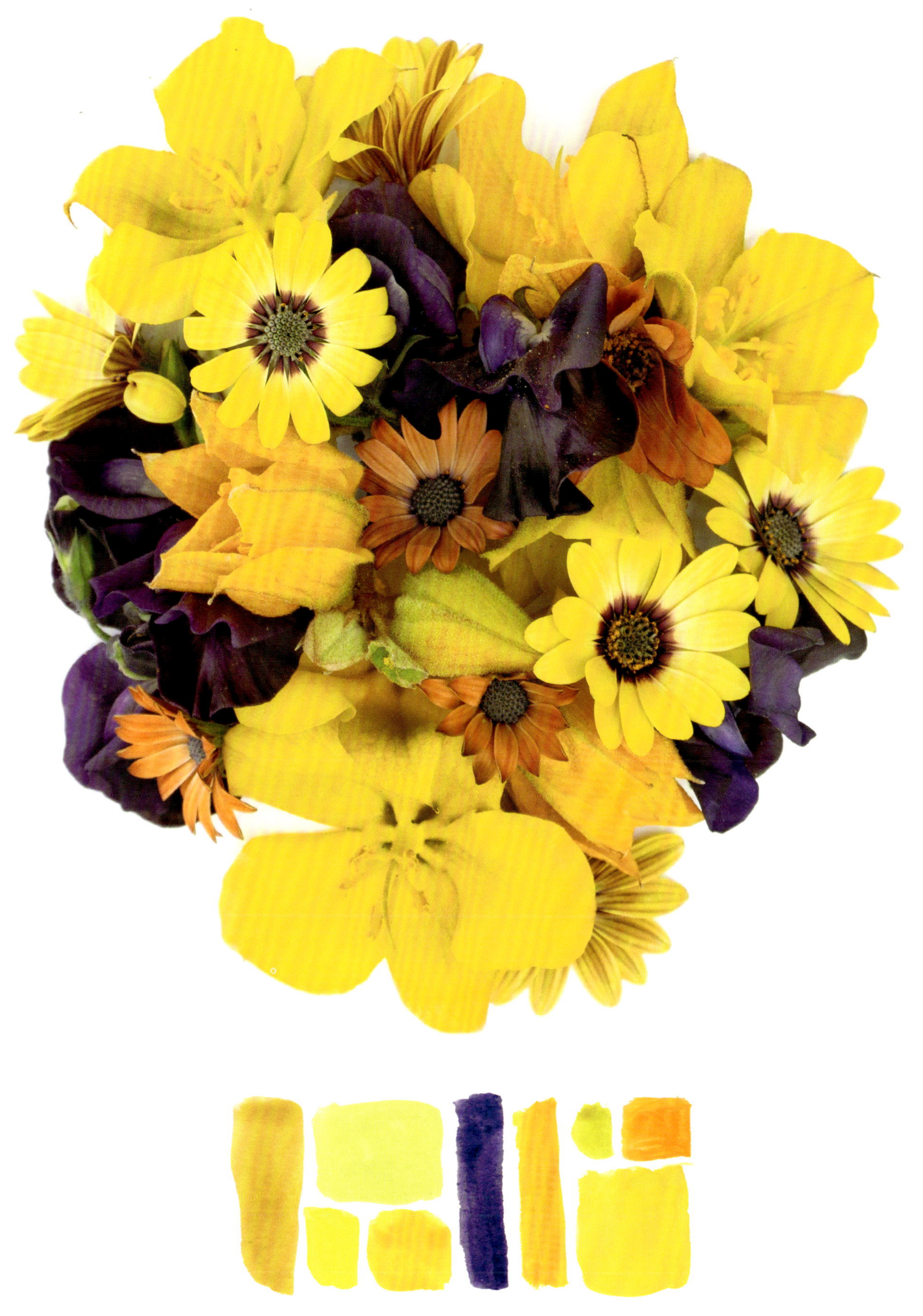

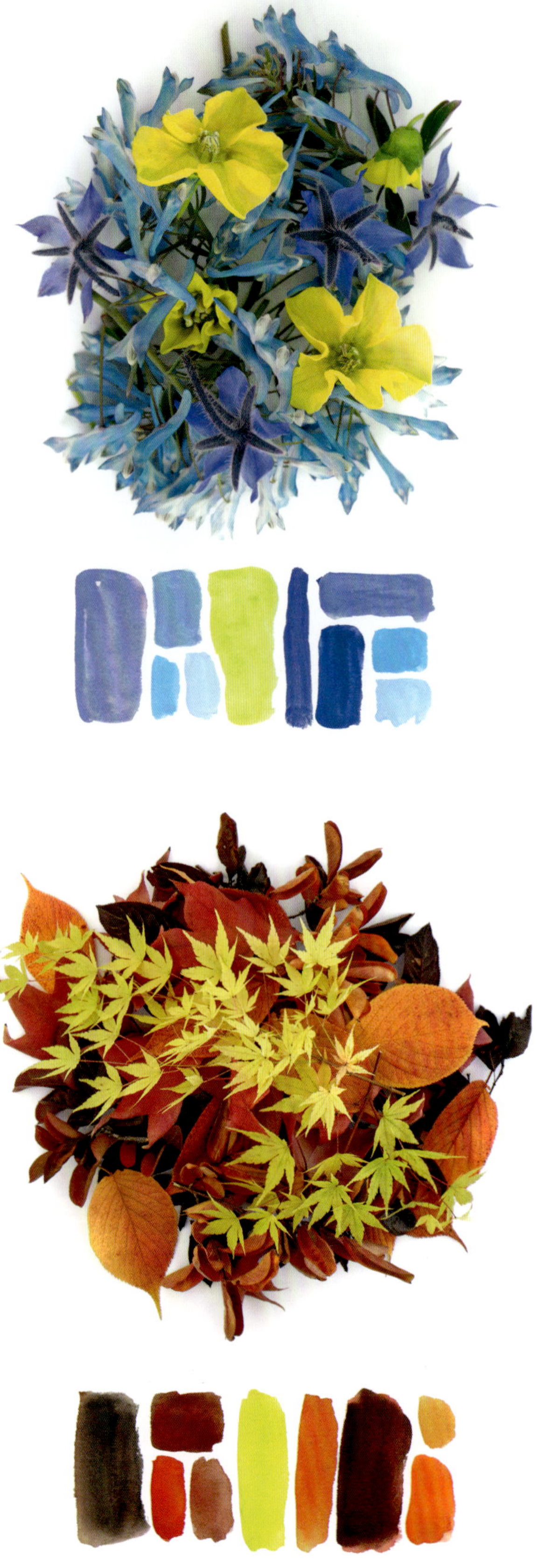

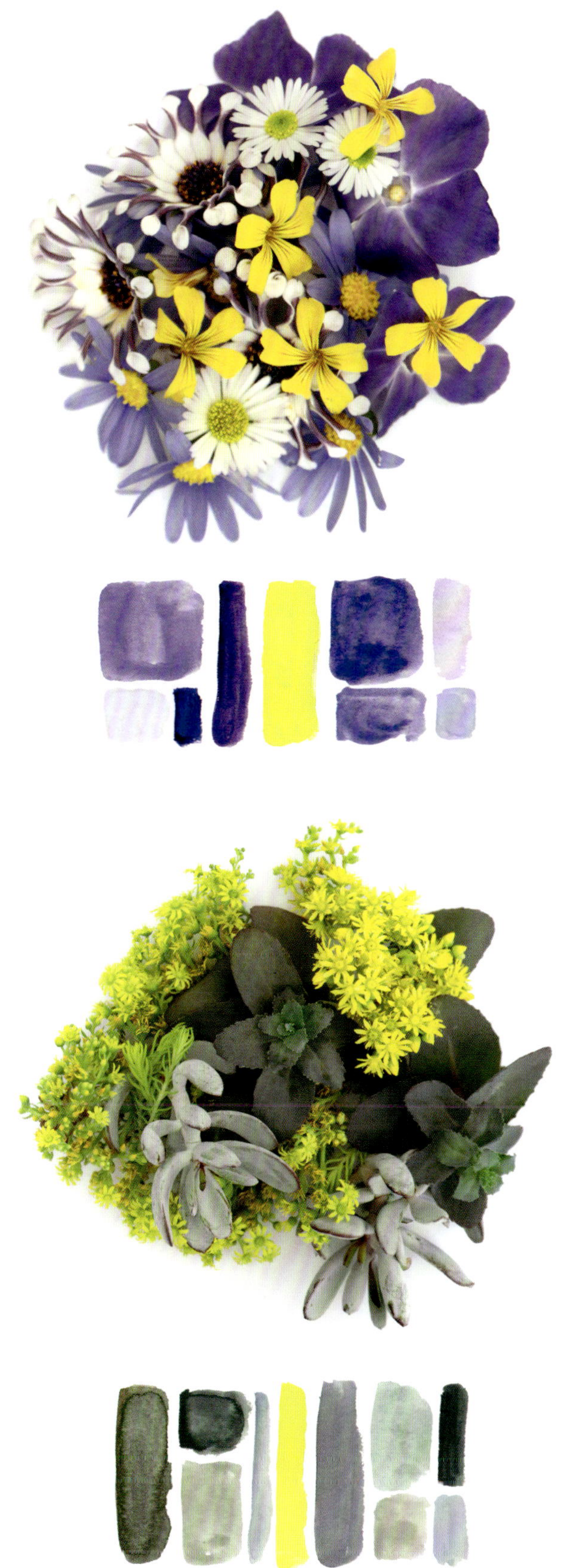

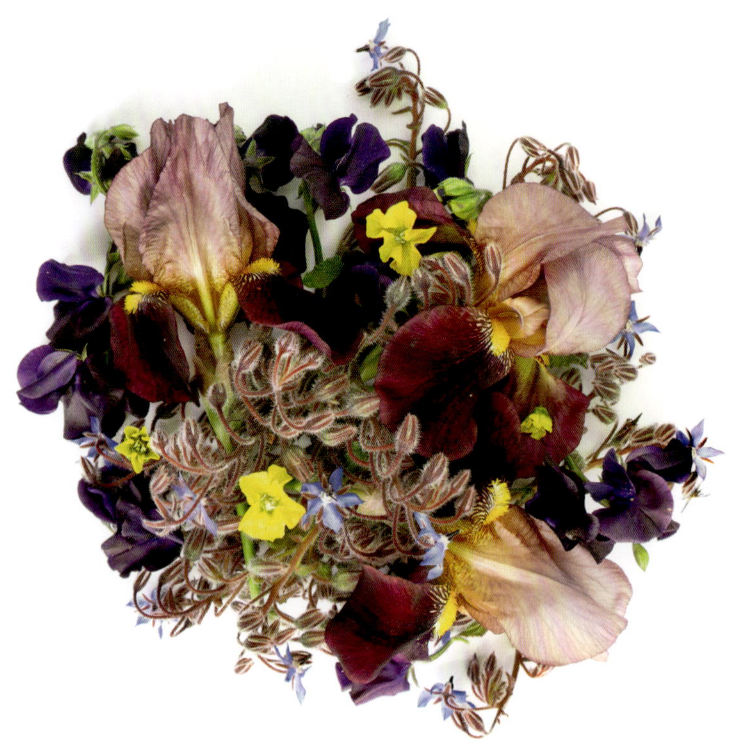
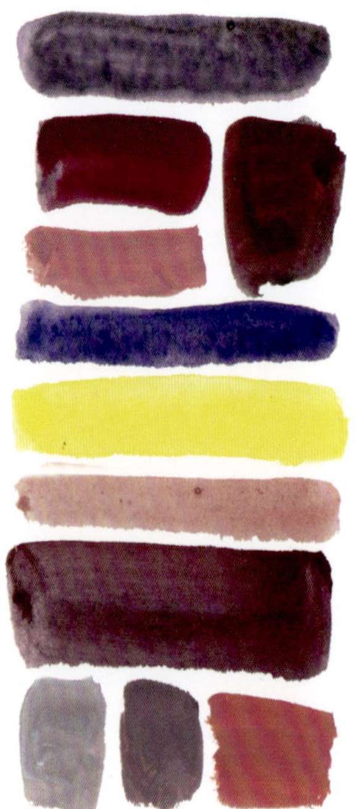
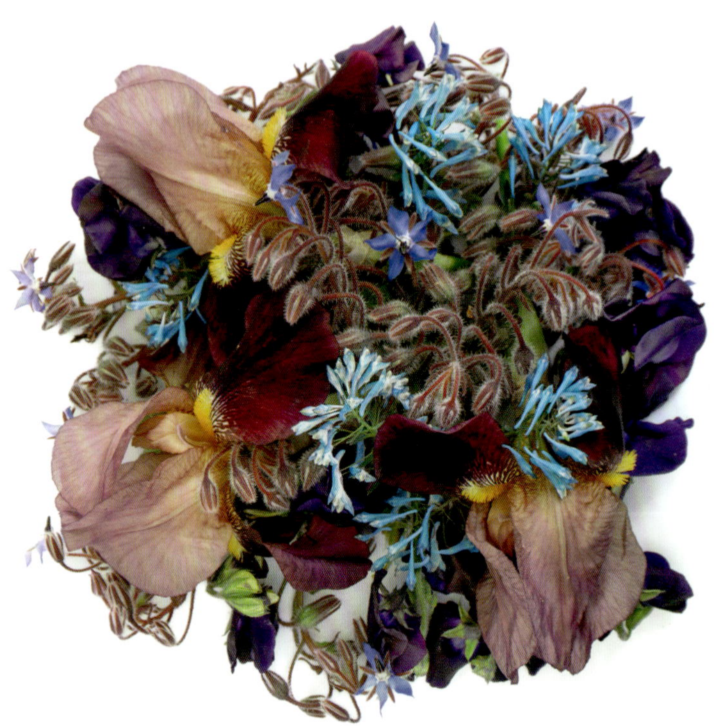

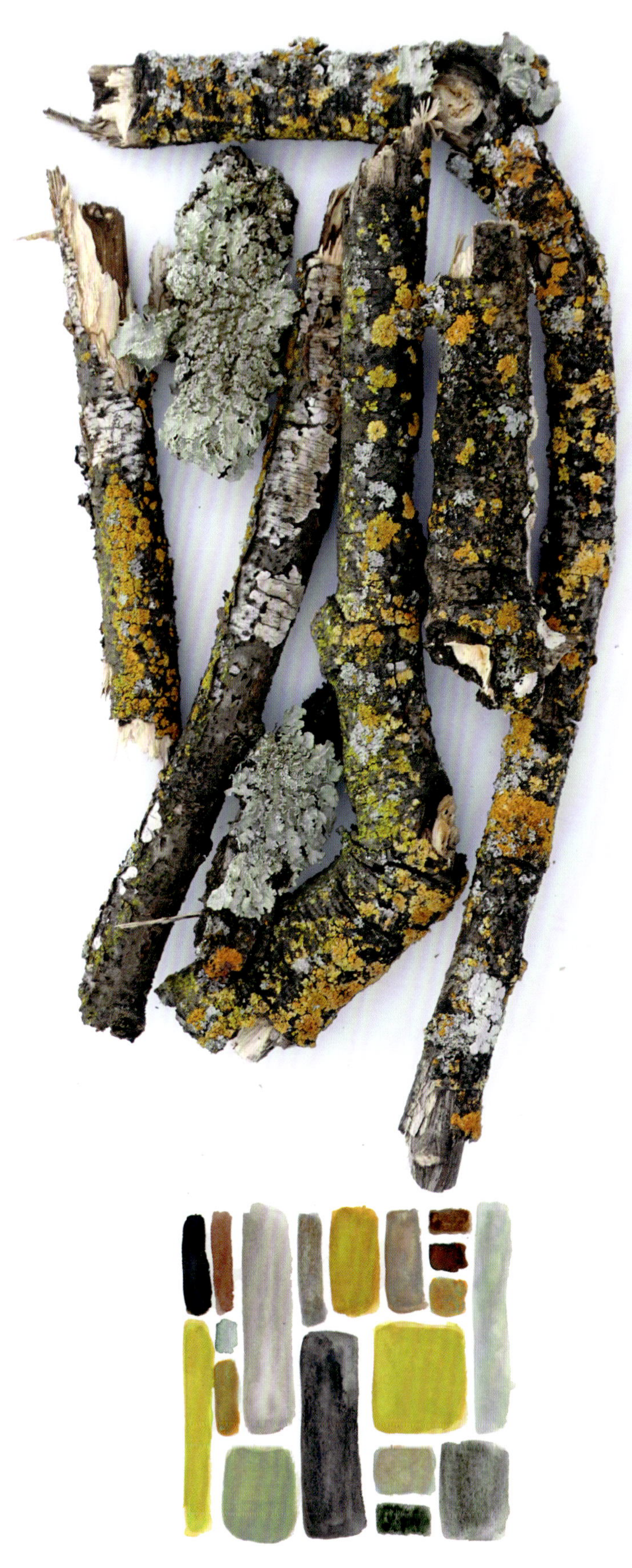

PROJECT

OBSERVE: Observe the many ways to create a pop of color. Observe this chapter's cover to see how the hot pink relates to all the neutrals. Revisit pages 196–205 with the photos of botanical groupings and their palettes for a closer look at how the different ways to create an accent work, and consider how the accent color, bright or dark, creates contrast and visual interest.

Look back at work you've done in the past, projects you like or even some pieces you are not really proud of for one reason or another. Look especially for pieces where the color palette is quite even: all neutrals, all muted colors, all deep dark tones, or all brights, where everything seems to have the same level of intensity as you reconsider them. Ask yourself whether they are perfect as is or whether they could benefit from a pop of color.

ANALYZE: Analyze your usual art materials—paints, fabric, threads, collage elements, ceramic glazes, whatever you use in your creative practice. Select your favorite medium and think of what might be the best way to "interrupt" each set of colors or materials. If you work with textiles in fashion or interior design, remember that the pop of color can be enhanced by a change of texture in the materials—for example, wool in neutral colors with bright-colored silk or cotton, or shiny silk onto which you add felting accents.

CREATE: Create an "interruption" with neon colors (or another highly saturated color) on an existing image to change its aesthetics or meaning. Some ideas you could try:

- **Find a vintage image:** On page 190, I used an old sepia photo of a circus poster) and add color accents to accentuate some details. This will be a merely aesthetic exercise.
- **Find vintage photos** and enhance and transform them into something different using only a neon or saturated color. You can add a dialogue box to create a cartoon with humor, you can overdecorate them, or you can add elements like more characters or an exaggeration. Think of when you used to draw a mustache or paint red lips on the portraits of your history book (at least, I did that, not proud of it ...).

  This will be an exercise in adding humor or narrative elements. I am using scans of these old portraits of members of my paternal family, which are mostly from the 1910s to the 1930s, and working digitally on them. The original photos are too precious to paint over.
- **Find an old painting** at a thrift store or flea market—it can be a still life or perhaps a vase of flowers or a portrait. Don't buy an expensive painting, because you will be paintcoloing over it! It can even be something a bit tacky, perhaps an imitation of an Old

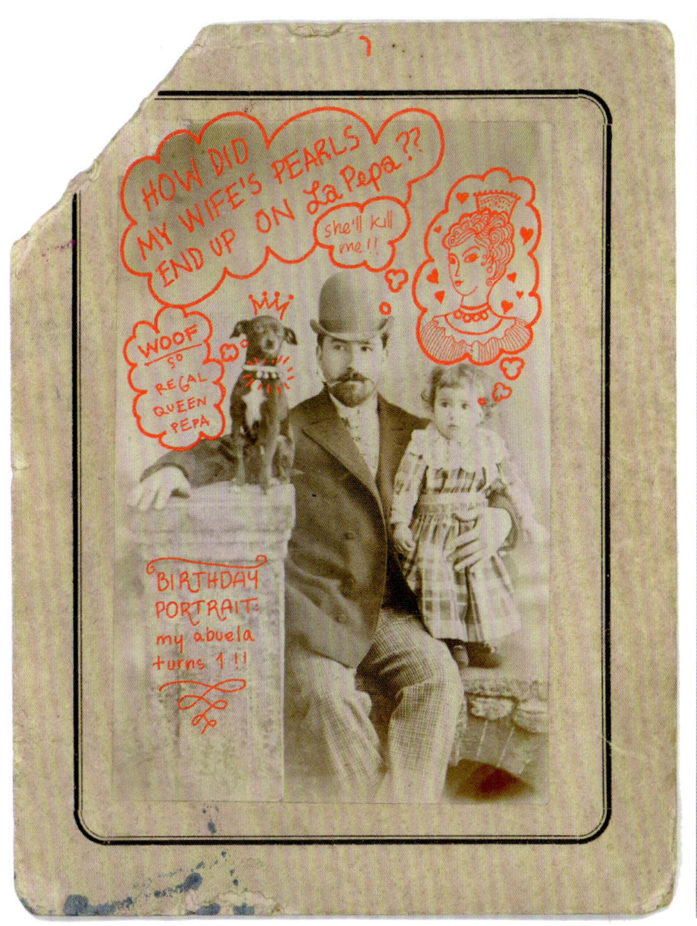

HOW DID MY WIFE'S PEARLS END UP ON La Pepa??
she'll kill me!!
WOOF SO REGAL QUEEN PEPA
BIRTHDAY PORTRAIT: my abuela turns 1!!

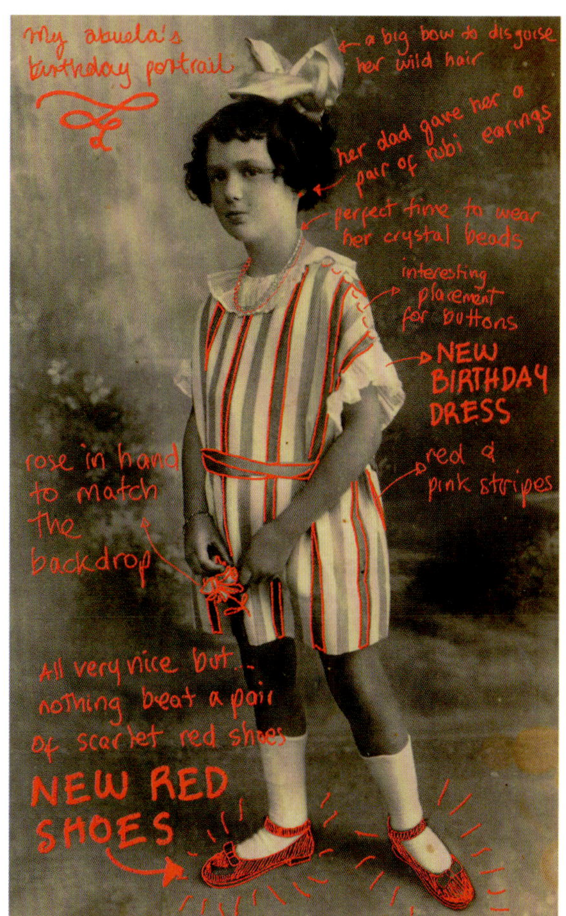

my abuela's birthday portrait
a big bow to disguise her wild hair
her dad gave her a pair of rubi earrings
perfect time to wear her crystal beads
interesting placement for buttons
NEW BIRTHDAY DRESS
red & pink stripes
rose in hand to match the backdrop
All very nice but... nothing beat a pair of scarlet red shoes
NEW RED SHOES

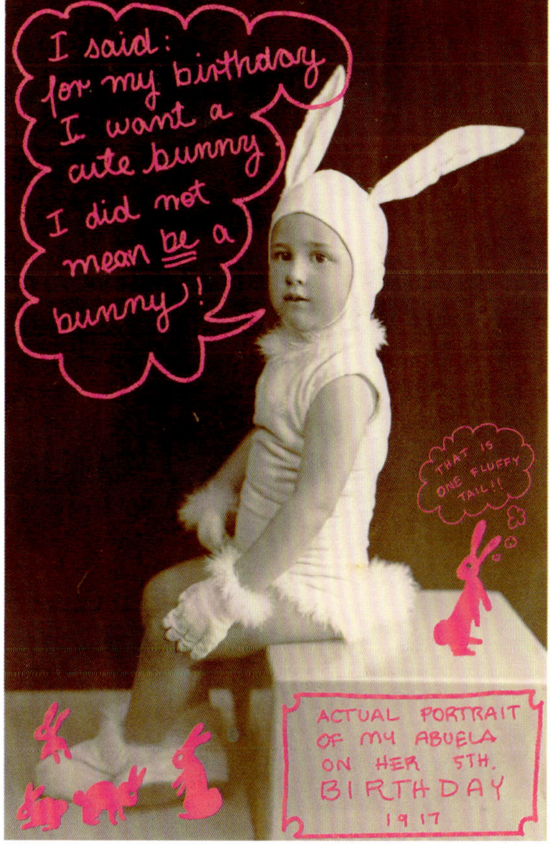

I said: for my birthday I want a cute bunny. I did not mean be a bunny!
THAT IS ONE FLUFFY TAIL!!
ACTUAL PORTRAIT OF MY ABUELA ON HER 5TH. BIRTHDAY 1917

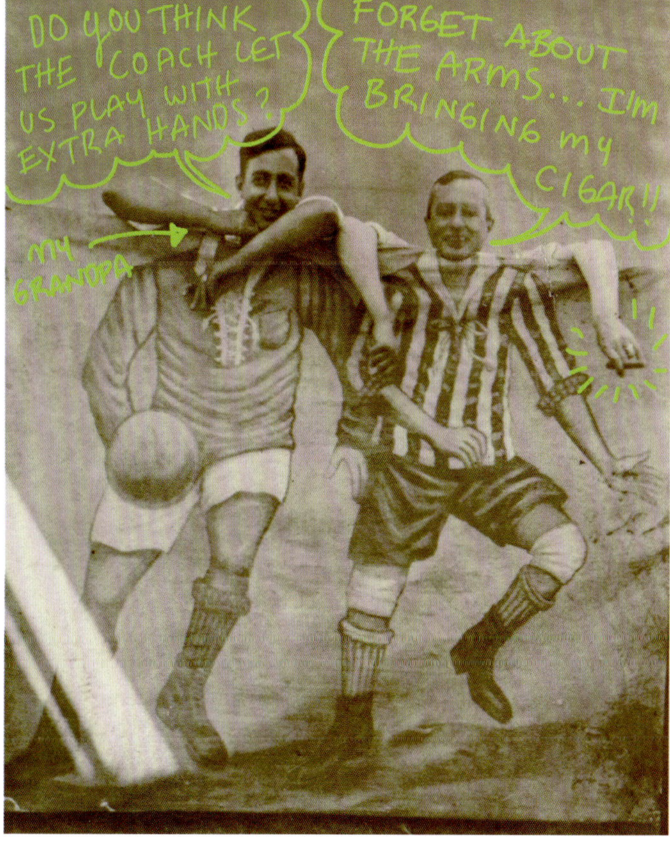

DO YOU THINK THE COACH LET US PLAY WITH EXTRA HANDS?
FORGET ABOUT THE ARMS... I'M BRINGING MY CIGAR!!
MY GRANDPA

Masters painting or something otherwise not very groundbreaking. If you can't find a painting, you can always download a high-resolution painting and either work digitally or print it out to paint over. Disrupt the harmony of this painting by overpainting it with a bright neon. The disruption can be a thing of beauty or an exaggeration, but the point is to try to turn an old, uninteresting painting into something arresting and contemporary. Use neon to change the meaning of the painting.

For this exercise, I found at the Alameda flea market a framed reproduction on canvas of a vase of yellow flowers painted by Rudolph Colao, an East Coast mid-century artist known for his landscapes and floral still lifes. By overpainting his yellow and ochre florals with a bright hot-pink color scheme and imagery of traditional candy from Mexico, the painting transforms and carries a different concept. Maine overpainted with Mexico.

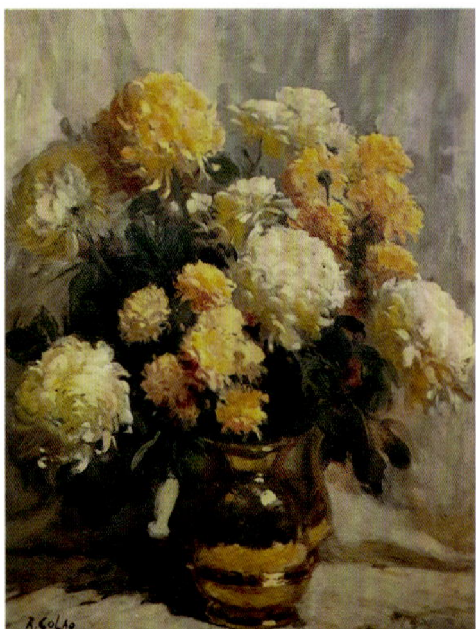 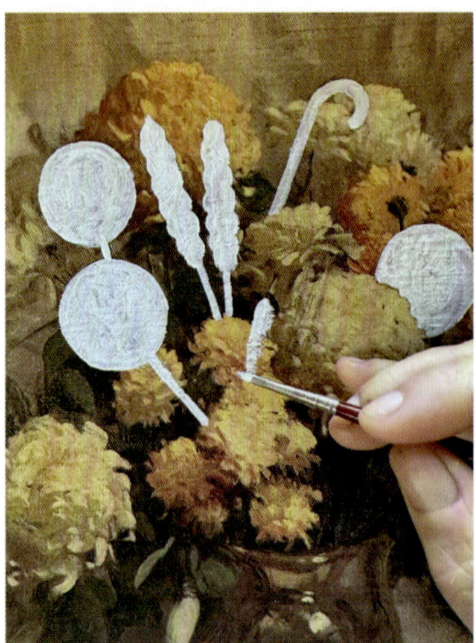

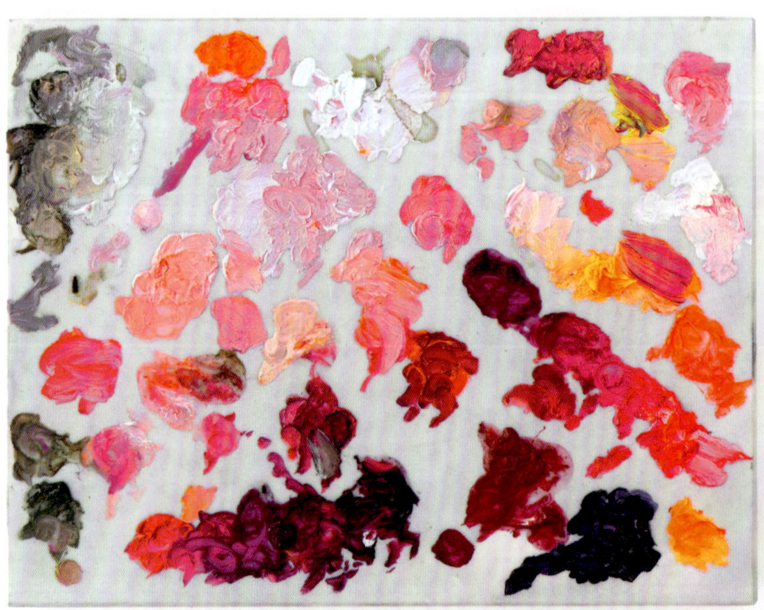

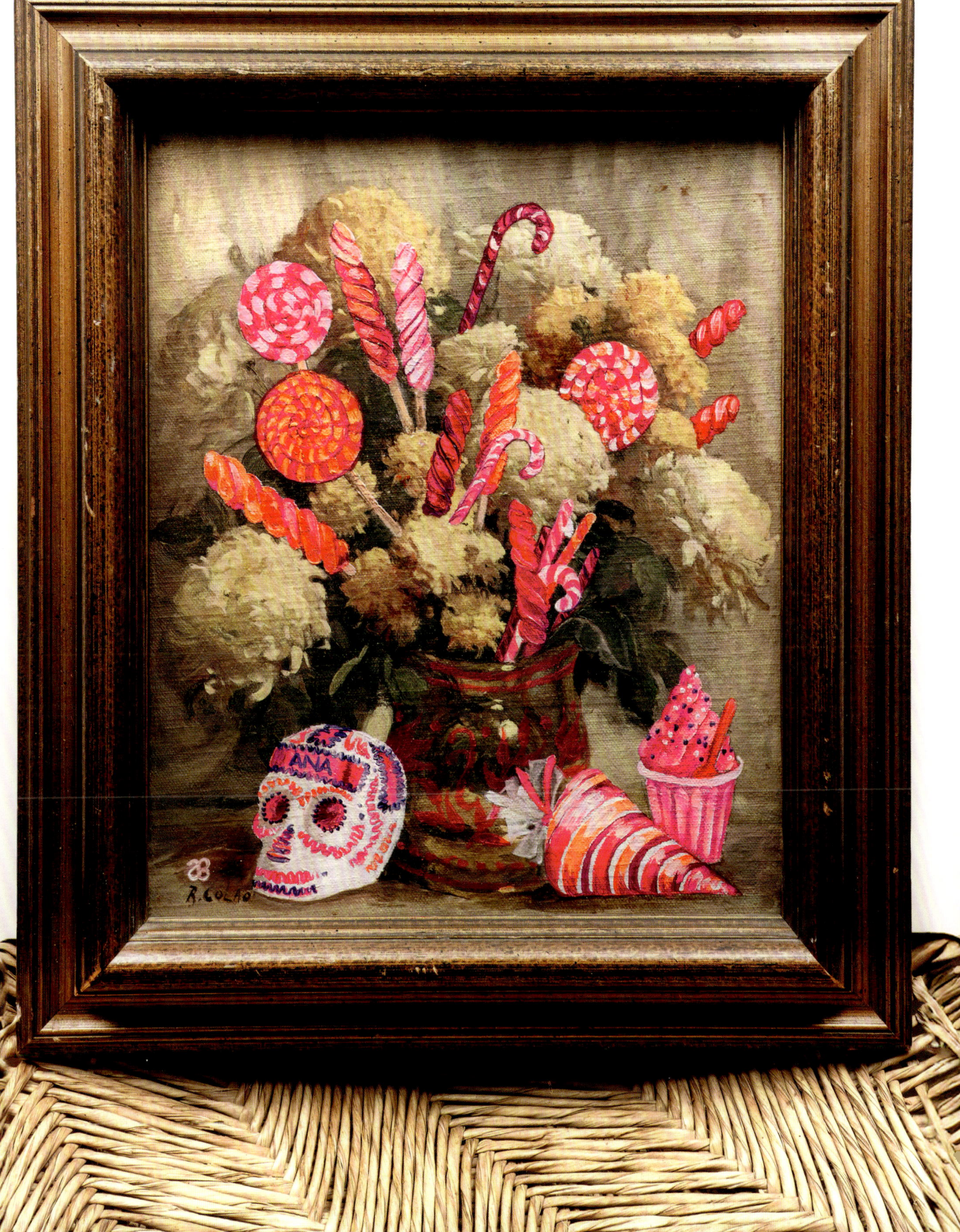

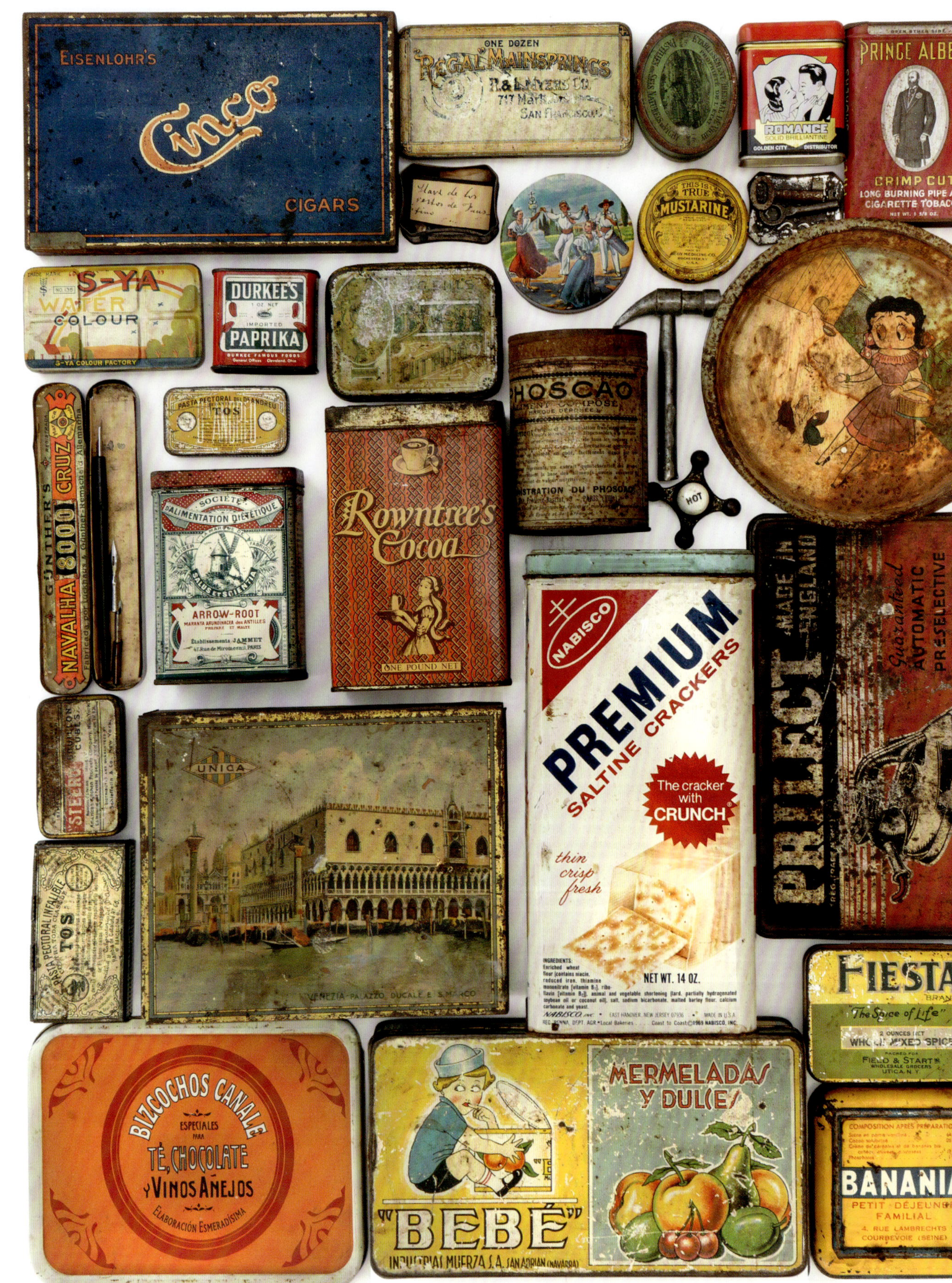

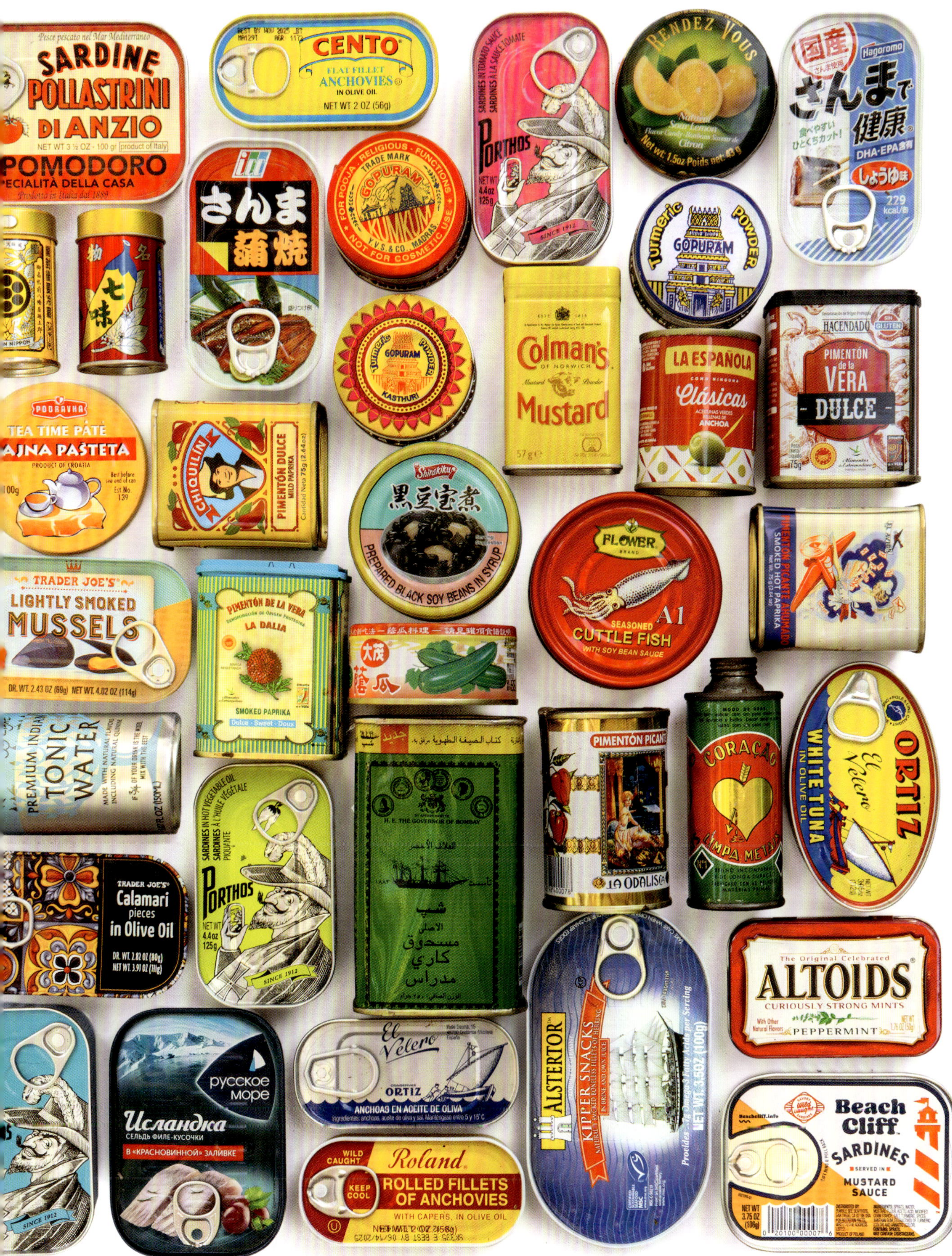

8.

THE PASSING OF TIME

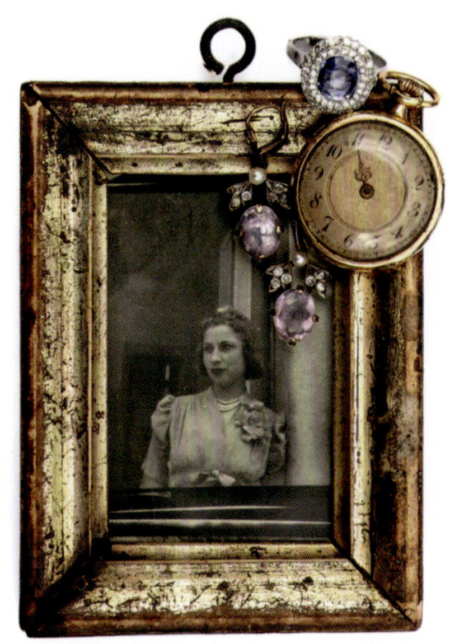

How Desaturating Color Can Convey a Sense of Time, Vintage Nostalgia, and History

W ashed out, faded, sun-washed, oxidized, dried, decomposed, dusty, dirty.

This is what happens to color as it ages. There is something that I've always found appealing about things that show the passing of time. Bright, new, and shiny is okay, but aged . . . I love it. It shows there's been a story, it sparks memories and nostalgia or, like they say in Portugal, saudade: a mix of sad, happy, and longing. Old things carry stories and make me wonder about previous owners. I think that is why I love flea markets and ephemera. Family heirlooms also hold the stories of people I knew or wish I'd met. In my family, somehow a lot of things were passed down, and a lot of them ended up in my house. I could make a family tree with five generations of handkerchiefs. There are embroidered tablecloths, some vintage clothes we used to play dress-up with, and a boxful of photos from as far back as the 1880s from both sides of my family.

All these old things also have the power to create a mood in a way new things just can't. Their colors don't exist in new things; that is why I love old colors. Right now, sitting at my desk I can see my two-tone green Singer sewing machine from the 1950s, a faded picture of me smiling and dressed as a peasant for a kindergarten performance in the '70s, and a few Polaroids of my daughter from when she was five. I see the framed charcoal drawings my great-great-great-granduncle made 130 years ago and a little technical graphite drawing my great-grandfather drew in the '40s, both on yellowed old paper. All this and more is within my eyesight, surrounding me with time-ripe colors that fill me with sentiment.

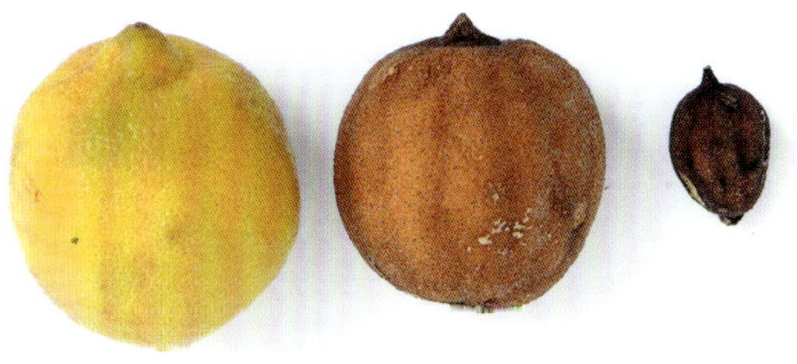

↑ From bright yellow to deep brown: Most colors change with age.

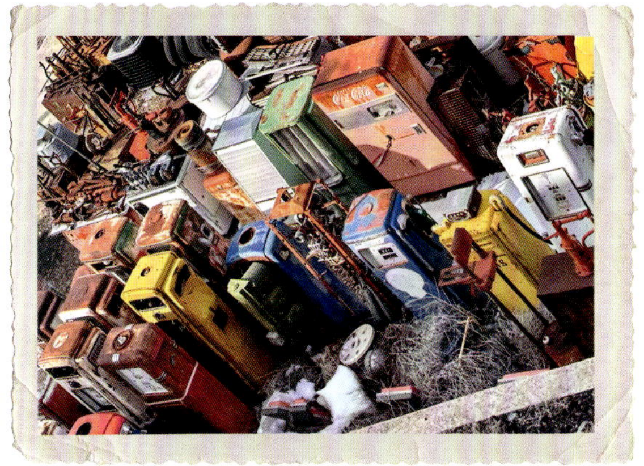

I've always had a tendency toward nostalgia. Not in a sad way, but in a really good way. I find the spark of storytelling there. I'm always collecting little trinkets, little cutout papers, and oxidized tins.

When I was in graduate school in Florence, I put all my little "treasure trash" to good use. I was an art student on a very tight budget, so I could not afford quality paints or canvases, but it was Italy, and there were little bits of treasure trash everywhere. I started collecting them: packaging with lovely typography, an old wooden mailbox, a cigar box, some computer circuits, a sun-bleached bone that I gilded, random bits and bobs and a few things that I did buy at the flea market, like half a dozen enamel watch faces. I spent my year making assemblages—collages with found objects and ephemera. Specifically, I made imaginary machines: a machine to recover conversations from the past, a miracle-making machine, and a time-traveling machine. These were all constructed inside old containers, or boxes I found or built and banged up to make them look old. All used carefully orchestrated vintage color. As I worked on these boxes, fellow students and teachers started referencing a great American artist I had not heard about before— Joseph Cornell—and while my curiosity to see his work was huge, I held back, waiting until my school year was over before researching his work and finally seeing it in New York City museums on my way back home. I was blown away, and he remains one of my favorite artists.

Cornell's collages of aged papers, his slightly dirty but beautiful whites, his labels on little jars, his various birds (especially the parrots) and dark blue skies with stars and faded maps in green and red . . . all are perfectly

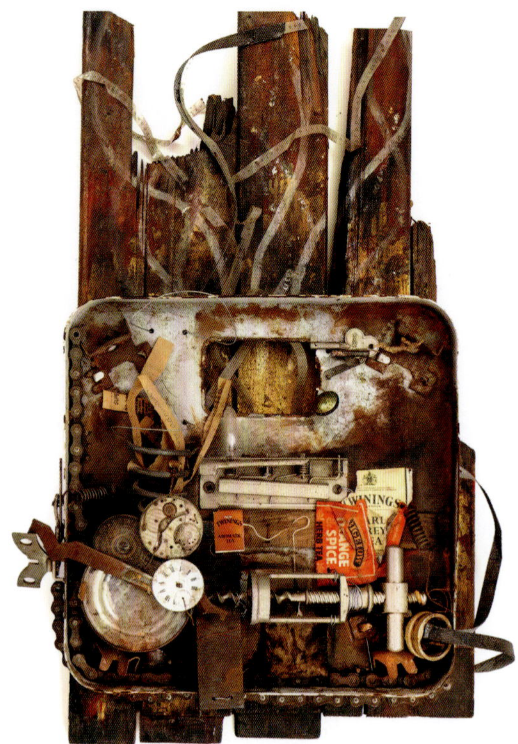

↑ This is the Conversation Retrieving Machine I made with junk found in the streets of Florence. It was meant to help retrieve memorable conversations from the past. The objects were old when I found them, and now the machine itself is twenty-five years old.

contained in beautifully composed boxes. They are a bit Victorian, a bit surreal, and a bit scientific. So evocative!

Cornell was a somewhat reclusive artist, living most of his life in the same house in Queens, New York. His private universe and his interest in psychology are reflected in his intimate boxes full of collected vintage elements, which he used to tell stories about childhood, dreams, and the cosmos at large.

Before Cornell (and the Surrealist and Dadaist movements), collage and assemblage were not considered fine art. However, Victorian ladies liked making little collages and scrapbooking as hobbies, and naturalists collected marvels in their cabinets of curiosities.

After Cornell, so many artists and illustrators, including myself, have used collage and assemblage in their work. What do I love most about collage and assemblage? The ready-made element of found objects already in perfectly aged colors, with no mixing necessary, and the built-in mood and nostalgia ready to be reshuffled into a new story.

VINTAGE COLOR HARVESTING

In my search for vintage colors, I have several favorite color-harvesting places:

- **Naturalist and botanical illustrations** from any century.
- **Vintage circus, carnival, and freak show posters**—the geometry of the tents, the costumes of the acrobats, the outrageous characters, and the animals.
- **Anything printed in chromolithography** (the technique that predates offset printing): fruit crate labels, seed packages, educational charts and maps, and calendars and books from the late nineteenth and early twentieth centuries where you can see the distinct dot patterns in various inks—not CMYK—creating all the nuances.
- **Old photos**—in black and white, sepia, and color. In particular, the Kodachrome film from my childhood and faded Polaroids. Just one childhood photo can be enough to base a whole color palette upon!
- **Old packaging**—tin or cardboard.
- **And anything else I see at the flea market!**

Observing vintage color is about understanding what time did to the pigments and how you can reproduce those colors to create a mood in whatever you are making.

There are nuances in these colors that aren't found in colors that read as brand new. Knowing how to desaturate the color without killing it takes practice and experimentation: lightening a color with an unbleached white; using midnight blue, indigo, aubergine, or sepia instead of black to darken other colors; aging colors by adding a barely there dab of burnt umber; or desaturating them using their complementary color. Try all this and see.

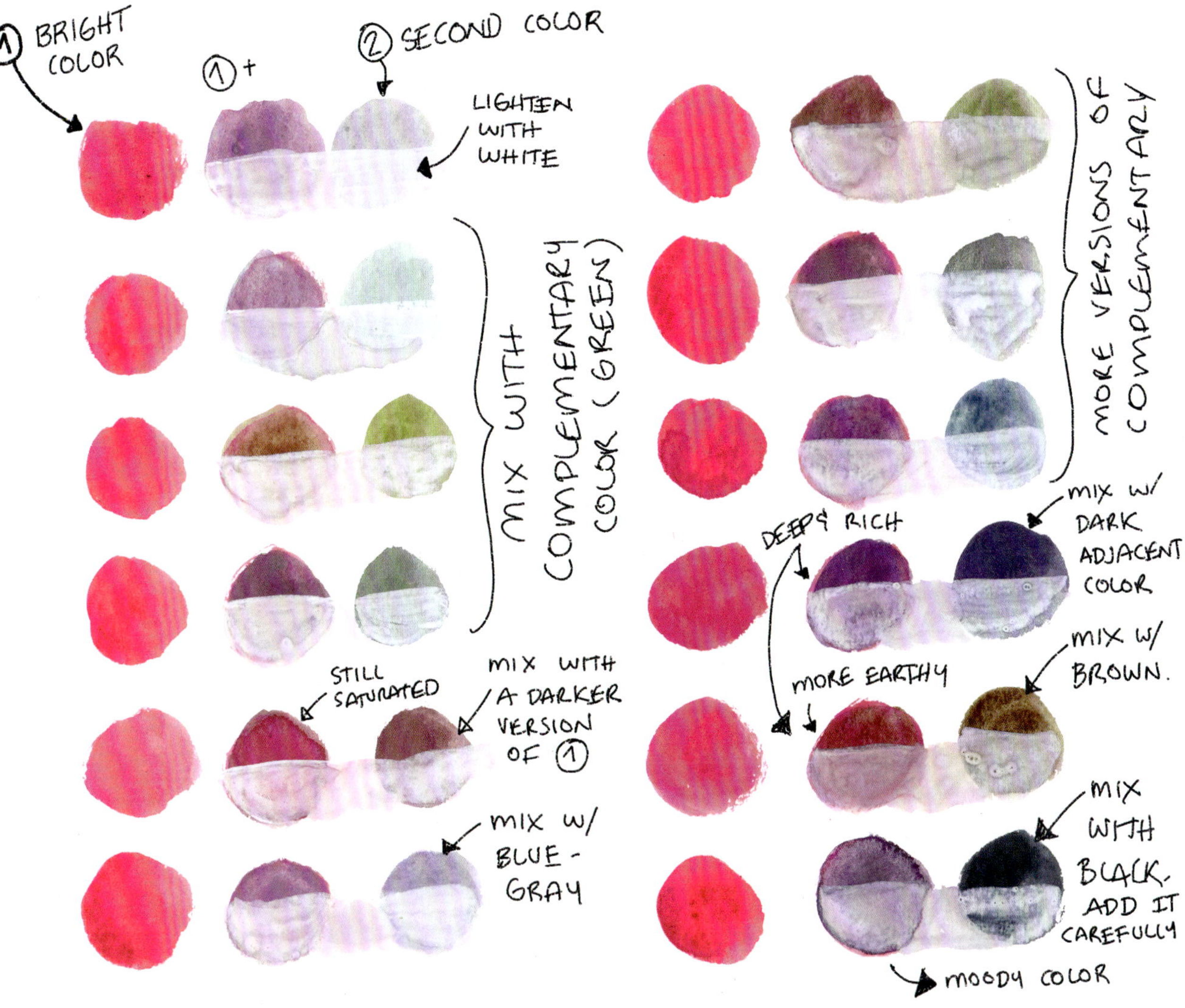

↑ **How to Desaturate a Color with Intention**

Using color straight from the tube is not very nuanced. Some colors can be used bright and saturated, but those same colors can take on a whole other life depending on what you need them for. Knowing how to take one of those hightly pigmented, saturated colors and make a whole range of tones, shades, and hues is in itself like alchemy.

Desaturating a color can be done in many ways. Your first thought may be to add black, gray, or white, but sometimes that results in muddy, murky, dirty colors, which may not be what you were looking for.

Take a look at this chart. In each column you will see, on the left, the starting point of each mix—a bright, saturated dot of opera pink—and on the right, the second color I added with the goal of transforming the pink into a more nuanced, desaturated, moody, earthy, aged version of itself. The result of the mix is the dot in the middle.

Then I topped it off with a brush of zinc white to show a lighter version of it. The variety of colors resulted from mixing the hot pink with

* A range of complementary colors,
* A muted darker version of itself,
* A neutral gray,
* A darker adjacent color like deep violet,
* A brown, and last but not least,
* A black, carefully.

There is no bad color in this chart; the right color comes from knowing what to mix your bright color with.

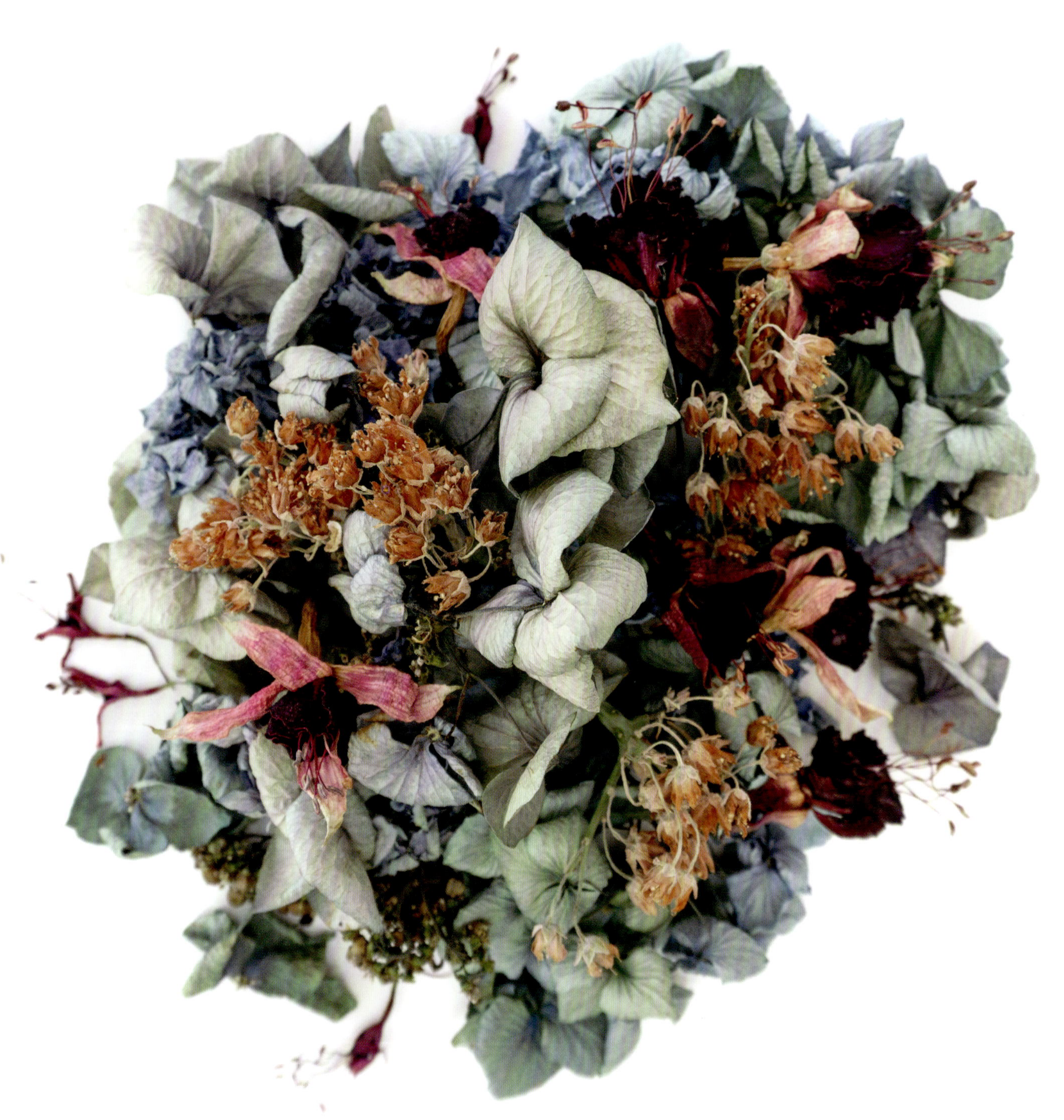

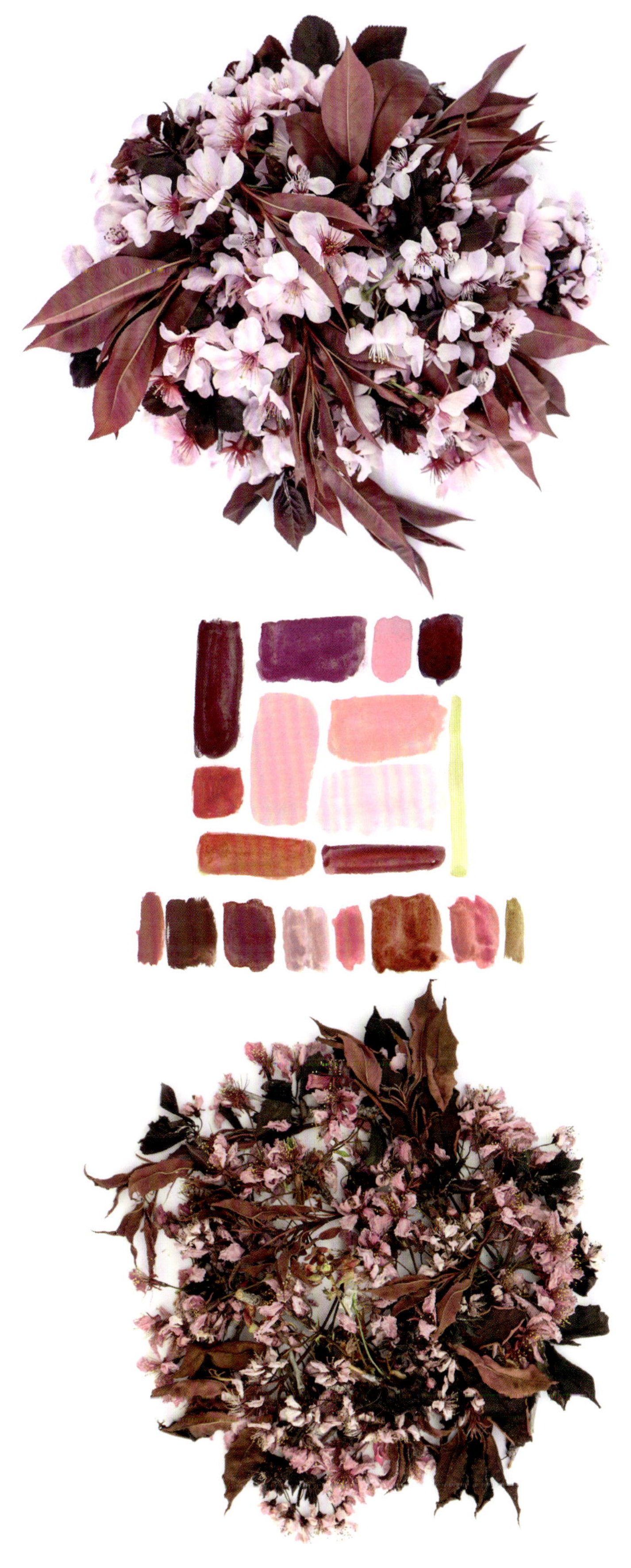

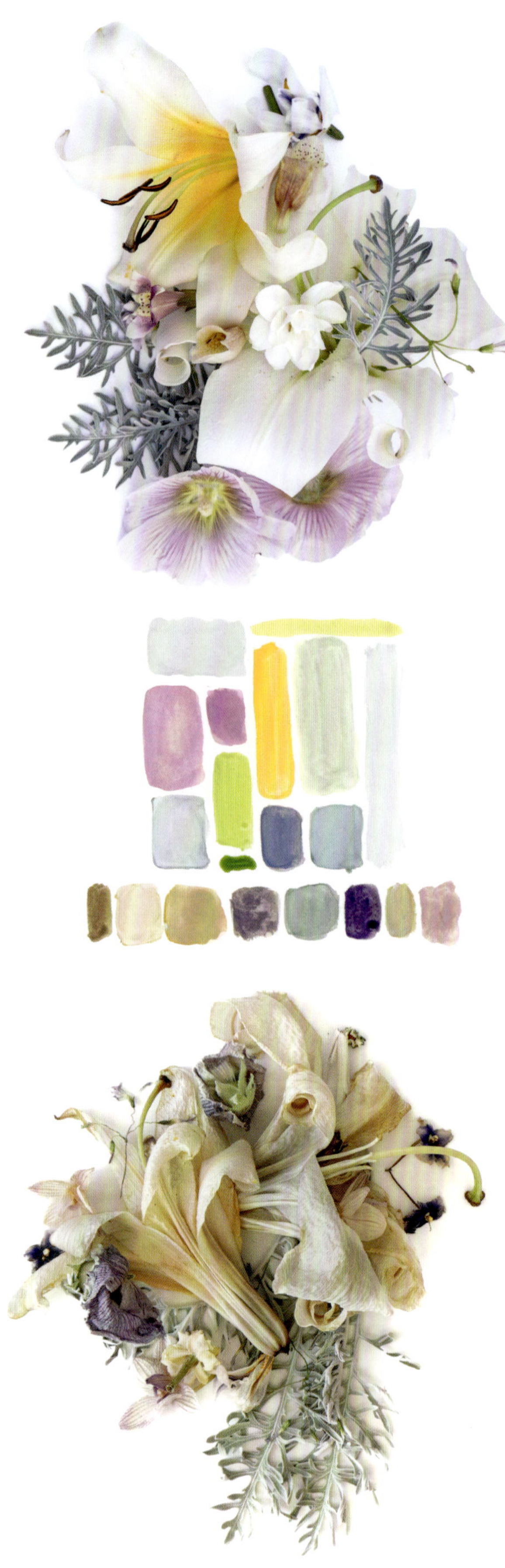

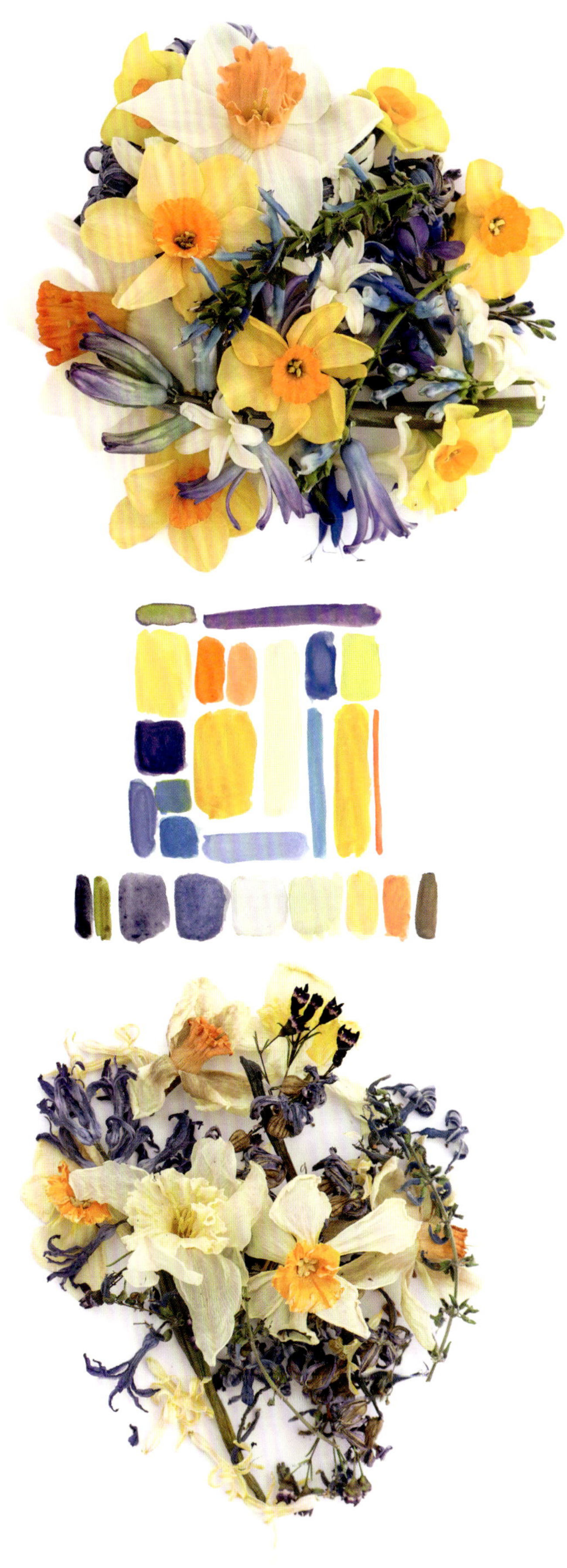

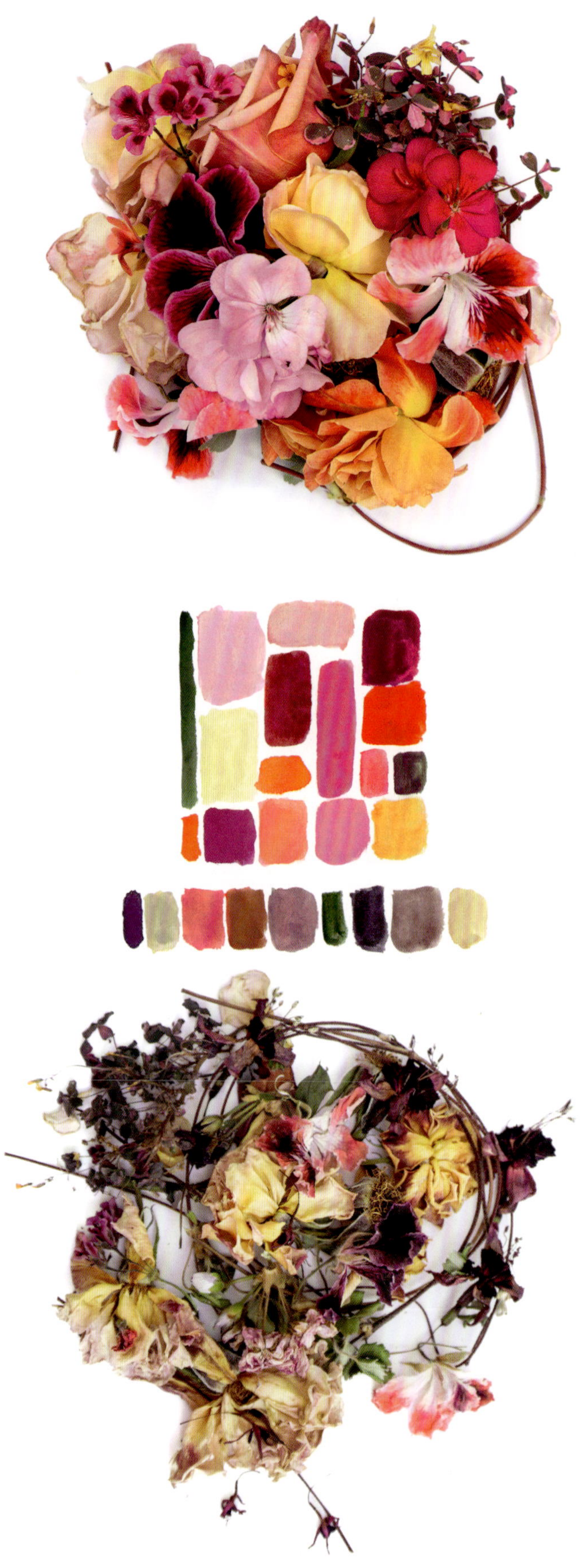

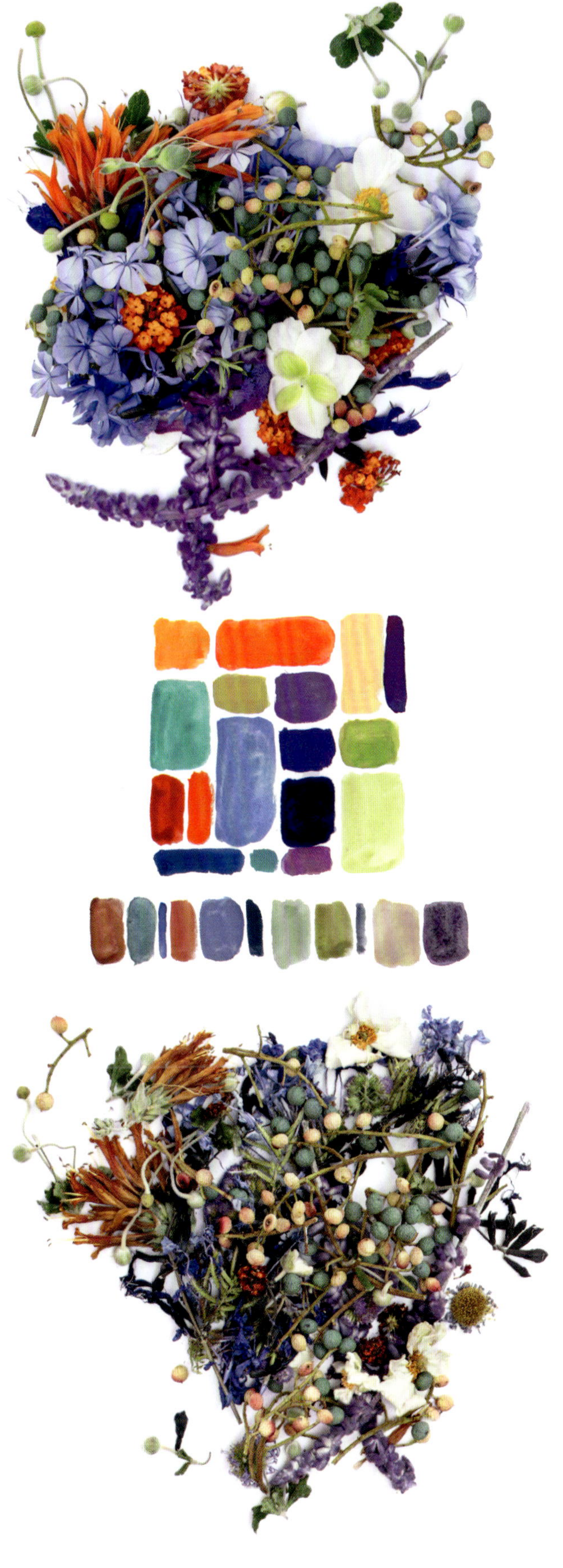

HISTORY IN COLOR

One cannot talk about time and color without talking about history. There are colors with deeply evocative names rooted in history, like the controversial mummy brown, made from ground-up Egyptian mummies and no longer in use since the nineteenth century, for obvious ethical reasons, and also called the wonderful and spooky caput mortuum (meaning *dead head* or, less literally, *worthless remains*, inspired by a term used in alchemy referring to the byproduct left from failing to sublimate gold), or the also magical dragon's blood (who doesn't want to paint with blood from a dragon?!).

Throughout history, each period seems to have a favored palette: the olive, ochre, and sepia we see in British drama series set between the World Wars; the jewel tones in late-Renaissance paintings; or the candy-sweet colors of the period before the French Revolution (yes, think Marie Antoinette and her love for ruffles, wigs, and cake).

Who doesn't love a period drama? I especially love it when historical color is reinvented in film, yet still manages to convey the period. Greta Gerwig does that brilliantly with the costumes and sets in *Little Women*, where colors are just a little bit brighter than other period movies and are stylized to reflect the personality of each of the sisters. *The Empress* uses color to reflect the arc of the main character, Sisi, moving from the whites and blues of her carefree girlhood through a series of golds, ochres, taupes, and aubergines as she grows into her role as Empress of

Austria to later grays and blues. And then, of course, there is *Bridgerton*, where even the families are color coded: the lovely Bridgerton family in their blues and lilacs, and the nouveau riche Featheringtons in their loud yellows and greens. This is not a historically accurate use of color, but instead a modernized eye-candy version of it. In reality, the Regency period was more subdued—soft pinks, dove grays, blues—but in the series, chromatic choices are used to carry the various storylines and delight the eye.

Color harvesting from the past to tell a contemporary story is nothing new; all through history, artists and designers of all kinds have looked to the past for inspiration. For example, let's take medieval tapestries and illuminated manuscripts: deep greens, rosy reds, ultramarine, and gold. This palette was revived in the nineteenth century by a group that called themselves the Pre-Raphaelites, since they were looking for inspiration in the era before Raphael and the Italian Renaissance. The Pre-Raphaelite artists, and the designers and architects of the Arts and Crafts movement, led by William Morris, were looking back into those medieval tapestries and textiles, those illuminated books, and all the details of gothic churches to create a new visual language in response to the ugliness of the Industrial Revolution. Their textiles, stained-glass pieces, posters, illustrations, paintings, and more bring back the ornamentation, floral motifs, and colors of medieval times. Similarly, nowadays I constantly see illustrators and surface-pattern designers creating new art for interiors, packaging, and fabrics that is clearly inspired by the Arts and Crafts movement.

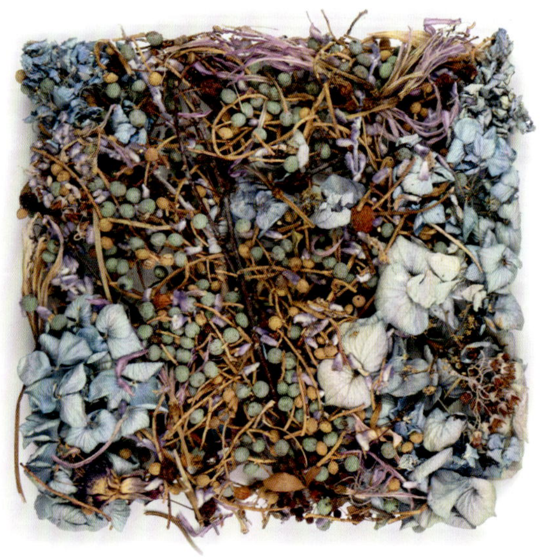

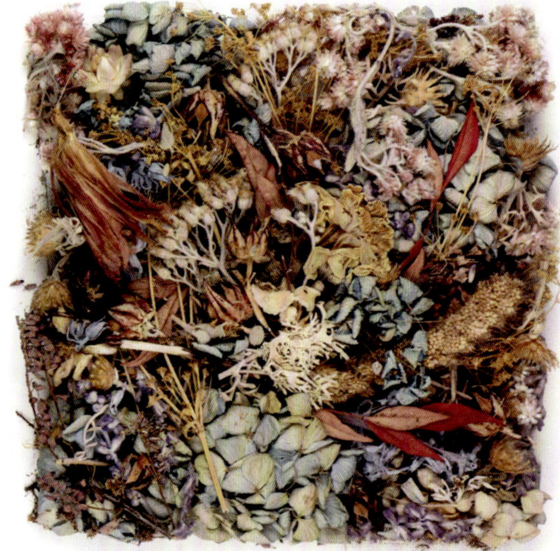

UNDER THE INFLUENCE: HOW TO COLOR HARVEST IN ART HISTORY BOOKS AND MUSEUMS

Now it is our turn as creatives to find influences in the past. As artists, designers, and all kinds of people interested in exploring our creative sides, we are constantly learning from what we see. Our minds are tickled by the muses of the artists who came before us. There is a whole world of art history inspiration out there. Color harvesting may occur in a book or on a day at a museum or during a trip. It can be a part of one's journey to enrich and educate oneself generally, or it can happen during research for a specific project.

I believe the more you observe, the richer your visual vocabulary gets. But observing is not copying and should never, ever get even remotely close to plagiarism or cultural appropriation.

So what can one do with all the inspiration—for colors, for shapes, for ways of drawing, for mood and feeling? How to do it right without appropriation?

About thirty years ago, my thesis advisor, the wise architect Fernando Rovalo, told me an anecdote that made the biggest impression and provided me with a North Star for managing my art history inspirations. The story is about the Mexican architect Luis Barragán and his creative process for designing the chapel for the Capuchin nuns in collaboration with the sculptor Mathias Goeritz in the 1950s. I may not be able to corroborate the specific details, but I will tell it as I remember since it is the memory of how it was told to me that made such a lasting impression:

As my teacher told it, Barragán wanted to design the chapel by drawing inspiration from Byzantine architecture. He was obviously not going to build a full-on Byzantine church in Mexico; instead, he wanted to capture the spirit of Byzantine architecture and recreate it in his own voice.

For this, as in other projects, he exposed himself not to one example but to many sources of inspiration. He collected books, postcards, prints, photographs, and any other visual references to not one but many Byzantine churches and buildings. Then he scattered them around his house: books open on tables and in the kitchen, photos on each step of the stairs, postcards on his bedside table and in the vanity behind his toothbrush. For weeks he walked around all these images, seeing them as he went about his day, from morning to evening, infusing his eyes with Byzantine art but not focusing too much on any particular one. Doing this allowed him to distill an essence: the use of space, the light and colors, the forms and volumes, but mostly, the spiritual and ethereal quality of these churches.

The finished chapel he designed looks nothing like a Byzantine church; it looks like a quintessential Barragán building. Yet knowing this story, you can see how close in mood and atmosphere it is to Byzantine churches. Instead of gold, there is Barragán's yellow and white. He used narrow and wide-open volumes like those churches, but in a minimalistic, modern way. And then there is the light. It comes into the chapel through narrow stained-

When the Mind's Eye Looks Back

Remembering *or recalling in Spanish is* recordar, *from the Latin* recordis, *formed from the roots* re, *meaning* repeat, *and* cordis, *related to the heart. So* recordis *means to pass again through the heart.*

This is how I like to do my visual research and manage inspiration.

glass windows that feature a simple geometric pattern designed by Goeritz that reflects on simple gilded surfaces and is filtered through thoroughly modern lattices. The light, the materials, the colors, the spaces all combine to make a masterpiece.

What did I get from this story? I got the practice of looking at many, many sources but none in particular when researching historical or world-culture art. I observe a lot of images and read and just fill myself up, then I usually take a nap or go to bed right after, and somehow in my dreams I process it all and wake up ready to draw or create something that is inspired by my research, but in my style, with my hand. When I sit down to make, I no longer consult the books, I work from what I remember.

I do this with the books on my bookshelf and those in bookstores and libraries. I browse, browse, browse, observe, maybe do a sketch, take some photos, or write some notes. If I am looking at medieval tapestries or illuminated manuscripts for inspiration, as the Pre-Raphaelites did, I notice the greens, indigos, and reds. I make mental notes on the specific flowers, little critters, and foliage, especially those acanthus leaves. I observe the curlicues, the gilded details, and the composition. Then I close the books and do my thing. Closing the books and separating myself, with space or with time, from the original sources gives me the chance to process, remember, and (I like to visualize this) send the images from my brain, through my heart, and down my arm to my hand.

What about art in museums and while traveling? I rarely photograph whole paintings or pieces of art; instead, my phone is exploding with photos of close-ups and cropped images. When I see a whole painting at a museum, I think of it through an intellectual, art-historian lens. When I come closer and focus on the details, the colors, the brushstrokes, I observe as an artist. That is how I learn from the past and become inspired and influenced by it, so that I can translate it through my mind and heart, my quirks and my eye, to make it in my style. Rather than copying, I am making it speak with my voice.

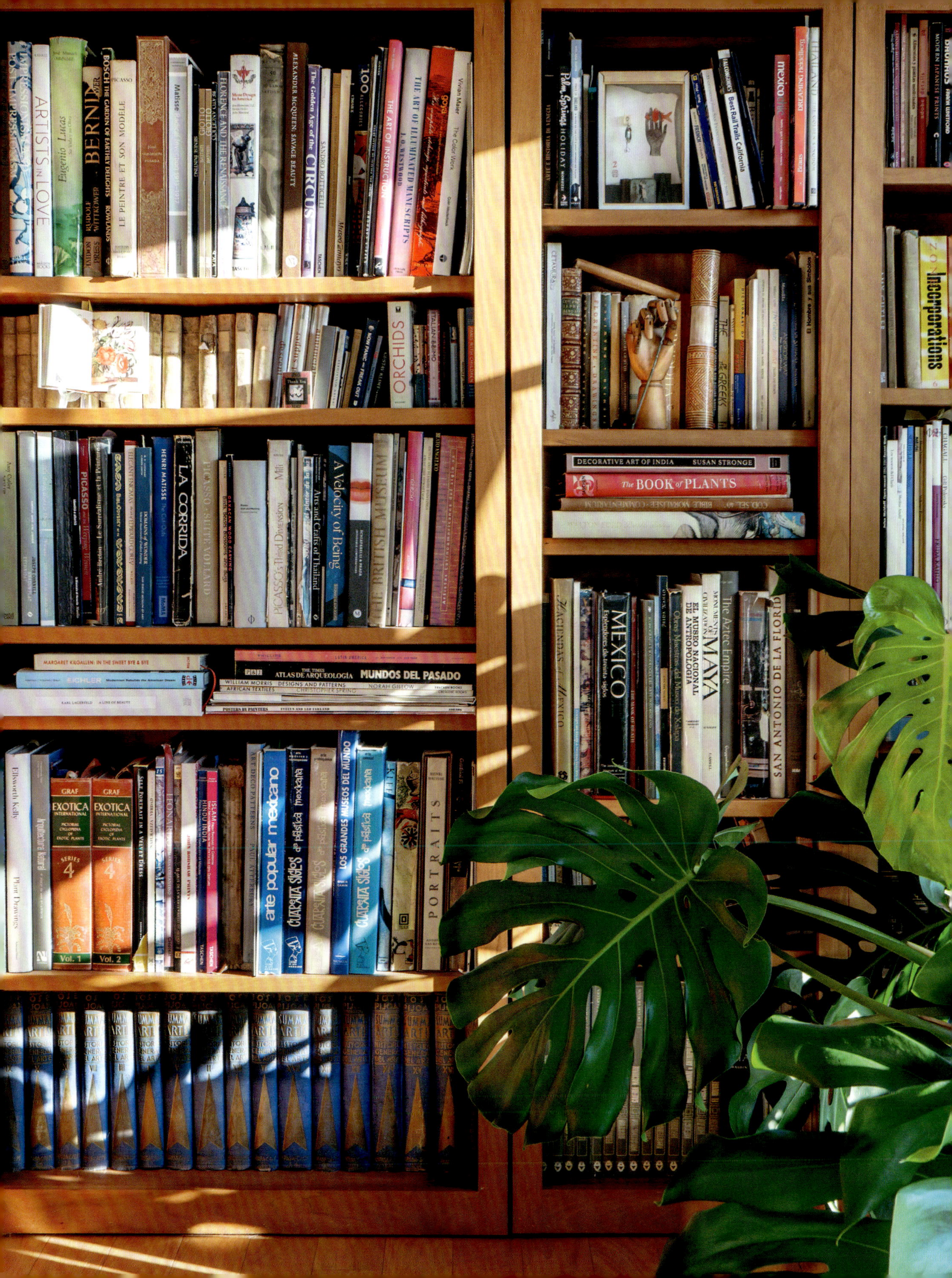

THE UK AND ITS COLOR HISTORY

IN CONVERSATION WITH JEHANE BODEN SPIERS

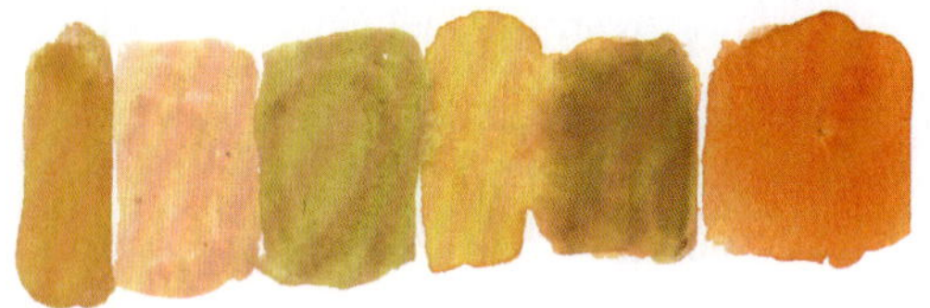

Jehane is the UK-based founder and creative director of her namesake illustration agency in Brighton, representing some of the most sought-after illustrators. She is also a successful artist and designer in her own right and an inspiration to the whole illustration industry through her courses, mentorships, and creative challenges.

You can find her and the artists of her agency at Jehane.com and @jehane_ltd.

Sign up for her mailing list to follow her creative challenges and more.

While looking back into history may not be relevant to all artists—they are to decide whether it is an important thing for them to do—in my case, I am hugely inspired by history to the point that my first creative business, Cloth of Gold, when I was twenty-two, was named after a very important historical event when Henry VIII traveled to France to meet Francis I, the king of France. Not much was achieved politically, but what was remarkable was the splendor of how the British monarch showed up: with a huge entourage equivalent to six full trains, all clad in full luxury to show his wealth and power. Catherine of Aragon, his first wife, donned a dress made with the cloth of gold, silk woven with actual gold threads. There was more golden fabric in the robes and tunics of dignitaries and in the tents that were put up for the three days of jousting and celebration.

There is a painting about this event called *The Field of the Cloth of Gold*.

I was designing and stitching pieces with lots of different types of gold thread in my own work, inspired by the history of the cloth of gold; there were cushions that featured the date of the event with a Tudor rose and a fleur-de-lis.

When exploring an idea and working with color or in any materials, it is not really about what you can do. It is about what matters to you. For me, that sort of historical reference provided the content for my designs. This is important to me.

Color-wise, I am interested in the links between Britain and India, and how that has come into our society still in the UK. It's interesting to see the historic trends in color, such as the Elizabethan palette with its deep purples, reds, and browns, and obviously Indian color, the arts, the textiles, the architecture. It is so rich!

One big advantage that the British—as artists and consumers of art, illustration, and design—have is the impact the Arts and Crafts movement had. It created an openness, a kind of subconscious natural understanding, acceptance, and value for the art and craftsmanship of everyday objects, not just fine art.

William Morris has had tremendous influence. Are artists overrepeating his work? Well, that is not a simple answer. Are we asking the question from a philosophical or a creative point of view? On one hand, is there tremendous demand for anything that looks like his patterns? Yes. Is it novel to create things in his style? Well, no. A lot of the work in the market now is too similar and thus too generic; people are not taking enough of a creative risk doing this, they are just playing it safe because there is market demand.

Is there a right way to do it? To work under the influence of others?

I think that when you are working very closely with a reference, any reference, for that matter, it is okay to look at it, maybe even draw from it, but then put all of it away and redraw it almost from memory. That new set of drawings becomes your starting point. Distancing yourself from the original material and then bringing in something that's your personal creative voice is what I encourage the artists in my agency to do.

When something is done with mindfulness and sensitivity, from a position of intentional respect and admiration for a culture and its heritage, I am comfortable with that as a source of influence. It is all about taking it back to a place of intent, creating the distance from the original, and bringing something of yours in. Also important to consider is that the newer the art is, or especially if it is contemporary, there is always the risk of copyright infringement.

"I am inspired by color and conversation."
–Jehane Boden Spiers

Elizabethan Colors

Digging around in history after my conversation with Jehane, I found a list of colors used in Elizabethan costumes from 1550–1580[17] full of interesting names that paint a picture of the times:

Bristol Red: A "pleasant" red
Cane Color: Yellowish tint
Carnation: Resembling raw flesh
Crane Color: Grayish white
Dead Spaniard: Pale grayish tan
Gingerline: Reddish violet
Goose-Turd: Yellowish green
Hair: Bright tan
Incarnate: Red
Isabella: Light buff
Lincoln Green: Bright green
Lustie-Gallant: Light red
Maiden Hair: Bright tan
Milk and Water: Bluish white
Murrey: Purplish red mulberry
Orange Tawney: Orangish brown
Plunket: Light blue
Popinjay: Bluish green
Primrose: Pale yellow
Puke: Dirty brown
Rat's Color: Dull gray
Sangyn: Blood red
Sheep's Color: Natural
Tawney: Brown tinged with yellow
Whey: Pale whitish blue
Willow: Light green

KEY TAKEAWAYS

1. Color degrades at different rates with time, and there are some colors that fade sooner than others. Notice these differences as you look at beautiful old things.

2. For me, old things evoke stories of other times. The colors bring back those stories. Notice what comes to mind when you see an old thing.

3. Different eras are associated with different colors and combinations. Maybe it has something to do with local color or the available pigments of the time, or maybe the style of the era. Observe history not as a dead thing, but think of other time periods as if they were alive and vibrant. For example, when you look at the ruins of Pompeii, imagine the people, their homes, and the landscape before the eruption of Mount Vesuvius.

4. Identify periods in history you are particularly interested in or curious about and practice the Barragán technique of filling yourself up with imagery, inspiration, and notions, then removing yourself from the source and working from your recollections, with your voice and style.

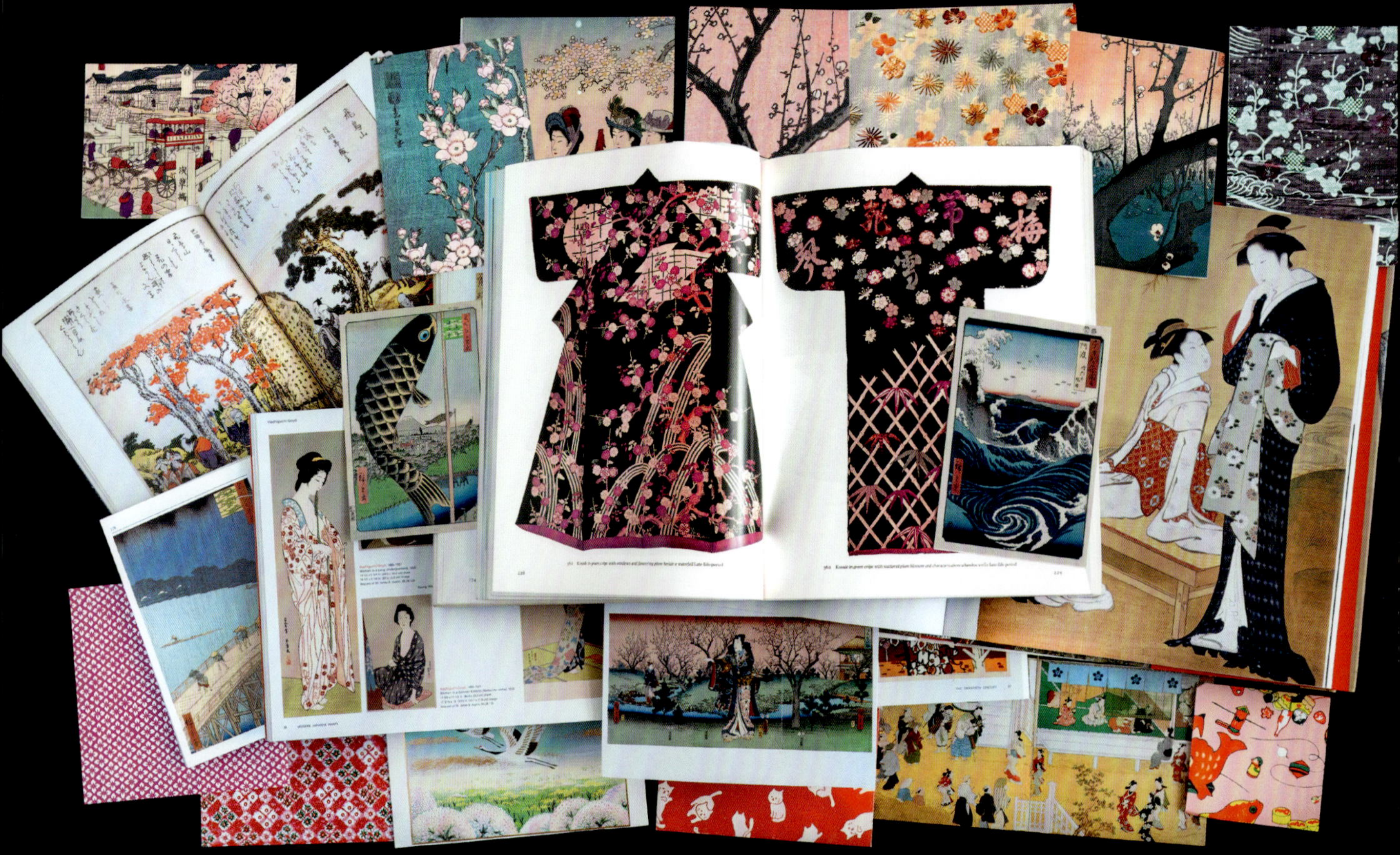

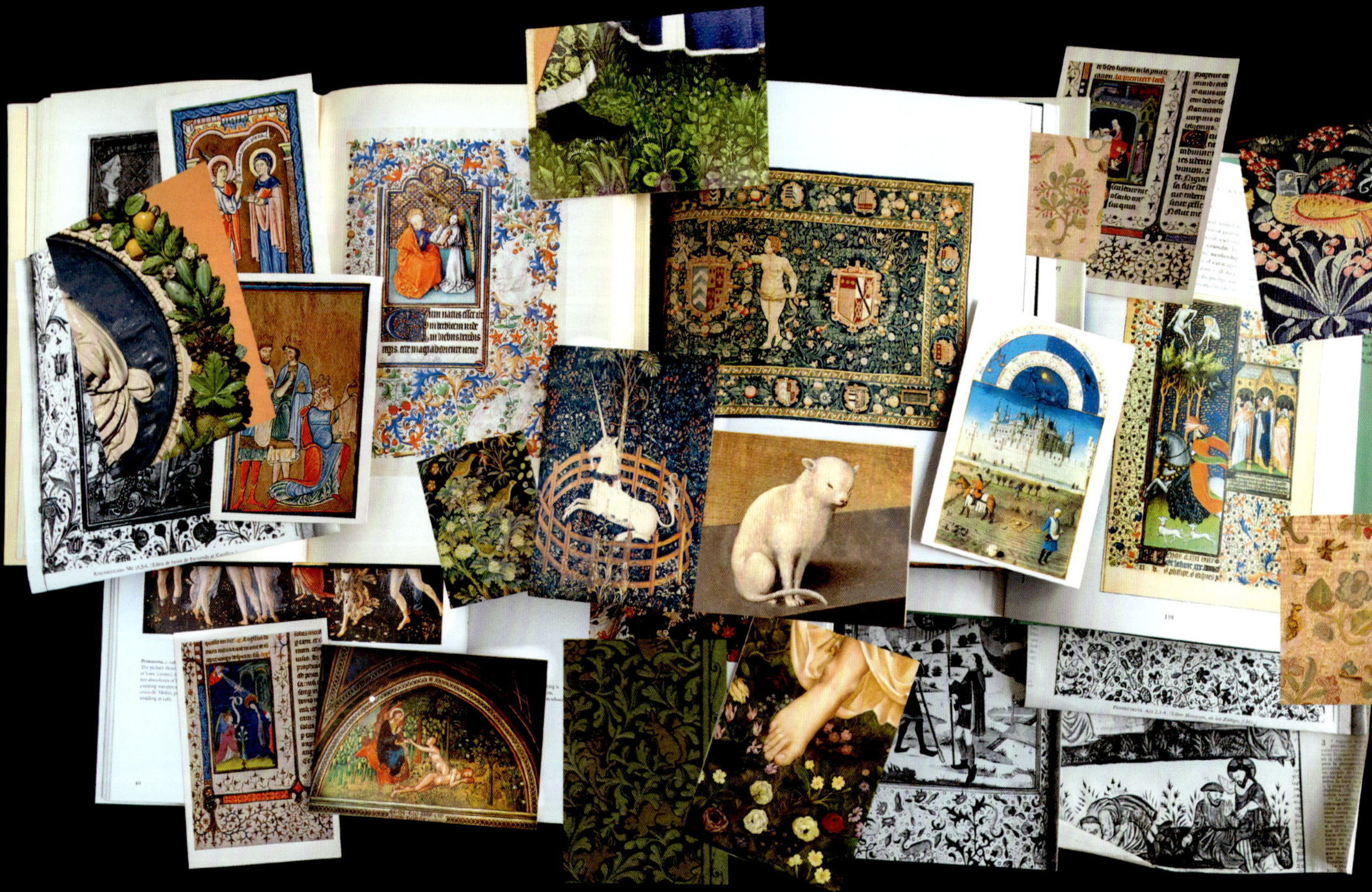

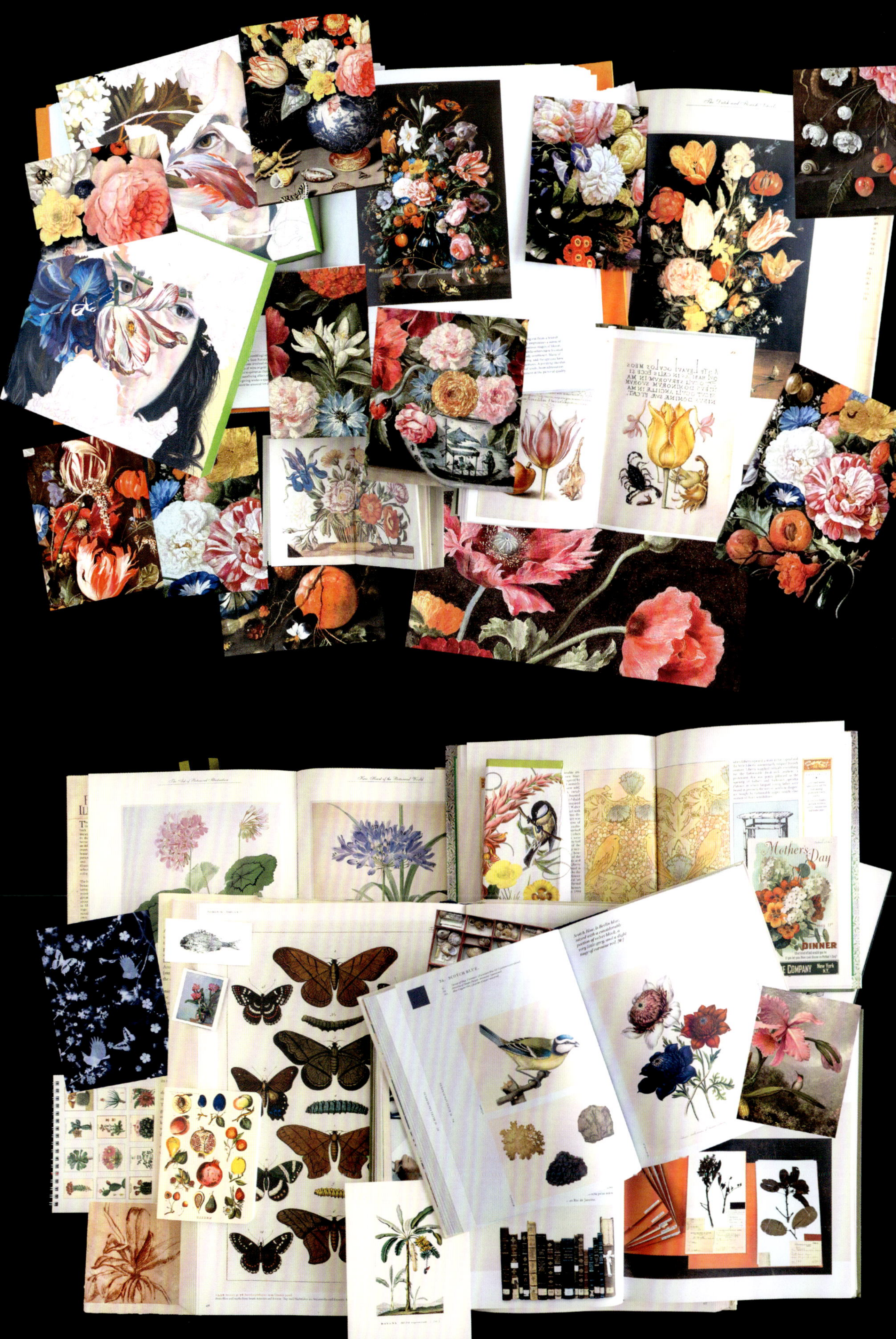

PROJECT

OBSERVE: Observe inspirational images from another era—use the ones I put together on pages 228–229 or choose your own. Observe the themes, the lines and style, the composition, and, especially, the colors. Observe their level of saturation or degradation. Consider whether those are the original colors or if time, grime, soot, sunlight, or other factors have changed them.

   If you like one of these particular periods, extend the visual search on your own to have more visual references.

ANALYZE: Analyze these colors by making a little palette. Be precise; desaturate, lighten, or darken as needed to really make the colors time ripe and period appropriate. When you see the palette, does it bring you back to the period? Are those colors currently different from how they would have been originally? Are those colors tarnished, faded, or dirty with soot, or maybe, like ancient Greek temples and statues, are their original painted colors now gone?

CREATE: Create one or more pieces that evoke the period in time you chose. You can use any technique and apply it to your area of creative expertise; the important thing is that the colors represent your chosen period and that the imagery shows thematic and stylistic influence but is clearly your creation.

   Time travel, but then come back and make something! Have fun!

   Over pages 231–233, you will see my four period-inspired pieces:

- A textile design on a wraparound dress from my illustrated clothing line for little girls, inspired by Edo Japan. The scene on the dress was made using a combination of watercolors and hand-carved rubber-stamp printing.
- A little chest of drawers featuring ephemera collage and decoupage inspired by Dutch florals but with a contemporary touch of humor.
- A pattern collection inspired by medieval tapestries, drawn with traditional media (watercolor, colored pencils, and gouache) and then digitized.
- White stoneware and porcelain plates with Victorian inspiration but made in a style I call Granny Moderne. The plates are all hand-built (I am awful at throwing on the wheel!) and hand-glazed.

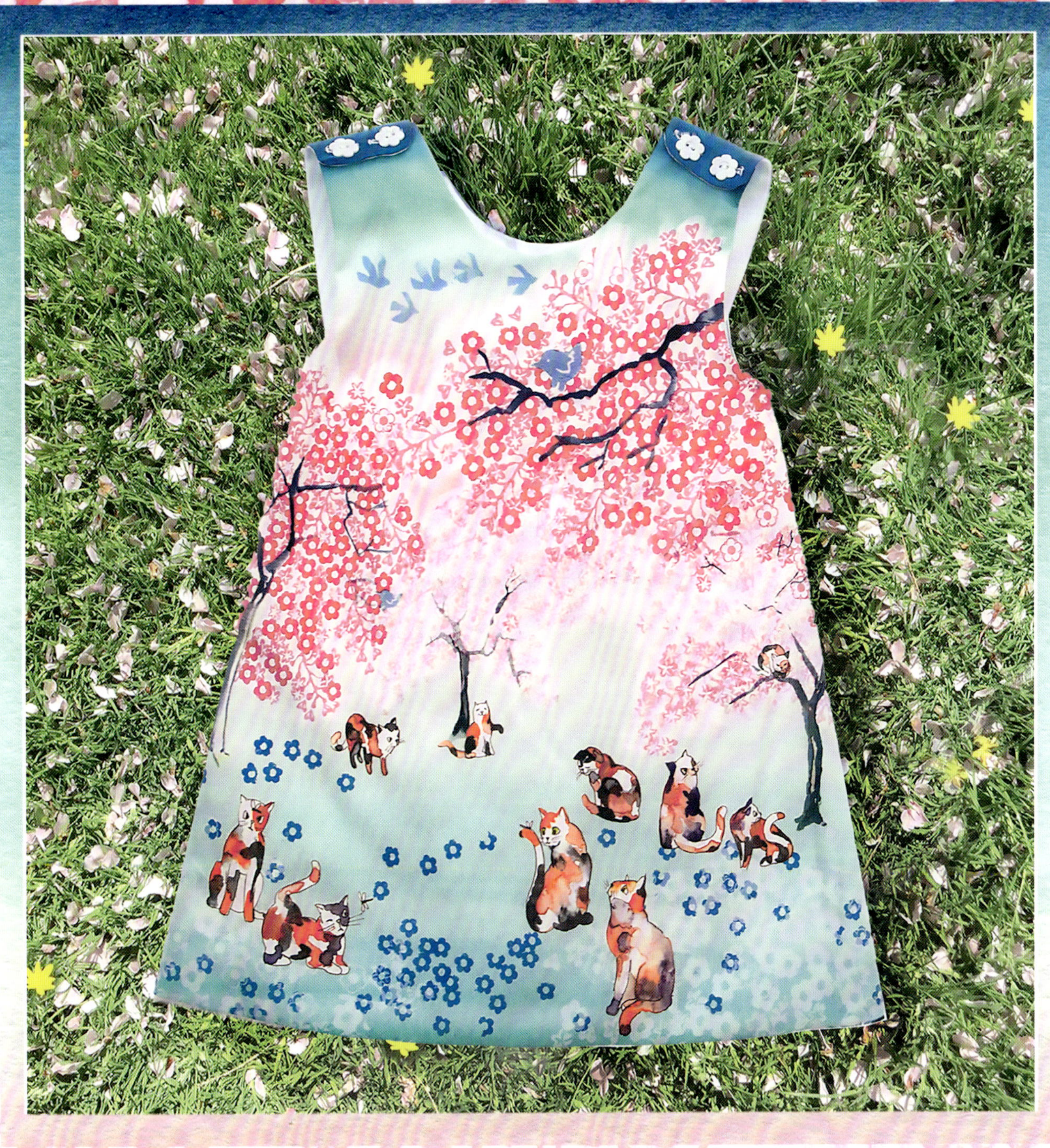

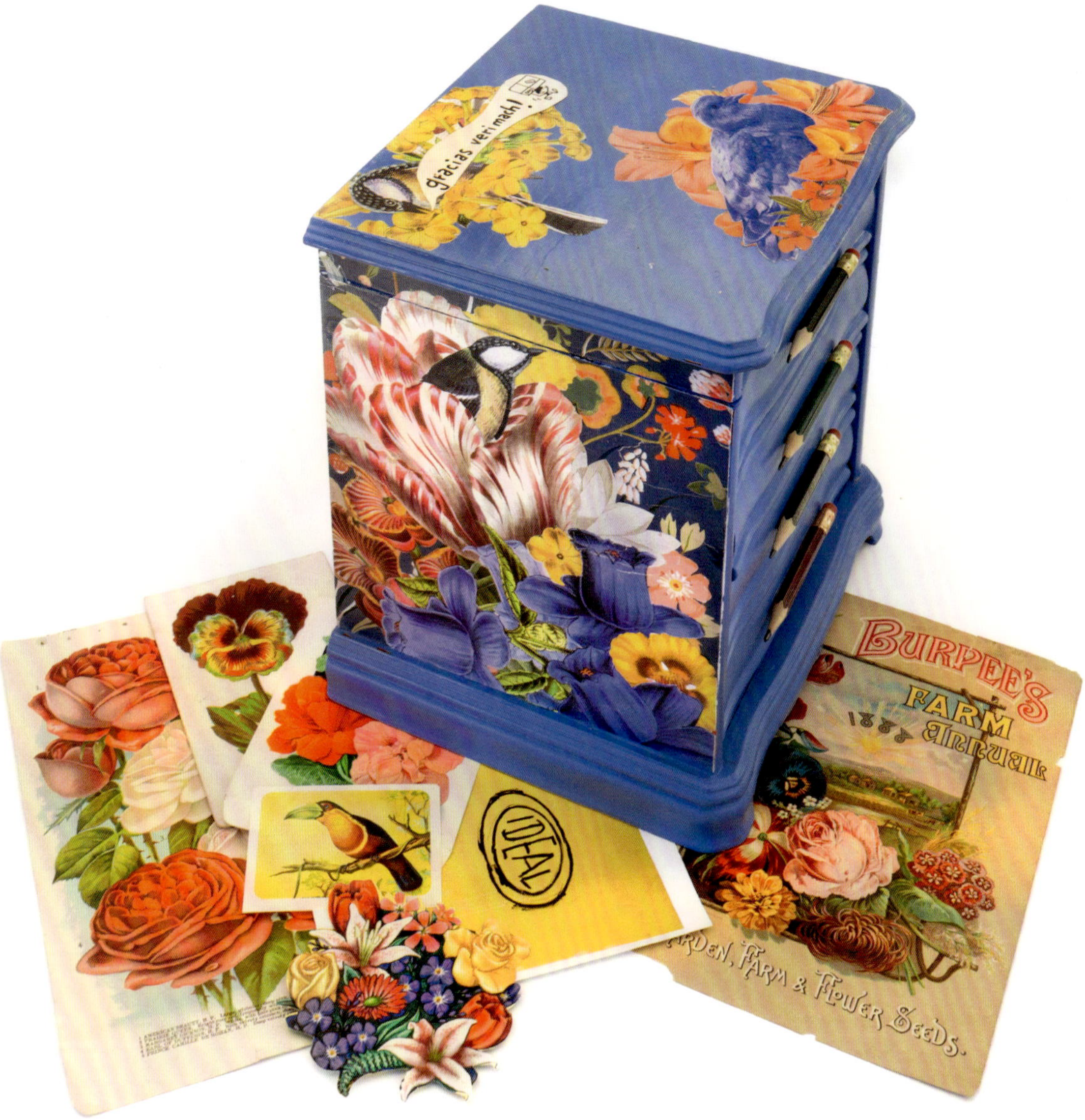

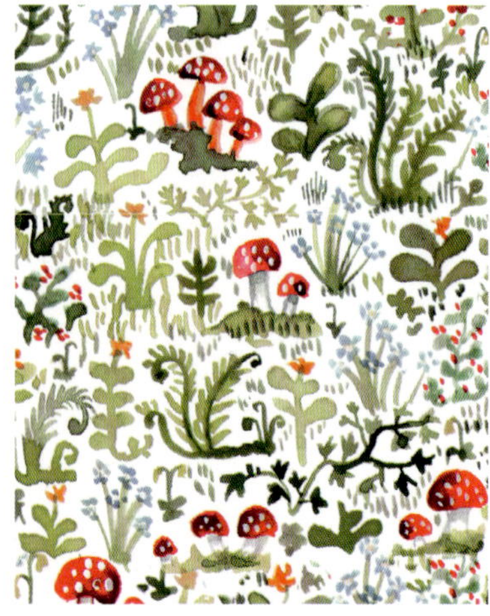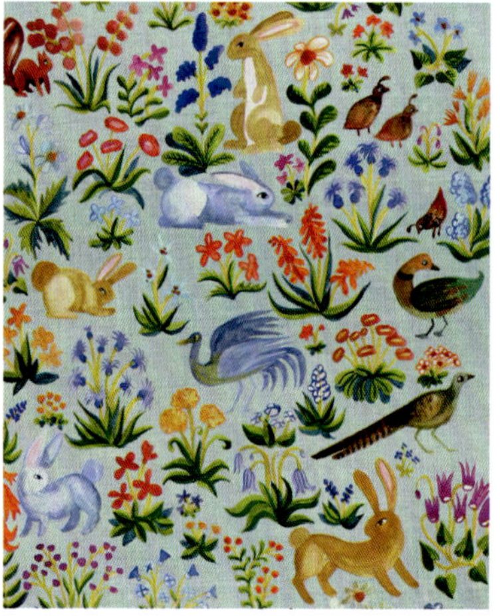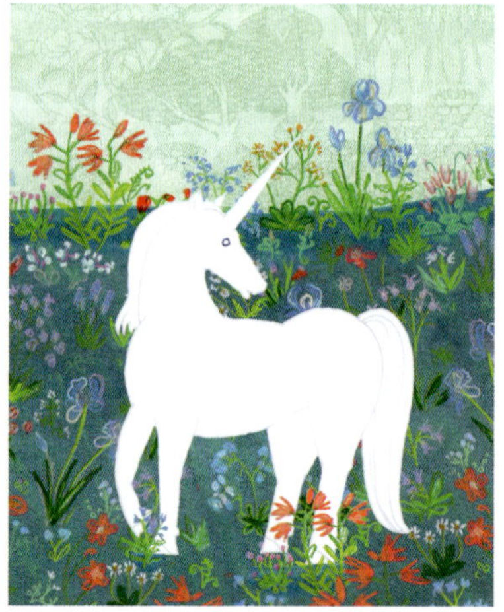

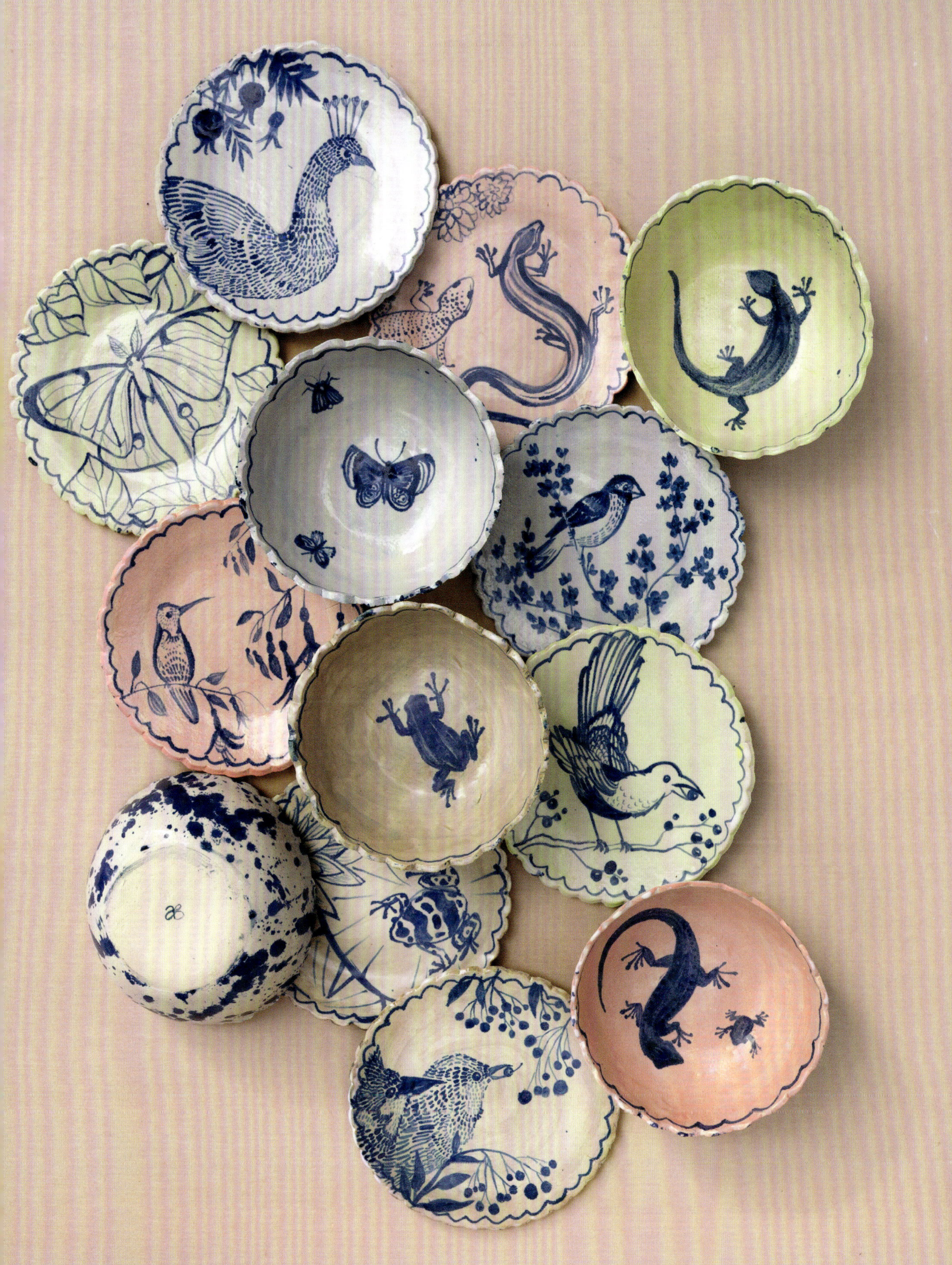

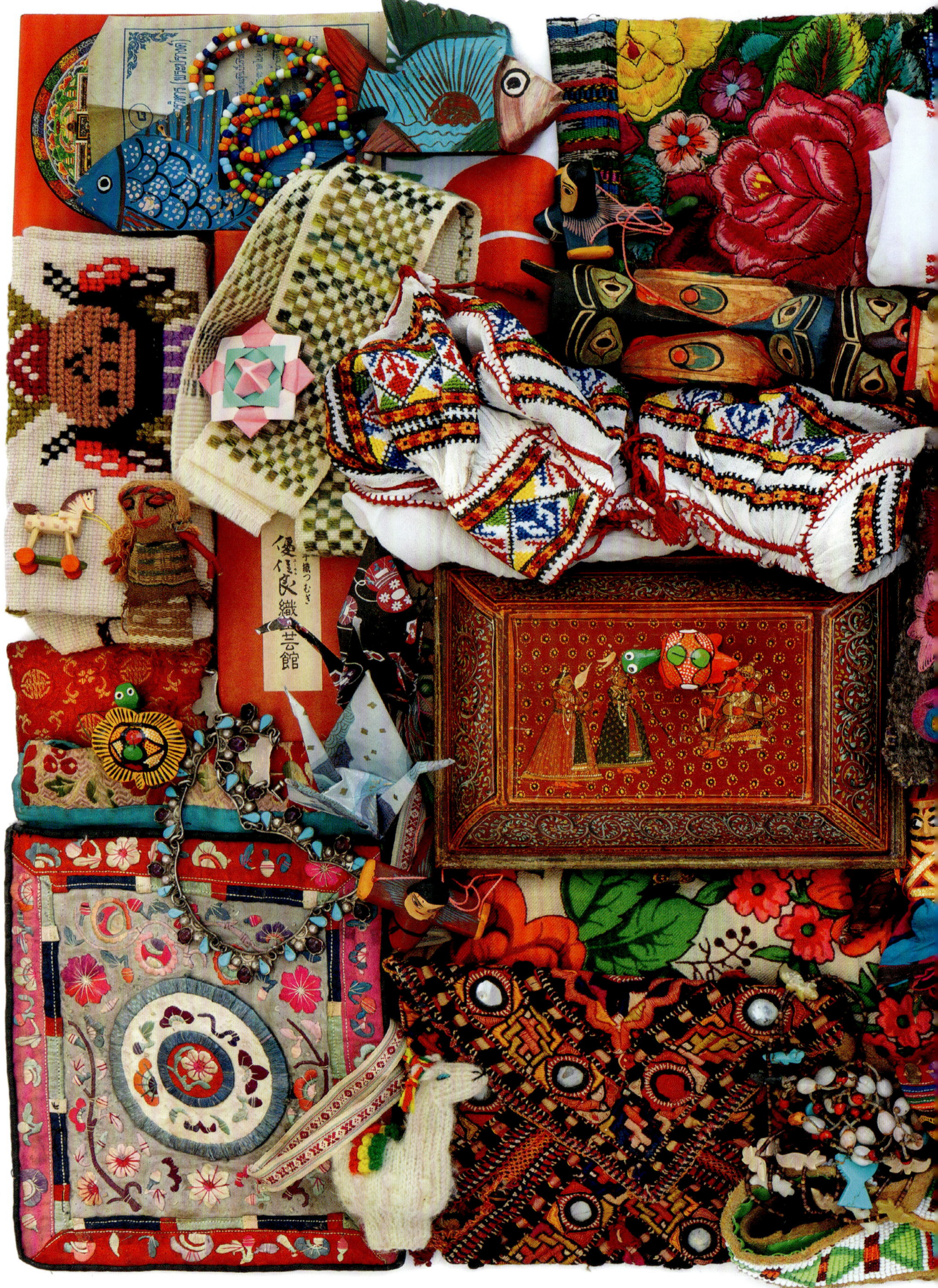

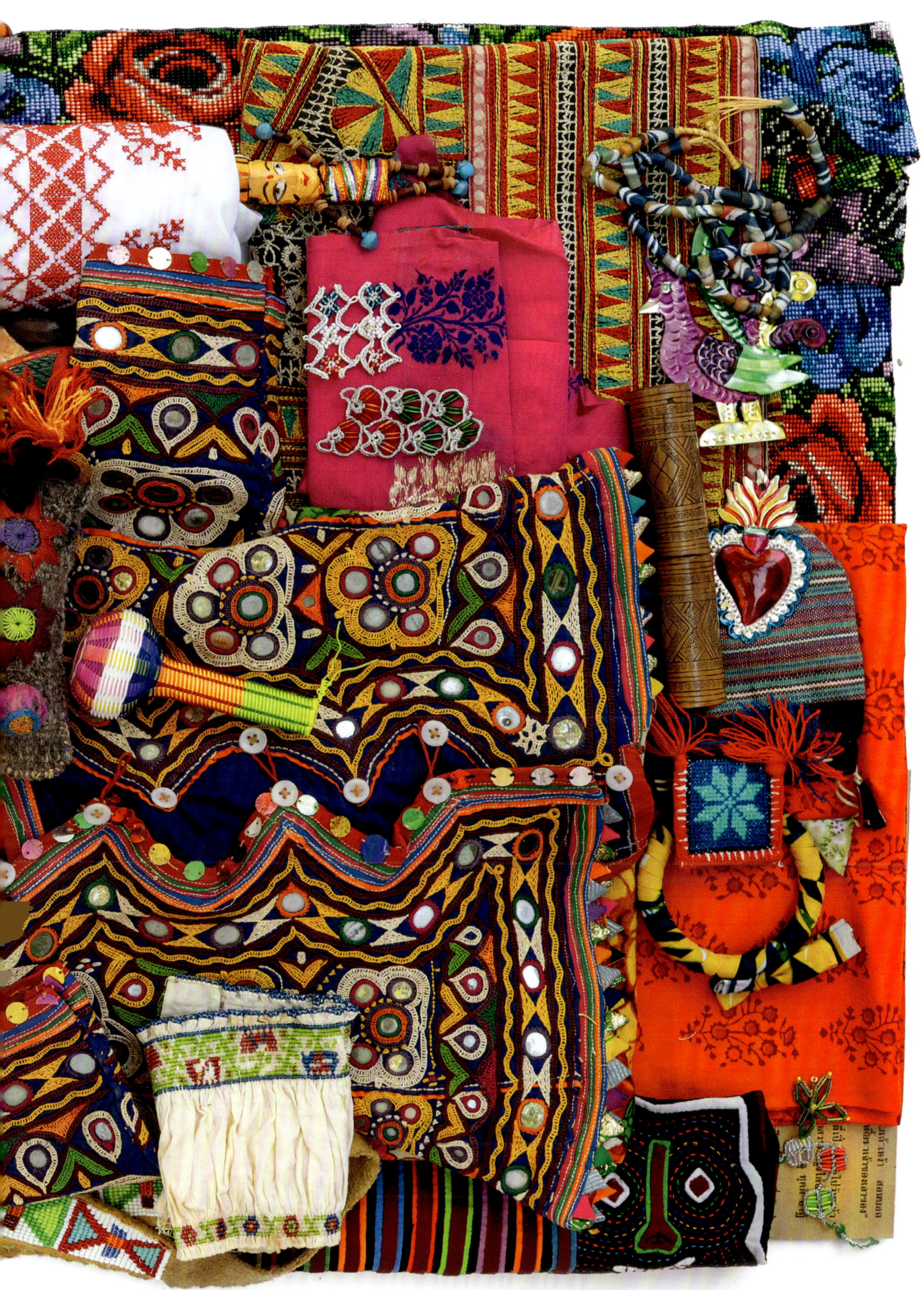

9.

THE COLOR OF A PLACE

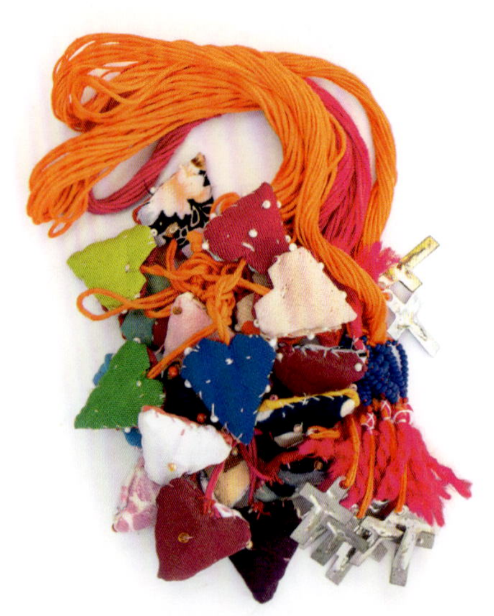

How to Be Inspired by a World Full of Color

W herever we go there is color, on the walls, in the food, in the landscape, and in the local history. Color is a cultural language; it comes across in traditional clothes and crafts as much as it is a result of the natural setting (besides the landscape, there may be animals or plants that imbue a place with a variety of hues). Even politics may come into regulating local color, with zoning laws dictating which color to use for the facades of the houses. Such is the case in Italy, where local regulations dictate that houses in Florence must be yellow and in Rome certain shades of oranges and reds.

I love the colors whose names come with a sense of place and a story. Sometimes, we buy a tube of paint that has deep connections to a place without even traveling or knowing about the origin story.

Those connections may have come about because that is where the colors are readily available, or because they've been used since ancient times and carried through history. While a lot of these colors are nowadays made synthetically, they retain the names that connect them to their place of origin.

First Things First: Thoughts on Cultural Appropriation

We live in a world that has become, rightfully so, much more aware of problematic cultural appropriation, the misuse of stereotypes, and the rights of artisans and crafters in small towns and communities around the world: those talented individuals whose names you would never know when you buy their crafts. I get enraged when I see artwork that I know comes from such communities suddenly being copied and used in all kinds of applications. One example is the long-stitch embroidered silhouettes of animals and flowers from the Otomí peoples in Tenango. Someone bought some pieces in Mexico and brought them back to the office, and the designers started churning out fashion and home decor items with these patterns. They have been copied and recopied either identically or very similarly. Do you think anyone asked for permission to use them? I am sure not. Are the Otomí people benefiting from it? I doubt it. At least these artisans got together and now their pieces do come with a certificate of authenticity. Too little too late, though, since now so many products have been made copying these patterns.

The same has happened with so many Mexican crafts, but also with crafts and traditional arts from around the world. Inspiration is not the same as plagiarism. In the same way that you would not copy a painting in a museum and pretend it was your own, you should not copy from other cultures and pretend it is your own creation.

So, now that you have your plane tickets and your camera and your eager eyes, how can you responsibly be inspired by the world?

Remember what I wrote in Chapter 8 about recordis? For me, one way to create a space where I can be thoroughly inspired by the world and still be respectful of the original authors, both in fine art and in traditional arts and crafts, is by going back to my memories of a place and allowing them to pass again through the heart. When I travel, I am all eyes (and nose and ears and tongue). I allow myself to be inspired by everything. The colors, the shapes, the typography, the materials, the figures, the patterns, the surfaces . . . everything goes into my mental notes or passes through my camera or sketchbook.

When I come back and go through my collected images, my sketches, and my visual souvenirs, I remember what I felt in the place. I remember what struck me as wonderful. As I recall the things I saw, they are passed from my memory, through my heart, and eventually to my hand and brush. Doing this process in full awareness creates a wide-enough creative playpen for me to create things inspired by travels, but far removed enough from the original source for it to be my own creation.

There may be many more ways—some looser, some stricter—for balancing inspiration and appropriation. This balancing game is fraught and delicate; regardless of how careful you are, it is entirely possible you may end up offending or annoying someone from the original culture. I get it, because I have been offended by people lifting or stereotyping my Mexican culture.

Besides the intimate act of using my recordis method, you can only proceed with true authenticity and honesty by learning as much as possible about the culture, the artisans, and the traditions. You can honor a place and a people by educating yourself about the things you saw in a trip. The more you learn, the less chance you have of being insensitive and becoming a visual thief.

THE WORLD IN A TUBE

Tyrian Purple

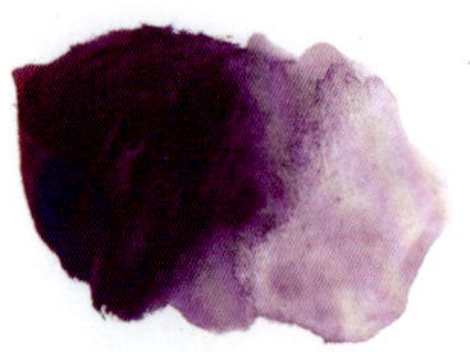

Also known as royal purple, this is a deep color worn by nobility in antiquity. It came from ancient Tyre, the Phoenician port where it was extracted from the glands of the Murex sea snail. Fermenting it in sunlight made the liquid turn from yellow to deep purple. The concentrate obtained was highly prized. Nowadays, there is a synthetic version.

Indigo

This deep blue dye, made from the leaves of a variety of plants, was independently created in India, China, and Egypt. But the name, derived from the Greek *indikon* meaning *from India*, was adopted as its use spread globally with the Silk Road and along the trade routes of the Dutch, English, and Spanish.

Egyptian Blue

This is one of the earliest synthetic colors. Ancient Egyptians made it by heating silica (present in sand) with copper (a readily available metal). It is a very stable and lightfast—important in the desert—pigment resulting in a range of intense blues. Widely used in ancient Egyptian artifacts and murals, it either represented divinity in a god figure or was used in depictions of the skies, the water, and ceremonial objects.

Prussian Blue

This synthetic blue pigment was accidentally discovered by the chemist Johann Jacob Diesbach in 1704. He was trying to create a different color when he stumbled upon this one and named it Prussian blue since he was based in Berlin, the capital of Prussia. It is also known as Berlin blue.

Mayan Blue

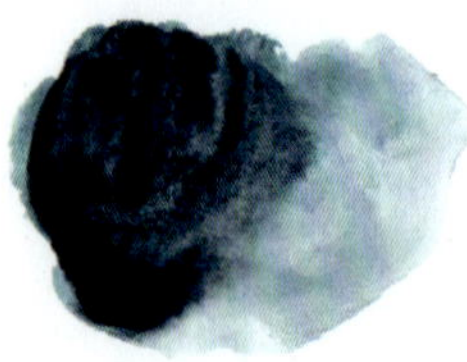

This particular tone of blue is associated with the beautiful Maya murals. It is the result of combining a native species of Indigo plant with a whitish local clay from the Yucatán Peninsula.

Turquoise

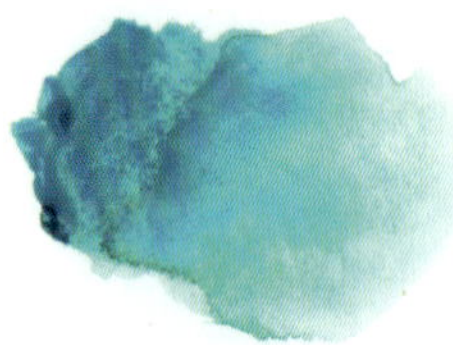

While the stone was highly valued in antiquity—ancient Egypt and Persia, where it originates, especially—both the stone and the color itself got their name from the French in the sixteenth century. The stones were introduced in France by Turkish merchants, and thus were called *the stone from Turkey.*

Paris Green

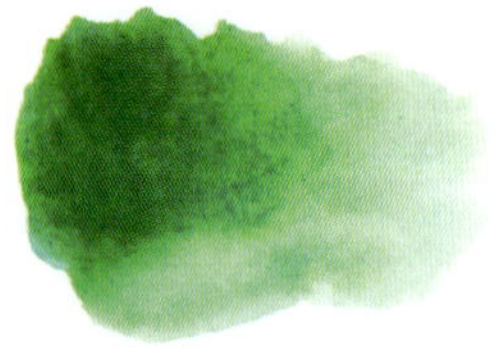

This intense green was all the rage in nineteenth-century France. It was used in wallpapers, textiles, and fine art. The rich and beautiful color was literally to die for since it contained a high dose of arsenic. Parisians figured this out because they were also using it as pest control for rats. Modern nontoxic substitutes include phthalo green, chromium-oxide green, and emerald green.

Chartreuse

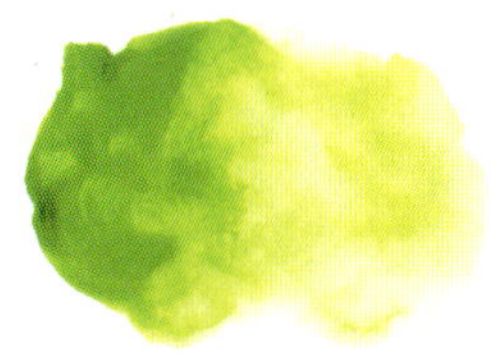

It is not named for a region or even for a town, but for a building: the Grande Chartreuse (the *grand cloister*) where the bright yellow-green liquor is still concocted by the silent and cloistered Carthusian monks following a secret centuries-old recipe including 130 botanicals. The color comes from the mix of green chlorophyll in the botanicals and yellow from the saffron.

Sienna

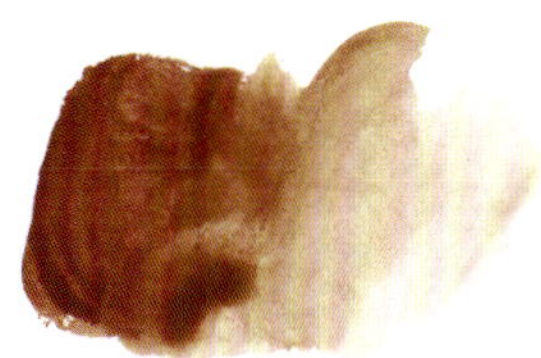

If you visit the Tuscan city of Sienna, you will understand where this color got its name. The whole medieval walled town is that shade. Raw sienna is the natural color of the local clay, which is high in iron oxide; burnt sienna is the color of the clay once it is fired, like in the bricks used to build the city. Technically these are among the many variations in the ochre family, but these two get to be named after the beautiful city from which they originate.

Sinope

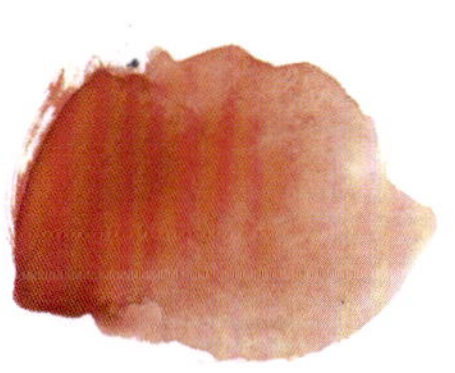

Also known as cinnabar, this is a rich orange red. It was used in Roman times and imported from the ancient city of Sinope (in Turkey), from which it got its name. In the Middle Ages and the Renaissance, it was used to sketch or trace, using handmade stencils called cartons, the outlines of figures on the walls before making a fresco. In Italy, the first sketch is still traditionally made in a vermilion color that gives a warm undertone to the painting, and the sketch is still called a sinopia even though the original pigment is not used anymore since its high content of mercury rendered it extremely toxic.

Kermes Red

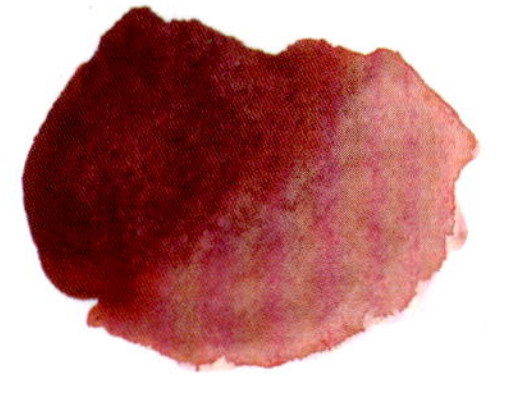

This color is made from little insects that live in a type of Mediterranean oak and were especially common in medieval times. The name is connected to Kermes, an ancient region in Asia Minor (modern-day Turkey), where production started before spreading around the Mediterranean basin. Kermes red was then substituted by grana cochinilla (cochineal) from the Americas.

Pompeian Red

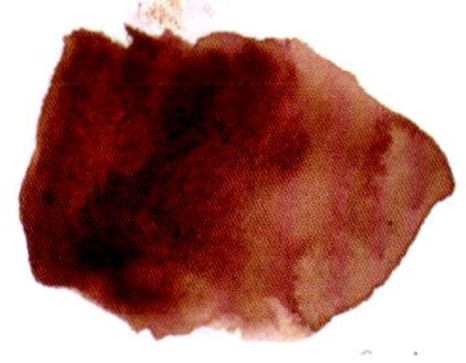

This is another red iron-oxide color, a red ochre, named after its city of origin. In ancient Pompeii and throughout the buildings of ancient Rome, it was extensively used for stucco finishes and murals.

Venetian Red

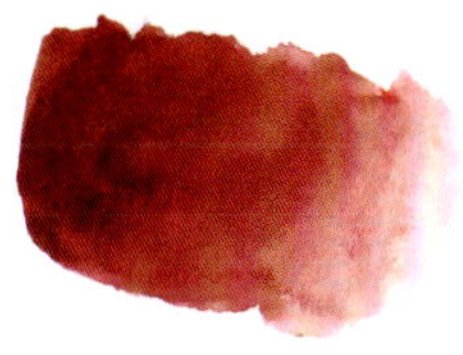

Similar in composition—with its use of red oxide—to Pompeian red, this deeper shade was especially loved by Renaissance artists and crafters in Venice.

Burgundy Red

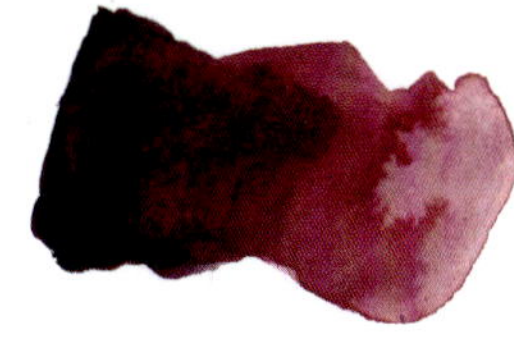

Cheers! Yes, this color is named after the wine from the Burgundy region of France. It is one of a few colors named after a wine region (another is pale yellow Champagne). Burgundy red was first used as a name for a color in the late nineteenth century. It is a deep red with purplish-brown undertones that evokes the aroma of red fruits and oak.

CAPTURING THE GENIUS LOCI

When I was in design school, every term we would take a trip somewhere in Mexico to gather inspiration for a graphic design assignment that would only be revealed after the trip. Our design theory teacher—the same Fernando Rovalo of the Barragán story—taught us the concept of genius loci. This is an ancient Roman concept referring to the spirit of a place: that collection of tangible and intangible qualities that make a place unique. He and our other design teachers would let us loose in the wonderful locations we visited with our cameras and sketchbooks. They made us sit in quiet corners and walk the streets collecting visual cues, sniffing the air, talking to locals, and savoring the food. We were doing everything we could with our senses to trap the essence of the place. At times, the genius loci felt to me like a flying spirit, colorful yet invisible, that I was chasing down the streets as it hid in the market stalls.

At the end of these trips, we would learn what the design project was: branding for a low-cost airline when we visited Real de Catorce, a former silver mining town, now a ghost town; a tourism campaign after visiting Oaxaca; food packaging after visiting Pátzcuaro; a textile collection after visiting the missions in the Sierra Gorda. By the time we sat down to design, we had all kinds of visual elements in mind: colors, motifs, typefaces that we had collected as we chased the spirit of the place. But mostly we had experienced the place with open minds and curious hearts. The place provided us a personal experience. The best grades went to those who struck the right balance, staying far away from copying anything directly yet holding the essence of the place and showing it in the designs.

This way of traveling and collecting inspiration has stayed with me. I continue to chase the genius loci wherever I go. When I travel, there are certain things I always do to collect the spirit of a place, in color and in a wider sense:

- **Photography:** I take tons of pictures, like we all do—digitally with a phone or camera, sometimes in film—but besides the obvious vistas and monuments, I try to be deliberate about what I shoot. I take photos with carefully cropped views—of people, places, things, art—that represent the essential colors of a place.

- **Sketches:** Sometimes I carry lots of art materials—an "artmobile"—but sometimes, after doing a bit of research ahead of time or anticipating colors for the landscape, I carry only a select few colors. That was the case on a train trip I took from California to Chicago with my daughter to capture the colors of the American West as they flew by us in the windows.

- **Objects:** I make a point of visiting markets, fleas, and galleries to find local artisans and understand the context and history of their crafts. I always assign myself a budget to buy these objects and try to choose them for their authentic representation of the place. As you know, there are a lot of inauthentic crafts everywhere that have nothing to do with the original work of the people. I try to buy crafts directly from the artisan or at a market or gallery that sells authentic pieces. This does not necessarily mean expensive; it can be super cheap. One of my treasured finds from Yucatán is a napkin, embroidered with bright threads, to wrap warm tortillas. I bought it from the Maya woman who made it, and she asked for three dollars. I normally don't bargain down a price unless it is part of the culture to do so.

- **Found objects:** Free souvenirs can range from paper, plastic, and fabric bits to a cut flower to a piece of peeled paint from a wall. These are everyday objects, not part of the art and traditional craft realms, that somehow catch my eye as reminiscent of the place. I have postcards, wrapping paper, and tickets. I have religious stamps from India and Latin America, packing paper from a bakery in Italy, and plastic wrestler figurines from Mexico. I have fabric and kitchenware and things found in thrift shops and flea markets. All this creates a random mix that somehow reminds me of the place and my experience there.

- **Things I collect with my other senses but somehow connect me to colors:** Aside from colors, I might collect travel mementos because of their scent, smell, or sound. Surprisingly, these memories can easily transform into visuals and colors: Warm colors relate to food and spices (saffron, curry, mole), or unseen flowers far off in a field might bring a scent of orange blossom that feels light green to me. Memories can come from either good or bad scents (jasmine in a woman's hair in Varanasi; cremation in Ganges, also in Varanasi). Evocative sounds can come from church bells in a concert written for the bells of the 175 churches in Cholula or in the praying room in a monastery in Tibet—similar metallic sounds that nonetheless bring different colors to my mind— or the sound of Vespas buzzing by in Rome, which in my mind I see in baby blue, minty green, and of course, bright red. These things that I experience through the other senses end up with color equivalents in my mind.

This is how I capture a place and make it mine; in my experience of it, I find inspiration to create art.

But what happens if I cannot travel or have not traveled to a certain place or experienced its culture firsthand? I embark on my research—online, in books, through documentaries—with the same spirit. I still try my best to capture the genius loci, even if it may be through the proxy of a book or a museum. As always, I aim to distance myself from the original, to find what is relevant from it in my heart and imagination, and transform it with my own hand as it becomes an expression of my creative voice, not a copy and paste.

COLOR HARVESTING IN THE WORLD

From pigment origins to folk stories and cultural history, from fine art to traditional craft, the world is full of color inspiration. No need to be a historian, just get your passport out and book a ticket to some faraway land. Your travel memories and photos, the objects you bring back, the foods and scents you experience, the people you meet, and the sights you see in museums, markets, and related books can be an endless source of inspiration. Travels are full of visual learning opportunities ready to be discovered and pursued.

"Why then, the world's mine oyster, which I with sword will open."
—William Shakespeare, The Merry Wives of Windsor, *1602*[18]

The world is your oyster: Shakespeare suggested cracking it open with a sword, but I suggest opening it with attention, curiosity, awe, and respect. Instead of a sword, use your pencils, your camera, and your watercolors or iPad.

I have always taken every opportunity to travel that has come my way. For me, the chance to see the world is something I relish. On every trip I feel like an artsy Marco Polo, bringing the wonders of my travels back to my studio. Sometimes I bring back just a bunch of curiosities I keep in my mind, sometimes it's crafts or random objects and the zillion photos I take or sketches I make. Every trip you go on enriches your visual vocabulary and develops your aesthetic sense. Travel fills you with ideas that you'll be eager to incorporate into your creative work.

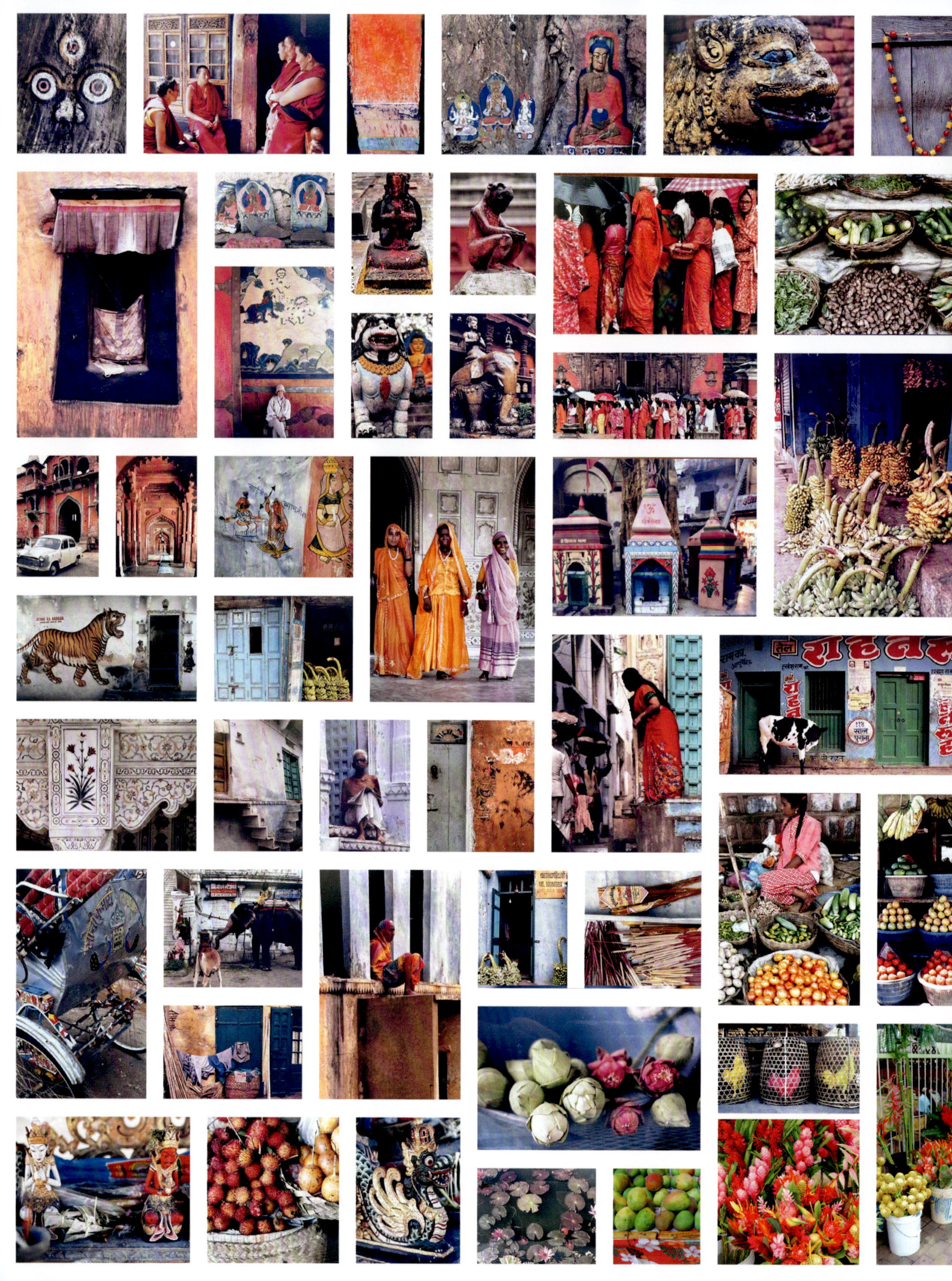

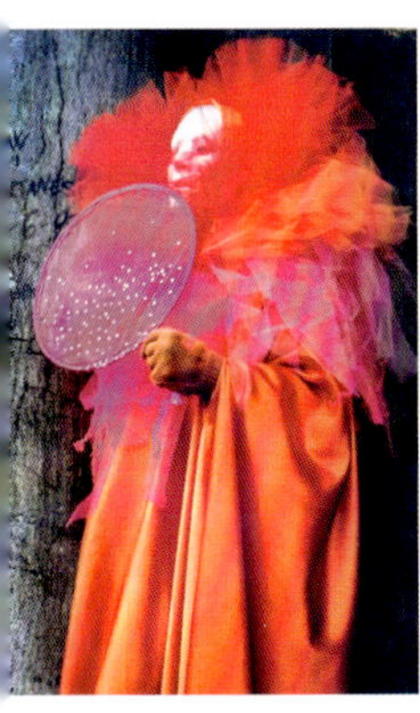
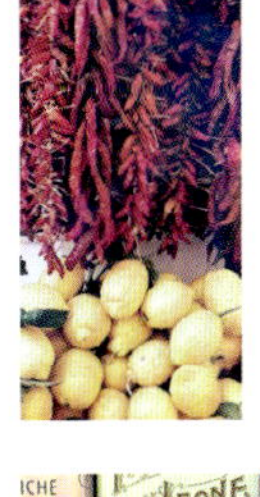
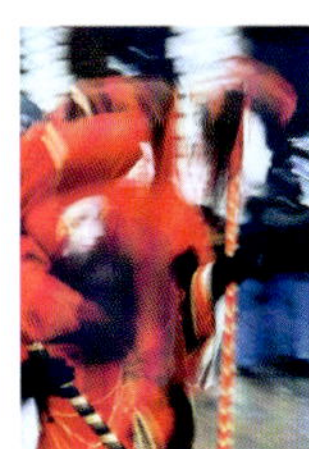
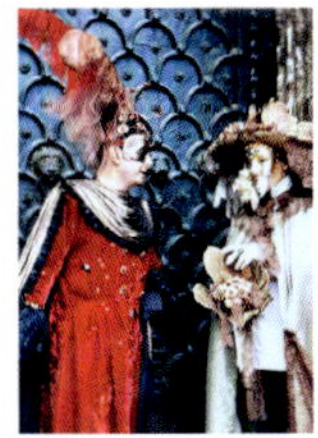
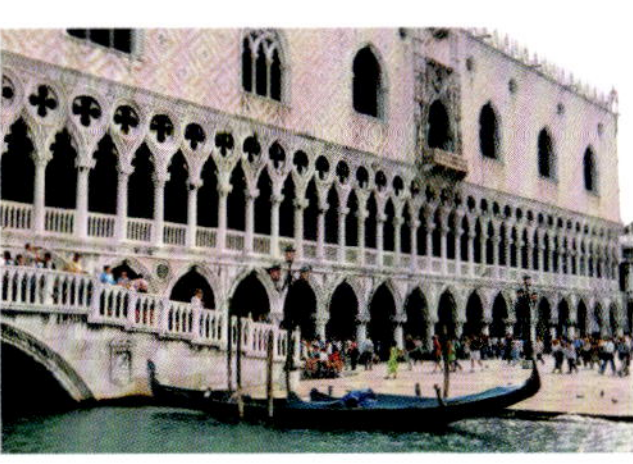
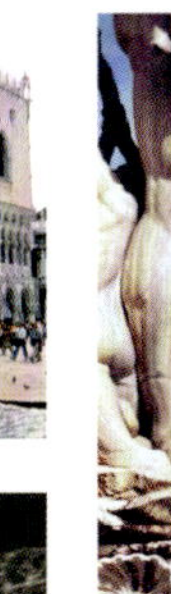
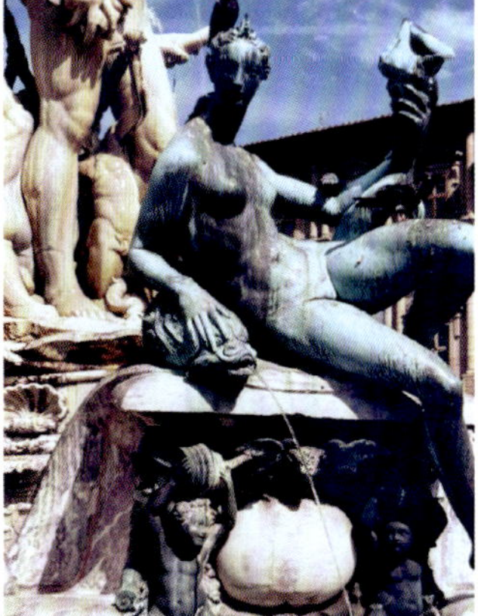
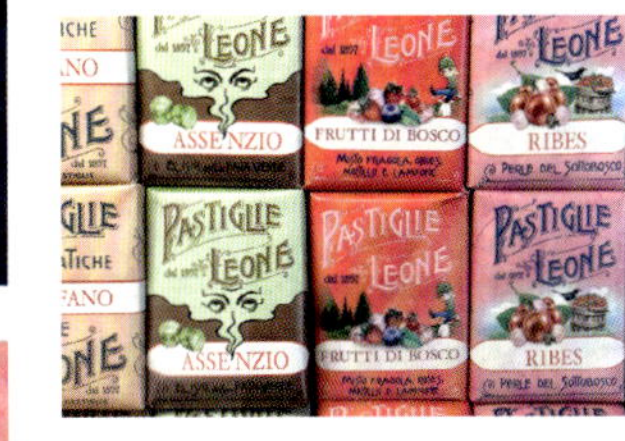
LEONE
LEONE
LEONE
ASSENZIO
FRUTTI DI BOSCO
RIBES
PASTIGLIE
PASTIGLIE
PASTIGLIE
LEONE
LEONE
LEONE
ASSENZIO
FRUTTI DI BOSCO
RIBES
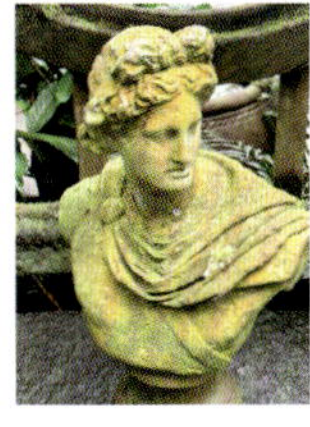
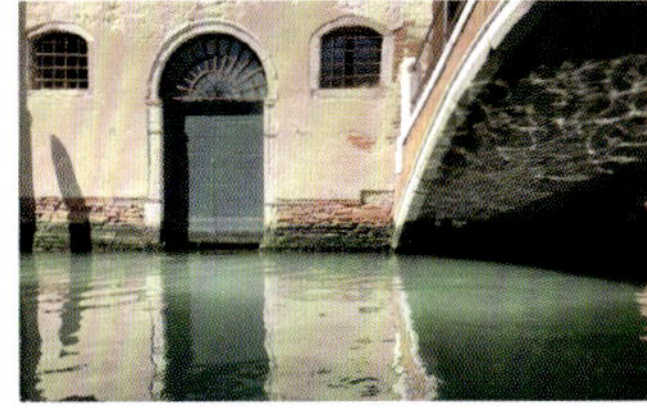
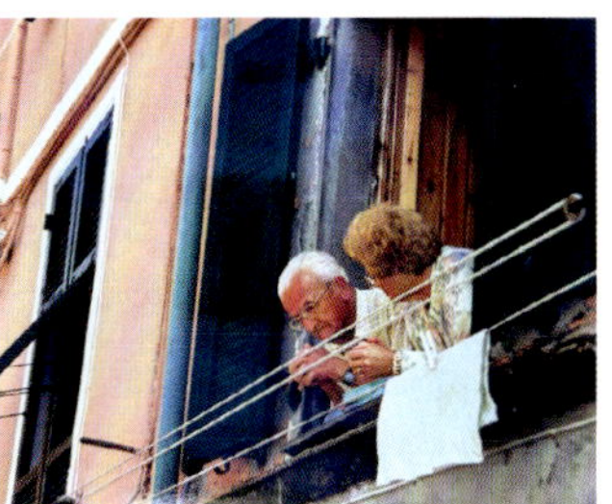
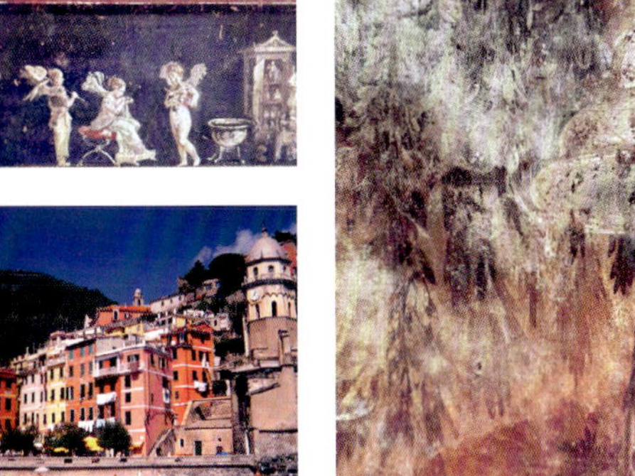
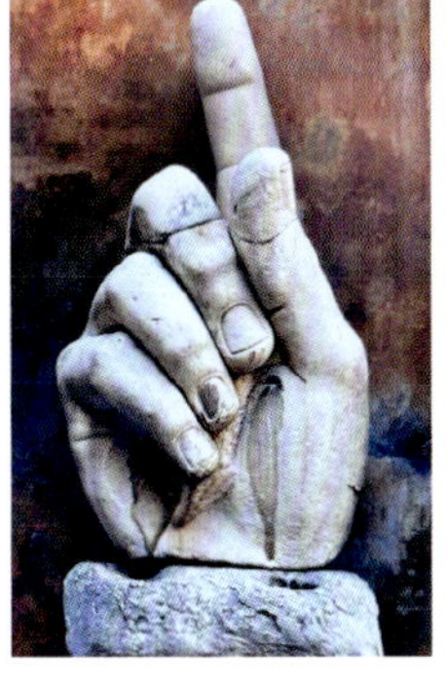
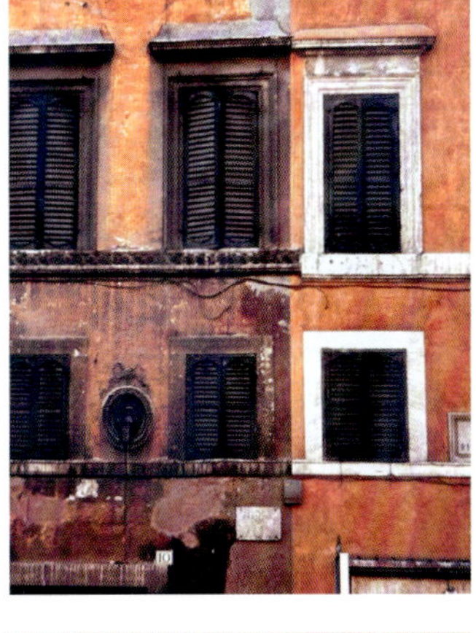
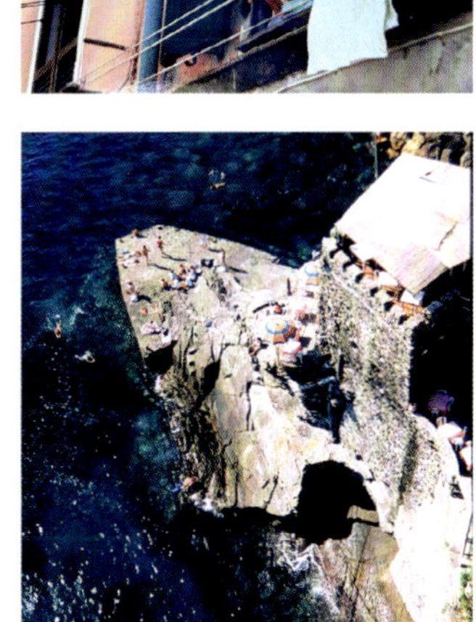
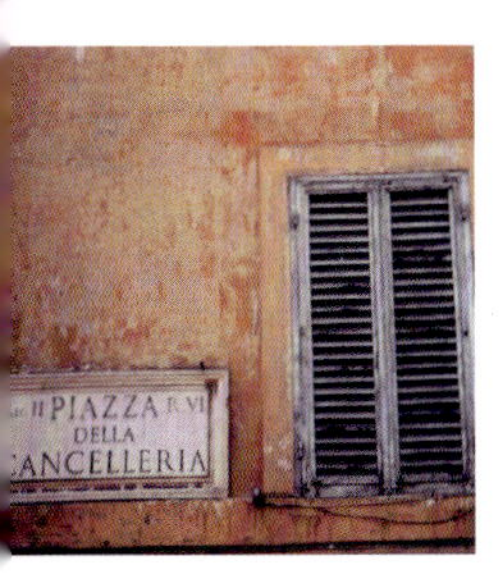
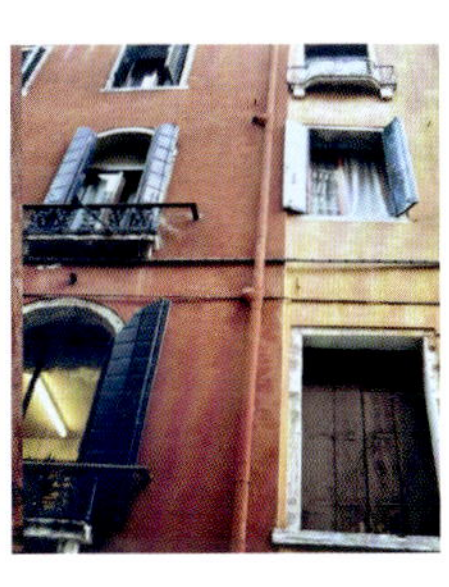
Il PIAZZA
DELLA
CANCELLERIA
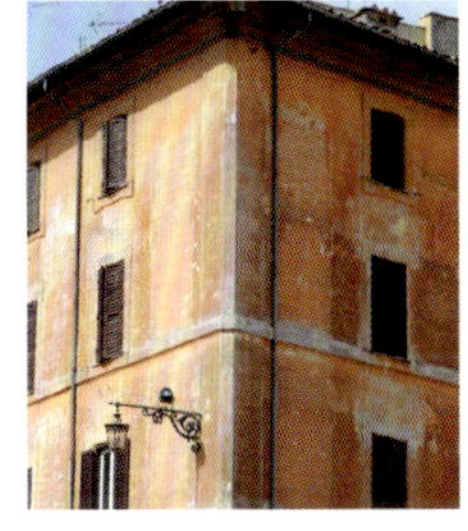
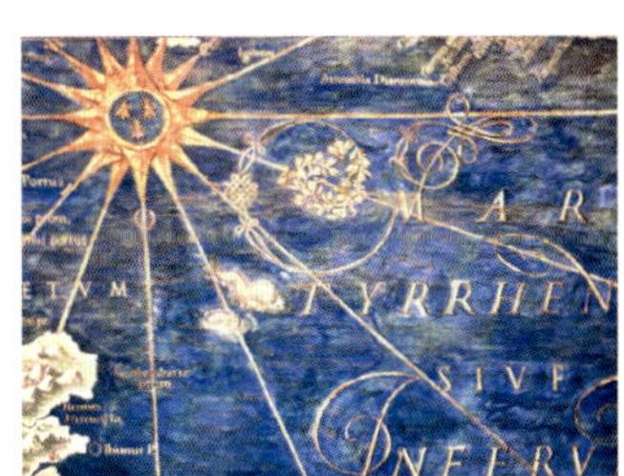
HERIA
OLIO - SEM
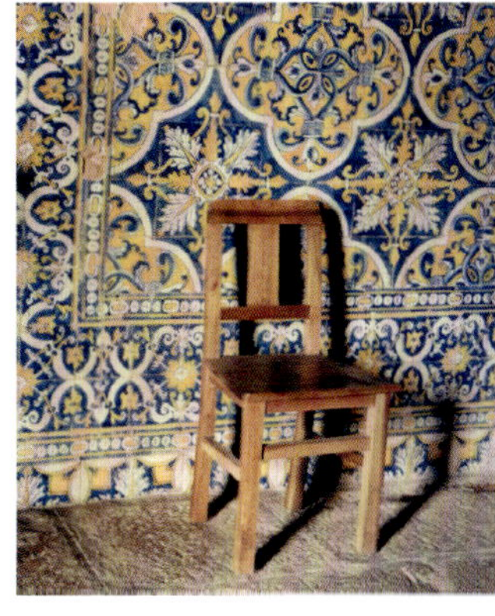
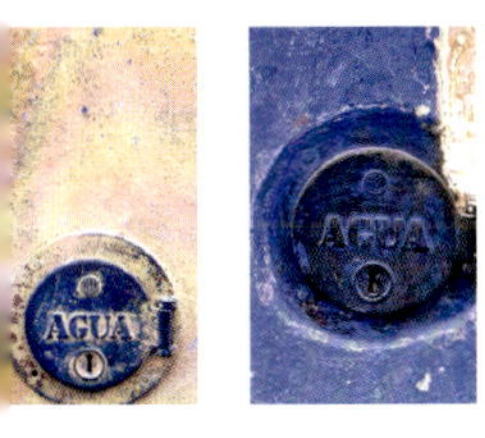
AGUA
AGUA
AGUA
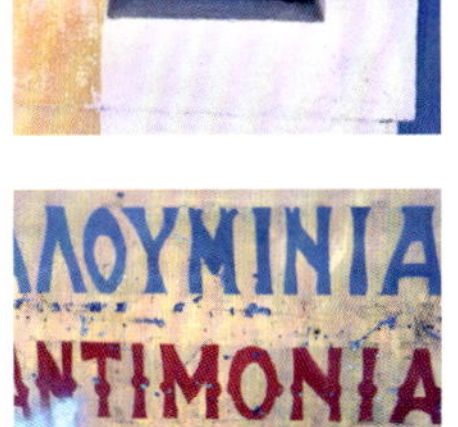
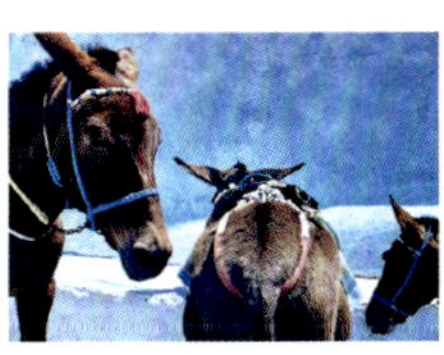
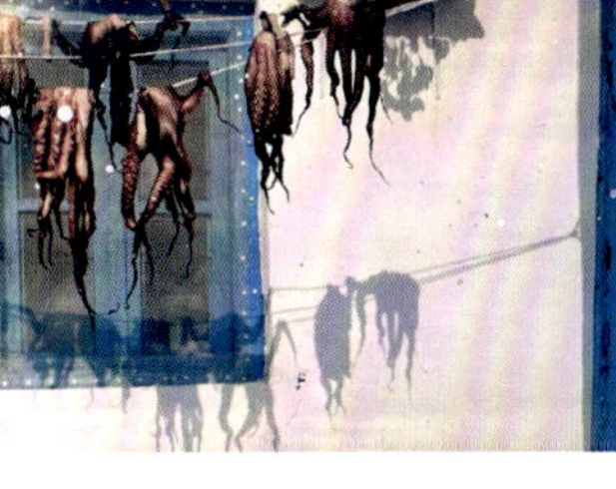
MAR
TYRRHEN
SIVE
INFERV
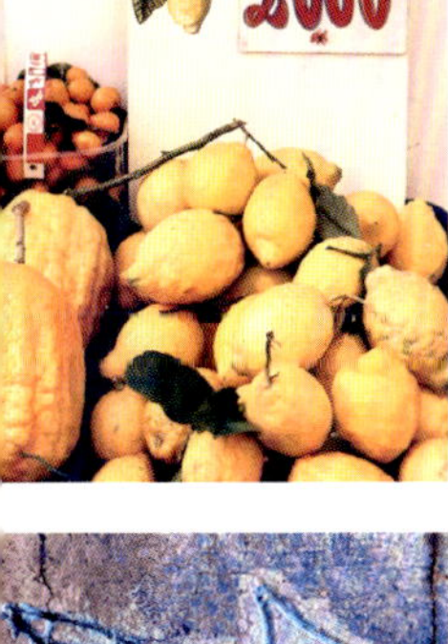
LIMONI DI
AMALFI
2000
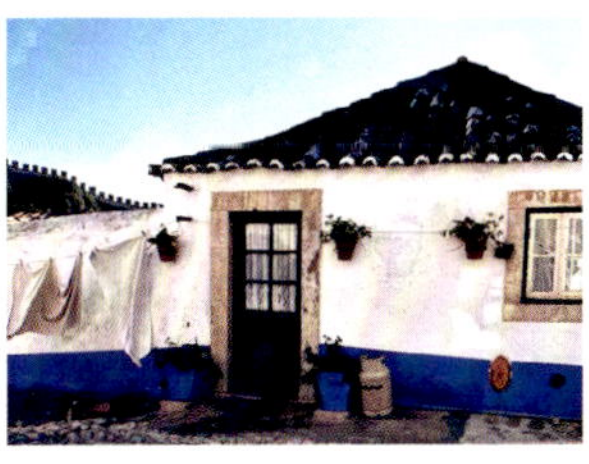
ΛΟΥΜΙΝΙΑ
ΑΝΤΙΜΟΝΙΑ
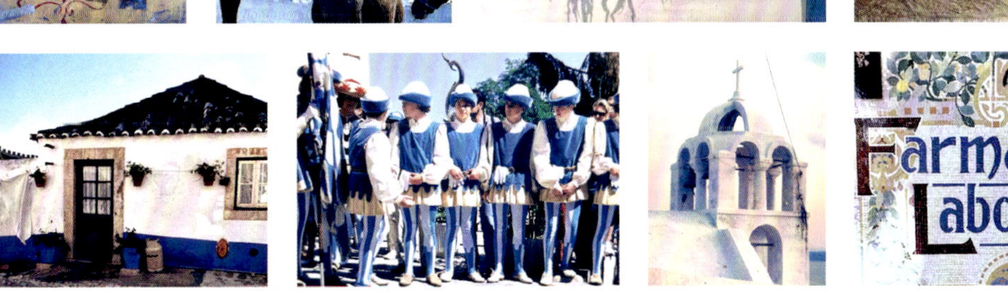
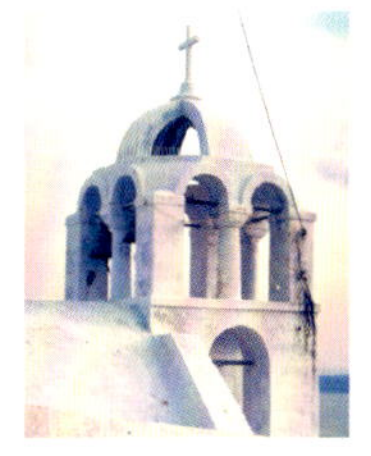
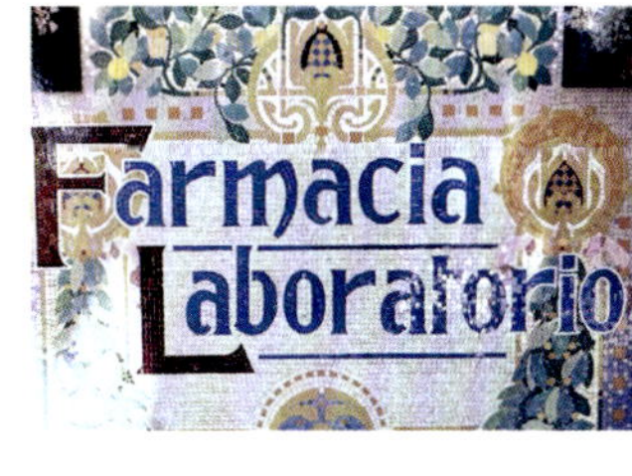
Farmacia
Laboratorio

THE COLOR STORIES OF FOUR ARTISTS FROM AROUND THE WORLD

Meenal Patel:
The Color of Home

Illustrator, children's book author, and designer
Based in Saint Paul, Minnesota
MeenalPatelStudio.com @meenalpatelstudio

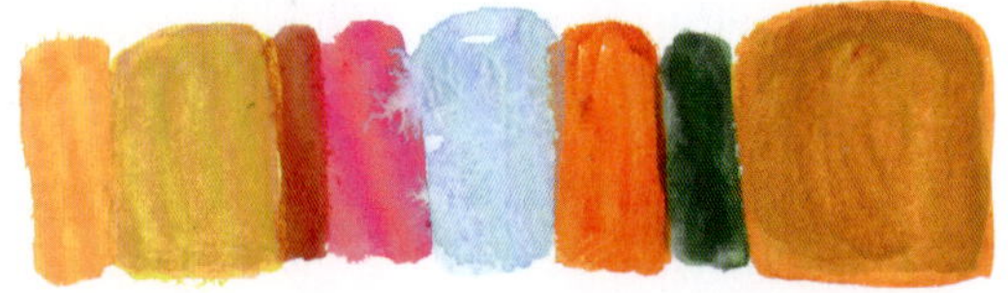

I grew up in an Indian American household, so my inspiration is multilayered, as is my lived cultural experience. I have lived my whole life in the United States, so there's also inspiration from the various places I've lived here. It is woven into my art just as it is woven within me.

My cultural backgrounds help me think about how colors interact and play with each other. It's an observation of places, cultural artifacts, and what types of color combinations thread them together. So rather than pulling specific colors from the cultures that I am a part of, I'm inspired by observing what overarching themes are happening in how colors play together—lush richness paired with earth tones, dusty pastels with bright pops of color. Thinking about color inspiration in this broader way helps me create more personal palettes.

When a color palette has a balance of bold and subdued, I feel a sense of calm and a feeling of contentment.

Color is perception and is rooted in each individual's experience. How is the way that I perceive or experience a color different from or similar to the person next to me?

I love it when there's a color that I don't quite know how to name in English—is it blue or green or gray? It reminds me of language and how some words don't translate directly to another language.

Andrea Pippins:
The Colors of Tropical Fruit

Illustrator, pattern design artist, and art educator
Based in Stockholm, Sweden
AndreaPippins.com @andreapippins

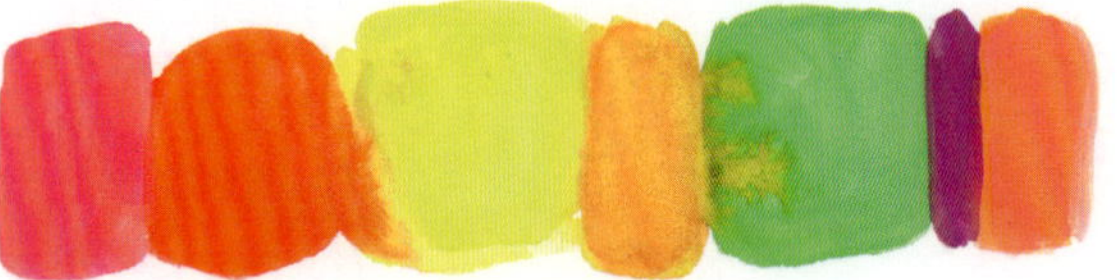

My cultural background is deeply rooted in my Brazilian heritage, but it is also very diverse. As a child I was surrounded by many different kinds of people from various backgrounds, which I loved. So with the exposure to many cultures, different people, and diverse ways of living, my work tends to reflect the richness in our differences while recognizing we are all people.

Some of my absolute favorite colors are a spicy orange, closer to chili-pepper red, its complementary color, seafoam green, and a bright acid yellow. I believe the inspiration for these colors comes from the vibrant dishes and fruit from my Brazilian background. My mother always kept fresh fruit available in our home, like oranges, mangoes, pineapples, guava, and papaya. She also loved cooking her favorite dishes from her home, which included colors from red peppers and tomatoes, fresh green salads and green peppers, and orange-colored sauces. I believe this influenced my attraction to color and how it can evoke a feeling.

Those three colors tend to pop up in most of my color palettes quite often. The orangey red and the acid yellow are eye-catching; they are vibrant colors that really make you stop and look. While the seafoam green allows the eye to rest bit, it is a great balance to the high energy of the other colors. Of all the colors, though, seafoam green is my favorite because it just feels calm, it reminds me of the clear blue waters of the sea, and it can act as a neutral.

Misha Zadeh:
The Colors of Southwest Asia

Illustrator and stationery, textile, and home wares designer
Based in Seattle, Washington
MishaZadeh.com @mishazadeh

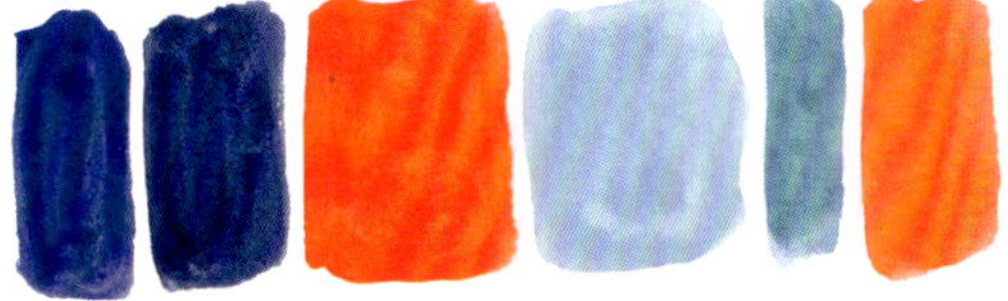

Although I don't feel much like it anymore, I am an immigrant to the US. I was born in Iran, and I came here with my family at age five. Although being Iranian is a very large part of my identity, I grew up in America and studied European and American art far more than art from my native Southwest Asia.

My design sensibility is very modern, clean—traits you would associate more with mid-century modern art from the West, or even maybe Japan. However, my color palettes tend to evoke Persian miniatures and carpet designs. This mix feels very comfortable to me and is very reflective of my life experience and my cultural heritage:

Turquoise—the first color used in the celebrated tile work of ancient Persians and Turks—made from ground-up turquoise stones! Along with lapis and yellow, this combination of three colors is found throughout the Middle East (we prefer to say Southwest Asia these days) and is a color palette that so many associate with the region. Turquoise can range from a robin's egg to quite green, and I am here for all of it. I love this color (and the history of it) so much that I named my first business Turquoise Creative.

Persian blue, or lapis lazuli, was the other blue incorporated into ancient Persian tile work. When I use acrylic inks, this is my most used color. I use it instead of black. The variation in tone gives the work a very warm and vintage feel. I use both the steel-blue and vibrant-blue ranges of this hue.

Poppy red (this is my name for it) is a warm orangey red, and very reminiscent of the poppy fields of Iran and Afghanistan. It is powerful, yet warm and inviting. Fun fact: In the housewares product world red colorways sell the best, then blues. If I were to be a color, I would be poppy red.

Geninne Zlatkis:
The Tale of Two Mexicos

Artist, illustrator, and maker of beautiful things
Based in Santa Fe, New Mexico
GeninnesArt.com @geninne

I was born in New York City but left when I was very little to spend most of my childhood in Latin America. In Mexico, my colors were super bright: lots of fuchsia, hot pink, and hot red oranges combined with cobalt and turquoise. It was the shock of the color that I was going for. I was very influenced by all the cultural aspects of living in Mexico, especially the beautiful crafts. I feel so moved just by the thought of how sensible and talented the artisans there are: They just know how to pick the right colors!

Then I came to New Mexico, and my colors changed. Here I became influenced by nature. My colors became more earthy. I started using browns, which I never used before; my greens became more olive, like the cacti. The desert landscape and everything that surrounds my adobe house ended up influencing my work. While I still love highly decorated Mexican crafts, here I only use the ones that are not decorated, the bare clay pieces.

Those reddish colors are present in so much of my work, my home, and all around me during my walks with Zorrito, my terracotta-colored dog. As I photograph and post these images on my Instagram, the colors are real, not a color filter!

My color palette stays the same, always consistent colors that I combine in a million ways.

My favorite color? Well, it has to be this range of blues that go from indigo to turquoise, a particular teal. That color has been a constant from Mexico to New Mexico to the point that once, a collector of my work in the UK sent me as a gift a little blue glass vase because it reminded her of my teal color so much. The vase contained a poem inside she had written and recited in front of two thousand people at a poetry festival there. The title of the poem was "Geninne's Blue."

THE COLOR OF LATIN AMERICA

A CHROMATIC CONVERSATION BETWEEN MEXICO AND PERU

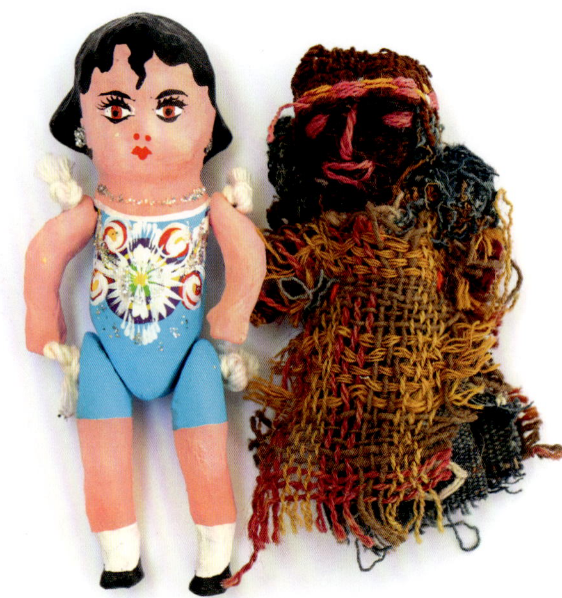

↑ Friends: a doll with articulated arms and legs from Mexico, made with the traditional papier-mâché technique called cartonería, and a traditional Peruvian rag doll from the Andes, made with Inca textile fragments.

It is common to think of Mexico as a colorful country: Its food, crafts, and art are usually quite vibrant, but across its rich history, not everything is in high-octane saturation. Mexico's culture is as nuanced by its rich history and layered in hues as it is in flavor and regional variety. The same is true of Peru. After all, both countries were the seats of vast ancient pre-Columbian empires, and later silver-rich capitals in colonialist times. Nowadays, both countries continue to keep their vibrant traditional arts alive thanks to the Indigenous communities who stay true to their crafts, collectors who appreciate them, and modern art galleries that carry new expressions inspired by tradition.

Something else that is common to both countries is their distinct love of color.

The following is a condensed conversation with Himi Saito, who, like me, is an artist, designer, and illustrator, and with whom I share thirty years of friendship since meeting in art school in Florence.

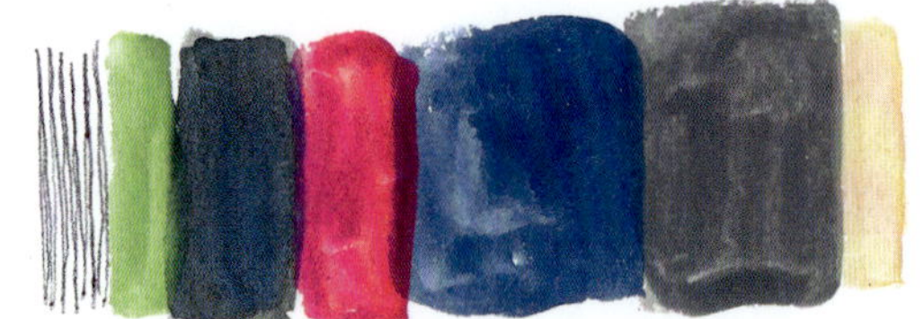

Himi Saito: The Color of Peru

Japanese Peruvian artist, designer, illustrator, and owner of Casa Ema in the Sacred Valley in Pisac, Peru
Based in Lima, Peru
HimiSaito.com @himisaito

ANA: We both were born in countries with rich history and color, you in Peru and I in Mexico, yet our families come from countries with a different color identity than our birth countries. My family from Spain, and yours from Japan. How does this dual nationality play into your favorite colors?

HIMI: I used to think that Japanese aesthetics were characterized by the use of neutral colors, while Peruvian aesthetics were vibrant and colorful. However, I now realize that both cultures express themselves in similar ways. In Peru, we also have sober expressions such as the use of stone, ceramics, and the purity of color in undyed alpaca fibers. Although Japan may seem more into neutral colors, it also has expressions of high chroma in its temples and celebrations.

In both cultures, I perceive a deeply rooted spirituality, not only through their symbolism but also in how they express themselves through color, depending on their respective mysticisms and festivals. Defining my favorite colors is a challenge given that each environment has its own palette and context. In my home, neutral tones predominate, and I feel that natural colors give me peace of mind. However, I can't help but admire the explosion of colors in the patron saint festivities, as well as the vibrant combinations worn by the women of the Andes. I feel that there is both experimentation and bravery in their choice of colors; this is an authentic expression of their essence and the lives they aspire to.

ANA: We've spent some time together traveling in Peru, and you are the host of Casa Ema in the Sacred Valley, decorated with beautiful crafts from the Cuzco region. What is your relationship with the artisans?

↓ This altarpiece, made and signed by Alfredo López Morales, follows the tradition of the Ayacucho polichromed altarpieces of Peru. By signing and taking ownership of his work for the world to see, Morales connects the viewer with the artist who made it.

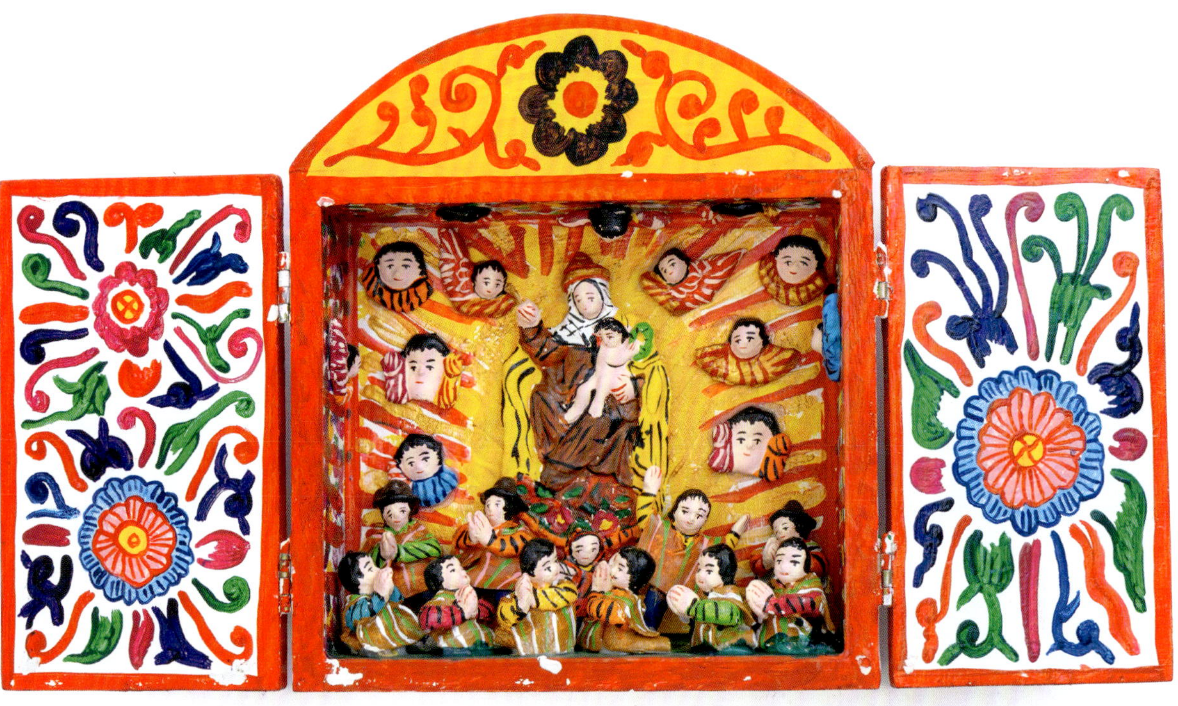

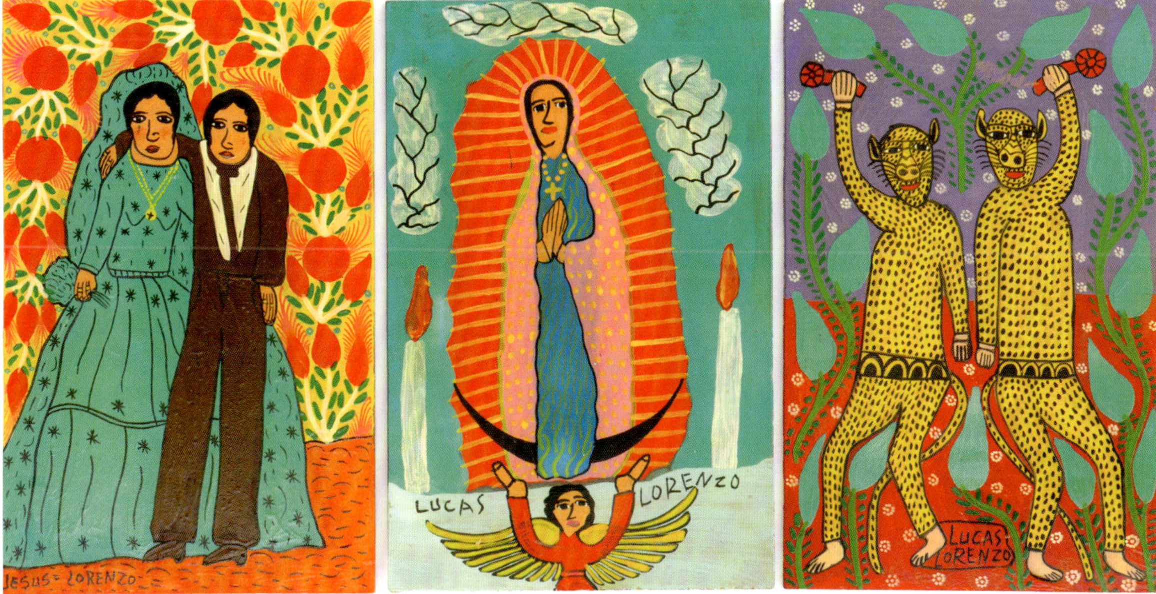

↑ These are some of the paintings from the Lorenzo family. Two were painted by the family patriarch, the late Lucas Lorenzo, and one by his son Jesús Lorenzo, following in his footsteps. Their paintings maintain a connection to and honor the traditional crafts of their hometown in Guerrero; however, they are also a departure, with their distinctive style and bright colors.

HIMI: Crafts constitute a medium for the transmission of traditions, stories, and values of a community, and they become a vehicle of cultural identity. I admire that a country keeps its artisan groups so alive.

ANA: Similarly, in Mexico, every region has its share of traditional crafts! All these traditions are usually not only region or town traditions, but knowledge passed through generations within a family. Some are derived from festivals and religious syncretism, and some are the result of beautified objects of daily life. There are whole towns dedicated to a single type of craft—ceramics in Tonalá, textiles in Teotítlan, and Talavera ceramics in Puebla.

Some traditions in Latin America are indigenous, and some are the result of the mix of Spanish and Indigenous populations, like the blue-and-white ceramics my ancestors were involved with when they first immigrated from Spain to Mexico in the late nineteenth century.

While popular art is often made by artisans and families known in their towns, most remain anonymous once their crafts leave their towns to be sold and enjoyed somewhere else. However, some artisans sign their pieces, so their pieces travel with their name. Sometimes it is the whole family that becomes well-known—like the Uriarte family in Mexico, whose exquisite Talavera-ware fetches high prices, or the more affordable and immensely colorful artwork from the Lorenzo family, whose art started with Lucas Lorenzo (1940–2020). Lucas Lorenzo was a traditional amate painter of scenes in Xalitla, Guerrero. He decided to break from tradition and started painting larger characters on masonite to make them more durable; he passed on this tradition to his children, Santiago, Jesús, Nicolás, Aureliano, and Carlota, and even his grandkid Fernando. Each piece is signed, and they leaped from market to galleries.

How do you see these leaps from artisan to artist in Peru?

HIMI: Perhaps the difference is that the artisan is often part of cultural and community traditions, passing down techniques from generation to generation, while the artist may operate in a more individualistic context, challenging established norms. However, the line between the two is very thin. During the last Venice Biennale exhibition, the Indigenous artists Santiago Yahuarcani from the Aimeni clan (the White Heron clan) of the Uitoto Nation of northern Amazonia and Violeta Quispe from the Quechua culture in the Ayacucho region of the Andean Peru were introduced, and both come from a more community-based path, while today they contribute their unique vision to contemporary art.

Closer to traditions is the Ayacucho artist Alfredo López Morales, an expert in creating pieces of imagery, such as polichromed altarpieces, crosses, and masks. He learned this trade from his grandfather, the renowned artist Joaquín López Antay, and continues the tradition while adding some contemporary elements. His fifty-plus-year career was recognized with a Meritorious Personality of Culture medal in 2009, and he is still creating. I hope you enjoy this piece of his that I got for you!

KEY TAKEAWAYS

1.	The whole world is a rich place for inspiration; color harvest with the right mix of curiosity, learning, and respect. Search for the true genius loci.
2.	Take every travel opportunity—on a plane, online, in a book—as a chance to learn and discover, to collect and expand your visual archive.
3.	Involve all your senses when you are on a journey. Scents, flavors, and sounds add dimension to the spirit of the place.
4.	Never copy what you find in the world; pass it through your heart—recordis—and apply it to your work only when you've found your personal meaning and connection with what inspired you.
5.	Color is culture; be aware of what colors may mean in different contexts.

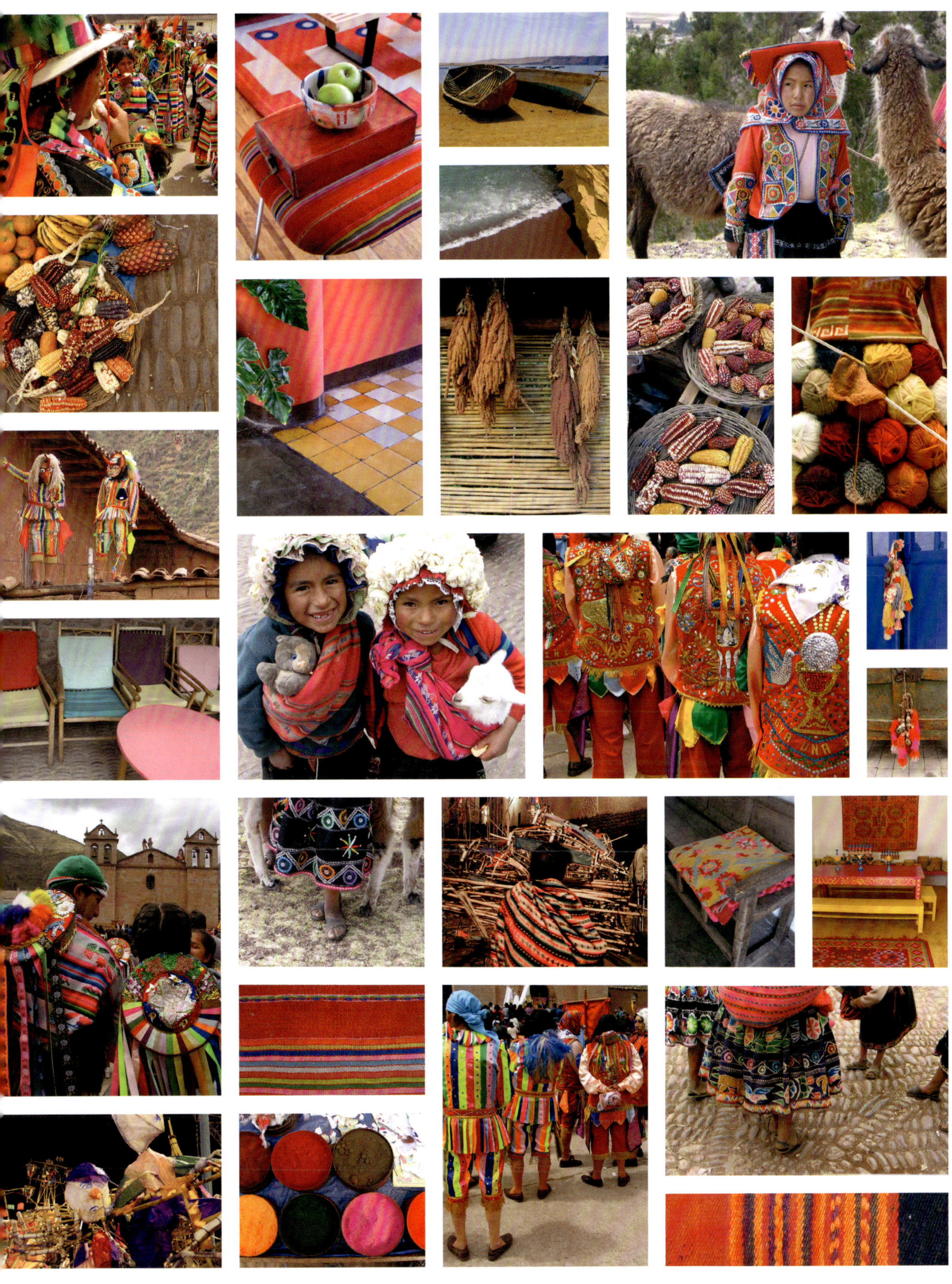

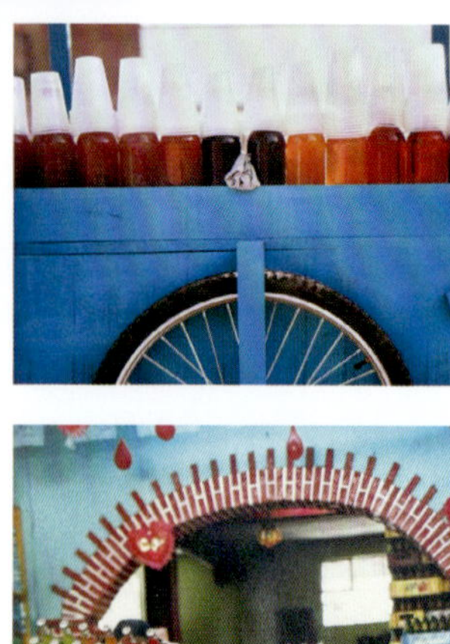
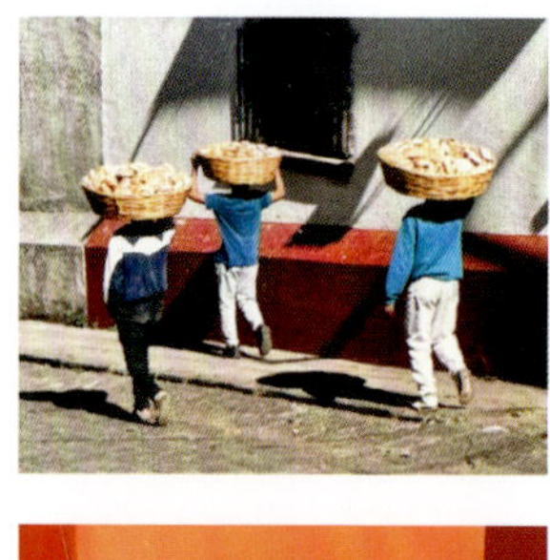
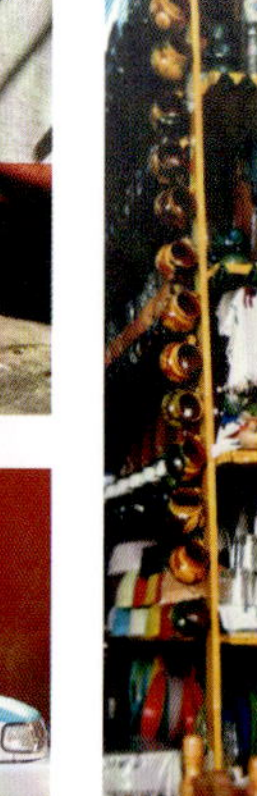
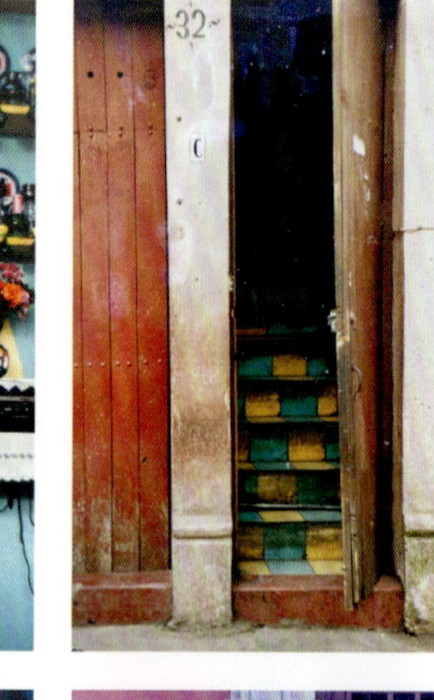
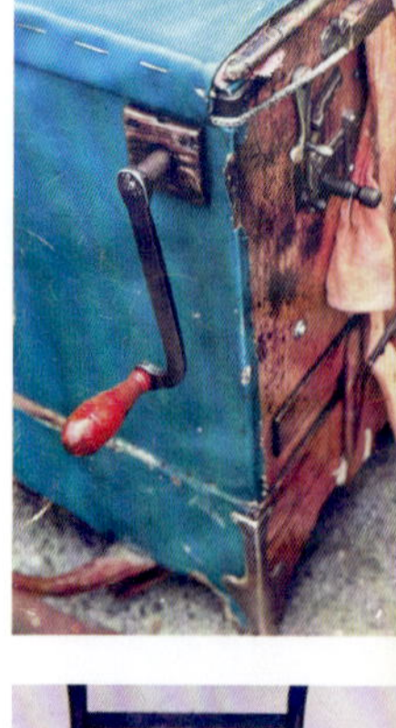
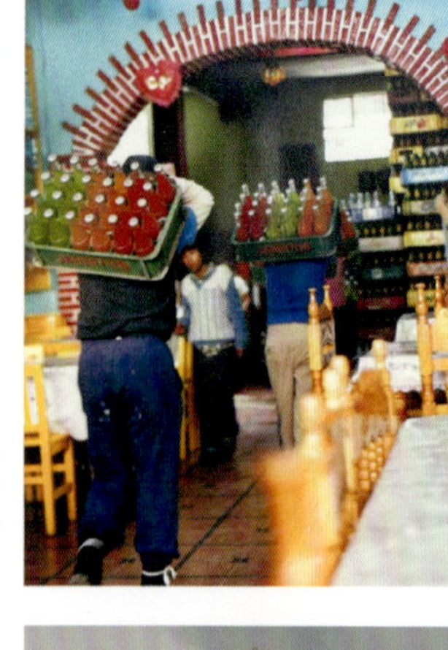
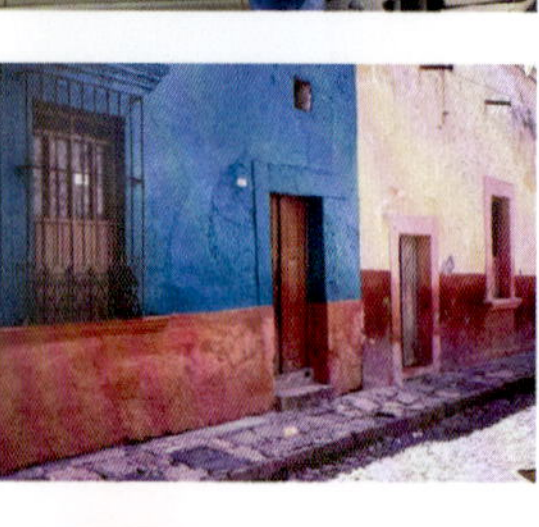
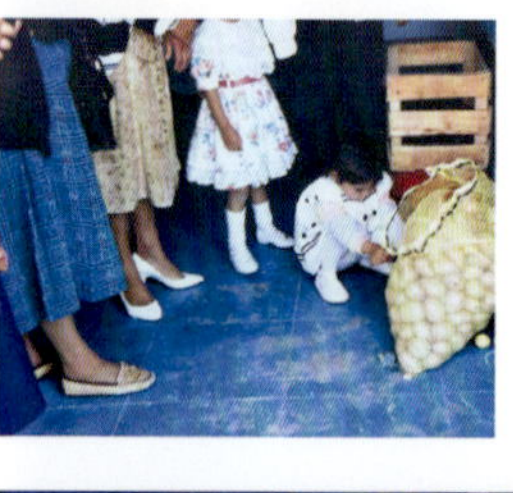
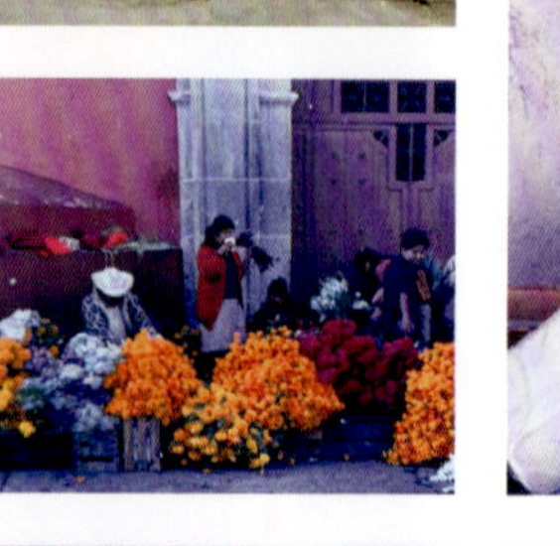
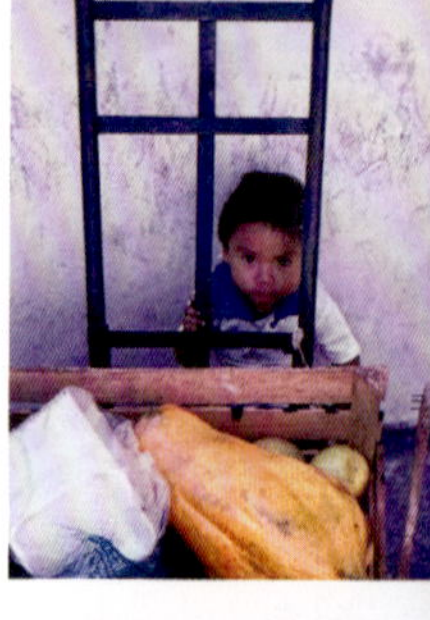
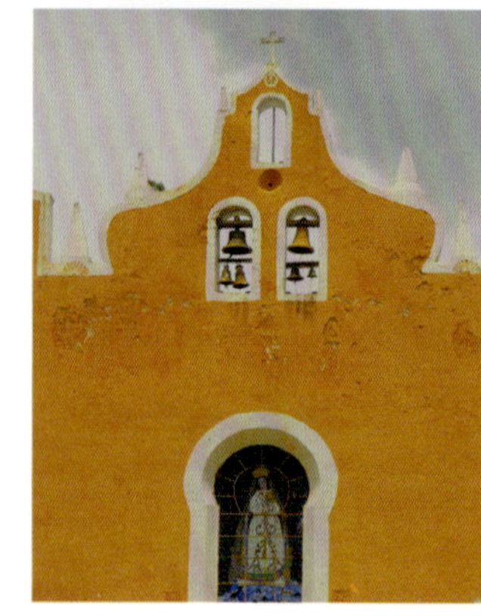
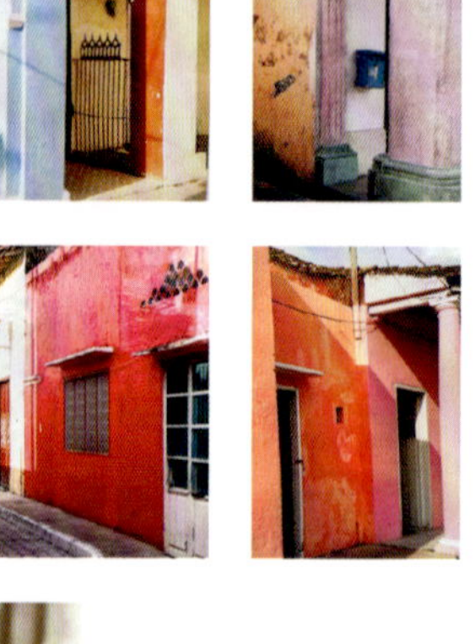
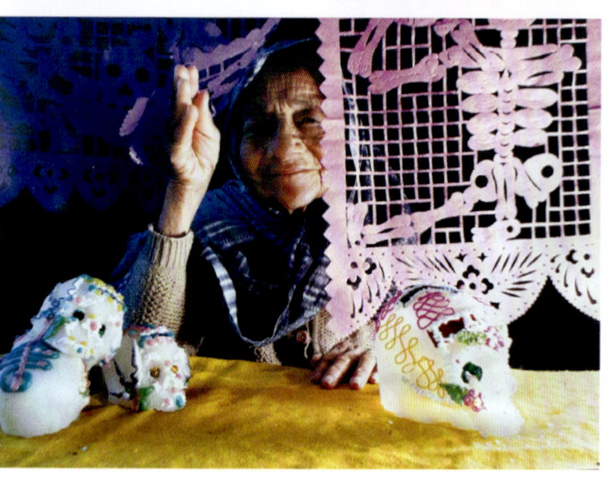
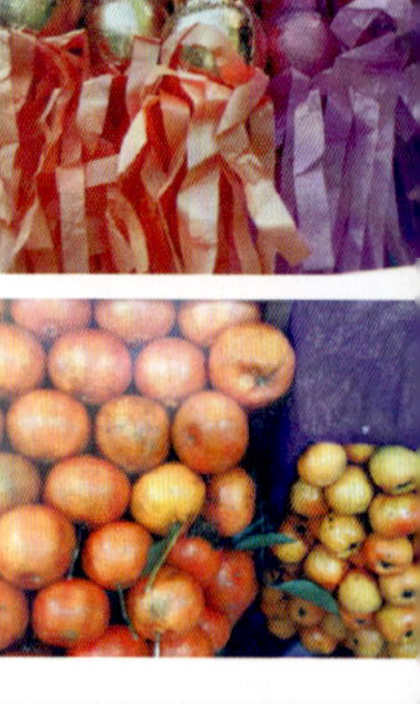
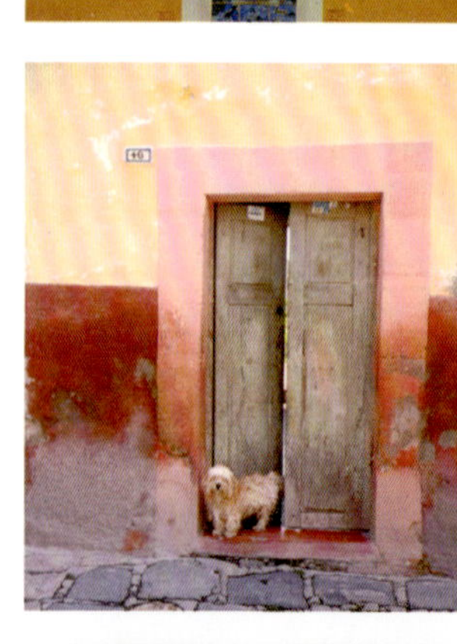
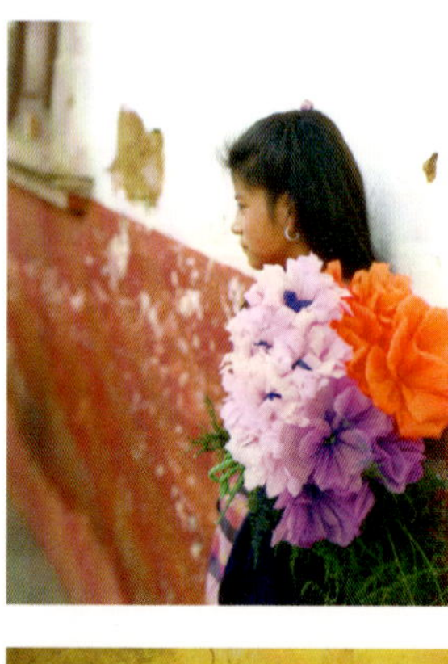
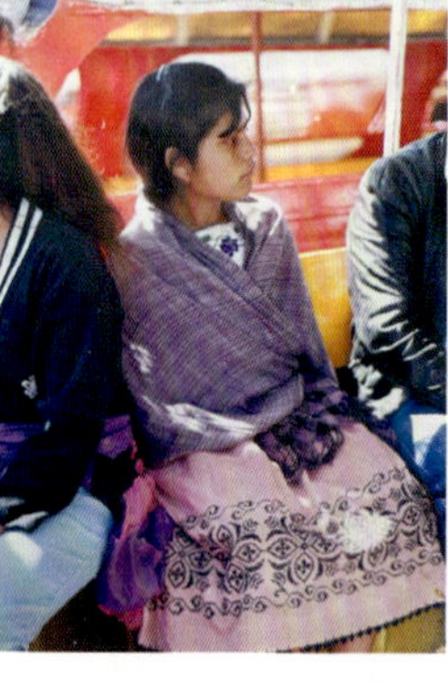
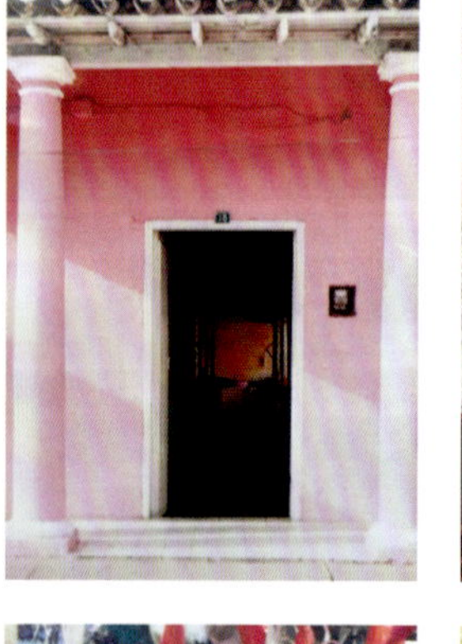
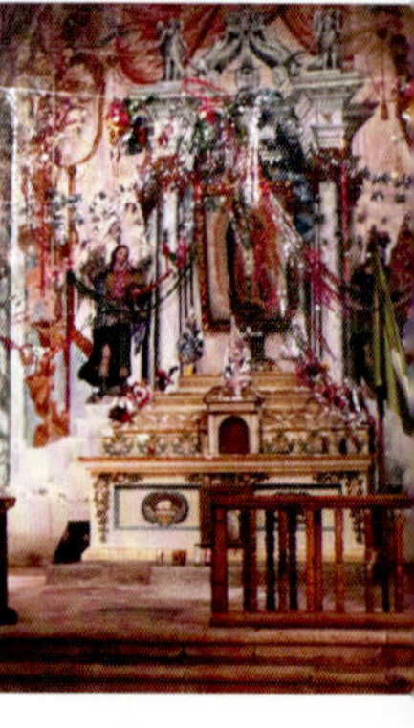
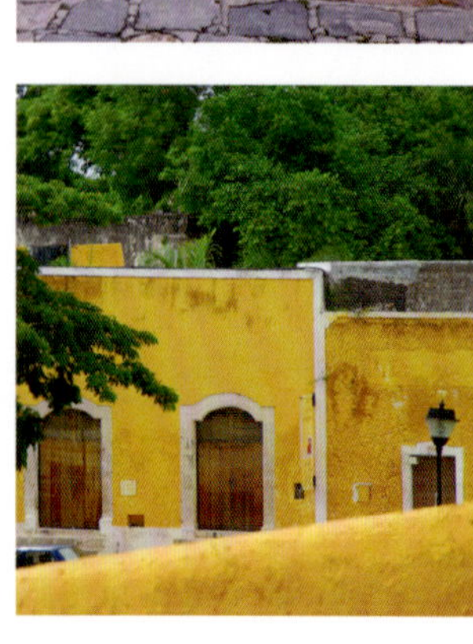
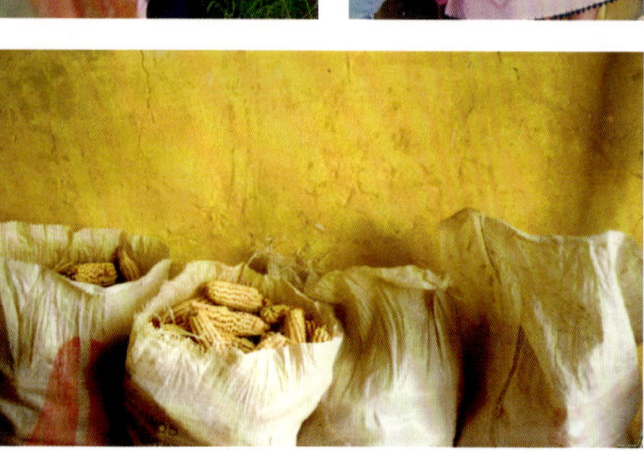
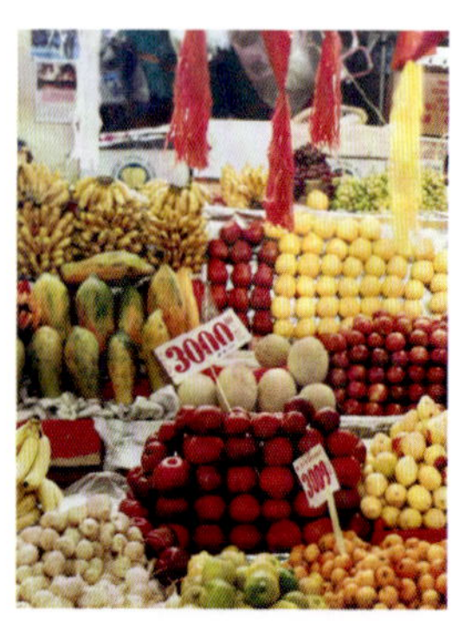
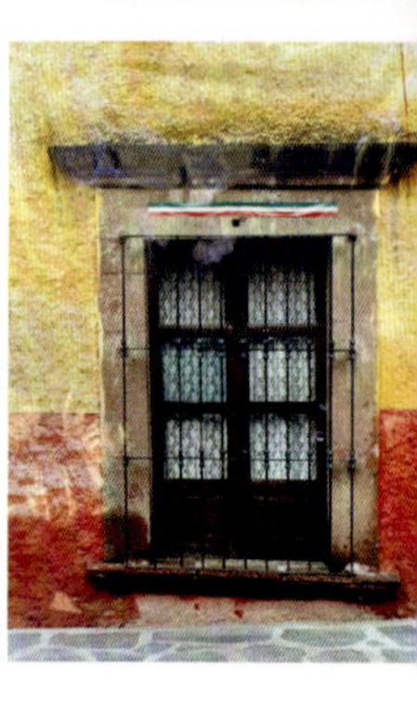

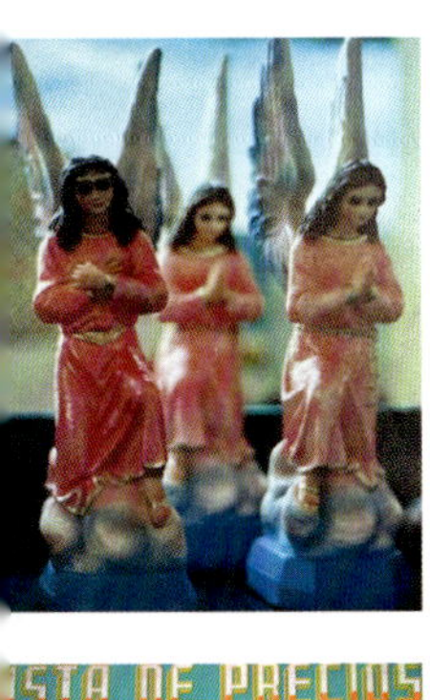
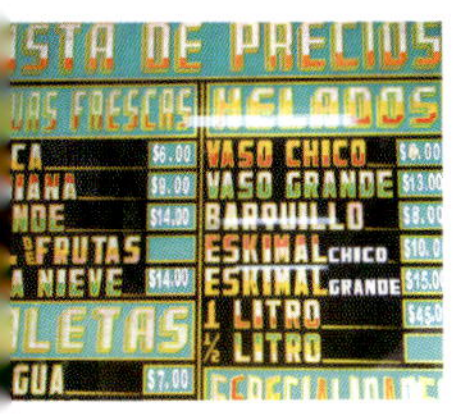
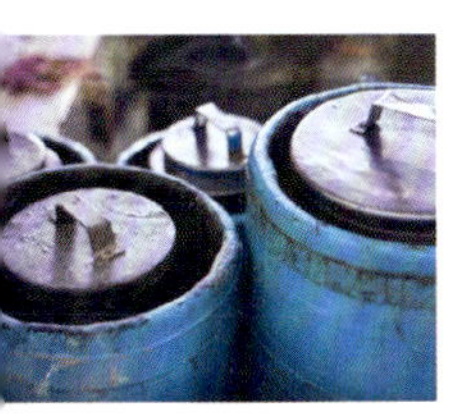
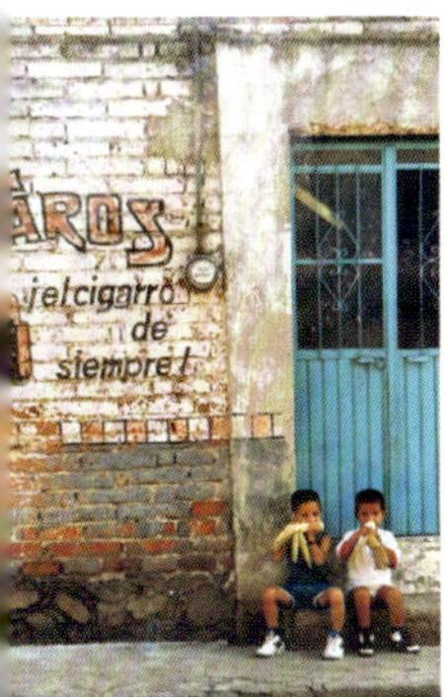
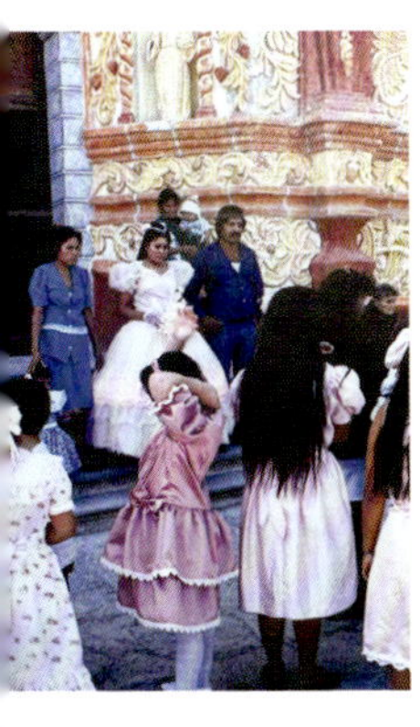
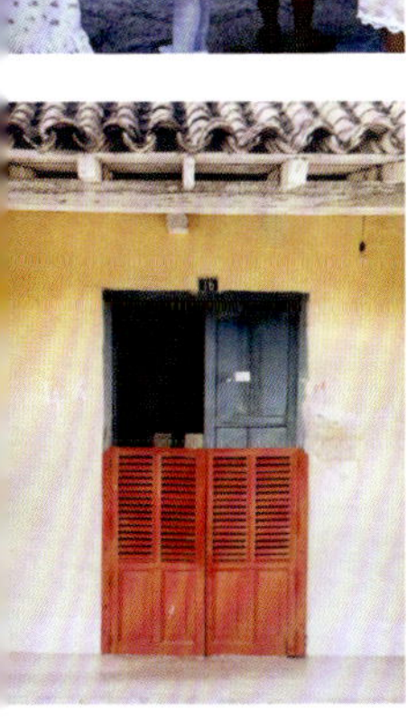
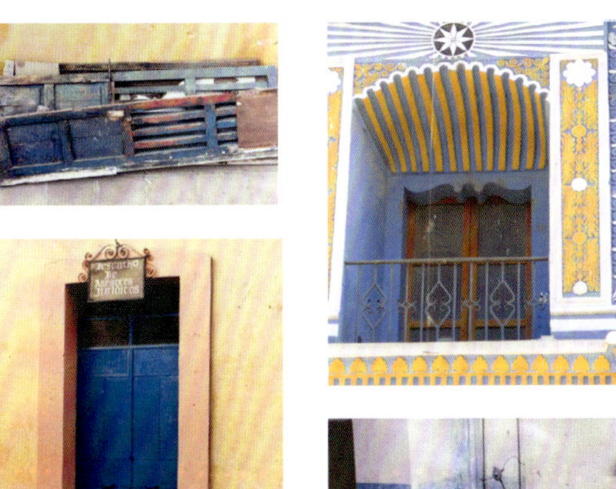
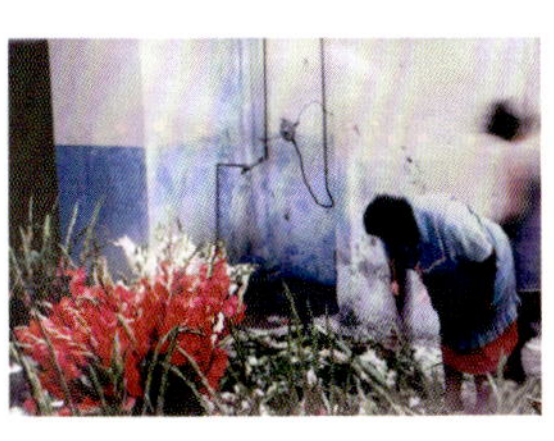
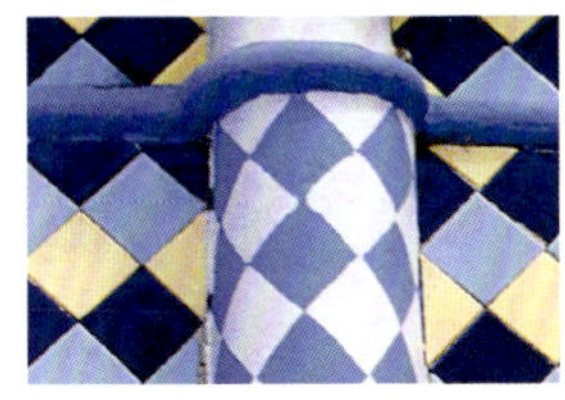
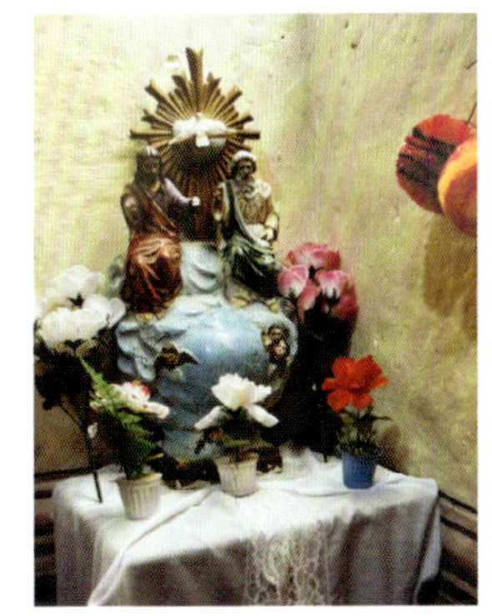
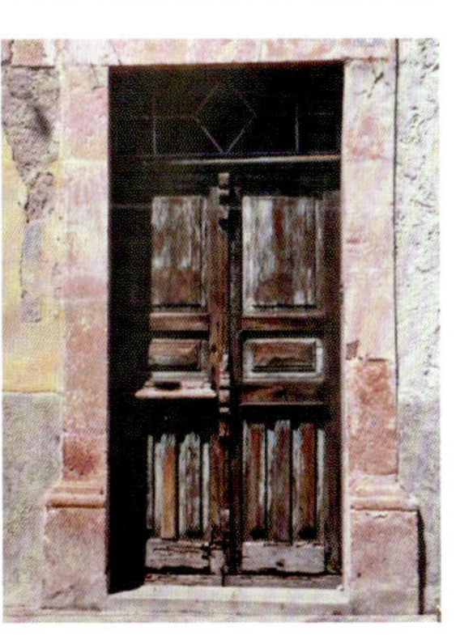
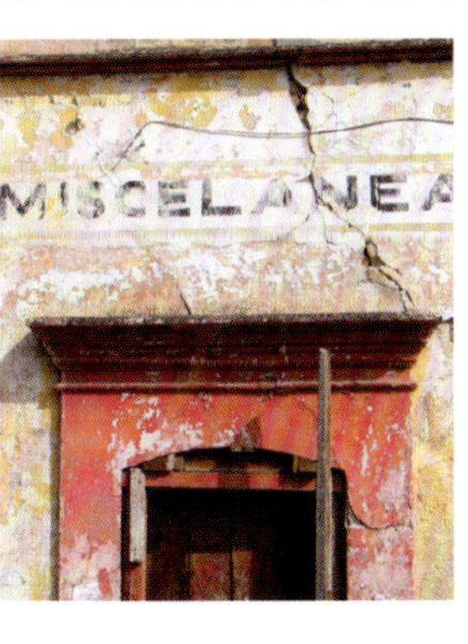
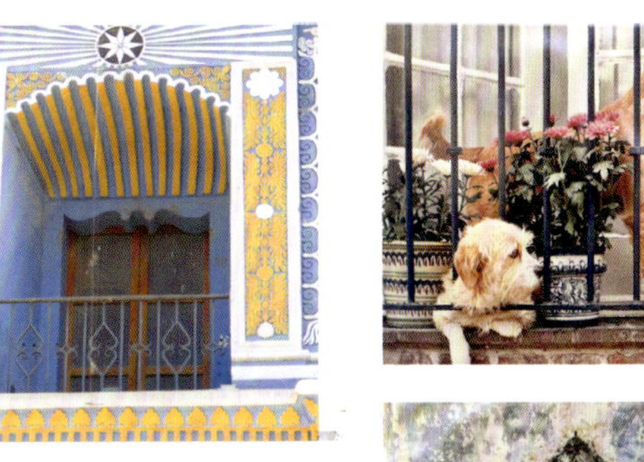
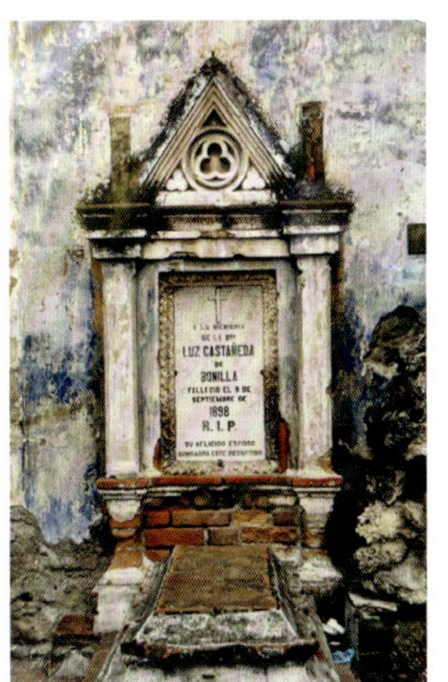
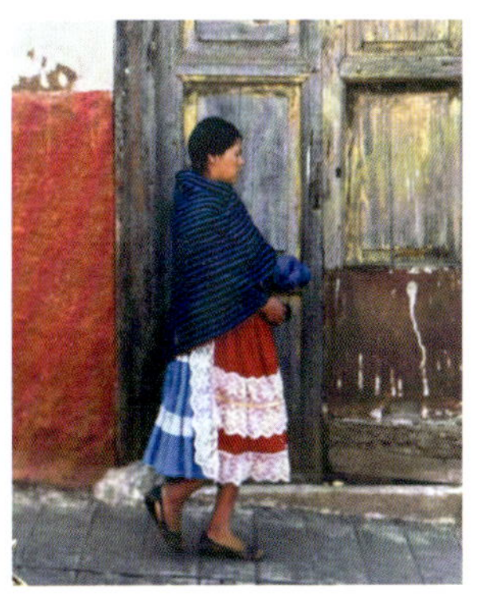
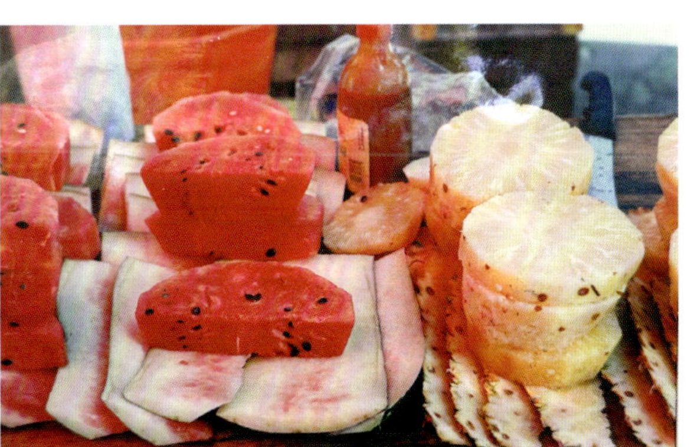
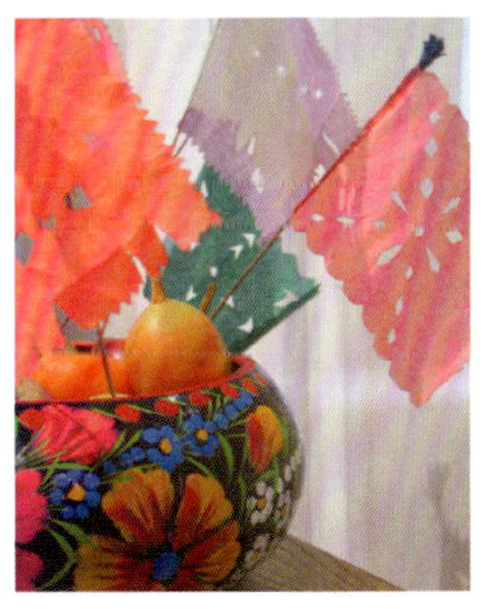
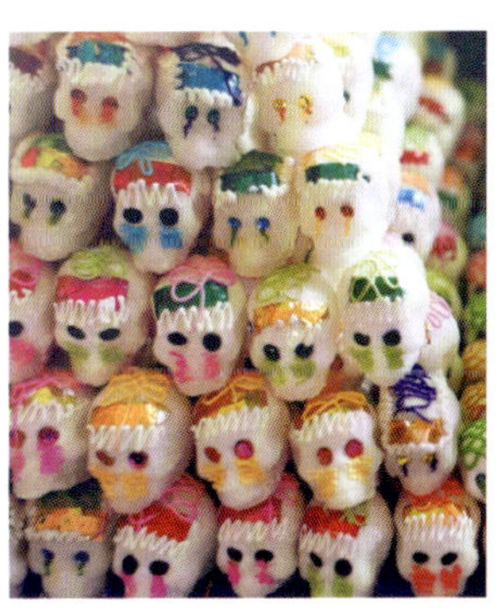
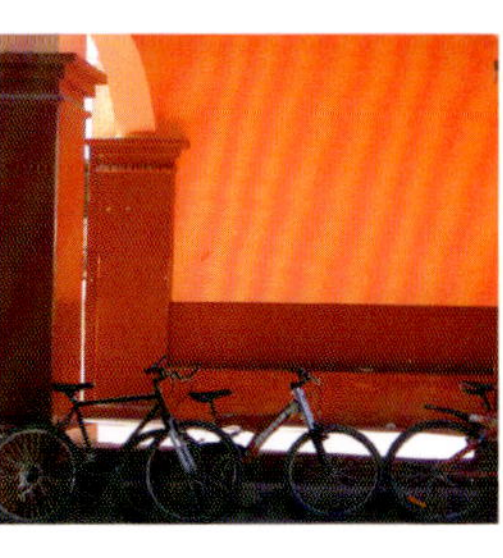
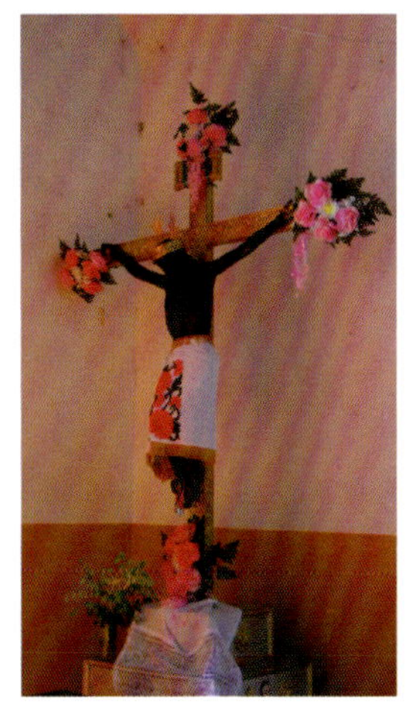
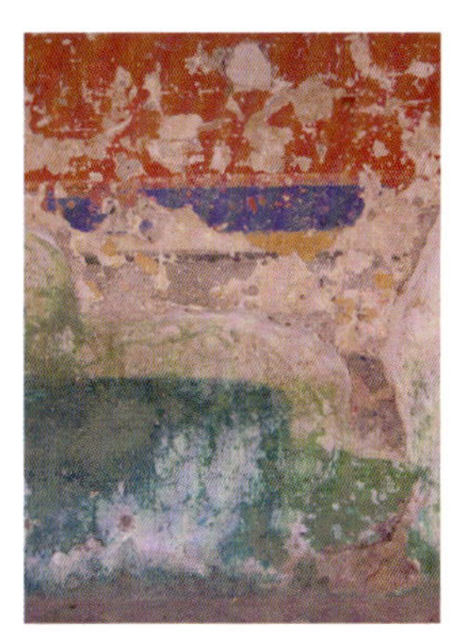
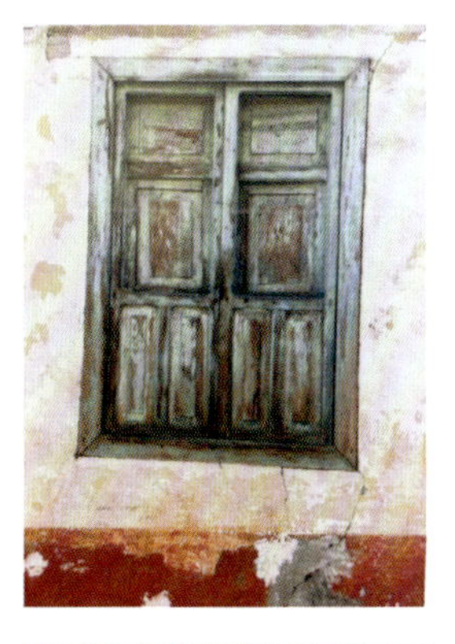
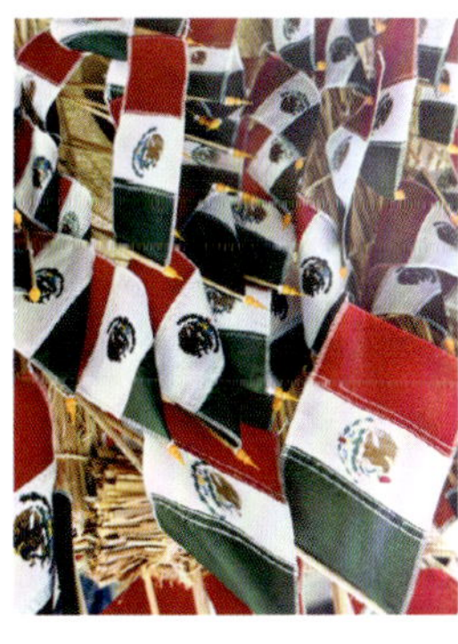

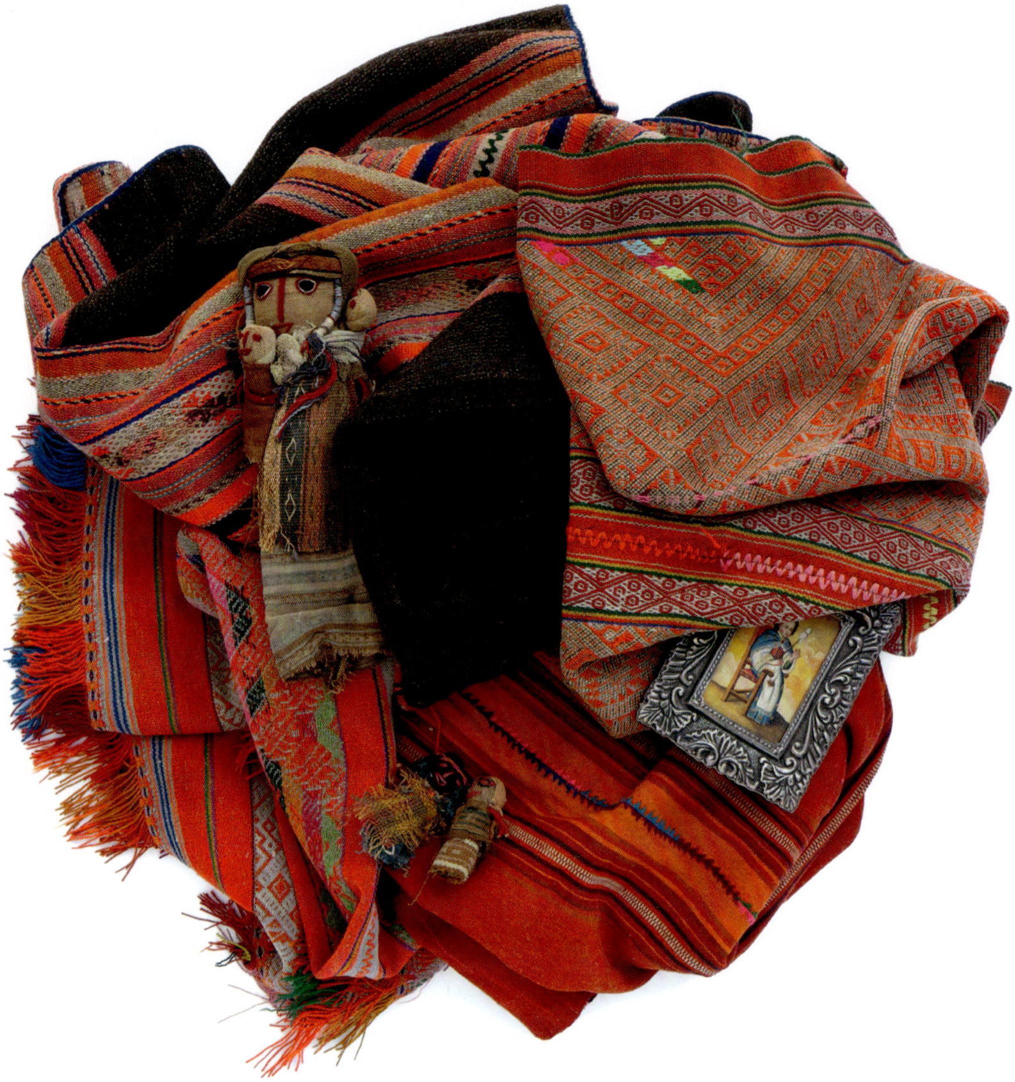

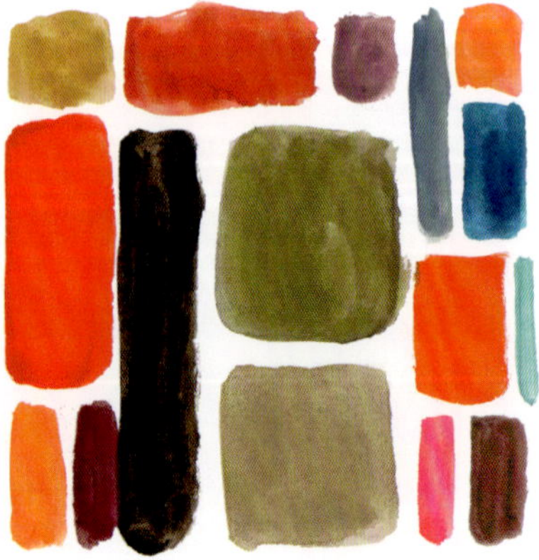

PERU | Traditional wool ponchos from the communities in the Sacred Valley and Cuzco in the Peruvian Andes. Inca textile dolls and colonial-style saint painting with silver frame.

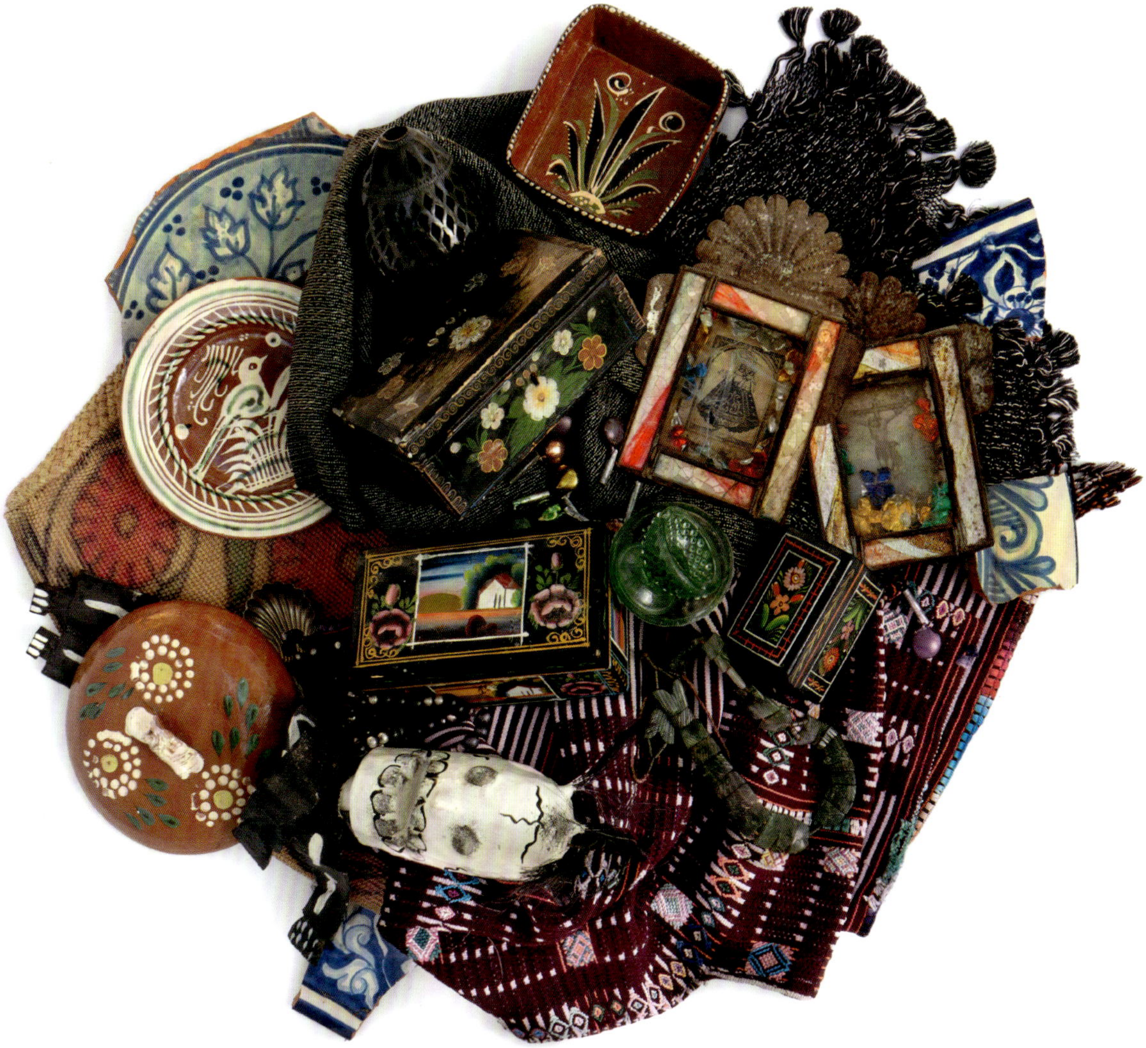

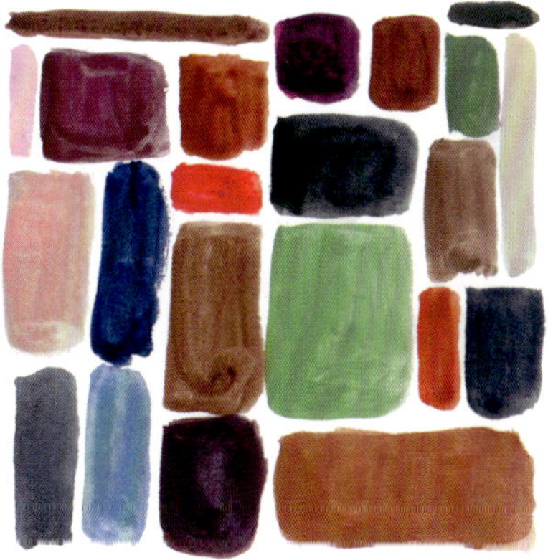

Muted traditional huipil textiles, Ixtle tote bag, Talavera and red-ware ceramics, lacquered boxes, cartonería skeleton, and tin altarpieces from the various regions in Mexico.

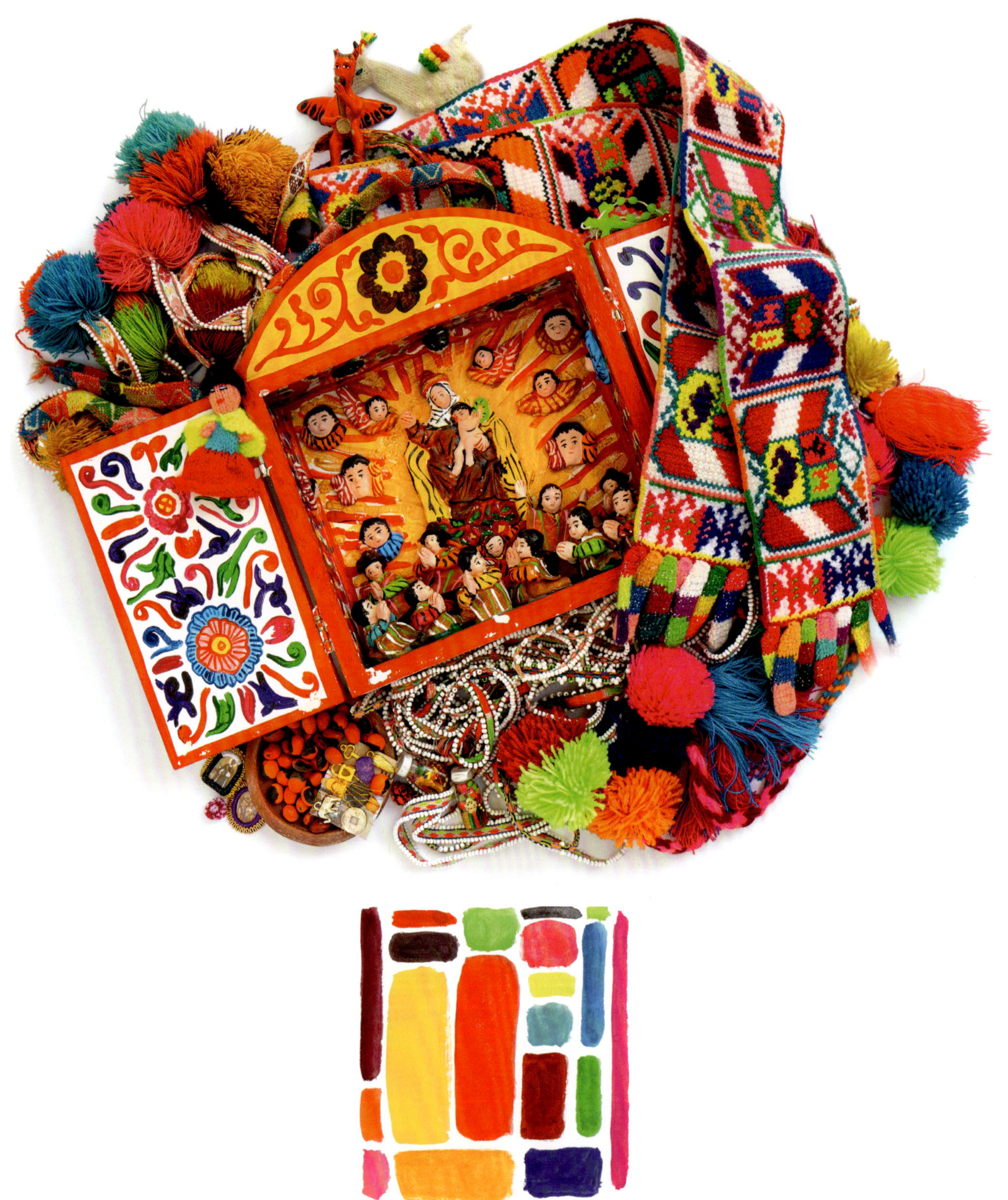

PERU | Multicolor textiles and beadwork traditionally worn by llamas in the Peruvian Andes, toys, and
huayruro red seeds, with the Alfredo López Morales altarpiece.

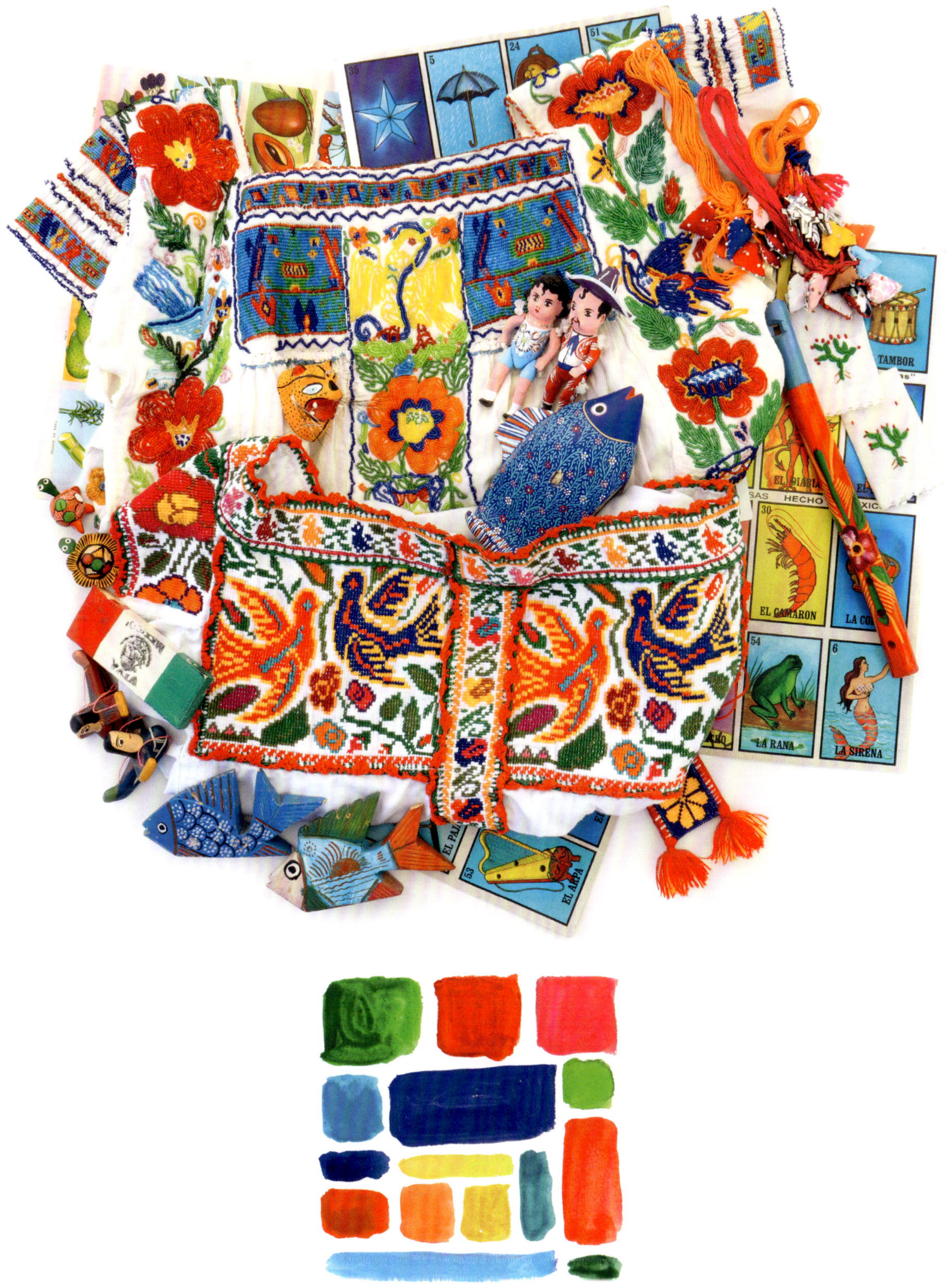

MEXICO | *Polichromed wood from Oaxaca and Guerrero, traditional toys and Lotería game, embroidered blouse from Oaxaca, and China poblana beaded blouse from the 1930s that belonged to my late abuela.*

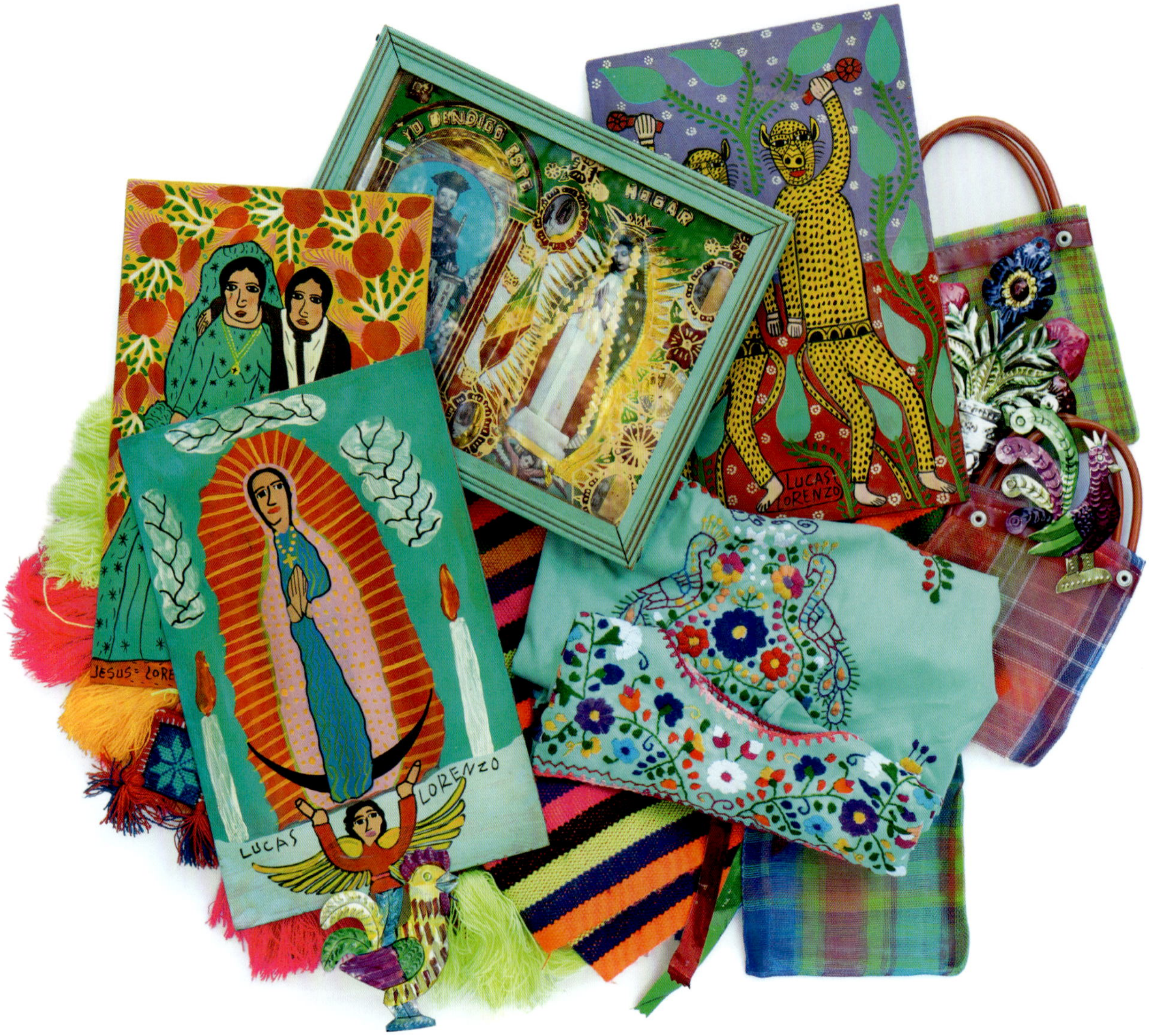

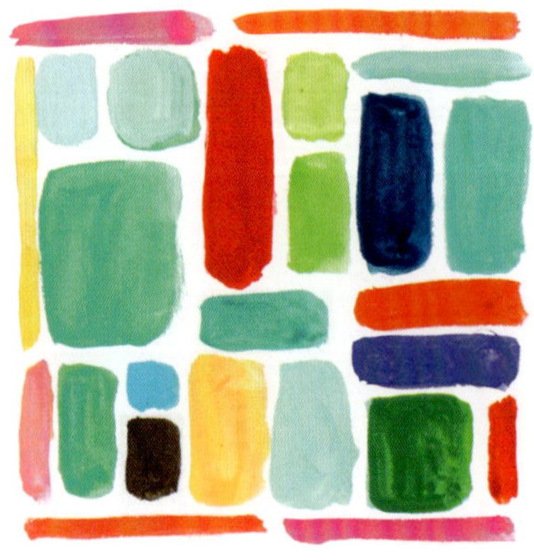

MEXICO | *Turquoise-centric textiles from various regions and paintings by the Lorenzo family.*

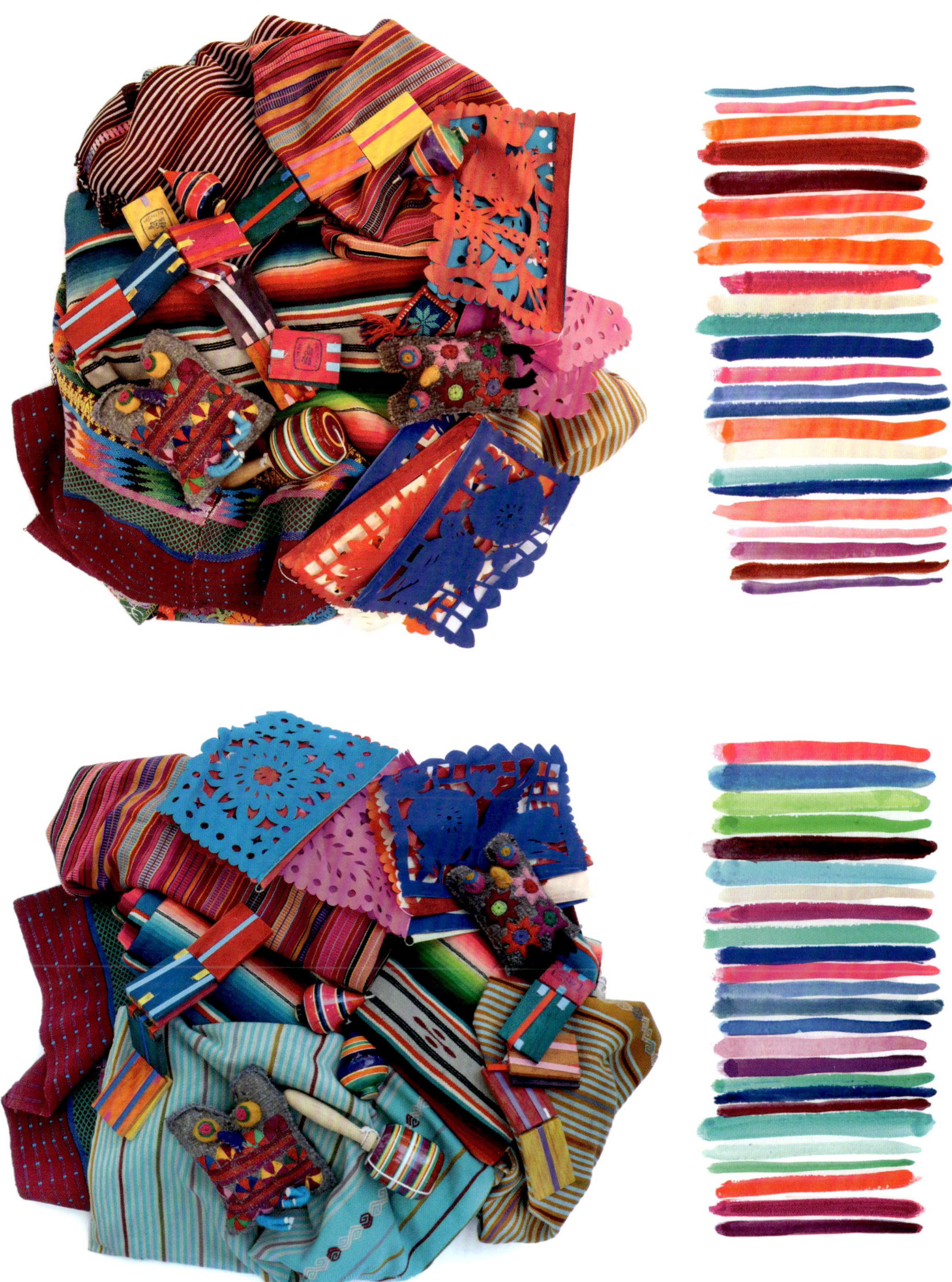

MEXICO | *Variations on striped textiles, traditional toys, and papel picado. Similar elements, two different palettes.*

PROJECT

OBSERVE: Observe objects and photos from your travels: Are there common colors, themes, and materials? Do you have memories captured with your other senses that have any associated color? Alternatively, if you are an immigrant or come from a mixed cultural background, observe the colors related to your heritage.

ANALYZE: Analyze these colors, forms, and motifs: Why do you like them? What do they make you feel or think of? Do they carry meaning? Does the experience of remembering those places—recordis—make them feel more personal or different from when you were in the location?

    If you do not live in the same country where you were born or where your family came from, analyze how your heritage culture informs your color choices and how the colors there might differ from the colors where you are now.

    Can you find the genius loci on your trip or in your cultural background? Making a list of adjectives and nouns related to the place is a good way to start.

CREATE: Once you have observed and analyzed your sources for inspiration, create some visual travel stories using one of the following techniques:

- **Make a collage**—with paper and glue or digitally—or shadow box combining knickknacks, ephemera, objects, and some extra pieces that you drew or painted to complete the piece. Be inspired by collage artists or by the boxes of Joseph Cornell, but create them in your style and fill them with your travel memories and mementos. Think of this not as a specific scene but as a group of things that together trap the genius loci. Use your list of nouns or adjectives.
- **Make a collection of little drawings, vignettes, or scenes,** from memories of the place or after looking at your photos and sources—monuments, sights, crafts, foods, things, landscapes, vegetation, people, or anything that makes you think of the place. Try preparing a color palette from your memories and draw your vignettes in the colors that you most associate with the place.

    As you start to create, ask yourself whether you are appropriating anything or whether the images carry a personal connection to you and are being rendered in homage to those places and their people in a respectful manner.

→ Paris: digital collage with iPhone travel photos. The city of style, such a beautiful city! As we walked its boulevards and little streets, collecting images of mosaic patterns, typefaces, and stone queens from past centuries, we encountered two women with the same graphic print dress in the same café! A few blocks later we saw another woman with the same dress, and over the six days we saw the infamous dress thirteen times! The perils of fast fashion in the city where Dior made masterpieces.

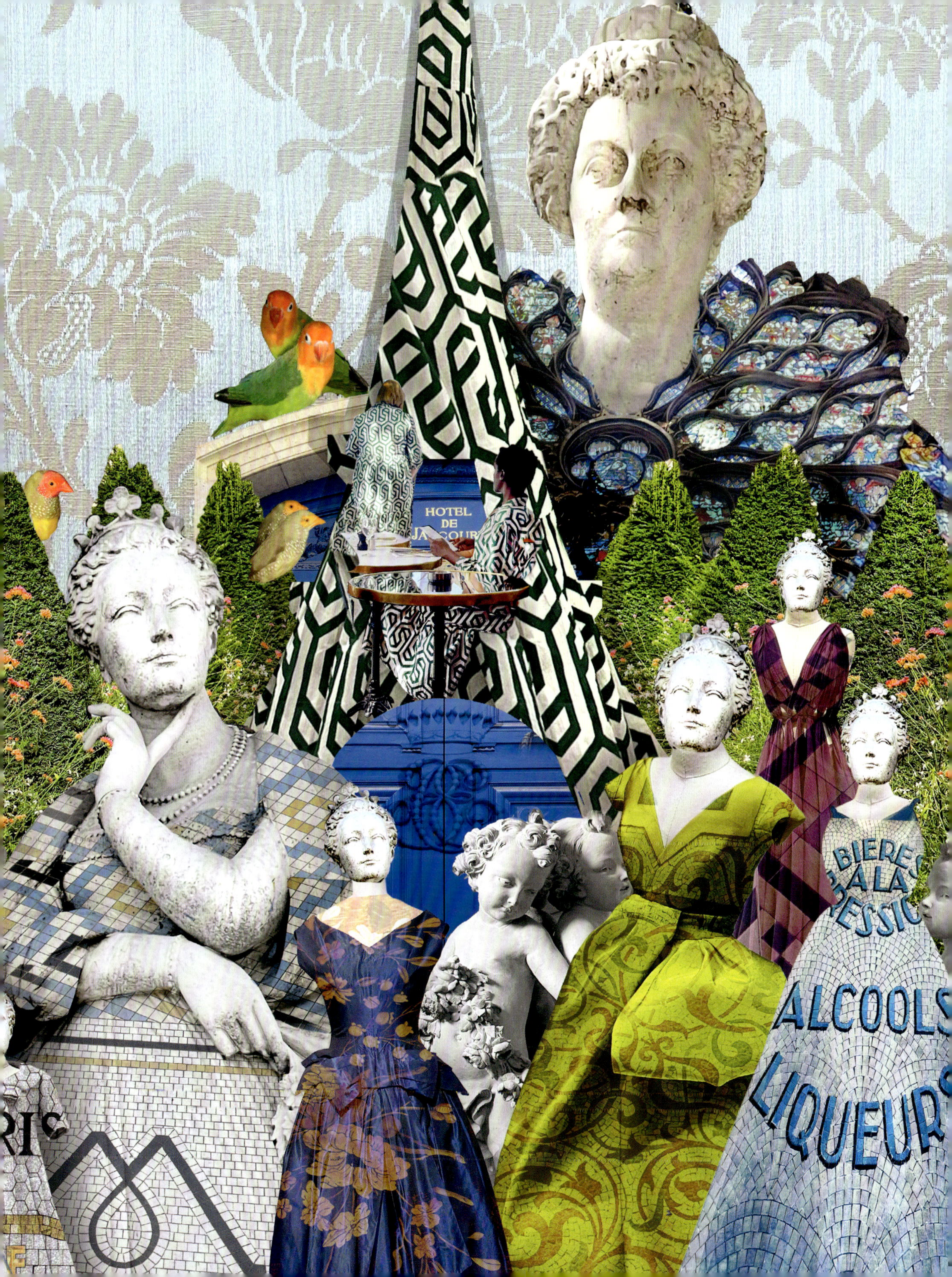

HOTEL
DE
LA COUR
BIERES
A LA
PRESSION
ALCOOLS
LIQUEURS
RIC

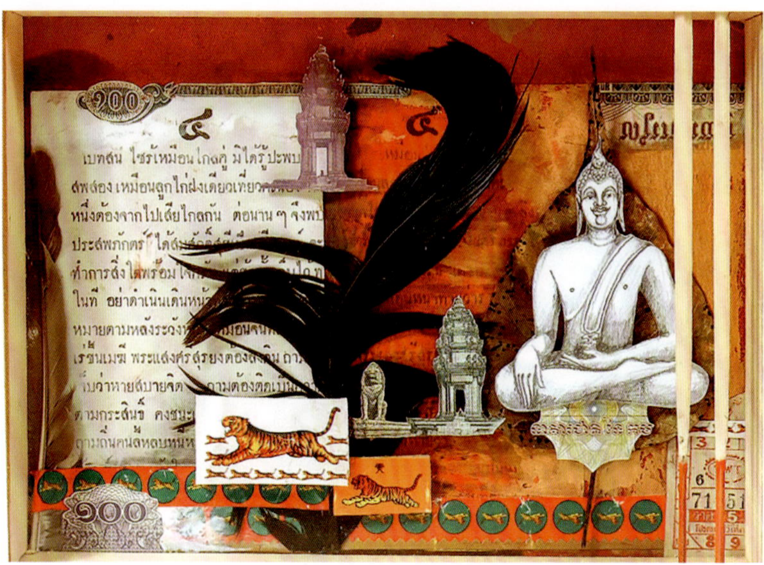

↑ Cambodia and Thailand: collage and assemblage inside a wooden box with collected ephemera from the trip. Lands full of Buddhas and the color orange. Typefaces full of curlicues like the smoke of the temple incense. Tired of walking, Tiger Balm.

→ Plaza Mágica: collection of watercolor and colored pencil illustrations. Every small town in Mexico has its plaza, and every region their traditional dresses. As I go over my photos and notes of three decades of trips around Mexico, I draw the people I have seen in those town central squares: the marchantas food vendors, the musicians, the danzantes, the kids and their animals, the young and the old, the town's fancy people, and even the muertos. I see the beautiful traditional clothes that are gradually disappearing from the streets but not from my memory, and I place them all together in this imaginary plaza.

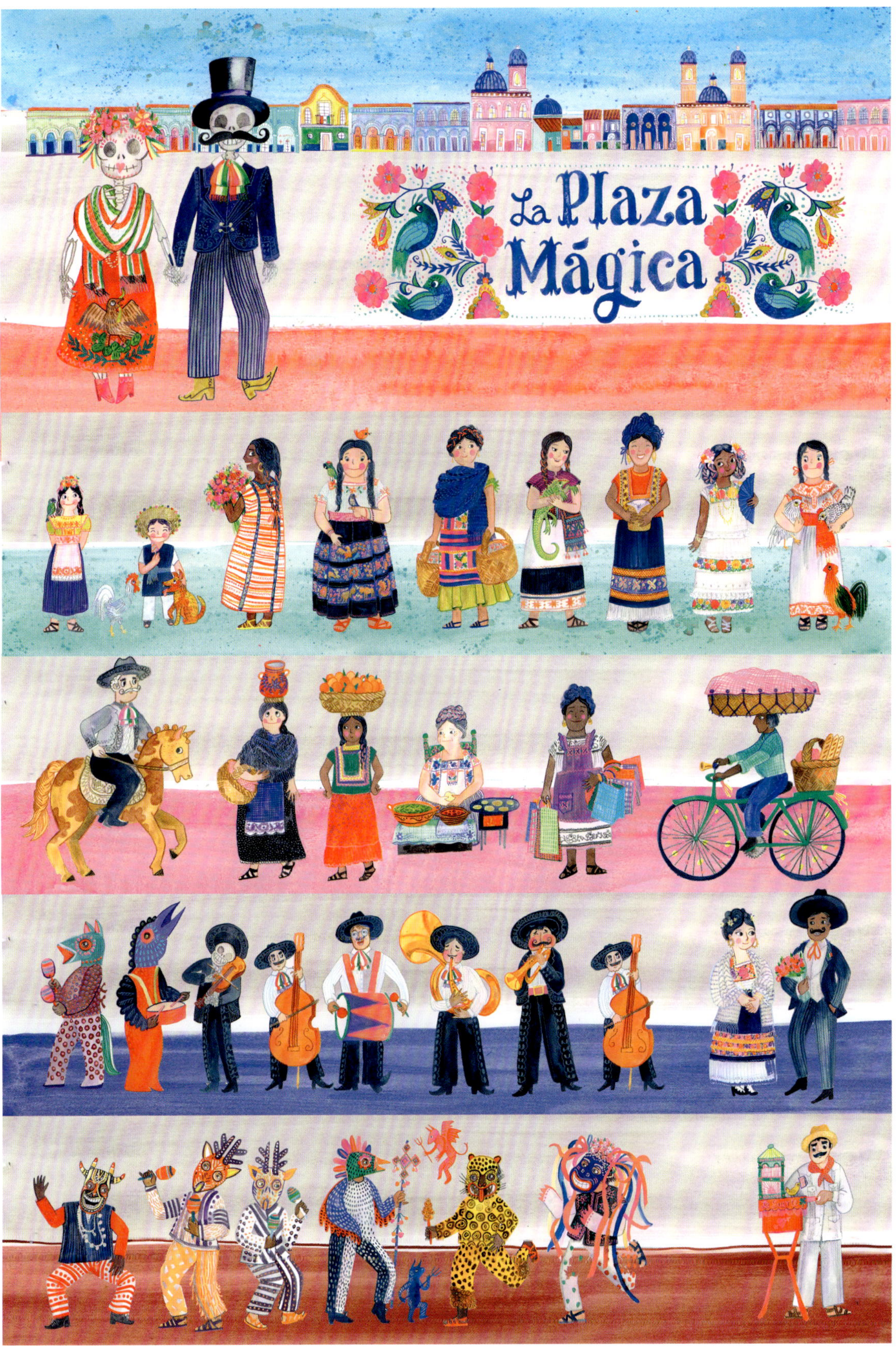
La Plaza
Mágica

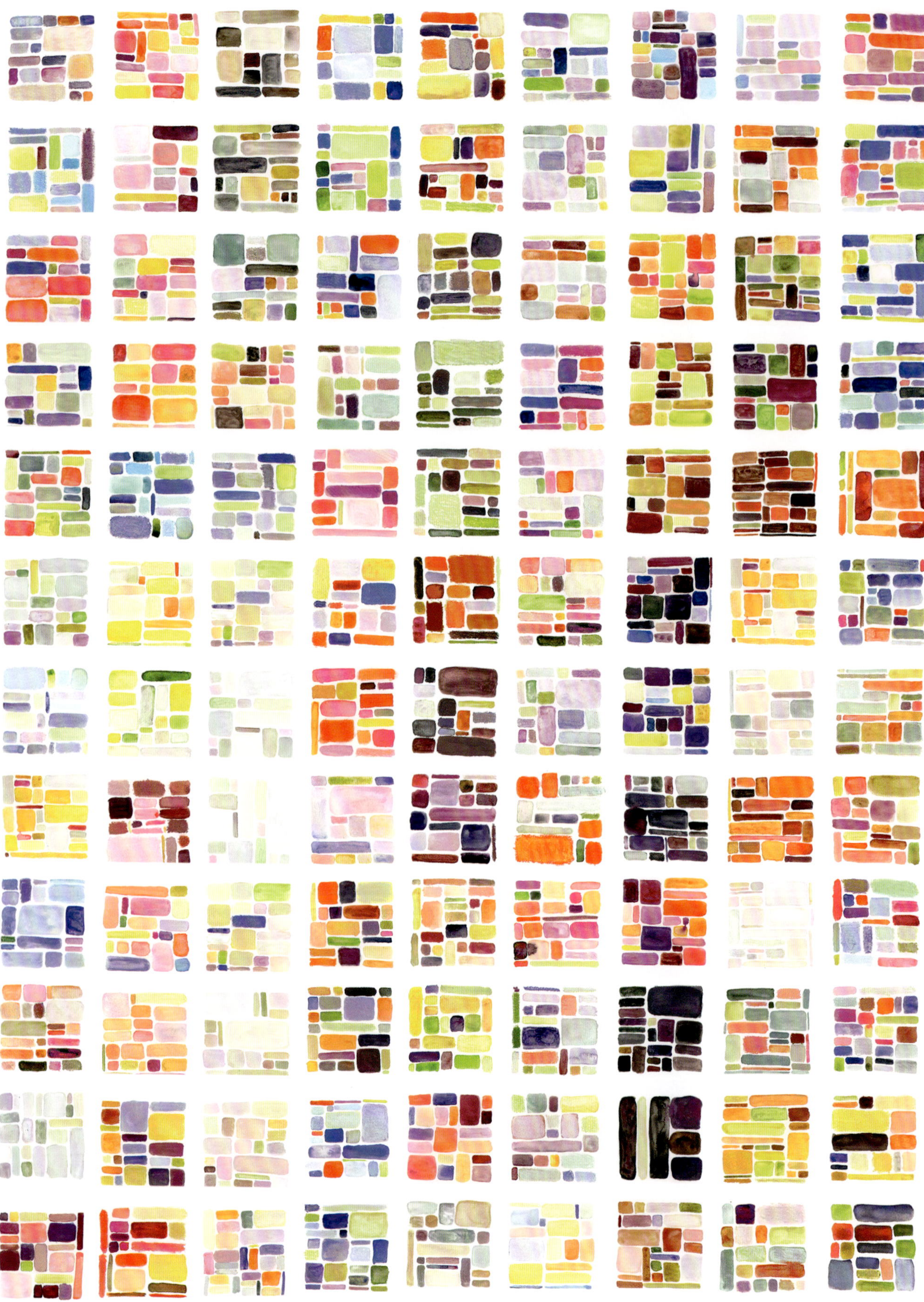

INTENTIONAL COLOR PALETTES

How to Create Color Palettes with Purpose and Intention

Regardless of where you are in your creative path or what your area of expertise is, color is one of the most important visual tools you have for making things and for expressing yourself. Think of a color palette as another way to make a self-portrait of you and your ideas. You would not want to be described in broad, generic terms, right? So your colors should not be generic; they should be as nuanced as your personality, as unique yet varied in their combinations as you are on a daily basis. The colors you choose to use should reflect the mood of your ideas, the moment of time you are in, and the path that brought you there.

Recently, I came across an article in *The New Yorker*[19] about Isabella Ducrot and became enamored by her artwork, her home, and the artist herself. She is a Neapolitan artist and textile connoisseur in her nineties. Her artwork can hardly be described as collage; it is more like she paints with bits and pieces of soft paper, silk, and other fabrics that are cut, pinned, and glued to form beautiful patterns and images of flowers and couples embracing. What I find extraordinary, besides her creative energy at her age, is how each of her art pieces is as delightfully colored as the objects of her home. Upon reading the *New Yorker* article and finding a delightful video interview online on *The World of Interiors*,[20] I could see her eye for color all over her magnificent apartment in Rome. If you were to walk around her home (or look at photos, as I did), you would find the same chromatic combinations as in her own art pieces also all around the home, in groupings of objects and vases with roses from the garden on tables, and in the eclectic art collection she built with her late husband featuring Italian baroque paintings—including one beautiful *Cleopatra* by Artemisia Gentileschi draped in deep teal—along with bright-colored Indian miniatures and an impressive collection of textiles from all over the world.

The dialogue between Ducrot's collections and her own creations is the result of a lifetime of color love and collecting things she found beautiful. She did not get there in a day, but developing your color voice does not need to take a lifetime when approached with attention and intention. That is why collecting is a great way to train your eye for color. Granted, not everyone can have an art collection like Ducrot's, but we can all collect images with our phones and cameras, or we can have treasure boxes of trinkets and paper cutouts, postcards, and random ephemera. What matters in collecting is training your eye to find those visual treasures that tickle your mind. It is about grabbing—physically or with our eyes and memories—those objects or images we love consistently over time. This recurrence will sharpen your eye and over time come to define your taste and, thus, your creative voice.

Become a serial collector! See whatever inspires you and notice what comes up over and over—which forms, themes, textures, and especially colors you gravitate toward, over and over. Look around your house or closet for recurrences and build upon that. Hoard colors, interesting bits, and inspiration in little treasure boxes! Let nobody tell you that fifty thousand photos on your phone is too much.

FINDING YOUR TRUE COLORS

Remember, there are no "bad" colors, nor is there a perfectly "good" color combo. What I like or my fellow color lovers like should not dictate what you love. Use this book to discover or evolve your own color voice. The content in these pages has covered many color topics that may nudge you to observe, analyze, and create differently, and in doing so your colors will become more intentional, more true to you. Sometimes the creative need comes from outside (a.k.a. client work or commissioned work), and it is the result of your inner drive for personal work. Regardless, push yourself to use colors and combinations you haven't used before. Experiment curiously. Go ahead and start creating palettes on your own or from the images in this book.

There are as many ways to put together a palette as there are artists and art educators on this planet. So I have enlisted four of my friends and fellow color lovers to have a conversation about intentional color palettes with me. The following are condensed versions of our color-love chats. Note that the hues of the text are their favorite colors, which I see these as their color voices.

THE POWER OF A LIMITED COLOR PALETTE

A limited color palette—three or four or even just two colors—can pack a punch! Take a minute to observe the artists, designers, and illustrators you love and, more often than not, you will notice that pieces you love most actually use quite a limited range of colors.

Over the years of working with color, this multicolor lover—me—has become enamored and amazed by the power of limiting the number of colors per piece. I still love opening my colored pencil box and seeing all those hues and shades at my disposal, I still get excited by sprinkles and confetti, and I feel skilled enough to be able to create things that include a wide range of color. But increasingly, I have been enjoying working with very limited hues in a piece and then squeezing all the juice and range I can from these limitations.

The realization that I could make good work with as few as two colors came when I discovered something called Coloricombo, a creative community and online challenge created by the artist, designer, and illustrator Esté MacLeod. Back in 2021, she launched, in collaboration with Lori Siebert, the first Coloricombo challenge with fifteen pairs of colors to be used in illustrations over a month. Esté's list of color pairs with inspiring, evocative names—lemon + elephant, aqua + oyster, cotton candy + avocado, cantaloupe + kohl, powder blue + chocolate—resulted in some of my favorite illustrations. Observing these illustrations and those made by other people following this challenge really got me thinking about the power of limited color palettes.

LIMITED COLOR PALETTES

A CONVERSATION WITH ESTÉ MACLEOD

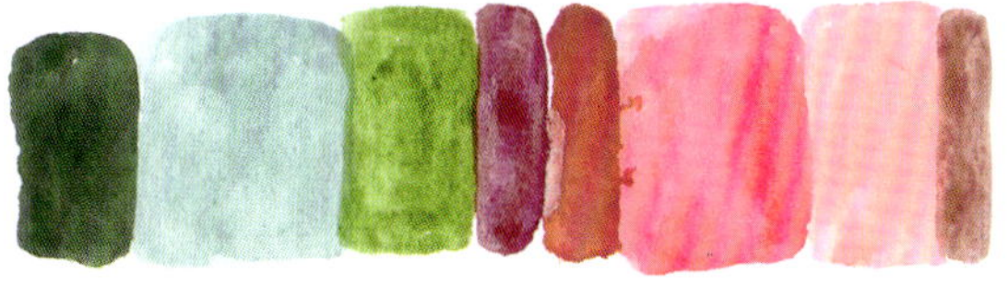

Esté MacLeod is a UK-based artist, surface designer, and art educator. Her #coloricombo challenges on social media and her beautiful weekly newsletter have inspired thousands to experiment with color. She also teaches at art retreats in far-flung places like Bali, Morocco, and Greece.

Find her on Instagram @estemacleod or her website at EsteMacLeod.com.

"Color is a catalyst for creativity. I think of myself as a colorist, since color is a central component in all my work regardless of subject!"
—Esté MacLeod

I love color; everyone can relate to color in some way or other. Over my career, I have used color in art and design to connect with people. In the past, color was used as the main component when I was an artist in residence at art fairs and festivals in the UK. I got people to paint interactive paintings using mixes of colors and shapes.

Social media opened new possibilities, and on Instagram I have been doing occasional color challenges since 2017. In 2021, Lori Siebert asked me to do a monthlong Instagram creative challenge with her. I proposed colors, and Coloricombo was born. Over the month, we shared fifteen combinations of two colors. I picked these to ensure variety and some unusual combinations. The idea was to create something in the color combination every second day during September. This challenge seemed so popular that I decided to turn it into a yearlong challenge in 2022, with fifty-two color prompts shared over the space of a year. I love doing

research into all things art, and to add to the challenge I decided to link colors to a featured artwork by an artist from the past, especially ones that were overlooked, obscure, or forgotten. In my research, I discovered many female artists who fit this category, and I make it a point to share their stories as well in these weekly prompts.

Coloricombo is now in its third year. It is an ongoing project to help people connect and engage with color, with an invitation to nurture their own creativity in their own authentic way. Coloricombo has grown over time; since January 2024, I have chosen a monthly theme for featured artworks to be linked to.

There are normally between three and five colors in each prompt. Along with the prompt's colors, you can add a dark color—maybe deep blue, black, or dark brown—as well as a neutral color such as a soft gray, buff, or similar. People are encouraged to use them in their own way or to create something linked to the monthly theme. The colors are a starting point, a catalyst to kickstart the processes. Members of the community use the colors to create in different media, from journaling to sketching, from painting to working in craft format, from embroidery to quilting, from pottery to crochet; everything works.

I wanted to present these bite-size weekly portions of colors to help all kinds of artists foster a creative habit and explore possibilities.

It is probably one of those open secrets: Limited colors often make for better art. I think it makes you more creative because you need to make the most out of the limited selection of colors. Having figured out a combination of three to five colors to use will help to keep the focus on the creative process and use the combination to your best ability. Based on what I have learned over years as a professional artist and a designer, my advice is to develop a library of painted color swatches from which you can pick a limited selection before adding more colors to a painting further along in the painting process.

Esté's favorite hack:
By using fewer, highly pigmented quality paints, you will be able to create a wide spectrum of colors. This is better than the alternative of acquiring dozens of tubes of hobby or student-grade paint. Because of the pigment concentration, you will get further with them and in the process learn how to mix wide ranges of colors.

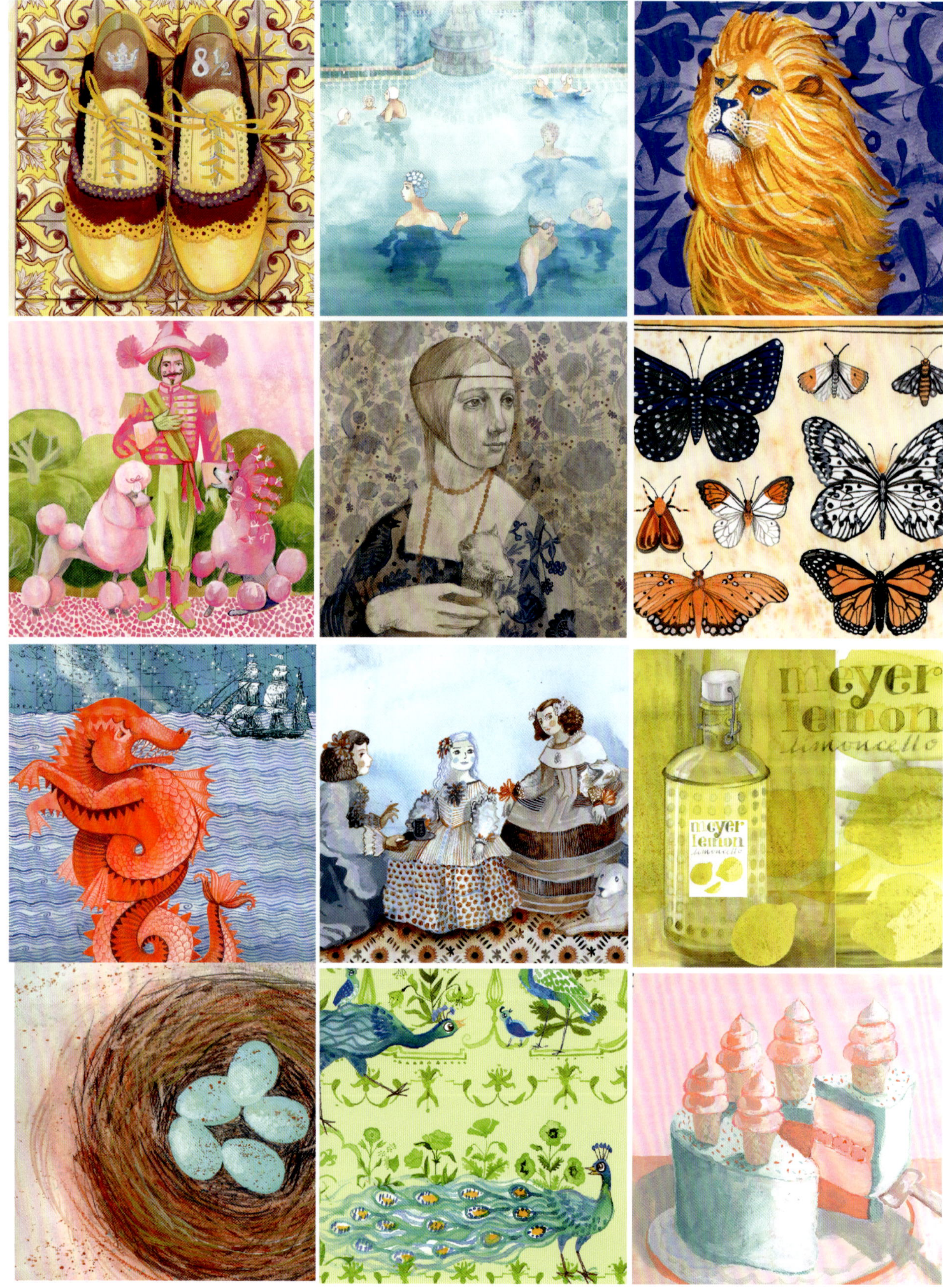

COLOR AND STYLE

The notion of "style" is a common theme across all creative professions. We all strive to find a personal voice and dress it in a recognizable style. This topic can take up whole books! Some of the elements of a recognizable style in visual arts and design are how you use shape and forms, or how your hand draws or your eye combines textures. It may comprise your choice of elements, themes, and composition, and it definitely includes how you use color. There are artists and designers so committed to some colors! Some go through periods of certain palettes that evolve over time, and some, like me, use all kinds of colors, but somehow there is a commonality, a certain temperature or saturation or play of combinations that ends up being cohesive and recognizable.

The use of these elements and how they come to form your voice and style does not happen overnight. It is not like you sit down at your art table one day and decide *these are my shapes, this is my rendering style, this is the quality of my line, and these are my colors*. It is really something that happens over time as you develop your eye and your creative language; it is the result of consistent art practice. This will sound odd, but since it evolves slowly, you will only discover it when you look back.

Let me explain: If you have been making art or design for a while, it is likely that you have been focusing your creative energy, going all in on each piece, and moving quickly from project to project. At some point, not necessarily after the proverbial ten thousand hours but when you have been doing this for a while, you'll benefit from taking a panoramic view of your work and finding recurrences and commonalities.

I have done this a few times, usually when my website is due for an update or when I am preparing for a trade show or even for this book. This is how I do it:

I collect all my artwork in a folder and create contact sheets in Photoshop (twelve images per page), print it all out, and cut the individual pieces. Then I spread them out on my dining table to look at them. I observe common themes, shapes, and ways of rendering. I group them,

discard some (whatever feels weaker or dissonant in that big panoramic table of my work), and find my favorites. I analyze what makes the best pieces good, and above all, when thinking about color, I find that there are indeed, even in my multicolor oeuvre, some common elements.

As I note the stronger pieces, their style and color, I know that is what I want to create more of. I may also find incipient ideas that I want to further explore. And I also find the "fakes" within my work, the inevitable pieces that are not true to my voice from when I was trying something cool I saw and it end up not feeling really like me. We all have these experiments; they have a place in our creative practice, but not when we are looking for our true voice and style. When you are selecting the top ten or twenty or fifty pieces, they should all have a similar level of quality, look good together, yet also display a range of themes, color, and spirit. This process is what helps me put together a portfolio, a book, or a social media page, website, or other promotional material for my work. Regardless of what project I have in mind, this is how I self-reflect on my creative voice, and above all, this is how I find what I am going to work on for the foreseeable future.

However, the most important notion about style, for me, is that it is not static. It will continue to evolve and change as my curious eye and mind follow a creative path.

Please don't get bogged down in the aim of having a signature style. Observe your body of work every now and then, stopping in the path to look back, notice the strongest, most joyous bits, and pick up the most promising, solid pieces to move forward in your creative journey. Remember that this only happens over time, and in the meantime, just keep swimming . . . and drawing . . . and making . . . and designing.

Do you maybe already have a current signature color palette? Observe and analyze it. After reading this book, you may feel like tweaking it. Then maybe you can create a piece with a new set of colors, or even redo a previous piece with this improved palette.

DEVELOPING YOUR COLOR VOICE

A CONVERSATION WITH LISA CONGDON

Lisa Congdon is an artist, product designer, illustrator, and author of multiple books based in Portland, Oregon. She had been a creative guide for me through her inspirational books, classes, and talks for years before I finally met her in person in 2021.

Find her on Instagram @lisacongdon or her website and beautiful online shop at LisaCongdon.com. Her books are also listed in the resource page at the end of this book.

"Color is so important to us; it infiltrates the clothes we wear, the way we decorate our house, and the things we are drawn to. Telling a color story is so ingrained in what we do that I don't even think we are conscious of it half the time. Color is everything. It changes the mood. It can transform what we create."
—Lisa Congdon

Color is so important! If my brand voice were a pie chart, my colors make up 35 percent, my shapes and lines another 35 percent, and my typography and messaging would be lumped together in the remaining 30 percent.

Color is a constant, even with nuances and variations in my work. When I am experimenting with new colors or when a client provides a specific color palette different from mine, I keep my shapes and forms consistent and recognizable. But occasionally, I find a new color—like now I am adding a purple or an orange—and while it is something I hadn't used before, people don't necessarily notice because the imagery is so iconic. By the same token, if a client needs me to draw things I normally don't or in a slightly different style, then I have to stay true to my signature colors, keeping it consistent across photographs, quilts, collages, digital drawings, and acrylic paintings. This makes my visual language cohesive and recognizable even when I apply it to different things or make variations.

I think back to when I first started painting and developing my visual vocabulary. I would mix colors together. Each color mixing was very intuitive, but certainly part of it was intentional, like my blues, which are a bit browner. I never liked a green straight from the tube because it was too bright, so I added yellow to make it more olive. I tend to make all my colors, including cool colors, a bit warmer.

What I did with paint I now do with my palettes on Procreate, since I now mostly work digitally. Color is something that has been consistent since the beginning of my career. We could say I have a primary palette—I guess you can call that one my signature color palette—and a secondary or multiple secondary palettes. Over time they all change a bit to evoke a certain energy or mood.

Growing up in the '70s caused me to be attracted to muted colors that were popular then. I have also always gravitated toward graphic design from that period. Those colors evoke a certain energy or mood.

My favorite color, and most consistent across my work, is red. I love red, I buy anything red and display it here in my studio. I never use pure white or pure black. My color palette is always accompanied by a warmer white or deep browns. Something else I like to pay attention to is background color. Playing with the background can make a piece! I ask myself, *What would this look like if it was on black or blue or pink?* Altering the background can completely change the look of an illustration.

One potential disadvantage of keeping a consistent color palette over time is monotony, but something I do is to slightly change certain hues and the temperature of colors. That keeps it varied for me, but still consistent and recognizable for people seeing my work.

I also like having constraints and making things work within those constraints. I feel that having a limited color palette is iconic for me. I don't ever use more than six to nine colors. When you intentionally choose a few colors and work with them, the piece simply becomes better. There is a certain nervous system regulation that a limited color palette provides; I don't have to make too many choices, and I can just focus on making this work within this limitation, and this calms me. I went through a whole year of just using blue, and I called it Experiments in Blue. From this constraint, I learned so much about color value, all the different shades and tones of blues, and how warm or cool blue can be. It was so fun! I found it really freeing.

"Trust your color intuition and let it happen organically. Trust yourself when you look at a color combination that feels right to you."
—Lisa Congdon

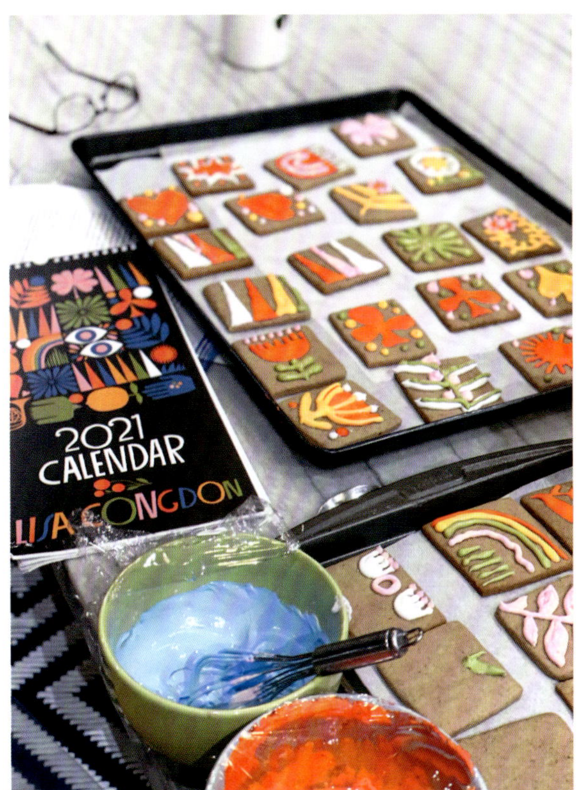

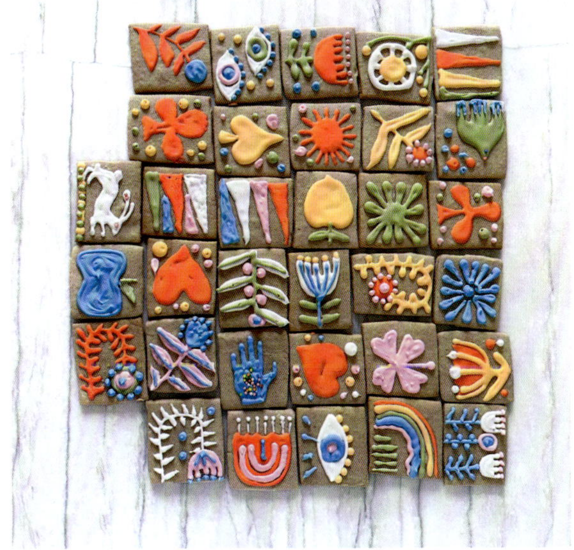

↑ I have been following and loving the work of Lisa Congdon for years, and along the way I also avidly read her books about art making, developing a creative voice, and aligning work and life with personal values. Her voice, kind and strong at the same time, has been the wind in my sails, and throughout, I have always loved and admired her use of color in her highly recognizable style. After years of following her and reading her books, we finally met in person in 2021 at her studio in Portland. I made her these cookies inspired by her art. It is the only time I have given myself permission to blatantly copy her—or any other artist's—work. It was an homage/gift for her.

COLOR AND BRANDING

A CONVERSATION WITH CLAUDE SALZBERGER

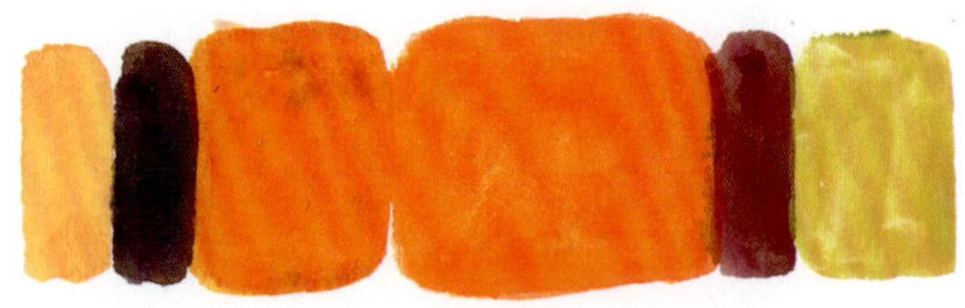

Regardless of whether we are observing your personal art brand (because artists, designers, illustrators, and crafters can benefit from thinking about their work in terms of having a personal brand) or we are talking about branding in a broader sense—for a company or a product—color plays a very important role.

One side of my creative practice has always been in graphic design and branding, from making brands, logos, and packaging for small businesses and food and beverage brands to working in a leading branding agency (yes, you have seen my design work . . .). All my brand work usually starts with defining the color story for the project: This guides me in finding the brand's story, its DNA, and it helps me convey the brand's emotional side.

Someone who has been with me for all those years in branding is Claude Salzberger. He was my first boss upon arriving in New York after offering me the job that brought me to the Big Apple from Mexico, and he is now one of my dearest friends. Together we worked on some of my favorite projects ever: namely, several airlines, including Air Canada (the one with the ice-blue plane) and American Airlines (the current striped livery design), for which I designed the liveries, created color palettes, and gave directions to the airplane paint company in their custom color formulations. Along the way, Claude Salzberger and I have had lots of color-related conversations.

With over four decades in branding, Claude is the original branding expert and guru. He's been creative director at Landor and founding partner and creative head at FutureBrand and MBLM agencies in New York City. We share twenty-five-plus years of collaboration in branding projects.

"A brand is the sum of all the associations and exp eriences you have with a product, tangible and intangible. It is not just the logo; that is just one of the pieces.

Color in a brand expresses something about the values, mission, and promise of the brand. It creates something evocative about what the brand stands for.

Color creates an indelible bridge between the product and you."
—Claude Salzberger

CLAUDE: When we talk about the logo, there are two components to it, the name and the design. But there is also, importantly, the color. It helps you identify, recognize, and remember that particular brand. Selecting the right color for the brand is an absolutely integral and subconscious part of the association you make with the brand. The thing about color is that the logo per se does not give you an emotional response, it is the color that ends up doing that.

It builds awareness, differentiation, and distinction. Just think of the role of color in these brands: blue Democrats, red Republicans; yellow Hertz, red Avis. Heineken is green, and Corona is yellow.

Color makes you *see* these brands, not just read the names. Color also tells you things about the brand or the category: Most banks' branding is blue to represent trustworthiness and stability. Over time, the mere color will remind you of the brand, and it will bring up all those emotional associations and evoke the moments and memories of when you interacted with the brand. Just think about that particular aqua blue of Tiffany's and what it brings to mind, or the sweet green of Ladurée.

Color in branding starts with the logo and the core color palette, and it extends to a secondary color palette, the colors of illustrations and brand photography. The core color palette may have a life of ten or twenty years, and the secondary colors may change more often, for a campaign, to freshen up the brand, or to announce a disruptive moment. All along, color has the power to trigger unconscious associations.

Now remember that those associations carry the promise of the brand too. You cannot have an earthy palette if your products are all synthetic, you cannot have an upscale palette if you deliver cheap mass-market products, you cannot be mega-colorful if you are a law firm or a bank.

There is always a balance between who you are as a brand, what the color permissions are in the category, and how you can stand out.

Brand colors, interestingly, may not even be expressed in the logo; I think of Apple as a multicolor brand. There is a lot of white for sure, but then there are the colors of the products. The colors of the products is what makes the white in the logo work.

ANA: That reminds me of how color can also serve as a way to disrupt a category. Think of cosmetics, for example, all those white, pearl, and golden little jars, Clinique's pale sage green, and the occasional blue. Now that I am a teen's mom, I go to Sephora and see the gorgeous packaging of Drunk Elephant. Like Apple, it has white combined with a plethora of punchy, saturated colors. A definite disrupter, and a standout on the shelf.

CLAUDE: Or think sunblocks in the pharmacy. What are each of those products communicating to people? The blue and orange one will connect with the sporty crowd, Banana Boat will remind you of a fun day at the beach, and a brand like Eucerin, with their white packages, looks really clinical, and you think, *This will really work*. When I recall those big containers of Castile soap, they all have bold solid colors and the same design, it is all very efficient and simple. Take the lavender one; it is well selected to make you evoke the scent, but it does not have illustrations that may direct you to think about your granny or the fields of France. You see the color and then you fill in the gap between the product and your own emotions or recollections regarding lavender.

ANA: Which color are you most curious about now?

CLAUDE: I have always loved orange. Orange is good! But lately I am very interested in mustard, because today's mustard is much more interesting than it used to be. Colors in branding and products have become much more nuanced, interesting, and sophisticated. People have indeed become more color conscious.

ANA: When you are working on a project, how do you balance your own favorite color or your color curiosities? How do you keep your personal color preferences as a creative separate from the colors that are best for the brand?

CLAUDE: I call you, Ana Bianchi.

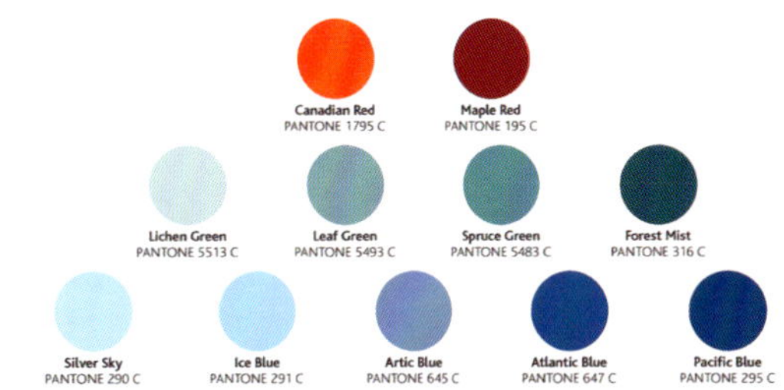

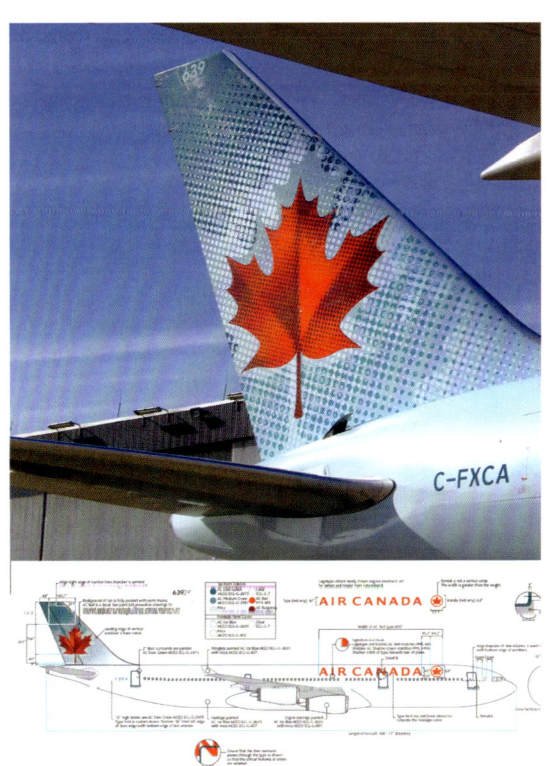

COLOR AND TRENDS

A CONVERSATION WITH MARGO TANTAU

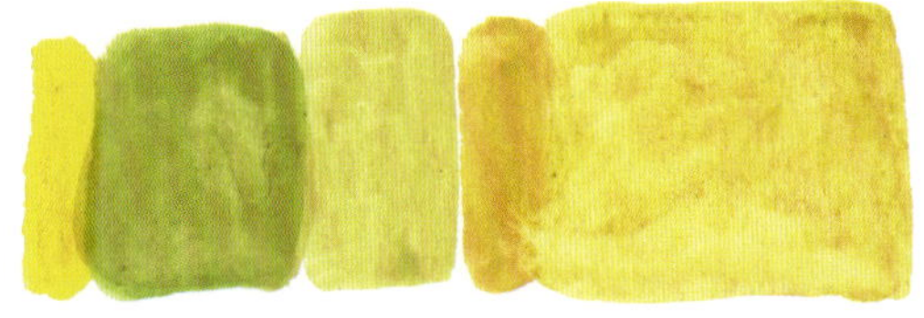

"You go to your closet and you select, I don't know, that lumpy blue sweater… but what you don't know is that that sweater is not just blue, it's not turquoise, it's not lapis, it's actually cerulean. And you're also blithely unaware of the fact that in 2002, Oscar de la Renta did a collection of cerulean gowns … And then it filtered down through the department stores, and then trickled on down into some tragic Casual Corner where you, no doubt, fished it out of some clearance bin. However, that blue represents millions of dollars and countless jobs. And it's sort of comical how you think that you've made a choice that exempts you from the fashion industry when, in fact, you're wearing a sweater that was selected for you by the people in this room."
—Miranda Priestly,
The Devil Wears Prada[21]

This quote is, hands down, the best way to introduce the topic of trends—where they start and how they trickle down from the upper echelons to the discount rack. Plus, I especially love that it is about a color: cerulean.

I will say it, I am not into following trends. I see them, I ponder them, I occasionally consider them, and unconsciously I may even follow some, but I am not a trend follower, so I reached out to my friend Margo Tantau—art director, art buyer, and podcaster for creative and creatively curious people—to talk about trends.

While she lives on Vashon Island off the coast of Washington State, Margo is really everywhere! She is the head of Tantau Studio art and illustration agency, plus an artist and crafter. Her podcast, *Windowsill Chats,* is for artists and creatives who are curious about what it's like to live, work, and walk on a creative path. It has been ranked one of the best podcasts for creatives.

Margo is like a beloved fairy godmother to artists in the home decor and illustration industry.

Find her at TantauStudio.com, @mtantau, and @windowsillchats, and listen to her podcast, *Windowsill Chats,* wherever you get your podcasts.

"Become your own trendspotter! Go out into the world—physically or virtually—with your eyes open to interesting and unique things that catch your attention, see the commonalities in what people are drawn to that is unique and original. Notice what interests you and combine all these observations to create from that."
—Margo Tantau

A trend is like fashion. It gets started by someone—usually trend companies like WGSN or Pantone or fashion houses. These trendspotters are out there in the world gathering inspiration by capturing whatever catches their eye, and then, by combining some of those observations, a trend gets started. It is very much a cycle. It starts with unique consumer behavior, like streetwear in Japan that someone captures on their phone, or a crossover from another industry, like interesting food, an archaeological find, colors from world cultures, or an art movement from the past. It all gets repackaged, and then people start designing from it. First you see it in upscale fashion houses, then it goes to home decor, and then it circles down to mass market and gift. You see it in a show in New York or Europe, and eventually, it is everywhere in Target.

It may be a color, mood, or theme. Years ago I was at Hallmark, and we were doing foxes and owls, when one of our designers, a fabulous Japanese designer, said "llamas." Nobody had seen that, it was so early! Eventually, they were everywhere. Now I think sardines are coming.

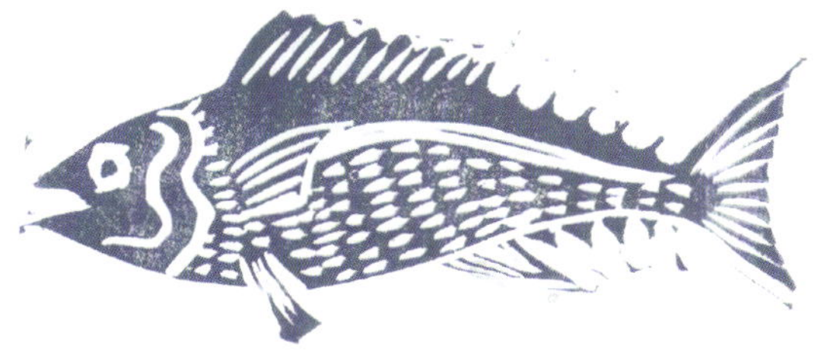

Good trends—set by trendspotters, influencers, or yourself—are always so multilayered and multidimensional. But at the end, it all depends on what kind of artist you want to be and what kind of work you want to put out into the world: Do you want to be setting the stage and standing out with your creative voice? Or do you want to simply follow?

I think the correct way to follow a trend is not verbatim; it is more the result of noticing what part of it is speaking to you so that what you produce has resonance with the true spirit of who you are as a creative.

Artists should get inspired by a lot of things, the same things that inspire the trendsetters. I think it is really about exposing yourself to a lot of visual things, not finished products in stores: imagery found on a trip, out in the streets, in books, or in movies. You notice something interesting repeating, something that catches your eye and leaves you thinking *I've never seen that before* or *That is so interesting!* And then you see it again and again. That is kind of *your* trend, your inspiration, your starting point.

When something keeps presenting itself to you, and it settles in your mind as something that feels interesting, that is the seed of a trend. It comes from conversation, from observation, from digging a bit, and from simply liking something. It is more about a gut check, what resonates with who you are. Getting together with peers and having conversations about what they've noticed or what is inspiring is also a great source of collective inspiration.

Color-wise, it is impossible to talk about trends and not talk about Pantone's Color of the Year. Remember, this is a fairly recent concept. It is something that was started as a marketing tool to make people aware of the Pantone system and sell more swatch books. Thus, I feel it should be taken with a grain of salt. However, people—the general public—have become more color aware as a result of this.

In looking at color choices, one important thing to consider is who you are creating for and what industry. Are you designing for the masses? Or for the top tier? That will certainly influence the quality of your color choices.

Margo's advice on timeless color:
In the home decor space, I think indigo is never going to go out of style, that deep, rich blue. A warm, sage-like green of some sort, and warm yellow or mustard, those are my favorite ones. And rich blacks: plum, deep green, espresso brown, and graphite. And of course all those beautiful natural colors that come from flowers and botanicals. Those never go away.

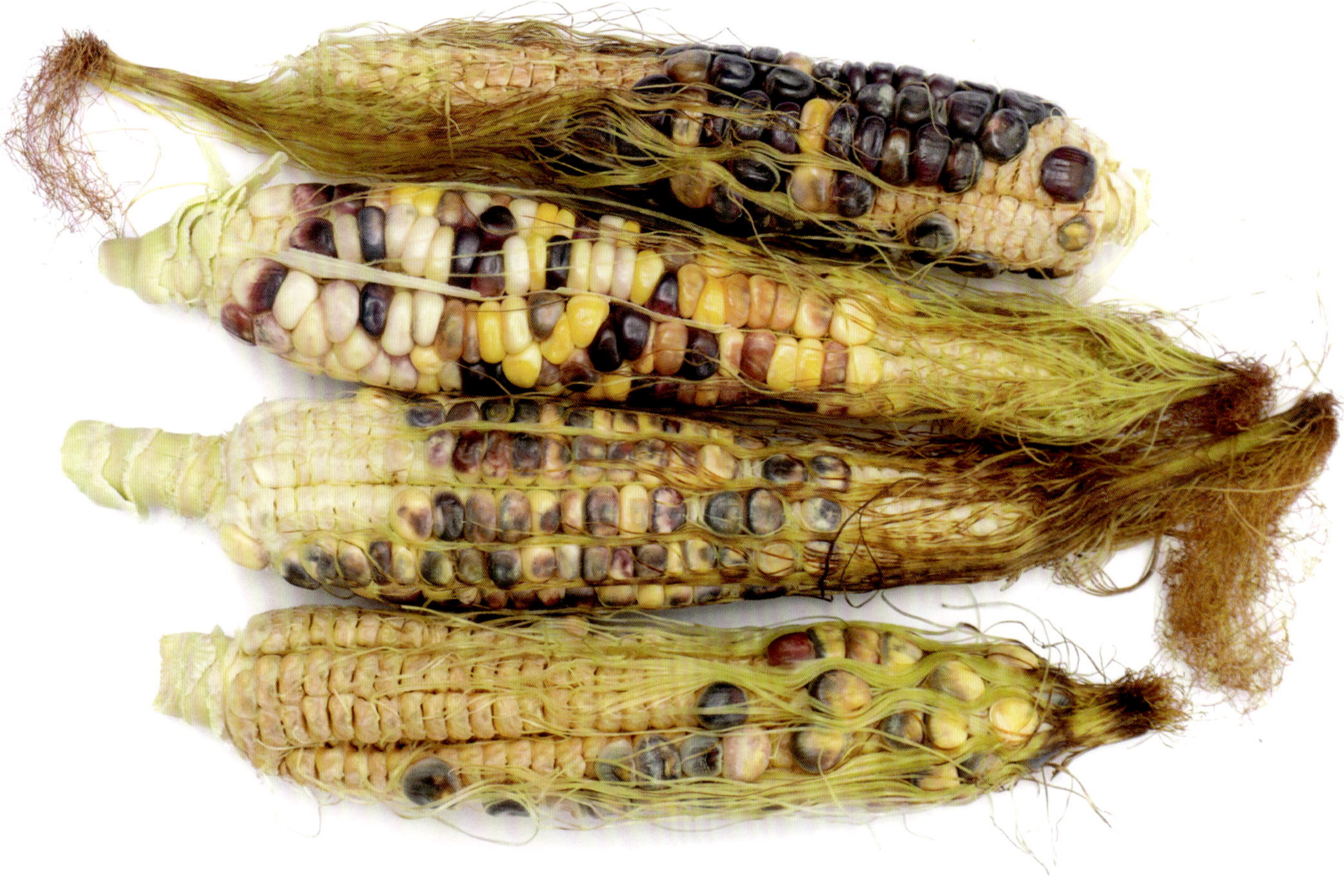

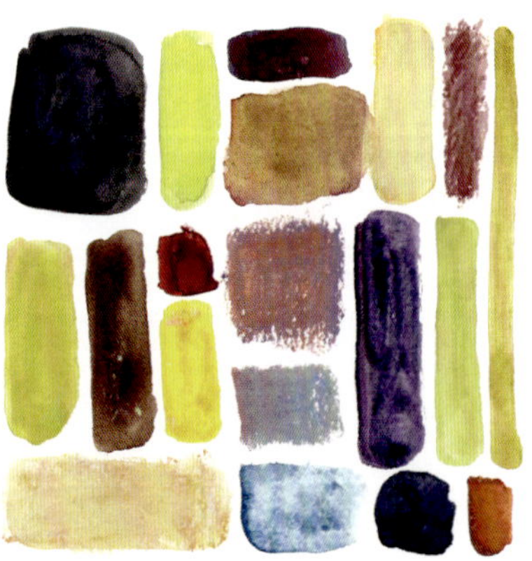

↑ Four years so far of color harvesting in the yard has yielded so many palettes! Some are the usual colors I love, but then comes that palette that surprises. This is one of those that really changed things for me; I had never used this palette, and now I find myself looking for opportunities to use it in my work. A failed heirloom corn crop yielded a lifetime of interesting color.

A FEW LAST TRICKS TO MAKE INTERESTING COLOR PALETTES

Experimenting with color combinations and palettes is never-ending for me. These are a few extra tricks I may play within my color-love search:

1. **Pick a color and play with it:** I may notice a new color, and I use that as a starting point to find matches: pairs, triads, or multicolor palettes, as in the leitmotif chapter.

2. **Skew your colors a bit:** I take a palette I have been using and "move" all the colors a bit in one direction or another. For example, if you usually use a bright red, try one that is more like a cherry red, or turn your cobalt blues into ceruleans.

    Perhaps tone them up and down, making some very pale and some deep and jewel-toned, or work the saturation level to let sweet pastels get amped up to neons.

3. **Make irrational color choices:** When making an illustration, I will do what I call an "irrational color trick." Inspired by Toulouse-Lautrec's green faces and Matisse's portrait of a lady with the green stripe in her face, along with the freedom of outsider artists and kids, I will break free from the obvious colors of things and work a palette using unexpected colors.

    I will, for example, start with a green sky, then use reds and magentas for the trees or make green and blue cherries with pink birds for a surface pattern.

4. **Enrich your color with texture:** Simply by combining art materials in an illustration or playing with texture in interior design or fashion, you can make your colors look different.

    When I do illustrations, I like to combine transparent media (watercolor) with opaque media (gouache or acrylic) and with something that has a grainy texture (colored pencils and pastels). This creates visual texture and enriches the piece. If working digitally, you can achieve the same thing by moving away from flat color. Interior design? Fashion? Simply getting dressed in the morning? Think of shiny—glass, tiles, ceramic—combined with matte things like rough textiles or unfinished wood. Think of wool next to silk, bouclé next to ribbon, fine-grain cotton next to thick, knotty linen.

5. **Go cinematic:** I love artsy movies and period pieces and series: The light! The costumes! The sets! I feel in those kinds of productions, colors are especially well orchestrated to tell the story, set the mood, and delight the eye.

    Think of what color does in Greta Gerwig's *Little Women* or *Barbie*. Think of the reds, greens, and blues of *Amélie* (or any other Jean-Pierre Jeunet movie). Note the color palette in any Wes Anderson film or the candy colors of *The Umbrellas of Cherbourg*. Think of the color coding of families and homes in *Bridgerton* and emotions and memories in *Inside Out*. Consider how nuanced the colors are in the dresses of *The Empress*, all those mauves, taupes, dusty blues, and mustards. Observe the careful color compositions in any Peter Greenaway movie. For blues and greens, look to *The Shape of Water* or *The Matrix*; for beautiful reds and greens, *The Scent of Green Papaya*.

    And of course, there are the movies in which color gives a sense of place, like in any Bollywood movie or *Farewell My Concubine*, directed by Chen Kaige, *Spirited Away* by Miyazaki, or the gorgeous *Dreams* of Akira Kurosawa.

    These visual delights gave me the idea of selecting color for any project as if I were producing a movie. I think of the story of the piece I am working on in terms of mood and atmosphere and then cast my color story "actors": Who are the main characters? Who are the supporting ones? What is the mood and color of their setting? What is the cadence of my color story? Maybe there is an explosion in the middle of an otherwise calm story; therefore I might use a neon among the blues. Maybe it all happens at dusk, and then that will dictate the mood of my colors.

    Whether it is a branding project or a kid-product illustration, whether you are doing interior or fashion design, thinking in movie terms while selecting a color palette is a useful trick.

    Let color help tell the story.

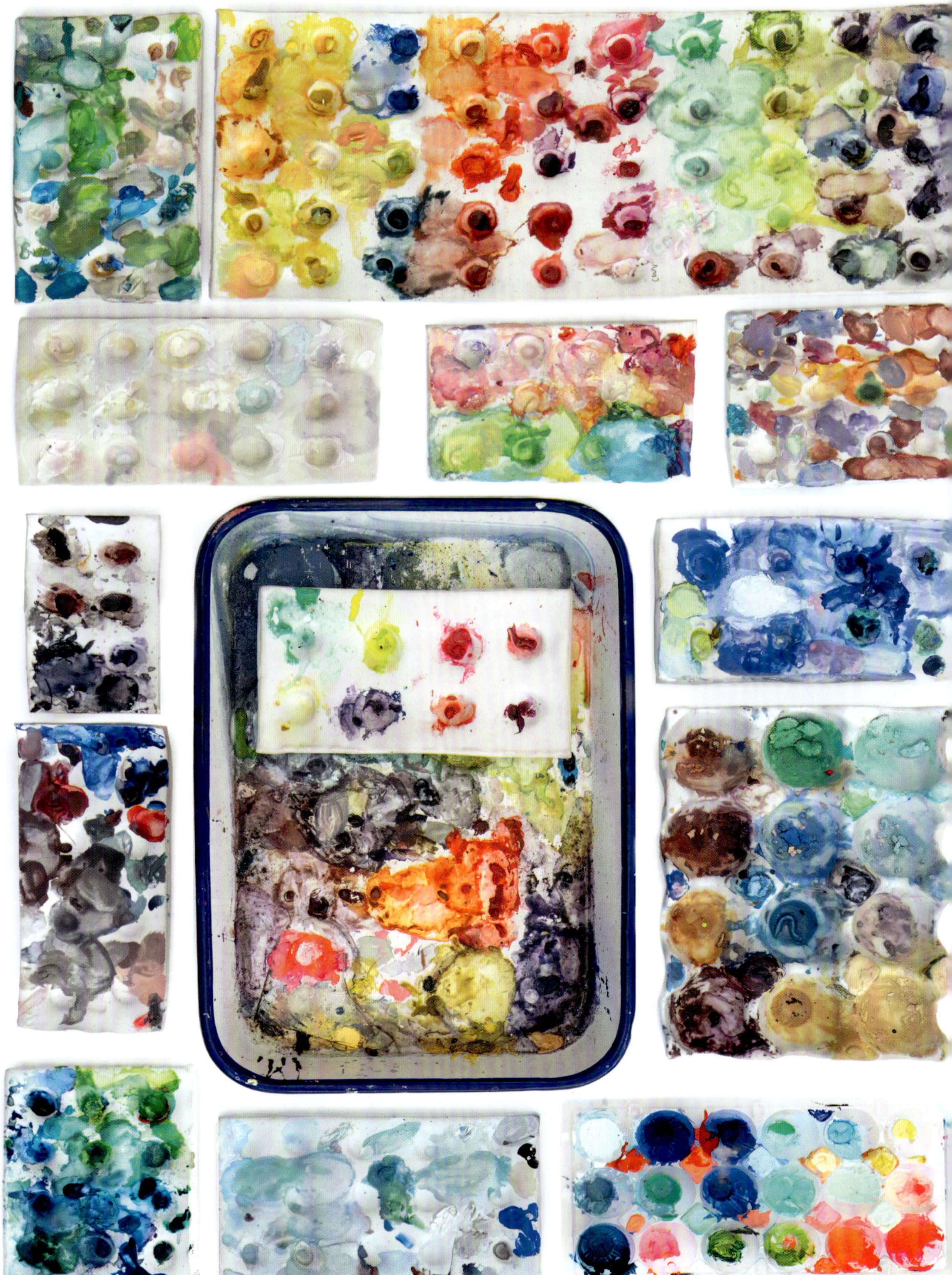

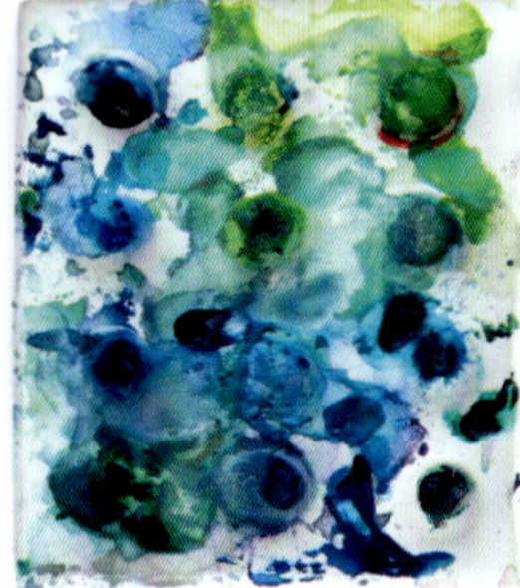
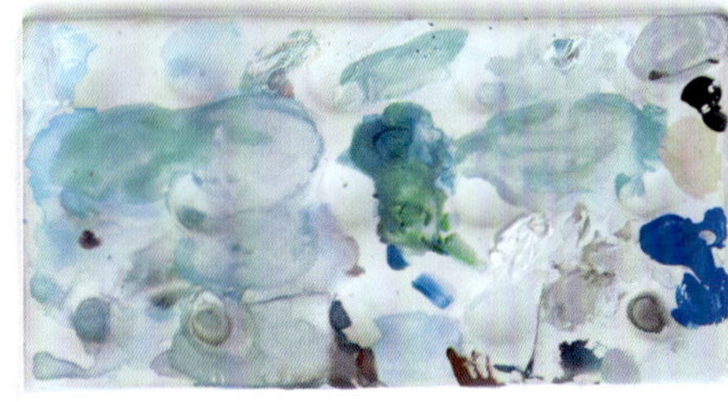
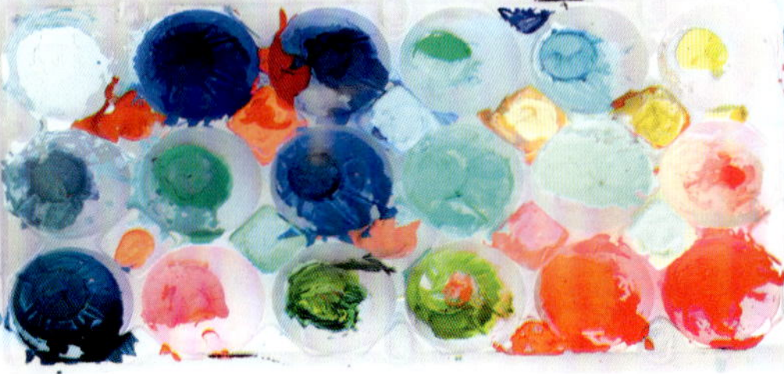

ONWARD

Inspiration for Using This Book to Continue Growing a Color Habit

*"I found the poems in the fields
And only wrote them down."
—John Clare*[22]

Inspiring color is everywhere. The simple act of noticing it already sets you on the right path to staying color curious. Observing and making a mental note is a wonderful daily practice in awareness. This is good for your eye, and for your brain. It makes you a more acute observer, it grounds you in the present, and it provides a tiny moment of joy and happiness, like a sprinkle of colorful pixie dust in your daily routine.

You may take your observation a step further and analyze in more detail. Why did this catch my eye? Why do these colors work together? What do these colors symbolize? What do they evoke? How can I mix this particular tone or hue in paint or other media? Remember, we do not have to get technical or scientific here; it is about understanding your personal experience.

For example, I was just in the kitchen, making ceviche, and as I pulled out the pink salt, I noticed the lemon pepper next to it in the spice bin: pale pink and light yellow green. So lovely! I let them sit together, then I carried on pulling out a range of dry herbs in various greens and went back for more reddish spices—sumac, dry chilis, paprika. Reds and greens, a whole range looking beautiful together. They all had a similar level of saturation, dry but still colorful, from the palest—the salt—to the darkest—the sumac.

I thought for a minute about their flavor too: Greens bring zest and fresh herbiness, even when dry, and the reds bring temperature and earthiness. Together they create contrast, visually and flavor-wise. Their colors do evoke their flavor!

This may be all the color harvesting one does in a day. That is plenty, because if this recurrent habit—observing and analyzing—is consistent, it is actually creating a color library in the brain, ready to be used when one has to choose colors to paint or decorate the house, dress in the morning, or get hands-on in creating a piece—whether personal or for a client.

Color curiosity and color love is ever evolving. You may love a certain green for a while. Experiment with it as a leitmotif and create multiple combinations with it. Then you may move on to a red. Your taste in color changes. You change settings—new house, new city, new country, new project, new vacation destination—and your color choices will change. Give yourself space for short-lived color infatuations and lifelong color loves. Keep it fluid, keep it varied, keep it interesting, mainly for yourself but ultimately to make your art better. The more interesting your color choices become in your creative practice, the more the observers—clients, collectors, friends, and family—will become enamored of your work. Remember how color is part of your unique creative voice and is also the most emotion-driven, evocative bridge for observers to connect with your work.

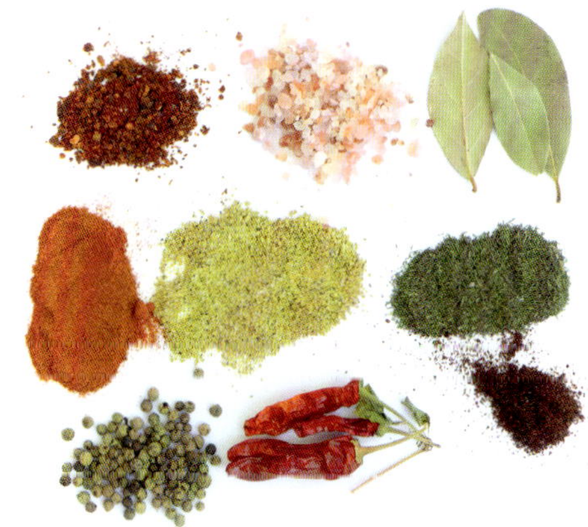

DOCUMENTING YOUR COLOR OBSERVATIONS

As you develop your color-harvesting habit, there are many ways to document your findings, many of which you have read throughout this book. By no means do you need to do all the color harvesting you have seen in these pages! Find and practice the methods that work best for you, but these are good places to start:

- **Keep a notebook** for noting down little color swatches, combinations, or palettes.
- **Photograph close-ups of color** that you find, in nature, out and about, in museums, and in books. The photos do not need to be perfect; phone cameras are fantastic for this kind of color collecting. For this purpose, do not photograph the whole landscape or the whole painting, but instead focus on a detail where you clearly note the colors that caught your eye.
- **Try grouping random things,** regardless of what they are, because of their colors.
- **Add written notes** to your photos or swatches, like a color cheat sheet, with the names of the color combinations you observe. For example, I catch Bonnie, my silver lab, surrounded by certain colors as I walk her. I may not be able to photograph her, but in my head, I will retain the image of Bonnie's gray and mustard with my red shoes and the pale pink and verdigris of *Eriogonum fasciculatum* (California buckwheat) on the sidewalk. Even noticing and thinking about color names in this way creates a memorable enough note in my head that I can later recall or write down and apply in future.
- **Make a wish list** of art materials in delicious colors.

A FINAL GIFT: THE CROP TOOL

In design school, they taught us a nifty little trick: the crop! Cropping the general view is a great way to focus and find interest, as it removes the extra noise and adds visual impact. Every time we designed a poster or a book cover, the teacher would come and crop an area: "That is your poster now," he would say.

You may have seen film directors or photographers connecting their index fingers with their thumbs to form a rectangular viewfinder. This viewfinder helps them find the right composition and framing for a scene.

When selecting the photos for this book and reviewing them for the umpteenth time, I would often notice that little area where I would just swoon over a specific green next to a purple or a single petal where a whole color transition was happening. That is where the cropping tool comes in handy. By isolating that little area or detail from the rest of the image, you can more easily grasp a whole new set of color observations, combinations, or ideas.

Use this crop tool to help you review the images in this book and extract new color inspiration that may be different from or simpler than the color palettes I created.

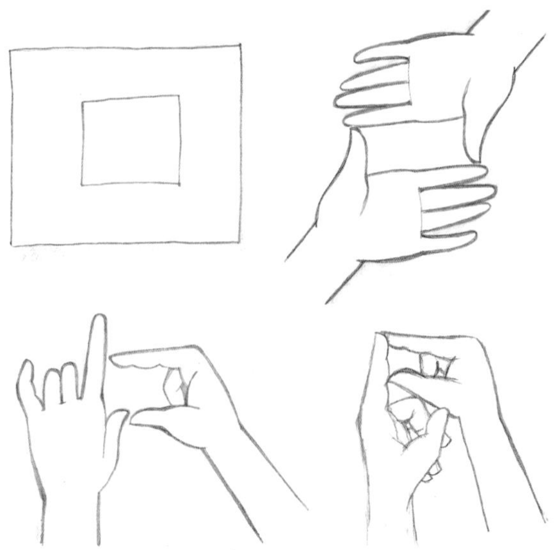

HOW TO KEEP USING THIS BOOK

This book has many layers, and it has been put together so that you can come back and peel back those layers as you need them. I threw into these pages so much of what inspires me, of what I have learned from others or discovered on my own. I have also filled the pages with so much color that I found inspiring and sometimes even revelatory. I know, it is a lot! But I also thought of this book as something you can come back to over and over. I hope it ends up like those cookbooks that are full of splashes of broth, oil, and tomato sauce because you have used them so much while actually cooking. The worst that can happen is that this book gets so covered with paint or even your annotations in the margins that you need to buy another one: "the clean copy."

Each of the layers and concepts I included in this book can be a gateway for discovery. Some of the ways you can go back into the book and keep on using it:

- **Rereading the essays** in each chapter and making a list of the art and design references I mention. Do more research on each of those—it can be a simple internet search to see more art by that artist or from the period mentioned, or you may be lucky to have a museum with the artist's work near you so that you can observe and analyze it in person, then maybe create something inspired by it. Seeing art in person is second to none.

- **Going back to the color-mixing charts** and trying to recreate them, with those colors or others. Learning how to mix colors intentionally for desired effect is one of the most important aspects of developing your color voice. It gives you fluency and control over your color choices.

- **Reviewing the interviews** and conversations I had with other artists, designers, art agents, and educators. Learn more about them or the themes they talk about.

- **Going on a shopping spree** with the art materials list or for the recommended books.

- **Taking a class** where you can experiment with colors; I've provided a few suggestions at the end of this book.

- **Observing with greater attention** the photographs of natural color (the Abstract Naturalism images of botanicals) and human-made color (the gatherings of trinkets, tchotchkes, textiles, and toys) in this book. Use the crop tool to zero in on a smaller area of colors you want to focus on. Find and gather your own favorite natural and human-made colors to work with.

- **Analyzing my or your own collections** in deeper detail, asking yourself questions and creating new color palettes from them.

- **Creating not the projects I suggested but the ones you normally work on** or new work you are curious to make, yet that somehow are inspired by all these color combinations. Create a thirty-day or one-hundred-day project around one of the themes or colors you find here. Use any and all of the images and palettes to inspire new work with colors you haven't tried.

- **Sharing your work.** Do not be shy about it! The more you share, the more encouraged and brave you will be at putting your creative voice out there in the world.

I wish you luck as you embark on your color-harvesting journey!

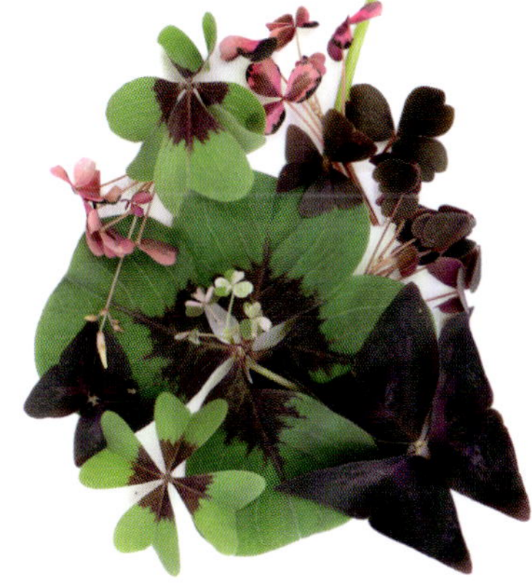

Chronicle Books, all the collaborators in this book, and I would be so happy to see what this book inspires you to create!

Please share with us, if you post it online, by tagging us: @AnaLovesColor @ChronicleBooks #AnaLovesColor #ChronicleBooks #ColorHarvesting #ColorCurious

COLOPHON

What Months of Constant Color Harvesting Did to Me

While I have been a color lover my whole life, it was while working on the images for this book that my color love really deepened. I started the first series, called Color/Flora, the one I also call Abstract Naturalism, in the early spring of 2020. As the world closed down due to the COVID pandemic and we were asked to stay home, I turned to my yard.

The first bits I collected were a variety of geraniums for a project during an online class with Lilla Rogers. That first photo had leaves and flowers organized in "platoon formation." I photographed them on white, beige, and other-colored backgrounds, created a palette, and used these for the class assignment. The idea of using botanicals for color lingered in my mind for a day or two before I embarked on a full-on color-harvesting journey through my garden. I decided to discard the backgrounds other than white, as they created too many variables, and after a few photos, I also discarded the platoon formations and favored just bunching up everything in apparent randomness. I say *apparent* because while the positioning of the elements in each picture is quite random, the colors combined are definitely intentional.

Since it was spring, there were lots of plants in bloom. (Did I mention I like to garden? A lot?)

So I decided to continue the series for the three weeks we would be in mandatory lockdown . . . and we all know what happened after those initial three weeks.

As we continued to isolate, the colors of spring changed into the fruits of summer—tomatoes, plums, berries, chiles—and I committed to completing the four seasons in this Color/Flora project. In the end, I completed a continuous eighteen months of color harvesting using whatever was growing, blooming, fruiting, drying, or decaying within the fence of my yard. Every few days, or as I gardened or relaxed out there, I would scout for color with my eyes. I even found these tiny (about four millimeters) black flowers I had never noticed in a bush! The power of a keen eye at peak training.

Let's talk about my yard. No, I do not live in a botanical garden. My yard is about a half acre on a steep, east-facing slope with a huge 250-year-old valley oak and a small vineyard. This is not so odd if you consider we live in the Bay Area, and the site where my town sits was full of orchards and vineyards before the highways were

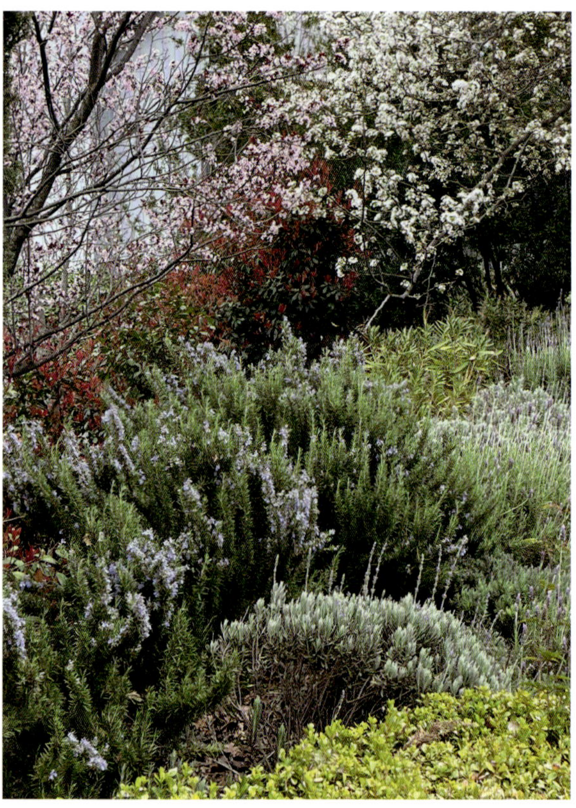

built. Typical of California, our seasons are divided into glorious spring (spring is glorious everywhere), a long, not-a-single-cloud-for-months, dry summer, followed by a dry, sometimes fire-smoked fall that with the first rains in months transitions into a wet, muddy winter. The vineyard and the oak were in my yard when we moved in 2017 from New York City, but the rest is an ongoing DIY project with my family. We do not have a gardener, but we do work with a winemaker. Some years I garden a lot, and some years, well, the garden does its wilder thing.

Since that initial eighteen-month project, I have continued to take photos of new groupings of natural color. My eye has come a long way since those first geranium photos: my colors less obvious, subtler, more adventurous in their combinations.

The search for color eventually led to looking at human-made color. I went from flora, fruit, and foliage to trinkets, tchotchkes, textiles, and toys as I color harvested every nook and cranny in my home and the glorious boxes of random things in the garage and closets. I am not a hoarder, but I am an heir to a family that loves collecting interesting and beautiful bits, books, and art.

Actually, all this grouping of color objects had a

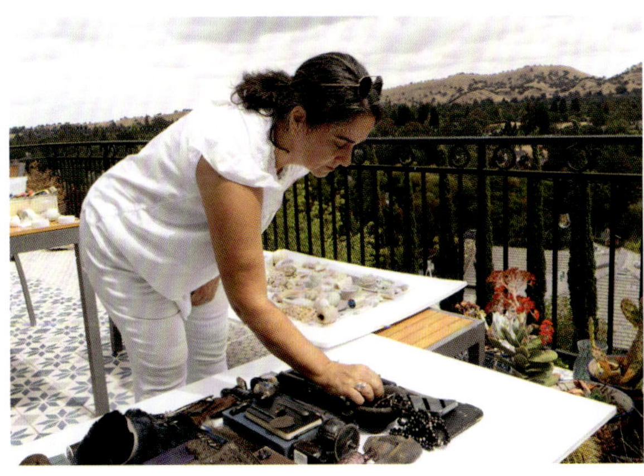

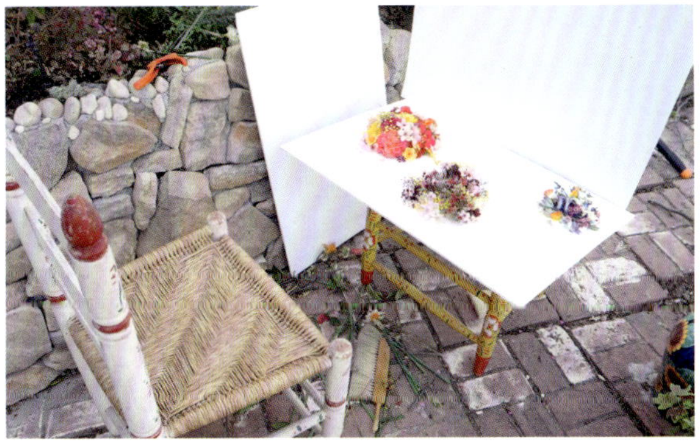

precursor that started by accident, years before the Color/Flora series. When we moved from New York City to California in 2017, as I packed my daughter's room, I would find the typical baskets of random toys mixed together. Because of the rush to pack, or because I can't help myself with colorful things, I actually bundled some of these random mixes together in off-white packing paper and, noticing how cool they looked together, before putting them in the movers' boxes, snapped a few photos of them on my phone with the idea of printing them and framing them in the new house.

The seed idea was there: random colorful objects that looked good together on a light, neutral background. The idea took four years to properly germinate and become the photo series for this book. I am so glad it did because everywhere in my house, I found a wealth of color.

So, what did I get from all these months and years of pointing my camera down at these colorful botanicals and human-made objects?

Above all, this series has taught me that there is always more to learn. Even with a subject matter like color, which has always been one of my passions, there is always more that I can learn and experiment with.

Through the process, my eye has become sharper when noticing and finding interesting colors everywhere I go. Every day, I make so many color notes in my head!

The colors found in my yard and my junk drawers have started appearing daringly in my artwork, in palettes and combinations I had never used before but with which now I feel more inspired to experiment.

The number of color conversations in my home has also increased, and these have deepened to the point that my teen daughter's artwork has also become very color brave!

Aside from the beneficial effect on my artwork is the impact color harvesting has had on my mind. The consistency with which I have continued to pay attention to my surroundings has brought me a lot of quiet joy, but it has also become a mindfulness practice of sorts. Looking for and at color puts me in the zone; it focuses and quiets the monkey in my mind. It settles me, even when I obsess so much about a color combination to the point of dreaming about it for three nights in a row. In the past, I had practiced calligraphy as a form of active meditation, but now, my color-harvesting habit provides me with the same benefits: being present and aware, cultivating unpunctual attention and focus, single-tasking, and finding an overall sense of calm.

Lastly, working on this series ultimately led me to Chronicle Books, the wonderful publishing house in San Francisco that I have loved and followed since the '80s when they first published the Griffin and Sabine series. This series was one of my first inspirations to become an illustrator.

I am incredibly thankful to Bridget Watson Payne, who with an open mind looked at the first, totally different iteration of this book and saw the potential the Color/Flora images carried. When she left Chronicle in 2023, she passed the baton to Mirabelle Korn, my brilliant editor, who became a marvelous sounding board and from day one enthusiastically championed the idea of using the images to talk about color differently.

To both of them, an ocean of gratitude. ❧

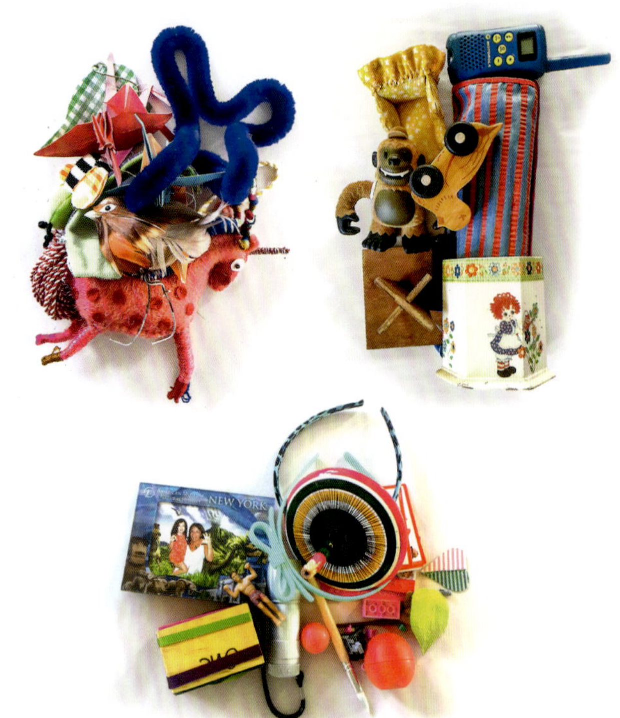

Photography Notes

"I myself have always stood in awe of the camera. I recognize it for the instrument that it is, part Stradivarius, part scalpel." —Irving Penn[23]

While I consider myself more of an artist, designer, and illustrator, photography has always been an important part of my creative practice. I got my first camera (a Nikon N2000) from my grandfather when I was thirteen, and I used it constantly through my teens, twenties, and midthirties, until I got a digital camera. I still shoot film occasionally with that camera or other vintage cameras, like our Rolleiflex. And of course, I photograph A LOT—like we all do—with my iPhone.

The smaller images in this book—the snapshots, the travel and museum photos—are mostly taken with either the film Nikon or my iPhone.

The main photos, the abstract naturalist Color/Flora series and all the object flat lays and color groupings, are taken with my Sony a6000, although I recently transitioned from that to a Sony Alpha 7 IV.

I always photograph outdoors, with natural light. It is all a very simple setting: the whiteboards with the color groupings on the floor outside my north-facing studio, in the shade created by the house, and me on a stool with the camera pointing down.

The real magic happens in the selection of the subject matter.

It is also important to note that later, in Adobe Lightroom and Photoshop, I aim to do the minimum possible in retouching. Mostly I do white balance, to neutralize the blues, greens, or golds that may have affected the natural daylight, and I do some adjustments of levels so that the background is pure white and everything looks crisp. I rarely modify the colors, as I want to stay true to their original hue, tint, chroma, and saturation.

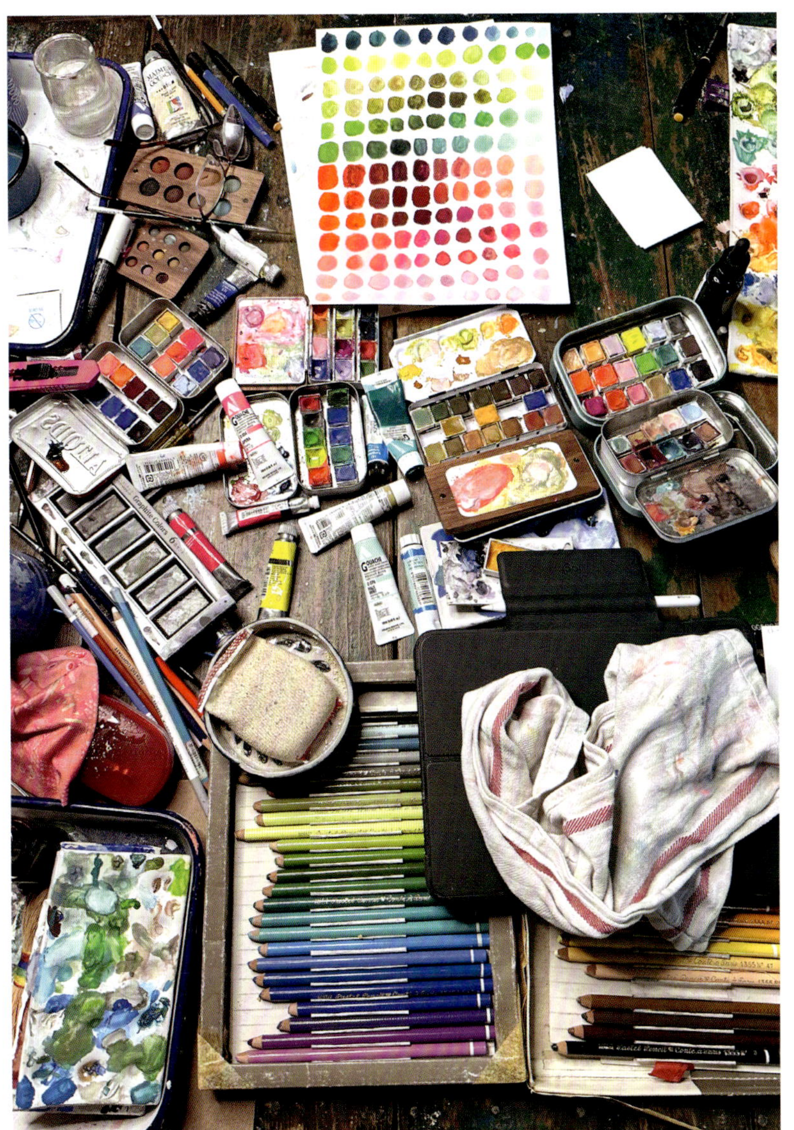
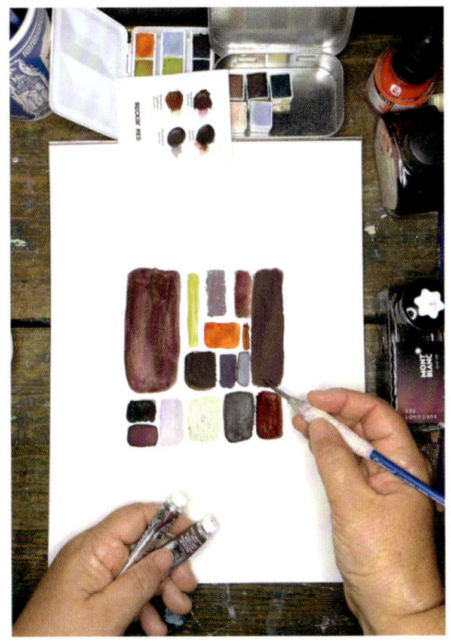
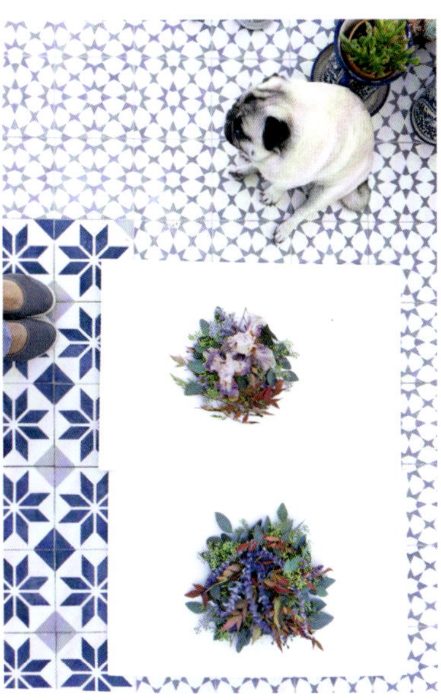
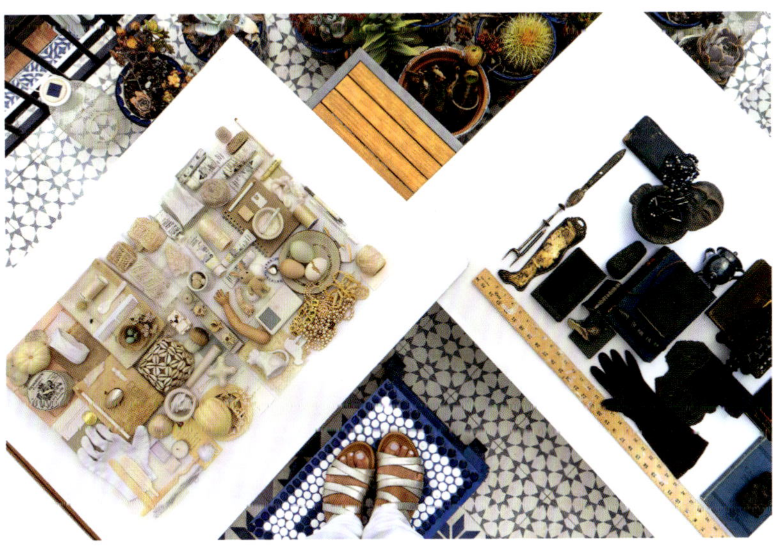
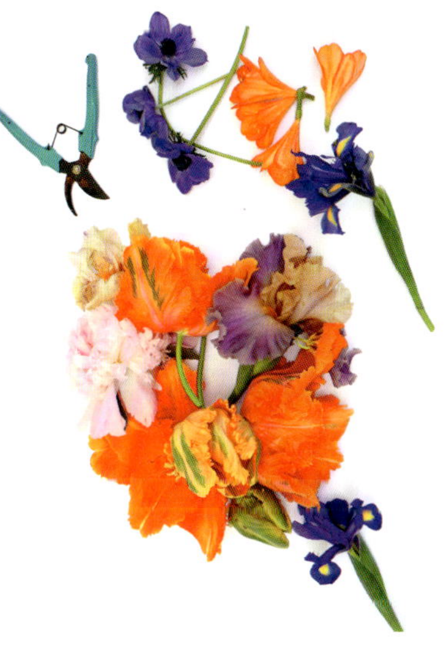

NOTES

1 O'Keeffe, Georgia. *Georgia O'Keefe*. The Viking Studio, 1976.

2 Ridgway, Robert. *Color Standards and Color Nomenclature*. Published by the author, 1912.

3 Hoffman, Mary Jo. *Still: The Art of Noticing*. The Monacelli Press, 2024.

4 Phillpotts, Eden. *A Shadow Passes*, Ulan Press, 2012.

5 Gustafson, Heidi. *Book of Earth: A Guide to Ochre, Pigment, and Raw Color*. Abrams, 2023.

6 Cennini, Cennino. *Il libro dell'Arte*, a book from the early Renaissance about pigments, techniques, and materials used at the time.

7 Cowart, Jack, Jack D. Flam, Dominique Fourcade, and John Hallmark Neff. *Henri Matisse: Paper Cut-Outs*. Detroit Institute of Arts, 1977.

8 and **9** Albers, Josef. *Interaction of Color: 50th Anniversary Edition*. Yale University Press, 2013. Original edition 1963.

10 Van Gogh, Vincent. "September 1888 letter to his brother Theo," from *Vincent van Gogh: A Life in Letters*. Thames & Hudson, 2020.

11 Daywalt, Drew and Oliver Jeffers (illustrator). *The Day the Crayons Quit*. Philomel Books, 2013.

12 and **13** Christopher Rothko (Mark Rothko's son) in the catalog for the Fondation Louis Vuitton *Mark Rothko* exhibit in Paris in 2023.

14 Vamos series by Raúl the Third, colorized by Elaine Bay. Versify.

15 For example: Isol. *Nocturne: Dream Recipes*. Groundwood Books, 2012.

16 For example: Alexander, Kwame and Melissa Sweet (illustrator). *How to Read a Book*. Harper, 2019.

17 Ladnier, Penny. 1996. "Color in Elizabethan Dress." Elizabethan Costumes. http://www.elizabethancostume.net/lizcolor.html. Excerpted from the paper "Color Names Throughout the Centuries."

18 Shakespeare, William. *The Merry Wives of Windsor*. 1602.

19 Mead, Rebecca. "An Artist Flowering in her Nineties." *The New Yorker*, July 22, 2024. https://www.newyorker.com/magazine/2024/07/29/an-artist-flowering-in-her-nineties.

20 Caracciolo Chia, Marella. "Thread and Thrum." *The World of Interiors*, June 6, 2024. https://www.worldofinteriors.com/story/isabella-ducrot-rome-apartment.

21 *The Devil Wears Prada*. Directed by David Frankel. Fox 2000 Pictures, 2006.

22 Clare, John. "Sighing for Retirement," in *The Later Poems of John Clare*. Oxford University Press, 1984.

23 Penn, Irving. Wall text for *Irving Penn* exhibition at the de Young Museum, San Francisco, 2024.

RECOMMENDATIONS

Books on Color

Werner's Nomenclature of Colours by Patrick Syme. Facsimile ed. Smithsonian Books, 2018; original ed. 1821.

Nature's Palettes: A Color Reference System from the Natural World. Princeton University Press, 2021.

An Atlas of Rare & Familiar Colour: The Harvard Art Museums' Forbes Pigment Collection. Atelier Éditions, 2019.

Three Hundred Years Before Color. Facsimile ed. of *Traité des couleurs servant à la peinture à l'eau* (Treatise on colors used for water painting) by A. Boogert. Galobart Books, 2019.

Kremer Pigmente Recipe Book. Kremer Pigmente, 2020.

On Color by David Scott Kastan with Stephen Farthing. Yale University Press, 2018.

The Secret Lives of Color by Kassia St. Clair. Penguin Books, 2017.

Color: A Natural History of the Palette by Victoria Finlay. Random House, 2004.

The Book of Colour Concepts by Sarah Lowengard and Alexandra Loske (ed.). Taschen, 2024.

A Dictionary of Color Combinations (vol. 1 and 2) by Sanzo Wada. Seigensha, 2010, based on an edition published in Japan in the 1930s.

Books on Creativity

Find Your Artistic Voice: The Essential Guide to Working Your Creative Magic by Lisa Congdon. Chronicle Books, 2019. (Plus any other book by Lisa Congdon, such as *Art., Inc., You Will Leave a Trail of Stars*, and, my favorite, *The Live Your Values Deck*, all from Chronicle.)

The Creative Habit: Learn It and Use It for Life by Twyla Tharp. Simon and Schuster, 2003.

Your Brain on Art: How the Arts Transform Us by Susan Magsamen and Ivy Ross. Random House, 2023.

My Favorite Art Material Brands

Case for Making for handmade watercolors, for their beautiful colors and delicious creaminess on application.

Daniel Smith watercolors, especially their mineral colors and the variety of quinacridone colors.

Gansa Tambi Kuretake for traditional Japanese pan watercolors, in sets and as individual colors (I must say, I love most Japanese art materials and stationery).

Holbein for anything and everything! I especially love their Acryla Gouache, watercolors, and oil paints. The colors are rich and saturated and smooth to work with.

Sennelier—also for everything, from printmaking inks to pastels. Especially if I can buy them in Paris because their shops are so historic.

La Maison du Pastel, also in Paris, has made the best handmade pastels since the time of the impressionists! This is the gold standard.

Staedtler for colored pencils, but above everything, their triangular neon Textsurfer dry pencils.

Derwent and **Prismacolor** for their creamy colored pencils, not in sets but for select colors.

Winsor & Newton for gouache and watercolors. Ubiquitous, trustworthy, and simply a classic.

Caran d'Ache for pastel pencils and especially watercolor pencils.

The Birmingham Pen Company for their interesting inks.

Vasari for high-quality oil paints handmade in New York.

Kremer Pigmente for pigments, in case you want to make your own colors. Their recipe book and their classes are great.

Precita Eyes, located in the Precita Eyes Muralist Center in San Francisco for acrylic paint for murals. While it is formulated for murals, I have used it on canvas and woodboard. I like that unlike most acrylics it is not gloppy and doesn't feel like plastic.

Last but not least, my various pencils: I always travel with a bicolor red-and-blue pencil, my Pilot Shaker mechanical pencil, various graphites (I love finding stores that sell graphite pencils from around the world, and I especially love Portuguese graphite pencils), and a water-soluble graphite.

ACKNOWLEDGMENTS

To the brilliant people who generously contributed a conversation for this book. **Thank you!**

Readers—do check out these people and their books, classes, products, and beautiful art:

→ **Lilla Rogers:** Everyone in illustration should take her classes on her website, Make Art That Sells. Especially do not miss my favorite MATS classes with Lilla and Riley Wilkinson on toy and character design.

→ **Esté MacLeod:** Check out her beautiful art and join her in her color-centric classes and her weekly Coloricombo Substack for inspiration.

→ **Jehane Boden Spiers:** Check out her work and the work of her agency's artists, and sign up for her newsletter for color and art inspiration, creative challenges, and more.

→ **Margo Tantau:** Listen to her inspiring conversations with creative people from all walks of life on her weekly podcast *Windowsill Chats* and sign up for her newsletter at Tantau Studio, as she always shares exciting things happening for the creative and the creatively curious community. Keep an eye on her agency artists at her website, Tantau Studio.

Thank you to my fellow artists:

→ **Misha Zadeh:** Visit her online store for all kinds of beautifully designed gifts and paper goods.

→ **Meenal Patel:** Don't miss her online store full of art, home and paper goods, and her various beautiful books.

→ **Elaine Bay (and Raúl the Third):** Through drawing, color, and storytelling in their multiple kids' books, they have created a really cool universe that Hispanic and specifically Mexican American kids can relate to. I especially love the Lowriders and Vamos series.

→ **Andrea Pippins:** Check out her beautiful books, take her brilliant classes, and read her blog, *Fly*.

→ **Geninne Zlatkis:** . . . Where do I start? Follow her on Instagram @geninne and you will see. Her books are super fun and inspiring, her gorgeous art is on products everywhere, and above all, her handcrafted products and jewelry simply evaporate the minute she makes them available on her Etsy store.

→ And with extra-special gratitude, **Lisa Congdon:** She has inspired so many people, including myself, over the years with her multiple books about creativity, illustration, having an art-centric business, and more, along with her fabulous products and beautiful art.

→ And with decades of friendship, creativity, culture, food, and art conversations, thank you especially to **Claude Salzberger and Himi Saito.**

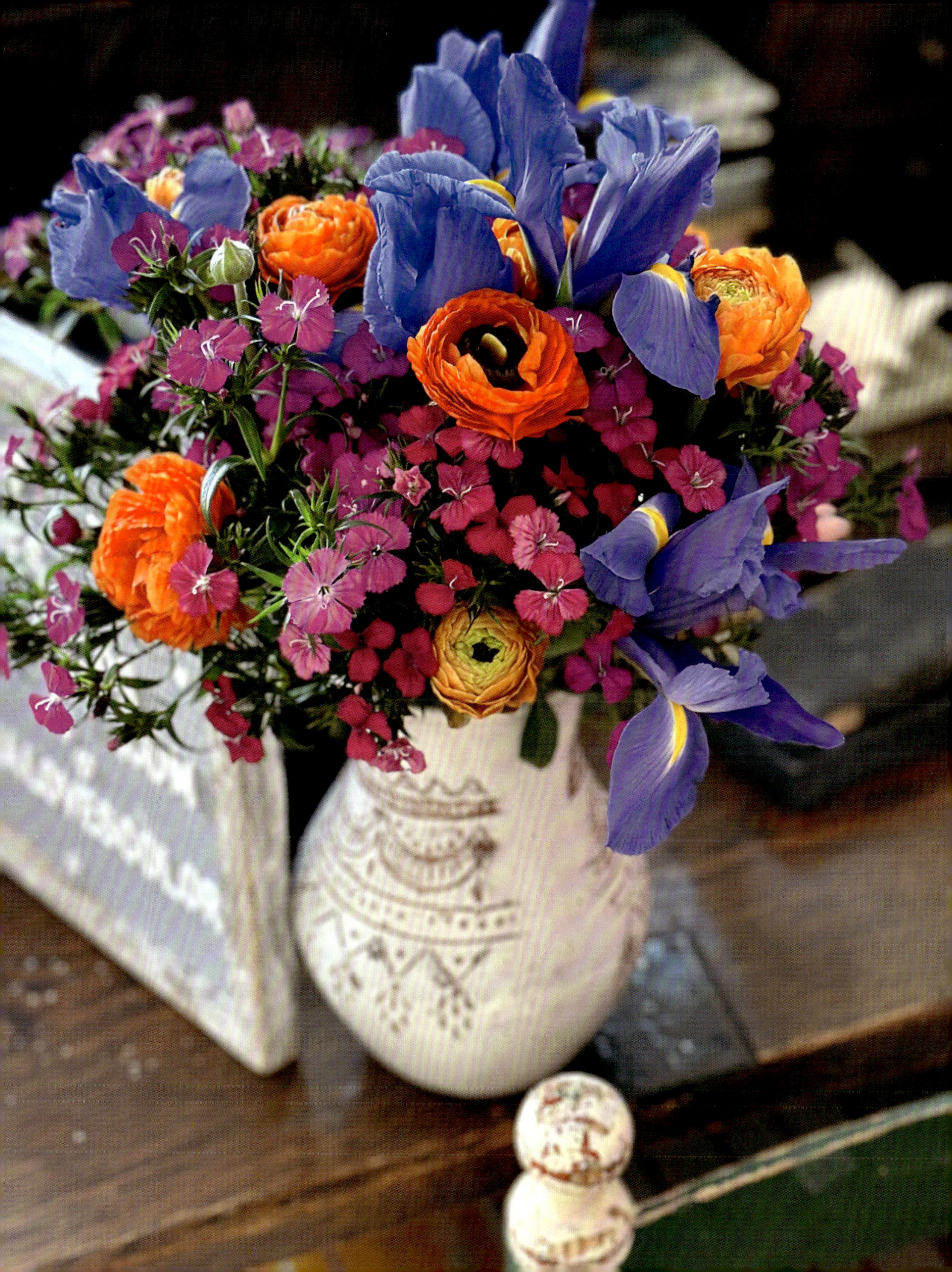

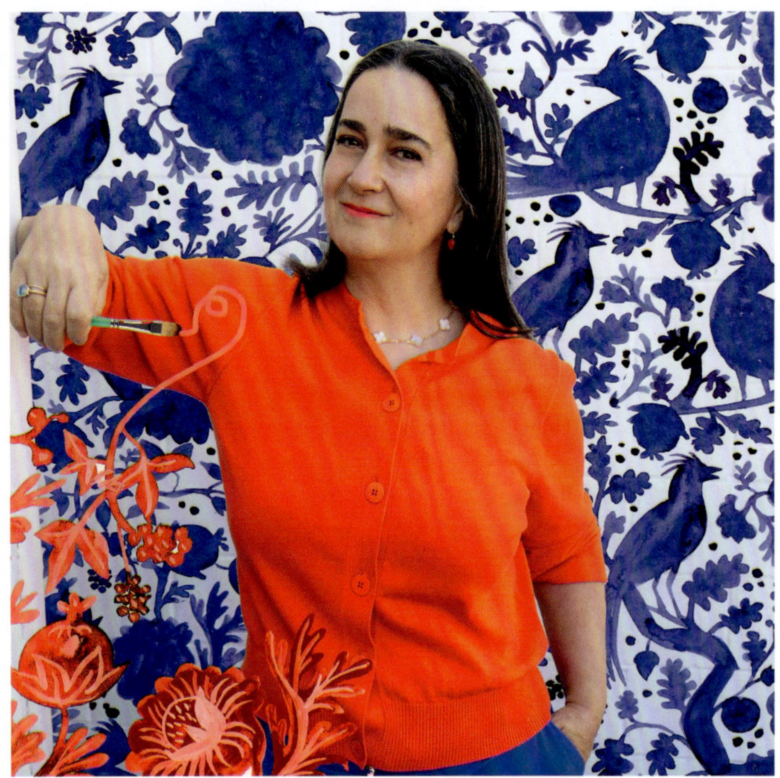

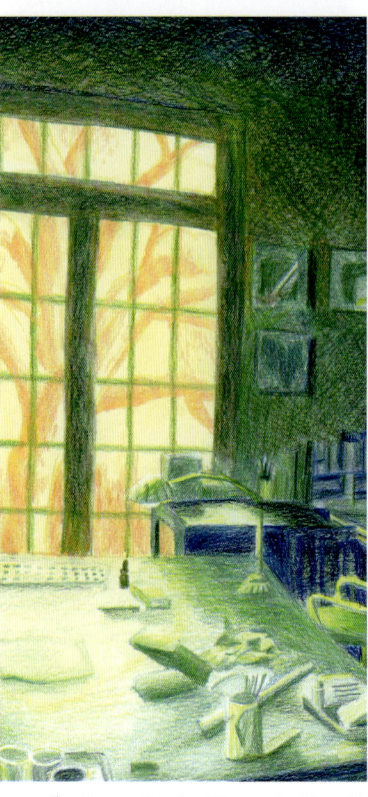

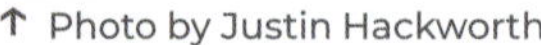
↑ Photo by Justin Hackworth

↑ Illustration by Florencia Bianchi

ABOUT THE AUTHOR

Originally from Mexico, Ana Bianchi is an artist, designer, illustrator, and twice-published children's book author and illustrator.

With degrees in both graphic design and fine arts, her thirty-five-plus years of creative work span disciplines ranging from printmaking and ceramics to illustration, surface design, and childrenswear to graphic design and branding for clients small and large, including local restaurants and major airlines.

Her art brand, Ana Loves Color, is where all these diverse projects live.

Her lifelong love of color is what connects it all and helps her comfortably move from one discipline to another and from one technique to another. On the pages of this book you can see her photography, illustrations, patterns, paintings, handmade ceramics, and colorful bakes, and as you read her text, you will discover her curiosity and deep interest in art history, world cultures, and the pursuit of creative ideas.

When not working in her Bay Area studio, Ana loves to cook and bake colorful things, tend to her garden—her other color studio—and spend time with her tiny family: Alberto, her husband; Florencia, her daughter; and Bonnie and PepaPug, their dogs.

To see her work, visit AnaLovesColor.com and @AnaLovesColor, and join her mailing list for more color love and to learn about upcoming presentations, products, workshops, and the latest colorful art.

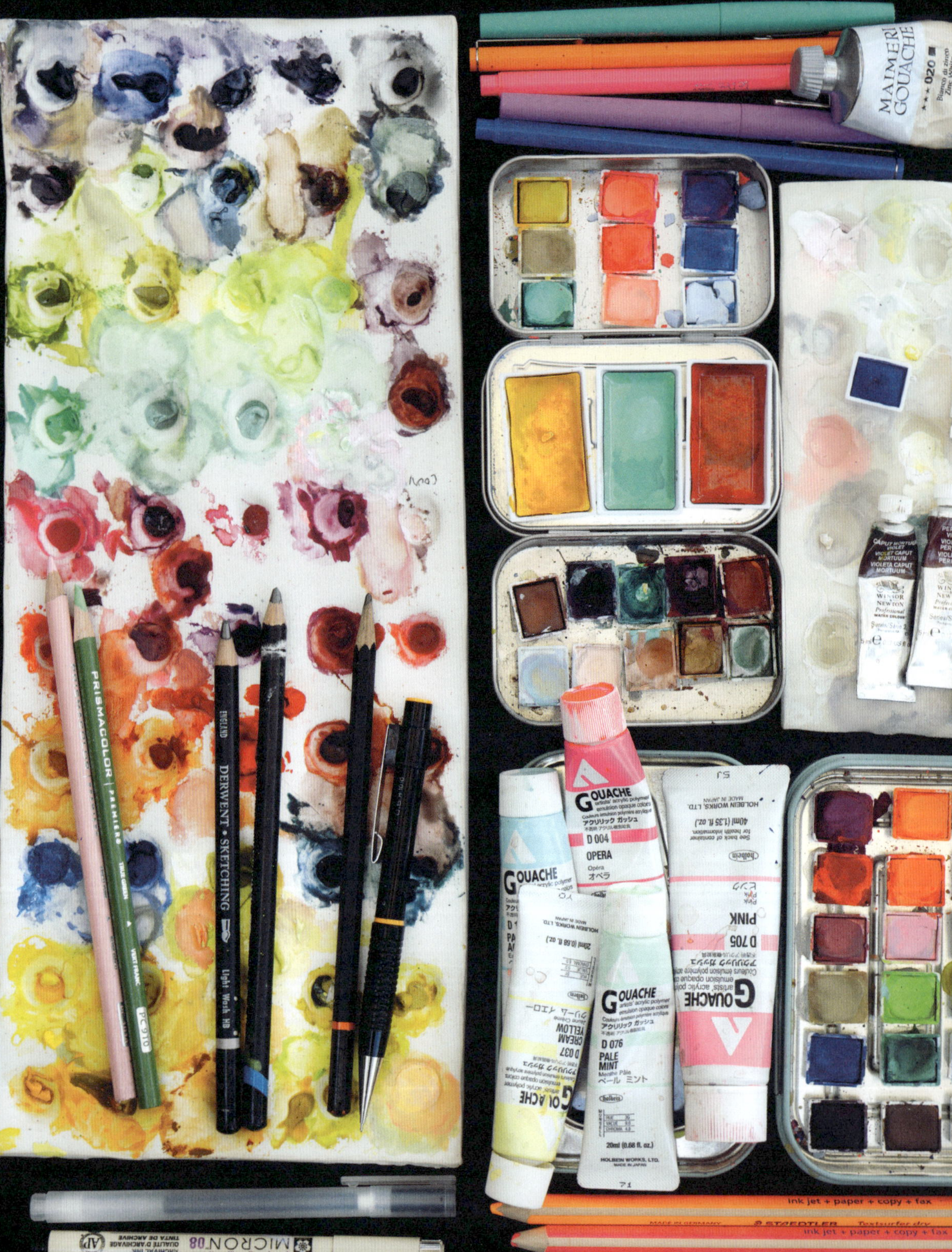

MAIMERI
GOUACHE
020
Bianco di zirco
Zinc White
gr.1
PRISMACOLOR | PREMIERE
TRUE GREEN
PC910
DERWENT · SKETCHING
ENGLAND
Light Wash HB
GOUACHE
artistic acrylic polymer
Couleurs emulsion opaque colors
アクリリック ガッシュ
D 004
OPERA
Opera
オペラ
HOLBEIN WORKS, LTD.
MADE IN JAPAN
40ml (1.35 fl. oz.)
See back of container
for health information.
PINK
D 705
GOUACHE
artists' acrylic polymer
emulsion opaque colors
Couleurs emulsion opaque co
GOUACHE
artistic acrylic polymer
Couleurs emulsion opaque colors
アクリリック ガッシュ
D 076
PALE
MINT
ペール ミント
20ml (0.68 fl. oz.)
HOLBEIN WORKS, LTD.
MADE IN JAPAN
71
GOUACHE
CREAM
YELLOW
D 037
CAPUT MORTUUM
VIOLET CAPUT
MORTUUM
VIOLETA CAPUT
MORTUUM
WINSOR
NEWTON
Professional
Water Colour
PERYLE
VIOLET
VIOLET
PERYLE
VIOLETA
PERLEN
WINSOR
NEWTON
Professional
Water Colour
ink jet + paper + copy + fax
STAEDTLER
ink jet + paper + copy + fax
STAEDTLER
MADE IN GERMANY
MICRON 08
SAKURA
PIGMA
AP
ARCHIVAL INK
QUALITÉ D'ARCHIVAGE
TINTA DE ARCHIVE
GELLY ROLL